GREENS
SHERIFF COURT RULES
2005/2006

AUSTRALIA
Law Book Co.
Sydney

CANADA and USA
Carswell
Toronto

HONG KONG
Sweet & Maxwell Asia

NEW ZEALAND
Brookers
Wellington

SINGAPORE and MALAYSIA
Sweet & Maxwell Asia
Singapore and Kuala Lumpur

Reprinted from the *Parliament House Book*, published in looseleaf form and updated five times a year by W. Green, the Scottish Law Publisher

The following paperback titles are also available in the series:
Annotated Rules of the Court of Session 2004/2005
Conveyancing, Property, Trusts and Succession Statutes 2005/2006
Solicitors Professional Handbook 2005/2006
and
Shiels & Bradley,
Criminal Procedure (Scotland) Act 1995, 4th edition

Parliament House Book consists of the following Divisions:
A Fees and Stamps
B Courts,Upper
C Rules of the Court of Session (annotated)
D Courts,Lower
E Licensing
F Solicitors
G Legal Aid
H Bankruptcy and other Mercantile Statutes
I Companies
J Conveyancing, Land Tenure and Registration
K Family Law
L Landlord and Tenant
M Succession, Trusts, Liferents and Judicial Factors
N Tribunals, Inquiries, etc.
O Valuation for Rating
P Practice and Procedures of the Scottish Parliament

GREENS
SHERIFF COURT RULES
2005/2006

Reprinted from
Division D (Courts, Lower)
of the *Parliament House Book*

THOMSON
™
W. GREEN

Published in 2005 by W. Green & Son Ltd
21 Alva Street
Edinburgh EH2 4PS

*Printed in Great Britain by TJ International Ltd,
Padstow, Cornwall*

No natural forests were destroyed to make this product;
only farmed timber was used and replanted

A CIP catalogue record for this book is available from the British Library

ISBN 0 414 01620 3

DIVISION D

Courts, Lower

Statutes

Acts of Sederunt, etc.

NOTE

Margin numbers in bold (e.g. **D 10**) are for cross-referencing purposes and refer to the current corresponding pages in Division D, Parliament House Book.

[1] Sheriff Courts (Scotland) Act 1907

(7 Edw. 7 c. 51)

An Act to regulate and amend the laws and practice relating to the D 10 civil procedure in sheriff courts in Scotland, and for other purposes. [28th August 1907]

NOTE

[1] As amended by the Sheriff Courts (Scotland) Act 1913 (2 & 3 Geo. V, c. 28). Applied by the Agricultural Holdings (Scotland) Act 1991 (c. 55), s.21(4), (5).

For the interpretation of the terms "sheriff" and "sheriff-substitute" throughout this Act, see now the Sheriff Courts (Scotland) Act 1971 (c. 58), s.4, and the Interpretation Act 1978 (c. 30), Sch.1.

PRELIMINARY

Short title

1. This Act may be cited for all purposes as the Sheriff Courts (Scotland) Act 1907.

2. [Repealed by the Statute Law Revision Act 1927, (c. 42).]

Interpretation

3. In construing this Act (unless where the context is repugnant to such construction)—

(*a*) "Sheriff" includes sheriff-substitute;

(*b*) "Tenant" includes sub-tenant;

(*c*) "Lease" includes sub-lease;

(*d*) "Action" or "cause" includes every civil proceeding competent in the ordinary sheriff court;

(*e*) "Person" includes company, corporation, or association and firm of any description nominate or descriptive, or any Board corporate or unincorporate;

(*f*) "Sheriff-clerk" includes sheriff-clerk depute;

(*g*) "Agent" means a law-agent enrolled in terms of the Law Agents (Scotland) Act 1873;

(*h*) "Final judgment" means an interlocutor which, by itself, or taken along with previous interlocutors, disposes of the subject-matter of the cause, notwithstanding that judgment may not have been pronounced on every question raised, and that the expenses found due may not have been modified, taxed or decerned for;

(*i*) [Repealed by the Sheriff Courts (Scotland) Act 1971 (c. 58), Sch.2.]

(*j*) "Small Debt Acts" means and includes the Small Debt (Scotland) Acts 1887 to 1889, and Acts explaining or amending the same;

(*k*) "Initial writ" means the statement of claim, petition, note of appeal, or other document by which the action is initiated;

(*l*) "Procurator-Fiscal" means procurator-fiscal in the sheriff court;

(*m*) [Repealed by the Statute Law (Repeals) Act 1989 (c. 43), Sch.1, Pt. I.]

(*n*) "Pursuer" means and includes any person making a claim or demand, or seeking any warrant or order competent in the sheriff court;

(*o*) "Defender" means and includes any person who is required to be called in any action;

(*p*) "Summary application" means and includes all applications of a summary nature brought under the common law jurisdiction of the sheriff, and all applications, whether by appeal or otherwise, brought under any Act of Parliament which provides, or, according to any practice in the sheriff court, which allows that the same shall be disposed of in a summary manner, but which does not more particularly define in what form the same shall be heard, tried, and determined;

(q) [Repealed by the Law Reform (Miscellaneous Provisions) (Scotland) Act 1980 (c. 55), Sch.3.]

JURISDICTION

Jurisdiction
[1] **4.** The jurisdiction of the sheriffs, within their respective sheriffdoms, shall extend to and include all navigable rivers, ports, harbours, creeks, shores, and anchoring grounds in or adjoining such sheriffdoms. And the powers and jurisdictions formerly competent to the High Court of Admiralty in Scotland in all maritime causes and proceedings, civil and criminal, including such as may apply to persons furth of Scotland, shall be competent to the sheriffs, provided the defender shall upon any legal ground of jurisdiction be amenable to the jurisdiction of the sheriff before whom such cause or proceeding may be raised, and provided also that it shall not be competent to the sheriff to try any crime committed on the seas which it would not be competent for him to try if the crime had been committed on land: Provided always that where sheriffdoms are separated by a river, firth, or estuary, the sheriffs on either side shall have concurrent jurisdictions over the intervening space occupied by water.

NOTE
[1] Repealed, so far as relating to criminal proceedings, by the Criminal Procedure (Scotland) Act 1975 (c. 21), Sch.10.

Extension of jurisdiction
[1] **5.** Nothing herein contained shall derogate from any jurisdiction, powers, or authority presently possessed or in use to be exercised by the sheriffs of Scotland, and such jurisdiction shall extend to and include—

[2] (1) Actions of declarator (except declarators of marriage or nullity of marriage);

(1A) [Repealed by the Law Reform (Parent and Child) (Scotland) Act 1986 (c. 9), Sch.2.]

[3] (2) Actions for aliment or separation (other than any action mentioned in subsection (2A) below):

[4] (2A) Actions, arising out of an application under section 31(1) of the Maintenance Orders (Reciprocal Enforcement) Act 1972, for the recovery of maintenance:

[5] (2B) Actions for divorce:

(2C) [Repealed by the Children (Scotland) Act 1995 (c. 36), Sch.5.]

(3) Actions of division of commonty and of division or division and sale of common property, in which cases the Act of 1695 concerning the division of commonties shall be read and construed as if it conferred jurisdiction upon the sheriff court in the same manner as upon the Court of Session:

(4) Actions relating to questions of heritable right or title (except actions of adjudication save in so far as now competent and actions of reduction) including all actions of declarator of irritancy and removing, whether at the instance of a superior against a vassal or of a landlord against a tenant:

(5) Suspension of charges or threatened charges upon the decrees of court granted by the sheriff or upon decrees of registration proceeding upon bonds, bills, contracts or other obligations registered in the books of the sheriff court, the books of council and session, or any others competent.

NOTES

[1] Explained (legal aid): see SI 1958/1872, r. 2(2). Excluded by the Land Registration **D 12** (Scotland) Act 1979 (c. 33), ss.21(6) and 22(7). As amended by the Law Reform (Miscellaneous Provisions) (Scotland) Act 1980 (c. 55), s.15(a) and Sch.3, and the Civil Jurisdiction and Judgments Act 1982 (c. 27), Sch.14.

[2] As amended by the Law Reform (Parent and Child) (Scotland) Act 1986 (c. 9), Sch.2.

[3] Substituted by the Family Law (Scotland) Act 1985 (c. 37), Sch.1, para.1. As amended by the Law Reform (Parent and Child) (Scotland) Act 1986 (c. 9), Sch.2. See the Domicile and Matrimonial Proceedings Act 1973 (c. 45), Sch.2.

[4] Inserted by the Domestic Proceedings and Magistrates' Courts Act 1978 (c. 22), Sch.2.

[5] Inserted by the Divorce Jurisdiction, Court Fees and Legal Aid (Scotland) Act 1983 (c. 12), s.1.

Power of sheriff to order sheriff clerk to execute deeds relating to heritage

[1] **5A.**—(1) This section applies where—

(a) an action relating to heritable property is before the sheriff; or

(b) it appears to the sheriff that an order under this section is necessary to implement a decree of a sheriff relating to heritable property.

(2) Where the grantor of any deed relating to the heritable property cannot be found or refuses or is unable or otherwise fails to execute the deed, the sheriff may—

(a) where subsection (1)(a) above applies, on application;

(b) where subsection (1)(b) above applies, on summary application,

by the grantee, make an order dispensing with the execution of the deed by the grantor and directing the sheriff clerk to execute the deed.

(3) Where in pursuance of an order under this section a deed is executed by the sheriff clerk, it shall have the like force and effect as if it had been executed by the grantor.

(4) In this section—

"grantor" means a person who is under an obligation to execute the deed; and

"grantee" means the person to whom that obligation is owed.

NOTE

[1] Inserted by the Law Reform (Miscellaneous Provisions) (Scotland) Act 1985 (c. 73), s.17.

Action competent in sheriff court

[1] **6.** Subject to section 8 of the Domicile and Matrimonial Proceedings Act 1973 and Chapter III of Part I of the Family Law Act 1986 any action competent in the sheriff court may be brought within the jurisdiction of the sheriff—

(a) Where the defender (or when there are several defenders over each of whom a sheriff court has jurisdiction in terms of this Act, where one of them) resides within the jurisdiction, or having resided there for at least forty days has ceased to reside there for less than forty days and has no known residence in Scotland:

(b) Where a defender carries on business, and has a place of business within the jurisdiction, and is cited either personally or at such place of business:

(c) Where the defender is a person not otherwise subject to the jurisdiction of the courts of Scotland, and a ship or vessel of which he is the owner or part owner or master, or goods, debts, money, or other moveable property belonging to him, have been arrested within the jurisdiction:

(d) Where the defender is the owner or part owner or tenant or joint tenant, whether individually or as a trustee of heritable property within the jurisdiction, and the action relates to such property or to his interest therein:

(e) Where the action is for interdict against an alleged wrong being committed or threatened to be committed within the jurisdiction:

D 12/1 (*f*) Where the action relates to a contract the place of execution or performance of which is within the jurisdiction, and the defender is personally cited there:

   (*g*) Where in an action of furthcoming or multiplepoinding the fund or subject *in medio* is situated within the jurisdiction; or the arrestee or holder of the fund is subject to the jurisdiction of the court:

   (*h*) Where the party sued is the pursuer in any action pending within the jurisdiction against the party suing:

  [2] (*i*) Where the action is founded on delict, and the delict forming the cause of action was committed within the jurisdiction:

   (*j*) Where the defender prorogates the jurisdiction of the court.

NOTES

[1] Excluded by the Civil Jurisdiction and Judgments Act 1982, s.20(3). This section ceases to have effect in relation to actions to which s.45 of the Administration of Justice Act 1956 applies; *ibid.* s.45(6).

As amended by the Domicile and Matrimonial Proceedings Act 1973, Sch.4 and by the Family Law Act 1986, Sch.1, para.3.

[2] Substituted by the Law Reform (Jurisdiction in Delict) (Scotland) Act 1971, s.1(2).

Privative jurisdiction in causes under fifteen hundred pounds value

D 13 [1] **7.** All causes not exceeding £1,500 in value exclusive of interest and expenses competent in the sheriff court shall be brought and followed forth in the sheriff court only, and shall not be subject to review by the Court of Session: Provided that nothing herein contained shall affect any right of appeal competent under any Act of Parliament in force for the time being.

NOTE

[1] As amended by the Sheriff Courts (Scotland) Act 1971 (c. 58), Sch.2, SI 1976/900, the Law Reform (Miscellaneous Provisions) (Scotland) Act 1980 (c. 55), Sch.3, and SI 1988/1993.

8. [Repealed by the Sheriff Courts (Scotland) Act 1971 (c. 58), Sch.2.]

9. [Repealed by the Sheriff Courts (Scotland) Act 1913 (c. 28), s.1.]

Privilege not to exempt from jurisdiction

10. No person shall be exempt from the jurisdiction of the sheriff court on account of privilege by reason of being a member of the College of Justice.

SHERIFFS

Appointment of sheriffs and salaried sheriffs-substitute

11. The right of appointing to the salaried offices of sheriff and salaried sheriff-substitute shall be vested in His Majesty, and shall be exercised on the recommendation of the Secretary for Scotland.

12, 13. [Repealed by the Sheriff Courts (Scotland) Act 1971 (c. 58), Sch.2.]

Salaries of sheriffs and sheriffs-substitute

[1] **14.** It shall be lawful to grant to any sheriff or sheriff-substitute such salary as to the Treasury may seem meet, and every such salary shall be paid quarterly or otherwise in every year as the Treasury may determine, and shall be charged upon and be payable out of the Consolidated Fund.

NOTE

[1] As amended by the Sheriffs' Pensions (Scotland) Act 1961 (c. 42), Sch.1.

15, 16. [Repealed by the Sheriff Courts (Scotland) Act 1971 (c. 58), Sch.2.]

Honorary sheriff-substitute

17. The sheriff may by writing under his hand appoint such persons as he thinks proper to hold the office of honorary sheriff-substitute within his sheriffdom during his pleasure, and for whom he shall be answerable. An honorary sheriff-substitute, during the subsistence of his commission, shall be entitled to exercise the powers and duties appertaining to the office of sheriff-substitute. An honorary sheriff-substitute shall hold office, notwithstanding the death, resignation, or removal of the sheriff, until his commission shall be recalled by a succeeding sheriff. In this section "sheriff" does not include sheriff-substitute.

18, 19. [Repealed by the Sheriff Courts (Scotland) Act 1971 (c. 58), Sch.2.]

20. [Repealed by the Sheriffs' Pensions (Scotland) Act 1961 (c. 42), Sch.2.]

21. [Repealed by the Sheriff Courts (Scotland) Act 1971 (c. 58), Sch.2.]

22–24. [Repealed by the Sheriff Courts and Legal Officers (Scotland) Act 1927 (c. 35), Sched.]

25, 26. [Repealed by the Sheriff Courts (Scotland) Act 1971 (c. 58), Sch.2.] **D 14**

APPEALS

Appeal to sheriff

[1] **27.** Subject to the provisions of this Act an appeal to the sheriff shall be competent against all final judgments of the sheriff-substitute and also against interlocutors—

    (a) Granting or refusing interdict, interim or final;
    (b) Granting interim decree for payment of money other than a decree for expenses, or making an order *ad factum praestandum*;
    (c) Sisting an action;
    (d) Allowing or refusing or limiting the mode of proof;
    (e) Refusing a reponing note; or
    (f) Against which the sheriff-substitute either *ex proprio motu* or on the motion of any party grants leave to appeal;

Provided always that notwithstanding the death, resignation, or removal of a sheriff, appeals may be taken from the judgment of the sheriff-substitute, which appeals shall be heard by the succeeding sheriff when he shall enter upon office. It shall be competent for the sheriff, when the action is before him on appeal on any point, to open the record *ex proprio motu* if the record shall appear to him not to have been properly made up, or to allow further proof.

NOTE
[1] As amended by the Law Reform (Miscellaneous Provisions) (Scotland) Act 1980 (c. 55), Sch.3.

Appeal to the Court of Session

[1] **28.**—(1) Subject to the provisions of this Act, it shall be competent to appeal to the Court of Session against a judgment either of a sheriff or of a sheriff-substitute if the interlocutor appealed against is a final judgment; or is an interlocutor—

    (a) Granting interim decree for payment of money other than a decree for expenses; or
    (b) Sisting an action; or
    (c) Refusing a reponing note; or
    (d) Against which the sheriff or sheriff-substitute, either *ex proprio motu* or on the motion of any party, grants leave to appeal.

(2) Nothing in this section nor in section 27 of this Act contained shall affect any right of appeal or exclusion of such right provided by any Act of Parliament in force for the time being.

NOTE
[1] See SI 1949/2062. As amended by the Sheriff Courts (Scotland) Act 1971 (c. 58), Sch.2.

Effect of appeal

29. An appeal shall be effectual to submit to review the whole of the interlocutors pronounced in the cause, and shall be available to and may be insisted in by all other parties in the cause notwithstanding they may not have noted separate appeals. An appeal shall not prevent immediate execution of a warrant of sequestration for rent, or of warrants to take inventories, or place effects in custody *ad interim*, or warrants for interim preservation, and an interim interdict, although appealed against, shall be binding till recalled.

30. [Repealed by the Law Reform (Miscellaneous Provisions) (Scotland) Act 1980 (c. 55), Sch.3.]

D 15   **31.** [Repealed by the Law Reform (Miscellaneous Provisions) (Scotland) Act 1980 (c. 55), s.11 and Sch.3.]

32. [Repealed by the Sheriff Courts (Scotland) Act 1913 (2 & 3 Geo. V, c. 28), s.1.]

33. [Repealed by the Juries Act 1949 (c. 27), Sch.3.]

[1] REMOVINGS

NOTE
[1] The provisions of this Act relating to removings are, in the case of an agricultural holding, subject to the Agricultural Holdings (Scotland) Act 1991 (c. 55), s.21: see subs.(4).

Removings

[1] **34.** Where lands exceeding two acres in extent are held under a probative lease specifying a term of endurance, and whether such lease contains an obligation upon the tenant to remove without warning or not, such lease, or an extract thereof from the books of any court of record shall have the same force and effect as an extract decree of removing obtained in an ordinary action at the instance of the lessor, or any one in his right, against the lessee or any party in possession, and such lease or extract shall along with authority in writing signed by the lessor or any one in his right or by his factor or law agent be sufficient warrant to any sheriff-officer or messenger-at-arms of the sheriffdom within which such lands or heritages are situated to eject such party in possession, his family, sub-tenants, cottars, and dependants, with their goods, gear, and effects, at the expiry of the term or terms of endurance of the lease: Provided that previous notice in writing to remove shall have been given—

    (*a*) When the lease is for three years and upwards not less than one year and not more than two years before the termination of the lease; and

    (*b*) In the case of leases from year to year (including lands occupied by tacit relocation) or for any other period less than three years, not less than six months before the termination of the lease (or where there is a separate ish as regards land and houses or otherwise before that ish which is first in date):

Provided that if such written notice as aforesaid shall not be given the lease shall be held to be renewed by tacit relocation for another year, and thereafter from year to year: Provided further that nothing contained in this section shall affect the right of the landlord to remove a tenant who has been sequestrated under the Bankruptcy (Scotland) Act 1913, or against whom a decree of cessio has been pronounced under the Debtors (Scotland) Act 1880, or who by failure to pay rent has incurred any irritancy of his lease or other liability to removal: Provided further that removal or ejectment in virtue of this section shall not be competent after six weeks from the date of the ish last in date: Provided further that nothing herein contained shall be construed to prevent proceedings under any lease in common form; and that the foregoing provisions as to notice shall not apply to any stipulations in a lease entitling the landlord to resume land for building, planting, feuing, or other purposes or to subjects let for any period less than a year.

NOTE
[1] Reference to the Bankruptcy (Scotland) Act 1913 inserted by virtue of the Interpretation Act 1889 (c. 63), s.38 (1). The 1913 Act was repealed by the Bankruptcy (Scotland) Act 1985 (c. 66): see s.5(1) and Sch.8.

Letter of removal
[1] **35.** Where any tenant in possession of any lands exceeding two acres in extent (whether with or without a written lease) shall, either at the date of entering upon the lease or at any other time, have granted a letter of removal, such letter of removal shall have the same force and effect as an extract decree of removing, and shall be a sufficient warrant for ejection to **D 16** the like effect as is provided in regard to a lease or extract thereof, and shall be operative against the granter of such letter of removal or any party in his right within the same time and in the same manner after the like previous notice to remove: Provided always that where such letter is dated and signed within twelve months before the date of removal or before the first ish, if there be more than one ish, it shall not be necessary that any notice of any kind shall be given by either party to the other.

NOTE
[1] As amended by the Requirements of Writing (Scotland) Act 1995 (c. 7) Sch.5 (effective 1st August 1995: s.15(2)).

Notice to remove
36. Where lands exceeding two acres in extent are occupied by a tenant without any written lease, and the tenant has given to the proprietor or his agent no letter of removal, the lease shall terminate on written notice being given to the tenant by or on behalf of the proprietor, or to the proprietor by or on behalf of the tenant not less than six months before the determination of the tenancy, and such notice shall entitle the proprietor, in the event of the tenant failing to remove, to apply for and obtain a summary warrant of ejection against the tenant and every one deriving right from him.

Notice of termination of tenancy
37. In all cases where houses, with or without land attached, not exceeding two acres in extent, lands not exceeding two acres in extent let without houses, mills, fishings, shootings, and all other heritable subjects (excepting land exceeding two acres in extent) are let for a year or more, notice of termination of tenancy shall be given in writing to the tenant by or on behalf of the proprietor or to the proprietor by or on behalf of the tenant: Provided always that notice under this section shall not warrant summary ejection from the subjects let to a tenant, but such notice, whether given to or by or on behalf of the tenant, shall entitle the proprietor to apply to the sheriff for a warrant for summary ejection in common form against the tenant and every one deriving right from him: Provided further that the notice provided for by this section shall be given at least forty days before the fifteenth day of May when the termination of the tenancy is the term of Whit-sunday, and

at least forty days before the eleventh day of November when the termination of the tenancy is the term of Martinmas.

SUMMARY REMOVINGS

Summary removing
[1] **38.** Where houses or other heritable subjects are let for a shorter period than a year, any person by law authorised may present to the sheriff a summary application for removing, and a decree pronounced in such summary cause shall have the full force and effect of a decree of removing and warrant of ejection. Where such a let is for a period not exceeding four months, notice of removal therefrom shall, in the absence of express stipulation, be given as many days before the ish as shall be equivalent to at least one-third of the full period of the duration of the let; and where the let exceeds four months, notice of removal shall, in the absence of express stipulation, be given at least forty days before the expiry of the said period. Provided that in no case shall notice of removal be given less than twenty-eight days before the date on which it is to take effect.

NOTE
[1] Proviso added by the Rent (Scotland) Act 1971 (c. 28), Sch.18.

Notice of termination in respect of dwelling-houses
[1] **38A.** Any notice of termination of tenancy or notice of removal given under sections 37 and 38 above in respect of a dwelling-house, on or after the date of the coming into operation of section 123 of the Housing Act 1974, shall be in writing and shall contain such information as may be pre-
D 17 scribed by virtue of section 131 of the Rent (Scotland) Act 1971, and Rule 112 of Schedule 1 to this Act shall no longer apply to any such notice under section 37 above.

NOTE
[1] Added by the Housing Act 1974 (c. 44), Sch.13, para.1. For rule 112 read rule 105 of the rules substituted by SI 1983/747, and rule 34.7 of the rules substituted by SI 1993/1956.

Lord Advocate as party to action for divorce
[1] **38B.**—(1) The Lord Advocate may enter appearance as a party in any action for divorce, and he may lead such proof and maintain such pleas as he thinks fit, and the sheriff shall, whenever he considers it necessary for the proper disposal of any such action, direct that the action shall be brought to the notice of the Lord Advocate in order that he may determine whether he should enter appearance therein.

(2) No expenses shall be claimable by or against the Lord Advocate in any action in which he has entered appearance under this section.

NOTE
[1] Inserted by the Court of Session Act 1988 (c. 36), Sch.1, para.2.

38C. [Repealed by the Children (Scotland) Act 1995 (c. 36), Sch.5.]

PROCEDURE RULES

Procedure rules
39. Subject to the provisions of any Act of Parliament in force after the passing of this Act, the procedure in all civil causes shall be conform to the rules of procedure set forth in Schedule 1 hereto annexed. Such rules shall be construed and have effect as part of this Act.

Court of Session to regulate fees, etc.
[1] **40.** The Court of Session may from time to time, by act of sederunt, make such regulations for regulating the fees of officers, shorthand writers,

and others: Provided that every such act of sederunt shall, within one week from the date thereof, be transmitted by the Lord President of the Court of Session to the Secretary of State, in order that it may be laid before the Houses of Parliament; and, if either of the Houses of Parliament shall within 36 days after it has been laid before them resolve that the whole or any part of such act of sederunt ought not to continue in force, the whole or such part thereof as shall be included in such resolution shall from and after the date of the passing of such resolution cease to be binding.

NOTE
[1] As amended by the Secretaries of State Act 1926 (c. 18), s.1(3), the Administration of Justice (Scotland) Act 1933 (c. 41), Sched., the Divorce Jurisdiction, Court Fees and Legal Aid (Scotland) Act 1983 (c. 12), Sch.1, para.7 and Sch.2, and the Law Reform (Miscellaneous Provisions) (Scotland) Act 1990 (c. 40), Sch.9 (effective March 1, 1997: SI 1996/2966). See the Statutory Instruments Act 1946 (c. 36), s.5(2).

41. [Repealed by the Administration of Justice (Scotland) Act 1933 (c. 41), Sch.]

Small Debts Acts

42–48. [Repealed by the Sheriff Courts (Scotland) Act 1971 (c. 58), Sch.2.]

Postal Charge

49. [Repealed by the Execution of Diligence (Scotland) Act 1926 (c. 16), **D 18** s.7.]

Summary Applications

Summary applications
[1] **50.** In summary applications (where a hearing is necessary) the sheriff shall appoint the application to be heard at a diet to be fixed by him, and at that or any subsequent diet (without record of evidence unless the sheriff shall order a record) shall summarily dispose of the matter and give his judgment in writing: Provided that wherever in any Act of Parliament an application is directed to be heard, tried, and determined summarily or in the manner provided by section 52 of the Sheriff Courts (Scotland) Act 1876, such direction shall be read and construed as if it referred to this section of this Act: Provided also that nothing contained in this Act shall affect any right of appeal provided by any Act of Parliament under which a summary application is brought.

NOTE
[1] "Rules 1, 3, 4, 5(3), 10 to 12 and 14 to 19 of the Ordinary Cause Rules shall apply to a summary application in so far as they are not inconsistent with section 50 of the Act of 1907": SI 1983/747, reg.5, as amended by SI 1988/1978. This regulation ceases to have effect in relation to causes commenced on or after January 1, 1994 by virtue of SI 1993/1956. See now SI 1993/3240.

The Poor's Roll

51. [Repealed by the Statute Law (Repeals) Act 1973 (c. 39).]

Repeal

52. [Repealed by the Statute Law Revision Act 1927 (c. 42).]

SCHEDULES

FIRST SCHEDULE

[1] ORDINARY CAUSE RULES 1993

[1] The Ordinary Cause Rules were amended *inter alia* by SI 1996/2445, effective November 1, 1996. The amendments made thereby apply equally to causes commenced before that date: see SI 1996/2586

D 44/31

Chapter 26

Transfer and Remit of Causes

Chapter 27

Caution and Security

D 44/33

Chapter 28

Recovery of Evidence

Chapter 29

Proof

Chapter 30

Decrees, Extracts and Execution

Chapter 31   **D 44/34**

Appeals

Chapter 32

Taxation of Expenses

SPECIAL PROVISIONS IN RELATION TO PARTICULAR CAUSES

Chapter 33

Family Actions

Part I

General Provisions

D 44/35

Part II

Undefended Family Actions

Part III

Defended Family Actions

Part IV

Applications and Orders Relating to Children in Certain Actions

Part V

Orders Relating to Financial Provision

Part XIII

Child Support Act 1991

Part XIV

Referrals to Principal Reporter

Part XV

Management of Money Payable to Children

Chapter 34

Actions Relating to Heritable Property

Part I

Sequestration for Rent

Part II

Removing

Chapter 35

Actions of Multiplepoinding

D 44/38/1

D 44/39   I̲NITIATION̲ ̲AND̲ ̲P̲ROGRESS̲ ̲OF̲ ̲C̲AUSES̲

C̲HAPTER̲ 1

C̲ITATION̲, I̲NTERPRETATION̲, R̲EPRESENTATION̲ ̲AND̲ F̲ORMS̲

Citation
1.1. These Rules may be cited as the Ordinary Cause Rules 1993.

Interpretation
1.2.—(1) In these Rules, unless the context otherwise requires—
"document" has the meaning assigned to it in section 9 of the Civil Evidence (Scotland) Act 1988;
"period of notice" means the period determined under rule 3.6 (period of notice after citation).
(2) For the purposes of these Rules—
(a) "affidavit" includes an affirmation and a statutory or other declaration; and
(b) an affidavit shall be sworn or affirmed before a notary public or any other competent authority.
(3) Where a provision in these Rules requires a party to intimate or send a document to another party, it shall be sufficient compliance with that provision if the document is intimated or sent to the solicitor acting in the cause for that party.
(4) Unless the context otherwise requires, anything done or required to be done under a provision in these Rules by a party may be done by the agent for that party acting on his behalf.
(5) Unless the context otherwise requires, a reference to a specified Chapter, Part, rule or form, is a reference to the Chapter, Part, rule, or form in Appendix 1, so specified in these Rules; and a reference to a specified paragraph, sub-paragraph or head is a reference to that paragraph

of the rule or form, that sub-paragraph of the paragraph or that head of the sub-paragraph, in which the reference occurs.

Representation
    1.3.—(1) Subject to paragraph (2), a party to any proceedings arising solely under the provisions of the Debtors (Scotland) Act 1987 shall be entitled to be represented by a person other than a solicitor or an advocate provided that the sheriff is satisfied that such person is a suitable representative and is duly authorised to represent that party.
    (2) Paragraph (1) shall not apply to an appeal to the Sheriff Principal.

Forms
    1.4. Where there is a reference to the use of a form in these Rules, that form in Appendix 1 or Appendix 2, as the case may be, to these Rules, or a form substantially to the same effect, shall be used with such variation as circumstances may require.

CHAPTER 2

RELIEF FROM COMPLIANCE WITH RULES

Relief from failure to comply with rules
    2.1.—(1) The sheriff may relieve a party from the consequences of failure to comply with a provision in these Rules which is shown to be due to mistake, oversight or other excusable cause, on such conditions as he thinks fit.
    (2) Where the sheriff relieves a party from the consequences of a failure to comply with a provision in these Rules under paragraph (1), he may make such order as he thinks fit to enable the cause to proceed as if the failure to comply with the provision had not occurred.

CHAPTER 3

COMMENCEMENT OF CAUSES

Form of initial writ
    3.1.—[1] (1) A cause shall be commenced—
      (a) in the case of an ordinary cause, by initial writ in Form G1; or
      (b) in the case of a commercial action within the meaning of Chapter 40, by initial writ in Form G1A.
    (2) The initial writ shall be written, typed or printed on A4 size paper of durable quality and **D 44/40** shall not be backed.
    (3) Where the pursuer has reason to believe that an agreement exists prorogating jurisdiction over the subject matter of the cause to another court, the initial writ shall contain details of that agreement.
    (4) Where the pursuer has reason to believe that proceedings are pending before another court involving the same cause of action and between the same parties as those named in the instance of the initial writ, the initial writ shall contain details of those proceedings.
    (5) An article of condescendence shall be included in the initial writ averring—
      (a) the ground of jurisdiction; and
      (b) the facts upon which the ground of jurisdiction is based.
    (6) Where the residence, registered office or place of business, as the case may be, of the defender is not known and cannot reasonably be ascertained, the pursuer shall set out in the instance that the whereabouts of the defender are not known and aver in the condescendence what steps have been taken to ascertain his present whereabouts.
    (7) The initial writ shall be signed by the pursuer or his solicitor (if any) and the name and address of that solicitor shall be stated on the back of every service copy of that writ.

NOTE
  [1] Inserted by the Act of Sederunt (Ordinary Cause Rules) Amendment (Commercial Actions) 2001 (SSI 2001/8) (effective March 1, 2001).

Actions relating to heritable property
    3.2.—(1) In an action relating to heritable property, it shall not be necessary to call as a defender any person by reason only of any interest he may have as the holder of a heritable security over the heritable property.
    (2) Intimation of such an action shall be made to the holder of the heritable security referred to in paragraph (1)—

(a) where the action relates to any heritable right or title; and

(b) in any other case, where the sheriff so orders.

[1] (3) In an action falling within section 1(1)(b) or (c) of the Mortgage Rights (Scotland) Act 2001, the initial writ shall include averments about those persons who appear to the pursuer to be entitled to apply for an order under section 2 of that Act and such persons shall, so far as known to the pursuer, be called as defenders for their interest.

NOTE

[1] Inserted by the Act of Sederunt (Amendment of Ordinary Cause Rules and Summary Applications, Statutory Applications and Appeals etc. Rules) (Applications under the Mortgage Rights (Scotland) Act 2001) 2002 (SSI 2002/7), para.2(2).

Warrants of citation

[1] **3.3.**—(1) The warrant of citation in any cause other than—

(a) a family action within the meaning of rule 33.1(1),

(b) an action of multiplepoinding,

(c) an action in which a time to pay direction under the Debtors (Scotland) Act 1987 may be applied for by the defender,

(d) an action to which rule 3.2(3) applies,

shall be in Form O1.

(2) In a cause in which a time to pay direction under the Debtors (Scotland) Act 1987 may be applied for by the defender, the warrant of citation shall be in Form O2.

(3) In a cause in which a warrant for citation in accordance with Form O2 is appropriate, there shall be served on the defender (with the initial writ and warrant) a notice in Form O3.

(4) In an action to which rule 3.2(3) applies, the warrant of citation shall be in Form O2A.

NOTE

[1] Inserted by the Act of Sederunt (Amendment of Ordinary Cause Rules and Summary Applications, Statutory Applications and Appeals etc. Rules) (Applications under the Mortgage Rights (Scotland) Act 2001) 2002 (SSI 2002/7), para.2(3).

Warrants for arrestment to found jurisdiction

3.4.—(1) Where an application for a warrant for arrestment to found jurisdiction may be made, it shall be made in the crave of the initial writ.

(2) Averments to justify the granting of such a warrant shall be included in the condescendence.

D 44/41 *Warrants and precepts for arrestment on dependence*

3.5.—(1) A copy of—

(a) an initial writ with warrant to cite which includes a warrant to arrest on the dependence,

(b) defences which include, or a minute of amendment which includes, a counterclaim with warrant granted to arrest on the dependence endorsed on that writ,

certified as a true copy by the pursuer or defender, as the case may be, or his solicitor, shall be sufficient warrant to arrest on the dependence if it is otherwise competent to do so.

[1] (2) A precept of arrestment may be issued by the sheriff on production to him of—

(a) an initial writ containing a crave for payment of money on which a warrant of citation has been issued;

(b) defences which include, or a minute of amendment which includes, a counterclaim containing a crave for payment of money; or

(c) a document of liquid debt.

[1] (3) Averments to justify the granting of a warrant to arrest on the dependence, or a precept of arrestment, shall be included in the condescendence of an initial writ or the statement of claim in a counterclaim.

NOTE

[1] As amended by the Act of Sederunt (Ordinary Cause, Summary Application and Small Claim Rules) Amendment (Miscellaneous) 2004 (SSI 2004/197) (effective May 21, 2004), para.2(2).

Period of notice after citation

3.6.—(1) Subject to rule 5.6(1) (service where address of person is not known) and to paragraph (2) of this rule, a cause shall proceed after one of the following periods of notice has been given to the defender:—

(a) where the defender is resident or has a place of business within Europe, 21 days after the date of execution of service; or

(b) where the defender is resident or has a place of business outside Europe, 42 days after the date of execution of service.

(2) Subject to paragraph (3), the sheriff may, on cause shown, shorten or extend the period of notice on such conditions as to the method or manner of service as he thinks fit.

(3) A period of notice may not be reduced to a period of less than 2 days.

(4) Where a period of notice expires on a Saturday, Sunday, or public or court holiday, the period of notice shall be deemed to expire on the next day on which the sheriff clerk's office is open for civil court business.

CHAPTER 4

CAVEATS

Orders against which caveats may be lodged
4.1. A person may lodge a caveat against—
(a) an interim interdict sought in an action before he has lodged a notice of intention to defend; or

(b) an interim order (other than an order under section 1 of the Administration of Justice (Scotland) Act 1972 (orders for inspection of documents and other property, etc.)) sought before the expiry of the period within which he could lodge a notice of intention to defend.

Form, lodging and renewal of caveats
4.2.—(1) A caveat shall be in Form G2 and shall be lodged with the sheriff clerk.

(2) A caveat shall remain in force for a period of one year from the date on which it was lodged and may be renewed on its expiry for a further period of one year and yearly thereafter.

(3) Where a caveat has been lodged and has not expired, no order in respect of which the caveat was lodged may be pronounced unless the sheriff is satisfied that all reasonable steps have been taken to afford the person lodging the caveat an opportunity of being heard; and the sheriff may continue the hearing on such an order until he is satisfied that such steps have been taken.

CHAPTER 5

CITATION, SERVICE AND INTIMATION

Signature of warrants
5.1.—[1](1) Subject to paragraph (2), a warrant for citation, or intimation may be signed by the sheriff or sheriff clerk.

(2) The following warrants shall be signed by the sheriff:— **D 44/42**
(a) a warrant containing an order shortening or extending the period of notice or any other order other than a warrant which the sheriff clerk may sign;
[1] (b) a warrant for arrestment to found jurisdiction;
[1] (ba) a warrant for arrestment on the dependence;
(c) a warrant for intimation ordered under rule 33.8 (intimation where improper association).

(3) Where the sheriff clerk refuses to sign a warrant which he may sign, the party presenting the initial writ may apply to the sheriff for the warrant.

NOTE
[1] Inserted by the Act of Sederunt (Ordinary Cause, Summary Application and Small Claim Rules) Amendment (Miscellaneous) 2004 (SSI 2004/197) (effective May 21, 2004), para.2(3).

Form of citation and certificate
[1] **5.2.**—(1) Subject to rule 5.6 (service where address of person is not known), in any cause other than—
(a) a family action within the meaning of rule 33.1(1),
(b) an action of multiplepoinding,
(c) an action in which a time to pay direction under the Debtors (Scotland) Act 1987 may be applied for by the defender, or
(d) an action to which rule 3.2(3) applies,
citation by any person shall be in Form O4 which shall be attached to a copy of the initial writ

and warrant of citation and shall have appended to it a notice of intention to defend in Form O7.

(2) In a cause in which a time to pay direction under the Debtors (Scotland) Act 1987 may be applied for by the defender, citation shall be in Form O5 which shall be attached to a copy of the initial writ and warrant of citation and shall have appended to it a notice of intention to defend in Form O7.

(2A) In an action to which rule 3.2(3) applies, citation shall be in Form O5A which shall be attached to a copy of the initial writ and warrant of citation and shall have appended to it a notice of intention to defend in Form O7.

(3) The certificate of citation in any cause other than a family action within the meaning of rule 33.1(1) or an action of multiplepoinding shall be in Form O6 which shall be attached to the initial writ.

(4) Where citation is by a sheriff officer, one witness shall be sufficient for the execution of citation.

(5) Where citation is by a sheriff officer, the certificate of citation shall be signed by the sheriff officer and the witness and shall state—
  (a) the method of citation; and
  (b) where the method of citation was other than personal or postal citation, the full name and designation of any person to whom the citation was delivered.

(6) Where citation is executed under paragraph (3) of rule 5.4 (depositing or affixing by sheriff officer), the certificate shall include a statement—
  (a) of the method of service previously attempted;
  (b) of the circumstances which prevented such service being executed; and
  (c) that a copy was sent in accordance with the provisions of paragraph (4) of that rule.

NOTE
[1] As amended by SI 1996/2445 (effective November 1, 1996) (clerical error) and further amended by the Act of Sederunt (Amendment of Ordinary Cause Rules and Summary Applications, Statutory Applications and Appeals etc. Rules) (Applications under the Mortgage Rights (Scotland) Act 2001) 2002 (SSI 2002/7), para.2(4).

Postal service or intimation
5.3.—(1) In any cause in which service or intimation of any document or citation of any person may be by recorded delivery, such service, intimation or citation shall be by the first class recorded delivery service.

(2) Notwithstanding the terms of section 4(2) of the Citation Amendment (Scotland) Act 1882 (time from which period of notice reckoned), where service or intimation is by post, the period of notice shall run from the beginning of the day after the date of posting.

(3) On the face of the envelope used for postal service or intimation under this rule there shall be written or printed the following notice:—
  "This envelope contains a citation to or intimation from (*specify the court*). If delivery cannot be made at the address shown it is to be returned immediately to:— The Sheriff Clerk (*insert address of sheriff clerk's office*)".

D 44/42/1

(4) The certificate of citation or intimation in the case of postal service shall have attached to it any relevant postal receipts.

Service within Scotland by sheriff officer
5.4.—(1) An initial writ, decree, charge, warrant or any other order or writ following upon such initial writ or decree served by a sheriff officer on any person shall be served—
  (a) personally; or
  (b) by being left in the hands of a resident at the person's dwelling place or an employee at his place of business.

(2) Where service is executed under paragraph (1)(b), the certificate of citation or service shall contain the full name and designation of any person in whose hands the initial writ, decree, charge, warrant or other order or writ, as the case may be, was left.

(3) Where a sheriff officer has been unsuccessful in executing service in accordance with paragraph (1), he may, after making diligent enquiries, serve the document in question—
  (a) by depositing it in that person's dwelling place or place of business; or
  (b) by affixing it to the door of that person's dwelling place or place of business.

(4) Subject to rule 6.1 (service of schedule of arrestment), where service is executed under paragraph (3), the sheriff officer shall, as soon as possible after such service, send a letter containing a copy of the document by ordinary first class post to the address at which he thinks it most likely that the person on whom service has been executed may be found.

[1] (5) Where the firm which employs the sheriff officer has in its possession—
  (a) the document or a copy of it certified as correct by the pursuer's solicitor, the sheriff

officer may serve the document upon the defender without having the document or certified copy in his possession, in which case he shall if required to do so by the person on whom service is executed and within a reasonable time of being so required, show the document or certified copy to the person; or

(b) a certified copy of the interlocutor pronounced allowing service of the document, the sheriff officer may serve the document without having in his possession the certified copy interlocutor if he has in his possession a facsimile copy of the certified copy interlocutor (which he shall show, if required, to the person on whom service is executed).

NOTE

[1] Inserted by the Act of Sederunt (Ordinary Cause, Summary Application, Summary Cause and Small Claim Rules) Amendment (Miscellaneous) 2003 (SSI 2003/26), para.2(3) (effective January 24, 2003).

Service on persons furth of Scotland

[1] **5.5.**—(1) Subject to the following provisions of this rule, an initial writ, decree, charge, warrant or any other order or writ following upon such initial writ or decree on a person furth of Scotland shall be served—

(a) at a known residence or place of business in England, Wales, Northern Ireland, the Isle of Man, the Channel Islands or any country with which the United Kingdom does not have a convention providing for service of writs in that country—

   (i) in accordance with the rules for personal service under the domestic law of the **D 44/43** place in which service is to be executed; or

   (ii) by posting in Scotland a copy of the document in question in a registered letter addressed to the person at his residence or place of business;

[2] (b) in a country which is a party to the Hague Convention on the Service Abroad of Judicial and Extra-Judicial Documents in Civil and Commercial Matters dated 15th November 1965 or the Convention in Schedule 1 or 3C to the Civil Jurisdiction and Judgments Act 1982—

   (i) by a method prescribed by the internal law of the country where service is to be executed for the service of documents in domestic actions upon persons who are within its territory;

   (ii) by or through the central, or other appropriate, authority in the country where service is to be executed at the request of the Secretary of State for Foreign and Commonwealth Affairs;

   (iii) by or through a British Consular Office in the country where service is to be executed at the request of the Secretary of State for Foreign and Commonwealth Affairs;

   (iv) where the law of the country in which the person resides permits, by posting in Scotland a copy of the document in a registered letter addressed to the person at his residence; or

   (v) where the law of the country in which service is to be executed permits, service by an huissier, other judicial officer or competent official of the country where service is to be executed; or

(c) in a country with which the United Kingdom has a convention on the service of writs in that country other than the conventions mentioned in sub-paragraph (b), by one of the methods approved in the relevant convention.

[3] (1A) In a country to which the Council Regulation applies, service—

(a) may be effected by the methods prescribed in paragraph (1)(b)(ii) and (iii) only in exceptional circumstances; and

(b) is effected only if the receiving agency has informed the person that acceptance of service may be refused on the ground that the document has not been translated in accordance with paragraph (6).

(2) Any document which requires to be posted in Scotland for the purposes of this rule shall be posted by a solicitor or a sheriff officer; and on the face of the envelope there shall be written or printed the notice set out in rule 5.3(3).

(3) In the case of service by a method referred to in paragraph (1)(b)(ii) and (iii), the pursuer shall—

(a) send a copy of the writ and warrant for service with citation attached, or other document, as the case may be, with a request for service by the method indicated in the request to the Secretary of State for Foreign and Commonwealth Affairs; and

(b) lodge in process a certificate signed by the authority which executed service stating that it has been, and the manner in which it was, served.

(4) In the case of service by a method referred to in paragraph (1)(b)(v), the pursuer or the sheriff officer, shall—

    (a) send a copy of the writ and warrant for service with citation attached, or other document, as the case may be, with a request for service by the method indicated in the request to the official in the country in which service is to be executed; and

    (b) lodge in process a certificate of the official who executed service stating that it has been, and the method in which it was, served.

(5) Where service is executed in accordance with paragraph (1)(a)(i) or (1)(b)(i) other than on another party in the United Kingdom, the Isle of Man or the Channel Islands, the party executing service shall lodge a certificate by a person who is conversant with the law of the country concerned and who practises or has practised law in that country or is a duly accredited representative of the Government of that country, stating that the method of service employed is in accordance with the law of the place where service was executed.

(6) Every writ, document, citation or notice on the face of the envelope mentioned in rule 5.3(3) shall be accompanied by a translation in

    [3] (a) an official language of the country in which service is to be executed; or

    (b) in a country to which the Council Regulation applies, a language of the member state of transmission that is understood by the person on whom service is being executed.

(7) A translation referred to in paragraph (6) shall be certified as correct by the person making it; and the certificate shall—

    (a) include his full name, address and qualifications; and

    (b) be lodged with the execution of citation or service.

    [3] (8) In this rule "the Council Regulation" means Council Regulation (EC) No. 1348/2000 on **D 44/44** the service in the Member States of judicial and extrajudicial documents in civil or commercial matters.

NOTE

[1] As amended by SI 1996/2445 (effective November 1, 1996) and the Act of Sederunt (Ordinary Cause, Summary Application, Summary Cause and Small Claim Rules) Amendment (Miscellaneous) 2003 (SSI 2003/26), para.2(4) (effective January 24, 2003).

[2] As amended by the Act of Sederunt (Ordinary Cause, Summary Application and Small Claim Rules) Amendment (Miscellaneous) 2004 (SSI 2004/197) (effective May 21, 2004), para.2(4).

[3] Inserted by the Act of Sederunt (Ordinary Cause, Summary Application and Small Claim Rules) Amendment (Miscellaneous) 2004 (SSI 2004/197) (effective May 21, 2004), para.2(4).

Service where address of person is not known

5.6.—(1) Where the address of a person to be cited or served with a document is not known and cannot reasonably be ascertained, the sheriff shall grant warrant for citation or service upon that person—

    (a) by the publication of an advertisement in Form G3 in a specified newspaper circulating in the area of the last known address of that person, or

    (b) by displaying on the walls of court a copy of the instance and crave of the initial writ, warrant of citation and a notice in Form G4;

and the period of notice fixed by the sheriff shall run from the date of publication of the advertisement or display on the walls of court, as the case may be.

(2) Where service requires to be executed under paragraph (1), the pursuer shall lodge a service copy of the initial writ and a copy of any warrant of citation with the sheriff clerk from whom they may be uplifted by the person for whom they are intended.

(3) Where a person has been cited or served in accordance with paragraph (1) and, after the cause has commenced, his address becomes known, the sheriff may allow the initial writ to be amended subject to such conditions as to re-service, intimation, expenses, or transfer of the cause as he thinks fit.

(4) Where advertisement in a newspaper is required for the purpose of citation or service under this rule, a copy of the newspaper containing the advertisement shall be lodged with the sheriff clerk by the pursuer.

(5) Where display on the walls of court is required under paragraph (1)(b), the pursuer shall supply to the sheriff clerk for that purpose a certified copy of the instance and crave of the initial writ and any warrant of citation.

Persons carrying on business under trading or descriptive name

[1] **5.7.**—(1) A person carrying on a business under a trading or descriptive name may sue or be sued in such trading or descriptive name alone; and an extract—

    (a) of a decree pronounced in the sheriff court, or

    (b) of a decree proceeding upon any deed, decree arbitral, bond, protest of a bill,

promissory note or banker's note or upon any other obligation or document on which execution may proceed, recorded in the sheriff court books,
against such person under such trading or descriptive name shall be a valid warrant for diligence against such person.

(2) An initial writ, decree, charge, warrant or any other order or writ following upon such initial writ or decree in a cause in which a person carrying on business under a trading or descriptive name sues or is sued in that name may be served—

(a) at any place of business or office at which such business is carried on within the sheriffdom of the sheriff court in which the cause is brought; or

(b) where there is no place of business within that sheriffdom, at any place where such business is carried on (including the place of business or office of the clerk or secretary of any company, corporation or association or firm).

NOTE
[1] As amended by SI 1996/2445 (effective November 1, 1996).

Endorsation unnecessary
5.8. An initial writ, decree, charge, warrant or any other order or writ following upon such initial writ or decree may be served, enforced or otherwise lawfully executed anywhere in Scotland without endorsation by a sheriff clerk; and, if executed by a sheriff officer, may be so executed by a sheriff officer of the court which granted it or by a sheriff officer of the sheriff court district in which it is to be executed.

Re-service   **D 44/45**
5.9. Where it appears to the sheriff that there has been any failure or irregularity in citation or service on a person, he may order the pursuer to re-serve the initial writ on such conditions as he thinks fit.

No objection to regularity of citation, service or intimation
5.10.—(1) A person who appears in a cause shall not be entitled to state any objection to the regularity of the execution of citation, service or intimation on him; and his appearance shall remedy any defect in such citation, service or intimation.

(2) Nothing in paragraph (1) shall preclude a party from pleading that the court has no jurisdiction.

CHAPTER 6

ARRESTMENT

Service of schedule of arrestment
[1] **6.1** If a schedule of arrestment has not been personally served on an arrestee, the arrestment shall have effect only if a copy of the schedule is also sent by registered post or the first class recorded delivery service to—

(a) the last known place of residence of the arrestee, or

(b) if such place of residence is not known, or if the arrestee is a firm or corporation, to the arrestee's principal place of business if known, or, if not known, to any known place of business of the arrestee;
and the sheriff officer shall, on the certificate of execution, certify that this has been done and specify the address to which the copy of the schedule was sent.

Arrestment on dependence before service   **D 44/46**
6.2.—(1) An arrestment on the dependence of a cause used before service shall cease to have effect unless—

(a) the initial writ is served within 20 days from the date of arrestment; and

(b) in the case of an undefended cause, decree in absence has been pronounced within 20 days after the expiry of the period of notice.

(2) After such an arrestment has been executed, the party who executed it shall forthwith report the execution to the sheriff clerk.

Movement of arrested property   **D 44/46/1**
6.3.—(1) Any person having an interest may apply by motion for a warrant authorising the movement of a vessel or cargo which are the subject of an arrestment to found jurisdiction or on the dependence of a cause.

(2) Where the court grants a warrant sought under paragraph (1), it may make such further order as it thinks fit to give effect to that warrant.

D 44/46/2

CHAPTER 7

UNDEFENDED CAUSES

Application of this Chapter
7.1. This Chapter applies to any cause other than an action in which the sheriff may not grant decree without evidence.

Minute for granting of decree without attendance
7.2.—(1) Subject to the following paragraphs, where the defender—
(a) does not lodge a notice of intention to defend,
(b) does not lodge an application for a time to pay direction under the Debtors (Scotland) Act 1987,
(c) has lodged such an application for a time to pay direction and the pursuer does not object to the application or to any recall or restriction of an arrestment sought in the application,
the sheriff may, on the pursuer endorsing a minute for decree on the initial writ, at any time after the expiry of the period for lodging that notice or application, grant decree in absence or other order in terms of the minute so endorsed without requiring the attendance of the pursuer in court.
(2) The sheriff shall not grant decree under paragraph (1)—
(a) unless it appears *ex facie* of the initial writ that a ground of jurisdiction exists under the Civil Jurisdiction and Judgments Act 1982; and
(b) the cause is not a cause—
(i) in which decree may not be granted without evidence;
(ii) to which paragraph (4) applies; or
¹ (iii) to which rule 33.31 (procedure in undefended family action for a section 11 order) applies.
(3) Where a defender is domiciled in another part of the United Kingdom or in another Contracting State, the sheriff shall not grant decree in absence until it has been shown that the defender has been able to receive the initial writ in sufficient time to arrange for his defence or that all necessary steps have been taken to that end; and for the purposes of this paragraph—
(a) the question whether a person is domiciled in another part of the United Kingdom shall be determined in accordance with sections 41 and 42 of the Civil Jurisdiction and Judgments Act 1982;
(b) the question whether a person is domiciled in another Contracting State shall be determined in accordance with Article 52 of the Convention in Schedule 1 or 3C to that Act; and
(c) the term "Contracting State" has the meaning assigned in section 1 of that Act.
(4) Where an initial writ has been served in a country to which the Hague Convention on the Service Abroad of Judicial and Extra-Judicial Documents in Civil or Commercial Matters dated 15th November 1965 applies, decree shall not be granted until it is established to the satisfaction of the sheriff that the requirements of Article 15 of that Convention have been complied with.

NOTE
¹ As amended by SI 1996/2167 (effective November 1, 1996) and SI 1996/2445 (effective November 1, 1996).

D 44/46/3 *Applications for time to pay directions in undefended causes*
7.3.—(1) This rule applies to a cause in which a time to pay direction may be applied for under the Debtors (Scotland) Act 1987.
(2) A defender in a cause which is otherwise undefended, who wishes to apply for a time to pay direction, and where appropriate, to have an arrestment recalled or restricted, shall complete and lodge with the sheriff clerk the appropriate part of Form O3 before the expiry of the period of notice.
(3) Where the pursuer does not object to the application of the defender made in accordance with paragraph (2), he shall minute for decree in accordance with rule 7.2; and the sheriff may grant decree or other order in terms of the application and minute.
(4) Where the pursuer objects to the application of the defender made in accordance with paragraph (2), he shall minute for decree in accordance with rule 7.2; and the sheriff clerk shall

thereafter fix a hearing on the application of the defender and intimate the hearing to the pursuer and defender.

(5) The sheriff may determine an application in which a hearing has been fixed under paragraph (4) whether or not any of the parties appear.

Decree for expenses
7.4. On granting decree in absence or thereafter, the sheriff may grant decree for expenses.

Finality of decree in absence
[1] **7.5.** Subject to section 9(7) of the Land Tenure Reform (Scotland) Act 1974 (decree in action of removing for breach of condition of long lease to be final when extract recorded in Register of Sasines), a decree in absence which has not been recalled or brought under review by suspension or by reduction shall become final and shall have effect as a decree *in foro contentioso*—

(a) on the expiry of six months from the date of the decree or from the date of a charge made under it, as the case may be, where the service of the initial writ or of the charge has been personal; and

(b) in any event, on the expiry of 20 years from the date of the decree.

NOTE
[1] As amended by SI 1996/2445 (effective November 1, 1996).

Amendment of initial writ
7.6.—(1) In an undefended cause, the sheriff may—

(a) allow the pursuer to amend the initial writ in any way permitted by rule 18.2 (powers of sheriff to allow amendment); and

(b) order the amended initial writ to be re-served on the defender on such period of notice as he thinks fit.

(2) The defender shall not be liable for the expense occasioned by any such amendment unless the sheriff so orders.

(3) Where an amendment has been allowed under paragraph (1), the amendment—

(a) shall not validate diligence used on the dependence of a cause so as to prejudice the rights of creditors of the party against whom the diligence has been executed who are interested in defeating such diligence; and

(b) shall preclude any objection to such diligence stated by a party or any person by virtue of a title acquired or in right of a debt contracted by him subsequent to the execution of such diligence.

Disapplication of certain rules
[1] **7.7** The following rules in Chapter 15 (motions) shall not apply to an action in which no notice of intention to defend has been lodged or to any action in so far as it proceeds as undefended—

rule 15.2 (intimation of motions),
rule 15.3 (opposition to motions),
rule 15.5 (hearing of motions).

NOTE
[1] Inserted by SI 1996/2445 (effective November 1, 1996).

CHAPTER 8

REPONING

D 44/46/4

Reponing
8.1.—(1) In any cause other than—

(a) a cause mentioned in rule 33.1(1)(a) to (h), (certain family actions), or

(b) a cause to which Chapter 37 (causes under the Presumption of Death (Scotland) Act 1977) applies,

the defender or any party with a statutory title or interest may apply to be reponed by lodging with the sheriff clerk, before implement in full of a decree in absence, a reponing note setting out his proposed defence or the proposed order or direction and explaining his failure to appear.

(2) A copy of the note lodged under paragraph (1) shall be served on the pursuer and any other party—

(3) The sheriff may, on considering the reponing note, recall the decree so far as not

D 44/47

implemented subject to such order as to expenses as he thinks fit; and the cause shall thereafter proceed as if—

    (a) the defender had lodged a notice of intention to defend and the period of notice had expired on the date on which the decree in absence was recalled; or

[2] (b) the party seeking the order or direction had lodged the appropriate application on the date when the decree was recalled.

(4) A reponing note, when duly lodged with the sheriff clerk and served upon the pursuer, shall have effect to sist diligence.

[1] (4A) Where an initial writ has been served on a defender furth of the United Kingdom under rule 5.5(1)(b) (service on persons furth of Scotland) and decree in absence has been pronounced against him as a result of his failure to enter appearance, the court may, on the defender applying to be reponed in accordance with paragraph (1) above, recall the decree and allow defences to be received if—

    (a) without fault on his part, he did not have knowledge of the initial writ in sufficient time to defend;

    (b) he has disclosed a prima facie defence to the action on the merits; and

    (c) the reponing note is lodged within a reasonable time after he had knowledge of the decree or in any event before the expiry of one year from the date of decree.

(5) Any interlocutor or order recalling, or incidental to the recall of, a decree in absence shall be final and not subject to appeal.

NOTE

  [1] Inserted by SSI 2000/239 (effective October 2, 2000).

  [2] Inserted by the Act of Sederunt (Ordinary Cause, Summary Application and Small Claim Rules) Amendment (Miscellaneous) 2004 (SSI 2004/197) (effective May 21, 2004), para.2(5).

CHAPTER 9

STANDARD PROCEDURE IN DEFENDED CAUSES

Notice of intention to defend

  9.1.—[1] (1) Subject to rules 33.34 (notice of intention to defend and defences in family action) and 35.8 (lodging of notice of appearance in action of multiplepoinding), where the defender intends to—

    (a) challenge the jurisdiction of the court,

    (b) state a defence, or

    (c) make a counterclaim,

he shall, before the expiry of the period of notice, lodge with the sheriff clerk a notice of intention to defend in Form O7 and, at the same time, send a copy to the pursuer.

(2) The lodging of a notice of intention to defend shall not imply acceptance of the jurisdiction of the court.

[2] (3) This Chapter shall not apply to a commercial action within the meaning of Chapter 40.

NOTE

  [1] As amended by the Act of Sederunt (Family Proceedings in the Sheriff Court) 1996 (SI 1996/2167) (effective November 1, 2000).

  [2] Inserted by the Act of Sederunt (Ordinary Cause Rules) Amendment (Commercial Actions) 2001 (SSI 2001/8) (effective March 1, 2001).

Fixing date for Options Hearing

  9.2.—[1] (1) Subject to paragraph (1A), on the lodging of a notice of intention to defend, the sheriff clerk shall fix a date and time for an Options Hearing which date shall be on the first suitable court day occurring not sooner than 10 weeks after the expiry of the period of notice.

[2] (1A) Where in a family action—

    (i) the only matters in dispute are an order in terms of section 11 of the Children (Scotland) Act 1995 (court orders relating to parental responsibilities etc.); or

    (ii) the matters in dispute include an order in terms of section 11 of that Act,

there shall be no requirement to fix an Options Hearing in terms of paragraph (1) above insofar as the matters in dispute relate to an order in terms of section 11(2) of the Children (Scotland) Act 1995.

(1B) In paragraph (1A) above, "family action" has the meaning given to it in rule 33.1(1).

(2) On fixing the date for the Options Hearing, the sheriff clerk shall—

    (a) forthwith intimate to the parties in Form G5—

      (i) the last date for lodging defences;

    (ii) the last date for adjustment; and

    (iii) the date of the Options Hearing; and

  (b) prepare and sign an interlocutor recording those dates.

[3] (3) The fixing of the date for the Options Hearing shall not affect the right of a party to make any incidental application to the court.

NOTE

[1] As amended by the Act of Sederunt (Sheriff Court Ordinary Cause Rules Amendment) (Miscellaneous) 2000 (SSI 2000/239) (effective October 2, 2000).

[2] Added by the Act of Sederunt (Sheriff Court Ordinary Cause Rules Amendment) (Miscellaneous) 2000 (SSI 2000/239) (effective October 2, 2000).

[3] As amended by the Act of Sederunt (Sheriff Court Ordinary Cause Rules Amendment) (Miscellaneous) 1996 (SI 1996/2445) (effective November 1, 1996).

Second or subsequent Options Hearing

[1] **9.2A.**—(1) Where for any reason a second or subsequent Options Hearing requires to be fixed and an Options Hearing has already been fixed but has not yet taken place, the sheriff shall fix a second or subsequent Options Hearing and discharge that earlier hearing.

  (2) The sheriff clerk shall forthwith intimate to all parties—

    (a) that the original Options Hearing has been discharged;

    (b) the last date for lodging defences, if appropriate;

    (c) the last date for adjustment; and

    (d) the date and time fixed for the second or subsequent Options Hearing.

  (3) Any reference in these Rules to an Options Hearing or a continuation of it shall include a reference to a second or subsequent Options Hearing ordered under this rule.

NOTE

[1] Inserted by the Act of Sederunt (Sheriff Court Ordinary Cause Rules Amendment) (Miscellaneous) 1996 (SI 1996/2445) (effective November 1, 1996).

Return of initial writ

9.3. Subject to rule 9.4 (lodging of pleadings before Options Hearing), the pursuer shall return the initial writ, unbacked and unfolded, to the sheriff clerk within 7 days after the expiry of the period of notice.

Lodging of pleadings before Options Hearing

9.4. Where any hearing, whether by motion or otherwise, is fixed before the Options Hearing, each party shall lodge in process a copy of his pleadings, or, where the pleadings have been adjusted, the pleadings as adjusted, not later than 2 days before the hearing.

Process folder

9.5.—(1) On receipt of the notice of intention to defend, the sheriff clerk shall prepare a process folder which shall include—

    (a) interlocutor sheets;

    (b) duplicate interlocutor sheets;

    (c) a production file;

    (d) a motion file; and

    (e) an inventory of process.

  (2) Any production or part of process lodged in a cause shall be placed in the process folder.

Defences

9.6.—(1) Where a notice of intention to defend has been lodged, the defender shall (subject to paragraph (3)) lodge defences within 14 days after the expiry of the period of notice.

  (2) Subject to rule 19.1(3) (form of defences where counterclaim included), defences shall be in the form of answers in numbered paragraphs corresponding to the articles of the condescendence, and shall have appended a note of the pleas-in-law of the defender.

[1] (3) In a family action (within the meaning of rule 33.1(1)), neither a crave nor averments need be made in the defences which relate to any order under section 11 of the Children (Scotland) Act 1995. **D 44/49**

NOTE

[1] Inserted by the Act of Sederunt (Family Proceedings in the Sheriff Court) 1996 (SI 1996/2167) (effective November 1, 2000)

Implied admissions

9.7. Every statement of fact made by a party shall be answered by every other party, and if such a statement by one party within the knowledge of another party is not denied by that other party, that other party shall be deemed to have admitted that statement of fact.

Adjustment of pleadings

9.8.—(1) Parties may adjust their pleadings until 14 days before the date of the Options Hearing or any continuation of it.

(2) Any adjustments shall be exchanged between parties and not lodged in process.

(3) Parties shall be responsible for maintaining a record of adjustments made during the period for adjustment.

(4) No adjustments shall be permitted after the period mentioned in paragraph (1) except with leave of the sheriff.

Effect of sist on adjustment

9.9.—(1) Where a cause has been sisted, any period for adjustment before the sist shall be reckoned as a part of the period for adjustment.

(2) On recall of the sist of a cause, the sheriff clerk shall—
  (a) fix a new date for the Options Hearing;
  (b) prepare and sign an interlocutor recording that date; and
  (c) intimate that date to each party.

Open record

9.10. The sheriff may, at any time before the closing of the record in a cause to which this Chapter applies, of his own motion or on the motion of a party, order any party to lodge a copy of the pleadings in the form of an open record containing any adjustments and amendments made as at the date of the order.

Record for Options Hearing

9.11.—(1) The pursuer shall, at the end of the period for adjustment referred to in rule 9.8(1), and before the Options Hearing, make a copy of the pleadings and any adjustments and amendments in the form of a record.

(2) Not later than 2 days before the Options Hearing, the pursuer shall lodge a certified copy of the record in process.

[1] (3) Where the Options Hearing is continued under rule 9.12(5), and further adjustment or amendment is made to the pleadings, a copy of the pleadings as adjusted or amended, certified by the pursuer, shall be lodged in process not later than 2 days before the Options Hearing so continued.

NOTE
[1] Inserted by SI 1996/2445 (effective November 1, 1996).

Options Hearing

9.12.—(1) At the Options Hearing the sheriff shall seek to secure the expeditious progress of the cause by ascertaining from parties the matters in dispute and information about any other matter referred to in paragraph (3).

(2) It shall be the duty of parties to provide the sheriff with sufficient information to enable him to conduct the hearing as provided for in this rule.

(3) At the Options Hearing the sheriff shall, except where the cause is ordered to proceed under the procedure in Chapter 10 (additional procedure), close the record and—
  (a) appoint the cause to a proof and make such orders as to the extent of proof, the lodging of a joint minute of admissions or agreement, or such other matter as he thinks fit;
  (b) after having heard parties and considered any note lodged under rule 22.1 (note of basis of preliminary plea), appoint the cause to a proof before answer and make such orders as to the extent of proof, the lodging of a joint minute of admissions or agreement, or such other matter as he thinks fit; or
  [1] (c) after having heard parties and considered any note lodged under rule 22.1, appoint the cause to debate if satisfied that there is a preliminary matter of law which if established following debate would lead to decree in favour of any party, or to limitation of proof to any substantial degree.

(4) At the Options Hearing the sheriff may, having heard parties—
  (a) of his own motion or on the motion of any party, and
  (b) on being satisfied that the difficulty or complexity of the cause makes it unsuitable for the procedure under this Chapter,

order that the cause proceed under the procedure in Chapter 10 (additional procedure).

(5) The sheriff may, on cause shown, of his own motion or on the motion of any party, allow a continuation of the Options Hearing on one occasion only for a period not exceeding 28 days or to the first suitable court day thereafter.

(6) On closing the record—

    (a) where there are no adjustments made since the lodging of the record under rule 9.11(2), that record shall become the closed record; and

    (b) where there are such adjustments, the sheriff may order that a closed record including such adjustments be lodged within 7 days after the date of the interlocutor closing the record.

(7) For the purposes of rules 16.2 (decrees where party in default) and 33.37 (decree by default in family action), an Options Hearing shall be a diet in accordance with those rules.

NOTE

[1] As amended by the Act of Sederunt (Ordinary Cause, Summary Application and Small Claim Rules) Amendment (Miscellaneous) 2004 (SSI 2004/197) (effective May 21, 2004), para.2(5).

Rules 9.13.–9.15. are omitted by the Act of Sederunt (Ordinary Cause, Summary Application and Small Claim Rules) Amendment (Miscellaneous) 2004 (SSI 2004/197) (effective May 21, 2004), para.2(5).

[1] CHAPTER 9A

DOCUMENTS AND WITNESSES

Application of this Chapter
9A.1. This Chapter applies to any cause proceeding under Chapters 9 and 10.

Inspection and recovery of documents
9A.2.—(1) Each party shall, within 14 days after the date of the interlocutor allowing proof or proof before answer, intimate to every other party a list of the documents, which are or have been in his possession or control and which he intends to use or put in evidence at the proof, including the whereabouts of those documents.

(2) A party who has received a list of documents from another party under paragraph (1) may inspect those documents which are in the possession or control of the party intimating the list at a time and place fixed by that party which is reasonable to both parties.

(3) A party who seeks to use or put in evidence at a proof a document not on his list intimated under paragraph (1) shall, if any other party objects to such document being used or put in evidence, seek leave of the sheriff to do so; and such leave may be granted on such conditions, if any, as the sheriff thinks fit.

(4) Nothing in this rule shall affect—

    (a) the law relating, or the right of a party to object, to the inspection of a document on the ground of privilege or confidentiality; or

    (b) the right of a party to apply under rule 28.2 for a commission and diligence for recovery of documents or an order under section 1 of the Administration of Justice (Scotland) Act 1972.

Exchange of lists of witnesses
9A.3.—(1) Within 28 days after the date of the interlocutor allowing a proof or proof before answer, each party shall—

    (a) intimate to every other party a list of witnesses, including any skilled witnesses, on whose evidence he intends to rely at proof; and

    (b) lodge a copy of that list in process.

(2) A party who seeks to rely on the evidence of a person not on his list intimated under paragraph (1) shall, if any other party objects to such evidence being admitted, seek leave of the sheriff to admit that evidence whether it is to be given orally or not; and such leave may be granted on such conditions, if any, as the sheriff thinks fit.

(3) The list of witnesses intimated under paragraph (1) shall include the name, occupation (where known) and address of each intended witness.

Applications in respect of time to pay directions, and arrestments   **D 44/50/1**
9A.4. An application for a time to pay direction under section 1(1) of the Debtors (Scotland) Act 1987, or for the recall or restriction of an arrestment under section 2(3) or 3(1) of that Act, in a cause which is defended, shall be made by motion lodged before the sheriff grants decree.

NOTE
[1] Inserted by the Act of Sederunt (Ordinary Cause, Summary Application and Small Claim Rules) Amendment (Miscellaneous) 2004 (SSI 2004/197) (effective May 21, 2004), para.2(8).

CHAPTER 10

ADDITIONAL PROCEDURE

Additional period for adjustment
10.1.—(1) Where, under rule 9.12(4) (order at Options Hearing to proceed under Chapter 10), the sheriff orders that a cause shall proceed in accordance with the procedure in this Chapter, he shall continue the cause for adjustment for a period of 8 weeks.

(2) Paragraphs (2) and (3) of rule 9.8 (exchange and record of adjustments) shall apply to a cause in which a period for adjustment under paragraph (1) of this rule has been allowed as they apply to the period for adjustment under that rule.

Effect of sist on adjustment period
10.2. Where a cause has been sisted, any period for adjustment before the sist shall be reckoned as part of the period for adjustment.

Variation of adjustment period
10.3.—(1) At any time before the expiry of the period for adjustment the sheriff may close the record if parties, of consent or jointly, lodge a motion seeking such an order.

(2) The sheriff may, if satisfied that there is sufficient reason for doing so, extend the period for adjustment for such period as he thinks fit, if any party—
(a) lodges a motion seeking such an order; and
(b) lodges a copy of the record adjusted to the date of lodging of the motion.

(3) A motion lodged under paragraph (2) shall set out—
(a) the reasons for seeking an extension of the period for adjustment; and
(b) the period for adjustment sought.

Order for open record
10.4. The sheriff may, at any time before the closing of the record in a cause to which this Chapter applies, of his own motion or on the motion of a party, order any party to lodge a copy of the pleadings in the form of an open record containing any adjustments and amendments made as at the date of the order.

Closing record
10.5.—(1) On the expiry of the period for adjustment, the record shall be closed and, without the attendance of parties, the sheriff clerk shall forthwith—
(a) prepare and sign an interlocutor recording the closing of the record and fixing the date of the Procedural Hearing under rule 10.6, which date shall be on the first suitable court day occurring not sooner than 21 days after the closing of the record; and
(b) intimate the date of the hearing to each party.

(2) The pursuer shall, within 14 days after the date of the interlocutor closing the record, lodge a certified copy of the closed record in process.

(3) The closed record shall contain only the pleadings of the parties.

Procedural Hearing
10.6.—(1) At the Procedural Hearing, the sheriff shall seek to secure the expeditious progress of the cause by ascertaining from parties the matters in dispute and information about any other matter referred to in paragraph (3).

(2) It shall be the duty of parties to provide the sheriff with sufficient information to enable him to conduct the hearing as provided for in this rule.

D 44/51   (3) At the Procedural Hearing the sheriff shall—
(a) appoint the cause to a proof and make such orders as to the extent of proof, the lodging of a joint minute of admissions or agreement, or such other matter as he thinks fit;
(b) after having heard the parties and considered any note lodged under rule 22.1 (note of basis of preliminary plea), appoint the cause to a proof before answer and make such orders as to the extent of proof, the lodging of a joint minute of admissions or agreement, or such other matter as he thinks fit; or
[1] (c) after having heard parties and considered any note lodged under rule 22.1, appoint the cause to a debate if satisfied that there is a preliminary matter of law which if

established following debate would lead to decree in favour of any party, or to limitation of proof to any substantial degree.

(4) For the purposes of rule 33.37 (decree by default in family action), a Procedural Hearing shall be a diet in accordance with that rule.

NOTE

[1] As amended by the Act of Sederunt (Ordinary Cause, Summary Application and Small Claim Rules) Amendment (Miscellaneous) 2004 (SSI 2004/197) (effective May 21, 2004), para.2(9).

CHAPTER 11

THE PROCESS

Form and lodging of parts of process
11.1. All parts of process shall be written, typed or printed on A4 size paper of durable quality and shall be lodged, unbacked and unfolded, with the sheriff clerk.

Custody of process
11.2.—(1) The initial writ, and all other parts of process lodged in a cause, shall be placed by the sheriff clerk in the process folder.

(2) The initial writ, interlocutor sheets, borrowing receipts and the process folder shall remain in the custody of the sheriff clerk.

(3) The sheriff clerk may, on cause shown, authorise the initial writ to be borrowed by the pursuer, his solicitor or the solicitor's authorised clerk.

Borrowing and returning of process
11.3.—(1) Subject to paragraph (3), a process, or any part of a process which may be borrowed, may be borrowed only by a solicitor or by his authorised clerk.

(2) All remedies competent to enforce the return of a borrowed process may proceed on the warrant of the court from the custody of which the process was obtained.

(3) A party litigant—
    (a) may borrow a process only—
        (i) with leave of the sheriff; and
        (ii) subject to such conditions as the sheriff may impose; or
    (b) may inspect a process and obtain copies, where practicable, from the sheriff clerk.

(4) The sheriff may, on the motion of any party, ordain any other party who has borrowed a part of process to return it within such time as the sheriff thinks fit.

Failure to return parts of process
11.4.—(1) Where a solicitor or party litigant has borrowed any part of process and fails to return it for any diet or hearing at which it is required, the sheriff may impose on such solicitor or party litigant a fine not exceeding £50, which shall be payable to the sheriff clerk; but an order imposing a fine may, on cause shown, be recalled by the sheriff.

(2) An order made under this rule shall not be subject to appeal.

Replacement of lost documents
11.5. Where any part of process is lost or destroyed, a copy of it, authenticated in such manner as the sheriff thinks fit, may be substituted for and shall, for the purposes of the cause to which the process relates, be treated as having the same force and effect as the original.

Intimation of parts of process and adjustments
[1] **11.6.**—(1) After a notice of intention to defend has been lodged, any party lodging a part of process or making an adjustment to his pleadings shall, at the same time, intimate such lodging or adjustment to every other party who has entered the process by delivering to every other party a copy of each part of process or adjustment, including, where practicable, copies of any documentary production.

(2) Unless otherwise provided in these Rules, the party required to give intimation under paragraph (1) shall deliver to every other party who has entered the process a copy of the part of **D 44/52** process or adjustment or other document, as the case may be, by—
    (a) any of the methods of service provided for in Chapter 5 (citation, service and intimation); or
    (b) where intimation is to a party represented by a solicitor—
        (i) personal delivery,

    (ii) facsimile transmission,
    (iii) first class ordinary post,
    (iv) delivery to a document exchange,
  to that solicitor.
  (3) Subject to paragraph (4), where intimation is given under—
    (a) paragraph (2)(b)(i) or (ii), it shall be deemed to have been given—
        (i) on the day of transmission or delivery where it is given before 5.00 p.m. on any day; or
        (ii) on the day after transmission or delivery where it is given after 5.00 p.m. on any day; or
    (b) paragraph (2)(b)(iii) or (iv), it shall be deemed to have been given on the day after posting or delivery.
  (4) Where intimation is given or, but for this paragraph, would be deemed to be given on a Saturday, Sunday or public or court holiday, it shall be deemed to have been given on the next day on which the sheriff clerk's office is open for civil court business.

NOTE
[1] As amended by SI 1996/2445 (effective November 1, 1996).

Retention and disposal of parts of process by sheriff clerk
  11.7.—(1) Where any cause has been finally determined and the period for marking an appeal has expired without an appeal having been marked, the sheriff clerk shall—
    (a) retain—
        (i) the initial writ;
        (ii) any closed record;
        (iii) the interlocutor sheets;
        (iv) any joint minute;
        (v) any offer and acceptance of tender;
        (vi) any report from a person of skill;
        (vii) any affidavit; and
        (viii) any extended shorthand notes of the proof; and
    (b) dispose of all other parts of process (except productions) in such a manner as seems appropriate.
  (2) Where an appeal has been marked on the final determination of the cause, the sheriff clerk shall exercise his duties mentioned in paragraph (1) after the final disposal of the appeal and any subsequent procedure.

Uplifting of productions from process
  11.8.—(1) Each party who has lodged productions in a cause shall—
    (a) within 14 days after the final determination of the cause, where no subsequent appeal has been marked, or
    (b) within 14 days after the disposal of any appeal marked on the final determination of the cause,
uplift the productions from process.
  (2) Where any production has not been uplifted as required by paragraph (1), the sheriff clerk shall intimate to—
    (a) the solicitor who lodged the production, or
    (b) where no solicitor is acting, the party himself or such other party as seems appropriate,
that if he fails to uplift the production within 28 days after the date of such intimation, it will be disposed of in such a manner as the sheriff directs.

CHAPTER 12

INTERLOCUTORS

Signature of interlocutors by sheriff clerk
  12.1. In accordance with any directions given by the Sheriff Principal, any interlocutor other than a final interlocutor may be written and signed by the sheriff clerk and—
    (a) any interlocutor written and signed by a sheriff clerk shall be treated for all purposes as if it had been written and signed by the sheriff; and
    (b) any extract of such an interlocutor shall not be invalid by reason only of its being written and signed by a sheriff clerk.

Further provisions in relation to interlocutors

12.2.—(1) The sheriff may sign an interlocutor when furth of his sheriffdom.

(2) At any time before extract, the sheriff may correct any clerical or incidental error in an interlocutor or note attached to it.

[1] (3) In any cause, other than a family action within the meaning of rule 33.1(1) which has proceeded as undefended, where at any stage evidence has been led, the sheriff shall—

(a) in the interlocutor, make findings in fact and law; and

(b) append to that interlocutor a note setting out the reasons for his decision.

[1] (4) In any other interlocutor, the sheriff may, and shall when requested by a party, append a note setting out the reasons for his decision.

(5) Where the sheriff reserves his decision and gives his decision at a date later than the date of the hearing outwith the presence of the parties—

(a) the date of the interlocutor of the sheriff shall be the date on which it is received by the sheriff clerk; and

(b) the sheriff clerk shall—

(i) enter that date in the interlocutor; and

(ii) forthwith send a copy of the interlocutor and any note attached to it free of charge to each party.

NOTE

[1] Substituted by SI 1996/2445 (effective November 1, 1996).

CHAPTER 13

PARTY MINUTER PROCEDURE

Person claiming title and interest to enter process as defender

13.1.—(1) A person who has not been called as a defender or third party may apply by minute for leave to enter a process as a party minuter and to lodge defences.

(2) A minute under paragraph (1) shall specify—

(a) the applicant's title and interest to enter the process; and

(b) the grounds of the defence he proposes to state.

(3) Subject to paragraph (4), after hearing the applicant and any party, the sheriff may—

(a) if he is satisfied that the applicant has shown title and interest to enter the process, grant the applicant leave to enter the process as a party minuter and to lodge defences; and

(b) make such order as to expenses or otherwise as he thinks fit.

(4) Where an application under paragraph (1) is made after the closing of the record, the sheriff shall only grant leave under paragraph (3) if he is satisfied as to the reason why earlier application was not made.

Procedure following leave to enter process

13.2.—[1] (1) Where a party minuter lodges answers, the sheriff clerk shall fix a date and time under rule 9.2 for a hearing under rule 9.12 (Options Hearing) as if the party minuter had lodged a notice of intention to defend and the period of notice had expired on the date for lodging defences.

(2) At the Options Hearing, or at any time thereafter, the sheriff may grant such decree or other order as he thinks fit.

(3) A decree or other order against the party minuter shall have effect and be extractable in the same way as a decree or other order against a defender.

NOTE

[1] As amended by SI 1996/2445 (effective November 1, 1996).

CHAPTER 14

D 44/54

APPLICATIONS BY MINUTE

Application of this Chapter

14.1.—(1) Where an application may be made by minute, the form of the minute and the procedure to be adopted shall, unless otherwise provided in these Rules, be in accordance with this Chapter.

[1] (2) This Chapter shall not apply to—

(a) a minute of amendment;

(b) a minute of abandonment; or

(c) a joint minute.

NOTE

[1] As amended by SI 1996/2445 (effective November 1, 1996).

Form of minute
  14.2. A minute to which this Chapter applies shall contain—
    (a) a crave;
    (b) where appropriate, a condescendence in the form of a statement of facts supporting the crave; and
    (c) where appropriate, pleas-in-law.

Lodging of minutes
  [1] **14.3.**—(1) Before intimating any minute, the minuter shall lodge the minute in process.
  (2) On the lodging of a minute, and any document under rule 21.1(1)(b) (lodging documents founded on or adopted), the sheriff—
    (a) may make an order for answers to be lodged;
    (b) may order intimation of the minute without making an order for answers; or
    (c) where he considers it appropriate for the expeditious disposal of the minute or for any other specified reason, may fix a hearing.
  (3) Any answers ordered to be lodged under paragraph (2)(a) shall, unless otherwise ordered by the sheriff, be lodged within 14 days after the date of intimation of the minute.
  (4) Where the sheriff fixes a hearing under paragraph (2)(c), the interlocutor fixing that hearing shall specify whether—
    (a) answers are to be lodged;
    (b) the sheriff will hear evidence at that hearing; and
    (c) the sheriff will allow evidence by affidavit.
  (5) Any answers or affidavit evidence ordered to be lodged under paragraph (4) shall be lodged within such time as shall be specified in the interlocutor of the sheriff.
  (6) The following rules shall not apply to any hearing fixed under paragraph (2)(c):—
    rule 14.7 (opposition where no order for answers made),
    rule 14.8 (hearing of minutes where no opposition or no answers lodged),
    rule 14.10 (notice of opposition or answers lodged).
D 44/55 (7) The sheriff clerk shall forthwith return the minute to the minuter with any interlocutor pronounced by the sheriff.

NOTE

[1] Substituted by SI 1996/2445 (effective November 1, 1996).

Intimation of minutes
  [1] **14.4.**—(1) The party lodging a minute shall, on receipt from the sheriff clerk of the minute, intimate to every other party including any person referred to in rule 14.13(1)—
    (a) a notice in Form G7A, G7B or G7C, as the case may be, by any of the methods provided for in rule 14.5 (methods of intimation); and
    (b) a copy of—
      (i) the minute;
      (ii) any interlocutor; and
      (iii) any document referred to in the minute.
  (2) The sheriff may, on cause shown, dispense with intimation.

NOTE

[1] Inserted by SI 1996/2445 (effective November 1, 1996).

Methods of intimation
  [1] **14.5.**—(1) Intimation of a minute may be given by—
    (a) any of the methods of service provided for in Chapter 5 (citation, service and intimation); or
    (b) where intimation is to a party represented by a solicitor, by—
      (i) personal delivery,
      (ii) facsimile transmission,
      (iii) first class ordinary post, or
      (iv) delivery to a document exchange,
      to that solicitor.

(2) Where intimation is given—
    (a) under paragraph (1)(b)(i) or (ii), it shall be deemed to have been given—
        (i) on the day of transmission or delivery where it is given before 5.00 p.m. on any day; or
        (ii) on the day after transmission or delivery where it is given after 5.00 p.m. on any day; or
    (b) under paragraph 1(b)(iii) or (iv), it shall be deemed to have been given on the day after the date of posting or delivery.

NOTE
  [1] Inserted by SI 1996/2445 (effective November 1, 1996).

Return of minute with evidence of intimation
  [1] **14.6.** Where intimation of any minute has been given, the minute and a certificate of intimation in Form G8 shall be returned to the sheriff clerk within 5 days after the date of intimation.

NOTE
  [1] Inserted by SI 1996/2445 (effective November 1, 1996).

Opposition where no order for answers made
  [1] **14.7.**—(1) Where a party seeks to oppose a minute lodged under rule 14.3 (lodging of minutes) in which no order for answers has been made under paragraph (2)(a) of that rule, that party shall, within 14 days after the date of intimation of the minute to him—
    (a) complete a notice of opposition in Form G9;
    (b) lodge the notice with the sheriff clerk; and
    (c) intimate a copy of that notice to every other party.

D 44/56

  (2) Rule 14.5 (methods of intimation) and rule 14.6 (return of minute with evidence of intimation) shall apply to intimation of opposition to a minute under paragraph (1)(c) of this rule as they apply to intimation of a minute.
  (3) The sheriff may, on cause shown, reduce or dispense with the period for lodging the notice mentioned in paragraph (1)(b).

NOTE
  [1] Inserted by SI 1996/2445 (effective November 1, 1996).

Hearing of minutes where no opposition or no answers lodged
  [1] **14.8.**—(1) Where no notice of opposition is lodged or where no answers have been lodged to the minute within the time allowed, the minute shall be determined by the sheriff in chambers without the attendance of parties, unless the sheriff otherwise directs.
  (2) Where the sheriff requires to hear a party on a minute, the sheriff clerk shall—
    (a) fix a date, time and place for the party to be heard; and
    (b) inform that party—
        (i) of that date, time and place; and
        (ii) of the reasons for the sheriff wishing to hear him.

NOTE
  [1] Inserted by SI 1996/2445 (effective November 1, 1996).

Intimation of interlocutor
  [1] **14.9.** Where a minute has been determined in accordance with rule 14.8 (hearing of minutes where no opposition or no answers lodged), the sheriff clerk shall intimate the interlocutor determining that minute to the parties forthwith.

NOTE
  [1] Inserted by SI 1996/2445 (effective November 1, 1996).

Notice of opposition or answers lodged
  [1] **14.10.**—(1) Where a notice of opposition has, or answers have, been lodged to the minute, the sheriff clerk shall—
    (a) assign a date, time and place for a hearing on the first suitable court day after the date of the lodging of the notice of opposition or answers, as the case may be; and
    (b) intimate that date, time and place to the parties.
  (2) The interlocutor fixing a hearing under paragraph (1) shall specify whether the sheriff will hear evidence at the hearing or receive evidence by affidavit.

NOTE
　[1] Inserted by SI 1996/2445 (effective November 1, 1996).

Procedure for hearing
　[1] **14.11.**—(1) A certified copy of the interlocutor assigning a hearing under this Chapter and

D 44/57 requiring evidence to be led shall be sufficient warrant to a sheriff officer to cite a witness on behalf of a party.

　(2) At the hearing, the sheriff shall hear parties on the minute and any answers lodged, and may determine the minute or may appoint such further procedure as he considers necessary.

NOTE
　[1] Inserted by SI 1996/2445 (effective November 1, 1996).

Consent to minute
　[1] **14.12.** Subject to paragraph (2) of rule 14.8 (hearing of minutes where no opposition or no answers lodged), where all parties to the action indicate to the sheriff, by endorsement of the minute or otherwise in writing, their intention to consent to the minute, the sheriff may forthwith determine the minute in chambers without the appearance of parties.

NOTE
　[1] Inserted by SI 1996/2445 (effective November 1, 1996).

Procedure following grant of minute
　[1] **14.13.**—(1) Where the minute includes a crave seeking leave—
　　(a)　for a person—
　　　　(i)　to be sisted as a party to the action, or
　　　　(ii)　to appear in the proceedings, or
　　(b)　for the cause to be transferred against the representatives of a party who has died or is under a legal incapacity,
the sheriff, on granting the minute, may order a hearing under rule 9.12 (Options Hearing) to be fixed or may appoint such further procedure as he thinks fit.
　(2) Where an Options Hearing is ordered under paragraph (1), the sheriff clerk shall—
　　(a)　fix a date and time for such hearing, which date, unless the sheriff otherwise directs, shall be on the first suitable court day occurring not sooner than 10 weeks after the date of the interlocutor of the sheriff ordering such hearing be fixed;
　　(b)　forthwith intimate to the parties in Form G5—
　　　　(i)　where appropriate, the last date for lodging defences;
　　　　(ii)　where appropriate, the last date for adjustment; and
　　　　(iii)　the date of the Options Hearing; and
　　(c)　prepare and sign an interlocutor recording those dates.
　(3) For the purpose of fixing the date for the Options Hearing referred to in paragraph (1), the date of granting the minute shall be deemed to be the date of expiry of the period of notice.

NOTE
　[1] Inserted by SI 1996/2445 (effective November 1, 1996).

[1] Chapter 15

NOTE
　[1] Substituted by SI 1996/2445 (effective November 1, 1996).

Motions

Lodging of motions
　15.1.—(1) A motion may be made—
　　(a)　orally with leave of the court during any hearing of a cause; or
　　(b)　by lodging a written motion in Form G6.
　(2) Subject to paragraph (3), a written motion shall be lodged with the sheriff clerk within 5 days after the date of intimation of the motion required by rule 15.2 (intimation of motions) with—
　　(a)　a certificate of intimation in Form G8; and
　　(b)　so far as practicable any document referred to in the written motion and not already lodged in process.

(3) Where the period for lodging opposition to the motion is varied under rule 15.2(4) (variation of and dispensing with period of intimation) to a period of 5 days or less, the written motion and certificate to be lodged in terms of paragraph (2) shall be lodged no later than the **D 44/58** day on which the period for lodging opposition expires.

Intimation of motions

15.2.—(1) Subject to paragraphs (4) and (7), a party intending to lodge a motion in accordance with rule 15.1(1)(b) (lodging written motion) shall intimate the motion in Form G7, and a copy of any document referred to in the motion, to every other party.

(2) Intimation of a motion may be given by—
- (a) any of the methods of service provided for in Chapter 5 (citation, service and intimation); or
- (b) where intimation is to a party represented by a solicitor, by—
  - (i) personal delivery,
  - (ii) facsimile transmission,
  - (iii) first class ordinary post, or
  - (iv) delivery to a document exchange,

  to that solicitor.

(3) Where intimation is given—
- (a) under paragraph (2)(b)(i) or (ii), it shall be deemed to have been given—
  - (i) on the day of transmission or delivery where it is given before 5.00 p.m. on any day; or
  - (ii) on the day after transmission or delivery where it is given after 5.00 p.m. on any day; or
- (b) under paragraph (2)(b)(iii) or (iv), it shall be deemed to have been given on the day after posting or delivery.

(4) The sheriff may, on the application of a party intending to lodge a written motion, vary the period of 7 days specified in rule 15.3(1)(c) for lodging opposition to the motion or dispense with intimation.

(5) An application under paragraph (4) shall be made in the written motion, giving reasons for such variation or dispensation.

(6) Where the sheriff varies the period within which notice of opposition is to be lodged under rule 15.3(1)(c), the form of intimation required under rule 15.2(1) (intimation of motion in Form G7) shall state the date by which such notice requires to be lodged.

(7) A joint motion by all parties lodged in Form G6 need not be intimated.

Opposition to motions **D 44/59**

15.3.—(1) Where a party seeks to oppose a motion made in accordance with rule 15.1(1)(b) (written motion), he shall—
- (a) complete a notice of opposition in Form G9;
- (b) intimate a copy of that notice to every other party; and
- (c) lodge the notice with the sheriff clerk within 7 days after the date of intimation of the motion or such other period as the sheriff may have determined under rule 15.2(6).

(2) Paragraphs (2) and (3) of rule 15.2 (methods and time of intimation of motions) shall apply to the intimation of opposition to a motion under paragraph (1)(b) of this rule as they apply to intimation under that rule.

Consent to motions

15.4. Where a party consents to a written motion, he shall endorse the motion, or give notice to the sheriff clerk in writing, of his consent.

Hearing of motions

15.5.—(1) Subject to paragraph (2), where no notice of opposition is lodged with the sheriff clerk within the period specified in rule 15.3(1)(c), or ordered by virtue of rule 15.2(4), the motion shall be determined by the sheriff in chambers without the appearance of parties, unless the sheriff otherwise directs.

(2) In accordance with any directions given by the sheriff principal, the sheriff clerk may determine any motion other than a motion which seeks a final interlocutor.

(3) Where the sheriff clerk considers that a motion dealt with by him under paragraph (2) should not be granted, he shall refer that motion to the sheriff who shall deal with it in accordance with paragraph (1).

(4) Where the sheriff requires to hear a party on a motion which is not opposed, the sheriff clerk shall—
- (a) fix a date, time and place for the party to be heard, and
- (b) inform that party—

(i) of that date, time and place; and

(ii) of the reasons for the sheriff wishing to hear him.

(5) Where a notice of opposition is lodged in accordance with rule 15.3(1), the sheriff clerk shall—

(a) assign a date, time and place, on the first suitable court day after the lodging of the notice of opposition, for the motion to be heard; and

(b) intimate that date, time and place to the parties.

(6) Where a motion has been determined under paragraph (1) or (2), the sheriff clerk shall intimate the interlocutor determining that motion to all parties forthwith.

(7) Where the sheriff, under paragraph (4) of rule 15.2, dispenses with intimation required by paragraph (1) of that rule, he shall make such order as he thinks fit for intimation of his determination of the motion to every party to the action in respect of whom intimation has been so dispensed with.

(8) Subject to paragraph (4), where all parties consent to a written motion, the sheriff may determine the motion in chambers without the appearance of parties.

(9) Subject to paragraph (4) where a joint motion of all parties in Form G6 is lodged with the sheriff clerk, the sheriff may determine the motion in chambers without the appearance of parties.

D 44/60 *Motions to sist*

[1] **15.6.**—(1) Where a motion to sist is made, either orally or in writing in accordance with rule 15.1(1)(a) or (b)—

(a) the reason for the sist shall be stated by the party seeking the sist; and

(b) that reason shall be recorded in the interlocutor.

(2) Where a cause has been sisted, the sheriff may, after giving parties an opportunity to be heard, recall the sist.

NOTE

[1] Inserted by SSI 2000/239 (effective October 2, 2000).

CHAPTER 16

DECREES BY DEFAULT

Application of this Chapter

[1] **16.1.** This Chapter applies to any cause other than—

(a) an action to which rule 33.37 (decree by default in family action) applies;

(b) an action of multiplepoinding;

(c) a cause under the Presumption of Death (Scotland) Act 1977; or

(d) a commercial action within the meaning of Chapter 40.

NOTE

[1] As amended by SSI 2001/8 (effective March 1, 2001).

Decrees where party in default

16.2.—(1) In a cause to which this Chapter applies, where a party fails—

(a) to lodge, or intimate the lodging of, any production or part of process within the period required under a provision in these Rules or an order of the sheriff,

(b) to implement an order of the sheriff within a specified period, or

(c) to appear or be represented at any diet,

that party shall be in default.

(2) Where a party is in default, the sheriff may grant decree as craved, decree of absolvitor or dismiss the cause, as the case may be, with expenses.

(3) Where no party appears at a diet, the sheriff may dismiss the cause.

(4) In this rule, "diet" includes—

(a) a hearing under rule 9.12 (Options Hearing);

(b) a hearing under rule 10.6 (Procedural Hearing);

(c) a proof or proof before answer; and

(d) a debate.

Prorogation of time where party in default

16.3. In an action to which this Chapter applies, the sheriff may, on cause shown, prorogate the time for lodging any production or part of process or for giving intimation or for implementing any order.

SUMMARY DECREES

Application of this Chapter
17.1. This Chapter applies to any action other than—
(a) a family action within the meaning of rule 33.1(1);
(b) an action of multiplepoinding; or
(c) an action under the Presumption of Death (Scotland) Act 1977.

Applications for summary decree
17.2.—(1) Subject to paragraphs (2) to (5) of this rule, a pursuer may, at any time after a defender has lodged defences, apply by motion for summary decree against that defender on the ground that there is no defence to the action, or part of it, disclosed in the defences.
(2) In applying for summary decree, the pursuer may move the sheriff—
(a) to grant decree in terms of all or any of the craves of the initial writ;
(b) to pronounce an interlocutor sustaining or repelling a plea-in-law; or
(c) to dispose of the whole or part of the subject-matter of the cause. **D 44/62**
(3) *[Repealed by SSI 2000/239 (effective October 2, 2000).]*
(4) On a motion under paragraph (1), the sheriff may—
(a) if satisfied that there is no defence to the action or to any part of it to which the motion relates, grant the motion for summary decree in whole or in part, as the case may be; or
(b) ordain any party, or a partner, director, officer or office-bearer of, any party—
(i) to produce any relevant document or article; or
(ii) to lodge an affidavit in support of any assertion of fact made in the pleadings or at the hearing of the motion.
(5) Notwithstanding the refusal of all or part of a motion for summary decree, a subsequent motion may be made where there has been a change of circumstances.

Application of summary decree to counterclaims, etc.
17.3.—(1) Where a defender has lodged a counterclaim—
(a) he may apply by motion for summary decree against the pursuer on that counterclaim on the ground that there is no defence to the counterclaim, or a part of it, disclosed in the answers to it; and
(b) paragraphs (2) to (5) of rule 17.2 shall, with the necessary modifications, apply to a motion by a defender under this paragraph as they apply to a motion by a pursuer under paragraph (1) of that rule.
(2) Where a defender or third party has made a claim against another defender or third party who has lodged defences or answers, as the case may be—
(a) he may apply by motion for summary decree against that other defender or third party on the ground that there is no defence to his claim, or a part of it, disclosed in the defences or answers, as the case may be; and
(b) paragraphs (2) to (5) of rule 17.2 shall, with the necessary modifications, apply to a motion by a defender or third party under this paragraph as they apply to a motion by a pursuer under paragraph (1) of that rule.

CHAPTER 18 **D 44/62/1**

AMENDMENT OF PLEADINGS

Alteration of sum sued for
18.1.—[1] (1) In a cause in which all other parties have lodged defences or answers, the pursuer may, before the closing of the record, alter any sum sued for by amending the crave of the initial writ, and any record.
(2) The pursuer shall forthwith intimate any such amendment in writing to every other party.

NOTE
[1] As amended by SI 1996/2445 (effective November 1, 1996).

Powers of sheriff to allow amendment **D 44/62/2**
18.2.—(1) The sheriff may, at any time before final judgment, allow an amendment mentioned in paragraph (2).
(2) Paragraph (1) applies to the following amendments:—
(a) an amendment of the initial writ which may be necessary for the purpose of

determining the real question in controversy between the parties, notwithstanding that in consequence of such amendment—

    (i) the sum sued for is increased or restricted after the closing of the record; or

    (ii) a different remedy from that originally craved is sought;

(b) an amendment which may be necessary—

    (i) to correct or supplement the designation of a party to the cause;

    (ii) to enable a party who has sued or has been sued in his own right to sue or be sued in a representative capacity;

    (iii) to enable a party who has sued or has been sued in a representative capacity to sue or be sued in his own right or in a different representative capacity;

    (iv) to add the name of an additional pursuer or person whose concurrence is necessary;

    (v) where the cause has been commenced or presented in the name of the wrong person, or it is doubtful whether it has been commenced or presented in the name of the right person, to allow any other person to be sisted in substitution for, or in addition to, the original person; or

    (vi) to direct a crave against a third party brought into an action under Chapter 20 (third party procedure);

(c) an amendment of a condescendence, defences, answers, pleas-in-law or other pleadings which may be necessary for determining the real question in controversy between the parties; and

(d) where it appears that all parties having an interest have not been called or that the cause has been directed against the wrong person, an amendment inserting in the initial writ an additional or substitute party and directing existing or additional craves, averments and pleas-in-law against that party.

D 44/62/4 *Applications to amend*

    18.3.—(1) A party seeking to amend shall lodge a minute of amendment in process setting out his proposed amendment and, at the same time, lodge a motion—

    (a) to allow the minute of amendment to be received; and

    (b) to allow—

      (i) amendment in terms of the minute of amendment and, where appropriate, to grant an order under rule 18.5(1)(a) (service of amendment for additional or substitute party); or

      (ii) where the minute of amendment may require to be answered, any other person to lodge answers within a specified period.

    (2) Where the sheriff has pronounced an interlocutor allowing a minute of amendment to be received and answered, he may allow a period of adjustment of the minute of amendment and answers and, on so doing, shall fix a date for parties to be heard on the minute of amendment and answers as adjusted.

    [1] (3) Any adjustment to any minute of amendment or answers shall be exchanged between parties and not lodged in process.

    [1] (4) Parties shall be responsible for maintaining a record of adjustment made and the date of their intimation.

    [1] (5) No adjustments shall be permitted after the period of adjustment allowed, except with leave of the sheriff.

    [1] (6) Each party shall, no later than 2 days before the hearing fixed in terms of paragraph (2), lodge in process a copy of their minute of amendment or answers with all adjustments made thereto in italic or bold type, or underlined.

NOTE

    [1] Inserted by SSI 2000/239 (effective October 2, 2000).

D 44/62/5 *Applications for diligence on amendment*

    18.4.—(1) Where a minute of amendment is lodged by a pursuer under rule 18.2(2)(d) (all parties not, or wrong person, called), he may apply by motion for warrant to use any form of diligence which could be used on the dependence of a separate action.

    (2) A copy certified by the sheriff clerk of the interlocutor granting warrant for diligence on the dependence applied for under paragraph (1) shall be sufficient authority for the execution of that diligence.

Service of amended pleadings

    18.5.—[1] (1) Where an amendment under rule 18.2(2)(b)(iv), (v) or (vi) (additional or substitute defenders added by amendment) or rule 18.2(2)(d) (all parties not, or wrong person, called) has been made—

(a) the sheriff shall order that a copy of the initial writ or record, as the case may be, as so amended be served by the party who made the amendment on that additional or substitute party with—
- (i) in a cause in which a time to pay direction under the Debtors (Scotland) Act 1987 may be applied for, a notice in Form O8 specifying the date by which a notice of intention must be lodged in process, a notice in Form O3 and a notice of intention to defend in Form O7; or
- (ii) in any other cause, a notice in Form O9 specifying the date by which a notice of intention to defend must be lodged in process and a notice of intention to defend in Form O7; and

(b) the party who made the amendment shall lodge in process—
- (i) a copy of the initial writ or record as amended;
- (ii) a copy of the notice sent in Form O8 or Form O9; and
- (iii) a certificate of service.

(2) When paragraph (1) has been complied with, the cause as so amended shall proceed in every respect as if that party had originally been made a party to the cause.

(3) Where a notice of intention to defend is lodged by virtue of paragraph (1)(a), the sheriff clerk shall fix a date for a hearing under rule 9.12 (Options Hearing).

NOTE
[1] As amended by SI 1996/2445 (effective November 1, 1996).

Expenses and conditions of amendment D 44/62/6
18.6. The sheriff shall find the party making an amendment liable in the expenses occasioned by the amendment unless it is shown that it is just and equitable that the expenses occasioned by the amendment should be otherwise dealt with, and may attach such other conditions as he thinks fit.

Effect of amendment on diligence
18.7. Where an amendment has been allowed, the amendment—
(a) shall not validate diligence used on the dependence of a cause so as to prejudice the rights of creditors of the party against whom the diligence has been executed who are interested in defeating such diligence; and
(b) shall preclude any objection to such diligence stated by a party or any person by virtue of a title acquired or in right of a debt contracted by him subsequent to the execution of such diligence.

Preliminary pleas inserted on amendment
18.8.—(1) Where a party seeks to add a preliminary plea by amendment or answers to an amendment, or by adjustment thereto, a note of the basis for the plea shall be lodged at the same time as the minute, answers or adjustment, as the case may be.

(2) If a party fails to comply with paragraph (1), that party shall be deemed to be no longer insisting on the preliminary plea and the plea shall be repelled by the sheriff.

If the minute of amendment or answers thereto seeks to add a preliminary plea, a note of the basis of that plea must be lodged at the same time as the minute, answers or adjustments thereto which introduces the plea (OCR 18.8(1))

CHAPTER 19 D 44/63

COUNTERCLAIMS

Counterclaims
19.1.—(1) In any action other than a family action within the meaning of rule 33.1(1) or an action of multiplepoinding, a defender may counterclaim against a pursuer—
(a) where the counterclaim might have been made in a separate action in which it would not have been necessary to call as defender any person other than the pursuer; and
(b) in respect of any matter—
- (i) forming part, or arising out of the grounds, of the action by the pursuer;
- (ii) the decision of which is necessary for the determination of the question in controversy between the parties; or
- (iii) which, if the pursuer had been a person not otherwise subject to the jurisdiction of the court, might have been the subject-matter of an action against that pursuer in which jurisdiction would have arisen by reconvention.

(2) A counterclaim shall be made in the defences—

(a) when the defences are lodged or during the period for adjustment;

(b) by amendment at any other stage, with the leave of the sheriff and subject to such conditions, if any, as to expenses or otherwise as the sheriff thinks fit.

(3) Defences which include a counterclaim shall commence with a crave setting out the counterclaim in such form as, if the counterclaim had been made in a separate action, would have been appropriate in the initial writ in that separate action and shall include—

(a) answers to the condescendence of the initial writ as required by rule 9.6(2) (form of defences);

(b) a statement of facts in numbered paragraphs setting out the facts on which the counterclaim is founded, incorporating by reference, if necessary, any matter contained in the defences; and

(c) appropriate pleas-in-law.

D 44/65 *Warrants for diligence on counterclaims*
19.2.—(1) A defender who makes a counterclaim may apply for a warrant for arrestment on the dependence which would have been permitted had the warrant been sought in an initial writ in a separate action.

[1] (2) An application for a warrant under paragraph (1) shall be made—

(a) at the time of making the counterclaim, by inserting after the crave of the counterclaim the words "Warrant for arrestment on the dependence applied for."; or

[2] (b) after the counterclaim has been made by application for a precept of arrestment.

[3] (3) An application for a warrant under paragraph (2)(a) may be granted by the sheriff by writing on the defences, defences as adjusted or minute of amendment, as the case may be, the words "Warrant granted as craved." after the warrant sought, and adding his signature and the date below those words.

(4) A warrant granted under paragraph (3) shall have the same effect as if the warrant had been in an initial writ.

NOTE
[1] As amended by SI 1996/2445 (effective November 1, 1996).
[2] As amended by the Act of Sederunt (Ordinary Cause, Summary Application and Small Claim Rules) Amendment (Miscellaneous) 2004 (SSI 2004/197) (effective May 21, 2004), para.2(10).

Form of record where counterclaim lodged
[1] **19.2A.** Where, under rule 9.10 (open record), 9.11 (record for Options Hearing), 10.4 (open record), or 10.5 (closed record), a record requires to be lodged in an action in which a counterclaim is included in the defences, the pleadings of the parties shall be set out in the record in the following order:—

(a) the crave of the initial writ;

(b) the condescendence and answers relating to the initial writ;

(c) the pleas-in-law of the parties relating to the crave of the initial writ;

(d) the crave of the counterclaim;

(e) the statement of facts and answers relating to the counterclaim; and

(f) the pleas-in-law of the parties relating to the counterclaim.

NOTE
[1] Inserted by SI 1996/2445 (effective November 1, 1996).

D 44/66 *Effect of abandonment of cause*
19.3.—(1) The right of a pursuer to abandon a cause under rule 23.1 shall not be affected by a counterclaim; and any expenses for which the pursuer is found liable as a condition of, or in consequence of, such abandonment shall not include the expenses of the counterclaim.

(2) Notwithstanding abandonment by the pursuer, a defender may insist in his counterclaim; and the proceedings in the counterclaim shall continue in dependence as if the counterclaim were a separate action.

Disposal of counterclaims
19.4. The sheriff may—

(a) deal with a counterclaim as if it had been stated in a separate action;

(b) regulate the procedure in relation to the counterclaim as he thinks fit; and

(c) grant decree for the counterclaim in whole or in part or for the difference between it and the sum sued for by the pursuer.

THIRD PARTY PROCEDURE

Applications for third party notice
   20.1.—(1) Where, in an action, a defender claims that—
   (a) he has in respect of the subject-matter of the action a right of contribution, relief or
        indemnity against any person who is not a party to the action, or
   (b) a person whom the pursuer is not bound to call as a defender should be made a party
        to the action along with the defender in respect that such person is—
        (i) solely liable, or jointly or jointly and severally liable with the defender, to the
             pursuer in respect of the subject-matter of the action, or
        (ii) liable to the defender in respect of a claim arising from or in connection with the
             liability, if any, of the defender to the pursuer,
he may apply by motion for an order for service of a third party notice upon that other person
in Form O10 for the purpose of convening that other person as a third party to the action.
   [1] (2) Where—
   (a) a pursuer against whom a counterclaim has been made, or
   (b) a third party convened in the action,
seeks, in relation to the claim against him, to make against a person who is not a party, a claim
mentioned in paragraph (1) as a claim which could be made by a defender against a third party,
he shall apply by motion for an order for service of a third party notice in Form O10 in the same
manner as a defender under that paragraph; and rules 20.2 to 20.6 shall, with the necessary
modifications, apply to such a claim as they apply in relation to such a claim by a defender.   **D 44/67**

NOTE
   [1] As amended by SI 1996/2445 (effective November 1, 1996).

Averments where order for service of third party notice sought
   20.2.—(1) Where a defender intends to apply by motion for an order for service of a third
party notice before the closing of the record, he shall, before lodging the motion, set out in his
defences, by adjustment to those defences, or in a separate statement of facts annexed to those
defences—
   (a) averments setting out the grounds on which he maintains that the proposed third party
        is liable to him by contribution, relief or indemnity or should be made a party to the
        action; and
   (b) appropriate pleas-in-law.
   (2) Where a defender applies by motion for an order for service of a third party notice after
the closing of the record, he shall, on lodging the motion, lodge a minute of amendment
containing—
   (a) averments setting out the grounds on which he maintains that the proposed third party
        is liable to him by contribution, relief or indemnity or should be made a party to the
        action, and
   (b) appropriate pleas-in-law,
unless those grounds and pleas-in-law have been set out in the defences in the closed record.
   (3) A motion for an order for service of a third party notice shall be lodged before the
commencement of the hearing of the merits of the cause.

Warrants for diligence on third party notice   **D 44/68**
   20.3.—(1) A defender who applies for an order for service of a third party notice may apply
for a warrant for arrestment to found jurisdiction or for arrestment on the dependence which
would have been permitted had the warrant been sought in an initial writ in a separate action.
   (2) Averments in support of the application for such a warrant shall be included in the
defences or the separate statement of facts referred to in rule 20.2(1).
   (3) An application for a warrant under paragraph (1) shall be made by motion—
   (a) at the time of applying for the third party notice; or
   (b) if not applied for at that time, at any stage of the cause thereafter.
   (4) A certified copy of the interlocutor granting warrant for diligence applied for under
paragraph (2) shall be sufficient authority for execution of the diligence.

Service on third party
   20.4.—(1) A third party notice shall be served on the third party within 14 days after the date
of the interlocutor allowing service of that notice.
   (2) Where service of a third party notice has not been made within the period specified in

paragraph (1), the order for service of it shall cease to have effect; and no service of the notice may be made unless a further order for service of it has been applied for and granted.

[1] (3) There shall be served with a third party notice—

(a) a copy of the pleadings (including any adjustments and amendments); and

(b) where the pleadings have not been amended in accordance with the minute of amendment referred to in rule 20.2, a copy of that minute.

(4) A copy of the third party notice, with a certificate of service attached to it, shall be lodged in process by the defender.

NOTE

[1] As amended by SSI 2003/26, reg.2 (effective from January 24, 2003).

Answers to third party notice

20.5.—(1) An order for service of a third party notice shall specify 28 days, or such other period as the sheriff on cause shown may specify, as the period within which the third party may lodge answers.

(2) Answers for a third party shall be headed "Answers for [E.F.], Third Party in the action at the instance of [A.B.], Pursuer against [C.D.], Defender" and shall include—

D 44/69

(a) answers to the averments of the defender against him in the form of numbered paragraphs corresponding to the numbered articles of the condescendence annexed to the summons and incorporating, if the third party so wishes, answers to the averments of the pursuer; or

(b) where a separate statement of facts has been lodged by the defender under rule 20.2(1), answers to the statement of facts in the form of numbered paragraphs corresponding to the numbered paragraphs of the statement of facts; and

(c) appropriate pleas-in-law.

Consequences of failure to amend pleadings

20.5A. Where the pleadings have not been amended in accordance with the minute of amendment referred to in rule 20.2, no motion for a finding, order or decree against a third party may be enrolled by the defender unless, at or before the date on which he enrols the motion, he enrols a motion to amend the pleadings in accordance with that minute.

NOTE

[1] As amended by SSI 2003/26, reg.2 (effective from January 24, 2003).

Procedure following answers

20.6.—(1) Where a third party lodges answers, the sheriff clerk shall fix a date and time under rule 9.2 for a hearing under rule 9.12 (Options Hearing) as if the third party had lodged a notice of intention to defend and the period of notice had expired on the date for lodging answers.

(2) At the Options Hearing, or at any time thereafter, the sheriff may grant such decree or other order as he thinks fit.

(3) A decree or other order against the third party shall have effect and be extractable in the same way as a decree or other order against a defender.

D 44/70   CHAPTER 21

DOCUMENTS FOUNDED ON OR ADOPTED IN PLEADINGS

Lodging documents founded on or adopted

21.1.—(1) Subject to any other provision in these Rules, any document founded on by a party, or adopted as incorporated, in his pleadings shall, so far as in his possession or within his control, be lodged in process as a production by him—

(a) when founded on or adopted in an initial writ, at the time of returning the initial writ under rule 9.3;

(b) when founded on or adopted in a minute, defences, counterclaim or answers, at the time of lodging that part of process; and

(c) when founded on or adopted in an adjustment to any pleadings, at the time when such adjustment is intimated to any other party.

(2) Paragraph (1) shall be without prejudice to any power of the sheriff to order the production of any document or grant a commission and diligence for recovery of it.

Consequences of failure to lodge documents founded on or adopted

21.2. Where a party fails to lodge a document in accordance with rule 21.1(1), he may be found liable in the expenses of any order for production or recovery of it obtained by any other party.

Objection to documents founded on **D 44/70/1**

21.3.—(1) Where a deed or writing is founded on by a party, any objection to it by any other party may be stated and maintained by exception without its being reduced.

(2) Where an objection is stated under paragraph (1) and an action of reduction would otherwise have been competent, the sheriff may order the party stating the objection to find caution or give such other security as he thinks fit.

CHAPTER 22 **D 44/71**

PRELIMINARY PLEAS

Note of basis of preliminary plea

22.1.—(1) A party intending to insist on a preliminary plea shall, not later than 3 days before the Options Hearing under rule 9.12 or the Procedural Hearing under rule 10.6—

(a) lodge in process a note of the basis for the plea; and

(b) intimate a copy of it to every other party.

[1] (2) Where the Options Hearing is continued under rule 9.12(5) and a preliminary plea is added by adjustment, a party intending to insist on that plea shall, not later than 3 days before the date of the Options Hearing so continued—

(a) lodge in process a note of the basis for the plea; and

(b) intimate a copy of it to every other party.

(3) If a party fails to comply with paragraph (1) or (2), he shall be deemed to be no longer insisting on the preliminary plea; and the plea shall be repelled by the sheriff at the Options Hearing or Procedural Hearing.

[2] (4) At any proof before answer or debate, parties may on cause shown raise matters in addition to those set out in the note mentioned in paragraph (1) or (2).

[1] (5) Where a note of the basis of a preliminary plea has been lodged under paragraph (1), and the Options Hearing is continued under rule 9.12(5), unless the basis of the plea has changed following further adjustment, it shall not be necessary for a party who is insisting on the plea to lodge a further note before the Options Hearing so continued.

NOTE

[1] Inserted by the Act of Sederunt (Sheriff Court Ordinary Cause Rules Amendment) (Miscellaneous) 1996 (SI 1996/2445) (effective November 1, 1996).

[2] As amended by the Act of Sederunt (Sheriff Court Ordinary Cause Rules Amendment) (Miscellaneous) 2000 (SSI 2000/239) (effective October 2, 2000).

CHAPTER 23 **D 44/72**

ABANDONMENT

Abandonment of causes

23.1.—(1) A pursuer may abandon a cause at any time before decree of absolvitor or dismissal by lodging a minute of abandonment and—

(a) consenting to decree of absolvitor; or

(b) seeking decree of dismissal.

[1] (2) The sheriff shall not grant decree of dismissal under paragraph (1)(b) unless full judicial expenses have been paid to the defender, and any third party against whom the pursuer has directed any crave, within 28 days after the date of taxation.

(3) If the pursuer fails to pay the expenses referred to in paragraph (2) to the party to whom they are due within the period specified in that paragraph, that party shall be entitled to decree of absolvitor with expenses.

NOTE

[1] As amended by SSI 2003/26, reg.2 (effective from January 24, 2003).

Application of abandonment to counterclaims **D 44/73**

23.2. Rule 23.1 shall, with the necessary modifications, apply to the abandonment by a defender of his counterclaim as it applies to the abandonment of a cause.

WITHDRAWAL OF SOLICITORS

Intimation of withdrawal to court
    24.1.—[1] (1) Subject to paragraph (3), where a solicitor withdraws from acting on behalf of a party, he shall intimate his withdrawal by letter to the sheriff clerk and to every other party.
    [1] (2) The sheriff clerk shall forthwith lodge such letter in process.
    [2] (3) Where a solicitor withdraws from acting on behalf of a party in open court and in the presence of the other parties to the action or their representatives, paragraph (1) shall not apply.

NOTES
    [1] As amended by the Act of Sederunt (Sheriff Court Ordinary Cause Rules Amendment) (Miscellaneous) 2000 (SSI 2000/239) (effective October 2, 2000).
    [2] Inserted by the Act of Sederunt (Sheriff Court Ordinary Cause Rules Amendment) (Miscellaneous) 2000 (SSI 2000/239) (effective October 2, 2000).

Intimation to party whose solicitor has withdrawn
    24.2.—[1] (1) Subject to paragraph (1A), the sheriff shall, of his own motion, or on the motion of any other party, pronounce an interlocutor ordaining the party whose solicitor has withdrawn from acting to appear or be represented at a specified diet fixed by the sheriff to state whether or not he intends to proceed, under certification that if he fails to do so the sheriff may grant decree or make such other order or finding as he thinks fit.
    [2] (1A) Where any previously fixed diet is to occur within 14 days from the date when the sheriff first considers the solicitor's withdrawal, the sheriff may either—
        (a) pronounce an interlocutor in accordance with paragraph (1);
          or
        (b) consider the matter at the previously fixed diet.
    (2) The diet fixed in the interlocutor under paragraph (1) shall not be less than 14 days after the date of the interlocutor unless the sheriff otherwise orders.
    (3) The party who has lodged the motion under paragraph (1), or any other party appointed by the sheriff, shall forthwith serve on the party whose solicitor has withdrawn a copy of the interlocutor and a notice in Form G10; and a certificate of service shall be lodged in process.

NOTES
    [1] As amended by the Act of Sederunt (Sheriff Court Ordinary Cause Rules Amendment) (Miscellaneous) 2000 (SSI 2000/239) (effective October 2, 2000).
    [2] Inserted by the Act of Sederunt (Sheriff Court Ordinary Cause Rules Amendment) (Miscellaneous) 2000 (SSI 2000/239) (effective October 2, 2000).

D 44/74 *Consequences of failure to intimate intention to proceed*
    24.3. Where a party on whom a notice and interlocutor has been served under rule 24.2(2) fails to appear or be represented at a diet fixed under rule 24.2(1) and to state his intention as required by that paragraph, the sheriff may grant decree or make such other order or finding as he thinks fit.

CHAPTER 25

MINUTES OF SIST AND TRANSFERENCE

Minutes of sist
    25.1. Where a party dies or comes under legal incapacity while a cause is depending, any person claiming to represent that party or his estate may apply by minute to be sisted as a party to the cause.

Minutes of transference
    [1] **25.2.** Where a party dies or comes under legal incapacity while a cause is depending and the provisions of rule 25.1 are not invoked, any other party may apply by minute to have the cause
D 44/75 transferred in favour of or against, as the case may be, any person who represents that party or his estate.

NOTE
    [1] As amended by the Act of Sederunt (Sheriff Court Ordinary Cause Rules Amendment) (Miscellaneous) 1996 (SI 1996/2445) (effective November 1, 1996).

CHAPTER 26

TRANSFER AND REMIT OF CAUSES

Transfer to another sheriff court
26.1.—(1) The sheriff may, on cause shown, remit any cause to another sheriff court.

(2) Subject to paragraph (4), where a cause in which there are two or more defenders has been brought in the sheriff court of the residence or place of business of one of them, the sheriff may transfer the cause to any other sheriff court which has jurisdiction over any of the defenders.

(3) Subject to paragraph (4), where a plea of no jurisdiction is sustained, the sheriff may transfer the cause to the sheriff court before which it appears to him the cause ought to have been brought.

(4) The sheriff shall not transfer a cause to another sheriff court under paragraph (2) or (3) except—
    (a) on the motion of a party; and
    (b) where he considers it expedient to do so having regard to the convenience of the parties and their witnesses.

(5) On making an order under paragraph (1), (2) or (3), the sheriff—
    (a) shall state his reasons for doing so in the interlocutor; and
    (b) may make the order on such conditions as to expenses or otherwise as he thinks fit.

(6) The court to which a cause is transferred under paragraph (1), (2) or (3) shall accept the cause.

(7) A transferred cause shall proceed in all respects as if it had been originally brought in the court to which it is transferred.

(8) An interlocutor transferring a cause may, with leave of the sheriff, be appealed to the sheriff principal but shall not be subject to appeal to the Court of Session.

Remit to Court of Session
26.2.—(1) The sheriff clerk shall, within four days after the sheriff has pronounced an interlocutor remitting a cause to the Court of Session, transmit the process to the Deputy Principal Clerk of Session.

(2) The sheriff clerk shall, within the period specified in paragraph (1), send written notice of **D 44/76** the remit to each party and certify on the interlocutor sheet that he has done so.

(3) Failure by a Sheriff Clerk to comply with paragraph (2) shall not affect the validity of a remit made under paragraph (1).

Remit from Court of Session
26.3. On receipt of the process in an action which has been remitted from the Court of Session under section 14 of the Law Reform (Miscellaneous Provisions) (Scotland) Act 1985, the sheriff clerk shall—
    (a) record the date of receipt on the interlocutor sheet;
    (b) fix a hearing to determine further procedure on the first court day occurring not earlier than 14 days after the date of receipt of the process; and
    (c) forthwith send written notice of the date of the hearing fixed under sub-paragraph (b) to each party.

CHAPTER 27   D 44/76/1

CAUTION AND SECURITY

Application of this Chapter
27.1. This Chapter applies to—
    (a) any cause in which the sheriff has power to order a person to find caution or give other security; and
    (b) security for expenses ordered to be given by the election court or the sheriff under section 136(2)(i) of the Representation of the People Act 1983 in an election petition.

Form of applications
27.2.—(1) An application for an order for caution or other security or for variation or recall of such an order, shall be made by motion.

(2) The grounds on which such an application is made shall be set out in the motion.

Orders
27.3. Subject to section 726(2) of the Companies Act 1985 (expenses by certain limited

companies), an order to find caution or give other security shall specify the period within which such caution is to be found or such security given.

D 44/76/2 *Methods of finding caution or giving security*

27.4.—(1) A person ordered—

(a) to find caution, shall do so by obtaining a bond of caution; or

(b) to consign a sum of money into court, shall do so by consignation under the Sheriff Court Consignations (Scotland) Act 1893 in the name of the sheriff clerk.

(2) The sheriff may approve a method of security other than one mentioned in paragraph (1), including a combination of two or more methods of security.

(3) Subject to paragraph (4), any document by which an order to find caution or give other security is satisfied shall be lodged in process.

(4) Where the sheriff approves a security in the form of a deposit of a sum of money in the joint names of the agents of parties, a copy of the deposit receipt, and not the principal, shall be lodged in process.

(5) Any document lodged in process, by which an order to find caution or give other security is satisfied, shall not be borrowed from process.

Cautioners and guarantors

[1] 27.5. A bond of caution or other security shall be given only by a person who is an "authorised person" within the meaning of section 31 of the Financial Services and Markets Act 2000.

NOTE

[1] As amended by the Act of Sederunt (Ordinary Cause Rules) Amendment (Caution and Security) 2005 (SSI 2005/20), para.2(2) (effective February 1, 2005).

Form of bonds of caution and other securities

27.6.—(1) A bond of caution shall oblige the cautioner, his heirs and executors to make payment of the sums for which he has become cautioner to the party to whom he is bound, as validly and in the same manner as the party, his heirs and successors, for whom he is cautioner, are obliged.

[1] (2) A bond of caution or other security document given by a person shall state whether that person is an "authorised person" within the meaning of section 31 of the Financial Services and Markets Act 2000.

NOTE

[1] As amended by the Act of Sederunt (Ordinary Cause Rules) Amendment (Caution and Security) 2005 (SSI 2005/20), para.2(3) (effective February 1, 2005).

Sufficiency of caution or security and objections

27.7.—(1) The sheriff clerk shall satisfy himself that any bond of caution, or other document lodged in process under rule 27.4(3), is in proper form.

(2) A party who is dissatisfied with the sufficiency or form of the caution or other security offered in obedience to an order of the court may apply by motion for an order under rule 27.9 (failure to find caution or give security).

Insolvency or death of cautioner or guarantor

27.8. Where caution has been found by bond of caution or security has been given by guarantee and the cautioner or guarantor, as the case may be—

D 44/76/3
(a) becomes apparently insolvent within the meaning assigned by section 7 of the Bankruptcy (Scotland) Act 1985 (constitution of apparent insolvency),

(b) calls a meeting of his creditors to consider the state of his affairs,

(c) dies unrepresented, or

(d) is a company and—

    (i) an administration or winding up order has been made, or a resolution for a voluntary winding up has been passed, with respect to it,

    (ii) a receiver of all or any part of its undertaking has been appointed, or

    (iii) a voluntary arrangement (within the meaning assigned by section 1(1) of the Insolvency Act 1986) has been approved under Part I of that Act,

the party entitled to benefit from the caution or guarantee may apply by motion for a new security or further security to be given.

Failure to find caution or give security

27.9. Where a party fails to find caution or give other security (in this rule referred to as "the party in default") any other party may apply by motion—

    (a) where he party in default is a pursuer, for decree of absolvitor; or

    (b) where the party in default is a defender or a third party, for decree by default or for such other finding or order as the sheriff thinks fit.

CHAPTER 28

RECOVERY OF EVIDENCE

Application and interpretation of this Chapter

28.1.—(1) This Chapter applies to the recovery of any evidence in a cause depending before the sheriff.

(2) In this Chapter, "the Act of 1972" means the Administration of Justice (Scotland) Act 1972.

Applications for commission and diligence for recovery of documents or for orders under section 1 of the Act of 1972

28.2.—(1) An application by a party for—

    (a) a commission and diligence for the recovery of a document, or

    (b) an order under section 1 of the Act of 1972,

shall be made by motion.

(2) At the time of lodging a motion under paragraph (1), a specification of— **D 44/76/4**

    (a) the document or other property sought to be inspected, photographed, preserved, taken into custody, detained, produced, recovered, sampled or experimented with or upon, as the case may be, or

    (b) the matter in respect of which information is sought as to the identity of a person who might be a witness or a defender,

shall be lodged in process.

[1] (3) A copy of the specification lodged under paragraph (2) and the motion made under paragraph (1) shall be intimated by the applicant to—

    (a) every other party;

    (b) in respect of an application under section 1(1) of the Act of 1972, any third party haver; and

    (c) where necessary, the Lord Advocate.

(4) Where the sheriff grants a motion under paragraph (1) in whole or in part, he may order the applicant to find such caution or give such other security as he thinks fit.

(5) The Lord Advocate may appear at the hearing of any motion under paragraph (1).

NOTE

[1] Substituted by SI 1996/2445 (effective November 1, 1996).

Optional procedure before executing commission and diligence **D 44/76/5**

28.3.—(1) The party who has obtained a commission and diligence for the recovery of a document under rule 28.2(1)(a) may, at any time before executing it against a haver, serve on the haver an order in Form G11 (in this rule referred to as "the order"); and if so, the provisions of this rule shall apply.

[1] (2) The order and a copy of the specification referred to in rule 28.2(2) as approved by the court shall be served on the haver or his known solicitor and shall be complied with by the haver in the manner and within the period specified in the order.

[1] (3) Not later than the day after the date on which the order, the certificate appended to Form G11 and any document is received by the sheriff clerk from a haver, he shall intimate that to each party.

(4) No party, other than the party who served the order, may uplift such a document until after the expiry of 7 days after the date of intimation under paragraph (3).

(5) Where the party who served the order fails to uplift such a document within 7 days after the date of intimation under paragraph (3), the sheriff clerk shall intimate that failure to every other party.

(6) Where no party has uplifted such a document within 14 days after the date of intimation under paragraph (5), the sheriff clerk shall return it to the haver who delivered it to him.

(7) Where a party who has uplifted such a document does not wish to lodge it, he shall return it to the sheriff clerk who shall—

    (a) intimate the return of the document to every other party; and

(b) if no other party uplifts the document within 14 days of the date of intimation, return it to the haver.

D 44/76/6 (8) If the party who served the order is not satisfied—

(a) that full compliance has been made with the order, or

(b) that adequate reasons for non-compliance have been given,

he may execute the commission and diligence under rule 28.4.

(9) Where an extract from a book of any description (whether the extract is certified or not) is produced under the order, the sheriff may, on the motion of the party who served the order, order that that party shall be allowed to inspect the book and take copies of any entries falling within the specification.

(10) Where any question of confidentiality arises in relation to a book ordered to be inspected under paragraph (9), the inspection shall be made, and any copies shall be taken, at the sight of the commissioner appointed in the interlocutor granting the commission and diligence.

[1] (11) The sheriff may, on cause shown, order the production of any book (not being a banker's book or book of public record) containing entries falling under a specification, notwithstanding the production of a certified extract from that book.

NOTE

[1] As amended by SI 1996/2445 (effective November 1, 1996).

Execution of commission and diligence for recovery of documents

28.4.—(1) The party who seeks to execute a commission and diligence for recovery of a document obtained under rule 28.2(1)(a) shall—

(a) provide the commissioner with a copy of the specification, a copy of the pleadings (including any adjustments and amendments) and a certified copy of the interlocutor of his appointment; and

(b) instruct the clerk and any shorthand writer considered necessary by the commissioner or any party; and

(c) be responsible for the fees of the commissioner and his clerk, and of any shorthand writer.

(2) The Commissioner shall, in consultation with the parties, fix a diet for the execution of the commission.

(3) The interlocutor granting such a commission and diligence shall be sufficient authority for citing a haver to appear before the commissioner.

[1] (4) A citation in Form G13 shall be served on the haver with a copy of the specification and, where necessary for a proper understanding of the specification, a copy of the pleadings (including any adjustments and amendments) and the party citing the haver shall lodge a certificate of citation in Form G12.

D 44/76/7 (5) The parties and the haver shall be entitled to be represented by a solicitor or person having a right of audience before the sheriff at the execution of the commission.

[1] (6) At the commission, the commissioner shall—

(a) administer the oath *de fideli administratione* to any clerk and any shorthand writer appointed for the commission; and

(b) administer to the haver the oath in Form G14, or, where the haver elects to affirm, the affirmation in Form G15.

(7) The report of the execution of the commission and diligence, any document recovered and an inventory of that document, shall be sent by the commissioner to the sheriff clerk.

(8) Not later than the day after the date on which such a report, document and inventory, if any, are received by the sheriff clerk, he shall intimate to the parties that he has received them.

(9) No party, other than the party who served the order, may uplift such a document until after the expiry of 7 days after the date of intimation under paragraph (8).

(10) Where the party who served the order fails to uplift such a document within 7 days after the date of intimation under paragraph (8), the sheriff clerk shall intimate that failure to every other party.

(11) Where no party has uplifted such a document within 14 days after the date of intimation under paragraph (10), the sheriff clerk shall return it to the haver.

(12) Where a party who has uplifted such a document does not wish to lodge it, he shall return it to the sheriff clerk who shall—

(a) intimate the return of the document to every other party; and

(b) if no other party uplifts the document within 14 days of the date of intimation, return it to the haver.

Note

[1] As amended by SI 1996/2445 (effective November 1, 1996).

Execution of orders for production or recovery of documents or other property under section 1(1) **D 44/76/8**
of the Act of 1972

28.5.—(1) An order under section 1(1) of the Act of 1972 for the production or recovery of a document or other property shall grant a commission and diligence for the production or recovery of that document or other property.

(2) Rules 28.3 (optional procedure before executing commission and diligence) and 28.4 (execution of commission and diligence for recovery of documents) shall apply to an order to which paragraph (1) applies as they apply to a commission and diligence for the recovery of a document.

Execution of orders for inspection etc. of documents or other property under section 1(1) of the Act of 1972

28.6.—(1) An order under section 1(1) of the Act of 1972 for the inspection or photographing of a document or other property, the taking of samples or the carrying out of any experiment thereon or therewith, shall authorise and appoint a specified person to photograph, inspect, take samples of, or carry out any experiment on or with, any such document or other property, as the case may be, subject to such conditions, if any, as the sheriff thinks fit.

(2) A certified copy of the interlocutor granting such an order shall be sufficient authority for the person specified to execute the order.

(3) When such an order is executed, the party who obtained the order shall serve on the haver a copy of the interlocutor granting it, a copy of the specification and, where necessary for a proper understanding of the specification, a copy of the pleadings (including any adjustments and amendments).

Execution of orders for preservation etc. of documents or other property under section 1(1) of the Act of 1972

[1] **28.7.**—(1) An order under section 1(1) of the Act of 1972 for the preservation, custody and detention of a document or other property shall grant a commission and diligence for the detention and custody of that document or other property.

(2) The party who has obtained an order under paragraph (1) shall—
- (a) provide the commissioner with a copy of the specification, a copy of the pleadings (including any adjustments and amendments) and a certified copy of the interlocutor of his appointment;
- (b) be responsible for the fees of the commissioner and his clerk; and
- (c) serve a copy of the order on the haver.

(3) The report of the execution of the commission and diligence, any document or other property taken by the commissioner and an inventory of such property, shall be sent by the commissioner to the sheriff clerk for the further order of the sheriff.

NOTE
[1] As amended by SI 1996/2445 (effective November 1, 1996).

Confidentiality **D 44/76/9**

[1] **28.8.**—(1) Where confidentiality is claimed for any evidence sought to be recovered under any of the following rules, such evidence shall, where practicable, be enclosed in a sealed packet:—

28.3 (optional procedure before executing commission and diligence),

28.4 (execution of commission and diligence for recovery of documents),

28.5 (execution of orders for production or recovery of documents or other property under section 1(1) of the Act of 1972),

28.7 (execution of orders for preservation etc. of documents or other property under section 1(1) of the Act of 1972).

(2) A motion to have such a sealed packet opened up or such recovery allowed may be lodged by—
- (a) the party who obtained the commission and diligence; or
- (b) any other party after the date of intimation by the sheriff clerk under rule 28.3(5) or 28.4(10) (intimation of failure to uplift documents).

(3) In addition to complying with rule 15.2 (intimation of motions), the party lodging such a motion shall intimate the terms of the motion to the haver by post by the first class recorded delivery service.

(4) The person claiming confidentiality may oppose a motion made under paragraph (2).

NOTE
[1] As amended by SI 1996/2445 (effective November 1, 1996).

Warrants for production of original documents from public records

28.9.—(1) Where a party seeks to obtain from the keeper of any public record production of the original of any register or deed in his custody for the purposes of a cause, he shall apply to the sheriff by motion.

(2) Intimation of a motion under paragraph (1) shall be given to the keeper of the public record concerned at least 7 days before the motion is lodged.

(3) In relation to a public record kept by the Keeper of the Registers of Scotland or the Keeper of the Records of Scotland, where it appears to the sheriff that it is necessary for the ends of justice that a motion under this rule should be granted, he shall pronounce an **D 44/76/10** interlocutor containing a certificate to that effect; and the party applying for production may apply by letter (enclosing a copy of the interlocutor duly certified by the sheriff clerk), addressed to the Deputy Principal Clerk of Session, for an order from the Court of Session authorising the Keeper of the Registers or the Keeper of the Records, as the case may be, to exhibit the original of any register or deed to the sheriff.

(4) The Deputy Principal Clerk of Session shall submit the application sent to him under paragraph (3) to the Lord Ordinary in chambers who, if satisfied, shall grant a warrant for production or exhibition of the original register or deed sought.

(5) A certified copy of the warrant granted under paragraph (4) shall be served on the keeper of the public record concerned.

(6) The expense of the production or exhibition of such an original register or deed shall be met, in the first instance, by the party who applied by motion under paragraph (1).

Commissions for examination of witnesses

28.10.—[1] (1) This rule applies to a commission—
   (a) to take the evidence of a witness who—
      (i) is resident beyond the jurisdiction of the court;
      (ii) although resident within the jurisdiction of the court, resides at some place remote from that court; or
      (iii) by reason of age, infirmity or sickness, is unable to attend the diet of proof;
   (b) in respect of the evidence of a witness which is in danger of being lost, to take the evidence to lie *in retentis*; or
   (c) on special cause shown, to take evidence of a witness on a ground other than one mentioned in sub-paragraph (a) or (b).

(2) An application by a party for a commission to examine a witness shall be made by motion; and that party shall specify in the motion the name and address of at least one proposed commissioner for approval and appointment by the sheriff.

(3) The interlocutor granting such a commission shall be sufficient authority for citing the witness to appear before the commissioner.

[1] (4) At the commission, the commissioner shall—
   (a) administer the oath *de fideli administratione* to any clerk and any shorthand writer appointed for the commission; and
   (b) administer to the witness the oath in Form G14, or where the witness elects to affirm, the affirmation in Form G15.

(5) Where a commission is granted for the examination of a witness, the commission shall proceed without interrogatories unless, on cause shown, the sheriff otherwise directs.

NOTE
[1] As amended by SI 1996/2445 (effective November 1, 1996).

D 44/76/11 *Commissions on interrogatories*

28.11.—(1) Where interrogatories have not been dispensed with, the party who obtained the commission to examine a witness under rule 28.10 shall lodge draft interrogatories in process.

(2) Any other party may lodge cross-interrogatories.

(3) The interrogatories and any cross-interrogatories, when adjusted, shall be extended and returned to the sheriff clerk for approval and the settlement of any dispute as to their contents by the sheriff.

(4) The party who has obtained the commission shall—
   (a) provide the commissioner with a copy of the pleadings (including any adjustments and amendments), the approved interrogatories and any cross-interrogatories and a certified copy of the interlocutor of his appointment;
   (b) instruct the clerk; and
   (c) be responsible, in the first instance, for the fee of the commissioner and his clerk.

(5) The commissioner shall, in consultation with the parties, fix a diet for the execution of the commission to examine the witness.

(6) The executed interrogatories, any document produced by the witness and an inventory of that document, shall be sent by the commissioner to the sheriff clerk.

(7) Not later than the day after the date on which the executed interrogatories, any document and an inventory of that document, are received by the sheriff clerk, he shall intimate to each party that he has received them.

(8) The party who obtained the commission to examine the witness shall lodge in process—
  (a) the report of the commission; and
  (b) the executed interrogatories and any cross-interrogatories.

Commissions without interrogatories
28.12.—(1) Where interrogatories have been dispensed with, the party who has obtained a commission to examine a witness under rule 28.10 shall—
  (a) provide the commissioner with a copy of the pleadings (including any adjustments and amendments) and a certified copy of the interlocutor of his appointment;
  (b) fix a diet for the execution of the commission in consultation with the commissioner and every other party;
  (c) instruct the clerk and any shorthand writer; and
  (d) be responsible for the fees of the commissioner, his clerk and any shorthand writer.

(2) All parties shall be entitled to be present and represented at the execution of the commission.

(3) The report of the execution of the commission, any document produced by the witness **D 44/76/12** and an inventory of that document, shall be sent by the commissioner to the sheriff clerk.

(4) Not later than the day after the date on which such a report, any document and an inventory of that document are received by the sheriff clerk, he shall intimate to each party that he has received them.

(5) The party who obtained the commission to examine the witness shall lodge the report in process.

Evidence taken on commission
28.13.—(1) Subject to the following paragraphs of this rule and to all questions of relevancy and admissibility, evidence taken on commission under rule 28.11 or 28.12 may be used as evidence at any proof of the cause.

(2) Any party may object to the use of such evidence at a proof; and the objection shall be determined by the sheriff.

(3) Such evidence shall not be used at a proof if the witness becomes available to attend the diet of proof.

(4) A party may use such evidence in accordance with the preceding paragraphs of this rule notwithstanding that it was obtained at the instance of another party.

Letters of request
28.14.—(1) This rule applies to an application for a letter of request to a court or tribunal outside Scotland to obtain evidence of the kind specified in paragraph (2), being evidence obtainable within the jurisdiction of that court or tribunal, for the purposes of a cause depending before the sheriff.

(2) An application to which paragraph (1) applies may be made in relation to a request—
  (a) for the examination of a witness,
  (b) for the inspection, photographing, preservation, custody, detention, production or recovery of, or the taking of samples of, or the carrying out of any experiment on or with, a document or other property, as the case may be,
  (c) for the medical examination of any person,   **D 44/76/13**
  (d) for the taking and testing of samples of blood from any person, or
  (e) for any other order for obtaining evidence,
for which an order could be obtained from the sheriff.

(3) Such an application shall be made by minute in Form G16 together with a proposed letter of request in Form G17.

(4) It shall be a condition of granting a letter of request that any solicitor for the applicant, or a party litigant, as the case may be, shall be personally liable, in the first instance, for the whole expenses which may become due and payable in respect of the letter of request to the court or tribunal obtaining the evidence and to any witness who may be examined for the purpose; and he shall consign into court such sum in respect of such expenses as the sheriff thinks fit.

(5) Unless the court or tribunal to which a letter of request is addressed is a court or tribunal in a country or territory—
  (a) where English is an official language, or
  (b) in relation to which the sheriff clerk certifies that no translation is required,

then the applicant shall, before the issue of the letter of request, lodge in process a translation of that letter and any interrogatories and cross-interrogatories into the official language of that court or tribunal.

(6) The letter of request when issued; any interrogatories and cross-interrogatories adjusted as required by rule 28.11 and the translations (if any), shall be forwarded by the sheriff clerk to the Foreign and Commonwealth Office or to such person and in such manner as the sheriff may direct.

NOTE
[1] As amended by SI 1996/2445 (effective November 1, 1996).

Citation of witnesses and havers
28.15. The following rules shall apply to the citation of a witness or haver to a commission under this Chapter as they apply to the citation of a witness for a proof:—
rule 29.7 (citation of witnesses) except paragraph 4,
rule 29.9 (second diligence against a witness,
rule 29.10 (failure of witness to attend).

D 44/76/14

<h1 style="text-align:center">CHAPTER 29</h1>

<h2 style="text-align:center">PROOF</h2>

Reference to oath
29.1.—(1) Where a party intends to refer any matter to the oath of his opponent he shall lodge a motion to that effect.

(2) If a party fails to appear at the diet for taking his deposition on the reference to his oath, the sheriff may hold him as confessed and grant decree accordingly.

Remit to person of skill
29.2.—(1) The sheriff may, on a motion by any party or on a joint motion, remit to any person of skill, or other person, to report on any matter of fact.

(2) Where a remit under paragraph (1) is made by joint motion or of consent of all parties, the report of such person shall be final and conclusive with respect to the subject-matter of the remit.

(3) Where a remit under paragraph (1) is made—
    (a) on the motion of one of the parties, the expenses of its execution shall, in the first instance, be met by that party; and
    (b) on a joint motion or of consent of all parties, the expenses shall, in the first instance, be met by the parties equally, unless the sheriff otherwise orders.

Written statements
[1] **29.3.** Where a statement in a document is admissible under section 2(1)(b) of the Civil Evidence (Scotland) Act 1988, any party who wishes to have that statement received in evidence shall—
    (a) docquet that document as follows:—
        "(*Place and date*)
        This document contains a statement admissible under section 2(1)(b) of the Civil Evidence (Scotland) Act 1988.
        (*Signed*)
        (*Designation and address*)";
    (b) lodge that document in process; and
    (c) provide all other parties with a copy of that document.

D 44/76/15 NOTE
[1] Inserted by the Act of Sederunt (Ordinary Cause, Summary Application and Small Claim Rules) Amendment (Miscellaneous) 2004 (SSI 2004/197) (effective May 21, 2004), para.2(11).

Renouncing probation
29.4.—(1) Where, on or at any time after, the closing of the record, the parties seek to renounce probation, they shall lodge in process a joint minute to that effect with or without a statement of admitted facts and any productions.

(2) On the lodging of a joint minute under paragraph (1), the sheriff may order a debate.

Orders for proof
29.5. Where proof is necessary in any cause, the sheriff shall fix a date for taking the proof and may limit the mode of proof.

Hearing parts of proof separately
29.6.—[1] (1) In any cause, the sheriff may—
(a) of his own motion, or
(b) on the motion of any party,
order that proof on liability or any specified issue be heard separately from proof on the question of the amount for which decree may be pronounced and determine the order in which **D 44/76/16** the proofs shall be heard.
(2) The sheriff shall pronounce such interlocutor as he thinks fit at the conclusion of the first proof of any cause ordered to be heard in separate parts under paragraph (1).

NOTE
[1] As amended by SI 1996/2445 (effective November 1, 1996).

Citation of witnesses
29.7.—(1) A witness shall be cited for a proof—
(a) by registered post or the first class recorded delivery service by the solicitor for the party on whose behalf he is cited; or
(b) by a sheriff officer—
    (i) personally;
    (ii) by a citation being left with a resident at the person's dwelling place or an employee at his place of business;
    (iii) by depositing it in that person's dwelling place or place of business;
    (iv) by affixing it to the door of that person's dwelling place or place of business; or
    (v) by registered post or the first class recorded delivery service.
(2) Where service is executed under paragraph (1)(b)(iii) or (iv), the sheriff officer shall, as soon as possible after such service, send, by ordinary post to the address at which he thinks it most likely that the person may be found, a letter containing a copy of the citation.
(3) A certified copy of the interlocutor allowing a proof shall be sufficient warrant to a sheriff officer to cite a witness on behalf of a party.
(4) A witness shall be cited on a period of notice of 7 days in Form G13 and the party citing the witness shall lodge a certificate of citation in Form G12.
(5) A solicitor who cites a witness shall be personally liable for his fees and expenses.
(6) In the event of a solicitor intimating to a witness that his citation is cancelled, the solicitor shall advise him that the cancellation is not to affect any other citation which he may have received from another party.

Citation of witnesses by party litigants
29.8.—(1) Where a party to a cause is a party litigant, he shall—
(a) not later than 4 weeks before the diet of proof, apply to the sheriff by motion to fix caution in such sum as the sheriff considers reasonable having regard to the number of witnesses he proposes to cite and the period for which they may be required to attend **D 44/76/17** court; and
(b) before instructing a sheriff officer to cite a witness, find caution for such expenses as can reasonably be anticipated to be incurred by the witness in answering the citation.
(2) A party litigant who does not intend to cite all the witnesses referred to in his application under paragraph (1)(a), may apply by motion for variation of the amount of caution.

Second diligence against a witness
29.9.—(1) The sheriff may, on the motion of a party, grant a second diligence to compel the attendance of a witness under pain of arrest and imprisonment until caution can be found for his due attendance.
(2) The warrant for a second diligence shall be effective without endorsation and the expenses of such a motion and diligence may be decerned for against the witness.

Failure of witness to attend
29.10.—(1) Where a witness fails to answer a citation after having been duly cited, the sheriff may, on the motion of a party and on production of a certificate of citation, grant warrant for the apprehension of the witness and for bringing him to court; and the expenses of such a motion and apprehension may be decerned for against the witness.
(2) Where a witness duly cited and after having demanded and been paid his travelling

expenses, fails to attend a diet, either before the sheriff or before a commissioner, the sheriff may—

(a) ordain the witness to forfeit and pay a penalty not exceeding £250 unless a reasonable excuse be offered and sustained; and

(b) grant decree for that penalty in favour of the party on whose behalf the witness was cited.

Lodging productions

29.11.—[1] (1) Where a proof has been allowed, all productions and affidavits which are intended to be used at the proof shall be lodged in process not later than 14 days before the diet of proof.

(2) A production which is not lodged in accordance with paragraph (1) shall not be used or put in evidence at a proof unless—

(a) by consent of parties; or

D 44/76/18 (b) with leave of the sheriff on cause shown and on such conditions, if any, as to expenses or otherwise as the sheriff thinks fit.

NOTE

[1] As amended by SSI 2000/239 (effective October 2, 2000).

Copy productions

29.12.—[1] (1) A copy of every documentary production, marked with the appropriate number of process of the principal production, shall be lodged for the use of the sheriff at a proof not later than 48 hours before the diet of proof.

(2) Each copy production consisting of more than one sheet shall be securely fastened together by the party lodging it.

NOTE

[1] As amended by SSI 2000/239 (effective October 2, 2000).

Returning borrowed parts of process and productions before proof

29.13. All parts of process and productions which have been borrowed shall be returned to process before 12.30 pm on the day preceding the diet of proof.

Notices to admit and notices of non-admission

29.14.—[1] (1) At any time after the record has closed, a party may intimate to any other party a notice or notices calling on him to admit for the purposes of that cause only—

(a) such facts relating to an issue averred in the pleadings as may be specified in the notice;

(b) that a particular document lodged in process and specified in the notice is—

(i) an original and properly authenticated document; or

(ii) a true copy of an original and properly authenticated document.

(2) Where a party on whom a notice is intimated under paragraph (1)—

(a) does not admit a fact specified in the notice, or

(b) does not admit, or seeks to challenge, the authenticity of a document specified in the notice,

he shall, within 21 days after the date of intimation of the notice under paragraph (1), intimate a notice of non-admission to the party intimating the notice to him under paragraph (1) stating that he does not admit the fact or document specified.

(3) A party who fails to intimate a notice of non-admission under paragraph (2) shall be

D 44/76/19 deemed to have admitted the fact or document specified in the notice intimated to him under paragraph (1); and such fact or document may be used in evidence at a proof if otherwise admissible in evidence, unless the sheriff, on special cause shown, otherwise directs.

(4) A party who fails to intimate a notice of non-admission under paragraph (2) within 14 days after the notice to admit intimated to him under paragraph (1) shall be liable to the party intimating the notice to admit for the expenses of proving the fact or document specified in that notice unless the sheriff, on special cause shown, otherwise directs.

(5) The party serving a notice under paragraph (1) or (2) shall lodge a copy of it in process.

(6) A deemed admission under paragraph (3) shall not be used against the party by whom it was deemed to be made other than in the cause for the purpose for which it was deemed to be made or in favour of any person other than the party by whom the notice was given under paragraph (1).

[2] (7) The sheriff may, at any time, allow a party to amend or withdraw an admission made by him on such conditions, if any, as he thinks fit.

[2] (8) A party may, at any time, withdraw in whole or in part a notice of non admission by intimating a notice of withdrawal.

Notes
¹ As amended by SSI 2000/239 (effective October 2, 2000).
² Inserted by SSI 2000/239 (effective October 2, 2000).

Instruction of shorthand writer
29.15. Where a shorthand writer is to record evidence at a proof, the responsibility for instructing a shorthand writer shall lie with the pursuer.

Administration of oath or affirmation to witnesses
29.16. The sheriff shall administer the oath to a witness in Form G14 or, where the witness elects to affirm, the affirmation in Form G15.

Proof to be taken continuously **D 44/76/20**
29.17. A proof shall be taken continuously so far as possible; but the sheriff may adjourn the diet from time to time.

Recording of evidence
¹ **29.18.**—(1) Evidence in a cause shall be recorded by—
  (a) a shorthand writer, to whom the oath *de fideli administratione* in connection with the sheriff court service generally shall have been administered, or
  (b) tape recording or other mechanical means approved by the court,
unless the parties, by agreement and with the approval of the sheriff, dispense with the recording of evidence.
(2) Where a shorthand writer is employed to record evidence, he shall, in the first instance, be paid by the parties equally.
(3) Where evidence is recorded by tape recording or other mechanical means, any fee payable shall, in the first instance, be paid by the parties equally.
(4) The solicitors for the parties shall be personally liable for the fees payable under paragraph (2) or (3), and the sheriff may make an order directing payment to be made.
(5) The record of the evidence at a proof shall include—
  (a) any objection taken to a question or to the line of evidence;
  (b) any submission made in relation to such an objection; and
  (c) the ruling of the court in relation to the objection and submission.
(6) A transcript of the record of the evidence shall be made only on the direction of the sheriff; and the cost shall, in the first instance, be borne—
  (a) in an undefended cause, by the solicitor for the pursuer; and
  (b) in a defended cause, by the solicitors for the parties in equal proportions.
(7) The transcript of the record of the evidence provided for the use of the court shall be certified as a faithful record of the evidence by—
  (a) the shorthand writer who recorded the evidence; or
  (b) where the evidence was recorded by tape recording or other mechanical means, by the person who transcribed the record.
(8) The sheriff may make such alterations to the transcript of the record of the evidence as appear to him to be necessary after hearing the parties; and, where such alterations are made, the sheriff shall authenticate the alterations.
(9) Where a transcript of the record of the evidence has been made for the use of the sheriff, copies of it may be obtained by any party from the person who transcribed the record on payment of his fee.
(10) Except with leave of the sheriff, the transcript of the record of the evidence may be borrowed from process only for the purpose of enabling a party to consider whether to appeal against the interlocutor of the sheriff on the proof.
(11) Where a transcript of the record of the evidence is required for the purpose of an appeal **D 44/76/21** but has not been directed to be transcribed under paragraph (6), the appellant—
  (a) may request such a transcript from the shorthand writer or as the case may be, the cost of the transcript being borne by the solicitor for the appellant in the first instance; and
  (b) shall lodge the transcript in process;
and copies of it may be obtained by any party from the shorthand writer or as the case may be, on payment of his fee.
(12) Where the recording of evidence has been dispensed with under paragraph (1), the sheriff, if called upon to do so, shall—
  (a) in the case of an objection to—
    (i) the admissibility of evidence on the ground of confidentiality, or
    (ii) the production of a document on any ground,
    note the terms in writing of such objections and his decision on the objection; and

(b) in the case of any other objection, record, in the note to his interlocutor disposing of the merits of the cause, the terms of the objection and his decision on the objection.

(13) This rule shall, with the necessary modifications, apply to the recording of evidence at a commission as it applies to the recording of evidence at a proof.

NOTE

[1] As amended by SI 1996/2445 (effective November 1, 1996).

Incidental appeal against rulings on confidentiality of evidence and production of documents
29.19.—(1) Where a party or any other person objects to the admissibility of oral or documentary evidence on the ground of confidentiality or to the production of a document on any ground, he may, if dissatisfied with the ruling of the sheriff on the objection, express immediately his formal dissatisfaction with the ruling and, with leave of the sheriff, appeal to the sheriff principal.

(2) The sheriff principal shall dispose of an appeal under paragraph (1) with the least possible delay.

(3) Except as provided in paragraph (1), no appeal may be made during a proof against any decision of the sheriff as to the admissibility of evidence or the production of documents.

D 44/76/22   (4) The appeal referred to in paragraph (1) shall not remove the cause from the sheriff who may proceed with the cause in relation to any issue which is not dependent on the ruling appealed against.

Parties to be heard at close of proof
29.20. At the close of the proof, or at an adjourned diet if for any reason the sheriff has postponed the hearing, the sheriff shall hear parties on the evidence and thereafter shall pronounce judgment with the least possible delay.

D 44/76/23

CHAPTER 30

DECREES, EXTRACTS AND EXECUTION

Interpretation of this Chapter
30.1. In this Chapter, "decree" includes any judgment, deliverance, interlocutor, act, order, finding or authority which may be extracted.

Taxes on funds under control of the court
30.2.—(1) Subject to paragraph (2), in a cause in which money has been consigned into court under the Sheriff Court Consignations (Scotland) Act 1893, no decree, warrant or order for payment to any person shall be granted until there has been lodged with the sheriff clerk a certificate by an authorised officer of the Inland Revenue stating that all taxes or duties payable to the Commissioners of Inland Revenue have been paid or satisfied.

(2) In an action of multiplepoinding, it shall not be necessary for the grant of a decree, warrant or order for payment under paragraph (1) that all of the taxes or duties payable on the estate of a deceased claimant have been paid or satisfied.

Decrees for payment in foreign currency
30.3.—(1) Where decree has been granted for payment of a sum of money in a foreign currency or the sterling equivalent, a party requesting extract of the decree shall do so by minute endorsed on or annexed to the initial writ stating the rate of exchange prevailing on the date of the decree sought to be extracted or the date, or within 3 days before the date, on which the extract is ordered, and the sterling equivalent at that rate for the principal sum and interest decerned for.

(2) A certificate in Form G18, from the Bank of England or a bank which is an institution authorised under the Banking Act 1987 certifying the rate of exchange and the sterling equivalent shall be lodged with the minute requesting extract of the decree.

(3) The extract decree issued by the sheriff clerk shall mention any certificate referred to in paragraph (2).

When decrees extractable
30.4.—[1] (1) Subject to the following paragraphs:—
  (a) subject to sub-paragraph (c), a decree in absence may be extracted after the expiry of 14 days from the date of decree;
  (b) subject to sub-paragraph (c), any decree pronounced in a defended cause may be extracted at any time after whichever is the later of the following:—

(i) the expiry of the period within which an application for leave to appeal may be made and no such application has been made;

(ii) the date on which leave to appeal has been refused and there is no right of appeal from such refusal;

(iii) the expiry of the period within which an appeal may be marked and no appeal has been marked; or

(iv) the date on which an appeal has been finally disposed of; and

(c) where, the sheriff has, in pronouncing decree, reserved any question of expenses, extract of that decree may be issued only after the expiry of 14 days from the date of the interlocutor disposing of the question of expenses unless the sheriff otherwise directs.

(2) The sheriff may, on cause shown, grant a motion to allow extract to be applied for and **D 44/77** issued earlier than a date referred to in paragraph (1).

(3) In relation to a decree referred to in paragraph (1)(b) or (c), paragraph (2) shall not apply unless—

(a) the motion under that paragraph is made in the presence of parties; or

(b) the sheriff is satisfied that proper intimation of the motion has been made in writing to every party not present at the hearing of the motion.

(4) Nothing in this rule shall affect the power of the sheriff to supersede extract.

NOTE
[1] As amended by SI 1996/2445 (effective November 1, 1996).

Extract of certain awards notwithstanding appeal

30.5. The sheriff clerk may issue an extract of an award of custody, access or aliment notwithstanding that an appeal had been made against an interlocutor containing such an award unless an order under rule 31.5 (appeals in connection with custody, access or aliment) has been made excusing obedience to or implement of that interlocutor.

Form of extract decree

30.6.—(1) The extract of a decree mentioned in Appendix 2 shall be in the appropriate form for that decree in Appendix 2.

(2) In the case of a decree not mentioned in Appendix 2, the extract of the decree shall be modelled on a form in that Appendix with such variation as circumstances may require.

Form of warrant for execution

30.7. An extract of a decree on which execution may proceed shall include a warrant for execution in the following terms:— "This extract is warrant for all lawful execution hereon.".

Date of decree in extract

30.8.—(1) Where the sheriff principal has adhered to the decision of the sheriff following an appeal, the date to be inserted in the extract decree as the date of decree shall be the date of the decision of the sheriff principal.

(2) Where a decree has more than one date it shall not be necessary to specify in an extract what was done on each date.

Service of charge where address of defender not known

30.9.—(1) Where the address of a defender is not known to the pursuer, a charge shall be deemed to have been served on the defender if it is—

(a) served on the sheriff clerk of the sheriff court district where the defender's last known address is located; and

(b) displayed by the sheriff clerk on the walls of court for the period of the charge.

(2) On receipt of such a charge, the sheriff clerk shall display it on the walls of court and it shall remain displayed for the period of the charge.

(3) The period specified in the charge shall run from the first date on which it was displayed on the walls of court.

(4) On the expiry of the period of charge, the sheriff clerk shall endorse a certificate on the charge certifying that it has been displayed in accordance with this rule and shall thereafter return it to the sheriff officer by whom service was executed.

CHAPTER 31

APPEALS

Time limit for appeal
31.1. Subject to the provisions of any other enactment, an interlocutor which may be appealed against may be appealed within 14 days after the date of the interlocutor unless it has been extracted following a motion under rule 30.4(2) (early extract).

Applications for leave to appeal
31.2.—(1) Where leave to appeal is required, applications for leave to appeal against an interlocutor of a sheriff shall be made within 7 days after the date of the interlocutor against which it is sought to appeal unless the interlocutor has been extracted following a motion under rule 30.4(2) (early extract).

(2) Subject to the provisions of any other enactment, where leave to appeal has been granted, an appeal shall be made within 7 days after the date when leave was granted.

D 44/78 (3) An application for leave to appeal from a decision in relation to a time to pay direction made under section 1 of the Debtors (Scotland) Act 1987 or the recall or restriction of an arrestment made under section 3(4) of that Act shall specify the question of law on which the appeal is made.

Form of appeal to Court of Session
[1] **31.3.**—(1) An appeal to the Court of Session shall be marked by writing a note of appeal—
  (a) on the interlocutor sheet or other written record containing the interlocutor appealed against, or
  (b) where the decision appealed against is not available or the proceedings appealed against are recorded in an official book, on a separate sheet lodged with the sheriff clerk,
in the following terms:—"The pursuer [*or* defender *or as the case may be*] appeals to the Court of Session.".

(2) A note of appeal under paragraph (1) shall—
  (a) be signed by the appellant or his solicitor;
  (b) bear the date on which it is signed; and
  (c) where the appellant is represented, specify the name and address of the solicitor or other agent who will be acting for him in the appeal.

NOTE
[1] Substituted by SI 1996/2445 (effective November 1, 1996).

Form of appeal to the sheriff principal
[1] **31.4.**—(1) An appeal to the sheriff principal shall be marked by lodging a note of appeal in Form A1.

(2) A note of appeal under paragraph (1) shall—
  (a) be signed by the appellant or his solicitor;
  (b) bear the date on which it is signed;
  (c) where the appellant is represented, specify the name and address of the solicitor or other agent who will be acting for him in the appeal; and
  (d) where a note has not been provided by the sheriff, request that the sheriff write a note setting out the reasons for his decision.

(3) The grounds of appeal in a note of appeal shall consist of brief specific numbered propositions stating the grounds on which it is proposed to submit that the appeal should be allowed or as the case may be.

(4) On making or lodging a note of appeal, the appellant shall send a copy of the note of appeal to every other party.

(5) An appellant—
  (a) may amend the grounds of appeal at any time up to 14 days before the date assigned for the hearing of the appeal; and
  (b) shall at the same time send or deliver a copy of such amendment to every other party.

(6) Where any party wishes to cross-appeal, he shall—
  (a) lodge a note of the grounds of appeal in accordance with paragraph (1) not less than 7 days before the date assigned for the hearing of the appeal; and
  (b) at the same time send a copy of the note to every other party.

(7) The sheriff principal may, on cause shown, shorten or dispense with the time limits mentioned in paragraphs (5) and (6).

(8) On a note of appeal being lodged, the sheriff clerk shall note on the interlocutor sheet that an appeal has been marked and the date of the appeal.

NOTE
¹ Substituted by SI 1996/2445 (effective November 1, 1996).

Transmission of process and notice to parties
¹ **31.5.**—(1) Where an appeal is marked in terms of rule 31.3 (appeal to Court of Session) or 31.4 (appeal to sheriff principal), the sheriff clerk shall transmit the process of the cause—
    (a) in an appeal to the sheriff principal, to him; or
    (b) in an appeal to the Court of Session, to the Deputy Principal Clerk of Session, within the period specified in rule 40.6 of the Rules of the Court of Session 1994.
(2) On transmitting the process in terms of paragraph (1), the sheriff clerk shall—
    (a) send written notice of the appeal to every party; and
    (b) certify on the interlocutor sheet that he has done so.
(3) Failure of the sheriff clerk to comply with paragraph (2) shall not invalidate the appeal.

NOTE
¹ Substituted by SI 1996/2445 (effective November 1, 1996).

Record of pleadings etc.   **D 44/79**
¹ **31.6** In an appeal to him, the sheriff principal may order the appellant to lodge a record of the pleadings containing all adjustments made in the cause with—
    (a) a copy of all relevant interlocutors;
    (b) any other document lodged in process by any party or produced by order of the sheriff, whether or not pursuant to the commission and diligence for its recovery; and
    (c) any other document to which reference is intended to be made in the appeal, by any party.

NOTE
¹ Substituted by SI 1996/2445 (effective November 1, 1996).

Determination of appeal
¹ **31.7.** In an appeal to him, the sheriff principal shall—
    (a) hear parties at an oral hearing; or
    (b) on the motion of the parties, and if he thinks fit, dispose of the appeal without ordering an oral hearing.

NOTE
¹ Substituted by SI 1996/2445 (effective November 1, 1996).

Fixing of Options Hearing or making other order following appeal
¹ **31.8.** On determination of an appeal from a decision of the sheriff made before or at an Options Hearing or any contribution of it, the sheriff principal may order the sheriff clerk to fix a new date for a hearing under rule 9.12 (options hearing) or may make such other order as he thinks fit.

NOTE
¹ Inserted by SI 1996/2445 (effective November 1, 1996).

Appeals in connection with orders under section 11 of the Children (Scotland) Act 1995 or aliment
¹ **31.9.** Where an appeal is marked against an interlocutor making an order under section 11 of the Children (Scotland) Act 1995 (court orders relating to parental responsibilities etc.) or in respect of aliment, the marking of that appeal shall not excuse obedience to or implement of that order unless by order of the sheriff, the sheriff principal or the Court of Session, as the case may be.

NOTE
¹ Inserted by SI 1996/2445 (effective November 1, 1996).

Interim possession etc. pending appeal
¹ **31.10.**—(1) Notwithstanding an appeal, the sheriff or sheriff principal from whose decision an appeal has been taken shall have power—

(a) to regulate all matters relating to interim possession;

(b) to make any order for the preservation of any property to which the action relates or for its sale if perishable;

(c) to make provision for the preservation of evidence; or

(d) to make any interim order which a due regard to the interests of the parties may require.

(2) An order made under paragraph (1) may be reviewed—

(a) by the sheriff principal, on an appeal to him; or

(b) the Court of Session, on an appeal to it.

NOTE
[1] Former rule 31.6 renumbered by SI 1996/2445 (effective November 1, 1996).

Abandonment of appeal
[1] **31.11.** After an appeal to the sheriff principal has been marked, the appellant shall not be entitled to abandon his appeal unless—

(a) of consent of all other parties; or

(b) with leave of the sheriff principal.

NOTE
[1] Former rule 31.7 renumbered by SI 1996/2445 (effective November 1, 1996).

D 44/80

CHAPTER 32

TAXATION OF EXPENSES

Taxation before decree for expenses
32.1. Expenses allowed in any cause, whether in absence or *in foro contentioso*, unless modified at a fixed amount, shall be taxed before decree is granted for them.

Order to lodge account of expenses
[1]**32.1A.** A party found liable in expenses may from 4 months after the date of the interlocutor finding him so liable apply by motion for an order ordaining the party entitled to expenses to lodge an account of those expenses in process.

NOTE
[1] Inserted by the Act of Sederunt (Ordinary Cause, Summary Application and Small Claim Rules) Amendment (Miscellaneous) 2004 (SSI 2004/197) (effective May 21, 2004), para.2(12).

Decree for expenses in name of solicitor
32.2. The sheriff may allow a decree for expenses to be extracted in the name of the solicitor who conducted the cause.

Procedure for taxation
32.3.—(1) Where an account of expenses awarded in a cause is lodged for taxation, the account and process shall be transmitted by the sheriff clerk to the auditor of court.

(2) The auditor of court shall—

(a) assign a diet of taxation not earlier than 7 days from the date he receives the account from the sheriff clerk; and

(b) intimate that diet forthwith to the party who lodged the account.

(3) The party who lodged the account of expenses shall, on receiving intimation from the auditor of court under paragraph (2)—

(a) send a copy of the account, and

(b) intimate the date, time and place of the diet of taxation,

to every other party.

(4) After the account has been taxed, the auditor of court shall transmit the process with the account and his report to the sheriff clerk.

(5) Where the auditor of court has reserved consideration of the account at the date of the taxation, he shall intimate his decision to the parties who attended the taxation.

(6) Where no objections are lodged under rule 32.4 (objections to auditor's report), the sheriff may grant decree for the expenses as taxed.

Objections to auditor's report

32.4.—(1) A party may lodge a note of objections to an account as taxed only where he attended the diet of taxation.

(2) Such a note shall be lodged within 7 days after—

    (a) the diet of taxation; or

    (b) where the auditor of court reserved consideration of the account under paragraph (5) of rule 32.3, the date on which the auditor of court intimates his decision under that paragraph.

(3) The sheriff shall dispose of the objection in a summary manner, with or without answers.

SPECIAL PROVISIONS IN RELATION TO PARTICULAR CAUSES

CHAPTER 33

FAMILY ACTIONS

PART I

GENERAL PROVISIONS

Interpretation of this Chapter

[1] **33.1.**—(1) In this Chapter, "family action" means—

    (a) an action of divorce;

    (b) an action of separation;   **D 44/80/1**

    (c) an action of declarator of legitimacy;

    (d) an action of declarator of illegitimacy;

    (e) an action of declarator of parentage;

    (f) an action of declarator of non-parentage;

    (g) an action of declarator of legitimation;

    (h) an action or application for, or in respect of, an order under section 11 of the Children (Scotland) Act 1995 (court orders relating to parental responsibilities etc.), except—

        (i) an application for the appointment of a judicial factor mentioned in section 11(2)(g) of the Act of 1995 to which Part I of the Act of Sederunt (Judicial Factors Rules) 1992 applies; and

        (ii) an application for the appointment or removal of a person as a guardian **D 44/81** mentioned in section 11(2)(h) of the Act of 1995 to which paragraph 4 of the Act of Sederunt (Family Proceedings in the Sheriff Court) 1996 applies;

    (i) an action of affiliation and aliment;

    (j) an action of, or application for or in respect of, aliment;

    (k) an action or application for financial provision after a divorce or annulment in an overseas country within the meaning of Part IV of the Matrimonial and Family Proceedings Act 1984;

    (l) an action or application for an order under the Act of 1981;

    (m) an application for the variation or recall of an order mentioned in section 8(1) of the Law Reform (Miscellaneous Provisions) (Scotland) Act 1966.

(2) In this Chapter, unless the context otherwise requires—

    "the Act of 1975" means the Children Act 1975;

    "the Act of 1976" means the Divorce (Scotland) Act 1976;

    "the Act of 1981" means the Matrimonial Homes (Family Protection) (Scotland) Act 1981;

    "the Act of 1985" means the Family Law (Scotland) Act 1985;

    "the Act of 1995" means the Children (Scotland) Act 1995;

    "contact order" has the meaning assigned in section 11(2)(d) of the Act of 1995;

    [2] "full gender recognition certificate" and "interim gender recognition certificate" mean the certificates issued as such under section 4 or 5 of the Gender Recognition Act 2004;

    [2] "Gender Recognition Panel" is to be construed in accordance with Schedule 1 to the Gender Recognition Act 2004;

    "local authority" means a council constituted under section 2 of the Local Government etc. (Scotland) Act 1994;

    "mental disorder" means mental illness or mental handicap however caused or manifested;

    "order for financial provision" means, except in Part VII of this Chapter (financial provision after overseas divorce or annulment), an order mentioned in section 8(1) of the Act of 1985;

    "parental responsibilities" has the meaning assigned in section 1(3) of the Act 1995;

    "parental rights" has the meaning assigned in section 2(4) of the Act of 1995;

"residence order" has the meaning assigned in section 11(2)(c) of the Act of 1995;
"section 11 order" means an order under section 11 of the Act of 1995.

(3) For the purposes of rules 33.2 (averments in actions of divorce or separation about other proceedings) and 33.3 (averments where section 11 order sought) and, in relation to proceedings in another jurisdiction, Schedule 3 to the Domicile and Matrimonial Proceedings Act 1973 (sisting of consistorial actions in Scotland), proceedings are continuing at any time after they have commenced and before they are finally disposed of.

NOTE

[1] As amended by SI 1996/2167 (effective November 1, 1996).

[2] Inserted by the Act of Sederunt (Ordinary Cause Rules) Amendment (Gender Recognition Act 2004) 2005 (SSI 2005/189), para.2 (effective April 4, 2005).

Averments in actions of divorce or separation about other proceedings

33.2.—(1) This rule applies to an action of divorce or separation.

(2) In an action to which this rule applies, the pursuer shall state in the condescendence of the initial writ—

    (a) whether to his knowledge any proceedings are continuing in Scotland or in any other country in respect of the marriage to which the initial writ relates or are capable of affecting its validity or subsistence; and

    (b) where such proceedings are continuing—

        (i) the court, tribunal or authority before which the proceedings have been commenced;

        (ii) the date of commencement;

        (iii) the names of the parties;

        (iv) the date, or expected date of any proof (or its equivalent) in the proceedings; and

        (v) such other facts as may be relevant to the question of whether or not the action before the sheriff should be sisted under Schedule 3 to the Domicile and Matrimonial Proceedings Act 1973.

(3) Where—

    (a) such proceedings are continuing;

    (b) the action before the sheriff is defended; and

    (c) either—

        (i) the initial writ does not contain the statement referred to in paragraph (2)(a), or

        (ii) the particulars mentioned in paragraph (2)(b) as set out in the initial writ are incomplete or incorrect,

D 44/82 any defences or minute, as the case may be, lodged by any person to the action shall include that statement and, where appropriate, the further or correct particulars mentioned in paragraph (2)(b).

Averments where section 11 order sought

[1] **33.3.**—(1) A party to a family action, who makes an application in that action for a section 11 order in respect of a child shall include in his pleadings—

    (a) where that action is an action of divorce or separation, averments giving particulars of any other proceedings known to him, whether in Scotland or elsewhere and whether concluded or not, which relate to the child in respect of whom the section 11 order is sought;

    (b) in any other family action—

        (i) the averments mentioned in paragraph (a); and

        (ii) averments giving particulars of any proceedings known to him which are continuing, whether in Scotland or elsewhere, and which relate to the marriage of the parents of that child.

(2) Where such other proceedings are continuing or have taken place and the averments of the applicant for such a section 11 order—

    (a) do not contain particulars of the other proceedings, or

    (b) contain particulars which are incomplete or incorrect,

any defences or minute, as the case may be, lodged by any party to the family action shall include such particulars or such further or correct particulars as are known to him.

(3) In paragraph (1)(b)(ii), "child" includes a child of the family within the meaning assigned in section 42(4) of the Family Law Act 1986.

NOTE

[1] As amended by SI 1996/2167 (effective November 1, 1996) and SI 1996/2445 (effective November 1, 1996) (clerical error).

Averments where identity or address of person not known

33.4. In a family action, where the identity or address of any person referred to in rule 33.7 as a person in respect of whom a warrant for intimation requires to be applied for is not known and cannot reasonably be ascertained, the party required to apply for the warrant shall include in his pleadings an averment of that fact and averments setting out what steps have been taken to ascertain the identity or address, as the case may be, of that person.

Averments about maintenance orders
    33.5. In a family action in which an order for aliment or periodical allowance is sought, or is sought to be varied or recalled, by any party, the pleadings of that party shall contain an averment stating whether and, if so, when and by whom, a maintenance order (within the meaning of section 106 of the Debtors (Scotland) Act 1987) has been granted in favour of or against that party or of any other person in respect of whom the order is sought.

Averments where aliment or financial provision sought
    [1] **33.6.**—(1) In this rule—
    "the Act of 1991" means the Child Support Act 1991;
    "child" has the meaning assigned in section 55 of the Act of 1991;
    "crave relating to aliment" means—
        (a) for the purposes of paragraph (2), a crave for decree of aliment in relation to a child or for recall or variation of such a decree; and
        (b) for the purposes of paragraph (3), a crave for decree of aliment in relation to a child or for recall or variation of such a decree or for the variation or termination of an agreement on aliment in relation to a child;
    "maintenance calculation" has the meaning assigned in section 54 of the Act of 1991.
    (2) A family action containing a crave relating to aliment and to which section 8(6), (7), (8) or (10) of the Act of 1991 (top up maintenance orders) applies shall—
        (a) include averments stating, where appropriate—
            (i) that a maintenance calculation under section 11 of that Act (maintenance calculations) is in force;
            (ii) the date of the maintenance calculation;
            (iii) the amount and frequency of periodical payments of child support maintenance fixed by the maintenance calculation; and
            (iv) the grounds on which the sheriff retains jurisdiction under section 8(6), (7), (8) or (10) of that Act; and
        (b) unless the sheriff on cause shown otherwise directs, be accompanied by any document issued by the Secretary of State to the party intimating the making of the maintenance calculation referred to in sub-paragraph (a).
    (3) A family action containing a crave relating to aliment, and to which section 8(6), (7), (8) or (10) of the Act of 1991 does not apply, shall include averments stating—
        (a) that the habitual residence of the absent parent, person with care or qualifying child, **D 44/83** within the meaning of section 3 of that Act, is furth of the United Kingdom;
        (b) that the child is not a child within the meaning of section 55 of that Act; or
        (c) where the action is lodged for warranting before 7th April 1997, the grounds on which the sheriff retains jurisdiction.
    (4) In an action for declarator of non-parentage or illegitimacy—
        (a) the initial writ shall include an article of condescendence stating whether the pursuer previously has been alleged to be the parent in an application for a maintenance calculation under section 4, 6 or 7 of the Act of 1991 (applications for maintenance calculation); and
        (b) where an allegation of paternity has been made against the pursuer, the Secretary of State shall be named as a defender in the action.
    (5) A family action involving parties in respect of whom a decision has been made in any application, review or appeal under the Act of 1991 relating to any child of those parties, shall—
        (a) include averments stating that such a decision has been made and giving details of that decision; and
        (b) unless the sheriff on cause shown otherwise directs, be accompanied by any document issued by the Secretary of State to the parties intimating that decision.

NOTE
    [1] As amended by the Act of Sederunt (Ordinary Cause, Summary Application, Summary Cause and Small Claim Rules) Amendment (Miscellaneous) 2003 (SSI 2003/26), para.2(8) (effective January 24, 2003).

Warrants and forms for intimation
    [1] **33.7.**—(1) Subject to paragraphs (5) and (7), in the initial writ in a family action, the pursuer shall include a crave for a warrant for intimation—

(a) in an action where the address of the defender is not known to the pursuer and cannot reasonably be ascertained, to—
  (i) every child of the marriage between the parties who has reached the age of 16 years; and
  (ii) one of the next-of-kin of the defender who has reached that age,
  unless the address of such a person is not known to the pursuer and cannot reasonably be ascertained, and a notice of intimation in Form F1 shall be attached to the copy of the initial writ intimated to any such person;

(b) in an action where the pursuer alleges that the defender has committed adultery with another person, to that person, unless—
  (i) that person is not named in the initial writ and, if the adultery is relied on for the purposes of section 1(2)(a) of the Act of 1976 (irretrievable breakdown of marriage by reason of adultery), the initial writ contains an averment that his or her identity is not known to the pursuer and cannot reasonably be ascertained; or
  (ii) the pursuer alleges that the defender has been guilty of rape upon or incest with, that named person,
  and a notice of intimation in Form F2 shall be attached to the copy of the initial writ intimated to any such person;

(c) in an action where the defender is a person who is suffering from a mental disorder, to—
  (i) those persons mentioned in sub-paragraph (a)(i) and (ii), unless the address of such person is not known to the pursuer and cannot reasonably be ascertained; and
  (ii) the *curator bonis* to the defender, if one has been appointed,
  and a notice of intimation in Form F3 shall be attached to the copy of the initial writ intimated to any such person;

(d) in an action relating to a marriage which was entered into under a law which permits polygamy where—
  (i) one of the decrees specified in section 2(2) of the Matrimonial Proceedings (Polygamous Marriages) Act 1972 is sought; and
  (ii) either party to the marriage in question has any spouse additional to the other party,
  to any such additional spouse, and a notice of intimation in Form F4 shall be attached to the initial writ intimated to any such person;

(e) in an action of divorce or separation where the sheriff may make a section 11 order in respect of a child—
  (i) who is in the care of a local authority, to that authority and a notice of intimation in Form F5 shall be attached to the initial writ intimated to that authority;
  (ii) who, being a child of one party to the marriage, has been accepted as a child of the family by the other party to the marriage and who is liable to be maintained by a third party, to that third party, and a notice of intimation in Form F5 shall be attached to the initial writ intimated to that third party; or
  (iii) in respect of whom a third party in fact exercises care and control, to that third party, and a notice of intimation in Form F6 shall be attached to the initial writ intimated to that third party;

(f) in an action where the pursuer craves a section 11 order, to any parent or guardian of the child who is not a party to the action, and a notice of intimation in Form F7 shall be attached to the initial writ intimated to any such parent or guardian;

(g) in an action where the pursuer craves a residence order in respect of a child and he is—
  (i) not a parent of that child; and
  (ii) resident in Scotland when the initial writ is lodged,
  to the local authority within which area the pursuer resides, and a notice of intimation in Form F8 shall be attached to the initial writ intimated to that authority;

(h) in an action which includes a crave for a section 11 order, to the child to whom such an order would relate if not a party to the action, and a notice of intimation in Form F9 shall be intimated to that child;

(i) in an action where the pursuer makes an application for an order under section 8(1)(aa) of the Act of 1985 (transfer of property) and—
  (i) the consent of a third party to such a transfer is necessary by virtue of an obligation, enactment or rule of law, or
  (ii) the property is subject to a security,
  to the third party or creditor, as the case may be, and a notice of intimation in Form F10 shall be attached to the initial writ intimated to any such person;

(j) in an action where the pursuer makes an application for an order under section 18 of the Act of 1985 (which relates to avoidance transactions), to—

(i) any third party in whose favour the transfer of, or transaction involving, the property is to be or was made, and

(ii) any other person having an interest in the transfer of, or transaction involving, the property,

and a notice of intimation in Form F11 shall be attached to the initial writ intimated to any such person;

(k) in an action where the pursuer makes an application for an order under the Act of 1981—

(i) where he is a non-entitled partner and the entitled partner has a spouse, to that spouse; or

(ii) where the application is under section 2(1)(e), 2(4)(a), 3(1), 3(2), 4, 7, 13 or 18 of that Act, and the entitled spouse or entitled partner is a tenant or occupies the matrimonial home by permission of a third party, to the landlord or the third party, as the case may be,

and a notice of intimation in Form F12 shall be attached to the initial writ intimated to any such person;

(l) in an action where the pursuer makes an application for an order under section 8(1)(ba) of the Act of 1985 (orders under section 12A of the Act of 1985 for pension lump sum), to the person responsible for the pension arrangement, and a notice of intimation in Form F12A shall be attached to the initial writ intimated to any such person; and

[2] (m) in an action where a pursuer makes an application for an order under section 8(1)(baa) of the Act of 1985 (pension sharing orders), to the person responsible for the pension arrangement and a notice of intimation in Form F12B shall be attached to the initial writ intimated to any such person.

(2) Expressions used in paragraph (1)(k) which are also used in the Act of 1981 have the same meaning as in that Act.

(3) A notice of intimation under paragraph (1) shall be on a period of notice of 21 days unless the sheriff otherwise orders; but the sheriff shall not order a period of notice of less than 2 days.

(4) In a family action, where the pursuer—

(a) craves a residence order in respect of a child,

(b) is not a parent of the child, and

(c) is not resident in Scotland when the initial writ is lodged for warranting,

he shall include a crave for an order for intimation in Form F8 to such local authority as the sheriff thinks fit.

(5) Where the address of a person mentioned in paragraph (1)(b), (d), (e), (f), (h), (i), (j), (k) or (l) is not known and cannot reasonably be ascertained, the pursuer shall include a crave in the initial writ to dispense with intimation; and the sheriff may grant that crave or make such other order as he thinks fit.

(6) Where the identity or address of a person to whom intimation of a family action is required becomes known during the course of the action, the party who would have been required to insert a warrant for intimation to that person shall lodge a motion for a warrant for **D 44/84/1** intimation to that person or to dispense with such intimation.

(7) Where a pursuer considers that to order intimation to a child under paragraph (1)(h) is inappropriate, he shall—

(a) include a crave in the initial writ to dispense with intimation to that child, and

(b) include in the initial writ averments setting out the reasons why such intimation is inappropriate;

and the sheriff may dispense with such intimation or make such other order as he thinks fit.

NOTE

[1] As amended by SI 1996/2167 (effective November 1, 1996) and SI 1996/2445 (effective November 1, 1996).

[2] Inserted by the Act of Sederunt (Ordinary Cause Rules) Amendment (No.2)(Pension Sharing on Divorce etc.) 2000 (SSI 2000/408), para.2(2)(b)(ii).

Intimation where improper association

33.8.—(1) In a family action where the pursuer alleges an improper association between the defender and another named person, the pursuer shall, immediately after the expiry of the period of notice, lodge a motion for an order for intimation to that person or to dispense with such intimation.

(2) In determining a motion under paragraph (1), the sheriff may—

(a) make such order for intimation as he thinks fit; or

(b) dispense with intimation; and

(c) where he dispenses with intimation, order that the name of that person be deleted from the condescendence of the initial writ.

(3) Where intimation is ordered under paragraph (2), a copy of the initial writ and an intimation in Form F13 shall be intimated to the named person.

(4) In paragraph (1), "improper association" means sodomy, incest or any homosexual relationship.

Productions in action of divorce or where section 11 order may be made
[1] **33.9.** Unless the sheriff otherwise directs—
- (a) in an action of divorce, a warrant for citation shall not be granted without there being produced with the initial writ an extract of the relevant entry in the register of marriages or an equivalent document; and
- (b) in an action which includes a crave for a section 11 order, a warrant for citation shall not be granted without there being produced with the initial writ an extract of the relevant entry in the register of births or an equivalent document.

NOTE
[1] As amended by SI 1996/2167 (effective November 1, 1996).

D 44/85 *Productions in action of divorce on ground of issue of interim gender recognition certificate*
[1] **33.9A.**—(1) This rule applies where, in an action of divorce, the ground on which decree of divorce may be granted is that an interim gender recognition certificate has, after the date of the marriage, been issued to either party to the marriage.

(2) Unless the sheriff otherwise directs, a warrant for citation shall not be granted without there being produced with the initial writ—
- (a) where the pursuer is the subject of the interim gender recognition certificate, the interim gender recognition certificate or, failing that, a certified copy of the interim gender recognition certificate; or
- (b) where the pursuer is the spouse of the person who is the subject of the interim gender recognition certificate, a certified copy of the interim gender recognition certificate.

(3) For the purposes of this rule, a certified copy of an interim gender recognition certificate shall be a copy of that certificate sealed with the seal of the Gender Recognition Panels and certified to be a true copy by an officer authorised by the President of Gender Recognition Panels.

Application for corrected gender recognition certificate
33.9B. An application for a corrected gender recognition certificate under section 6 of the Gender Recognition Act 2004 by—
- (a) the person to whom a full gender recognition certificate has been issued; or
- (b) the Secretary of State,

shall be made by minute in the process of the action pursuant to which the full gender recognition certificate was issued.

NOTE
[1] Inserted by the Act of Sederunt (Ordinary Cause Rules) Amendment (Gender Recognition Act 2004) 2005 (SSI 2005/189), para.2 (effective April 4, 2005).

Warrant of citation
33.10. The warrant of citation in a family action shall be in Form F14.

Form of citation and certificate
33.11.—(1) Subject to rule 5.6 (service where address of person is not known), citation of a defender shall be in Form F15, which shall be attached to a copy of the initial writ and warrant of citation and shall have appended to it a notice of intention to defend in Form F26.

(2) The certificate of citation shall be in Form F16 which shall be attached to the initial writ.

Execution of service on, or intimation to, local authority
[1] **33.12.**—(1) Where a local authority referred to in rule 33.7(1)(g) (residence order sought by non-parent resident in Scotland) or 33.7(4) (residence order sought by pursuer not resident in Scotland) is named as a defender in an initial writ at the time it is lodged, service of the initial writ on that local authority shall be executed within 7 days after the date of granting of the warrant of citation.

(2) Where in a family action—
- (a) to which rule 33.7(1)(g) applies, or
- (b) in which a motion under rule 33.7(4) is required,

the local authority referred to in that provision is named as a defender in the initial writ at the time it is lodged, a notice in Form F8 shall be attached to the copy of the initial writ served on that local authority.

(3) In any family action, the sheriff may, if he thinks fit, order intimation to a local authority; and such intimation shall be in Form F8.

(4) Where, by virtue of paragraph 3 of this rule or rule 33.7(1)(g) or 33.7(4), intimation of an application for a residence order is to be made to a local authority, intimation to that local authority shall be given within 7 days after the date on which a warrant for citation, or an order for intimation, as the case may be, has been granted.

NOTE
[1] As amended by SI 1996/2167 (effective November 1, 1996).

Service in cases of mental disorder of defender
33.13.—(1) In a family action where the defender suffers or appears to suffer from mental disorder and is resident in a hospital or other similar institution, citation shall be executed by registered post or the first class recorded delivery service addressed to the medical officer in charge of that hospital or institution; and there shall be included with the copy of the initial writ—

    (a) a citation in Form F15;   **D 44/86**

    (b) any notice required by rule 33.14(1);

    (c) a request in Form F17;

    (d) a form of certificate in Form F18 requesting the medical officer to—

        (i) deliver and explain the initial writ, citation and any notice or form of notice of consent required under rule 33.14(1) personally to the defender; or

        (ii) certify that such delivery or explanation would be dangerous to the health or mental condition of the defender; and

    (e) a stamped envelope addressed for return of that certificate to the pursuer or his solicitor, if he has one.

(2) The medical officer referred to in paragraph (1) shall send the certificate in Form F18 duly completed to the pursuer or his solicitor, as the case may be.

(3) The certificate mentioned in paragraph (2) shall be attached to the certificate of citation.

(4) Where such a certificate bears that the initial writ has not been delivered to the defender, the sheriff may, at any time before decree—

    (a) order such further medical inquiry, and

    (b) make such order for further service or intimation,

as he thinks fit.

Notices in certain actions of divorce or separation
33.14.—(1) In the following actions of divorce or separation there shall be attached to the copy of the initial writ served on the defender—

    (a) in an action relying on section 1(2)(d) of the Act of 1976 (no cohabitation for two years with consent of defender to decree)—

        (i) which is an action of divorce, a notice in Form F19 and a notice of consent in Form F20;

        (ii) which is an action of separation, a notice in Form F21 and a form of notice of consent in Form F22;

    (b) in an action relying on section 1(2)(e) of the Act of 1976 (no cohabitation for five years)—

        (i) which is an action of divorce, a notice in Form F23;

        (ii) which is an action of separation, a notice in Form F24.

[1] (2) The certificate of citation of an initial writ in an action mentioned in paragraph (1) shall state which notice or form mentioned in paragraph (1) has been attached to the initial writ.

NOTE
[1] As amended by SI 1996/2445 (effective November 1, 1996).

Orders for intimation
33.15.—(1) In any family action, the sheriff may, at any time—

    (a) subject to paragraph (2), order intimation to be made on such person as he thinks fit;

    (b) postpone intimation, where he considers that such postponement is appropriate and, in that case, the sheriff shall make such order in respect of postponement of intimation as he thinks fit; or

    (c) dispense with intimation, where he considers that such dispensation is appropriate.

(2) Where the sheriff is considering whether to make a section 11 order by virtue of section 12 of the Act of 1995 (restrictions on decrees for divorce, separation or annulment affecting

children), he shall, subject to paragraph (1)(c) and without prejudice to paragraph (1)(b) of this rule, order intimation in Form F9 to the child to whom the section 11 order would relate unless—

    (a) intimation has been given to the child under rule 33.7(1)(h); or

    (b) the sheriff considers that the child is not of sufficient age or maturity to express his views.

(3) Where a party makes a crave or averment in a family action which, had it been made in an initial writ, would have required a warrant for intimation under rule 33.7, that party shall include a crave in his writ for a warrant for intimation or to dispense with such intimation; and rule 33.7 shall, with the necessary modifications, apply to a crave for a warrant under this paragraph as it applies to a crave for a warrant under that rule.

Appointment of curators ad litem to defenders

33.16.—(1) This rule applies to an action of divorce or separation where it appears to the court that the defender is suffering from a mental disorder.

(2) In an action to which this rule applies, the sheriff shall—

    (a) appoint a curator *ad litem* to the defender;

    (b) where the facts set out in section 1(2)(d) of the Act of 1976 (no cohabitation for two years with consent of defender to decree) are relied on—

D 44/87

        (i) make an order for intimation of the ground of the action to the Mental Welfare Commission for Scotland; and

        (ii) include in such an order a requirement that the Commission sends to the sheriff clerk a report indicating whether in its opinion the defender is capable of deciding whether or not to give consent to the granting of decree.

[1] (3) Within 7 days after the appointment of a curator *ad litem* under paragraph (2)(a), the pursuer shall send to him—

    (a) a copy of the initial writ and any defences (including any adjustments and amendments) lodged; and

    (b) a copy of any notice in Form G5 sent to him by the sheriff clerk.

(4) On receipt of a report required under paragraph (2)(b)(ii), the sheriff clerk shall—

    (a) lodge the report in process; and

    (b) intimate that this has been done to—

        (i) the pursuer;

        (ii) the solicitor for the defender, if known; and

        (iii) the curator *ad litem*.

(5) The curator *ad litem* shall lodge in process one of the writs mentioned in paragraph (6)—

    (a) within 14 days after the report required under paragraph (2)(b)(ii) has been lodged in process; or

    (b) where no such report is required, within 21 days after the date of his appointment under paragraph (2)(a).

(6) The writs referred to in paragraph (5) are—

    (a) a notice of intention to defend;

    (b) defences to the action;

    (c) a minute adopting defences already lodged; and

    (d) a minute stating that the curator *ad litem* does not intend to lodge defences.

(7) Notwithstanding that he has lodged a minute stating that he does not intend to lodge defences, a curator *ad litem* may appear at any stage of the action to protect the interests of the defender.

(8) If, at any time, it appears to the curator *ad litem* that the defender is not suffering from mental disorder, he may report that fact to the court and seek his own discharge.

(9) The pursuer shall be responsible, in the first instance, for payment of the fees and outlays of the curator *ad litem* incurred during the period from his appointment until—

    (a) he lodges a minute stating that he does not intend to lodge defences;

    (b) he decides to instruct the lodging of defences or a minute adopting defences already lodged; or

    (c) being satisfied after investigation that the defender is not suffering from mental disorder, he is discharged.

NOTE

[1] As amended by SI 1996/2445 (effective November 1, 1996).

Applications for sist

33.17. An application for a sist, or the recall of a sist, under Schedule 3 to the Domicile and Matrimonial Proceedings Act 1973 shall be made by written motion.

Notices of consent to divorce or separation

33.18.—(1) Where, in an action of divorce or separation in which the facts in section 1(2)(d) of the Act of 1976 (no cohabitation for two years with consent of defender to decree) are relied on, the defender wishes to consent to the grant of decree of divorce or separation he shall do so by giving notice in writing in Form F20 (divorce) or Form F22 (separation), as the case may be, to the sheriff clerk.

(2) The evidence of one witness shall be sufficient for the purpose of establishing that the signature on a notice of consent under paragraph (1) is that of the defender.

(3) In an action of divorce or separation where the initial writ includes, for the purposes of section 1(2)(d) of the Act of 1976, an averment that the defender consents to the grant of decree, the defender may give notice by letter sent to the sheriff clerk stating that he has not so consented or that he withdraws any consent which he has already given.

(4) On receipt of a letter under paragraph (3), the sheriff clerk shall intimate the terms of the letter to the pursuer.

(5) On receipt of any intimation under paragraph (4), the pursuer may, within 14 days after the date of the intimation, if none of the other facts mentioned in section 1(2) of the Act of 1976 is averred in the initial writ, lodge a motion for the action to be sisted.

(6) If no such motion is lodged, the pursuer shall be deemed to have abandoned the action and the action shall be dismissed.

(7) If a motion under paragraph (5) is granted and the sist is not recalled or renewed within a period of 6 months from the date of the interlocutor granting the sist, the pursuer shall be deemed to have abandoned the action and the action shall be dismissed.

Procedure in respect of children **D 44/88**

[1] **33.19.**—(1) In a family action, in relation to any matter affecting a child, where that child has—

    (a) returned to the sheriff clerk Form F9, or

    (b) otherwise indicated to the court a wish to express views on a matter affecting him,

the sheriff shall not grant any order unless an opportunity has been given for the views of that child to be obtained or heard.

(2) Where a child has indicated his wish to express his views, the sheriff shall order such steps to be taken as he considers appropriate to ascertain the views of that child.

(3) The sheriff shall not grant an order in a family action, in relation to any matter affecting a child who has indicated his wish to express his views, unless due weight has been given by the sheriff to the views expressed by that child, having due regard to his age and maturity.

NOTE

[1] As substituted by SI 1996/2167 (effective November 1, 1996).

Recording of views of the child

[1] **33.20**—(1) This rule applies where a child expresses a view on a matter affecting him whether expressed personally to the sheriff or to a person appointed by the sheriff for that purpose or provided by the child in writing.

(2) The sheriff, or the person appointed by the sheriff, shall record the views of the child in writing; and the sheriff may direct that such views, and any written views, given by a child shall—

    (a) be sealed in an envelope marked "Views of the child—confidential";

    (b) be kept in the court process without being recorded in the inventory of process;

    (c) be available to a sheriff only;

    (d) not be opened by any person other than a sheriff; and

    (e) not form a borrowable part of the process.

NOTE

[1] As substituted by SI 1996/2167 (effective November 1, 1996).

Appointment of local authority or reporter to report on a child

[1] **33.21.**—(1) This rule applies where, at any stage of a family action, the sheriff appoints—

    (a) a local authority under section 11(1) of the Matrimonial Proceedings (Children) Act 1958 (reports as to arrangements for future care and upbringing of children) or otherwise, or

    (b) another person (referred to in this rule as a "reporter"), whether under a provision mentioned in sub-paragraph (a) or otherwise,

to investigate and report to the court on the circumstances of a child and on proposed arrangements for the care and upbringing of the child.

(2) On making an appointment referred to in paragraph (1), the sheriff shall direct that the

party who sought the appointment or, where the court makes the appointment of its own motion, the pursuer or minuter, as the case may be, shall—
- (a) instruct the local authority or reporter; and
- (b) be responsible, in the first instance, for the fees and outlays of the local authority or reporter appointed.

(3) Where a local authority or reporter is appointed—
- (a) the party who sought the appointment, or
- (b) where the sheriff makes the appointment of his own motion, the pursuer or minuter, as the case may be,

shall, within 7 days after the date of the appointment, intimate the name and address of the local authority or reporter to any local authority to which intimation of the family action has been made.

(4) On completion of a report referred to in paragraph (1), the local authority or reporter, as the case may be, shall send the report, with a copy of it for each party, to the sheriff clerk.

(5) On receipt of such a report, the sheriff clerk shall send a copy of the report to each party.

(6) Where a local authority or reporter has been appointed to investigate and report in respect of a child, an application for a section 11 order in respect of that child shall not be determined until the report of the local authority or reporter, as the case may be, has been lodged.

NOTE
[1] As amended by SI 1996/2167 (effective November 1, 1996).

D 44/89 *Referral to family mediation*
[1] **33.22.** In any family action in which an order in relation to parental responsibilities or parental rights is in issue, the sheriff may, at any stage of the action, where he considers it appropriate to do so, refer that issue to a mediator accredited to a specified family mediation organisation.

NOTE
[1] As substituted by SI 1996/2167 (effective November 1, 1996).

Child Welfare Hearing
[1] **33.22A.**—(1) Where—
- (a) on the lodging of a notice of intention to defend in a family action in which the initial writ seeks or includes a crave for a section 11 order, a defender wishes to oppose any such crave or order, or seeks the same order as that craved by the pursuer,
- (b) on the lodging of a notice of intention to defend in a family action, the defender seeks a section 11 order which is not craved by the pursuer, or
- (c) in any other circumstances in a family action, the sheriff considers that a Child Welfare Hearing should be fixed and makes an order (whether at his own instance or on the motion of a party) that such a hearing shall be fixed,

the sheriff clerk shall fix a date and time for a Child Welfare Hearing on the first suitable court date occurring not sooner than 21 days after the lodging of such notice of intention to defend, unless the sheriff directs the hearing to be held on an earlier date.

(2) On fixing the date for the Child Welfare Hearing, the sheriff clerk shall intimate the date of the Child Welfare Hearing to the parties in Form F41.

(3) The fixing of the date of the Child Welfare Hearing shall not affect the right of a party to make any other application to the court whether by motion or otherwise.

(4) At the Child Welfare Hearing (which may be held in private), the sheriff shall seek to secure the expeditious resolution of disputes in relation to the child by ascertaining from the parties the matters in dispute and any information relevant to that dispute, and may—
- (a) order such steps to be taken, or
- (b) make such order, if any, or
- (c) order further procedure,

as he thinks fit.

(5) All parties (including a child who has indicated his wish to attend) shall, except on cause shown, attend the Child Welfare Hearing personally.

(6) It shall be the duty of the parties to provide the sheriff with sufficient information to enable him to conduct the Child Welfare Hearing.

NOTE
[1] As inserted by SI 1996/2167 (effective November 1, 1996).

Applications for orders to disclose whereabouts of children
33.23.—(1) An application for an order under section 33(1) of the Family Law Act 1986 (which relates to the disclosure of the whereabouts of a child) shall be made by motion.

(2) Where the sheriff makes an order under section 33(1) of the Family Law Act 1986, he may ordain the person against whom the order has been made to appear before him or to lodge an affidavit.

Applications in relation to removal of children
[1] **33.24.**—(1) An application for leave under section 51(1) of the Act of 1975 (authority to remove a child from the care and possession of the applicant for a residence order) or for an order under section 35(3) of the Family Law Act 1986 (application for interdict or interim interdict prohibiting removal of child from jurisdiction) shall be made—
(a) by a party to the action, by motion; or
(b) by a person who is not a party to the action, by minute.

(2) An application under section 35(3) of the Family Law Act 1986 need not be served or intimated.

(3) An application under section 23(2) of the Child Abduction and Custody Act 1985 (declarator that removal of child from United Kingdom was unlawful) shall be made—
(a) in an action depending before the sheriff—
(i) by a party, in the initial writ, defences or minute, as the case may be, or by motion; or
(ii) by any other person, by minute; or
(b) after final decree, by minute in the process of the action to which the application relates.

NOTE
[1] As amended by SI 1996/2167 (effective November 1, 1996).

Intimation to local authority before supervised contact order **D 44/90**
33.25. Where the sheriff, at his own instance or on the motion of a party, is considering making a contact order or an interim contact order subject to supervision by the social work department of a local authority, he shall ordain the party moving for such an order to intimate to the Chief Executive of that local authority (where not already a party to the action and represented at the hearing at which the issue arises)—
(a) the terms of any relevant motion;
(b) the intention of the sheriff to order that the contact order be supervised by the social work department of that local authority; and
(c) that the local authority shall, within such period as the sheriff has determined—
(i) notify the sheriff clerk whether it intends to make representations to the sheriff; and
(ii) where it intends to make representations in writing, to do so within that period.

NOTE
[1] As amended by SI 1996/2167 (effective November 1, 1996).

Joint minutes
[1] **33.26.** Where any parties have reached agreement in relation to—
(a) a section 11 order,
(b) aliment for a child, or
(c) an order for financial provision,
a joint minute may be entered into expressing that agreement; and, subject to rule 33.19(3) (no order before views of child expressed), the sheriff may grant decree in respect of those parts of the joint minute in relation to which he could otherwise make an order, whether or not such a decree would include a matter for which there was no crave.

NOTE
[1] As amended by SI 1996/2167 (effective November 1, 1996).

Affidavits
33.27. The sheriff may accept evidence by affidavit at any hearing for an order or interim order.

PART II

UNDEFENDED FAMILY ACTIONS

Evidence in certain undefended family actions
[1] **33.28.**—(1) This rule—
(a) subject to sub-paragraph (b), applies to all family actions in which no notice of intention to defend has been lodged, other than a family action—
    (i) for a section 11 order or for aliment;
    (ii) of affiliation and aliment;
    (iii) for financial provision after an overseas divorce or annulment within the meaning of Part IV of the Matrimonial and Family Proceedings Act 1984; or
    (iv) for an order under the Act of 1981;
(b) applies to a family action in which a curator *ad litem* has been appointed under rule 33.16 where the curator *ad litem* to the defender has lodged a minute intimating that he does not intend to lodge defences;
(c) applies to any family action which proceeds at any stage as undefended where the sheriff so directs;
(d) applies to the merits of a family action which is undefended on the merits where the sheriff so directs, notwithstanding that the action is defended on an ancillary matter.
(2) Unless the sheriff otherwise directs, evidence shall be given by affidavits.
(3) Unless the sheriff otherwise directs, evidence relating to the welfare of a child shall be given by affidavit, at least one affidavit being emitted by a person other than a parent or party to the action.
(4) Evidence in the form of a written statement bearing to be the professional opinion of a duly qualified medical practitioner, which has been signed by him and lodged in process, shall be admissible in place of parole evidence by him.

NOTE
[1] As amended by SI 1996/2167 (effective November 1, 1996).

D 44/91 *Procedure for decree in actions under rule 33.28*
33.29.—(1) In an action to which rule 33.28 (evidence in certain undefended family actions) applies, the pursuer shall at any time after the expiry of the period for lodging a notice of intention to defend—
(a) lodge in process the affidavit evidence; and
(b) endorse a minute in Form F27 on the initial writ.
(2) The sheriff may, at any time after the pursuer has complied with paragraph (1), without requiring the appearance of parties—
(a) grant decree in terms of the motion for decree; or
(b) remit the cause for such further procedure, if any, including proof by parole evidence, as the sheriff thinks fit.

Extracts of undefended decree
33.30. In an action to which rule 33.28 (evidence in certain undefended family actions) applies, the sheriff clerk shall, after the expiry of 14 days after the grant of decree under rule 33.29 (procedure for decree in cases under rule 33.28), issue to the pursuers and the defender an extract decree.

Procedure in undefended family action for section 11 order
[1] **33.31.**—(1) Where no notice of intention to defend has been lodged in a family action for a section 11 order, any proceedings in the cause shall be dealt with by the sheriff in chambers.
(2) In an action to which paragraph (1) applies, decree may be pronounced after such inquiry as the sheriff thinks fit.

NOTE
[1] As amended by SI 1996/2167 (effective November 1, 1996).

No recording of evidence
33.32. It shall not be necessary to record the evidence in any proof in a family action which is not defended.

Disapplication of Chapter 15
[1] **33.33.** Other than rule 15.1(1), Chapter 15 (motions) shall not apply to a family action in

which no notice of intention to defend has been lodged, or to a family action in so far as it proceeds as undefended.

NOTE
[1] As amended by SI 1996/2445 (effective November 1, 1996).

Notice of intention to defend and defences
[1] **33.34.**—(1) This rule applies where the defender in a family action seeks—
  (a) to oppose any crave in the initial writ;
  (b) to make a claim for—
      (i) aliment;
      (ii) an order for financial provision within the meaning of section 8(3) of the Act of 1985; or
      (iii) a section 11 order; or
  (c) an order—
      (i) under section 16(1)(b) or (3) of the Act of 1985 (setting aside or varying agreement as to financial provision);
      (ii) under section 18 of the Act of 1985 (which relates to avoidance transactions); or
      (iii) under the Act of 1981; or
  (d) to challenge the jurisdiction of the court.
  (2) In an action to which this rule applies, the defender shall—
  (a) lodge a notice of intention to defend in Form F26 before the expiry of the period of notice; and
  (b) make any claim or seek any order referred to in paragraph (1), as the case may be, in those defences by setting out in his defences—
      (i) craves;
      (ii) averments in the answers to the condescendence in support of those craves; and
      (iii) appropriate pleas-in-law.
  (3) Where a defender intends to make an application for a section 11 order which, had it been **D 44/92** made in an initial writ, would have required a warrant for intimation under rule 33.7, the defender shall include a crave in his notice of intention to defend for a warrant for intimation or to dispense with such intimation; and rule 33.7 shall, with the necessary modifications, apply to a crave for a warrant under this paragraph as it applies to a crave for a warrant under that rule.

NOTE
[1] As amended by SI 1996/2167 (effective November 1, 1996).

Abandonment by pursuer
33.35. Notwithstanding abandonment by a pursuer, the court may allow a defender to pursue an order or claim sought in his defences; and the proceedings in relation to that order or claim shall continue in dependence as if a separate cause.

Attendance of parties at Options Hearing
33.36. All parties shall, except on cause shown, attend personally the hearing under rule 9.12 (Options Hearing).

Decree by default
33.37.—[1] (1) In a family action in which the defender has lodged a notice of intention to defend, where a party fails—
  (a) to lodge, or intimate the lodging of, any production or part of process,
  (b) to implement an order of the sheriff within a specified period, or
  (c) to appear or be represented at any diet,
that party shall be in default.
  (2) Where a party is in default under paragraph (1), the sheriff may—
  (a) where the family action is one mentioned in rule 33.1(1)(a) to (h), allow the cause to proceed as undefended under Part II of this Chapter; or
  (b) where the family action is one mentioned in rule 33.1(1)(i) to (m), grant decree as craved; or
  (c) grant decree of absolvitor; or
  (d) dismiss the family action or any claim made or order sought; and

(e) award expenses.

(3) Where no party appears at a diet in a family action, the sheriff may dismiss that action.

(4) In a family action, the sheriff may, on cause shown, prorogate the time for lodging any production or part of process, or for intimating or implementing any order.

NOTE
[1] As amended by SI 1996/2445 (effective November 1, 1996) (clerical error).

PART IV

APPLICATIONS AND ORDERS RELATING TO CHILDREN IN CERTAIN ACTIONS

Application and interpretation of this Part
[1] **33.38.** This Part applies to an action of divorce or separation.

NOTE
[1] As amended by SI 1996/2167 (effective November 1, 1996).

Applications in actions to which this Part applies
[1] **33.39.**—(1) An application for an order mentioned in paragraph (2) shall be made—
    (a) by a crave in the initial writ or defences, as the case may be, in an action to which this Part applies; or
    (b) where the application is made by a person other than the pursuer or defender, by minute in that action.
(2) The orders referred to in paragraph (1) are—
    (a) an order for a section 11 order; and
    (b) an order for aliment for a child.

NOTE
[1] As amended by SI 1996/2167 (effective November 1, 1996).

33.40. [Repealed by SI 1996/2167 (effective November 1, 1996).]

33.41. [Repealed by SI 1996/2167 (effective November 1, 1996).]

33.42. [Repealed by SI 1996/2167 (effective November 1, 1996).]

D 44/93 *Applications in depending actions by motion*
[1] **33.43.** An application by a party in an action depending before the court to which this Part applies for, or for variation of, an order for—
    (a) interim aliment for a child under the age of 18, or
    (b) a residence order or a contact order,
shall be made by motion.

NOTE
[1] As amended by SI 1996/2167 (effective November 1, 1996).

Applications after decree relating to a section 11 order
[1] **33.44.**—[2] (1) An application after final decree for, or for the variation or recall of, a section 11 order or in relation to the enforcement of such an order shall be made by minute in the process of the action to which the application relates.

(2) Where a minute has been lodged under paragraph (1), any party may apply by motion for any interim order which may be made pending the determination of the application.

NOTE
[1] As amended by SI 1996/2167 (effective November 1, 1996).
[2] As amended by SSI 2000/239 (effective October 2, 2000).

Applications after decree relating to aliment
33.45.—(1) An application after final decree for, or for the variation or recall of, an order for aliment for a child shall be made by minute in the process of the action to which the application relates.

(2) Where a minute has been lodged under paragraph (1), any party may lodge a motion for any interim order which may be made pending the determination of the application.

Applications after decree by persons over 18 years for aliment

33.46.—(1) A person—

(a) to whom an obligation of aliment is owed under section 1 of the Act of 1985,

(b) in whose favour an order for aliment while under the age of 18 years was made in an action to which this Part applies, and

(c) who seeks, after attaining that age, an order for aliment against the person in that action against whom the order for aliment in his favour was made,

shall apply by minute in the process of that action.

(2) An application for interim aliment pending the determination of an application under paragraph (1) shall be made by motion.

(3) Where a decree has been pronounced in an application under paragraph (1) or (2), any application for variation or recall of any such decree shall be made by minute in the process of the action to which the application relates.

Part V

Orders Relating to Financial Provision

Application and interpretation of this Part

33.47.—(1) This Part applies to an action of divorce.

(2) In this Part, "incidental order" has the meaning assigned in section 14(2) of the Act of 1985.

Applications in actions to which this Part applies

33.48.—(1) An application for an order mentioned in paragraph (2) shall be made—

(a) by a crave in the initial writ or defences, as the case may be, in an action to which this Part applies; or

(b) where the application is made by a person other than the pursuer or defender, by minute in that action.

(2) The orders referred to in paragraph (1) are—

(a) an order for financial provision within the meaning of section 8(3) of the Act of 1985;

(b) an order under section 16(1)(b) or (3) of the Act of 1985 (setting aside or varying agreement as to financial provision);

(c) an order under section 18 of the Act of 1985 (which relates to avoidance transactions); and

(d) an order under section 13 of the Act of 1981 (transfer or vesting of tenancy).

Applications in depending actions relating to incidental orders **D 44/94**

33.49.—(1) In an action depending before the sheriff to which this Part applies—

(a) the pursuer, notwithstanding rules 33.34(2) (application by defender for order for financial provision) and 33.48(1)(a) (application for order for financial provision in initial writ or defences), may apply by motion for an incidental order; and

(b) the sheriff shall not be bound to determine such a motion if he considers that the application should properly be by a crave in the initial writ or defences, as the case may be.

(2) In an action depending before the sheriff to which this Part applies, an application under section 14(4) of the Act of 1985 for the variation or recall of an incidental order shall be made by minute in the process of the action to which the application relates.

Applications relating to interim aliment

33.50. An application for, or for the variation or recall of, an order for interim aliment for the pursuer or the defender shall be made by motion.

Applications relating to orders for financial provision

33.51.—(1) An application—

(a) after final decree under any of the following provisions of the Act of 1985—

(i) section 8(1) for periodical allowance,

(ii) section 12(1)(b) (payment of capital sum or transfer of property),

(iii) section 12(4) (variation of date or method of payment of capital sum or date of transfer of property), or

(iv) section 13(4) (variation, recall, backdating or conversion of periodical allowance), or

(b) after the grant or refusal of an application under—

(i) section 8(1) or 14(3) for an incidental order, or

    (ii) section 14(4) (variation or recall of incidental order),
shall be made by minute in the process of the action to which the application relates.

(2) Where a minute is lodged under paragraph (1), any party may lodge a motion for any interim order which may be made pending the determination of the application.

[1] (3) An application under—

    (a) paragraph (5) of section 12A of the Act of 1985 (recall or variation of order in respect of a pension lump sum),

    (b) paragraph (7) of that section (variation of order in respect of pension lump sum to substitute trustees or managers), or

    (c) section 28(10) or 48(9) of the Welfare Reform and Pensions Act 1999,

shall be made by minute in the process of the action to which the application relates.

NOTE

[1] Inserted by SI 1996/2445 (effective November 1, 1996) and as amended by the Act of Sederunt (Ordinary Cause, Summary Application, Summary Cause and Small Claim Rules) Amendment (Miscellaneous) 2003 (SSI 2003/26), para.2(9) (effective January 24, 2003).

Applications after decree relating to agreements and avoidance transactions
33.52. An application for an order—

    (a) under section 16(1)(a) or (3) of the Act of 1985 (setting aside or varying agreement as to financial provision), or

    (b) under section 18 of the Act of 1985 (which relates to avoidance transactions),

made after final decree shall be made by minute in the process of the action to which the application relates.

PART VI

APPLICATIONS RELATING TO AVOIDANCE TRANSACTIONS

Form of applications
33.53.—(1) An application for an order under section 18 of the Act of 1985 (which relates to avoidance transactions) by a party to an action shall be made by including in the initial writ, defences or minute, as the case may be, appropriate craves, averments and pleas-in-law.

(2) An application for an order under section 18 of the Act of 1985 after final decree in an action, shall be made by minute in the process of the action to which the application relates.

D 44/95   PART VII

FINANCIAL PROVISION AFTER OVERSEAS DIVORCE OR ANNULMENT

Interpretation of this Part
33.54. In this Part—

    "the Act of 1984" means the Matrimonial and Family Proceedings Act 1984;

    "order for financial provision" has the meaning assigned in section 30(1) of the Act of 1984;

    "overseas country" has the meaning assigned in section 30(1) of the Act of 1984.

[1] *Applications for financial provision after overseas divorce or annulment*
33.55.—(1) An application under section 28 of the Act of 1984 for an order for financial provision after a divorce or annulment in an overseas country shall be made by initial writ.

(2) An application for an order in an action to which paragraph (1) applies made before final decree under—

    (a) section 13 of the Act of 1981 (transfer of tenancy of matrimonial home),

    (b) section 29(4) of the Act of 1984 for interim periodical allowance, or

    (c) section 14(4) of the Act of 1985 (variation or recall of incidental order),

shall be made by motion.

(3) An application for an order in an action to which paragraph (1) applies made after final decree under—

    (a) section 12(4) of the Act of 1985 (variation of date or method of payment of capital sum or date of transfer of property),

    (b) section 13(4) of the Act of 1985 (variation, recall, backdating or conversion of periodical allowance), or

    (c) section 14(4) of the Act of 1985 (variation or recall of incidental order),

shall be made by minute in the process of the action to which the application relates.

² (4) An application under—
- (a) paragraph (5) of section 12A of the Act of 1985 (recall or variation of order in respect of a pension lump sum), or
- (b) paragraph (7) of that section (variation of order in respect of pension lump sum to substitute trustees or managers),

shall be made by minute in the process of the action to which the application relates.

(5) Where a minute has been lodged under paragraph (3), any party may apply by motion for an interim order pending the determination of the application.

NOTES
¹ Heading amended by SI 1996/2445 (effective November 1, 1996).
² Inserted by SI 1996/2445 (effective November 1, 1996).

Part VIII

Actions of Aliment

Interpretation of this Part
33.56. In this Part, "action of aliment" means a claim for aliment under section 2(1) of the Act of 1985.

Undefended actions of aliment
33.57.—(1) Where a motion for decree in absence under Chapter 7 (undefended causes) is lodged in an action of aliment, the pursuer shall, on lodging the motion, lodge all documentary evidence of the means of the parties available to him in support of the amount of aliment sought.

(2) Where the sheriff requires the appearance of parties, the sheriff clerk shall fix a hearing.

Applications relating to aliment
33.58.—(1) An application for, or for variation of, an order for interim aliment in a depending action of aliment shall be made by motion.

(2) An application after final decree for the variation or recall of an order for aliment in an action of aliment shall be made by minute in the process of the action to which the application relates.

(3) A person—
- (a) to whom an obligation of aliment is owed under section 1 of the Act of 1985,
- (b) in whose favour an order for aliment while under the age of 18 years was made in an action of aliment, or
- (c) who seeks, after attaining that age, an order for aliment against the person in that action against whom the order for aliment in his favour was made,

shall apply by minute in the process of that action.

(4) An application for interim aliment pending the determination of an application under **D 44/96** paragraph (2) or (3) shall be made by motion.

(5) Where a decree has been pronounced in an application under paragraph (2) or (3), any application for variation or recall of any such decree shall be made by minute in the process of the action to which the application relates.

Applications relating to agreements on aliment
33.59.—(1) Subject to paragraph (2), an application under section 7(2) of the Act of 1985 (variation or termination of agreement on aliment) shall be made by summary application.

(2) In a family action in which a crave for aliment may be made, an application under section 7(2) of the Act of 1985 shall be made by a crave in the initial writ or in defences, as the case may be.

Part IX

Applications for Orders under Section 11 of the Children (Scotland) Act 1995

Application of this Part
¹ **33.60.** This Part applies to an application for a section 11 order in a family action other than in an action of divorce or separation.

NOTE
¹ Substituted by SI 1996/2167 (effective November 1, 1996).

Form of applications
[1] **33.61.** Subject to any other provision in this Chapter, an application for a section 11 order shall be made—
  (a) by an action for a section 11 order;
  (b) by a crave in the initial writ or defences, as the case may be, in any other family action to which this Part applies; or
  (c) where the application is made by a person other than a party to an action mentioned in paragraph (a) or (b), by minute in that action.

NOTE
[1] As amended by SI 1996/2167 (effective November 1, 1996).

Defenders in action for a section 11 order
[1] **33.62.** In an action for a section 11 order, the pursuer shall call as a defender—
  (a) the parents or other parent of the child in respect of whom the order is sought;
  (b) any guardian of the child;
  (c) any person who has treated the child as a child of his family;
  (d) any person who in fact exercises care or control in respect of the child; and
 [2] (e) [*Repealed by SSI 2000/239 (effective October 2, 2000).*]

NOTE
[1] Substituted by SI 1996/2167 (effective November 1, 1996). Clerical error corrected by SI 1996/2445 (effective November 1, 1996).

Applications relating to interim orders in depending actions
[1] **33.63.** An application, in an action depending before the sheriff to which this Part applies, for, or for the variation or recall of, an order for an interim residence order or an interim contact order shall be made—
  (a) by a party to the action, by motion; or
  (b) by a person who is not a party to the action, by minute.

NOTE
[1] As amended by SI 1996/2167 (effective November 1, 1996).

33.64. [Repealed by SI 1996/2167 (effective November 1, 1996).]

Applications after decree
[1] **33.65.**—(1) An application after final decree for variation or recall of a section 11 order shall be made by minute in the process of the action to which the application relates.
  (2) Where a minute has been lodged under paragraph (1), any party may apply by motion for an interim order pending the determination of the application.

NOTE
[1] As amended by SI 1996/2167 (effective November 1, 1996).

D 44/97   PART X

ACTIONS UNDER THE MATRIMONIAL HOMES (FAMILY PROTECTION) (SCOTLAND) ACT 1981

Interpretation of this Part
33.66. Unless the context otherwise requires, words and expressions used in this Part which are also used in the Act of 1981 have the same meaning as in that Act.

Form of applications
33.67.—(1) Subject to any other provision in this Chapter, an application for an order under the Act of 1981 shall be made—
  (a) by an action for such an order;
  (b) by a crave in the initial writ or in defences, as the case may be, in any other family action; or
  (c) where the application is made by a person other than a party to any action mentioned in paragraph (a) or (b), by minute in that action.
 [1] (2) An application under section 7(1) (dispensing with consent of non-entitled spouse to a dealing) or section 11 (application in relation to attachment) shall, unless made in a depending family action, be made by summary application.

NOTE
[1] As amended by the Act of Sederunt (Debt Arrangement and Attachment (Scotland) Act 2002) 2002 (SSI 2002/560), art.4, Sch.3 (effective December 30, 2002).

Defenders
33.68. The applicant for an order under the Act of 1981 shall call as a defender—
    (a) where he is seeking an order as a spouse, the other spouse;
    (b) where he is a third party making an application under section 7(1) dispensing with consent of non-entitled spouse to a dealing), or 8(1) (payment from non-entitled spouse in respect of loan), of the Act of 1981, both spouses; and
    (c) where the application is made under section 18 of the Act of 1981 (occupancy rights of cohabiting couples), or is one to which that section applies, the other partner.

Applications by motion
33.69.—(1) An application under any of the following provisions of the Act of 1981 shall be made by motion in the process of the depending action to which the application relates:—
    (a) section 3(4) (interim order for regulation of rights of occupancy, etc.);
    (b) section 4(6) (interim order suspending occupancy rights);
    (c) section 7(1) (dispensing with consent of non-entitled spouse to a dealing);
    (d) section 15(1) (order attaching power of arrest), if made after application for matrimonial interdict; and
    (e) the proviso to section 18(1) (extension of period of occupancy rights).
  (2) Intimation of a motion under paragraph (1) shall be given—
    (a) to the other spouse or partner, as the case may be;
    (b) where the motion is under paragraph (1)(a), (b) or (e) and the entitled spouse or partner is a tenant or occupies the matrimonial home by the permission of a third party, to the landlord or third party, as the case may be; and
    (c) to any other person to whom intimation of the application was or is to be made by virtue of rule 33.7(1)(k) (warrant for intimation to certain persons in actions for orders under the Act of 1981) or 33.15 (order for intimation by sheriff).

Applications by minute
33.70.—(1) An application for an order under—
    (a) section 5 of the Act of 1981 (variation and recall of orders regulating occupancy rights and of exclusion order), or
    (b) section 15(2) and (5) of the Act of 1981 (variation and recall of matrimonial interdict and power of arrest),
shall be made by minute.
  (2) A minute under paragraph (1) shall be intimated—
    (a) to the other spouse or partner, as the case may be;
    (b) where the entitled spouse or partner is a tenant or occupies the matrimonial home by the permission of a third party, to the landlord or third party, as the case may be; and
    (c) to any other person to whom intimation of the application was or is to be made by virtue of rule 33.7(1)(k) (warrant for intimation to certain persons in actions for orders under the Act of 1981) or 33.15 (order for intimation by sheriff).

Sist of actions to enforce occupancy rights
33.71. Unless the sheriff otherwise directs, the sist of an action by virtue of section 7(4) of the Act of 1981 (where action raised by non-entitled spouse to enforce occupancy rights) shall apply **D 44/98** only to such part of the action as relates to the enforcement of occupancy rights by a non-entitled spouse.

Certificates of delivery of documents to chief constable
33.72.—(1) Where an applicant is required to comply with section 15(4) or (5), as the case may be, of the Act of 1981 (delivery of documents to chief constable where power of arrest attached to matrimonial interdict is granted, varied or recalled), he shall, after such compliance, lodge in process a certificate of delivery in Form F30.
  [1] (2) Where a matrimonial interdict to which a power of arrest under section 15(1) of the Act of 1981 has been attached ceases to have effect by reason of a decree of divorce being pronounced by the sheriff, the pursuer shall send—
    (a) to the chief constable of the police area in which the matrimonial home is situated, and
    (b) if the applicant spouse (within the meaning of section 15(6) of the Act of 1981) resides in another police area, to the chief constable of that other police area,
a copy of the interlocutor granting decree; and lodge in process a certificate of delivery in Form F30.

NOTE

[1] As amended by SI 1996/2445 (effective November 1, 1996) (clerical error).

PART XI

SIMPLIFIED DIVORCE APPLICATIONS

Application and interpretation of this Part
33.73.—(1) This Part applies to an application for divorce by a party to a marriage made in the manner prescribed in rule 33.74 (form of applications) if, but only if—
>   (a) that party relies on the facts set out in section 1(2)(d) (no cohabitation for two years with consent of defender to decree), or section 1(2)(e) (no cohabitation for five years), of the Act of 1976;
>   (b) in an application under section 1(2)(d) of the Act of 1976, the other party consents to decree of divorce being granted;
>   (c) no other proceedings are pending in any court which could have the effect of bringing the marriage to an end;
>   (d) there are no children of the marriage under the age of 16 years;
>   (e) neither party to the marriage applies for an order for financial provision on divorce; and
>   (f) neither party to the marriage suffers from mental disorder.

(2) If an application ceases to be one to which this Part applies at any time before final decree, it shall be deemed to be abandoned and shall be dismissed.

(3) In this Part "simplified divorce application" means an application mentioned in paragraph (1).

Form of applications
33.74.—[1] (1) A simplified divorce application in which the facts set out in section 1(2)(d) of the Act of 1976 (no cohabitation for two years with consent of defender to decree) are relied on shall be made in Form F31 and shall only be of effect if—
>   (a) it is signed by the applicant; and
>   (b) the form of consent in Part 2 of Form F31 is signed by the party to the marriage giving consent.

(2) A simplified divorce application in which the facts set out in section 1(2)(e) of the Act of 1976 (no cohabitation for five years) are relied on shall be made in Form F33 and shall only be of effect if it is signed by the applicant.

NOTE

[1] As amended by SI 1996/2445 (effective November 1, 1996) (clerical error).

Lodging of applications
33.75. The applicant shall send a simplified divorce application to the sheriff clerk with—
>   (a) an extract or certified copy of the marriage certificate; and
>   (b) the appropriate fee.

Citation and intimation
33.76.—(1) This rule is subject to rule 33.77 (citation where address not known).

(2) It shall be the duty of the sheriff clerk to cite any person or intimate any document in connection with a simplified divorce application.

(3) The form of citation—

D 44/99
>   (a) in an application relying on the facts in section 1(2)(d) of the Act of 1976 shall be in Form F34; and
>   (b) in an application relying on the facts in section 1(2)(e) of the Act of 1976 shall be in Form F35.

[1] (4) The citation or intimation required by paragraph (2) shall be made—
>   (a) by the sheriff clerk by registered post or the first class recorded delivery service in accordance with 5.3 (postal service or intimation);
>   (b) on payment of an additional fee, by a sheriff officer in accordance with rule 5.4(1) and (2) (service within Scotland by sheriff officer); or
>   (c) where necessary, by the sheriff clerk in accordance with rule 5.5 (service on persons furth of Scotland).

[2] (5) Where citation or intimation is made in accordance with paragraph (4)(c), the translation into an official language of the country in which service is to be executed required by rule 5.5(6) shall be provided by the party lodging the simplified divorce application.

NOTES
¹ Substituted by SSI 2000/239 (effective October 2, 2000).
² Inserted by SSI 2000/239 (effective October 2, 2000).

Citation where address not known
33.77.—(1) In a simplified divorce application in which the facts in section 1(2)(e) of the Act of 1976 (no cohabitation for five years) are relied on and the address of the other party to the marriage is not known and cannot reasonably be ascertained—
    (a) citation shall be executed by displaying a copy of the application and a notice in Form F36 on the walls of court on a period of notice of 21 days; and
    (b) intimation shall be made to—
        (i) every child of the marriage between the parties who has reached the age of 16 years, and
        (ii) one of the next of kin of the other party to the marriage who has reached that age, unless the address of such person is not known and cannot reasonably be ascertained.
(2) Intimation to a person referred to in paragraph (1)(b) shall be given by intimating a copy of the application and a notice of intimation in Form F37.

Opposition to applications
33.78.—(1) Any person on whom service or intimation of a simplified divorce application has been made may give notice by letter sent to the sheriff clerk that he challenges the jurisdiction of the court or opposes the grant of decree of divorce and giving the reasons for his opposition to the application.
(2) Where opposition to a simplified divorce application is made under paragraph (1), the sheriff shall dismiss the application unless he is satisfied that the reasons given for the opposition are frivolous.
(3) The sheriff clerk shall intimate the decision under paragraph (2) to the applicant and the respondent.
(4) The sending of a letter under paragraph (1) shall not imply acceptance of the jurisdiction of the court.

Evidence
33.79. Parole evidence shall not be given in a simplified divorce application.

Decree
33.80.—(1) The sheriff may grant decree in terms of the simplified divorce application on the expiry of the period of notice if such application has been properly served provided that, when the application has been served in a country to which the Hague Convention on the Service Abroad of Judicial and Extra-Judicial Documents in Civil and Commercial Matters dated November 15, 1965 applies, decree shall not be granted until it is established to the satisfaction of the sheriff that the requirements of Article 15 of that Convention have been complied with.
(2) The sheriff clerk shall, not sooner than 14 days after the granting of decree in terms of paragraph (1), issue to each party to the marriage an extract of the decree of divorce in Form F38.

Appeals
33.81. Any appeal against an interlocutor granting decree of divorce under rule 33.80 (decree) may be made, within 14 days after the date of decree, by sending a letter to the court giving reasons for the appeal.

Applications after decree   **D 44/100**
33.82. Any application to the court after decree of divorce has been granted in a simplified divorce application which could have been made if it had been made in an action of divorce shall be made by minute.

PART XII

VARIATION OF COURT OF SESSION DECREES

Application and interpretation of this Part
33.83.—(1) This Part applies to an application to the sheriff for variation or recall of any order to which section 8 of the Act of 1966 (variation of certain Court of Session orders) applies.

(2) In this Part, the "Act of 1966" means the Law Reform (Miscellaneous Provisions) (Scotland) Act 1966.

Form of application and intimation to Court of Session
33.84.—(1) An application to which this Part applies shall be made by initial writ.

(2) In such an application there shall be lodged with the initial writ a copy of the interlocutor, certified by a clerk of the Court of Session, which it is sought to vary.

(3) Before lodging the initial writ, a copy of the initial writ certified by the pursuer or his solicitor shall be lodged, or sent by first class recorded delivery post to the Deputy Principal Clerk of Session to be lodged in the process of the cause in the Court of Session in which the original order was made.

(4) The pursuer or his solicitor shall attach a certificate to the initial writ stating that paragraph (3) has been complied with.

¹ (5) The sheriff may, on cause shown, prorogate the time for lodging the certified copy of the interlocutor required under paragraph (2).

NOTE
¹ As amended by SI 1996/2445 (effective November 1, 1996) (clerical error).

Defended actions
33.85.—(1) Where a notice of intention to defend has been lodged and no request is made under rule 33.87 (remit of application to Court of Session), the pursuer shall within 14 days after the date of the lodging of a notice of intention to defend or within such other period as the sheriff may order, lodge in process the following documents (or copies) from the process in the cause in the Court of Session in which the original order was made:—
  (a) the pleadings;
  (b) the interlocutor sheets;
  (c) any opinion of the court; and
  (d) any productions on which he seeks to found.

(2) The sheriff may, on the joint motion of parties made at any time after the lodging of the documents mentioned in paragraph (1)—
  (a) dispense with proof;
  (b) whether defences have been lodged or not, hear the parties; and
  (c) thereafter, grant decree or otherwise dispose of the cause as he thinks fit.

Transmission of process to Court of Session
33.86.—(1) Where decree has been granted or the cause otherwise disposed of—
  (a) and the period for marking an appeal has elapsed without an appeal being marked, or
  (b) after the determination of the cause on any appeal,
the sheriff clerk shall transmit to the Court of Session the sheriff court process and the documents from the process of the cause in the Court of Session which have been lodged in the sheriff court process.

(2) A sheriff court process transmitted under paragraph (1) shall form part of the process of the cause in the Court of Session in which the original order was made.

Remit of application to Court of Session
33.87.—(1) A request for a remit to the Court of Session under section 8(3) of the Act of 1966 shall be made by motion.

(2) The sheriff shall, in respect of any such motion, order that the cause be remitted to the Court of Session; and, within 4 days after the date of such order, the sheriff clerk shall transmit the whole sheriff court process to the Court of Session.

(3) A cause remitted to the Court of Session under paragraph (2) shall form part of the process of the cause in the Court of Session in which the original order was made.

PART XIII

CHILD SUPPORT ACT 1991

Interpretation of this Part
¹ **33.88.** In this Part—
  "the Act of 1991" means the Child Support Act 1991;
  "child" has the meaning assigned in section 55 of the Act of 1991;
  "maintenance calculation" has the meaning assigned in section 54 of the Act of 1991.

NOTE
[1] As amended by SI 1996/2445 (effective November 1, 1996) and the Act of Sederunt (Ordinary Cause, Summary Application, Summary Cause and Small Claim Rules) Amendment (Miscellaneous) 2003 (SSI 2003/26), para.2(10) (effective January 24, 2003).

Restriction of expenses
33.89. Where the Secretary of State is named as a defender in an action for declarator of non-parentage or illegitimacy, and the Secretary of State does not defend the action, no expenses shall be awarded against the Secretary of State.

Effect of maintenance calculations
[1] **33.90.**—(1) The sheriff clerk shall, on receiving notification that a maintenance calculation has been made, cancelled or has ceased to have effect so as to affect an order of a kind prescribed for the purposes of section 10 of the Act of 1991, endorse on the interlocutor sheet relating to that order a certificate, in Form F39 or F40, as the case may be.

NOTE
[1] As amended by the Act of Sederunt (Ordinary Cause, Summary Application, Summary Cause and Small Claim Rules) Amendment (Miscellaneous) 2003 (SSI 2003/26), para.2(11) (effective January 24, 2003).

Effect of maintenance calculations on extracts relating to aliment
[1] **33.91.**—(1) Where an order relating to aliment is affected by a maintenance calculation, any extract of that order issued by the sheriff clerk shall be endorsed with the following certificate:—
    "A maintenance calculation having been made under the Child Support Act 1991 on (*insert date*), this order, in so far as it relates to the making or securing of periodical payments to or for the benefit of (*insert name(s) of child/children*), ceases to have effect from (*insert date 2 days after the date on which the maintenance calculation was made*)."
(2) Where an order relating to aliment has ceased to have effect on the making of a maintenance calculation, and that maintenance calculation is later cancelled or ceases to have effect, any extract of that order issued by the sheriff clerk shall be endorsed also with the following certificate:—
    "The jurisdiction of the child support officer under the Child Support Act 1991 having terminated on (*insert date*), this order, in so far as it relates to (*insert name(s) of child/children*), again shall have effect as from (*insert date of termination of child support officer's jurisdiction*).".

NOTE
[1] As amended by the Act of Sederunt (Ordinary Cause, Summary Application, Summary Cause and Small Claim Rules) Amendment (Miscellaneous) 2003 (SSI 2003/26), para.2(12) (effective January 24, 2003).

[1] PART XIV

NOTE
[1] Inserted by SI 1996/2167 (effective November 1, 1996).

REFERRALS TO PRINCIPAL REPORTER

Application and interpretation of this Part
33.92.—(1) This Part applies where a sheriff, in a family action, refers a matter to the Principal Reporter under section 54 of the Act of 1995 (reference to the Principal Reporter by court).
(2) In this Part, "Principal Reporter" has the meaning assigned in section 93(1) of the Act of 1995.

Intimation to Principal Reporter   **D 44/102**
33.93. Where a matter is referred by the sheriff to the Principal Reporter under section 54 of the Act of 1995, the interlocutor making the reference shall be intimated by the sheriff clerk forthwith to the Principal Reporter; and that intimation shall specify which of the conditions in paragraph (2)(a) to (h), (j), (k) or (l) of that section it appears to the sheriff has been satisfied.

Intimation of decision by Principal Reporter

33.94.—(1) Where a matter has been referred by the sheriff to the Principal Reporter under section 54 of the Act of 1995 and the Principal Reporter, having made such investigation as he thinks appropriate and having reached the view that compulsory measures of supervision are necessary, arranges a children's hearing under section 69 of that Act (continuation or disposal of referral by children's hearing), the Principal Reporter shall intimate to the court which referred the matter to him—

    (a) the decision to arrange such children's hearing;

    (b) where there is no appeal made against the decision of that children's hearing once the period for appeal has expired, the outcome of the children's hearing; and

    (c) where such an appeal has been made, that an appeal has been made and, once determined, the outcome of that appeal.

(2) Where a matter has been referred by the sheriff to the Principal Reporter under section 54 of the Act of 1995 and the Principal Reporter, having made such investigation as he thinks appropriate and having considered whether compulsory measures of supervision are necessary, decides not to arrange a children's hearing under section 69 of that Act, the Principal Reporter shall intimate that decision to the court which referred the matter to him.

[1] PART XV

NOTE
   [1] Inserted by SI 1996/2167 (effective November 1, 1996).

MANAGEMENT OF MONEY PAYABLE TO CHILDREN

33.95. Where the sheriff has made an order under section 13 of the Act of 1995 (awards of damages to children), an application by a person for an order by virtue of section 11(1)(d) of that Act (administration of child's property) may be made in the process of the cause in which the order under section 13 of that Act was made.

CHAPTER 34

ACTIONS RELATING TO HERITABLE PROPERTY

PART I

SEQUESTRATION FOR RENT

[1] *Actions craving payment of rent*

34.1.—(1) In an action for sequestration and sale—

    (a) for non-payment of rent,

    (b) for recovery of rent, or

    (c) in security of rent,

whether brought before or after the term of payment, payment of rent may be craved; and decree for payment of such rent or part of it, when due and payable, may be pronounced and extracted in common form.

(2) There shall be served on the defender in such an action, with the initial writ, warrant and citation, a notice in Form H1.

NOTE
   [1] As amended by SI 1996/2445 (effective November 1, 1996) (clerical error).

Warrant to inventory and secure

34.2.—(1) In the first deliverance on an initial writ for sequestration and sale, the sheriff may sequestrate the effects of the tenant, and grant warrant to inventory and secure them.

   [1] (2) A warrant to sequestrate, inventory, sell, eject or relet shall include authority to open shut and lockfast places for the purpose of executing such warrant.

D 44/102/1 NOTE
   [1] As amended by SI 1996/2445 (effective November 1, 1996) (clerical error).

Sale of effects

34.3.—(1) In an action for sequestration and sale, the sheriff may order the sequestrated effects to be sold by a sheriff officer or other named person.

(2) Where a sale follows an order under paragraph (1), the sale shall be reported within 14 **D 44/103** days after the date of the sale and the pursuer shall lodge with the sheriff clerk the roup rolls or certified copies of them and a state of debt.

(3) In the interlocutor approving the report of sale, or by separate interlocutor, the sheriff may grant decree against the defender for any balance remaining due.

Care of effects
34.4. The sheriff may, at any stage of an action for sequestration and sale appoint a fit person to take charge of the sequestrated effects, or may require the tenant to find caution that they shall be made available.

PART II

REMOVING

Action of removing where fixed term of removal
34.5.—(1) Subject to section 21 of the Agricultural Holdings (Scotland) Act 1991 (notice to quit and notice of intention to quit)—
  (a) where the tenant has bound himself to remove by writing, dated and signed—
     (i) within 12 months after the term of removal; or
     (ii) where there is more than one ish, after the ish first in date to remove;
    an action of removing may be raised at any time; and
  (b) where the tenant has not bound himself, an action of removing may be raised at any time, but—
     (i) in the case of a lease of lands exceeding two acres in extent for three years and upwards, an interval of not less than one year nor more than two years shall elapse between the date of notice of removal and the term of removal first in date;
     (ii) in the case of a lease of lands exceeding two acres in extent, whether written or verbal, held from year to year or under tacit relocation, or for any other period less than three years, an interval of not less than six months shall elapse between the date of notice of removal and the term of removal first in date; and
     (iii) in the case of a house let with or without land attached not exceeding two acres in extent, as also of land not exceeding two acres in extent without houses, as also of mills, fishings, shootings, and all other heritable subjects excepting land exceeding two acres in extent, and let for a year or more, 40 days at least shall elapse between the date of notice of removal and the term of removal first in date.

(2) In any defended action of removing the sheriff may order the defender to find caution for violent profits.

(3) In an action for declarator of irritancy and removing by a superior against a vassal, the pursuer shall call as parties the last entered vassal and such heritable creditors and holders of postponed ground burdens as are disclosed by a search for 20 years before the raising of the action, and the expense of the search shall form part of the pursuer's expenses of process.

Form of notice of removal
34.6.—[1] (1) A notice under the following sections of the Sheriff Courts (Scotland) Act 1907 shall be in Form H2:—
  (a) section 34 (notice in writing to remove where lands exceeding two acres held on probative lease),
  (b) section 35 (letter of removal where tenant in possession of lands exceeding two acres), and
  (c) section 36 (notice of removal where lands exceeding two acres occupied by tenant without written lease).
(2) A letter of removal shall be in Form H3.

NOTE
[1] As amended by SI 1996/2445 (effective November 1, 1996).

Form of notice under section 37 of the Act of 1907
[1] **34.7.** A notice under section 37 of the Sheriff Courts (Scotland) Act 1907 (notice of termination of tenancy) shall be in Form H4.

NOTE
[1] As amended by SI 1996/2445 (effective November 1, 1996).

D 44/104 *Giving notice of removal*
    [1] **34.8.**—(1) A notice under section 34, 35, 36, 37 or 38 of the Sheriff Courts (Scotland) Act 1907 (which relate to notices of removal) may be given by—
        (a) a sheriff officer
        (b) the person entitled to give such notice, or
        (c) the solicitor or factor of such person,
posting the notice by registered post or the first class recorded delivery service at any post office within the United Kingdom in time for it to be delivered at the address on the notice before the last date on which by law such notice must be given, addressed to the person entitled to receive such notice, and bearing the address of that person at the time, if known, or, if not known, to the last known address of that person.
    (2) A sheriff officer may also give notice under a section of the Sheriff Courts (Scotland) Act 1907 mentioned in paragraph (1) in any manner in which he may serve an initial writ; and, accordingly, rule 5.4 (service within Scotland by sheriff officer) shall, with the necessary modifications, apply to the giving of notice under this paragraph as it applies to service of an initial writ.

NOTE
    [1] As amended by SI 1996/2445 (effective November 1, 1996).

Evidence of notice to remove
    34.9.—(1) A certificate of the sending of notice under rule 34.8 dated and endorsed on the lease or an extract of it, or on the letter of removal, signed by the sheriff officer or the person sending the notice, his solicitor or factor, or an acknowledgement of the notice endorsed on the lease or an extract of it, or on the letter of removal, by the party in possession or his agent, shall be sufficient evidence that notice has been given.
    (2) Where there is no lease, a certificate of the sending of such notice shall be endorsed on a copy of the notice or letter of removal.

Applications under Part II of the Conveyancing and Feudal Reform (Scotland) Act 1970
    34.10.—(1) An application or counter-application to the sheriff under any of the following provisions of Part II of the Conveyancing and Feudal Reform (Scotland) Act 1970 (which relates to the standard security) shall be made by initial writ where any other remedy is craved:—
        (a) section 18(2) (declarator that obligations under contract performed);
        (b) section 20(3) (application by creditor for warrant to let security subjects);
        (c) section 22(1) (objections to notice of default);
        (d) section 22(3) (counter-application for remedies under the Act);
        (e) section 24(1) (application by a creditor for warrant to exercise remedies on default); and
        (f) section 28(1) (decree of foreclosure).
    (2) An interlocutor of the sheriff disposing of an application or counter-application under paragraph (1) shall be final and not subject to appeal except as to a question of title or any other remedy granted.

Service on unnamed occupiers
    [1] **34.11.**—(1) Subject to paragraph (2), this rule applies only to a crave for removing in an action of removing against a person or persons in possession of heritable property without right or title to possess the property.
    (2) This rule shall not apply with respect to a person who has or had a title or other right to occupy the heritable property and who has been in continuous occupation since that title or right is alleged to have come to an end.
    (3) Where this rule applies, the pursuer may apply by motion to shorten or dispense with the period of notice or other period of time in these Rules relating to the conduct of the action or the extracting of any decree.
    (4) Where the name of a person in occupation of the heritable property is not known and cannot reasonably be ascertained, the pursuer shall call that person as a defender by naming him as an "occupier".
    (5) Where the name of a person in occupation of the heritable property is not known and cannot reasonably be ascertained, the initial writ shall be served (whether or not it is also served on a named person), unless the court otherwise directs, by a sheriff officer—
        (a) affixing a copy of the initial writ and a citation in Form H5 addressed to "the occupiers" to the main door or other conspicuous part of the premises, and if practicable, depositing a copy of each of those documents in the premises; or
D 44/105   (b) in the case of land only, inserting stakes in the ground at conspicuous parts of the

occupied land to each of which is attached a sealed transparent envelope containing a copy of the initial writ and a citation in Form H5 addressed to "the occupiers".

NOTE
[1] Inserted by the Act of Sederunt (Sheriff Court Ordinary Cause Rules Amendment) (Miscellaneous) 2000 (SSI 2000/239) (effective October 2, 2000).

[1] *Applications under the Mortgage Rights (Scotland) Act 2001*
34.12.—(1) In an action to which rule 3.2(3) applies, an application under either of the following provisions of the Mortgage Rights (Scotland) Act 2001 shall be made by minute in the action—
    (a) section 1(2) (application to the court for an order under section 2);
    (b) section 2(5) (application to vary or revoke an order or to further continue proceedings).
(2) Any such minute may be lodged by a person who is entitled to make an application even although that person has not been called as a defender and such a person may appear or be represented at any hearing to determine the application.

NOTE
[1] Inserted by the Act of Sederunt (Amendment of Ordinary Cause Rules and Summary Applications, Statutory Applications and Appeals etc. Rules) (Applications under the Mortgage Rights (Scotland) Act 2001) 2002 (SSI 2002/7), para.2(5).

CHAPTER 35

ACTIONS OF MULTIPLEPOINDING

Application of this Chapter   D 44/106
    35.1.—(1) This Chapter applies to an action of multiplepoinding.

Application of Chapters 9 and 10
    35.2. Chapter 10 (additional procedure) and the following rules in Chapter 9 (standard procedure in defended causes) shall not apply to an action of multiplepoinding:—
    rule 9.1   (notice of intention to defend),
    rule 9.2   (fixing date for Options Hearing),
    rule 9.4   (lodging of pleadings before Options Hearing),
    rule 9.8   (adjustment of pleadings),
    rule 9.9   (effect of sist on adjustment),
    rule 9.10   (open record),
    rule 9.11   (record for Options Hearing),
    rule 9.12   (Options Hearing),
    rule 9.15   (applications for time to pay directions).

Parties
    35.3.—(1) An action of multiplepoinding may be brought by any person holding, or having an interest in, or claim on, the fund *in medio*, in his own name.
(2) The pursuer shall call as defenders to such an action—
    (a) all persons so far as known to him as having an interest in the fund *in medio*; and
    (b) where he is not the holder of the fund, the holder of that fund.

Condescendence of fund in medio   D 44/106/1
    35.4.—(1) Where the pursuer is the holder of the fund *in medio*, he shall include a detailed statement of the fund in the condescendence in the initial writ.
(2) Where the pursuer is not the holder of the fund *in medio*, the holder shall, before the expiry of the period of notice—
    (a) lodge in process—
        (i) a condescendence of the fund *in medio*, stating any claim or lien which he may profess to have on that fund;
        (ii) a list of all persons known to him as having an interest in the fund; and
    (b) intimate a copy of the condescendence and list to any other party.

"Warrant of citation in multiplepoindings
    35.5. The warrant of citation of the initial writ in an action of multiplepoinding shall be in Form M1.

D 44/106/2 *Citation*

    35.6.—(1) Subject to rule 5.6 (service where address of person is not known), citation of any person in an action of multiplepoinding shall be in Form M2 which shall be attached to a copy of the initial writ and warrant of citation and shall have appended to it a notice of appearance in Form M4.

    (2) The certificate of citation shall be in Form M3 and shall be attached to the initial writ.

Advertisement

    35.7. The sheriff may make an order for advertisement of the action in such newspapers as he thinks fit.

Lodging of notice of appearance

    35.8. Where a party intends to lodge—

        (a) defences to challenge the jurisdiction of the court or the competency of the action,

        (b) objections to the condescendence of the fund *in medio*, or

        (c) a claim on the fund,

he shall, before the expiry of the period of notice, lodge a notice of appearance in Form M4.

D 44/106/3 *Fixing date for first hearing*

    35.9. Where a notice of appearance, or a condescendence on the fund *in medio* and list under rule 35.4(2)(a) has been lodged, the sheriff clerk shall—

        (a) fix a date and time for the first hearing, which date shall be the first suitable court day occurring not sooner than 4 weeks after the expiry of the period of notice;

        (b) on fixing the date for the first hearing forthwith intimate that date in Form M5 to each party; and

        (c) prepare and sign an interlocutor recording the date of the first hearing.

D 44/106/4 *Hearings*

    35.10.—(1) The sheriff shall conduct the first, and any subsequent hearing, with a view to securing the expeditious progress of the cause by ascertaining from parties the matters in dispute.

    (2) The parties shall provide the sheriff with sufficient information to enable him to conduct the hearing as provided for in this Chapter.

    (3) At the first, or any subsequent hearing, the sheriff shall fix a period within which defences, objections or claims shall be lodged, and appoint a date for a second hearing.

    (4) Where the list lodged under rule 35.4(2)(a) contains any person who is not a party to the action, the sheriff shall order—

        (a) the initial writ to be amended to add that person as a defender;

        (b) service of the pleadings so amended to be made on that person, with a citation in Form M6; and

        (c) intimation to that person of any condescendence of the fund *in medio* lodged by a holder of the fund who is not the pursuer.

    (5) Where a person to whom service has been made under paragraph (4) lodges a notice of appearance under rule 35.8, the sheriff clerk shall intimate to him in Form M5 the date of the next hearing fixed in the action.

Lodging defences, objections and claims

    35.11.—(1) Defences, objections and claims by a party shall be lodged with the sheriff clerk in a single document under separate headings.

    (2) Each claimant shall lodge with his claim any documents founded on in his claim, so far as they are within his custody or power.

Disposal of defences

    35.12.—(1) Where defences have been lodged, the sheriff may order the initial writ and defences to be adjusted and thereafter close the record and regulate further procedure.

    (2) Unless the sheriff otherwise directs, defences shall be disposed of before any further procedure in the action.

D 44/106/5 *Objections to fund* in medio

    35.13.—(1) Where objections to the fund *in medio* have been lodged, the sheriff may, after disposal of any defences, order the condescendence of the fund and objections to be adjusted, and thereafter close the record and regulate further procedure.

    (2) If no objections to the fund *in medio* have been lodged, or if objections have been lodged and disposed of, the sheriff may, on the motion of the holder of the fund, and without ordering intimation to any party approve the condescendence of the fund and find the holder liable only in one single payment.

Preliminary pleas in multiplepoindings

35.14.—(1) A party intending to insist on a preliminary plea shall, not later than 3 days before any hearing to determine further procedure following the lodging of defences, objections or claims, lodge with the sheriff clerk a note of the basis of the plea.

(2) Where a party fails to comply with the provisions of paragraph (1), he shall be deemed to be no longer insisting on the plea and the plea shall be repelled by the sheriff at the hearing referred to in paragraph (1).

(3) If satisfied that there is a preliminary matter of law which justifies a debate, the sheriff shall, after having heard parties and considered the note lodged under this rule, appoint the action to debate.

Consignation of the fund and discharge of holder   **D 44/107**

35.15.—(1) At any time after the condescendence of the fund *in medio* has been approved, the sheriff may order the whole or any part of the fund to be sold and the proceeds of the sale consigned into court.

(2) After such consignation the holder of the fund *in medio* may apply for his exoneration and discharge.

(3) The sheriff may allow the holder of the fund *in medio*, on his exoneration and discharge, his expenses out of the fund as a first charge on the fund.

Further service or advertisement

35.16. The sheriff may at any time, of his own motion or on the motion of any party, order further service on any person or advertisement.

Ranking of claims

35.17.—(1) After disposal of any defences, and approval of the condescendence of the fund *in medio*, the sheriff may, where there is no competition on the fund, rank and prefer the claimants and grant decree in terms of that ranking.   **D 44/108**

(2) Where there is competition on the fund, the sheriff may order claims to be adjusted and thereafter close the record and regulate further procedure.

Remit to reporter

35.18.—(1) Where several claims have been lodged, the sheriff may remit to a reporter to prepare a scheme of division and report.

(2) The expenses of such remit, when approved by the sheriff, shall be made a charge on the fund, to be deducted before division.

CHAPTER 36   **D 44/108/1**

ACTIONS OF DAMAGES

PART I

INTIMATION TO CONNECTED PERSONS IN CERTAIN ACTIONS OF DAMAGES

Application and interpretation of this Part

36.1.—(1) This Part applies to an action of damages in which, following the death of any person from personal injuries, damages are claimed—

    (a) by the executor of the deceased, in respect of the injuries from which the deceased died; or

    (b) by any relative of the deceased, in respect of the death of the deceased.

(2) In this Part—

    "connected person" means a person, not being a party to the action, who has title to sue the defender in respect of the personal injuries from which the deceased died or in respect of his death;

    "relative" has the meaning assigned to it in Schedule 1 to the Damages (Scotland) Act 1976.

Averments

36.2. In an action to which this Part applies, the pursuer shall aver in the condescendence, as the case may be—

    (a) that there are no connected persons;

    (b) that there are connected persons, being the persons specified in the crave for intimation;

(c) that there are connected persons in respect of whom intimation should be dispensed with on the ground that—
    (i) the names or whereabouts of such persons are not known to, and cannot reasonably be ascertained by, the pursuer; or
    (ii) such persons are unlikely to be awarded more than £200 each.

Warrants for intimation

36.3.—(1) Where the pursuer makes averments under rule 36.2(b) (existence of connected persons), he shall include a crave in the initial writ for intimation to any person who is believed to have title to sue the defender in an action in respect of the death of the deceased or the personal injuries from which the deceased died.

(2) A notice of intimation in Form D1 shall be attached to the copy of the initial writ where intimation is given on a warrant under paragraph (1).

Applications to dispense with intimation

36.4.—(1) Where the pursuer makes averments under rule 36.2(c) (dispensing with intimation to connected persons), he shall apply by crave in the initial writ for an order to dispense with intimation.

(2) In determining an application under paragraph (1), the sheriff shall have regard to—
    (a) the desirability of avoiding a multiplicity of actions; and
    (b) the expense, inconvenience or difficulty likely to be involved in taking steps to ascertain the name or whereabouts of the connected person.

(3) Where the sheriff is not satisfied that intimation to a connected person should be dispensed with, he may—
    (a) order intimation to a connected person whose name and whereabouts are known;
    (b) order the pursuer to take such further steps as he may specify in the interlocutor to ascertain the name or whereabouts of any connected person; and
    (c) order advertisement in such manner, place and at such times as he may specify in the interlocutor.

Subsequent disclosure of connected persons

36.5. Where the name or whereabouts of a person, in respect of whom the sheriff has dispensed with intimation on a ground specified in rule 36.2(c) (dispensing with intimation to connected persons), subsequently becomes known to the pursuer, the pursuer shall apply to the sheriff by motion for a warrant for intimation to such a person; and such intimation shall be made in accordance with rule 36.3(2).

D 44/108/2 *Connected persons entering process*

36.6.—(1) A connected person may apply by minute craving leave to be sisted as an additional pursuer to the action.

(2) Such a minute shall also crave leave of the sheriff to adopt the existing grounds of action, and to amend the craves, condescendence and pleas-in-law.

(3) The period within which answers to a minute under this rule may be lodged shall be 14 days from the date of intimation of the minute.

[1] (4) Rule 14.13 (procedure following grant of minute) shall not apply to a minute to which this rule applies.

NOTE
[1] As amended by SI 1996/2445 (effective November 1, 1996).

Failure to enter process

36.7. Where a connected person to whom intimation is made in accordance with this Part—
    (a) does not apply to be sisted as an additional pursuer to the action,
    (b) subsequently raises a separate action against the same defender in respect of the same personal injuries or death, and
    (c) would, apart from this rule, be awarded the expenses or part of the expenses of that action,
he shall not be awarded those expenses except on cause shown.

PART II

INTERIM PAYMENTS OF DAMAGES

Application and interpretation of this Part
36.8.—(1) This Part applies to an action of damages for personal injuries or the death of a person in consequence of personal injuries.
(2) In this Part—
"defender" includes a third party against whom the pursuer has a crave for damages;
"personal injuries" includes any disease or impairment of a physical or mental condition.

Applications for interim payment of damages
36.9.—(1) In an action to which this Part applies, a pursuer may, at any time after defences have been lodged, apply by motion for an order for interim payment of damages to him by the defender or, where there are two or more of them, by any one or more of them.
(2) The pursuer shall intimate a motion under paragraph (1) to every other party on a period of notice of 14 days. **D 44/109**
(3) On a motion under paragraph (1), the sheriff may, if satisfied that—
  (a) the defender has admitted liability to the pursuer in the action, or
  (b) if the action proceeded to proof, the pursuer would succeed in the action on the question of liability without any substantial finding of contributory negligence on his part, or on the part of any person in respect of whose injury or death the claim of the pursuer arises, and would obtain decree for damages against any defender,
ordain that defender to make an interim payment to the pursuer of such amount as the sheriff thinks fit, not exceeding a reasonable proportion of the damages which, in the opinion of the sheriff, are likely to be recovered by the pursuer.
(4) Any such payment may be ordered to be made in one lump sum or otherwise as the sheriff thinks fit.
[1] (5) No order shall be made against a defender under this rule unless it appears to the sheriff that the defender is—
  (a) a person who is insured in respect of the claim of the pursuer;
  (b) a public authority;
  (c) a person whose means and resources are such as to enable him to make the interim payment; or
  (d) the person's liability will be met by—
    (i) an insurer under section 151 of the Road Traffic Act 1988; or
    (ii) an insurer acting under the Motor Insurers Bureau Agreement, or the Motor Insurers Bureau where it is acting itself.
(6) Notwithstanding the grant or refusal of a motion for an interim payment, a subsequent motion may be made where there has been a change of circumstances.
(7) Subject to Part IV (management of damages payable to persons under legal disability) an interim payment shall be paid to the pursuer unless the sheriff otherwise directs.
(8) This rule shall, with the necessary modifications, apply to a counterclaim for damages for personal injuries made by a defender as it applies to an action in which the pursuer may apply for an order for interim payment of damages.

NOTE
[1] Amended by the Act of Sederunt (Ordinary Cause, Summary Application and Small Claim Rules) Amendment (Miscellaneous) 2004 (SSI 2004/197) (effective May 21, 2004), para.2(13).

Adjustment on final decree
36.10. Where a defender has made an interim payment under rule 36.9, the sheriff may, when final decree is pronounced, make such order with respect to the interim payment as he thinks fit to give effect to the final liability of that defender to the pursuer; and in particular may order—
  (a) repayment by the pursuer of any sum by which the interim payment exceeds the amount which that defender is liable to pay to the pursuer; or
  (b) payment by any other defender or a third party, of any part of the interim payment which the defender who made it is entitled to recover from him by way of contribution or indemnity or in respect of any remedy or relief relating to, or connected with, the claim of the pursuer.

Provisional Damages for Personal Injuries

Application and interpretation of this Part
36.11.—(1) This Part applies to an action of damages for personal injuries.
(2) In this Part—
  "the Act of 1982" means the Administration of Justice Act 1982;
  "further damages" means the damages referred to in section 12(4)(b) of the Act of 1982;
  "provisional damages" means the damages referred to in section 12(4)(a) of the Act of
    1982.

Applications for provisional damages
36.12. An application under section 12(2)(a) of the Act of 1982 for provisional damages for personal injuries shall be made by including in the initial writ—
  (a) a crave for provisional damages;
  (b) averments in the condescendence supporting the crave, including averments—
    (i) that there is a risk that, at some definite or indefinite time in the future, the pursuer will, as a result of the act or omission which gave rise to the cause of action, develop some serious disease or suffer some serious deterioration of his physical or mental condition; and
    (ii) that the defender was, at the time of the act or omission which gave rise to the cause of action, a public authority, public corporation or insured or otherwise indemnified in respect of the claim; and
  (c) an appropriate plea-in-law.

D 44/110

Applications for further damages
36.13.—(1) An application for further damages by a pursuer in respect of whom an order under section 12(2)(b) of the Act of 1982 has been made shall be made by minute in the process of the action to which it relates and shall include—
  (a) a crave for further damages;
  (b) averments in the statement of facts supporting that crave; and
  (c) appropriate pleas-in-law.
(2) On lodging such a minute in process, the pursuer shall apply by motion for warrant to serve the minute on—
  (a) every other party; and
  (b) where such other party is insured or otherwise indemnified, his insurer or indemnifier, if known to the pursuer.
(3) Any such party, insurer or indemnifier may lodge answers to such a minute in process within 28 days after the date of service on him.
(4) Where answers have been lodged under paragraph (3), the sheriff may, on the motion of any party, make such further order as to procedure as he thinks fit.

Part IV

Management of Damages Payable to Persons under Legal Disability

Orders for payment and management of money
[1] **36.14.**—(1) In an action of damages in which a sum of money becomes payable, by virtue of a decree or an extra-judicial settlement, to or for the benefit of a person under legal disability (other than a person under the age of 18 years), the sheriff shall make such order regarding the payment and management of that sum for the benefit of that person as he thinks fit.
(2) An order under paragraph (1) shall be made on the granting of decree for payment or of absolvitor.

NOTE
[1] As amended by SI 1996/2167 (effective November 1, 1996).

Methods of management
36.15. In making an order under rule 36.14(1), the sheriff may—
  (a) appoint a judicial factor to apply, invest or otherwise deal with the money for the benefit of the person under legal disability;
  (b) order the money to be paid to—
    (i) the Accountant of Court, or

    (ii) the guardian of the person under legal disability,
as trustee, to be applied, invested or otherwise dealt with and administered under the directions of the sheriff for the benefit of the person under legal disability;
  (c) order the money to be paid to the sheriff clerk of the sheriff court district in which the person under legal disability resides, to be applied, invested or otherwise dealt with and administered, under the directions of the sheriff of that district, for the benefit of the person under legal disability; or
  (d) order the money to be paid directly to the person under legal disability.

Subsequent orders
    36.16.—(1) Where the sheriff has made an order under rule 36.14(1), any person having an interest may apply for an appointment or order under rule 36.15, or any other order for the payment or management of the money, by minute in the process of the cause to which the application relates.
    (2) An application for directions under rule 36.15(b) or (c) may be made by any person having an interest by minute in the process of the cause to which the application relates.

Management of money paid to sheriff clerk
    36.17.—(1) A receipt in Form D2 by the sheriff clerk shall be a sufficient discharge in respect of the amount paid to him under this Part.
    (2) The sheriff clerk shall, at the request of any competent court, accept custody of any sum of money in an action of damages ordered to be paid to, applied, invested or otherwise dealt with by him, for the benefit of a person under legal disability.
    (3) Any money paid to the sheriff clerk under this Part shall be paid out, applied, invested or otherwise dealt with by the sheriff clerk only after such intimation, service and enquiry as the sheriff may order.
    (4) Any sum of money invested by the sheriff clerk under this Part shall be invested in a   **D 44/111** manner in which trustees are authorised to invest by virtue of the Trustee Investments Act 1961.

[1] Part IV A

PRODUCTIONS IN CERTAIN ACTIONS OF DAMAGES

    36.17A. This Part applies to an action of damages for personal injuries or the death of a person in consequence of personal injuries.

Averments of medical treatment
    36.17B. The condescendence of the initial writ in an action to which this Part applies shall include averments naming—
  (a) every general medical practitioner or general medical practice from whom; and
  (b) every hospital or other institution in which,
the pursuer or, in an action in respect of the death of a person, the deceased received treatment for the injuries sustained, or disease suffered, by him.

Lodging of medical reports
    36.17C.—(1) In an action to which this Part applies, the pursuer shall lodge as productions, with the initial writ when it is presented for warranting in accordance with rule 5.1, all medical reports on which he intends, or intends to reserve the right, to rely in the action.
    (2) Where no medical report is lodged as required by paragraph (1), the defender may apply by motion for an order specifying a period within which such a report shall be lodged in process.

NOTE
[1] Inserted by the Act of Sederunt (Sheriff Court Ordinary Cause Rules Amendment) (Miscellaneous) 2000 (SSI 2000/239) (effective October 2, 2000).

PART V

SEX DISCRIMINATION ACT 1975

Causes under section 66 of the Act of 1975
    36.18.—(1) In a cause in which a breach of statutory duty under section 66(1) of the Sex Discrimination Act 1975 (proceedings for act of discrimination) is averred, the sheriff may, of his own motion or on the motion of any party, appoint an assessor.
    [1] (2) An assessor appointed under paragraph (1) shall be a person who the sheriff considers

has special qualifications to be of assistance in determining a cause referred to in that paragraph.

(3) In a cause referred to in paragraph (1), the pursuer should send a copy of the initial writ by post by the first class recorded delivery service to the Equal Opportunities Commission.

NOTE
[1] As amended by the Act of Sederunt (Sheriff Court Ordinary Cause Rules Amendment) (Miscellaneous) 1996 (SI 1996/2445) (effective November 1, 1996) (clerical error).

CHAPTER 37

CAUSES UNDER THE PRESUMPTION OF DEATH (SCOTLAND) ACT 1977

Interpretation of this Chapter
37.1. In this Chapter—
　　"the Act of 1977" means the Presumption of Death (Scotland) Act 1977;
　　"action of declarator" means an action under section 1(1) of the Act of 1977;
　　"missing person" has the meaning assigned in section 1(1) of the Act of 1977.

Parties to, and service and intimation of, actions of declarator
37.2.—[1,2] (1) In an action of declarator—
　　(a) the missing person shall be named as the defender;
　　(b) subject to paragraph (2), service on that person shall be executed by advertisement in such newspaper or other publication as the sheriff thinks fit of such facts relating to the missing person and set out in the initial writ as the sheriff may specify; and
　　(c) the period of notice shall be 21 days from the date of publication of the advertisement unless the sheriff otherwise directs.
　[2] (2) The advertisement mentioned in paragraph (1) shall be in Form P1.

D 44/112　　(3) Subject to paragraph (5), in an action of declarator, the pursuer shall include a crave for a warrant for intimation to—
　　(a) the missing person's—
　　　　(i) spouse, and
　　　　(ii) children, or, if he has no children, his nearest relative known to the pursuer,
　　(b) any person, including any insurance company, who so far as known to the pursuer has an interest in the action, and
　　(c) the Lord Advocate,
in the following terms:— "For intimation to (*name and address*) as [husband *or* wife, child *or* nearest relative] [a person having an interest in the presumed death] of (*name and last known address of the missing person*) and to the Lord Advocate.".

　[3] (4) A notice of intimation in Form P2 shall be attached to the copy of the initial writ where intimation is given on a warrant under paragraph (3).

(5) The sheriff may, on the motion of the pursuer, dispense with intimation on a person mentioned in paragraph (3)(a) or (b).

(6) An application by minute under section 1(5) of the Act of 1977 (person interested in seeking determination or appointment not sought by pursuer) shall contain a crave for the determination or appointment sought, averments in the answers to the condescendence in support of that crave and an appropriate plea-in-law.

(7) On lodging a minute under paragraph (6), the minuter shall—
　　(a) send a copy of the minute by registered post or the first class recorded delivery service to each person to whom intimation of the action has been made under paragraph (2); and
　　(b) lodge in process the Post Office receipt or certificate of posting of that minute.

NOTE
[1] As amended by the Act of Sederunt (Sheriff Court Ordinary Cause Rules Amendment) (Miscellaneous) 1996 (SI 1996/2445) (effective November 1, 1996) (clerical error).
[2] Substituted by the Act of Sederunt (Sheriff Court Ordinary Cause Rules Amendment) (Miscellaneous) 2000 (SSI 2000/239) (effective October 2, 2000).
[3] As amended by the Act of Sederunt (Sheriff Court Ordinary Cause Rules Amendment) (Miscellaneous) 2000 (SSI 2000/239) (effective October 2, 2000).

Further advertisement
37.3. Where no minute has been lodged indicating knowledge of the present whereabouts of the missing person, at any time before the determination of the action, the sheriff may, of his own motion or on the motion of a party, make such order for further advertisement as he thinks fit.

Applications for proof
37.4.—(1) In an action of declarator where no minute has been lodged, the pursuer shall, after such further advertisement as may be ordered under rule 37.3, apply to the sheriff by motion for an order for proof.

(2) A proof ordered under paragraph (1) shall be by affidavit evidence unless the sheriff otherwise directs.

Applications for variation or recall of decree
37.5.—(1) An application under section 4(1) of the Act of 1977 (variation or recall of decree) shall be made by minute in the process of the action to which it relates.

(2) On the lodging of such a minute, the sheriff shall make an order—
(a) for service on the missing person, where his whereabouts have become known;
(b) for intimation to those persons mentioned in rule 37.2(3) or to dispense with intimation to a person mentioned in rule 37.2(3)(a) or (b); and
(c) for any answers to the minute to be lodged in process within such period as the sheriff thinks fit.

(3) An application under section 4(3) of the Act of 1977 (person interested seeking determination or appointment not sought by applicant for variation order) shall be made by lodging answers containing a crave for the determination or appointment sought.

(4) A person lodging answers containing a crave under paragraph (3) shall, as well as sending a copy of the answers to the minuter—
(a) send a copy of the answers by registered post or the first class recorded delivery service to each person on whom service or intimation of the minute was ordered; and
(b) lodge in process the Post Office receipt or certificate of posting of those answers.

Appointment of judicial factors
37.6.—(1) The Act of Sederunt (Judicial Factors Rules) 1992 shall apply to an application for the appointment of a judicial factor under section 2(2)(c) or section 4(2) of the Act of 1977 as it applies to a petition for the appointment of a judicial factor.

(2) In the application of rule 37.5 (applications for variation or recall of decree) to an **D 44/112/1** application under section 4(1) of the Act of 1977 in a cause in which variation or recall of the appointment of a judicial factor is sought, for reference to a minute there shall be substituted references to a note.

CHAPTER 38

EUROPEAN COURT

Interpretation of this Chapter
38.1.—(1) In this Chapter—
"appeal" includes an application for leave to appeal;
"the European Court" means the Court of Justice of the European Communities;
"reference" means a reference to the European Court for
[1] (a) a preliminary ruling under Article 234 of the E.E.C. Treaty, Article 150 of the Euratom Treaty or Article 41 of the E.C.S.C. Treaty; or
(b) a ruling on the interpretation of the Conventions, as defined in section 1(1) of the Civil Jurisdiction and Judgments Act 1982, under Article 3 of Schedule 2 to that Act.

(2) The expressions "E.E.C. Treaty", "Euratom Treaty" and "E.C.S.C. Treaty" have the meanings assigned respectively in Schedule 1 to the European Communities Act 1972.

NOTE
[1] As amended by the Act of Sederunt (Sheriff Court Ordinary Cause Rules Amendment) (Miscellaneous) 2000 (SSI 2000/239) (effective October 2, 2000).

Applications for reference
38.2.—(1) A reference may be made by the sheriff of his own motion or on the motion of a party.
(2) [*Repealed by SSI 2000/239 (effective October 2, 2000).*]

Preparation of case for reference

38.3.—(1) Where the sheriff decides that a reference shall be made, he shall continue the cause for that purpose and, within 4 weeks after the date of that continuation, draft a reference.

[1] (1A) Except in so far as the sheriff may otherwise direct, a reference shall be prepared in accordance with Form E1, having regard to the guidance set out in the Notes for Guidance issued by the Court of Justice of the European Communities.

(2) On the reference being drafted, the sheriff clerk shall send a copy to each party.

(3) Within 4 weeks after the date on which copies of the draft have been sent to parties, each party may—

(a) lodge with the sheriff clerk, and

(b) send to every other party,

a note of any adjustments he seeks to have made in the draft reference.

(4) Within 14 days after the date on which any such note of adjustments may be lodged, the sheriff, after considering any such adjustments, shall make and sign the reference.

(5) The sheriff clerk shall forthwith intimate the making of the reference to each party.

NOTE

[1] Inserted by the Act of Sederunt (Sheriff Court Ordinary Cause Rules Amendment) (Miscellaneous) 2000 (SSI 2000/239) (effective October 2, 2000).

Sist of cause

38.4.—(1) Subject to paragraph (2), on a reference being made, the cause shall, unless the sheriff when making such a reference otherwise orders, be sisted until the European Court has given a preliminary ruling on the question referred to it.

(2) The sheriff may recall a sist made under paragraph (1) for the purpose of making an interim order which a due regard to the interests of the parties may require.

Transmission of reference

38.5.—(1) Subject to paragraph (2), a copy of the reference, certified by the sheriff clerk, shall be transmitted by the sheriff clerk to the Registrar of the European Court.

(2) Unless the sheriff otherwise directs, a copy of the reference shall not be sent to the Registrar of the European Court where an appeal against the making of the reference is pending.

D 44/112/2 (3) For the purpose of paragraph (2), an appeal shall be treated as pending—

(a) until the expiry of the time for making that appeal; or

(b) where an appeal has been made, until that appeal has been determined.

CHAPTER 39

PROVISIONS IN RELATION TO CURATORS AD LITEM

Fees and outlays of curators ad litem in respect of children

[1] **39.1.**—(1) This rule applies to any civil proceedings whether or not the child is a party to the action.

(2) In an action where the sheriff appoints a curator ad litem to a child, the pursuer shall in the first instance, unless the court otherwise directs, be responsible for the fees and outlays of the curator ad litem incurred during the period from his appointment until the occurrence of any of the following events:

(a) he lodges a minute stating that he does not intend to lodge defences or to enter the process;

(b) he decides to instruct the lodging of defences or a minute adopting defences already lodged; or(c) the discharge, before the occurrence of the events mentioned in sub paragraphs (a) and (b), of the curator.

NOTE

[1] Inserted by the Act of Sederunt (Sheriff Court Ordinary Cause Rules Amendment) (Miscellaneous) 2000 (SSI 2000/239) (effective October 2, 2000).

COMMERCIAL ACTIONS

NOTE
¹ Inserted by the Act of Sederunt (Ordinary Cause Rules) Amendment (Commercial Actions) 2001 (SSI 2001/8).

Application and interpretation of this Chapter
40.1.—(1) This Chapter applies to a commercial action.
(2) In this Chapter—
    (a) "commercial action" means—an action arising out of, or concerned with, any transaction or dispute of a commercial or business nature including, but not limited to, actions relating to—
        (i) the construction of a commercial document;
        (ii) the sale or hire purchase of goods;
        (iii) the export or import of merchandise;
        (iv) the carriage of goods by land, air or sea;
        (v) insurance;
        (vi) banking;
        (vii) the provision of services;
        (viii) a building, engineering or construction contract; or
        (ix) a commercial lease; and
    (b) "commercial action" does not include an action in relation to consumer credit transactions.
(3) A commercial action may be raised only in a sheriff court where the Sheriff Principal for the sheriffdom has directed that the procedure should be available.

Proceedings before a nominated sheriff   **D 44/112/2/2**
40.2. All proceedings in a commercial action shall be brought before—
    (a) a sheriff of the sheriffdom nominated by the Sheriff Principal; or
    (b) where a nominated sheriff is not available, any other sheriff of the sheriffdom.

Procedure in commercial actions
40.3.—(1) In a commercial action the sheriff may make such order as he thinks fit for the progress of the case in so far as not inconsistent with the provisions in this Chapter.
(2) Where any hearing is continued, the reason for such continuation shall be recorded in the interlocutor.

Election of procedure for commercial actions
40.4. The pursuer may elect to adopt the procedure in this Chapter by bringing an action in Form G1A.

Transfer of action to be a commercial action   **D 44/112/2/3**
40.5.—(1) In an action within the meaning of rule 40.1(2) in which the pursuer has not made an election under rule 40.4, any party may apply by motion at any time to have the action appointed to be a commercial action.
(2) An interlocutor granted under paragraph (1) shall include a direction as to further procedure.

Appointment of a commercial action as an ordinary cause
40.6.—(1) At any time before, or at the Case Management Conference, the sheriff shall appoint a commercial action to proceed as an ordinary cause—
    (a) on the motion of a party where—
        (i) detailed pleadings are required to enable justice to be done between the parties; or
        (ii) any other circumstances warrant such an order being made; or
    (b) on the joint motion of parties.
(2) If a motion to appoint a commercial action to proceed as an ordinary action is refused, no subsequent motion to appoint the action to proceed as an ordinary cause shall be considered except on a material change of circumstances.
(3) Where the sheriff orders that a commercial action shall proceed as an ordinary cause the interlocutor granting such shall prescribe—
    (a) a period of adjustment, if appropriate; and
    (b) the date, time and place for any options hearing fixed.

(4) In determining what order to make in deciding that a commercial action proceed as an ordinary cause the sheriff shall have regard to the periods prescribed in rule 9.2.

D 44/112/2/4 *Special requirements for initial writ in a commercial action*

40.7.—(1) Where the construction of a document is the only matter in dispute no pleadings or pleas-in-law require to be included in the initial writ.

(2) There shall be appended to an initial writ in Form G1A a list of the documents founded on or adopted as incorporated in the initial writ.

Notice of Intention to Defend

40.8.—(1) Where the defender intends to—

(a) challenge the jurisdiction of the court;

(b) state a defence; or

(c) make a counterclaim,

he shall, before the expiry of the period of notice lodge with the sheriff clerk a notice of intention to defend in Form O7 and shall, at the same time, send a copy to the pursuer.

(2) The lodging of a notice of intention to defend shall not imply acceptance of the jurisdiction of the court.

Defences

40.9.—(1) Where a notice of intention to defend has been lodged, the defender shall lodge defences within 7 days after the expiry of the period of notice.

(2) There shall be appended to the defences a list of the documents founded on or adopted as incorporated in the defences.

(3) Subject to the requirement that each article of condescendence in the initial writ need not be admitted or denied, defences shall be in the form of answers that allow the extent of the dispute to be identified and shall have appended a note of the pleas in law of the defender.

D 44/112/2/5 *Fixing date for Case Management Conference*

40.10.—(1) On the lodging of defences, the sheriff clerk shall fix a date and time for a Case Management Conference, which date shall be on the first suitable court day occurring not sooner than 14 days, nor later than 28 days after the date of expiry of the period of notice.

(2) On fixing the date for the Case Management Conference, the sheriff clerk shall—

(a) forthwith intimate to the parties the date and time of the Case Management Conference; and

(b) prepare and sign an interlocutor recording that information.

(3) The fixing of the date of the Case Management Conference shall not affect the right of a party to make application by motion, to the court.

D 44/112/2/6 *Applications for summary decree in a commercial action*

40.11. Where a pursuer, in terms of rule 17.2(1) (applications for summary decree), or a defender in terms of rule 17.3(1) (application of summary decree to counterclaims), applies for summary decree in a commercial action, the period of notice mentioned in rule 17.2(3) shall be 48 hours.

Case Management Conference

40.12.—(1) At the Case Management Conference in a commercial action the sheriff shall seek to secure the expeditious resolution of the action.

(2) Parties shall be prepared to provide such information as the sheriff may require to determine—

(a) whether, and to what extent, further specification of the claim and defences is required; and

(b) the orders to make to ensure the expeditious resolution of the action.

(3) The orders the sheriff may make in terms of paragraph 2(b) may include but shall not be limited to—

(a) the lodging of written pleadings by any party to the action which may be restricted to particular issues;

(b) the lodging of a statement of facts by any party which may be restricted to particular issues;

(c) allowing an amendment by a party to his pleadings;

(d) disclosure of the identity of witnesses and the existence and nature of documents relating to the action or authority to recover documents either generally or specifically;

(e) the lodging of documents constituting, evidencing or relating to the subject matter of the action or any invoices, correspondence or similar documents;

(f) the exchanging of lists of witnesses;

(g) the lodging of reports of skilled persons or witness statements;

(h) the lodging of affidavits concerned with any of the issues in the action;

(i) the lodging of notes of arguments setting out the basis of any preliminary plea;

(j) fixing a debate or proof, with or without any further preliminary procedure, to determine the action or any particular aspect thereof;

(k) the lodging of joint minutes of admission or agreement;

(l) recording admissions made on the basis of information produced; or

(m) any order which the sheriff thinks will result in the speedy resolution of the action (including the use of alternative dispute resolution), or requiring the attendance of parties in person at any subsequent hearing.

(4) In making any order in terms of paragraph (3) the sheriff may fix a period within which such order shall be complied with.

(5) The sheriff may continue the Case Management Conference to a specified date where he considers it necessary to do so—

(a) to allow any order made in terms of paragraph (3) to be complied with; or

(b) to advance the possibility of resolution of the action.

(6) Where the sheriff makes an order in terms of paragraph (3) he may ordain the pursuer **D 44/112/2/7** to—

(a) make up a record; and

(b) lodge that record in process,

within such period as he thinks fit.

Lodging of productions **D 44/112/2/8**

40.13. Prior to any proof or other hearing at which the documents listed in terms of rules 40.7(2) and 40.9(2) are to be referred to parties shall, in addition to lodging the productions in terms of rule 21.1, prepare, for the use of the sheriff, a working bundle in which the documents are arranged chronologically or in another appropriate order.

Hearing for further procedure

40.14. At any time before final judgement, the sheriff may—

(a) of his own motion or on the motion of any party, fix a hearing for further procedure; and

(b) make such other order as he thinks fit.

Failure to comply with rule or order of sheriff

40.15. Any failure by a party to comply timeously with a provision in this Chapter or any order made by the sheriff in a commercial action shall entitle the sheriff, of his own motion—

(a) to refuse to extend any period for compliance with a provision in these Rules or an order of the court;

(b) to dismiss the action or counterclaim, as the case may be, in whole or in part;

(c) to grant decree in respect of all or any of the craves of the initial writ or counterclaim, as the case may be; or

(d) to make an award of expenses,

as he thinks fit.

Determination of action **D 44/112/2/9**

40.16. It shall be open to the sheriff, at the end of any hearing, to restrict any interlocutor to a finding.

Parts of Process

40.17. All parts of process lodged in a commercial action shall be clearly marked "Commercial Action".

[1] CHAPTER 41 **D 44/112/2/11**

PROTECTION FROM ABUSE (SCOTLAND) ACT 2001

NOTE

[1]Inserted by the Act of Sederunt (Ordinary Cause Rules) Amendment (Applications under the Protection from Abuse (Scotland) Act 2001) 2002 (SSI 2002/128), para.2.

Interpretation

41.1.—(1) In this Chapter a section referred to by number means the section so numbered in the Protection from Abuse (Scotland) Act 2001.

(2) Words and expressions used in this Chapter which are also used in the Protection from Abuse (Scotland) Act 2001 have the same meaning as in that Act.

Attachment of power of arrest to interdict

[1] **41.2.**—(1) An application under section 1(1) (application for attachment of power of arrest to interdict)—

(a) shall be made in the crave in the initial writ, defences or counterclaim in which the interdict to which it relates is applied for, or, if made after the application for interdict, by motion in the process of the action in which the interdict was sought, or by minute, with answers if appropriate, should the sheriff so order; and

(b) shall be intimated to the person against whom the interdict is sought or was obtained.

(2) Where the sheriff attaches a power of arrest under section 1(2) (order attaching power of arrest) the following documents shall be served along with the power of arrest in accordance with section 2(1) (documents to be served along with power of arrest)—

(a) a copy of the application for interdict;

(b) a copy of the interlocutor granting interdict; and

(c) where the application to attach the power of arrest was made after the interdict was granted, a copy of the certificate of service of the interdict.

(3) After the power of arrest has been served, the following documents shall be delivered by the person who obtained the power to the chief constable in accordance with section 3(1) (notification to police)—

(a) a copy of the application for interdict;

(b) a copy of the interlocutor granting interdict;

(c) a copy of the certificate of service of the interdict; and

(d) where the application to attach the power of arrest was made after the interdict was granted—

(i) a copy of the application for the power of arrest;

(ii) a copy of the interlocutor granting it; and

(iii) a copy of the certificate of service of the power of arrest and the documents that required to be served along with it in accordance with section 2(1).

NOTE

[1] As amended by the Act of Sederunt (Ordinary Cause, Summary Application, Summary Cause and Small Claim Rules) Amendment (Miscellaneous) 2003 (SSI 2003/26), para.2(13) (effective January 24, 2003).

Extension or recall of power of arrest

41.3.—(1) An application under either of the following provisions shall be made by minute in the process of the action in which the power of arrest was attached—

(a) section 2(3) (extension of duration of power of arrest);

(b) section 2(7) (recall of power of arrest).

(2) Where the sheriff extends the duration of, or recalls, a power of arrest, the person who obtained the extension or recall must deliver a copy of the interlocutor granting the extension or recall in accordance with section 3(1).

Documents to be delivered to chief constable in relation to recall or variation of interdict

41.4. Where an interdict to which a power of arrest has been attached under section 1(2) is varied or recalled, the person who obtained the variation or recall must deliver a copy of the interlocutor varying or recalling the interdict in accordance with section 3(1).

D 44/112/2/12 *Certificate of delivery of documents to chief constable*

41.5.—Where a person is in any circumstances required to comply with section 3(1) he shall, after such compliance, lodge in process a certificate of delivery in Form PA1.".

(3) In Appendix 1 (forms), after Form E1 insert Form PA1 as set out in the Schedule to this Act of Sederunt.

CHAPTER 42[1]

NOTE

[1] Inserted by the Act of Sederunt (Ordinary Cause Rules) Amendment (Competition Appeal Tribunal) 2004 (SSI 2004/350), para.2 (effective August 20, 2004).

COMPETITION APPEAL TRIBUNAL

Interpretation
42.1. In this Chapter—
"the 1998 Act" means the Competition Act 1998; and
"the Tribunal" means the Competition Appeal Tribunal established by section 12 of the Enterprise Act 2002.

Transfer of proceedings to the Tribunal
42.2.—(1) A party in proceedings for a monetary claim to which section 47A of the 1998 Act applies may apply by motion to the sheriff for an order transferring the proceedings, or any part of them, to the Tribunal.
(2) Where the sheriff orders that such proceedings (or any part of them) are transferred to the Tribunal, the sheriff clerk shall, within 7 days from the date of such order—
  (a) transmit the process (or the appropriate part) to the clerk of the Tribunal;
  (b) notify each party to the proceedings in writing of the transmission under sub paragraph (a); and
  (c) certify, by making an appropriate entry on the interlocutor sheet, that he has made all notifications required under sub paragraph (b).
(3) Transmission of the process under paragraph (2)(a) shall be valid notwithstanding any failure by the sheriff clerk to comply with paragraph (2)(b) and (c).

APPENDIX 1   **Rule 1.4   D 44/112/3**

FORMS

Rule 3.1(1)(a)   FORM G1

Form of initial writ

INITIAL WRIT

SHERIFFDOM OF (*insert name of sheriffdom*)
AT (*insert place of sheriff court*)

[A.B.] (*design and state any special capacity in which the pursuer is suing*). Pursuer.
Against
[C.D.] (*design and state any special capacity in which the defender is being sued*). Defender.

The Pursuer craves the court (*here state the specific decree, warrant or order sought*).

CONDESCENDENCE
(*State in numbered paragraphs the facts which form the ground of action*)

PLEAS-IN-LAW
(*State in numbered sentences*)

Signed
[A.B.], Pursuer.
or [X.Y.], Solicitor for the pursuer (*state designation and business address*)

Rule 3.1(1)(b) and 40.4   [1] FORM G1A

Form of initial writ in a commercial action

SHERIFFDOM OF (*insert name of sheriffdom*)
AT (*insert place of sheriff court*)

COMMERCIAL ACTION

[A.B.] (*design and state any special capacity in which the pursuer is being sued*). Pursuer.
Against
[C.D.] (*design and state any special capacity in which the defender is being sued*). Defender.

[A.B.] for the Pursuer craves the court (*specify the orders sought*)

CONDESCENDENCE
(provide the following, in numbered paragraphs—

*information sufficient to identify the transaction or dispute from which the action arises;
a summary of the circumstances which have resulted in the action being raised; and
details setting out the grounds on which the action proceeds.)*

*Note: Where damages are sought, the claim may be summarised in the pleadings—
in the form of a statement of damages; or
by lodging with the initial writ a schedule detailing the claim.*

PLEAS-IN-LAW
(state in numbered sentences)

> Signed
> [A.B.], Pursuer
> *or* [X.Y.], Solicitor for the Pursuer *(state
> designation and business address)*

D 44/112/4 NOTE
     [1] Inserted by the Act of Sederunt (Ordinary Cause Rules) Amendment (Commercial Actions)
2001 (SSI 2001 |No.8) (effective March 1, 2001).

Rule 4.2(1)   FORM G2

Form of caveat

SHERIFFDOM OF *(insert name of sheriffdom)*
AT *(insert place of sheriff court)*

CAVEAT for [A.B.] *(insert designation and address***)*

Should any application be made for *(here specify the nature of the application(s) to which this
caveat is to apply)* before the lodging of a notice of intention to defend, it is requested that
intimation be made to the caveator before any order is pronounced.

Date *(insert date)*   Signed
                              [A.B.]
                              or [X.Y.] Solicitor for [A.B.] *(add designation and
                              business address)*

Caveator's telephone and fax number *(insert where caveat is not lodged by solicitor)*

Solicitor *(insert name and address, telephone and fax number and reference)*

Out of hours contacts:
                    1. *(insert name and telephone number)*
                    2. *(insert name and telephone number)*

     * State whether the caveat is lodged in an individual capacity, or a specified representative
capacity (e.g. as trustee of a named trust) or both. Where appropriate, state also the nature of
the caveator's interest (e.g. shareholder, debenture holder).

Rule 5.6(1)(a)   FORM G3

Form of advertisement

NOTICE TO [C.D.]   Court ref. no.
An action has been raised in   Sheriff Court by [A.B.], Pursuer, calling as a Defender
[C.D.] whose last known address was *(insert last known address of defender)*. If [C.D.] wishes to
defend the action *[where notice is given in a family action add*: or make any claim or seek any
order]* he *[or she]* should immediately contact the sheriff clerk at *(insert address)* from whom the
service copy initial writ may be obtained. If he *[or she]* fails to do so decree may be granted
against him *[or her]*.

> Signed
> [X.Y.], *(add designation and business
> address)*
> Solicitor for the pursuer

or [P.Q.], (*add business address*)
Sheriff officer

Rule 5.6(1)(b) FORM G4

Form of notice for walls of court

NOTICE TO [C.D.] Court ref. no.
An action has been raised in Sheriff Court by [A.B.], Pursuer, calling as a Defender
[C.D.] whose last known address was (*insert last known address of defender*). If [C.D.] wishes to
defend the action [*where notice is to be given in a family action add*: or make any claim or seek
any order] he [*or* she] should immediately contact the sheriff clerk at (*insert address*) from whom
the service copy initial writ may be obtained. If he [*or* she] fails to do so decree may be granted
against him [*or* her].

Date (*insert date*) (*Signed*)
Sheriff clerk (depute)
Telephone no. (*insert telephone number of sheriff clerk's
office*)

Rules 9.2(2)(a) and 33.16(3)(b) [1] FORM G5 **D 44/112/5**

Form of intimation of Options Hearing

Sheriff Court (*insert address and telephone number*) Court ref. no.

[A.B.] (*design*) Pursuer against [C.D.] (*design*) Defender

You are given notice that in this action:—

| (*insert date*) | is the last day for lodging defences; |

| (*insert date*) | is the last day for making adjustments to the writ or defences; |

| (*insert date, time and place*) | is the date, time and place for the Options Hearing. |

Date (*insert date*) (*Signed*)
Sheriff clerk (depute)

NOTE:
If you fail to comply with the terms of this notice or with any of the rules 9.3, 9.4, 9.6, 9.10
and 9.11 of the Standard Procedure of the Ordinary Cause Rules of the Sheriff Court or, where
applicable, rule 33.37 (decree by default in a family action), decree by default may be granted in
terms of rule 16.2(2) of those Rules.

NOTE TO BE ADDED WHERE PARTY UNREPRESENTED

NOTE
IF YOU ARE UNCERTAIN WHAT ACTION TO TAKE you should consult a solicitor.
You may be eligible for legal aid depending on your income, and you can get information
from any Citizens Advice Bureau or other advice agency.

NOTE
[1] As amended by SI 1996/2445 (effective November 1, 1996).

Rule 15.1(1)(b) FORM G6

Form of motion

SHERIFFDOM OF (*insert name of sheriffdom*) Court ref. no.
AT (*insert place of sheriff court*)

MOTION FOR THE PURSUER [*or* DEFENDER]
in the cause
[A.B.] (*insert designation and address*)
Pursuer
against
[C.D.] (*insert designation and address*)
Defender

The (*insert description of party*) moves the court to (*insert details of motion and, where appropriate, the reason(s) for seeking the order*).

List the documents or parts of process lodged with the motion:—
(*Insert description of document or name part of process*)
Date (*insert date*)   (*Signed*)
                                                       Party (*insert name and
                                                       description of party*)
                                                       or Solicitor for party
                                                       (*insert designation and business
                                                       address*)

D 44/112/6 Rule 15.2(1)   [1] **FORM G7**

Form of intimation of motion

SHERIFFDOM OF (*insert name of sheriffdom*)   Court ref. no.
AT (*insert place of sheriff court*)

in the cause

[A.B.] (*insert name and address*)
Pursuer
against
[C.D.] (*insert name and address*)
Defender

LAST DATE FOR LODGING NOTICE OF OPPOSITION:

APPLICATION IS MADE BY MOTION FOR THE ORDER(S) SOUGHT IN THE ATTACHED FORM (*attach a copy of the motion in Form G6*)

* A copy of the document(s) or part(s) of process referred to in Form G6 is/are attached.

OPPOSITION TO THE MOTION MAY BE MADE by completing Form G9 (notice of opposition to motion) and lodging it with the sheriff clerk at (*insert address*) on or before the last date for lodging notice of opposition. A copy of the notice of opposition must be sent immediately to any other party in the action.

IN THE EVENT OF A NOTICE OF OPPOSITION BEING LODGED the sheriff clerk will assign a date, time and place for hearing parties on the motion. Intimation of this hearing will be sent to parties by the sheriff clerk.

IF NO NOTICE OF OPPOSITION IS LODGED, the motion may be considered by the sheriff without the attendance of parties.

Date (*insert date*)   (*Signed*)
                                            Pursuer (*or as the case may be*)
                                            [*or* Solicitor for pursuer [*or as the case may be*]
                                            (*insert name and business address*)]

EXPLANATORY NOTE TO BE ADDED WHERE PARTY TO WHOM INTIMATION IS MADE IS NOT LEGALLY REPRESENTED

IF YOU ARE UNCERTAIN WHAT ACTION TO TAKE you should consult a solicitor. You may also obtain advice from a Citizens Advice Bureau or other advice agency.

NOTE: If YOU intend to oppose the motion you must appear or be represented on the date of the hearing. If you return Form G9 (notice of opposition to motion) and then fail to attend or be represented at the court hearing, the court may consider the motion in your absence and may grant the order(s) sought.

* Delete if not applicable

NOTE
¹ Substituted by SI 1996/2445 (effective November 1, 1996).

Rule 14.4(1)(a)   ¹ FORM G7A

Form of intimation of minute (answers lodged)

SHERIFFDOM OF (*insert name of sheriffdom*)   Court ref. no.
AT (*insert place of sheriff court*)

in the cause

[A.B.] (*insert name and address*)
Pursuer

against   **D 44/112/7**

[C.D.] (*insert name and address*)
Defender

LAST DATE FOR LODGING ANSWERS:

APPLICATION IS MADE BY MOTION FOR THE ORDER(S) SOUGHT IN THE MINUTE ATTACHED (*attach a copy of minute and interlocutor*)

* A copy of the document(s) or part(s) of process referred to in the minute is/are attached.

IN THE EVENT OF ANSWERS BEING LODGED the sheriff clerk will assign a date, time and place for hearing parties on the minute and answers. Intimation of this hearing will be sent to parties by the sheriff clerk.

IF NO ANSWERS ARE LODGED, the motion may be considered by the sheriff without the attendance of parties.

Date (*insert date*)   (*Signed*)
Pursuer (*or as the case may be*)
[*or* Solicitor for pursuer [*or as the case may be*]
(*Add name and business address*)]

EXPLANATORY NOTE TO BE ADDED WHERE PARTY TO WHOM INTIMATION IS MADE IS NOT LEGALLY REPRESENTED

IF YOU ARE UNCERTAIN WHAT ACTION TO TAKE you should consult a solicitor. You may also obtain advice from a Citizens Advice Bureau or other advice agency.

NOTE: If you intend to oppose the minute you must appear or be represented on the date of the hearing. If you return Form G9 (notice of opposition to minute) and then fail to attend or be represented at the court hearing, the court may consider the minute in your absence and may grant the order(s) sought.

* Delete if not applicable

NOTE
¹ Inserted by SI 1996/2445 (effective November 1, 1996).

Rule 14.4(1)(a)   ¹ FORM G7B

Form of intimation of minute (no order for answers or no hearing fixed)

SHERIFFDOM OF (*insert name of sheriffdom*)   Court ref. no.
AT (*insert place of sheriff court*)

in the cause

[A.B.] (*insert name and address*)
Pursuer

against
[C.D.] (*insert name and address*)
Defender

LAST DATE FOR LODGING NOTICE OF OPPOSITION:

APPLICATION IS MADE BY MINUTE FOR THE ORDER(S) SOUGHT IN THE MINUTE ATTACHED (*attach a copy of minute and interlocutor*)

* A copy of the document(s) or part(s) of process referred to in the minute is/are attached.

OPPOSITION TO THE MOTION MAY BE MADE by completing Form G9 (notice of opposition to motion) and lodging it with the sheriff clerk at (*insert address*) on or before the last date for lodging notice of opposition. A copy of the notice of opposition must be sent immediately to any other party in the action.

IN THE EVENT OF A NOTICE OF OPPOSITION BEING LODGED the sheriff clerk will
D 44/112/8 assign a date, time and place for hearing parties on the minute. Intimation of this hearing will be sent to parties by the sheriff clerk.

IF NO NOTICE OF OPPOSITION IS LODGED, the minute may be considered by the sheriff without the attendance of parties.

Date (*insert date*)   (*Signed*)
Pursuer (*or as the case may be*)
[*or* Solicitor for pursuer [*or as the case may be*]
(*Add name and business address*)]

EXPLANATORY NOTE TO BE ADDED WHERE PARTY TO WHOM INTIMATION IS MADE IS NOT LEGALLY REPRESENTED

IF YOU ARE UNCERTAIN WHAT ACTION TO TAKE you should consult a solicitor. You may also obtain advice from a Citizens Advice Bureau or other advice agency.

NOTE: If YOU intend to oppose the minute you must appear or be represented on the date of the hearing. If you return Form G9 (notice of opposition to minute) and then fail to attend or be represented at the court hearing, the court may consider the motion in your absence and may grant the order(s) sought.

* Delete if not applicable

NOTE
[1] Inserted by SI 1996/2445 (effective November 1, 1996).

Rule 14.4(1)(a)   [1] FORM G7C

Form of intimation of minute (hearing fixed)

SHERIFFDOM OF (*insert name of sheriffdom*)   Court ref. no.
AT (*insert place of sheriff court*)

in the cause

[A.B.] (*insert name and address*)
Pursuer
against
[C.D.] (*insert name and address*)
Defender

DATE AND TIME FOR HEARING MINUTE:

*DATE FOR LODGING ANSWERS OR AFFIDAVIT EVIDENCE:

APPLICATION IS MADE FOR THE ORDER(S) SOUGHT IN THE MINUTE ATTACHED (*attach a copy of minute and interlocutor*)

* A copy of the document(s) or part(s) of process referred to in the minute is/are attached.

IF YOU WISH TO OPPOSE THE MINUTE OR MAKE ANY REPRESENTATIONS you must attend or be represented at (*insert name and address of court*) on the date and time referred to above.

* If an order has been made for you to lodge answers or affidavit evidence these must be lodged with the sheriff clerk (*insert address*) on or before the above date.

IF YOU FAIL TO ATTEND OR BE REPRESENTED the minute may be determined in your absence.

Date (*insert date*) (*Signed*)
Pursuer (*or as the case may be*)
[*or* Solicitor for pursuer [*or as the case may be*]
(*Add name and business address*)]

EXPLANATORY NOTE TO BE ADDED WHERE PARTY TO WHOM INTIMATION IS MADE IS NOT LEGALLY REPRESENTED

IF YOU ARE UNCERTAIN WHAT ACTION TO TAKE you should consult a solicitor. You may also obtain advice from a Citizens Advice Bureau or other advice agency.

D 44/112/9

NOTE: If you intend to oppose the minute you must appear or be represented on the date of the hearing. If you return Form G9 (notice of opposition to minute) and then fail to attend or be represented at the court hearing, the court may consider the minute in your absence and may grant the order(s) sought.

* Delete if not applicable

NOTE
[1] Inserted by SI 1996/2445 (effective November 1, 1996).

Rules 14.6 and 15.1(2) [1] FORM G8

Form of certificate of intimation of motion or minute

CERTIFICATE OF INTIMATION OF MOTION [*or* MINUTE]

I certify that intimation of the motion [*or* minute] was made to (*insert names of parties or solicitors for the parties, as appropriate*) by (*insert method of intimation; where intimation is by facsimile transmission, insert fax number to which intimation sent*) on (*insert date of intimation*).

Date (*insert date*) (*Signed*)
Solicitor [*or* Sheriff Officer]
(*Add name and business address*)

NOTE
[1] Substituted by SI 1996/2445 (effective November 1, 1996).

Rules 14.7(1)(a) and 15.3(1)(a) [1] FORM G9

Form of notice of opposition to motion or minute

NOTICE OF OPPOSITION TO MOTION [*or* MINUTE]

SHERIFFDOM OF (*insert name of sheriffdom*) Court ref. no.:
AT (*insert place of sheriff court*)

in the cause

[A.B.] (*insert name and address*)
Pursuer

against

[C.D.] (*insert name and address*)
Defender

Notice of opposition to motion [*or* minute] given by (*insert name of party opposing motion*) to (*insert names of all other parties, or solicitors for the parties, to the action*) by (*insert method of *intimation; where intimation is made by facsimile transmission, insert fax number to which notice of opposition sent*) on (*insert date of intimation*).

Date (*insert date*)   (*Signed*)

Pursuer (*or as the case may be*)
(*insert name and address of party*)
[*or* Solicitor for Pursuer [*or as the case may be*]
(*Add name and business address*)]

NOTE
[1] Substituted by SI 1996/2445 (effective November 1, 1996).

D 44/112/10 Rule 24.2(3)   [1] FORM G10

Form of intimation to a party whose solicitor has withdrawn

SHERIFFDOM OF (*insert name of sheriffdom*)
AT (*insert place of sheriff court*)

in the cause

[A.B.] (*insert designation*)
Pursuer
against

[C.D.] (*insert designation*)
Defender

Court ref. no.

The court has been informed that your solicitors have ceased to act for you.

As a result the sheriff has ordered that you appear or be represented on (*insert date and time*) within the Sheriff Court at the above address. A copy of the order is attached.

When you appear you will be asked by the sheriff to state whether you intend to proceed with your action [*or* defences *or* answers].

> **NOTE:**
> **IF YOU ARE UNCERTAIN WHAT ACTION TO TAKE** you should consult a solicitor. You may also obtain advice from a Citizens Advice Bureau or other advice agency.

NOTE
[1] As amended by SI 1996/2445 (effective November 1, 1996).

Rule 28.3(1) and (3)   FORM G11

Form of notice in optional procedure for commission and diligence

Court ref. no.

Order by the Sheriff Court at (*insert address*)

In the cause

[A.B.] (*design*) Pursuer
against

[C.D.] (*design*) Defender

To (*insert name and designation of party or parties or haver, from whom documents are sought to be recovered*)

You are given notice that you are required to produce to the sheriff clerk at the above address within seven days of (*insert date on which service was executed. N.B. Rule 5.3(2) relating to postal service or intimation*):

(1) this order; which must be produced intact;
(2) a certificate signed and completed in terms of the form appended to this notice; and
(3) all documents in your possession falling within the enclosed specification, with an inventory of such documents signed by you relating to this order and your certificate.

Production may be made by lodging the documents with the sheriff clerk at the above address, by posting them by registered post or the first class recorded delivery service addressed to the sheriff clerk at the above address.

Date (*insert date*)   (*Signed*)
                                                      Solicitor for party (*add designation and business address of the solicitor for the party in whose favour commission and diligence granted*)

NOTE

If you claim confidentiality for any of the documents produced by you, such documents must nevertheless be produced, but may be placed in a special sealed packet by themselves, marked "confidential".

CERTIFICATE   **D 44/112/11**

I hereby certify with reference to the order of the Sheriff Court at (*insert place of sheriff court*) in the cause (*insert court ref. no.*) and the relative specification of documents, served upon me and marked respectively X and Y:

(1) that the documents which are produced and which are numbered in the inventory signed by me and marked Z, are the whole documents in my possession falling under the specification [*or* that I have no documents in my possession falling within the specification];

(2) that, to the best of my knowledge and belief, there are in existence other documents falling within the specification, but not in my possession, namely (*describe them by reference to one or more of the descriptions of documents in the specification*), which were last seen by me on or about (*insert date*), at (*insert place*), in the hands of (*insert name and address of the person*) [*or* that I know of the existence of no documents in the possession of any person, other than myself, which fall within the specification].

Signed

Rules 28.4(4) and 29.7(4)   FORM G12

Form of certificate of citation of witness or haver

I certify that on (*insert date of citation*)   I duly cited [K.L.], (*design*) to attend at (*insert name of sheriff court*) Sheriff Court on (*insert date*) at (*insert time*) as a witness for the pursuer [*or* defender] in the action at the instance of [A.B.] (*design*), Pursuer, against [C.D.] (*design*), Defender, [and I required him [*or* her] to bring with him [*or* her] (*specify documents*)]. This I did by (*state mode of citation*).

Date (*insert date*)   (*Signed*)
                                                      [P.Q.], Sheriff officer;
                                                      or [X.Y.], (*add designation and business address*)
                                                      Solicitor for the pursuer [*or* defender]

Rules 28.4(4) and 29.7(4)   [1] FORM G13

Form of citation of witness or haver

CITATION

SHERIFFDOM OF (*insert name of sheriffdom*)
AT (*insert place of sheriff court*)

To [K.L.] (*design*)

You are required to attend the above sheriff court on (*insert date*) at (*insert time*) as a witness for the pursuer [*or* defender] in the action by [A.B.] (*design*), Pursuer, against [C.D.] (*design*), Defender, [and to bring with you (*specify documents*)].

If you fail to attend, warrant may be granted for your arrest.

Date (*insert date*)   Signed
                                        [P.Q.], Sheriff Officer,
                                        or [X.Y.], (*add designation and business
                                        address*)
                                        Solicitor for the pursuer [*or
                                        defender*]

NOTE
Claims for necessary outlays and loss of earnings within certain specified limits will be paid. Claims should be made to the person who has cited you to attend court. Proof of any loss of earnings should be given to that person.

If you wish your travelling expenses to be paid prior to your attendance you should apply for payment to the person who has cited you.

D 44/112/12   **If you fail to attend without reasonable cause, having requested and been paid your travelling expenses, you may be ordered to pay a penalty not exceeding £250.**

NOTE
[1] Substituted by SSI 2000/239 (effective October 2, 2000).

Rules 28.4(6)(b), 28.10(4)(b)   FORM G14
and 29.16

Form of oath for witness

The witness to raise his right hand and repeat after the sheriff [*or* commissioner]: "I swear by Almighty God that I will tell the truth, the whole truth and nothing but the truth".

Rules 28.4(6)(b), 28.10(4)(b)   FORM G15
and 29.16

Form of affirmation for witness

The witness to repeat after the sheriff [*or* commissioner]: "I solemnly, sincerely and truly declare and affirm that I will tell the truth, the whole truth and nothing but the truth".

D 44/113   FORM G16   **Rule 28.14(3)**

Form of minute for letter of request

SHERIFFDOM OF (*insert name of sheriffdom*)
AT (*insert place of sheriff court*)

MINUTE FOR PURSUER [*or* DEFENDER]

in the cause

[A.B.] (*insert designation and address*)
                                        Pursuer
                    against

[C.D.] (*insert designation and address*)
                                        Defender

                                        Court ref. no.

The Minuter states that the evidence specified in the attached letter of request is required for the purpose of these proceedings and craves the court to issue a letter of request to (*specify the court or tribunal having powers to obtain the evidence*) to obtain the evidence specified.

Date (*insert date*)   Signed
                                        Solicitor for the pursuer [*or* defender *or*
                                        third party] (*add designation and business
                                        address*)

FORM G17   Rule 28.14(3)

Form of letter of request

LETTER OF REQUEST

1. Sender   (*insert name and address*)

2. Central authority of the requested state   (*insert name and address*)

3. Person to whom the executed request is to   (*insert name and address*)
be returned

4. The undersigned applicant has the honour to submit the following request:

5. a. Requesting judicial authority   (*insert name and address*)

   b. To the competent authority   (*insert name of requested state*)

6. Names and addresses of the parties and
their representatives

   a. Pursuer

   b. Defender

   c. Other parties

7. Nature and purpose of the proceedings
and summary of facts

8. Evidence to be obtained or other judicial
act to be performed

(*Items to be completed where applicable*)

9. Identity and address of any person to be
examined

10. Questions to be put to the persons to be   (*or see attached list*)
examined or statement of the subject-matter
about which they are to be examined

11. Documents or other property to be   (*specify whether it is to be produced, copied,*
inspected   *valued, etc.*)

12. Any requirement that the evidence be   (*in the event that the evidence cannot be taken* **D 44/114**
given on oath or affirmation and any special   *in the manner requested, specify whether it is to*
form to be used   *be taken in such manner as provided by local*
                                               law for the formal taking of evidence)

13. Special methods or procedure to be
followed

14. Request for notification of the time and
place for the execution of the request and
identity and address of any person to be
notified

15. Request for attendance or participation
of judicial personnel of the requesting authority at the execution of the letter of request

16. Specification of privilege or duty to refuse
to give evidence under the law of the state of
origin

17. The fees and expenses (costs) incurred   (*insert name and address*)
will be borne by

(*Items to be included in all letters of request*)

18. Date of request

19. Signature and seal of the requesting
authority

FORM G18 Rule 30.3(2)

Form of certificate of rate of exchange

CERTIFICATE OF RATE OF EXCHANGE

I (*insert designation and address*) certify that the rates current in London for the purchase of (*state the unit of currency in which the decree is expressed*) on (*insert date*) was (*state rate of exchange*) to the £ sterling and at this rate the sum of (*state the amount of the sum in the decree*) amounts to (*insert sterling equivalent*).

Date (*insert date*) Signed
For and on behalf of the bank manager or other official

FORM O1 Rule 3.3(1)

Form of warrant of citation

(*Insert place and date*) Grants warrant to cite the defender (*insert name and address*) by serving upon him [*or* her] a copy of the writ and warrant on a period of notice of (*insert period of notice*) days, and ordains him [*or* her], if he [*or* she] intends to defend the action or make any claim, to lodge a notice of intention to defend with the sheriff clerk at (*insert place of sheriff court*) within the said period of notice after such service [and grants warrant to arrest on the dependence].

[Meantime grants interim interdict; *or* grants warrant to arrest to found jurisdiction; *or* sequestrates and grants warrant to inventory; *or otherwise, as the case may be*.]

Signed
Sheriff [*or* sheriff clerk]

D 44/115 FORM O2 **Rule 3.3(2)**

Form of warrant of citation where time to pay direction may be applied for

(*Insert place and date*) Grants warrant to cite the defender (*insert name and address*) by serving a copy of the writ and warrant, with Form O3, on a period of notice of (*insert period of notice*) days and ordains him [*or* her] if he [*or* she]—

(a) intends to defend the action or make any claim, to lodge a notice of intention to defend; or
(b) admits the claim and intends to apply for a time to pay direction [and apply for recall or restriction of an arrestment] to lodge the appropriate part of Form O3 duly completed;

with the sheriff clerk at (*insert place of sheriff court*) within the said period of notice after such service [and grants warrant to arrest on the dependence].

[Meantime grants interim interdict, *or* grants warrant to arrest to found jurisdiction; *or* sequestrates and grants warrant to inventory; *or otherwise, as the case may be*.]

Signed
Sheriff [*or* sheriff clerk]

[1] FORM O2A **Rule 3.3(4)**

Form of warrant in an action to which rule 3.2(3) applies

(*Insert place and date*) Grants warrant to cite the defender (*insert name and address*) by serving a copy of the writ and warrant and Form O7 on a period of notice of (*insert period of notice*) days and ordains him [*or* her] if he [*or* she]—

(a) intends to defend the action or make any claim, to lodge a notice of intention to defend with the sheriff clerk at (*insert place of sheriff court*) within the said period of notice after such service [and grants warrant to arrest on the dependence]; or

(b) intends to apply for an order under section 2 of the Mortgage Rights (Scotland) Act 2001, to lodge a minute applying for an order under that section before the conclusion of the proceedings.

[Meantime grants interim interdict *or otherwise as the case may be.*]

NOTE
[1] Inserted by the Act of Sederunt (Amendment of Ordinary Cause Rules and Summary Applications, Statutory Applications and Appeals etc. Rules) (Applications under the Mortgage Rights (Scotland) Act 2001) 2002 (SSI 2002/7), para.5.

FORM O3 **Rules 3.3(3), 7.3(2) and 18.5(1)(a)**

Form of notice to be served on defender in ordinary action where time to pay direction may be applied for

ACTION RAISED BY

PURSUER   DEFENDER

AT   SHERIFF COURT

(Including address)

COURT REF. NO.   _____   DATE OF EXPIRY OF
                                  _____   PERIOD OF NOTICE

THIS SECTION MUST BE COMPLETED BY THE PURSUER BEFORE SERVICE   **D 44/116**

The Debtors (Scotland) Act 1987 gives you the right to apply to the court for a "time to pay direction" which is an order permitting you to pay any sum of money you are ordered to pay to the pursuer (which may include interest and court expenses) either by way of instalments or deferred lump sum. A deferred lump sum means that you must pay all the amount at one time within a period specified by the court.

When making a time to pay direction the court may recall or restrict an arrestment made on your property by the pursuer in connection with the action or debt (for example your bank account may have been frozen).

HOW TO APPLY FOR A TIME TO PAY DIRECTION WHERE YOU ADMIT THE CLAIM AND YOU DO NOT WANT TO DEFEND THE ACTION

1 Attached to this notice at pages 3 and 4 is an application for a time to pay direction, and for recall or restriction of an arrestment, if appropriate. If you want to make an application you should lodge the completed application with the sheriff clerk at the above address before the expiry of the period of notice, the date of which is given above. No court fee is payable when lodging the application.

2 Before completing the application please read carefully the notes overleaf on page 2. In the event of difficulty you may contact the court's civil department at the address above or any sheriff clerk's office, solicitor, Citizens Advice Bureau or other advice agency.

NOTE
Where this form is being served on a defender along with Form O9 (notice to additional defender) the reference to "date of expiry of period of notice" should be amended to "date for lodging of defences or an application for a time to pay direction" and the reference to "before the expiry of the period of notice" should be amended to "on or before the date for lodging of defences or an application for a time to pay direction".

HOW TO COMPLETE THE APPLICATION

PLEASE WRITE IN INK USING BLOCK CAPITALS

PART A of the application will have been completed in advance by the pursuer and gives details of the pursuer and you as the defender.

PART B—If you wish to apply to pay by instalments enter the amount and tick the appropriate box at B3(1). If you wish to apply to pay the full sum due in one deferred payment enter the period of deferment you propose at B3(2).

PART C—Give full details of your financial position in the space provided.

PART D—If you wish the court, when making the time to pay direction, to recall or restrict an arrestment made in connection with the action, enter the appropriate details about what has been arrested and the place and date of the arrestment at D5, and attach the schedule of arrestment or copy.

Sign the application where indicated and detach pages 3 and 4. Retain the copy initial writ and pages 1 and 2 of this form as you may need them at a later stage. You should ensure that your application arrives at the court before the expiry of the period of notice.

WHAT WILL HAPPEN NEXT

If the pursuer objects to your application, a hearing will be fixed and the court will advise you in writing of the date and time.

If the pursuer does not object to your application, a copy of the court order for payment (called an extract decree) will be served on you by the pursuer's solicitor advising when instalment payments should commence or deferred payment be made.

Court ref. no.

D 44/117

APPLICATION FOR A TIME TO PAY DIRECTION

UNDER THE DEBTORS (SCOTLAND) ACT 1987

*PART A   By   _____

_____

_____

_____

DEFENDER

***(This section must be completed
by pursuer before service)**

In an action raised by

_____

_____

_____

PURSUER

PART B

1 The applicant is a defender in the action brought by the above named pursuer.
2 The defender admits the claim and applies to the court for a time to pay direction.
3 The defender applies   (1) To pay by instalments of £

(Tick one box only) EACH WEEK ☐   FORTNIGHT ☐   MONTH ☐

OR

(2) To pay the sum ordered in one payment within
WEEKS/MONTHS

PART C

4 Defender's financial position

My outgoings are:	weekly	fortnightly	monthly	My income is:	weekly	fortnightly	monthly

Rent/mortgage	£	Wages/pensions	£
Heating	£	Social security	£
Food	£	Other	£
HP	£		
Other	£		
Total	£	Total	£

Dependants: Children - how many [ ]   Dependant relatives - how many [ ]

Here list all capital (if any) e.g. value of house; amounts in bank or building society accounts; shares or other investments:

Here list any outstanding debts:

PART D

5   The defender seeks to recall or restrict an arrestment of which the details are as follows (*please state, and attach the schedule of arrestment or copy*):

6   This application is made under sections 1(1) and 2(3) of the Debtors (Scotland) Act 1987.

Therefore the defender asks the court

> *a. to make a time to pay direction.
> *b. to recall the above arrestment.
> *c. to restrict the above arrestment (*in which case state restriction wanted*):-

* Delete what does not apply   **D 44/118**

Date (*insert date*)   Signed
                                                    Defender

Rule 5.2(1)   [1] FORM 04

Form of Citation

CITATION

SHERIFFDOM OF (*insert name of Sheriffdom*)
AT (*insert place of sheriff court*)

[A.B.], (*insert designation and address*), Pursuer, against [C.D.], (*insert designation and address*), Defender

                                                    Court Ref No:

(*Insert place and date*). You [C.D.], are hereby served with this copy writ and warrant, with Form 07 (notice of intention to defend).

> **Form 07** is served on you for use should you wish to intimate an intention to defend this action.
>
> **IF YOU WISH TO DEFEND THIS ACTION** you should consult a solicitor with a view to lodging a notice of intention to defend (Form 07). The notice of intention to defend, together with the court fee of £ (*insert amount*) must be lodged with the Sheriff Clerk at the above address within 21 days (*or insert the appropriate period of notice*) of (*insert the date on which service was executed NB. Rule 5.3(2) relating to postal service*).

A copy of any notice of intention to defend should be sent to the Solicitor for the pursuer at the same time as your notice of intention to defend is lodged with the Sheriff Clerk.

IF YOU ARE UNCERTAIN WHAT ACTION TO TAKE you should consult a solicitor. You may be eligible for legal aid depending on your income, and you can get information about legal aid from a solicitor. You may also obtain advice from any Citizens' Advice Bureau or other advice agency.

PLEASE NOTE THAT IF YOU DO NOTHING IN ANSWER TO THIS DOCUMENT the court may regard you as admitting the claim made against you and the pursuer may obtain decree against you in your absence.

Signed
[P.Q.], Sheriff Officer
or [X.Y.] (*add designation and business address*)
Solicitor for the Pursuer

NOTE
[1] Substituted by the Act of Sederunt (Sheriff Court Ordinary Cause Rules Amendment) (Miscellaneous) 2000 (SSI 2000/239) (effective October 2, 2000).

Rule 5.2(2) [1] FORM 05

Form of citation where time to pay direction may be applied for

CITATION

SHERIFFDOM OF (*insert name of Sheriffdom*)
AT (*insert place of Sheriff Court*)

[A.B.], (*insert designation and address*) Pursuer against [C.D.], (*insert designation and address*) Defender

Court Ref No:

(*insert place and date*). You [C.D.], are hereby served with this copy writ and warrant, together with the following forms—

D 44/119
Form 03 (application for time to pay direction); and
Form 07 (notice of intention to defend).

Form 03 is served on you because it is considered that you may be entitled to apply for a time to pay direction [and for the recall or restriction of an arrestment used on the dependence of the action or in security of the debt referred to in the copy writ]. See Form 03 for further details.

IF YOU ADMIT THE CLAIM AND WISH TO APPLY FOR A TIME TO PAY DIRECTION, you must complete Form 03 and return it to the Sheriff Clerk at (*insert address*) within 21 days (*or insert the appropriate period of notice*) of (*insert the date on which service was executed. NB Rule 5.3 (2) relating to postal service*).

IF YOU ADMIT THE CLAIM AND WISH TO AVOID A COURT ORDER BEING MADE AGAINST YOU, the whole sum claimed including interest and any expense due should be paid to the pursuer or his solicitor in good time before the expiry of the period of notice.

Form 07 is served on you for use should you wish to intimate an intention to defend the action.

IF YOU WISH TO DEFEND THIS ACTION you should consult a solicitor with a view to lodging a notice of intention to defend (Form 07). The notice of intention to defend, together with the court fee of £ (*insert amount*) must be lodged with the Sheriff Clerk at the above address within 21 days (*or insert the appropriate period of notice*) of (*insert the date on which service was executed. NB Rule 5.3(2) relating to postal service*).

A copy of any notice of intention to defend should be sent to the Solicitor for the pursuer at the same time as your notice of intention to defend is lodged with the Sheriff Clerk.

IF YOU ARE UNCERTAIN WHAT ACTION TO TAKE you should consult a solicitor. You may be eligible for legal aid depending on your income, and you can get information about legal aid from a solicitor. You may also obtain advice from any Citizens' Advice Bureau or other advice agency.

> **PLEASE NOTE THAT IF YOU DO NOTHING IN ANSWER TO THIS DOCUMENT** the court may regard you as admitting the claim made against you and the pursuer may obtain decree against you in your absence.

Signed
[P.Q.], Sheriff Officer
or [X.Y.] (*add designation and business address*)
Solicitor for the Pursuer

NOTE
[1] Substituted by the Act of Sederunt (Sheriff Court Ordinary Cause Rules Amendment) (Miscellaneous) 2000 (SSI 2000/239) (effective October 2, 2000).

Rule 5.2(2A)   [1] FORM O5A

Form of citation in an action to which rule 3.2(3) applies

CITATION

SHERIFFDOM OF (*insert name of Sheriffdom*)
AT (*insert place of Sheriff Court*)

[A.B.], (*insert designation and address*) Pursuer against [C.D.], (*insert designation and address*), Defender

Court Ref No:

(*Insert place and date*). You [C.D.], are hereby served with this copy writ and warrant, with Form O7 (notice of intention to defend).

Form O7 is served on you for your use should you wish to intimate an intention to defend this action.

IF YOU WISH TO DEFEND THIS ACTION you should consult a solicitor with a view to **D 44/120** lodging a notice of intention to defend (Form O7). The notice of intention to defend, together with the court fee of £ (*insert amount*), must be lodged with the Sheriff Clerk at the above address within 21 days (*or insert the appropriate period of notice*) of (*insert the date on which service was executed NB Rule 5.3(2) relating to postal service*).

A copy of any notice of intention to defend should be sent to the Solicitor for the pursuer at the same time as your notice of intention to defend is lodged with the Sheriff Clerk.

IF YOU WISH TO MAKE AN APPLICATION FOR AN ORDER UNDER SECTION 2 OF THE MORTGAGE RIGHTS (SCOTLAND) ACT 2001 you should consult a solicitor with a view to lodging a minute applying for an order under that section. The minute, together with the court fee of £ (*insert amount*), must be lodged with the Sheriff Clerk at the above address before the conclusion of the proceedings.

IF YOU ARE UNCERTAIN AS TO WHAT ACTION TO TAKE you should consult a solicitor. You may be eligible for legal aid depending on your income, and you can get information about legal aid from a solicitor. You may also obtain advice from any Citizens' Advice Bureau, or other advice agency.

PLEASE NOTE THAT IF YOU DO NOTHING IN ANSWER TO THIS DOCUMENT the court may regard you as admitting the claim made against you and the pursuer may obtain decree against you in your absence.

Signed
[P.Q.], Sheriff Officer,
or [X.Y.] (*add designation and business address*)
Solicitor for the Applicant

NOTE
[1] Inserted by the Act of Sederunt (Amendment of Ordinary Cause Rules and Summary Applications, Statutory Applications and Appeals etc. Rules) (Applications under the Mortgage Rights (Scotland) Act 2001) 2002 (SSI 2002/7), para.2(6).

Rule 5.2(3)   [1] FORM O6

Form of certificate of citation

CERTIFICATE OF CITATION

(*Insert place and date*) I, hereby certify that upon the day of I duly cited [C.D.], Defender, to answer to the foregoing writ. This I did by (*state method of service; if by officer and not by post, add*: in presence of [L.M.], (*insert designation*), witness hereto with me subscribing; *and where service executed by post state whether by registered post or the first class recorded delivery service*).

(*In actions in which a time to pay direction may be applied for, state whether Form O2 and Form O3 were sent in accordance with rule 3.3*).

(*In actions to which rule 3.2(3) applies, state whether Form O2A was sent in accordance with rule 3.3*).

> Signed
> [P.Q.], Sheriff officer
> [L.M.], witness
> *or* [X.Y.]. (*add designation and business address*)
> Solicitor for the pursuer

NOTE
[1] Substituted by the Act of Sederunt (Amendment of Ordinary Cause Rules and Summary Applications, Statutory Applications and Appeals etc. Rules) (Applications under the Mortgage Rights (Scotland) Act 2001) 2002 (SSI 2002/7), para.2(6).

D 44/120/1 **Rules 5.2(1) and 9.1(1)**   [1] FORM O7

Form of notice of intention to defend

NOTICE OF INTENTION TO DEFEND

*PART A   in an action raised at   Sheriff Court
Court Ref No

(*Insert name and business address of solicitor for the Pursuer*)	
	Pursuer
Solicitor for the pursuer	
	Defender

*(This section to be completed by the Pursuer before service)

DATE OF SERVICE: DATE OF EXPIRY OF PERIOD OF NOTICE:

PART B

(This section to be completed by the defender or defender¿s solicitors, and both parts of this form to be returned to the Sheriff Clerk (*insert address of Sheriff Clerk*) on or before the date of expiry of the period of notice referred to in PART A above. At the same time a copy of the form should be sent to the Solicitor for the Pursuer).

(*Insert place and date*)

[C.D.], (*insert designation and address*), Defender, intends to defend the action raised by [A.B.], (*insert designation and address*), Pursuer, against him (and others).

Signed
[C.D.], Defender
or [X.Y.], (*add designation and business address*)
Solicitor for the defender

NOTE
[1] Substituted by the Act of Sederunt (Sheriff Court Ordinary Cause Rules Amendment) (Miscellaneous) 2000 (SSI 2000/239) (effective October 2, 2000).

Rule 18.5(1)(a)(i)   FORM O8

Form of notice to additional or substitute defender where time to pay direction may be applied for

SHERIFFDOM OF (*insert name of sheriffdom*)
AT (*insert place of sheriff court*)

To [E.F.] (*insert designation and address of additional* [or *substitute*] defender)   Court ref. no.

You [E.F.] are given notice that in this action in which [A.B.] is the pursuer and [C.D.] is the defender, your name has, by order of the court dated (*insert date of court order*) been added [*or* substituted] as a defender to the said action; and the action, originally against [C.D.] is now [*or* also] directed against you.

Enclosed with this notice are the following documents—
Copies of the [*insert as appropriate*, pleadings as adjusted *or* closed record];
Form O3 (application for a time to pay direction); and
Form O7 (notice of intention to defend).

Form O3 is served on you because it is considered that you may be entitled to apply for a time to pay direction [and for the recall or restriction of an arrestment used on the dependence of the action or in security of the debt referred to in the copy writ]. See Form O3 for further details.

IF YOU ADMIT THE CLAIM AND WISH TO APPLY FOR A TIME TO PAY DIRECTION, you must complete Form O3 and return it to the sheriff clerk at (*insert address*) within 21 days (*or insert the appropriate period of notice*) of (*insert the date on which service was executed. N.B. Rule 5.3(2) relating to postal citation*).

IF YOU ADMIT THE CLAIM AND WISH TO AVOID A COURT ORDER BEING MADE AGAINST YOU, the whole sum claimed including interest and any expenses due should be paid to the pursuer or his solicitor in good time before the expiry of the period of notice.

Form O7 is served on you for use should you wish to intimate an intention to defend the action.

IF YOU WISH TO DEFEND THIS ACTION you should consult a solicitor with a view to lodging a notice of intention to defend (Form O7). The notice of intention to defend, together with the court fee of £ (*insert amount*) must be lodged with the sheriff clerk at the above address within 21 days (*or insert the appropriate period of notice*) of (*insert the date on which service was executed. N.B. See Rule 5.3(2) relating to postal service*).

IF YOU ARE UNCERTAIN WHAT ACTION TO TAKE you should consult a solicitor. You may be eligible for legal aid depending on your income, and you can get information about legal aid from a solicitor. You may also obtain advice from any Citizens Advice Bureau or other advice agency.

PLEASE NOTE THAT IF YOU DO NOTHING IN ANSWER TO THIS DOCUMENT the court may regard you as admitting the claim made against you and the pursuer may obtain decree against you in your absence.

D 44/120/2

Signed
[P.Q.], Sheriff officer
or [X.Y.] (*add designation and business address*)
Solicitor for the pursuer [*or* defender]

Rule 18.5(1)(a)(ii)   FORM O9

Form of notice to additional or substitute defender

SHERIFFDOM OF (*insert name of sheriffdom*)
AT (*insert place of sheriff court*)

To [E.F.] (*insert designation and address of additional* [or *substitute*] defender)   Court ref. no.

You [E.F.] are given notice that in this action in which [A.B.] is the pursuer and [C.D.] is the defender, your name has, by order of the court dated (*insert date of court order*) been added [*or* substituted] as a defender to the said action; and the action, originally against the said [C.D.] is now [*or* also] directed against you.

Enclosed with this notice are the following documents—
    Copies of the [*insert as appropriate* pleadings as adjusted *or* closed record]; and
D 44/121   Form O7 (notice of intention to defend).

Form O7 is served on you for use should you wish to intimate an intention to defend the action.

IF YOU WISH TO DEFEND THIS ACTION you should consult a solicitor with a view to lodging a notice of intention to defend (Form O7). The notice of intention to defend, together with the court fee of £ (*insert amount*) must be lodged with the sheriff clerk at the above address with 28 days (*or insert the appropriate period of notice*) of (*insert the date on which service was executed. N.B. Rule 5.3(2) relating to postal service*).

IF YOU ARE UNDERTAIN WHAT ACTION TO TAKE you should consult a solicitor. You may be eligible for legal aid depending on your income, and you can get information about legal aid from a solicitor. You may also obtain advice from any Citizens Advice Bureau or other advice agency.

PLEASE NOTE THAT IF YOU DO NOTHING IN ANSWER TO THIS DOCUMENT the court may regard you as admitting the claim made against you and the pursuer may obtain decree against you in your absence.

                            Signed
                            [P.Q.], Sheriff officer
                            or [X.Y.] (*add designation and business* address)
                            Solicitor for the pursuer [*or* defender]

Rule 20.1   [1] FORM O10

Form of third party notice

SHERIFFDOM OF (*insert name of sheriffdom*)   Court ref. no.
AT (*insert place of sheriff court*)

THIRD PARTY NOTICE
in the cause

[A.B.], (*insert designation and address*), Pursuer
against
[C.D.], (*insert designation and address*), Defender

To [E.F.]

You are given notice by [C.D.] of an order granted by Sheriff (*insert name of sheriff*) in this action in which [A.B.] is the pursuer and [C.D.] the defender. In the action the pursuer claims against the defender the sum of £ as damages in respect of (*insert brief account of the circumstances of the claim*) as more fully appears in the [*insert as appropriate*, pleadings as adjusted *or* amended *or* closed record] enclosed.

        *The defender admits [*or* denies] liability to the pursuer but claims that, if he [*or* she] is liable to the pursuer, you are liable to relieve him [*or* her] wholly [*or* partially] of his [*or* her] liability because (*set forth contract or other right of contribution, relief, or indemnity*) as more fully appears from the defences lodged by him [*or* her] in the action.
                    or

*Delete as
appropriate.

*The defender denies liability for the injury claimed to have been suffered by
the pursuer and maintains that liability, if any, to the pursuer rests solely on
you [along with (*insert names of any other person whom defender maintains is
liable to him [or her] by way of contribution, relief or indemnity*)] as more fully
appears from the defences lodged by him [*or* her] in the action.

or

*The defender denies liability for the injury said to have been suffered by the
pursuer but maintains that if there is any liability he [*or* she] shares that with you,
as more fully appears from the defences lodged by him [*or* her] in the action.

or

*The defender admits liability in part for the injury suffered by the pursuer   **D 44/122**
but disputes the amount of damages and maintains that liability falls to be
shared by you, as more fully appears from the defences lodged by him [*or* her]
in the action.

or

*The defender admits liability in part for the injury suffered by the pursuer
and for the damages claimed but maintains that liability falls to be shared by
you, as more fully appears from the defences lodged by him [*or* her] in the
action.

or

*(*Otherwise as the case may be*)

IF YOU WISH TO resist either the claim of the pursuer against the defender, or the claim of the
defender against you, you must lodge answers with the sheriff clerk at the above address within
28 days of (*insert the date on which service was executed. N.B. Rule 5.3(2) relating to postal
service*). You must also pay the court fee of £ (*insert amount*).

Date (*insert date*)   (*Signed*)
                                               Solicitor for the defender.

NOTE
[1] As amended by SI 1996/2445 (effective November 1, 1996) (clerical error).

Rule 31.4(1)   [1] FORM A1

Form of note of appeal to the sheriff principal

SHERIFFDOM OF (*insert name of sheriffdom*)

AT (*insert name of sheriff court*)

Court ref. no.

in the cause

[A.B.] (*insert name and address*)
                                               Pursuer [*or as the case may be*]
                       against

[C.D.] (*insert name and address*)
                                               Defender [*or as the case may be*]

The pursuer (*or defender or as the case may be*) appeals to the sheriff principal on the following
grounds:—

(*state grounds on which appeal is to proceed*)

[and requests the sheriff to write a note].

Date (*insert date*)   (*Signed*)
                                               [*or* Solicitor for pursuer [*or
                                               as the case may be*]
                                               (*add name and business address*)]

NOTE
[1] Inserted by SI 1996/2445 (effective November 1, 1996).

Rule 33.7(1)(a)   FORM F1

Form of intimation to children and next-of-kin in an action of divorce or separation
where the defender's address is not known

Court ref. no.

To (*insert name and address as in warrant*)

You are given NOTICE that an action of divorce [*or* separation] has been raised against (*insert name*) your (*insert relationship, e.g. father, mother, brother or other relative as the case may be*). If you know of his [*or* her] present address, you are requested to inform the sheriff clerk (*insert address of sheriff clerk*) in writing immediately. If you wish to appear as a party you must lodge a minute with the sheriff clerk for leave to do so. Your minute must be lodged within 21 days of (*insert date on which intimation was given. N.B. Rule 5.3(2) relating to postal service or intimation*).

D 44/123   Date (*insert date*)   (*Signed*)
                                                Solicitor for the pursuer (*add designation
                                                and business address*)

NOTE
If you decide to lodge a minute it may be in your best interest to consult a solicitor. The minute should be lodged with the sheriff clerk together with the appropriate fee of (*insert amount*) and a copy of this intimation.

IF YOU ARE UNCERTAIN WHAT ACTION TO TAKE you should consult a solicitor. You may be entitled to legal aid depending on your financial circumstances, and you can get information about legal aid from a solicitor. You may also obtain advice from any Citizens Advice Bureau or other advice agency.

Rule 33.7(1)(b)   FORM F2

Form of intimation to alleged adulterer in action of divorce or separation

To (*insert name and address as in warrant*)   Court ref. no.

You are given NOTICE that in this action, you are alleged to have committed adultery. A copy of the initial writ is attached. If you wish to dispute the truth of the allegation made against you, you must lodge a minute with the sheriff clerk (*insert address of sheriff clerk*) for leave to appear as a party. Your minute must be lodged within 21 days of (*insert date on which intimation was given. N.B. Rule 5.3(2) relating to postal service or intimation*).

Date (*insert date*)   (*Signed*)
                                        Solicitor for the pursuer

---
NOTE
If you decide to lodge a minute it may be in your best interest to consult a solicitor. The minute should be lodged with the sheriff clerk together with the appropriate fee of (*insert amount*) and a copy of this intimation.

IF YOU ARE UNCERTAIN WHAT ACTION TO TAKE you should consult a solicitor. You may be entitled to legal aid depending on your financial circumstances, and you can get information about legal aid from a solicitor. You may also obtain advice from any Citizens Advice Bureau or other advice agency.

Rule 33.7(1)(c)   FORM F3

Form of intimation to children, next-of-kin and *curator bonis* in an action of divorce or separation where the defender suffers from a mental disorder

To (*insert name and address as in warrant*)   Court ref. no.

You are given NOTICE that an action of divorce [*or* separation] has been raised against (*insert name and designation*) your (*insert relationship, e.g. father, mother, brother or other relative, or ward, as the case may be*). A copy of the initial writ is enclosed. If you wish to appear as a party, you must lodge a minute with the sheriff clerk (*insert address of sheriff clerk*), for leave to do so.

Your minute must be lodged within 21 days of (*insert date on which intimation was given. N.B. Rule 5.3(2) relating to postal service or intimation*).

Date (*insert date*)   (*Signed*)
          Solicitor for the pursuer (*insert designation and business address*)

NOTE
If you decide to lodge a minute it may be in your best interest to consult a solicitor. The minute should be lodged with the sheriff clerk together with the appropriate fee of (*insert amount*) and a copy of this intimation.

IF YOU ARE UNCERTAIN WHAT ACTION TO TAKE you should consult a solicitor. You may be entitled to legal aid depending on your financial circumstances, and you can get information about legal aid from a solicitor. You may also obtain advice from any Citizens Advice Bureau or other advice agency.

Rule 33.7(1)(d)   FORM F4   **D 44/124**

Form of intimation to additional spouse of either party in proceedings relating to a polygamous marriage

To (*name and address as in warrant*)   Court ref. no.

You are given NOTICE that this action for divorce [*or* separation], involves (*insert name and designation*) your spouse. A copy of the initial writ is attached. If you wish to appear as a party, you must lodge a minute with the sheriff clerk (*insert address of sheriff clerk*) for leave to do so. Your minute must be lodged within 21 days of (*insert date on which intimation was given. N.B. Rule 5.3(2) relating to postal service or intimation*).

Date (*insert date*)   (*Signed*)
          Solicitor for the pursuer

NOTE
If you decide to lodge a minute it may be in your best interest to consult a solicitor. The minute should be lodged with the sheriff clerk together with the appropriate fee of (*insert amount*) and a copy of this intimation.

IF YOU ARE UNCERTAIN WHAT ACTION TO TAKE you should consult a solicitor. You may be entitled to legal aid depending on your financial circumstances, and you can get information about legal aid from a solicitor. You may also obtain advice from any Citizens Advice Bureau or other advice agency.

Rule 33.7(1)(e)(i) and (ii)   [1] FORM F5

Form of intimation to a local authority or third party who may be liable to maintain a child

To (*insert name and address as in warrant*)   Court ref. no.

YOU ARE GIVEN NOTICE that in this action, the court may make an order under section 11 of the Children (Scotland) Act 1995 in respect of (*insert name and address*), a child in your care [*or* liable to be maintained by you]. A copy of the initial writ is attached. If you wish to appear as a party, you must lodge a minute with the sheriff clerk (*insert address of sheriff clerk*) for leave to do so. Your minute must be lodged within 21 days of (*insert date on which intimation was given. N.B. Rule 5.3(2) relating to postal service or intimation*).

Date (*insert date*)   (*Signed*)
          Solicitor for the pursuer

NOTE
If you decide to lodge a minute it may be in your best interests to consult a solicitor. The minute should be lodged with the sheriff clerk together with the appropriate fee of (*insert amount*) and a copy of this intimation.

IF YOU ARE UNCERTAIN WHAT ACTION TO TAKE you should consult a solicitor. You may be entitled to legal aid depending on your financial circumstances, and you can get information about legal aid from a solicitor. You may also obtain advice from any Citizens Advice Bureau or other advice agency.

NOTE
[1] Substituted by SI 1996/2167 (effective November 1, 1996).

Rule 33.7(1)(e)(iii)   [1] **FORM F6**

Form of intimation to person who in fact exercises care or control of a child

To (*insert name and address as in warrant*)   Court ref. no.

YOU ARE GIVEN NOTICE that in this action, the court may make an order under section 11 of the Children (Scotland) Act 1995 in respect of (*insert name and address*) a child at present in your care or control. A copy of the initial writ is attached. If you wish to appear as a party, you must lodge a minute with the sheriff clerk (*insert address of sheriff clerk*) for leave to do so. Your minute must be lodged within 21 days of (*insert date on which intimation was given. N.B. Rule 5.3(2) relating to postal service or intimation*).

Date (*insert date*)   (*Signed*)
                    Solicitor for the pursuer

D 44/125

NOTE
If you decide to lodge a minute it may be in your best interests to consult a solicitor. The minute should be lodged with the sheriff clerk together with the appropriate fee of (*insert amount*) and a copy of this intimation.

IF YOU ARE UNCERTAIN WHAT ACTION TO TAKE you should consult a solicitor. You may be entitled to legal aid depending on your financial circumstances, and you can get information about legal aid from a solicitor. You may also obtain advice from any Citizens Advice Bureau or other advice agency.

NOTE
[1] Substituted by SI 1996/2167 (effective November 1, 1996).

Rule 33.7(1)(f)   [1] **FORM F7**

Form of notice to parent or guardian in action for a section 11 order in respect of a child

1. YOU ARE GIVEN NOTICE that in this action, the pursuer is applying for an order under section 11 of the Children (Scotland) Act 1995 in respect of the child (*insert name of child*). A copy of the initial writ is served on you and is attached to this notice.

2. If you wish to oppose this action, or oppose the granting of any order applied for by the pursuer in respect of the child, you must lodge a notice of intention to defend (Form F26). See Form F26 attached for further details.

Date (*insert date*)   (*Signed*)
                    Pursuer
                    or Solicitor for the pursuer (*add designation and business address*)

NOTE: IF YOU ARE UNCERTAIN WHAT ACTION TO TAKE you should consult a solicitor. You may be entitled to legal aid depending on your financial circumstances, and you can get information about legal aid from a solicitor. You may also obtain advice from any Citizens Advice Bureau or other advice agency.

NOTE
[1] Substituted by SI 1996/2167 (effective November 1, 1996).

Rules 33.7(1)(g), 33.7(4)   [1] FORM F8
and 33.12(2) and (3)

Form of notice to local authority requesting a report in respect of a child

To (*insert name and address*)   Court ref. no.

1. YOU ARE GIVEN NOTICE that in an action in the Sheriff Court at (*insert address*) the pursuer has applied for a residence order in respect of the child (*insert name of child*). A copy of the initial writ is enclosed.

2. You are required to submit to the court a report on all the circumstances of the child and on the proposed arrangements for the care and upbringing of the child.

Date (*insert date*)   (*Signed*)
                                       Solicitor for the pursuer (*add designation
                                       and business address*)

NOTE
[1] Substituted by SI 1996/2167 (effective November 1, 1996).

Rule 33.7(1)(h)   [1] FORM F9

Form of intimation in an action which includes a crave for a section 11 order

PART A   Court ref. No.

This part must be completed by the Pursuer's solicitor in language a child is capable of understanding.

To (1)   **D 44/126**

The Sheriff (the person who has to decide about your future) has been asked by (2)   to decide:—

    (a) (3) and (4)

    (b) (5)

    (c) (6)

If you want to tell the Sheriff what you think about the things your (2)   has asked the Sheriff to decide about your future you should complete Part B of this form and send it to the Sheriff Clerk at (7) by (8)   . An envelope which does not need a postage stamp is enclosed for you to use to return the form.

IF YOU DO NOT UNDERSTAND THIS FORM OR IF YOU WANT HELP TO COMPLETE IT you may get help from a SOLICITOR or contact the SCOTTISH CHILD LAW CENTRE ON the FREE ADVICE TELEPHONE LINE ON 0800 328 8970.

If you return the form it will be given to the Sheriff. The Sheriff may wish to speak with you and may ask you to come and see him or her.

NOTES FOR COMPLETION

(1) Insert name and address of child.	(2) Insert relationship to the child of party making the application to court.
(3) Insert appropriate wording for residence order sought.	(4) Insert address.
(5) Insert appropriate wording for contact order sought.	(6) Insert appropriate wording for any other order sought.
(7) Insert address of sheriff clerk.	(8) Insert the date occurring 21 days after the date on which intimation is given. N.B. Rule 5.3(2) relating to intimation and service.
(9) Insert court reference number.	(10) Insert name and address of parties to the action.

PART B

IF YOU WISH THE SHERIFF TO KNOW YOUR VIEWS ABOUT YOUR FUTURE YOU SHOULD COMPLETE THIS PART OF THE FORM

To the Sheriff Clerk, (7)

Court Ref. No. (9)

(10) ....

QUESTION (1): DO YOU WISH THE SHERIFF TO KNOW WHAT YOUR VIEWS ARE ABOUT YOUR FUTURE?

(PLEASE TICK BOX)

Yes	
No	

If you have ticked YES please also answer Question (2) *or* (3)

QUESTION (2): WOULD YOU LIKE A FRIEND, RELATIVE OR OTHER PERSON TO TELL THE SHERIFF YOUR VIEWS ABOUT YOUR FUTURE?

(PLEASE TICK BOX)

Yes	
No	

D 44/127 If you have ticked YES please write the name and address of the person you wish to tell the Sheriff your views in Box (A) below. You should also tell that person what your views are about your future.

BOX A:	(NAME) ....
	(ADDRESS) ....
	....
	Is this person:— A friend? A relative?
	A teacher? Other?

OR

QUESTION (3): WOULD YOU LIKE TO WRITE TO THE SHERIFF AND TELL HIM WHAT YOUR VIEWS ARE ABOUT YOUR FUTURE?

(PLEASE TICK BOX)

Yes	
No	

If you decide that you wish to write to the Sheriff you can write what your views are about your future in Box (B) below or on a separate piece of paper. If you decide to write your views on a separate piece of paper you should send it along with this form to the Sheriff Clerk in the envelope provided.

BOX B: WHAT I HAVE TO SAY ABOUT MY FUTURE:—

NAME: ....

ADDRESS: ....

DATE: ....

NOTE
[1] Substituted by SI 1996/2167 (effective November 1, 1996) and amended by SSI 2003/26 (effective January 24, 2003).

Rule 33.7(1)(a)   FORM F10

Form of intimation to creditor in application for order for the transfer of property under
section 8 of the Family Law (Scotland) Act 1985

To (*insert name and address as in warrant*)   Court ref. no.

You are given NOTICE that in this action an order is sought for the transfer of property
(*specify the order*), over which you hold a security. A copy of the initial writ is attached. If you
wish to appear as a party, you must lodge a minute with the sheriff clerk (*insert address of sheriff
clerk*) for leave to do so. Your minute must be lodged within 21 days of (*insert date on which
intimation was given. N.B. Rule 5.3(2) relating to postal service or intimation*).

Date (*insert date*)   (*Signed*)
                                         Solicitor for the pursuer

---

NOTE

If you decide to lodge a minute it may be in your best interests to consult a solicitor. The
minute should be lodged with the sheriff clerk together with the appropriate fee of (*insert
amount*) and a copy of this intimation.

IF YOU ARE UNCERTAIN WHAT ACTION TO TAKE you should consult a solicitor.
You may be entitled to legal aid depending on your financial circumstances, and you can get
information about legal aid from a solicitor. You may also obtain advice from any Citizens
Advice Bureau or other advice agency.

Rule 33.7(1)(j)   FORM F11   **D 44/128**

Form of intimation in an action where the pursuer makes an application for an order under
section 18 of the Family Law (Scotland) Act 1985

To (*insert name and address as in warrant*)   Court ref. no.

You are given NOTICE that in this action, the pursuer craves the court to make an order under
section 18 of the Family Law (Scotland) Act 1985. A copy of the initial writ is attached. If you
wish to appear as a party, you must lodge a minute with the sheriff clerk (*insert address of sheriff
clerk*) for leave to do so. Your minute must be lodged within 21 days of (*insert date on which
intimation was given. N.B. Rule 5.3(2) relating to postal service or intimation*).

Date (*insert date*)   (*Signed*)
                                         Solicitor for the pursuer

---

NOTE

If you decide to lodge a minute it may be in your best interests to consult a solicitor. The
minute should be lodged with the sheriff clerk together with the appropriate fee of (*insert
amount*) and a copy of this intimation.

IF YOU ARE UNCERTAIN WHAT ACTION TO TAKE you should consult a solicitor.
You may be entitled to legal aid depending on your financial circumstances, and you can get
information about legal aid from a solicitor. You may also obtain advice from any Citizens
Advice Bureau or other advice agency.

Rule 33.7(1)(k)   FORM F12

Form of intimation in an action where a non-entitled pursuer makes an application for an order
under the Matrimonial Homes (Family Protection) (Scotland) Act 1981

To (*insert name and address as in warrant*)   Court ref. no.

You are given NOTICE that in this action, the pursuer craves the court to make an order under
section   (*insert the section under which the order(s) is sought*) of the Matrimonial Homes
(Family Protection) (Scotland) Act 1981. A copy of the initial writ is attached. If you wish to
appear as a party, you must may lodge a minute with the sheriff clerk (*insert address of sheriff
clerk*) for leave to do so. Your minute must be lodged within 21 days of (*insert date on which
intimation was given. N.B. Rule 5.3(2) relating to postal service or intimation*).

Date (*insert date*)   (*Signed*)
                                              Solicitor for the pursuer

---

NOTE

If you decide to lodge a minute it may be in your best interests to consult a solicitor. The minute should be lodged with the sheriff clerk together with the appropriate fee of (*insert amount*) and a copy of this intimation.

IF YOU ARE UNCERTAIN WHAT ACTION TO TAKE you should consult a solicitor. You may be entitled to legal aid depending on your financial circumstances, and you can get information about legal aid from a solicitor. You may also obtain advice from any Citizens Advice Bureau or other advice agency.

Rule 33.7(1)(l)   [1] FORM F12A

Form of intimation to person responsible for pension arrangement in relation to order for payment in respect of pension lump sum under section 12A of the Family Law (Scotland) Act 1985

To (*insert name and address as in warrant*)   Court ref. no.

You are given NOTICE that in this action the pursuer has applied for an order under section 8 of the Family Law (Scotland) Act 1985 for a capital sum in circumstances where the **D 44/129** matrimonial property includes rights in a pension scheme under which a lump sum is payable. The relevant pension scheme is (*give brief details, including number, if known*). If you wish to apply to appear as a party, you must lodge a minute with the sheriff clerk (*insert address of sheriff clerk*) for leave to do so. Your minute must be lodged within 21 days of (*insert date on which intimation was given. N.B. rule 5.3(2) relating to postal service or intimation.*)

Date (*insert date*)   (*Signed*)
                                              Solicitor for the pursuer
                                              (*add designation and business address*)

NOTE

If you decide to lodge a minute it may be in your best interests to consult a solicitor. The minute should be lodged with the sheriff clerk together with the appropriate fee of (*insert amount*) and a copy of this intimation.

IF YOU ARE UNCERTAIN WHAT ACTION TO TAKE you should consult a solicitor. You may be entitled to legal aid depending on your financial circumstances, and you can get information about legal aid from a solicitor. You may also obtain advice from any Citizens Advice Bureau or other advice agency.

NOTE
[1] Inserted by SI 1996/2445 (effective November 1, 1996) and amended by the Act of Sederunt (Ordinary Cause Rules) Amendment (No.2)(Pension Sharing on Divorce etc.) 2000 (SSI 2000/ 408) para.2(3)(a).

Rule 33.7(1)(m)   [1] FORM F12B

Form of intimation to person responsible for the pension arrangement in relation to pension sharing order under section 8(1)(baa) of the Family Law (Scotland) Act 1985.

Court ref. no.

To (*insert name and address as in warrant*)

You are given NOTICE that in this action the pursuer has applied under section 8 of the Family Law (Scotland) Act 1985 for a pension sharing order in circumstances where the matrimonial property includes rights in a pension scheme. The relevant pension scheme is (*give brief details, including number, if known*). If you wish to apply to appear as a party, you must lodge a minute with the sheriff clerk (*insert address of sheriff clerk*) for leave to do so. Your minute must be lodged within 21 days of (*insert date on which intimation was given, N.B. rule 5.3(2) relating to postal service or intimation.*)

Date (*insert date*)   (*Signed*)
                                         Solicitor for the pursuer
                                         (*add designation and business address*)

NOTE
If you decide to lodge a minute it may be in your best interests to consult a solicitor. The minute should be lodged with the sheriff clerk together with the appropriate fee of (insert amount) and a copy of this intimation.

IF YOU ARE UNCERTAIN WHAT ACTION TO TAKE you should consult a solicitor. You may be entitled to legal aid depending on your financial circumstances, and you can get information about legal aid from a solicitor. You may also obtain advice from any Citizens Advice Bureau or other advice agency.

NOTE
[1] Inserted by the Act of Sederunt (Ordinary Cause Rules) Amendment (No.2)(Pension Sharing on Divorce etc.) 2000 (SSI 2000/408) para.2(3)(b).

Rule 33.8(3)   FORM F13   **D 44/130**

Form of intimation to person with whom an improper association is alleged to have occurred

To (*insert name and address as in warrant*)   Court ref. no.

You are given NOTICE that in this action, the defender is alleged to have had an improper association with you. A copy of the initial writ is attached. If you wish to dispute the truth of the allegation made against you, you must lodge a minute with the sheriff clerk (*insert address of sheriff clerk*) for leave to appear as a party. Your minute must be lodged within 21 days of (*insert date on which intimation was given. N.B. Rule 5.3(2) relating to postal service or intimation*).

Date (*insert date*)   (*Signed*)
                                         Solicitor for the pursuer

---

NOTE
If you decide to lodge a minute it may be in your best interests to consult a solicitor. The minute should be lodged with the sheriff clerk together with the appropriate fee of (*insert amount*) and a copy of this intimation.

IF YOU ARE UNCERTAIN WHAT ACTION TO TAKE you should consult a solicitor. You may be entitled to legal aid depending on your financial circumstances, and you can get information about legal aid from a solicitor. You may also obtain advice from any Citizens Advice Bureau or other advice agency.

Rule 33.10   FORM F14

Form of warrant of citation in family action

(*Insert place and date*)

Grants warrant to cite the defender (*insert name and address of defender*) by serving upon him [*or* her] a copy of the writ and warrant upon a period of notice of (*insert period of notice*) days, and ordains the defender to lodge a notice of intention to defend with the sheriff clerk at (*insert address of sheriff court*) if he [*or* she] wishes to:
  (a) challenge the jurisdiction of the court;
  (b) oppose any claim made or order sought;
  (c) make any claim or seek any order.

[Meantime grants interim interdict, *or* warrant to arrest on the dependence].

Rules 33.11(1) and 33.13(1)(a)   FORM F15

Form of citation in family action

CITATION

SHERIFFDOM OF (*insert name of sheriffdom*)
AT (*insert place of sheriff court*)

[A.B.], (*insert designation and address*), Pursuer, against [C.D.], (*insert designation and address*), Defender.

(*Insert place and date*)   Court ref. no.

You [C.D.], are hereby served with this copy writ and warrant, with Form F26 (notice of intention to defend) [and (*insert details of any other form of notice served, e.g. any of the forms served in accordance with rule 33.14.*)].

D 44/130/1

Form F26 is served on you for use should you wish to intimate an intention to defend the action.

IF YOU WISH TO—
(a) challenge the jurisdiction of the court;
(b) oppose any claim made or order sought;
(c) make any claim or seek any order; or
(d) seek any order;

you should consult a solicitor with a view to lodging a notice of intention to defend (Form F26). The notice of intention to defend, together with the court fee of £ (*insert amount*) must be lodged with the sheriff clerk at the above address within 21 days (*or insert appropriate period of notice*) of (*insert the date on which service was executed. N.B. Rule 5.3(2) relating to postal service or intimation*).

IF YOU ARE UNCERTAIN WHAT ACTION TO TAKE you should consult a solicitor. You may be entitled to legal aid depending on your financial circumstances, and you can get information about legal aid from a solicitor. You may also obtain advice from any Citizens Advice Bureau or other advice agency.

PLEASE NOTE THAT IF YOU DO NOTHING IN ANSWER TO THIS DOCUMENT the court may regard you as admitting the claim made against you and the pursuer may obtain decree against you in your absence.

Signed
[P.Q.], Sheriff officer
or
[X.Y.], (*add designation and business address*)
Solicitor for the pursuer

Rule 33.11(2)   FORM F16

Form of certificate of citation in family action

CERTIFICATE OF CITATION

(*Insert place and date*) I,   hereby certify that upon the   day of   I duly cited [C.D.], Defender, to answer to the foregoing writ. This I did by (*state method of service; if by officer and not by post, add*: in presence of [L.M.], (*insert designation*), witness hereto with me subscribing; and (*insert details of any forms of intimation or notice sent including details of the person to whom intimation sent and the method of service*).

Signed
[P.Q.], Sheriff officer
[L.M.], witness
or
[X.Y.] (*add designation and business address*)
Solicitor for the pursuer

Form of request to medical officer of hospital or similar institution

To (*insert name and address of medical officer*)

In terms of rule 33.13(1)(c) of the Ordinary Cause Rules of the Sheriff Court a copy of the initial writ at the instance of (*insert name and address of pursuer*), Pursuer, against (*insert name and address of defender*), Defender, is enclosed and you are requested to

(a) deliver it personally to (*insert name of defender*), and

(b) explain the contents to him or her,

unless you are satisfied that such delivery or explanation would be dangerous to his or her health or mental condition. You are further requested to complete and return to me in the enclosed stamped addressed envelope the certificate appended hereto, making necessary deletions.

Date (*insert date*)　　　　　(*Signed*)
　　　　　　　　　　　　Solicitor for the pursuer (*add designation and business address*)

Rules 33.13(1)(d) and 33.13(2)　　　FORM F18

Form of certificate by medical officer of hospital or similar institution

Court ref. no.

I (*insert name and designation*) certify that I have received a copy initial writ in an action of (*type of family action to be inserted by the party requesting service*) at the instance of (*insert name and designation*), Pursuer, against (*insert name and designation*), Defender, and that

* I have on the　　day of　　personally delivered a copy thereof to the said defender who is under my care at (*insert address*) and I have explained the contents or purport thereof to him or her, *or*
* I have not delivered a copy thereof to the said defender who is under my care at (*insert address*) and I have not explained the contents or purport thereof to him or her because (*state reasons*).

Date (*insert date*)　　　　　(*Signed*)
　　　　　　　　　　　　Medical officer (*add designation and address*)

　　　* Delete as appropriate.

Rule 33.14(1)(a)(i)　　　¹ FORM F19

Form of notice to defender where it is stated that defender consents to the granting of decree of divorce

YOU ARE GIVEN NOTICE that the copy initial writ served on you with this notice states that you consent to the grant of decree of divorce.

1. If you do so consent the consequences for you are that:—

(a) provided the pursuer establishes the fact that he [*or* she] has not cohabited with you at any time during a continuous period of two years after the date of your marriage and immediately preceding the bringing of this action and that you consent, a decree of divorce will be granted;

(b) on the grant of a decree of divorce you may lose your rights of succession to the pursuer's estate; and

(c) decree of divorce will end the marriage thereby affecting any right to such pension as may depend on the marriage continuing, or, on your being left a widow the state widow's pension will not be payable to you when the pursuer dies.

Apart from these, there may be other consequences for you depending upon your particular circumstances.

D 44/132 2. You are entitled, whether or not you consent to the grant of decree of divorce in this action, to apply to the sheriff in this action—

> (a) to make financial or other provision for you under the Family Law (Scotland) Act 1985;
> (b) for an order under section 11 of the Children (Scotland) Act 1995 in respect of any child of the marriage, or any child accepted as such, who is under 16 years of age; or
> (c) for any other competent order.

3. IF YOU WISH TO APPLY FOR ANY OF THE ABOVE ORDERS you should consult a solicitor with a view to lodging a notice of intention to defend (Form F26).

4. If, after consideration, you wish to consent to the grant of decree of divorce in this action, you should complete and sign the attached notice of consent (Form F20) and send it to the sheriff clerk at the sheriff court referred to in the initial writ within 21 days of (*insert the date on which service was executed. N.B. Rule 5.3(2) relating to postal service*).

5. If at a later stage, you wish to withdraw your consent to decree being granted against you in this action, you must inform the sheriff clerk immediately in writing.

Date (*insert date*)   (*Signed*)
                                        Solicitor for the pursuer (*add designation and business address*)

NOTE
[1] Substituted by SI 1996/2167 (effective November 1, 1996).

Rules 33.14(1)(a)(i) and 33.18(1)   FORM F20

Form of notice of consent in actions of divorce under section 1(2)(d) of the Divorce (Scotland) Act 1976

                                                    Court ref. no.

[A.B.], (*insert designation and address*), Pursuer, against [C.D.], (*insert designation and address*), Defender.

I (*full name and address of the defender to be inserted by pursuer or pursuer's solicitor before sending notice*) have received a copy of the initial writ in the action against me at the instance of (*full name and address of pursuer to be inserted by pursuer or pursuer's solicitor before sending notice*). I understand that it states that I consent to the grant of decree of divorce in this action. I have considered the consequences for me mentioned in the notice (Form F19) sent to me with this notice. I consent to the grant of decree of divorce in this action.

Date (*insert date*)   (*Signed*)
                                        Defender

Rule 33.14(1)(a)(ii)   [1] FORM F21

Form of notice to defender where it is stated that defender consents to the granting of decree of separation

YOU ARE GIVEN NOTICE that the copy initial writ served on you with this notice states that you consent to the grant of decree of separation.

1. If you do so consent the consequences for you are that—

> (a) provided the pursuer establishes the fact that he [*or she*] has not cohabited with you at any time during a continuous period of two years after the date of your marriage and immediately preceding the bringing of this action and that you consent, a decree of separation will be granted;
> (b) on the grant of a decree of separation you will be obliged to live apart from the pursuer but the marriage will continue to subsist; you will continue to have a legal obligation to support your wife [*or husband*] and children;

Apart from these, there may be other consequences for you depending upon your particular circumstances.

2. You are entitled, whether or not you consent to the grant of decree of separation in this **D 44/133**
action, to apply to the sheriff in this action—

    (a) to make financial or other provision for you under the Family Law (Scotland) Act
        1985;

    (b) for an order under Section 11 of the Children (Scotland) Act 1995 in respect of any
        child of the marriage, or any child accepted as such, who is under 16 years of age; or

    (c) for any other competent order.

3. IF YOU WISH TO APPLY FOR ANY OF THE ABOVE ORDERS you should consult a
solicitor with a view to lodging a notice of intention to defend (Form F26).

4. If, after consideration, you wish to consent to the grant of decree of separation in this action,
you should complete and sign the attached notice of consent (Form F22) and send it to the
sheriff clerk at the sheriff court referred to in the initial writ and other papers within 21 days of
(*insert the date on which service was executed. N.B. Rule 5.3(2) relating to postal service or
intimation*).

5. If at a later stage you wish to withdraw your consent to decree being granted against you in
this action, you must inform the sheriff clerk immediately in writing.

Date (*insert date*)   (*Signed*)
                              Solicitor for the pursuer (*add designation
                              and business address*)

NOTE
  [1] Substituted by SI 1996/2167 (effective November 1, 1996).

Rules 33.14(1)(a)(ii) and 33.18(1)   FORM F22

Form of notice of consent in actions of separation under section 1(2)(d) of the Divorce
(Scotland) Act 1976

                                             Court ref. no.

[A.B.], (*insert designation and address*), Pursuer against [C.D.], (*insert designation and address*),
Defender.

I (*full name and address of the defender to be inserted by pursuer or pursuer's solicitor before
sending notice*) confirm that I have received a copy of the initial writ in the action against me at
the instance of (*full name and address of pursuer to be inserted by pursuer or pursuer's solicitor
before sending notice*). I understand that it states that I consent to the grant of decree of
separation in this action. I have considered the consequences for me mentioned in the notice
(Form F21) sent together with this notice. I consent to the grant of decree of separation in this
action.

Date (*insert date*)   (*Signed*)
                              Defender

Rule 33.14(1)(b)(i)   [1] FORM F23

Form of notice to defender in an action of divorce where it is stated there has been five
years' non-cohabitation

YOU ARE GIVEN NOTICE that—

1. The copy initial writ served on you with this notice states that there has been no cohabitation
between you and the pursuer at any time during a continuous period of five years after the date
of the marriage and immediately preceding the commencement of this action. If the pursuer
establishes this as a fact and the sheriff is satisfied that the marriage has broken down
irretrievably, a decree will be granted, unless the sheriff is of the opinion that to grant decree
would result in grave financial hardship to you.

2. Decree of divorce will end the marriage thereby affecting any right to such pension as may
depend on the marriage continuing, or, on your being left a widow the state widow's pension
will not be payable to you when the pursuer dies. You may also lose your rights of succession to
the pursuer's estate.

D 44/134 3. You are entitled, whether or not you dispute that there has been no such cohabitation during that five year period, to apply to the sheriff in this action—

    (a) to make financial or other provision for you under the Family Law (Scotland) Act 1985;
    (b) for an order under section 11 of the Children (Scotland) Act 1995 in respect of any child of the marriage, or any child accepted as such, who is under 16 years of age; or
    (c) for any other competent order.

4. IF YOU WISH TO APPLY FOR ANY OF THE ABOVE ORDERS you should consult a solicitor with a view to lodging a notice of intention to defend (Form F26).

Date (*insert date*)   (*Signed*)
                      Solicitor for the pursuer (*add designation and business address*)

NOTE
[1] Substituted by SI 1996/2167 (effective November 1, 1996).

Rule 33.14(1)(b)(ii)   [1] FORM F24

Form of notice to defender in an action of separation where it is stated there has been five years' non-cohabitation

YOU ARE GIVEN NOTICE that—

1. The copy initial writ served on you together with this notice states that there has been no cohabitation between you and the pursuer at any time during a continuous period of five years after the date of the marriage and immediately preceding the commencement of this action and that if the pursuer establishes this as a fact, and the sheriff is satisfied that there are grounds justifying decree of separation, a decree will be granted, unless the sheriff is of the opinion that to grant decree would result in grave financial hardship to you.

2. On the granting of decree of separation you will be obliged to live apart from the pursuer but the marriage will continue to subsist. You will continue to have a legal obligation to support your wife [*or* husband] and children.

3. You are entitled, whether or not you dispute that there has been no such cohabitation during that five year period, to apply to the sheriff in this action—

    (a) to make provision under the Family Law (Scotland) Act 1985;
    (b) for an order under section 11 of the Children (Scotland) Act 1995 in respect of any child of the marriage, or any child accepted as such, who is under 16 years of age; or
    (c) for any other competent order.

4. IF YOU WISH TO APPLY FOR ANY OF THE ABOVE ORDERS you should consult a solicitor with a view to lodging a notice of intention to defend (Form F26).

Date (*insert date*)   (*Signed*)
                      Solicitor for the pursuer (*add designation and business address*)

NOTE
[1] Substituted by SI 1996/2167 (effective November 1, 1996).

FORM F25

[Removed by SI 1996/2167 (effective November 1, 1996).]

Rules 33.11(1) and 33.34(2)(a) [1] **FORM F26** D 44/135

Form of notice of intention to defend in family action

NOTICE OF INTENTION TO DEFEND

PART A
(This section to be completed
by the pursuer's solicitor before
service.)

Court ref. No.

[Insert name and business address of solicitor for the pursuer]

In an action brought in   Sheriff Court

....
....
....

Pursuer

....
....

Defender

Date of service: Date of expiry of period of notice

PART B

(This section to be completed by the defender or defender¿s solicitor, and both parts of the form to be returned to the Sheriff Clerk at the above Sheriff Court on or before the date of expiry of the period of notice referred to in Part A above.)

(*Insert place and date*)

[C.D.] (Insert designation and address), Defender, intends to
    (a) challenge the jurisdiction of the court;
    (b) oppose a crave in the initial writ;
    (c) make a claim;
    (d) seek an order;
in the action against him [or her] raised by [A.B.], (*insert designation and address*), Pursuer.

PART C

(This section to be completed by the defender or the defender's solicitor where an order under section 11 of the Children (Scotland) Act 1995 in respect of a child is sought by the pursuer or is to be sought by the defender)

DO YOU WISH TO OPPOSE THE MAKING OF ANY ORDER CRAVED BY THE PURSUER IN RESPECT OF A CHILD?

YES/NO*
*delete as appropriate

If you answered YES to the above question, please state here the order(s) which you wish to oppose and the reasons why the court should not make such order(s).

DO YOU WISH THE COURT TO MAKE ANY ORDER UNDER SECTION 11 OF THE CHILDREN (SCOTLAND) ACT 1995 IN RESPECT OF A CHILD?

YES/NO*
*delete as appropriate

If you answered YES to the above question, please state here the order(s) which you wish the court to make and the reasons why the court should make such order(s).

D 44/136 PART D

IF YOU HAVE COMPLETED PART C OF THIS FORM YOU MUST INCLUDE EITHER CRAVE (1) OR (2) BELOW (*delete as appropriate)

(1)* Warrant for intimation of notice in terms of Form F9 on the child(ren) (*insert full name(s) and date(s) of birth*) **is sought.**

(2)* I seek to dispense with intimation on the child(ren) (*insert full name(s) and date(s) of birth*) **for the following reasons:—**

Signed

[C.D.] Defenderor [X.Y.] (*add designation and business address*)

Solicitor for Defender

NOTE
[1] Substituted by SSI 2000/239 (effective October 2, 2000).

Rule 33.29(1)(b)   FORM F27

Form of minute for decree in family action to which rule 33.28 applies

(*Insert name of solicitor for the pursuer*) having considered the evidence contained in the affidavits and the other documents all as specified in the schedule hereto, and being satisfied that upon the evidence a motion for decree (in terms of the crave of the initial writ) [*or in such restricted terms as may be appropriate*] may properly be made, moves the court accordingly.

In respect whereof

Signed

Solicitor for the Pursuer (*add designation and business address*)

SCHEDULE

(*Number and specify documents considered*)

Rules 33.40(c) and 33.64(1)(c)   FORM F28

Form of notice of intimation to local authority or third party to whom care of a child
is to be given

To (*name and address as in warrant*)   Court ref. no.

You are given NOTICE that in this action, the sheriff proposes to commit to your care the child (*insert name and address*). A copy of the initial writ is attached. If you wish to appear as a party, you must lodge a minute with the sheriff clerk (*insert address of sheriff clerk*) for leave to do so. Your minute must be lodged within 21 days of (*insert date on which intimation was given. N.B. Rule 5.3(2) relating to postal service or intimation*).

Date (*insert date*)   (*Signed*)
                    Solicitor for the pursuer

NOTE
If you decide to lodge a minute it may be in your best interest to consult a solicitor. The minute should be lodged with the sheriff clerk together with the appropriate fee of (*insert amount*) and a copy of this intimation.

IF YOU ARE UNCERTAIN WHAT ACTION TO TAKE you should consult a solicitor. You may be entitled to legal aid depending on your financial circumstances, and you can get information about legal aid from a solicitor. You may also obtain advice from any Citizens Advice Bureau or other advice agency.

Form of notice of intimation to local authority of supervision order

[A.B.], (*insert designation and address*), Pursuer, against [C.D.], (*insert designation and address*), Defender.

To (*insert name and address of local authority*) Court ref. no.

You are given NOTICE that on (*insert date*) in the Sheriff Court at (*insert place*) the sheriff made a supervision order under section 12 of the Matrimonial Proceedings (Children) Act 1958 [*or* section 11(1)(b) of the Guardianship Act 1973] placing the child (*insert name and address of child*) under your supervision. A certified copy of the sheriff's interlocutor is attached.

Date (*insert date*) (*Signed*)
Sheriff clerk (depute)

Rules 33.72(1) and 33.72(2) FORM F30

Form of certificate of delivery of documents to chief constable

(*Insert place and date*) I, hereby certify that upon the day of I duly delivered to (*insert name and address*) chief constable of (*insert name of constabulary*) (*insert details of the documents delivered*). This I did by (*state method of service*).

Signed
Solicitor for the pursuer
(*add designation and business address*)

Rule 33.74(1) [1] FORM F31

Form of simplified divorce application under section 1(2)(d) of the Divorce (Scotland) Act 1976

Sheriff Clerk
Sheriff Court House

....

....

(Telephone) ....

APPLICATION FOR DIVORCE WITH CONSENT OF OTHER PARTY TO THE MARRIAGE (HUSBAND AND WIFE HAVING LIVED APART FOR AT LEAST TWO YEARS)

Before completing this form, you should have read the leaflet entitled "Do it yourself Divorce", which explains the circumstances in which a divorce may be sought by this method. If simplified procedure appears to suit your circumstances, you may use this form to apply for divorce. Below you will find directions designed to assist you with your application. Please follow them carefully. In the event of difficulty, you may contact any sheriff clerk's office or Citizens Advice Bureau.

Directions for making application

WRITE IN INK, USING BLOCK CAPITALS

Application (Part 1)
1. Complete and sign Part 1 of the form (pages 3–7), paying particular attention to the notes opposite each section.

Consent of husband/wife (Part 2)
2. When you have completed Part 1 of the form, attach the (blue) instruction sheet SP3 to it and send both documents to your spouse for completion of the consent at Part 2 (page 9).

NOTE: If your spouse does NOT complete and sign the form of consent, your application cannot proceed further under the simplified procedure. In that event, if you still wish to obtain a divorce, you should consult a solicitor.

Affidavit (Part 3)
3. When the application has been returned to you with the consent (Part 2) duly completed and signed, you should take the form to a Justice of the Peace, Notary Public, Commissioner for Oaths or other duly authorised

person so that your affidavit at Part 3 (page 10) may be completed and sworn.

D 44/138 Returning completed application form to court

4. When directions 1–3 above have been complied with, your application is now ready to be sent to the sheriff clerk at the above address. With it you must enclose:

(i) your marriage certificate (the document headed "Extract of an entry in a Register of Marriages", which will be returned to you in due course), and

(ii) either a cheque or postal order in respect of the court fee, crossed and made payable to "the Sheriff Clerk",

    or   a completed form SP15, claiming exemption from the court fee.

5. Receipt of your application will be promptly acknowledged. Should you wish to withdraw the application for any reason, please contact the sheriff clerk immediately.

PART 1

WRITE IN INK, USING BLOCK CAPITALS

1. NAME AND ADDRESS OF APPLICANT

Surname ....
Other name(s) in full ....
....

Present address ....
....

Daytime telephone number (if any)
....

2. NAME AND ADDRESS OF SPOUSE

Surname ....
Other name(s) in full ....
....

Present address ....
....

Daytime telephone number (if any) ....

3. JURISDICTION

Please indicate with a tick (✔) in the appropriate box or boxes which of the following apply:

PART A

(i) My spouse and I are habitually resident in Scotland

(ii) My spouse and I were last habitually resident in Scotland, and one of us still resides there

(iii) My spouse is habitually resident in Scotland

(iv) I am habitually resident in Scotland having resided there for at least a year immediately before this application was made

(v) I am habitually resident in Scotland having resided there for at least six months immediately before this application was made and am domiciled in Scotland

(vi) My spouse and I are domiciled in Scotland

Part B applies where the defender is not a national of a Contracting State (other than the UK or Ireland) or domiciled in Ireland

PART B

    (i)   I consider myself to be domiciled in Scotland

    (ii) My spouse considers himself or herself to be domiciled in Scotland   **D 44/139**

AND

    (iii) No court of a Contracting State has jurisdiction under the
Council Regulation

PART C

    (i)   I have lived at the address shown above for at least 40 days
immediately before the date I signed this application

    (ii) My spouse has lived at the address shown above for at least
40 days immediately before the date I signed this application

4. DETAILS OF PRESENT MARRIAGE

Place of Marriage .... (Registration District)

Date of Marriage: Day .... month .... year ....

5. PERIOD OF SEPARATION

    (i)   Please the date on which you ceased to live with your
spouse. (If more than 2 years, just give the month and
year)
Day ...... Month ...... Year ......

    (ii) Have you lived with your spouse since that date?   *[YES/NO]

    (iii) If yes, for how long in total did you live together before
finally separating again?
.... months

6. RECONCILIATION

Is there any reasonable prospect of reconciliation with your   *[YES/NO]
spouse?

Do you consider that the marriage has broken down   *[YES/NO]
irretrievably?

7. CONSENT

Does your spouse consent to a divorce being granted?   *[YES/NO]

8. MENTAL DISORDER

Is your spouse suffering from any mental disorder (whether   *[YES/NO]
illness or handicap?)

9. CHILDREN

Are there any children of the marriage under the age of 16?   *[YES/NO]

10. OTHER COURT ACTIONS

Are you aware of any court actions currently proceeding in any   *[YES/NO]
country (including Scotland) which may affect your
marriage?   (If yes, give details)   *Delete as appropriate

11. REQUEST FOR DIVORCE AND DISCLAIMER OF FINANCIAL PROVISION

I confirm that the facts stated in paragraphs 1–10 above apply to my marriage.

I do NOT ask the sheriff to make any financial provision in connection with this application.

I request the sheriff to grant decree of divorce from my spouse.

Date   Signature of applicant's spouse ....

IMPORTANT
Part 1 MUST be completed, signed and dated before sending the application form to your spouse.

D 44/140   PART 2

NOTICE TO CONSENTING SPOUSE

(Insert name and address of consenting spouse)

CONSENT TO APPLICATION FOR DIVORCE (HUSBAND AND WIFE HAVING LIVED APART FOR AT LEAST TWO YEARS)

In Part 1 of the enclosed application form your spouse is applying for divorce on the ground that the marriage has broken down irretrievably because you and he [*or* she] have lived apart for at least two years and you consent to the divorce being granted.

Such consent must be given formally in writing at Part 2 of the application form. BEFORE completing that part, you are requested to read it over carefully so that you understand the effect of consenting to divorce. Thereafter if you wish to consent—

(a) check the details given by the Applicant at Part 1 of the form to ensure that they are correct to the best of your knowledge;

(b) complete Part 2 (Consent by Applicant's spouse to divorce) by entering your name and address at the appropriate place and adding your signature and the date; and

(c) return the whole application form to your spouse at the address given in Part 1.

Once your husband or wife has completed the remainder of the form and has submitted it to the court, a copy of the whole application (including your consent) will later be served upon you formally by the sheriff clerk.

In the event of the divorce being granted, you will automatically be sent a copy of the extract decree. (Should you change your address before receiving the copy extract decree, please notify the sheriff clerk immediately.)

If you do NOT wish to consent please return the application form, with Part 2 uncompleted, to your spouse and advise him or her of your decision.

The sheriff will NOT grant a divorce on this application if Part 2 of the form is not completed by you.

Sheriff clerk (depute)
Sheriff Court (*insert address*)

CONSENT BY APPLICANT'S SPOUSE TO DIVORCE

NOTE: Before completing this part of the form, please read the notes opposite (page 8)

I, ...
(Insert full name, in BLOCK letters, of Applicant's spouse)

residing at
....
(Insert address, also in BLOCK letters)

....
....

HEREBY STATE THAT

(a) I have read Part 1 of this application;
(b) the Applicant has lived apart from me for a continuous period of two years immediately preceding the date of the application (paragraph 11 of Part 1);
(c) I do not ask the sheriff to make any financial provision for me including—
 (i) the payment by the Applicant of a periodical allowance (i.e. a regular payment of money weekly or monthly, etc. for maintenance);
 (ii) the payment by the Applicant of a capital sum (i.e. a lump sum payment);
(d) I understand that divorce may result in the loss to me of property rights; and

(e) I CONSENT TO DECREE OF DIVORCE BEING GRANTED IN RESPECT OF THIS APPLICATION.

Date   Signature ....

NOTE: You may withdraw your consent, even after giving it, at any time before divorce is granted by the sheriff. Should you wish to do so, please contact the sheriff clerk immediately.

PART 3   **D 44/141**

APPLICANT'S AFFIDAVIT

To be completed by the Applicant only after Parts 1 and 2 have been signed and dated.

I, (*insert Applicant's full name*) ....
residing at (*insert Applicant's present home address*) ....
....
....

SWEAR that to the best of my knowledge and belief:

    (1) the facts stated in Part 1 of this Application are true; and
    (2) the signature in Part 2 of this Application is that of my *husband/wife.

Signature of Applicant ....

To be completed by Justice of the Peace, Notary Public or Commissioner for Oaths	SWORN at (*insert place*) .... this .... day of ....19........ before me (*insert full name*) .... (*insert full address*) .... Signature .... *Justice of the Peace/Notary Public/Commissioner for Oaths *Delete as appropriate

NOTE
[1] As amended by SI 1996/2445 (effective November 1, 1996) and the Act of Sederunt (Ordinary Cause Rules) Amendment (Form of Simplified Divorce Application) 2003 (SSI 2003/25), para.2(2)(a) (effective January 31, 2003).

FORM F32

[Repealed by SI 1996/2445 (effective November 1, 1996).]

Rule 33.74(2)   [1] FORM F33

Form of simplified divorce application under section 1(2)(e) of the Divorce (Scotland) Act 1976

Sheriff Clerk
Sheriff Court House

....
....

(Telephone) ....

APPLICATION FOR DIVORCE (HUSBAND AND WIFE HAVING LIVED APART FOR AT LEAST FIVE YEARS)

Before completing this form, you should have read the leaflet entitled "Do it yourself Divorce", which explains the circumstances in which a divorce may be sought by this method. If the simplified procedure appears to suit your circumstances, you may use this form to apply for divorce.

Below you will find directions to assist you with your application. Please follow them carefully. In the event of difficulty, you may contact any sheriff clerk's office or Citizens Advice Bureau.

Directions for making application

WRITE IN INK, USING BLOCK CAPITALS

Application (Part 1)	1. Complete and sign Part 1 of the form (pages 3–7), paying particular attention to the notes opposite each section.
Affidavits (Part 2)	2. When you have completed Part 1, you should take the form to a Justice of the Peace, Notary Public, Commissioner for Oaths or other duly authorised person in order that your affidavit in Part 2 (page 8) may be completed and sworn.
D 44/142 Returning completed application form to court	3. When directions 1 and 2 above have been complied with, your application is now ready to be sent to the sheriff clerk at the above address. With it you must enclose:

    (i) your marriage certificate (the document headed "Extract of an entry in a Register of Marriages", which will be returned to you in due course). Check the notes on page 2 to see if you need to obtain a letter from the General Register Office stating that there is no record of your spouse having divorced you, and

    (ii) either a cheque or postal order in respect of the court fee, crossed and made out to "the Sheriff Clerk".

4. Receipt of your application will be promptly acknowledged. Should you wish to withdraw the application for any reason, please contact the sheriff clerk immediately.

PART 1

WRITE IN INK, USING BLOCK CAPITALS

1. NAME AND ADDRESS OF APPLICANT

Surname ....
Other name(s) in full ....
Present address ....
....
....
Daytime telephone number (if any) ....

2. NAME OF SPOUSE

Surname ....
Other name(s) in full ....

3. ADDRESS OF SPOUSE (if the address of your spouse is not known, please enter "not known" in this paragraph and proceed to paragraph 4)

Present address ....
....
....
Daytime telephone (if any) ....

4. Only complete this paragraph if you do not know the present address of your spouse

NEXT-OF-KIN

Name ....
Address ....
....
....
Relationship to your spouse ....

CHILDREN OF THE MARRIAGE

Names and dates of birth   Addresses

....

....

....

....

....

....

If insufficient space is available to list all the children of the marriage, please continue on a separate sheet and attach to this form.

5. JURISDICTION   Please indicate with a tick (✔) in the appropriate box or boxes which of **D 44/143** the following apply:

PART A

(i)   My spouse and I are habitually resident in Scotland

(ii) My spouse and I were last habitually resident in Scotland, and one of us still resides there

(iii) My spouse is habitually resident in Scotland

(iv) I am habitually resident in Scotland having resided there for at least a year immediately before this application was made

(v) I am habitually resident in Scotland having resided there for at least six months immediately before this application was made and am domiciled in Scotland

(vi) My spouse and I are domiciled in Scotland

Part B applies where the defender is not a national of a Contracting State (other than the UK or Ireland) or domiciled in Ireland

PART B

(i)   I consider myself to be domiciled in Scotland

(ii) My spouse considers himself or herself to be domiciled in Scotland

AND

(iii) No court of a Contracting State has jurisdiction under the Council Regulation

PART C

(i)   I have lived at the address shown above for at least 40 days immediately before the date I signed this application

(ii) My spouse has lived at the address shown above for at least 40 days immediately before the date I signed this application

6. DETAILS OF PRESENT MARRIAGE

Place of Marriage .... (Registration District)

Date of Marriage: Day .... month .... year ....

7. PERIOD OF SEPARATION

(i)   Please state the date on which you ceased to live with your spouse. (If more than 5 years, just give the month and year) Day .... Month .... Year ....

(ii) Have you lived with your spouse since that date?   *[YES/NO]

(iii) If yes, for how long in total did you live together before finally separating again?

.... months

8. RECONCILIATION

Is there any reasonable prospect of reconciliation with your spouse? *[YES/NO]

Do you consider that the marriage has broken down irretrievably? *[YES/NO]

D 44/144 ### 9. MENTAL DISORDER

Is your spouse suffering from any mental disorder (whether illness or handicap?) (If yes, give details) *[YES/NO]

10. CHILDREN

Are there any children of the marriage under the age of 16? *[YES/NO]

11. OTHER COURT ACTIONS

Are you aware of any court actions currently proceeding in any country (including Scotland) which may affect your marriage? *[YES/NO]
(If yes, give details)

*Delete as appropriate

12. DECLARATION AND REQUEST FOR DIVORCE

I confirm that the facts stated in paragraphs 1–12 above apply to my marriage.

I do NOT ask the sheriff to make any financial provision in connection with this application.

I believe that no grave financial hardship will be caused to my spouse as a result of the granting of this application.

I request the sheriff to grant decree of divorce from my husband or wife.

Date ....
Signature of Applicant ....

PART 2

APPLICANT'S AFFIDAVIT

(To be completed by the Applicant only after Part 1 has been signed and dated.)

I, (*insert full name*) ....

residing at (*insert present home address*) ....

....

SWEAR that to the best of my knowledge and belief the facts stated in Part 1 of this Application are true.

Signature of Applicant ....

	SWORN at (*insert place*)
To be completed by Justice of the Peace, Notary Public or Commissioner for Oaths	this .... day of .... 19.........
	before me (*insert full name*) ....
	of (*insert full address*) ....
	....
	....
	Signature ....
	*Justice of the Peace/Notary Public/Commissioner for Oaths
	*Delete as appropriate

NOTE
[1] As amended by SI 1996/2445 (effective November 1, 1996) and the Act of Sederunt (Ordinary Cause Rules) Amendment (Form of Simplified Divorce Application) 2003 (SSI 2003/25), para.2(2)(b) (effective January 31, 2003).

Rule 33.76(3)(a)　　　　　　FORM F34　　　　　　**D 44/144/1**

Form of citation in application relying on the facts in section 1(2)(d) of the Divorce (Scotland) Act 1976

(*Insert name and address of non-applicant spouse*)

APPLICATION FOR DIVORCE (HUSBAND AND WIFE HAVING LIVED APART FOR AT LEAST TWO YEARS WITH CONSENT OF OTHER PARTY)

> Your spouse has applied to the sheriff for divorce on the ground that the marriage has broken down irretrievably because you and he or she have lived apart for a period of at least two years and you consent to divorce being granted.

A copy of the application is hereby served upon you.

1. Please note:
    (a)　that the sheriff may not make financial provision under this procedure and that your spouse is making no claim for—
        (i)　the payment by you of a periodical allowance (i.e. a regular payment of money weekly or monthly, etc. for maintenance);
        (ii)　the payment by you of a capital sum (i.e. a lump sum payment);
    (b)　that your spouse states that you will not suffer grave financial hardship in the event of decree of divorce being granted.

2. Divorce may result in the loss to you of property rights (e.g. the right to succeed to the Applicant's estate on his or her death) or the right, where appropriate, to a widow's pension.

3. If you wish to oppose the granting of a divorce, you should put your reasons in writing and send your letter to the address shown below. Your letter must reach the sheriff clerk before (*insert date*).

4. In the event of the divorce being granted, you will be sent a copy of the extract decree. Should you change your address before receiving the copy extract decree, please notify the sheriff clerk immediately.

> Signed
> Sheriff clerk (depute)
> (*insert address and telephone number of the sheriff clerk*)
> *or* Sheriff officer

NOTE: If you wish to exercise your right to make a claim for financial provision you should immediately advise the sheriff clerk that you oppose the application for that reason, and thereafter consult a solicitor.

Rule 33.76(3)(b)　　　　　　FORM F35　　　　　　**D 44/145**

Form of citation in application relying on the facts in section 1(2)(e) of the Divorce (Scotland) Act 1976

(*Insert name and address of non-applicant spouse*)

APPLICATION FOR DIVORCE (HUSBAND AND WIFE HAVING LIVED APART FOR AT LEAST FIVE YEARS)

> Your spouse has applied to the sheriff for divorce on the ground that the marriage has broken down irretrievably because you and he or she have lived apart for a period of at least five years.

A copy of the application is hereby served upon you.

1. Please note:
    (a)　that the sheriff may not make financial provision under this procedure and that your spouse is making no claim for—

> (i) the payment by you of a periodical allowance (i.e. a regular payment of money weekly or monthly, etc., for maintenance);
>
> (ii) the payment by you of a capital sum (i.e. a lump sum payment);
>
> (b) that your spouse states that you will not suffer grave financial hardship in the event of decree of divorce being granted.

2. Divorce may result in the loss to you of property rights (e.g. the right to succeed to the Applicant's estate on his or her death) or the right, where appropriate, to a widow's pension.

3. If you wish to oppose the granting of a divorce, you should put your reasons in writing and send your letter to the address shown below. Your letter must reach the sheriff clerk before (*insert date*).

4. In the event of the divorce being granted, you will be sent a copy of the extract decree. Should you change your address before receiving the copy extract decree, please notify the sheriff clerk immediately.

Signed
Sheriff clerk (depute)
(*insert the address and telephone*
number of the sheriff court)
or Sheriff officer

NOTE: If you wish to exercise your right to make a claim for financial provision you should immediately advise the sheriff clerk that you oppose the application for that reason, and thereafter consult a solicitor.

Rule 33.77(1)(a)   FORM F36

Form of intimation of simplified divorce application for display on the walls of court

Court ref. no.

An application for divorce has been made in this sheriff court by [A.B.], (*insert designation and address*), Applicant, naming [C.D.], (*insert designation and address*) as Respondent.

If [C.D.] wishes to oppose the granting of decree of divorce he [*or* she] should immediately contact the sheriff clerk from whom he [*or* she] may obtain a copy of the application.

Date (*insert date*)

Signed
Sheriff clerk (depute)

Rule 33.77(2)   FORM F37

Form of intimation to children and next-of-kin in simplified divorce application

To (*insert name and address*)   Court ref. no.

You are hereby given NOTICE that an application for divorce has been made against (*insert name of respondent*) your (*insert relationship e.g. father, mother, brother or other relative as the case may be*). A copy of this application is attached.

D 44/146   If you know of his or her present address, you are requested to inform the sheriff clerk (*insert address of sheriff clerk*) in writing immediately. You may also, if you wish, oppose the granting of decree of divorce by sending a letter to the court giving your reasons for your opposition to the application. Your letter must be sent to the sheriff clerk within 21 days of (*insert date on which intimation was given. N.B. Rule 5.3(2) relating to postal service or intimation*).

Date (*insert date*)

Signed
Sheriff clerk (depute)

NOTE
IF YOU ARE UNCERTAIN WHAT ACTION TO TAKE you should consult a solicitor. You may be entitled to legal aid depending on your financial circumstances, and you can get information about legal aid from a solicitor. You may also obtain advice from any Citizens Advice Bureau or other advice agency.

Rule 33.80(2) FORM F38

Form of extract decree of divorce in simplified divorce application

At (*insert place and date*)
in an action in the Sheriff Court of the Sheriffdom of (*insert name of sheriffdom*) at (*insert place of sheriff court*)

at the instance of [A.B.], (*insert full name of applicant*), Applicant,

against (*insert full name of respondent*), Respondent,

who were married at (*insert place*) on (*insert date*),

the sheriff pronounced decree divorcing the Respondent from the Applicant.

Extracted at (*insert place and date*)

by me, sheriff clerk of the Sheriffdom of (*insert name of sheriffdom*).

Signed
Sheriff clerk (depute)

Rule 33.90 FORM F39

Form of certificate relating to the making of a maintenance assessment under the Child Support Act 1991

Sheriff Court (*insert address*)
Date (*insert date*)

I certify that notification has been received from the Secretary of State under section 10 of the Child Support Act 1991 of the making of a maintenance assessment under that Act which supersedes the decree or order granted on (*insert date*) in relation to aliment for (*insert the name(s) of child(ren)*) with effect from (*insert date*).

Signed
Sheriff clerk (depute)

Rule 33.90 FORM F40

Form of certificate relating to the cancellation or ceasing to have effect of a maintenance assessment under the Child Support Act 1991

Sheriff Court (*insert address*)
Date (*insert date*)

I certify that notification has been received from the Secretary of State under section 10 of the Child Support Act 1991 that the maintenance assessment made on (*insert date*) has been cancelled [*or ceased to have effect*] on (*insert date*).

Signed
Sheriff clerk (depute)

Rule 33.22A(2) [1] FORM F41 D 44/146/1

Form of intimation to parties of a Child Welfare Hearing

Sheriff Court (*insert address and telephone number*) Court Ref No:

In the action [A.B.], (*design*), Pursuer against [C.D.], (*design*), Defender

YOU ARE GIVEN NOTICE that a Child Welfare Hearing has been fixed for (*insert time*) on (*insert date*) at (*insert place*).

Date (*insert date*) Signed . . . .
Sheriff Clerk (Depute)

NOTE
Please note that in terms of Rule 33.22A(5) parties to the action must attend personally

---

*IF YOU ARE UNCERTAIN WHAT ACTION TO TAKE you should consult a solicitor. You may be eligible for legal aid depending on your financial circumstances, and you can get information about legal aid from a solicitor. You may also obtain information from any Citizens' Advice Bureau or other advice agency.

---

*This section to be deleted where service is to be made on a solicitor.

NOTE
[1] Substituted by SSI 2000/239 (effective October 2, 2000).

Rule 34.1(2)   FORM H1

Form of notice informing defender of right to apply for certain orders under the Debtors (Scotland) Act 1987 on sequestration for rent

Sheriff Court (*insert address*)   Court ref. no.

You are given NOTICE that, where articles are sequestrated for rent you have the right to apply to the sheriff for certain orders under the Debtors (Scotland) Act 1987.

    1. You may apply to the sheriff within fourteen days after the date the articles are sequestrated for an order releasing any article on the ground that:
        (a) it is exempt from sequestration for rent (articles which are exempt are listed in section 16 of the Debtors (Scotland) Act 1987); or
        (b) its inclusion in the sequestration for rent or its subsequent sale is unduly harsh.
    2. Where a mobile home, such as a caravan, is your only or principal residence and it has been sequestrated for rent you may apply to the sheriff before a warrant to sell is granted for an order that for a specified period no further steps shall be taken in the sequestration.

Any enquiry relating to the above rights should be made to a solicitor, Citizens Advice Bureau or other advice centre or to the sheriff clerk at the above address.

Rule 34.6(1)   FORM H2

Form of notice of removal

To (*insert name, designation, and address of party in possession*). You are required to remove from (*describe subjects*) at the term of (*or if different terms, state them and the subjects to which they apply*), in terms of lease (*describe it*) [*or* in terms of your letter of removal dated (*insert date*)] [*or otherwise as the case may be*].

Date (*insert date*)   Signed
                                  (*add designation and address*)

Rule 34.6(2)   FORM H3

Form of letter of removal

To (*insert name and designation of addressee*)
(*Insert place and date*) I am to remove from (*state subjects by usual name or short description sufficient for identification*) at the term of (*insert term and date*)

                        [K.L.] (*add designation and address*).
(*If not holograph, to be attested thus—*)   [M.N.] (*add designation and address*),
                                  witness.)

Rule 34.7 FORM H4 **D 44/146/2**

Form of notice of removal under section 37 of the 1907 Act

NOTICE OF REMOVAL UNDER SECTION 37 OF THE SHERIFF COURTS (SCOT-
LAND) ACT 1907

To (*insert designation and address*).
You are required to remove from (*insert description of heritable subjects, land, ground, etc.*) at
the term of [Whitsunday *or* Martinmas], (*insert date*)

Date (*insert date*) Signed
(*add designation and address*)

Rule 34.11(4) [1] FORM H5

Form of citation of unnamed occupiers

CITATION

SHERIFFDOM OF (*insert name of sheriffdom*)

AT (insert place of sheriff court)

[A.B.] (*insert designation and address*)

Pursuer

against

The Occupier[s] of (*address*)

Defender

An action has been brought in the above Sheriff Court by [A.B.]. [A.B.] calls as a defender the
occupier[s] of the property at (*insert address*). If the occupier[s] [or any of them] wish[es] to
challenge the jurisdiction of the court or to defend the action, he [or she [or it] [or they]] should
contact the sheriff clerk at (*insert address of sheriff court*) immediately and in any event by (*date
on which period of notice expires*).

Signed
Sheriff [or Sheriff Clerk]

NOTE
[1] Inserted by SSI 2000/239 (effective October 2, 2000).

Rule 35.5 FORM M1

Form of warrant of citation in an action of multiplepoinding

(*Insert place and date*) Grants warrant to cite the defender (*insert name and address*) by serving a
copy of the writ and warrant upon a period of notice of (*insert period of notice*) days, and
ordains him [*or* her], if he [*or* she] intends to lodge:—
(a) defences challenging the jurisdiction of the court or the competence of the action; or
(b) objections to the condescendence on the fund *in medio*; or
(c) a claim on the fund;
to lodge a notice of appearance with the sheriff clerk at (*insert name and address of sheriff court*)
within the said period of notice after such service [and grants warrant to arrest on the
dependence].

[*Where the holder of the fund in medio is a defender, insert:* Appoints the holder of the fund *in
medio* to
(a) lodge with the sheriff clerk at (*insert place of sheriff court*) within the said period of notice
after such service
 (i) a detailed condescendence on the fund *in medio*; and
 (ii) a list of parties having an interest in the fund; and
(b) intimate to all parties to the action a copy of the condescendence and list.]

Form of citation in an action of multiplepoinding

CITATION

SHERIFFDOM OF (*insert name of sheriffdom*)   Court ref. no.
AT (*insert place of sheriff court*)

[A.B.], (*insert designation and address*), Pursuer, against [C.D.], (*insert designation and address*), Defender.

(*Insert place and date*) You [C.D.] are hereby served with this copy writ and warrant, together with Form M4 (notice of appearance).

[*Where the defender is the holder of the fund in medio, insert the following paragraph:–*
As holder of the fund *in medio* you must lodge with the sheriff clerk at the above address within (*insert period of notice*)   days of (*insert date on which service was executed. N.B. Rule 5.3(2) relating to postal service*)—
(a) a detailed condescendence on the fund *in medio*; and
(b) a list of parties having an interest in the fund.
You must at the same time intimate to all other parties to the action a copy of
(a) the detailed condescendence on the fund; and
(b) the list of parties having an interest in the fund.]

Form M4 is served on you for use should you wish to intimate that you intend to lodge:—

(a) defences challenging the jurisdiction of the court or the competence of the action; or
(b) objections to the condescendence on the fund *in medio*; or
(c) a claim on the fund.

IF YOU WISH TO APPEAR IN THIS ACTION you should consult a solicitor with a view to lodgng a notice of appearnce (Form M4). The notice of appearance, together with the court fee of £(*insert amount*) must be lodged with the sheriff clerk at the above address within (*insert the appropriat period of notice*)   days of (*insert the date on which service was executed. N.B. Rule 5.3(2) relating to postal service*).

IF YOU ARE UNCERTAIN WHAT ACTION TO TAKE you should consult a solicitor. You may be eligible for legal aid depending on your income. You can get information about legal aid from a solicitor. You may also obtain advice from any Citizens Advice Bureau or other advice agency.

PLEASE NOTE THAT IF YOU DO NOTHING IN ANSWER TO THIS DOCUMENT the court may regard you as having no interest in the fund *in medio* and will proceed accordingly.

                              Signed
                                [P.Q.], Sheriff officer,
                                or [X.Y.] (*add designation and business address*)
                                Solicitor for the pursuer

FORM M3   Rule 35.6(2)

Form of certificate of citation in an action of multiplepoinding

CERTIFICATE OF CITATION

(*Insert place and date*) I,   hereby certify that upon the   day of

I duly cited [C.D.], Defender, to answer to the foregoing writ. This I did by (*state method of service; if by officer and not by post, add:* in presence of [L.M.], (*insert designation*), witness hereto with me subscribing *and where service is executed by post state whether made by registered post of the first class recorded delivery service*):

                              Signed
                                [P.Q.], Sheriff officer
                                [L.M.], witness
                                or [X.Y.] (*add designation and business address*)
                                Solicitor for the pursuer

FORM M4   Rules 35.6(1) and 35.8 **D 44/148**

Form of notice of appearance in an action of multiplepoinding

NOTICE OF APPEARANCE (MULTIPLEPOINDING)

*PART A

Court Ref. No.

(*insert name and business address of solicitor for the pursuer*)	in an action raised at Sheriff Court

        Pursuer

Defender

          Solicitor for the pursuer

*(**This section to be completed by the pursuer before service**)

DATE OF SERVICE: DATE OF EXPIRY OF PERIOD OF NOTICE:

*PART B

*This section to be completed by the defender or the defender's solicitor and both parts of this form returned to the sheriff clerk at (*insert address of sheriff clerk*) on or before the expiry of the period of notice referred to in PART A above)**

(*Insert place and date*)

[C.D.] (*design*), Defender, intends to lodge:

Tick the appropriate boxes

   defences challenging the jurisdiction of the court or the competence of the action.

   objections to the condescendence on the fund *in medio*

   a claim on the fund *in medio*.

        Signed
          [C.D.] Defender,
          or [X.Y.] (*add designation and business address*)
          Solicitor for the defender

FORM M5   Rules 35.9(b) and 35.10(5)

Form of intimation of first hearing in an action of multiplepoinding

SHERIFFDOM OF (*insert name of sheriffdom*)   Court ref. no.

AT (*insert place of sheriff court*)

[A.B.] (*insert designation and address*), Pursuer, against [C.D.] (*insert designation and address*), Defender.

You are given notice that in this action of multiplepoinding

   (*Insert date, time and place*)   is the date, time and place for the first hearing.

D 44/149 Date (*insert date*)   Signed
                                                         Sheriff clerk (dispute)

> **NOTE**
> If the pursuer fails to return the writ in terms of rule 9.3 of the Ordinary Cause Rules of the Sheriff Court or any party fails to comply with the terms of this notice or to provide the sheriff at the hearing with sufficient information to enable it to be conducted it in terms of rule 35.10 of these rules, the sheriff may make such order or finding against that party so failing as he thinks fit.

NOTE TO BE ADDED WHERE PARTY UNREPRESENTED

> **NOTE**
>
> **IF YOU ARE UNCERTAIN WHAT ACTION TO TAKE** you should consult a solicitor. You may be eligible for legal aid depending on your income. You can get information about legal aid from a solicitor. You may also obtain advice from any Citizens Advice Bureau or other advice agency.

FORM M6   Rule 35.10(4)(b)

Form of citation of person having an interest in the fund in an action of multiplepoinding

CITATION

SHERIFFDOM OF (*insert name of sheriffdom*)   Court ref. no.
AT (*insert place of sheriff court*)

[A.B.], (*insert designation and address*), Pursuer, against [C.D.], (*insert designation and address*), Defender.

(*Insert place and date*) In the above action the court has been advised that you (*insert name and address*) have an interest in (*insert details of the fund in medio*). You are hereby served with a copy of the pleadings in this action, together with Form M4 (notice of appearance).

> Form M4 is served on you for use should you wish to intimate that you intend to lodge:
>
> (a) defences challenging the jurisdiction of the court or the competence of the action; or
> (b) objections to the condescendence on the fund *in medio*; or
> (c) a claim on the fund.

> **IF YOU WISH TO APPEAR IN THIS ACTION** you should consult a solicitor with a view to lodging a notice of appearance (Form M4). The notice of appearance, together with the court fee of £ (*insert amount*) must be lodged with the sheriff clerk at the above address within   days of (*insert date on which service was executed N.B. Rule 5.3(2) relating to postal service*).

> **NOTE:**
> **IF YOU ARE UNCERTAIN WHAT ACTION TO TAKE** you should consult a solicitor. You may be eligible for legal aid depending on your income. You can get information about legal aid from a solicitor. You may also obtain advice from any Citizens Advice Bureau or other advice agency.
>
> **PLEASE NOTE THAT IF YOU DO NOTHING IN ANSWER TO THIS DOCUMENT** the court may regard you as having no interest in the fund *in medio* and will proceed accordingly.

D 44/150   Signed
                                                     [P.Q.], Sheriff officer,
                                                     or [X.Y.] (*add designation and business address*)
                                                     Solicitor for the pursuer

FORM D1   Rule 36.3(2)

Form of intimation to connected person in damages action

SHERIFFDOM OF (*insert name of sheriffdom*)   Court ref.no.
AT (*insert place of sheriff court*)

You are given NOTICE that an action has been raised in the above sheriff court by (*insert name and designation of pursuer*) against (*insert name and designation of defender*).
A copy of the initial writ is attached.

It is believed that you may have a title or interest to sue the said (*insert name of defender*) in an action based upon [the injuries from which the late (*insert name and designation*) died] [or the death of the late (*insert name and designation*)]. You may therefore be entitled to enter this action as an additional pursuer. If you wish to do so, you may apply by lodging a minute with the sheriff clerk at the above address to be sisted as an additional pursuer within (*insert the appropriate period of notice*) days of (*insert the date on which service was executed N.B. Rule 5.3(2) relating to postal service*).

Signed
Solicitor for the pursuer

NOTE
The minute must be lodged with the sheriff clerk with the court fee of (*insert amount*) and a motion seeking leave for the minute to be received and for answers to be lodged. When lodging the minute you must present to the sheriff clerk a copy of the initial writ and this intimation.

IF YOU ARE UNCERTAIN WHAT ACTION TO TAKE you should consult a solicitor. You may be eligible for legal aid depending on your income, and you can obtain information about legal aid from any solicitor. You may also obtain advice from any Citizens Advice Bureau or other advice agency.

FORM D2   Rule 36.17(1)

Form of receipt for payment into court

RECEIPT

In the Sheriff Court of (*insert name of sheriffdom*) at (*insert place of sheriff court*) in the cause, (*state names of parties or other appropriate description*) [A.B.] (*insert designation*) has this day paid into court the sum of (*insert sum concerned*) being a payment into court in terms of rule 36.14 of the Ordinary Cause Rules of the Sheriff Court of money which in an action of damages, has become payable to a person under legal disability.

[*If the payment is made under rule 36.15(c) add:* [the custody of which money has been accepted at the request of (*insert name of court making request*).]

Date (*insert date*)   Signed
Sheriff clerk (depute)

[1] **FORM P1**   Rule 37.2(2)

Form of advertisement in an action of declarator under section 1(1) of the Presumption of Death (Scotland) Act 1977

(insert such facts relating to the missing person as set out in the initial writ as the sheriff may specify).

Sheriff Court (*insert address*)   Court ref. no.

An action has been raised in (*insert name of sheriff court*) by [A.B.], Pursuer, to declare that [C.D.], Defender, whose last known address was (*insert last known address of [C.D.]*) is dead.

Any person wishing to defend the action must apply to do so by (*insert date, being [21] days* **D 44/151** *after the date of the advertisement*) by lodging a minute seeking to be sisted a a party to the action with the sheriff clerk at the above address.

A copy of the initial writ may be obtained from the sheriff clerk at the above address.

Date (*insert date*)

Signed

> [X.Y.] (*add designation and business address*) Solicitor for the pursuer *or* [P.Q.] Sheriff officer

NOTE
[1] As amended by the Act of Sederunt (Sheriff Court Ordinary Cause Rules Amendment) (Miscellaneous) 2000 (SSI 2000/239) (effective October 2, 2000).

FORM P2   Rule 37.2(4)

Form of intimation to missing person's spouse and children or nearest known relative

To (*insert name and address as in warrant*)   Court ref. no.

You are given notice that in this action the pursuer craves the court to declare that (*insert the name and last known address of missing person*) is dead. A copy of the initial writ is enclosed.

If you wish to appear as a party, and make an application under section 1 (5) of the Presumption of Death (Scotland) Act 1977 craving the court to make any determination or appointment not sought by the pursuer, you must lodge a minute with the sheriff clerk at (*insert address of sheriff clerk*).

Your minute must be lodged within [   ] days of (*insert the date on which intimation was given N.B. Rule 5.3(2) relating to postal service or intimation*).

Date (*insert date*)

Signed

> Solicitor for the pursuer
> (*add designation and business address*)

NOTE
If you decide to lodge a minute it may be in your best interest to consult a solicitor. The minute should be lodged with the sheriff clerk with the appropriate fee of £ (*insert amount*) and a copy of this intimation.

IF YOU ARE UNCERTAIN WHAT ACTION TO TAKE you should consult a solicitor. You may be entitled to legal aid depending on your financial circumstances. You can get information about legal aid from a solicitor. You may also obtain advice from any Citizen's Advice Bureau or other advice agency.

Rule 38.3(1A)   [1]FORM E1

Form of reference to the European Court

REQUEST
for
PRELIMINARY RULING
of
THE COURT OF JUSTICE OF THE EUROPEAN COMMUNITIES
from
THE SHERIFFDOM OF *insert name of sheriffdom* at (*insert place of court*)
in the cause
[A.B.] (*insert designation and address*), Pursuer
against
[C.D.] (*insert designation and address*), Defender

[Here set out a clear and succinct statement of the case giving rise to the request for the ruling of the European Court in order to enable the European Court to consider and understand the issues of Community law raised and to enable governments of Member States and other interested parties to submit observations. The statement of the case should include:
    (a) particulars of the parties;
    (b) the history of the dispute between the parties;
    (c) the history of the proceedings;
    (d) the relevant facts as agreed by the parties or found by the court or, failing such agreement or finding, the contentions of the parties on such facts;

(e) the nature of the issues of law and fact between the parties;

(f) the Scots law, so far as relevant;

(g) the Treaty provisions or other acts, instruments or rules of Community law concerned; and

(h) an explanation of why the reference is being made.]

The preliminary ruling of the Court of Justice of the European Communities is accordingly requested on the following questions:

1, 2, etc. [Here set out the question on which the ruling is sought, identifying the Treaty provisions or other acts, instruments or rules of Community law concerned.]

Dated the day of 20 .

NOTE

[1] Substituted by the Act of Sederunt (Sheriff Court Ordinary Cause Rules Amendment) (Miscellaneous) 2000 (SSI 2000/239) (effective October 2, 2000).

Rule 41.5 [1]FORM PA1

Form of certificate of delivery of documents to chief constable

(*Insert place and date*) I, hereby certify that upon the day of I duly delivered to (insert name and address) chief constable of (*insert name of constabulary*) (*insert details of the documents delivered*). This I did by (*state method of delivery*).

Signed

Solicitor/sheriff officer

(*add designation and business address*)

NOTE

[1] Inserted by the Act of Sederunt (Ordinary Cause Rules) (Applications under the Protection from Abuse (Scotland) Act 2001) 2002 (SSI 2002/128), para.2(3) and Sched.

Rule 30.6(1) APPENDIX 2

FORMS FOR EXTRACT DECREES

FORM 1

Form of extract decree for payment

EXTRACT DECREE FOR PAYMENT

Sheriff Court   Court ref. no.

Date of decree   * In absence

Pursuer(s)   Defender(s)

The sheriff granted decree against the   for payment to the   of the undernoted sums.

Sum decerned for £   with interest at   per cent a year from   until payment and expenses against the   of £ .

* A time to pay direction was made under section 1(1) of the Debtors (Scotland) Act 1987.

* The amount is payable by instalments of £   per   commencing **D 44/152/1** within   of intimation of this extract decree.

* The amount is payable by lump sum within   of intimation of this extract decree.

This extract is warrant for all lawful execution hereon.

Date   Sheriff clerk (depute)

    * Delete as appropriate.

FORM 2

Form of extract decree ad factum praestandum

EXTRACT DECREE *AD FACTUM PRAESTANDUM*

Sheriff Court   Court ref. no.

Date of decree   * In absence

Pursuer(s)   Defender(s)

D 44/153 The sheriff ordained the defender(s)

and granted decree against the   for payment of expenses of £   .

            This extract is warrant for all lawful execution hereon.

Date   Sheriff clerk (depute)

* Delete as appropriate.

FORM 3

Form of extract decree of removing

EXTRACT DECREE OF REMOVING

Sheriff Court   Court ref. no.

Date of decree   * In absence

Pursuer(s)   Defender(s)

The sheriff ordained the defender(s) to remove* himself/herself/themselves and his/her/their sub-tenants, dependents and others, and all effects from the premises at the undernoted address and to leave those premises vacant** [and that after a charge of   days].

In the event that the defender(s) fail(s) to remove the sheriff granted warrant to sheriff officers to eject the defender(s), sub-tenants, dependents and others, with all effects, from those premises so as to leave them vacant.

The Sheriff granted decree against the   for payment of expenses of £   .

Full address of premises:—

            This extract is warrant for all lawful execution hereon.

Date   Sheriff clerk (depute)

        ** Delete as appropriate.
        ** Delete if period of charge is not specified in the decree.

FORM 4

Form of extract decree of declarator

EXTRACT DECREE OF DECLARATOR

Sheriff Court   Court ref. no.

Date of decree   * In absence

Pursuer(s)   Defender(s)

The sheriff found and declared that   **D 44/154**

and granted decree against the   for payment of expenses of £   .

This extract is warrant for all lawful execution hereon.

Date   Sheriff clerk (depute)

* Delete as appropriate.

FORM 5

Form of extract decree of furthcoming

EXTRACT DECREE OF FURTHCOMING

Sheriff Court   Court ref. no.

Date of decree   * In absence

Date of original decree

Pursuer(s)   Defender(s)/Arrestee(s)

Common Debtor(s)

The sheriff granted against the arrestee(s) for payment of the undernoted sums.

Sum decerned for £   or such other sum(s) as may be owing by the arrestee(s) to the common debtor(s) by virtue of the original decree dated above in favour of the pursuer(s) against the common debtor(s).

Expenses of £   * payable out of the arrested fund / payable by the common debtor(s).

This extract is warrant for all lawful execution hereon.

Date   Sheriff clerk (depute)

* Delete as appropriate.

FORM 6

Form of extract decree of absolvitor

EXTRACT DECREE OF ABSOLVITOR

Sheriff Court   Court ref. no.

Date of first warrant   Date of decree

Pursuer(s)   Defender(s)

D 44/155

(*Insert the nature of crave(s) in the above action*)

The sheriff absolved the   defender(s)

and granted decree against the   for payment of expenses of £   .

This extract is warrant for all lawful execution hereon.

Date   Sheriff clerk (depute)

FORM 7

Form of extract decree of dismissal

EXTRACT DECREE OF DISMISSAL

Sheriff Court   Court ref. no.

Date of first warrant   Date of decree

Pursuer(s)   Defender(s)

The sheriff dismissed the action against the   defender(s)

and granted decree against the   for payment of expenses of £   .

* This extract is warrant for all lawful execution hereon.

Date   Sheriff clerk (depute)

        * Delete as appropriate.

FORM 8

[Repealed by the Act of Sederunt (Sheriff Court Ordinary Cause Rules Amendment) (Miscellaneous) 1996 (SI 1996/2445) (effective November 1, 1996).]

FORM 9

Form of extract decree

EXTRACT DECREE

Sheriff Court   Court ref. no.

Date of decree   * In absence

Pursuer(s)   Defender(s)

The sheriff

and granted decree against the   for payment of expenses of £   . **D 44/156**

This extract is warrant for all lawful execution hereon.

Date   Sheriff clerk (depute)

   * Delete as appropriate.

[1] FORM 10

Form of extract decree of divorce

EXTRACT DECREE OF DIVORCE

Sheriff Court   Court Ref No

Date of Decree   *In absence

Pursuer   Defender

Date of parties marriage   Place of parties marriage

The sheriff granted decree

(1) divorcing the defender from the Pursuer;

*(2) ordering that the following child(ren):

         Full name(s)   Date(s) of birth

Reside with the *pursuer/defender and finding the *pursuer/defender entitled to be in contact with the following child(ren): as follows:

All in terms of the Children (Scotland) Act 1995.

*(3) ordaining payment
   *(a) by the   to the   of a periodical allowance of £ per
   *(b) by the   to the   of a capital sum of £
   *(c) by the   to the   of £   per   as aliment for each child until that
        child attains years of age, said sum payable in advance and beginning at the date of this
        decree with interest thereon at the rate of per cent a year until payment;
   *(d) by the   to the   of £ of expenses;

*(4) finding the   liable to the   in expenses as the same may be subsequently taxed.

This extract is warrant for all lawful execution hereon.

Date: (*insert date*)   Sheriff Clerk (depute)
   *Delete as appropriate.

¹ FORM 11

Form of extract decree of separation and aliment

EXTRACT DECREE OF SEPARATION AND ALIMENT

Sheriff Court   Court Ref No

Date of Decree   *In absence

Pursuer   Defender

D 44/157   The sheriff found and declared that the pursuer is entitled to live separately from the defender from the date of decree and for all time thereafter.

The Sheriff ordered that the following child(ren):

                    Full name(s)   Date(s) of birth

Reside with the *pursuer/defender

And found the *pursuer/defender entitled to be in contact with the following child(ren):

as follows:

All in terms of the Children (Scotland) Act 1995.

*The sheriff ordained payment by the   to the   of £   per   as aliment for the   , said sum payable in advance and beginning at the date of this decree with interest thereon at   per cent a year until payment.

*The sheriff ordained payment by the   to the   of £   per   as aliment for each child, until that child attains   years of age, said sum payable in advance and beginning at the date of this decree with interest thereon at   per cent a year until payment;

and granted decree against the   for payment of £   .

            This extract is warrant for all lawful execution hereon.

Date: (*insert date*)   Sheriff Clerk (Depute)*Delete as appropriate.

¹ FORM 12

Form of extract decree: Residence Order/Contact Order and aliment

EXTRACT DECREE OF RESIDENCE ORDER/CONTACT ORDER AND ALIMENT

Sheriff Court   Court Ref No

Date of Decree   *In absence

Pursuer   Defender

The Sheriff granted decree against the *pursuer/defender.

The Sheriff ordered that the following child(ren):

                    Full name(s)   Date(s) of birth

reside with the *pursuer/defender and found the *pursuer/defender entitled to be in contact with the following child(ren):

as follows:

All in terms of the Children (Scotland) Act 1995.

*The sheriff ordained payment by the   to the of £   per   as aliment for each child, until that child attains   years of age, said sum payable in advance and beginning at the date of this decree with interest thereon at   per cent a year until payment;

and granted decree with interest thereon at per cent a year until payment;and granted decree against the for payment of expenses of £   .

This extract is warrant for all lawful execution hereon.

Date: (*insert date*)   Sheriff Clerk (Depute)

*Delete as appropriate.

NOTE
[1] Substituted by the Act of Sederunt (Sheriff Court Ordinary Cause Rules Amendment) (Miscellaneous) 2000 (SSI 2000/239) (effective October 2, 2000).

Sheriff Courts (Civil Jurisdiction and Procedure) (Scotland) Act 1963   D 69

(1963 c. 22)

An Act to increase the amount by reference to which actions are classified as summary causes in the sheriff court in Scotland; to increase the amount by reference to which the small debt jurisdiction of the sheriff is limited; to amend the law with regard to the bringing of actions between spouses for interim aliment of small amounts in the sheriff's small debt court and with regard to the jurisdiction of the sheriff in such actions brought as aforesaid; and for purposes connected with the matters aforesaid.
[10th July 1963]

1, 2. [*Repealed by the Sheriff Courts (Scotland) Act 1971, Sch.2.*]

Actions for aliment of small amounts
[1] **3.**—(1) An action under section 2 of the Family Law (Scotland) Act 1985 for aliment only (whether or not expenses are also sought) may be brought before the sheriff as a summary cause if the aliment claimed in the action does not exceed—
  (a) in respect of a child under the age of 18 years, the sum of £35 per week; and
  (b) in any other case, the sum of £70 per week;
and any provision in any enactment limiting the jurisdiction of the sheriff in a summary cause by reference to any amount, or limiting the period for which a decree granted by him shall have effect, shall not apply in relation to such an action.
  (2) [*Repealed by the Civil Jurisdiction and Judgments Act 1982, Sch.14.*]
  [2] (3) The Secretary of State may by order vary the amounts prescribed in paragraphs (a) and (b) of subsection (1) above.
  (4) The power to make an order under subsection (3) above shall be exercisable by statutory instrument subject to annulment in pursuance of a resolution of either House of Parliament and shall include power to vary or revoke any order made thereunder.

NOTES
[1] Substituted by the Family Law (Scotland) Act 1985, s.23.
[2] As amended by SI 1999/678, art.2, Sch. (effective May 19, 1999).

Citation, construction and commencement
  4.—(1) This Act may be cited as the Sheriff Courts (Civil Jurisdiction and Procedure) (Scotland) Act 1963.

(2) In this Act the expression "the principal Act" means the Sheriff Courts (Scotland) Act 1907, as amended by any other enactment, and the principal Act and this Act shall be construed together as one.

(3) This Act shall come into operation on 1st October 1963.

D 74

Sheriff Courts (Scotland) Act 1971

(1971 c. 58)

An Act to amend the law with respect to sheriff courts in Scotland, and for purposes connected therewith.   [27th July 1971]

PART I

CONSTITUTION, ORGANISATION AND ADMINISTRATION

General duty of the Secretary of State

Secretary of State to be responsible for organisation and administration of sheriff courts

1. Subject to the provisions of this Act, the Secretary of State shall be
D 75 under a duty to secure the efficient organisation and administration of the sheriff courts, and for the purpose of carrying out that duty shall have, in addition to any functions conferred on him by or under any other enactment, the functions conferred on him by the following provisions of this Act.

Sheriffdoms

Power of Secretary of State to alter sheriffdoms

2.—(1) The Secretary of State may by order alter the boundaries of sheriffdoms, form new sheriffdoms, or provide for the abolition of sheriffdoms existing at the time of the making of the order.

(2) An order under subsection (1) above may contain all such provisions as appear to the Secretary of State to be necessary or expedient for rendering the order of full effect and any incidental, supplemental or consequential provisions which appear to him to be necessary or expedient for the purposes of the order, including, but without prejudice to the generality of the foregoing words—

(a) provision for the abolition of any office,

(b) provisions amending, repealing or revoking any enactment (whether passed or made before or after the commencement of this Act, and including any enactment contained in or made under this Act).

(3) Where an order under subsection (1) above includes, by virtue of subsection (2)(a) above, provision for the abolition of any office, then—

(a) that provision shall have effect notwithstanding the provisions of any enactment (including any enactment contained in this Act), or of any instrument in terms of which any person holds that office;

¹ (b) the Secretary of State may, with the concurrence of the Minister for the Civil Service, pay to or in respect of any person who suffers loss of employment, or loss or diminution of emoluments, which is attributable to the said provision such amount by way of compensation as may appear to the Secretary of State to be reasonable in all the circumstances but no payment shall be made under this provision to or in respect of any person who is mentioned in section 51(2) of the Scotland Act 1998.

(4) The power to make orders under subsection (1) above shall be exercisable by statutory instrument, but no order shall be made under that

subsection unless a draft of the order has been laid before Parliament and approved by a resolution of each House of Parliament.

NOTE
[1] As amended by SI 1999/1820, art.4, Sch.2, para.50 (effective July 1, 1999).

Sheriff court districts and places where sheriff courts are to be held

Sheriff court districts and places where sheriff courts are to be held
3.—(1) Subject to any alterations made by an order under section 2(1) of this Act or under subsection (2) below—
  (a) the sheriff court districts existing immediately before the commencement of this Act shall continue to exist after such commencement, and
  (b) sheriff courts shall, after such commencement, continue to be held at the places at which they were in use to be held immediately before such commencement.
  (2) The Secretary of State may by order—
  (a) alter the boundaries of sheriff court districts, form new districts, or provide for the abolition of districts existing at the time of the making of the order;
  (b) provide that sheriff courts shall be held, or shall cease to be held, at any place.
  (3) An order under subsection (2) above may contain all such provisions **D 76** as appear to the Secretary of State to be necessary or expedient for rendering the order of full effect and any incidental, supplemental or consequential provisions which appear to him to be necessary or expedient for the purposes of the order, including, but without prejudice to the generality of the foregoing words, provisions amending, repealing or revoking any enactment (whether passed or made before or after the commencement of this Act, and including any enactment contained in or made under this Act).
  [1] (4) The Secretary of State may, with the concurrence of the Minister for the Civil Service, pay to or in respect of any person who suffers loss of employment, or loss or diminution of emoluments, which is attributable to an order under subsection (2) above such amount by way of compensation as may appear to the Secretary of State to be reasonable in all the circumstances but no payment shall be made under this provision to or in respect of any person who is mentioned in section 51(2) of the Scotland Act 1998.
  (5) The power to make orders under subsection (2) above shall be exercisable by statutory instrument.
  (6) Without prejudice to subsection (1) above, any enactment or other instrument in force immediately before the commencement of this Act shall, to the extent that it fixes sheriff court districts or the places at which sheriff courts are to be held, cease to have effect.

NOTE
[1] As amended by SI 1999/1820, art.4, Sch.2, para.50 (effective July 1, 1999).

Sheriffs principal and sheriffs

Offices of sheriff principal and sheriff
4.—(1) The office of sheriff (that is to say, the office known formerly as the office of sheriff depute, but known immediately before the commencement of this Act as the office of sheriff) shall be known as the office of sheriff principal, the office of sheriff substitute shall be known as the office of sheriff, and the office of honorary sheriff substitute shall be known as the office of honorary sheriff.
  (2) Accordingly, any enactment or other document in force or having

effect at the commencement of this Act which refers whether expressly or by implication, or which falls to be construed as referring, or as including a reference, to the office of sheriff (as defined in subsection (1) above), or to the office of sheriff substitute, or to the holder of any of the said offices, shall be construed in accordance with subsection (1) above.

[1] (3) Section 28 of the Interpretation Act 1889, shall not apply for the interpretation of this Act.

NOTE
[1] As amended by the Interpretation Act 1978 (c. 30), Sch.3. For definition of "sheriff" to include sheriff principal, see now Sch.1 to the 1978 Act, Division N, *infra*.

Qualification for offices of sheriff principal and sheriff

5.—(1) A person shall not be appointed to the office of sheriff principal or sheriff unless he is, and has been for at least ten years, legally qualified.

For the purposes of this subsection, a person shall be legally qualified if he is an advocate or a solicitor.

[1] (2) Without prejudice to sections 11(3) and 11A of this Act, in this section "sheriff principal" does not include a temporary sheriff principal and "sheriff" does not include a part-time sheriff or an honorary sheriff.

NOTE
[1] As amended by the Bail, Judicial Appointments etc. (Scotland) Act 2000 (asp 9), s.12 and Sch., para.1.

D 77 **[Retiring age for sheriff principal and sheriff]**

[1] **5A.**—(1) A sheriff principal or sheriff shall vacate his office on the day on which he attains the age of 70.

(2) Subsection (1) above is subject to section 26(4) to (6) of the Judicial Pensions and Retirement Act 1993 (power to authorise continuance in office up to the age of 75).]

[3] (3) Without prejudice to sections 11(4A) and (4B) and 11B(3) of this Act, in this section, "sheriff principal" does not include a temporary sheriff principal and "sheriff" does not include a part-time sheriff.

NOTE
[1] Inserted by the Judicial Pensions and Retirement Act 1993 (c.8), Sch.6, para.10 (effective March 31, 1995).
[3] Inserted by the Bail, Judicial Appointments etc. (Scotland) Act 2000 (asp 9), s.12 and Sch., para.1.

Disqualification of sheriffs principal and sheriffs

6.—(1) A sheriff principal to whom this subsection applies, or a sheriff, shall not, so long as he holds office as such—

(a) engage, whether directly or indirectly, in any private practice or business, or be in partnership with or employed by, or act as agent for, any person so engaged;

(b) [*Repealed by the Law Reform (Miscellaneous Provisions) (Scotland) Act 1985 (c. 73), s.20 and Sch.4.*]

(2) Subsection (1) above shall apply to any person holding the office of sheriff principal who is appointed to that office after the commencement of this Act and on whose appointment the Secretary of State directs that that subsection shall apply to him.

(3) The sheriff principal of any sheriffdom, not being either a sheriff principal who is restricted by the terms of his appointment from engaging in private practice or a sheriff principal to whom subsection (1) above applies, shall not, so long as he holds office as such, advise, or act as an advocate in any court, in any cause civil or criminal arising within or coming from that sheriffdom.

(4) Any reference in any enactment passed before the commencement of

this Act to a sheriff principal who is restricted by the terms of his appointment from engaging in private practice shall be construed as including a reference to a sheriff principal to whom subsection (1) above applies.

(5) Without prejudice to the giving of any direction under section 11 (5) of this Act, in this section "sheriff principal" does not include a temporary sheriff principal and "sheriff" does not include a part-time sheriff or an honorary sheriff.

NOTE
[1] As amended by the Bail, Judicial Appointments etc. (Scotland) Act 2000 (asp 9), s.12 and Sched., para.1.

Jurisdiction of sheriff
[1] **7.** For removal of doubt it is hereby declared that a sheriff by virtue of his appointment as such, has and is entitled to exercise the jurisdiction and powers attaching to the office of sheriff in all parts of the sheriffdom for which he is appointed.

[1] (2) Without prejudice to section 11A(4) of this Act, in this section, "sheriff" does not include a part-time sheriff.

NOTE
[1] Inserted by the Bail, Judicial Appointments etc. (Scotland) Act 2000 (asp 9), s.12 and Sched., para.1.

Sheriff may be appointed to assist Secretary of State   D 78
8. Notwithstanding anything in section 6 of this Act, a person holding the office of sheriff principal or sheriff may, without relinquishing that office, be appointed by the Secretary of State to assist him to discharge the functions vested in him in relation to the organisation and administration of the sheriff courts, but a person so appointed shall not perform his duties as the holder of the office of sheriff principal or sheriff, as the case may be, while he retails that appointment.

Functions of Secretary of State in relation to sheriffs principal, sheriffs, etc.

Power of Secretary of State to give administrative directions
[1] **9.**—(1) For the purpose of securing the efficient organisation and administration of the sheriff courts and, in particular, the speedy and efficient disposal of business in those courts, the Secretary of State may give such directions of an administrative nature as appear to him to be necessary or expedient, and any sheriff principal or sheriff, and any officer or servant engaged in the administration of the sheriff courts, to whom a direction is given under this section shall, subject to the provisions of this Act, give effect to that direction.

[1] (2) In this section, "sheriff" does not include a part-time sheriff.

NOTE
[1] Inserted by the Bail, Judicial Appointments etc. (Scotland) Act 2000 (asp 9), s.12 and Sched., para.1.

Scottish Ministers may authorise sheriff principal or direct sheriff to act in another sheriffdom
10.—[1,2] (1) Where a vacancy occurs in the office of sheriff principal of any sheriffdom the Scottish Ministers may, if it appears to them expedient so to do in order to avoid delay in the administration of justice in that sheriffdom, authorise the sheriff principal of any other sheriffdom to perform the duties of sheriff principal in the first-mentioned sheriffdom (in addition to his own duties) until the Scottish Ministers otherwise decide.

[1,2] (1A) Where the sheriff principal of any sheriffdom is unable to perform, or rules that he is precluded from performing, all of, or some part

of, his duties as sheriff principal the Scottish Ministers may authorise the sheriff principal of any other sheriffdom to perform the duties of sheriff principal, or as the case may be that part of those duties, in the first-mentioned sheriffdom (in addition to his own duties) until the Scottish Ministers otherwise decides.

[2] (2) Where as regards any sheriffdom—
  (a) a sheriff is by reason of illness or otherwise unable to perform his duties as sheriff, or
  (b) a vacancy occurs in the office of sheriff, or
  (c) any other reason it appears to the Scottish Ministers expedient so to do in order to avoid delay in the administration of justice in that sheriffdom,

the Scottish Ministers may direct a sheriff appointed for any other sheriffdom to perform, in accordance with the terms of the direction, the duties of sheriff in the first-mentioned sheriffdom (in addition to or in place of his own duties) until otherwise directed by the Scottish Ministers, and any sheriff to whom a direction is given under this subsection shall give effect to that direction.

(3) A sheriff principal authorised, or a sheriff directed, under this section to perform duties in any sheriffdom shall for that purpose, without the necessity of his receiving a commission in that behalf, have and be entitled to exercise the jurisdiction and powers attaching to the office of sheriff principal or, as the case may be, sheriff in that sheriffdom.

D 79 [2] (4) The Scottish Ministers may, pay to a sheriff principal or a sheriff, in respect of any duties performed by that sheriff principal or sheriff (in addition to his own duties) in pursuance of an authority or direction under this section, such remuneration and allowances as may appear to the Secretary of State, with the consent of the Treasury to be reasonable in all the circumstances.

[3] (5) In this section "sheriff" does not include an honorary or a part-time sheriff.

NOTES

[1] Subss (1) and (1A) substituted for subs.(1) by the Law Reform (Miscellaneous Provisions) (Scotland) Act 1980, s.10(a).
[2] As amended by SI 1999/1820, Art. 4, Sched. para.50 (effective July 1, 1999).
[3] As amended by the Bail, Judicial Appointments etc. (Scotland) Act 2000 (asp 9), s.12 and Sched., para.1.

Secretary of State may appoint temporary sheriffs principal and sheriffs
  11.—[1] (1) Where a vacancy occurs in the office of sheriff principal of any sheriffdom the Secretary of State may, if it appears to him expedient so to do in order to avoid delay in the administration of justice in that sheriffdom, appoint a person to act as sheriff principal of the sheriffdom.
  [1] (1A) Where the sheriff principal of any sheriffdom is unable to perform, or rules that he is precluded from performing, all of, or some part of, his duties as sheriff principal the Secretary of State may appoint a person to act as sheriff principal of the sheriffdom, or as the case may be to perform that part of the duties of the sheriff principal.
  [1] (1B) A person appointed under subsection (1) or (1A) above shall be known as a temporary sheriff principal.
  [2] (2) Where as regards any sheriffdom—
    (a) a sheriff is by reason of illness or otherwise unable to perform his duties as sheriff, or
    (b) a vacancy occurs in the office of sheriff, or
    (c) for any other reason it appears to the Secretary of State expedient so to do in order to avoid delay in the administration of justice in that sheriffdom,

the Secretary of State may appoint a person (to be known as a temporary sheriff) to act as a sheriff for the sheriffdom.

[2] (3) A person shall not be appointed to be a temporary sheriff principal unless he is legally qualified and has been so qualified—

(a) for at least ten years;

For the purposes of this subsection, a person shall be legally qualified if he is an advocate or a solicitor.

[2] (4) The appointment of a temporary sheriff principal shall subsist until recalled by the Secretary of State.

[2,3] (4A) No appointment under this section of a person to be a temporary sheriff principal shall extend beyond the day on which the person reaches the age of 70.

[3] (4B) Subsection (4A) above is subject to section 26(4) to (6) of the Judicial Pensions and Retirement Act 1993 (power to authorise continuance in office up to the age of 75).

[2] (5) If the Secretary of State, on appointing any person to be a temporary sheriff principal, so directs, the provisions of section 6(1) of this Act shall apply in relation to that person as they apply in relation to a person holding the office of sheriff.

[2] (6) A person appointed to be temporary sheriff principal of any sheriffdom shall for the purposes of his appointment, without the necessity of his receiving a commission in that behalf, have and be entitled to exercise the jurisdiction and powers attaching to the office of sheriff principal or sheriff in that sheriffdom.

(7) The appointment of any person holding the office of sheriff to be a temporary sheriff principal shall not affect the commission held by that person as sheriff, but he shall not, while his appointment as a temporary D 80 sheriff principal subsists, perform any duties by virtue of the said commission.

[2] (8) The Secretary of State may pay to any person appointed to be a temporary sheriff principal such remuneration and allowances as the Treasury, on the recommendation of the Secretary of State, may determine.

Appointment of part-time sheriffs

[4] **11A.**—(1) The Scottish Ministers may, under this section, appoint persons to act as sheriffs, and persons so appointed shall be known as "part-time sheriffs".

(2) In making those appointments, the Scottish Ministers shall comply with such requirements as to procedure and consultation as may be prescribed by regulations made by them.

(3) A person shall not be appointed a part-time sheriff unless qualified under section 5(1) of this Act to be appointed to the office of sheriff.

(4) A part-time sheriff shall, without the necessity of receiving a commission in that behalf, be entitled to exercise in every sheriffdom the jurisdiction and powers attaching to the office of sheriff.

(5) The number of persons holding appointments as part-time sheriffs shall not, at any one time, exceed 60 or such other number as may be fixed in substitution by order made by the Scottish Ministers.

(6) A part-time sheriff shall be subject to such instructions, arrangements and other provisions as fall to be made under this Act by the sheriff principal of the sheriffdom in which the part-time sheriff is sitting.

(7) In the performance of their functions under this Act, sheriffs principal shall together have regard to the desirability of securing that every part-time sheriff—

(a) is given the opportunity of sitting on not fewer than 20 days; and

(b) does not sit for more than 100 days,

in each successive period of 12 months beginning with the day of the part-time sheriff's appointment as such.

(8) The Scottish Ministers shall pay to part-time sheriffs such remuneration and allowances as they determine.

Limitation, termination etc. of appointment of part-time sheriffs

[4] **11B.**—(1) An appointment as a part-time sheriff shall, subject to subsections (2) to (4) below, last for 5 years.

(2) A part-time sheriff may resign at any time by giving notice to that effect to the Scottish Ministers.

(3) An appointment of a person as a part-time sheriff shall not extend beyond the day when the person reaches the age of 70.

(4) A part-time sheriff's appointment shall come to an end upon the part-time sheriff's being removed from office under section 11C of this Act.

(5) A part-time sheriff whose appointment comes to an end by operation of subsection (1) above may be reappointed and, except in the circumstances set out in subsection (6) below, shall be reappointed.

(6) The circumstances mentioned in subsection (5) above are that—

  (a) the part-time sheriff has declined that reappointment;
  (b) the part-time sheriff is aged 69 or over;
  (c) a sheriff principal has made a recommendation to the Scottish Ministers against the reappointment;
  (d) the part-time sheriff has not sat for a total of 50 or more days in the preceding five year period; or
  (e) the Scottish Ministers have, since the part-time sheriff was last appointed, made an order under section 11A(5) of this Act reducing the number of persons who may hold appointment as part-time sheriffs.

D 81   (7) A part-time sheriff whose appointment comes to an end by resignation under subsection (2) above may be reappointed.

(8) The provisions of section 11A and this section of this Act apply to a reappointment under subsections (5) and (7) above as they apply to an appointment.

(9) A part-time sheriff who is a solicitor in practice shall not carry out any function as a part-time sheriff in a sheriff court district in which his or her main place of business as such solicitor is situated.

Removal of part-time sheriffs from office

[4] **11C.**—(1) A part-time sheriff may be removed from office by and only by order of the tribunal constituted by and under subsection (3) below ("the tribunal").

(2) The tribunal may order the removal from office of a part-time sheriff only if, after investigation carried out at the request of the Scottish Ministers, it finds that the part-time sheriff is unfit for office by reason of inability, neglect of duty or misbehaviour.

(3) The tribunal shall consist of the following three members, who shall be appointed by the Lord President of the Court of Session—

  (a) either a Senator of the College of Justice or a sheriff principal (who shall preside);
  (b) a person who is, and has been for at least ten years, legally qualified within the meaning of section 5(1) of this Act; and
  (c) one other person.

(4) Regulations, made by the Scottish Ministers—

  (a) may make provision enabling the tribunal, at any time during an investigation, to suspend a part-time sheriff from office and providing as to the effect and duration of such suspension; and
  (b) shall make such further provision as respects the tribunal as the Scottish Ministers consider necessary or expedient, including provision for the procedure to be followed by and before it.

Regulations and orders under sections 11A and 11C

⁴ **11D**—(1) Regulations under section 11A or section 11C and orders under section 11A of this Act shall be made by statutory instrument.

(2) No such regulations or order shall be made unless laid in draft before, and approved by a resolution of, the Scottish Parliament.".

NOTES

¹ Subsections (1), (1A) and (1B) substituted for subs.(1) by the Law Reform (Miscellaneous Provisions) (Scotland) Act 1980 (c. 55), s.10(*b*). As amended by the Bail, Judicial Appointments etc. (Scotland) Act 2000 (asp 9), s.6, s.12 and Sched., para.1.

² Repealed by the Bail, Judicial Appointments etc. (Scotland) Act 2000 (asp 9), s.12 and Sched., para.1.

³ Inserted by the Judicial Pensions and Retirement Act 1993 (c. 8), Sch.6, para.11.

⁴ Inserted by the Bail, Judicial Appointments etc. (Scotland) Act 2000 (asp 9), s.7.

Removal from office, and suspension, of sheriff principal or sheriff

¹ **12.**—(1) The Lord President of the Court of Session and the Lord Justice Clerk may of their own accord and shall, if they are requested so to do by the Secretary of State, undertake jointly an investigation into the fitness for office of any sheriff principal or sheriff and, as soon as practicable after completing that investigation, shall report in writing to the Secretary of State either—

(*a*) that the sheriff principal or sheriff is fit for office, or

(*b*) that the sheriff principal or sheriff is unfit for office by reason of inability, neglect of duty or misbehaviour,

and shall in either case include in their report a statement of their reasons for so reporting.

(2) The Secretary of State may, if a report is made to him under subsection (1) above to the effect that any sheriff principal or sheriff is unfit **D 82** for office by reason of inability, neglect of duty or misbehaviour, make an order removing that sheriff principal or sheriff from office.

(3) An order under subsection (2) above—

(*a*) shall be made by statutory instrument, which shall be subject to annulment in pursuance of a resolution of either House of Parliament,

(*b*) shall not be made so as to come into operation before the expiry, in relation to the order, of the period of forty days mentioned in section 5(1) of the Statutory Instruments Act 1946.

(4) The Lord President of the Court of Session and the Lord Justice Clerk may, on undertaking an investigation under subsection (1) above or at any time during the course of such an investigation, if they think it proper so to do, recommend in writing to the Secretary of State that the sheriff principal or sheriff who is the subject of the investigation be suspended from office, and the Secretary of State may, on receiving such a recommendation as aforesaid, suspend that sheriff principal or sheriff from office.

(5) A sheriff principal or a sheriff suspended from office under subsection (4) above shall remain so suspended until the Secretary of State otherwise directs.

(6) The suspension from office of a sheriff principal or a sheriff under subsection (4) above shall not affect the payment to him of his salary in respect of the period of his suspension.

² (7) In this section "sheriff principal" does not include a temporary sheriff principal and "sheriff" does not include a part-time sheriff or an honorary sheriff.

NOTE

¹ Extended by the District Courts (Scotland) Act 1975 (c. 20), s.5(8).

² As amended by the Bail, Judicial Appointments etc. (Scotland) Act 2000 (asp 9), s.12 and Sched., para.1.

Functions of Secretary of State with respect to residence and leave of absence of sheriffs principal

13.—(1) The Secretary of State may require any sheriff principal (being a sheriff principal who is restricted by the terms of his appointment from engaging in private practice or to whom section 6(1) of this Act applies) to reside ordinarily at such place as the Secretary of State may specify.

(2) The Secretary of State may approve such leave of absence for any sheriff principal (being a sheriff principal who is restricted by the terms of his appointment from engaging in private practice or to whom section 6(1) of this Act applies) as appears to the Secretary of State to be proper, but the amount of leave so approved (other than leave granted on account of ill-health) shall not, unless the Secretary of State for special reasons otherwise permits, exceed seven weeks in any year.

Functions of Secretary of State with respect to number, residence and place of duties of sheriffs

14.—(1) The Secretary of State may, with the approval of the Treasury, by order prescribe the number of sheriffs to be appointed for each sheriffdom.

(2) The Secretary of State may require any sheriff to reside ordinarily at such place as the Secretary of State may specify.

(3) The Secretary of State—

> (a) shall, on the appointment of a person to hold the office of sheriff for any sheriffdom,
>
> (b) may, at any subsequent time while the said person holds that office,

give to that person a direction designating the sheriff court district or districts in which he is to perform his duties as sheriff:

Provided that a direction given to a sheriff under this subsection shall be

D 83 subject to any instruction given to that sheriff under section 15 of this Act by the sheriff principal of the sheriffdom, being an instruction given for the purpose of giving effect to any special provision made by the sheriff principal under section 16(1)(b) of this Act.

(4) If for the purpose of securing the efficient organisation and administration of the sheriff courts, and after consultation with the Lord President of the Court of Session the Secretary of State by order so directs, a person holding the office of sheriff for any sheriffdom shall, on such date as may be specified in the order, cease to hold that office and shall, on and after that date, without the necessity of his receiving a commission in that behalf, hold instead the office of sheriff for such other sheriffdom as may be so specified; and on making an order under this subsection with respect to any person the Secretary of State shall give to that person a direction under subsection (3) above designating the sheriff court district or districts in which he is to perform his duties as sheriff.

[1] (5) In this section "sheriff" does not include an honorary or a part-time sheriff.

NOTE
[1] As amended by the Bail, Judicial Appointments etc. (Scotland) Act 2000 (asp 9), s.12 and Sched., para.1.

Functions of the sheriff principal in relation to sheriffs, etc.

General functions of sheriff principal

15.—(1) Subject generally to the provisions of this Act, and in particular to the provisions of this or any other Act conferring functions on the Secretary of State or anything done under any such provision, the sheriff principal of each sheriffdom shall be under a duty to secure the speedy and efficient disposal of business in the sheriff courts of that sheriffdom, and for the purpose of carrying out that duty shall have, in addition to any functions conferred on him by or under any other enactment, the functions conferred on him by the following provisions of this Act.

[1] (2) For the purpose of securing the effective discharge of any of the said functions the sheriff principal of any sheriffdom may give such instructions of an administrative nature as appear to him to be necessary or expedient, and any sheriff appointed for that sheriffdom any part-time sheriff, and any officer or servant engaged in the administration of the sheriff courts in the sheriffdom, to whom an instruction is given under this section shall, subject to the provisions of this Act, give effect to that instruction.

NOTE
[1] As amended by the Bail, Judicial Appointments etc. (Scotland) Act 2000 (asp 9), s.12 and Sched., para.1.

Functions of sheriff principal with respect to duties and leave of absence of sheriffs

16.—[1] (1) The sheriff principal of each sheriffdom shall make such arrangements as appear to him necessary or expedient for the purpose of securing the speedy and efficient disposal of business in the sheriff courts of that sheriffdom and in particular, but without prejudice to the generality of the foregoing words, may—

(a) subject to any direction given by the Secretary of State under section 9 of this Act, provide for the division of such business as aforesaid between the sheriff principal, the sheriffs appointed for the sheriffdom and any part-time sheriffs, and for the distribution of the business (so far as allocated to the sheriffs) amongst those sheriffs;

(b) where any of those sheriffs is by reason of illness or otherwise unable to perform his duties as sheriff, or a vacancy occurs in the office of sheriff in the sheriffdom, or for any other reason it appears to the **D 84** sheriff principal expedient so to do in order to avoid delay in the administration of justice in the sheriffdom, make special provision of a temporary nature for the disposal of any part of the said business either by the sheriff principal or by any of the sheriffs appointed for the sheriffdom or by any part-time sheriffs, in addition to or in place of the sheriff principal's or, as the case may be, that sheriff's own duties;

so, however, that nothing done under this subsection shall enable a sheriff or part-time sheriff to dispose of business which he does not otherwise have power to dispose of.

(2) The sheriff principal of any sheriffdom may approve such leave of absence for any sheriff appointed for that sheriffdom as appears to the sheriff principal to be proper, but the amount of leave so approved (other than leave granted on account of ill-health) shall not, unless the Secretary of State for special reasons otherwise permits, exceed seven weeks in any year.

[1] (3) In subsection (2) above "sheriff" shall not include a part-time or an honorary sheriff.

NOTE
[1] As amended by the Bail, Judicial Appointments etc. (Scotland) Act 2000 (asp 9), s.12 and Sched., para.1.

Sheriff principal may fix sittings and business of sheriff courts in sheriffdom, and sessions for civil business

17.—(1) The sheriff principal of each sheriffdom may by order prescribe—

(a) the number of sheriff courts to be held at each of the places within that sheriffdom at which a court is required under or by virtue of this Act to be held,

[1] (b) subject to section 25(2) of this Act, the days on which and the times at which those courts are to be held,

(*c*) the descriptions of business to be disposed of at those courts.

(2) The sheriff principal of each sheriffdom shall by order prescribe the dates of the sessions to be held in the sheriff courts of that sheriffdom for the disposal of civil business, and may prescribe different dates in relation to different courts, so however that—

(*a*) there shall be held in the courts of each sheriffdom three sessions in each year for the disposal of civil business, that is to say, a winter session, a spring session and a summer session;

(*b*) the dates of the sessions prescribed under this subsection shall not be such as to allow, in any court, a vacation of longer than two weeks at Christmas time, four weeks in the spring and eight weeks in the summer.

(3) The sheriff principal of each sheriffdom shall, before the end of the spring session in each year, fix in respect of each sheriff court in that sheriffdom at least one day during the vacation immediately following that session for the disposal of civil business in that court, and shall, before the end of the summer session in each year, fix in respect of each court at least two days during the vacation immediately following that session for the said purpose; but civil proceedings in the sheriff courts may proceed during vacation as during session, and interlocutors may competently be pronounced during vacation in any such proceedings.

(4) A sheriff principal shall give notice of any matter prescribed or fixed by him under the foregoing provisions of this section in such manner as he may think sufficient for bringing that matter to the attention of all persons having an interest therein.

(5) Subject to anything done under subsection (1) above, or by an order under section 2(1) or section 3(2) of this Act, after the commencement of this Act—

D 85
(*a*) there shall be held at each of the places at which a sheriff court was in use to be held immediately before such commencement the same number of courts as was in use to be held there immediately before such commencement;

(*b*) the court days and times in use to be observed in any sheriff court immediately before such commencement (whether in pursuance of any enactment or other instrument or otherwise) shall continue to be observed in that court;

(*c*) the descriptions of business in use to be dealt with on court days in any sheriff court immediately before such commencement shall continue to be dealt with on those days.

(6) Without prejudice to subsection (5) above, any enactment or other instrument in force immediately before the commencement of this Act shall, to the extent that it contains provisions with respect to any matter which the sheriff principal has power to prescribe under subsection (1) above, cease to have effect.

NOTE

[1] See the Bail etc. (Scotland) Act 1980 (c. 44), s.10(2).

Secretary of State may exercise certain functions of sheriff principal in certain circumstances

18. If in any case the Secretary of State considers—

(*a*) that the exercise by the sheriff principal of any sheriffdom of any of the functions conferred on him by sections 15 to 17 of this Act, or

(*b*) that the failure of the sheriff principal of any sheriffdom to exercise any of the said functions,

is prejudicial to the speedy and efficient disposal of business in the sheriff courts of that sheriffdom or to the efficient organisation or administration of the sheriff courts generally, or is otherwise against the interests of the public, the Secretary of State may—

(i) (in the circumstances mentioned in paragraph (a) above) rescind that exercise of that function by the sheriff principal and, if he thinks fit, himself exercise that function in that case;

(ii) (in the circumstances mentioned in paragraph (b) above) himself exercise that function in that case,

and the exercise of any function of a sheriff principal by the Secretary of State under this section shall have effect as if it were an exercise of that function by the sheriff principal.

Miscellaneous

Travelling allowances for sheriffs principal

19. The Secretary of State may pay to any sheriff principal, in addition to the salary of that sheriff principal, such allowances as the Secretary of State, with the concurrence of the Treasury, may determine in respect of the travelling expenses incurred by the sheriff principal in the performance of the duties of his office.

Extension of purposes for which Lord Advocate may give instructions to procurators fiscal

20. The purposes for which the Lord Advocate may issue instructions to procurators fiscal under section 8(1) of the Sheriff Courts and Legal Officers (Scotland) Act 1927 shall include, in addition to the purpose mentioned in the said section 8(1), the speedy and efficient disposal of business in the sheriff courts.

21. [Repealed by the House of Commons Disqualification Act 1975 (c. 24), Sch.3.]

Saving for existing functions D 86

22. Nothing in the foregoing provisions of this Act shall affect the discharge by any person of any function lawfully held by him immediately before the commencement of this Act, except in so far as the discharge of that function is or would be inconsistent with any of those provisions or anything done thereunder.

Part II

Court Houses, Buildings and Offices

23–30. [Not reproduced.]

Part III

Civil Jurisdiction, Procedure and Appeals

Civil Jurisdiction

Upper limit to privative jurisdiction of sheriff court to be £500

[1] **31.** Section 7 of the Sheriff Courts (Scotland) Act 1907 (which provides that all causes not exceeding £50 in value which are competent in the sheriff court are to be brought in that court only, and are not to be subject to review by the Court of Session) shall have effect as if for the words "£50" there were substituted the words "£1,500".

NOTE
[1] As amended by SI 1976/900 and by SI 1988/1993, in relation to proceedings commenced on or after November 30, 1988.

Regulation of procedure in civil proceedings

Power of Court of Session to regulate civil procedure in sheriff court

[1] **32.**—[2] (1) Subject to the provisions of this section, the Court of Session may by act of sederunt regulate and prescribe the procedure and practice to be followed in any civil proceedings in the sheriff court (including any matters incidental or relating to any such procedure or practice), and, without prejudice to the generality of the foregoing words, the power conferred on the Court of Session by this section shall extend to—

(a) regulating the procedure to be followed in connection with execution or diligence following on any civil proceedings;

(b) prescribing the manner in which, the time within which, and the conditions on which, an appeal may be taken to the sheriff principal from an interlocutor of a sheriff, or to the Court of Session from an interlocutor of a sheriff principal or a sheriff (including an interlocutor applying the verdict of a jury), or any application may be made to the sheriff court, or anything required or authorised to be done in relation to any civil proceedings shall or may be done;

(c) prescribing the form of any document to be used in, or for the purposes of, any civil proceedings or any execution or diligence following thereon, and the person by whom, and the manner in which, any such document as aforesaid is to be authenticated;

(d) regulating the procedure to be followed in connection with the production and recovery of documents;

[3] (e) providing in respect of any category of civil proceedings for written statements (including affidavits) and reports, admissible under section 2(1)(b) of the Civil Evidence (Scotland) Act 1988, to be received in evidence, on such conditions as may be prescribed, without being spoken to by a witness;

[6] [(ea) regulating the procedure to be followed in connection with the making of orders under sections 12(1) and (6) and 13(2) of theVulnerable Witnesses (Scotland) Act 2004 (asp 3) ("the 2004 Act");

(eb) regulating, so far as not regulated by the 2004 Act, the use of special measures authorised by virtue of that Act to be used;]

(f) making such provision as may appear to the Court of Session to be necessary or expedient with respect to the payment, investment or application of any sum of money awarded to or in respect of a person under legal disability in any action in the sheriff court;

(g) regulating the summoning, remuneration and duties of assessors;

(h) making such provision as may appear to the Court of Session to be necessary or expedient for carrying out the provisions of this Act or of any enactment conferring powers or imposing duties on sheriffs principal or sheriffs or relating to proceedings in the sheriff courts;

(i) regulating the expenses which may be awarded by the sheriff to parties in proceedings before him;

[4] (j) permitting a person who is not an advocate or solicitor and is not represented by an advocate or solicitor to transmit, whether orally or in writing, the views of a child to the sheriff for the purposes of any enactment which makes provision (however expressed) for the sheriff to have regard to those views;

[5] (k) prescribing the procedure to be followed in appointing a person under section 3(4) of the Adults with Incapacity (Scotland) Act 2000 (asp 4) and the functions of such a person.

Provided that nothing contained in an act of sederunt made under this section shall derogate from—

(i) the provisions of sections 35 to 38 of this Act (as amended by the Law Reform (Miscellaneous Provisions) (Scotland) Act 1985) with respect to summary causes, or

(ii) the provisions of subsection (8) of section 20 of the Race Relations

Act 1968 with respect to the remuneration to be paid to assessors appointed under subsection (7) of that section.

(2) An act of sederunt under this section may contain such incidental, supplemental or consequential provisions as appear to the Court of Session to be necessary or expedient for the purposes of that act, including, but without prejudice to the generality of the foregoing words, provisions amending, repealing or revoking any enactment (whether passed or made before or after the commencement of this Act) relating to matters with respect to which an act of sederunt may be made under this section.

(3) Before making an act of sederunt under this section with respect to any matter the Court of Session shall (unless that act embodies, with or without modifications, draft rules submitted to them by the Sheriff Court Rules Council under section 34 of this Act) consult the said Council, and shall take into consideration any views expressed by the Council with respect to that matter.

(4) Section 34 of the Administration of Justice (Scotland) Act 1933 (power of Court of Session to regulate civil procedure in sheriff court) shall cease to have effect, but any act of sederunt made under or having effect by virtue of that section shall, if and so far as it is in force immediately before the commencement of this Act, continue in force and shall have effect, and be treated, as if it had been made under this section.

NOTES

[1] See also the Maintenance Orders (Reciprocal Enforcement) Act 1972 (c. 18), ss.19 and 31(3) (Division **K**, *infra*). Extended: see the Children Act 1975 (c. 72), s.66, the Banking Act 1979 (c. 37), s.31(7)(b), the Debtors (Scotland) Act 1987 (c. 18), s.97 (Division **B**, *supra*) and the Child Support Act 1991 (c. 48), ss.39(2) and 49 and the Children (Scotland) Act 1995 (c. 36), s.91, (effective October 1, 1996: SI 1996/2203), Division **K** *infra*. Applied: see the Children Act 1975 (c. 72), s.78. See also the Presumption of Death (Scotland) Act 1977 (c. 27), s.15(1) (Division **M**, *infra*).

[2] As amended by the Law Reform (Miscellaneous Provisions) (Scotland) Act 1985 (c. 73), Sch.2, para.12.

[3] Substituted by the Civil Evidence (Scotland) Act 1988 (c. 32), s.2(4).

[4] Inserted by the Children (Scotland) Act 1995 (c. 36), Sch.4, para.18(2) (effective November **D 86/2** 1, 1995: SI 1995/2787).

[5] Inserted by the Adults with Incapacity (Scotland) Act 2000 (asp 4), s.88 and Sch.5, para.13.

[6] As amended by the Vulnerable Witnesses (Scotland) Act 2004 (asp 3), s.14, and brought into force by the Vulnerable Witnesses (Scotland) Act 2004 Commencement Order 2005 (SSI 2005/168) (effective April 1, 2005) but only in respect of proceedings in the sheriff court under Part II of the Children (Scotland) Act 1995 in respect of appeals under section 51(1) and applications under sections 68 and 85 of that Act and only in respect of child witnesses.

Sheriff Court Rules Council

33.—[0] (1) There shall be established a body (to be known as the Sheriff Court Rules Council, and hereafter in this section and section 34 called "the Council") which shall have the functions conferred on it by section 34, and which shall consist of—

(a) two sheriffs principal, three sheriffs, one advocate, five solicitors and two whole-time sheriff clerks, all appointed by the Lord President of the Court of Session, after consultation with such persons as appear to him to be appropriate;

(b) two persons appointed by the Lord President after consultation with the Secretary of State, being persons appearing to the Lord President to have—
   (i) a knowledge of the working procedures and practices of the civil courts;
   (ii) a knowledge of consumer affairs; and
   (iii) an awareness of the interests of litigants in the civil courts; and

(c) one person appointed by the Secretary of State, being a person appearing to the Secretary of State to be qualified for such appointment.

(2) The members of the Council shall, so long as they retain the respective qualifications mentioned in subsection (1) above, hold office for three years and be eligible for re-appointment.

(3) Any vacancy in the membership of the Council occurring by reason of death, resignation or other cause before the expiry of the period for which the member whose place is so vacated was appointed shall be filled—

[0] (a) if the member was appointed by the Lord President of the Court of Session, by the appointment by the Lord President, after such consultation as is mentioned in paragraph (a) or, as the case may be, (b) of subsection (1) above, of a person having the same qualifications as that member,

 (b) if the member was appointed by the Secretary of State, by the appointment by the Secretary of State of another person appearing to the Secretary of State to have qualifications suitable for such appointment,

and a person so appointed to fill a vacancy shall hold office only until the expiry of the said period.

[1] (4) The Lord President of the Court of Session shall appoint one of the two sheriffs principal who are members of the Council as chairman thereof, and the Secretary of State shall appoint a secretary to the Council.

(5) The Council shall have power to regulate the summoning of meetings of the Council and the procedure at such meetings, so however that—

 (a) the Council shall meet within one month of its being established and thereafter at intervals of not more than six months, and shall meet at any time on a requisition in that behalf made by the chairman of the Council or any three members thereof, and

 (b) at any meeting of the Council six members shall be a quorum.

(6) The Rules Council for the sheriff court established under section 35 of the Administration of Justice (Scotland) Act 1933 is hereby dissolved, and the said section 35 shall cease to have effect.

D 86/3 NOTES

[0] As amended by the Law Reform (Miscellaneous Provisions) (Scotland) Act 1990 (c. 40), Sch.8, para.26.

[1] As amended by the Law Reform (Miscellaneous Provisions) (Scotland) Act 1985 (c. 73), Sch.2, para.13 and Sch.4.

Functions of Sheriff Court Rules Council

34.—(1) As soon as practicable after it has been established the Council shall review generally the procedure and practice followed in civil proceedings in the sheriff court (including any matters incidental or relating to that procedure or practice) and, in the light of that review and of the provisions of this Act, shall prepare and submit to the Court of Session draft rules, being rules which—

 (a) are designed to regulate and prescribe that procedure and practice (including any such matters as aforesaid), and

 (b) are such as the Court of Session have power to make by act of sederunt under section 32 of this Act,

and the Court of Session shall make an act of sederunt under the said section 32 embodying those rules with such modifications, if any, as they think expedient.

(2) After submitting draft rules to the Court of Session under subsection (1) above the Council shall keep under review the procedure and practice followed in civil proceedings in the sheriff court (including any matters incidental or relating to that procedure or practice), and the Council may prepare and submit to the Court of Session draft rules designed to deal with any of the matters relating to the sheriff court which the Court of Session have power under section 32 of this Act to regulate or prescribe by act of sederunt, and the Court of Session shall consider any draft rules so

submitted and shall, if they approve the rules, make an act of sederunt under the said section 32 embodying those rules with such modifications if any, as they think expedient.

(3) For the purpose of assisting it in the discharge of its functions under the foregoing provisions of this section the Council may invite representations on any aspect of the procedure or practice in civil proceedings in the sheriff court (including any matters incidental or relating to that procedure or practice), and shall consider any such representations received by it, whether in response to such an invitation as aforesaid or otherwise.

Summary causes

Summary causes

35.—(1) The definition of "summary cause" contained in paragraph (i) of section 3 of the Sheriff Courts (Scotland) Act 1907 shall cease to have effect, and for the purposes of the procedure and practice in civil proceedings in the sheriff court there shall be a form of process, to be known as a "summary cause", which shall be used for the purposes of all civil proceedings brought in that court, being proceedings of one or other of the following descriptions, namely—

[1] (a) actions for payment of money not exceeding £1,500[1a] in amount (exclusive of interest and expenses);

[1] (b) actions of multiplepoinding, actions of furthcoming and actions of sequestration for rent, where the value of the fund *in medio*, or the value of the arrested fund or subject, or the rent in respect of which sequestration is asked, as the case may be, does not exceed £1,500[1a] (exclusive of interest and expenses);

[2] (c) actions *ad factum praestandum* and actions for the recovery of **D 87** possession of heritable or moveable property, other than actions in which there is claimed in addition, or as an alternative, to a decree *ad factum praestandum* or for such recovery, as the case may be, a decree for payment of money exceeding £1,500[1a] in amount (exclusive of interest and expenses);

(d) proceedings which, according to the law and practice existing immediately before the commencement of this Act, might competently be brought in the sheriff's small debt court or where required to be conducted and disposed of in the summary manner in which proceedings were conducted and disposed of under the Small Debt Acts;

and any reference in the following provisions of this Act, or in any other enactment (whether passed or made before or after the commencement of this Act) relating to civil procedure in the sheriff court, to a summary cause shall be construed as a reference to a summary cause within the meaning of this subsection.

[3] (1A) For the avoidance of doubt it is hereby declared that nothing in subsection (1) above shall prevent the Court of Session from making different rules of procedure and practice in relation to different descriptions of summary cause proceedings.

[4,5] (2) There shall be a form of summary cause process, to be known as a "small claim", which shall be used for the purposes of such descriptions of summary cause proceedings as are prescribed by the Secretary of State by order.

[4] (3) No enactment or rule of law relating to admissibility or corroboration of evidence before a court of law shall be binding in a small claim.

[4] (4) An order under subsection (2) above shall be by statutory instrument but shall not be made unless a draft of it has been approved by a resolution of each House of Parliament.

NOTES

[1] As amended by SI 1976/900 and SI 1981/842.

[1a] As amended by SI 1988/1993, in relation to proceedings commenced on or after 30th November 1988.

[2] As amended by SI 1976/900 and SI 1981/842. Excluded by the Land Tenure Reform (Scotland) Act 1974 (c. 38), s.9(6).

[3] Inserted by the Law Reform (Miscellaneous Provisions) (Scotland) Act 1985 (c. 73), Sch.2, para.14, with effect from 30th December 1985.

[4] New subss (2)–(4) substituted for subs.(2) by the Law Reform (Miscellaneous Provisions) (Scotland) Act 1985 (c. 73), s.18(1).

[5] As amended by SI 1999/678, Art. 2, Sched. (effective May 19, 1999).

Procedure in summary causes

36.—(1) In relation to summary causes the power conferred on the Court of Session by section 32 of this Act shall extend to the making of rules permitting a party to such a cause, in such circumstances as may be specified in the rules, to be represented by a person who is neither an advocate nor a solicitor.

(2) A summary cause shall be commenced by a summons in, or as nearly as is practicable in, such form as may be prescribed by rules under the said section 32.

[1] (3) The evidence, if any, given in a summary cause shall not be recorded.

(4) [Repealed by the Debtors (Scotland) Act 1987 (c. 18), Sched. 8.]

NOTE

[1] Excluded by the Maintenance Orders (Reciprocal Enforcement) Act 1972 (c. 18), s.4(4)(b).

D 88 Further provisions as to small claims

[1] **36A.** Where the pursuer in a small claim is not—

(a) a partnership or a body corporate; or

(b) acting in a representative capacity,

he may require the sheriff clerk to effect service of the summons on his behalf.

NOTE

[1] Inserted by the Law Reform (Miscellaneous Provisions) (Scotland) Act 1985 (c. 73), s.18(2).

Expenses in small claims

[1] **36B.**—[2] (1) No award of expenses shall be made in a small claim in which the value of the claim does not exceed such sum as the Secretary of State shall prescribe by order.

[2] (2) Any expenses which the sheriff may award in any other small claim shall not exceed such sum as the Secretary of State shall prescribe by order.

(3) Subsections (1) and (2) above do not apply to a party to a small claim—

(a) who being a defender—

(i) has not stated a defence; or

(ii) having stated a defence, has not proceeded with it; or

(iii) having stated and proceeded with a defence, has not acted in good faith as to its merits; or

(b) on whose part there has been unreasonable conduct in relation to the proceedings or the claim;

nor do they apply in relation to an appeal to the sheriff principal.

(4) An order under this section shall be by statutory instrument but shall not be made unless a draft of it has been approved by a resolution of each House of Parliament.

NOTES

[1] Inserted by the Law Reform (Miscellaneous Provisions) (Scotland) Act 1985 (c. 73), s.18(2).

[2] As amended by SI 1999/678, Art. 2, Sched. (effective May 19, 1999).

Remits

[5] **37.**—[1] (1) In the case of any ordinary cause brought in the sheriff court the sheriff—

    (a) shall at any stage, on the joint motion of the parties to the cause, direct that the cause be treated as a summary cause, and in that case the cause shall be treated for all purposes (including appeal) as a summary cause and shall proceed accordingly;

    (b) may, subject to section 7 of the Sheriff Courts (Scotland) Act 1907, on the motion of any of the parties to the cause, if he is of the opinion that the importance or difficulty of the cause make it appropriate to do so, remit the cause to the Court of Session.

(2) In the case of any summary cause, the sheriff at any stage—

    (a) shall, on the joint motion of the parties to the cause, and

    (b) may, on the motion of any of the parties to the cause, if he is of the opinion that the importance or difficulty of the cause makes it appropriate to do so,

direct that the cause be treated as an ordinary cause, and in that case the cause shall be treated for all purposes (including appeal) as an ordinary cause and shall proceed accordingly:

Provided that a direction under this subsection may, in the case of an action for the recovery of possession of heritable or moveable property, be given by the sheriff of his own accord.

[2] (2A) In the case of any action in the sheriff court, being an action for divorce or an action in relation to the custody, guardianship or adoption of a child the sheriff may, of his own accord, at any stage remit the action to the Court of Session.

[4] (2B) In the case of any small claim the sheriff at any stage—   **D 88/1**

    (a) may, if he is of the opinion that a difficult question of law or a question of fact of exceptional complexity is involved, of his own accord or on the motion of any party to the small claim;

    (b) shall, on the joint motion of the parties to the small claim,

direct that the small claim be treated as a summary cause (not being a small claim) or ordinary cause, and in that case the small claim shall be treated for all purposes (including appeal) as a summary cause (not being a small claim) or ordinary cause as the case may be.

[4] (2C) In the case of any cause which is not a small claim by reason only of any monetary limit applicable to a small claim or to summary causes, the sheriff at any stage shall, on the joint motion of the parties to the cause, direct that the cause be treated as a small claim and in that case the cause shall be treated for all purposes (including appeal) as a small claim and shall proceed accordingly.

[5] (2D) In the case of any action in the sheriff court where the matter to which the action relates could competently be determined by the Land Court by virtue of the Agricultural Holdings (Scotland) Act 1991 (c.55) or the Agricultural Holdings (Scotland) Act 2003 (asp 11), the sheriff may (of his own accord or on the motion of any of the parties) at any stage remit the case to the Land Court if he is of the opinion that it is appropriate to do so.

[3] (3) A decision—

    (a) to remit, or not to remit, under subsection (2A), (2B) or (2C) above; or

    (b) to make, or not to make, a direction by virtue of paragraph (b) of, or the proviso to, subsection (2) above,

shall not be subject to review; but from a decision to remit, or not to remit, under subsection (1)(b) above an appeal shall lie to the Court of Session.

(4) In this section "sheriff" includes a sheriff principal.

NOTES

[1] As amended by the Law Reform (Miscellaneous Provisions) (Scotland) Act 1980 (c. 55), s.16(a). See the Land Tenure Reform (Scotland) Act 1974 (c. 38), s.9(6).

[2] Added by the Law Reform (Miscellaneous Provisions) (Scotland) Act 1980 (c. 55), s.16(b). As amended by the Divorce Jurisdiction, Court Fees and Legal Aid (Scotland) Act 1983 (c. 12), Sch.1, para.12, the Law Reform (Parent and Child) (Scotland) Act 1986 (c. 9), Sch.1, para.11, the Age of Legal Capacity (Scotland) Act 1991 (c. 50), Sch.1, para.35, and the Children (Scotland) Act 1995 (c. 36), Sch.4, para.18(3), *infra*, Division **K** (effective April 1, 1997: SI 1996/3201).

[3] As substituted by the Law Reform (Miscellaneous Provisions) (Scotland) Act 1980 (c. 55), s.16(c). As amended by the Law Reform (Miscellaneous Provisions) (Scotland) Act 1985 (c. 73), s.18(3)(b).

[4] Added by the Law Reform (Miscellaneous Provisions) (Scotland) Act 1988, s.18(3).

[5] Amended and inserted by the Agricultural Holdings (Scotland) Act 2003 (asp 11), Pt 7, s.86(1) (effective November 27, 2003).

Appeal in summary causes

[1] **38.** In the case of—

(a) any summary cause an appeal shall lie to the sheriff principal on any point of law from the final judgment of the sheriff; and

(b) any summary cause other than a small claim an appeal shall lie to the Court of Session on any point of law from the final judgment of the sheriff principal, if the sheriff principal certifies the cause as suitable for such an appeal,

but save as aforesaid an interlocutor of the sheriff or the sheriff principal in any such cause shall not be subject to review.

NOTE

[1] As amended by the Law Reform (Miscellaneous Provisions) (Scotland) Act 1985 (c. 73), s.18(4). Excluded by the Debtors (Scotland) Act 1987 (c. 18), s.103(1).

D 88/2   *Miscellaneous and supplemental*

39, 40. [*Repealed by the Law Reform (Miscellaneous Provisions) (Scotland) Act 1980 (c. 55), Sch.3.*]

Power of Her Majesty to vary limit to privative jurisdiction of sheriff court, etc.

[1] **41.**—(1) If it appears to Her Majesty in Council that the sum of £250 specified in any provisions of this Act mentioned in subsection (2) below (or such other sum as may be specified in that provision by virtue of an Order in Council under this section) should be varied, Her Majesty may by Order in Council, specifying the provision and the sum in question, direct that the provision shall be amended so as to substitute for that sum such other sum as may be specified in the Order.

(2) The provisions referred to in subsection (1) above are—
   section 31,
   paragraphs (a), (b) and (c) of section 35.

(3) An Order in Council under this section may contain such incidental, supplemental or consequential provisions as appear to Her Majesty in Council to be necessary or expedient for the purposes of the Order.

(4) Any Order in Council made under this section may be revoked by a subsequent Order in Council under this section which substitutes another sum for the sum specified in the Order which is thereby revoked.

(5) No recommendation shall be made to Her Majesty in Council to make an Order under this section unless a draft of the Order has been laid before Parliament and approved by resolution of each House of Parliament.

NOTE

[1] As amended by the Law Reform (Miscellaneous Provisions) (Scotland) Act 1980 (c. 55), Sch.3.

Application of provisions regarding jurisdiction and summary causes

42. The following provisions of this Act, namely—
   section 31,

sections 35 to 40,
section 46(2) so far as relating to the enactments mentioned in Part II of D 89
    Schedule 2,
    Schedule 1 (except paragraph 1),
shall not apply in relation to any proceedings commenced before the
commencement of this Act.

Part IV

Miscellaneous and General

Orders, etc.
    43.—(1) Any power conferred by this Act to make an order shall include a
power exercisable in the like manner and subject to the like conditions (if
any) to vary or revoke the order by a subsequent order.
    (2) It is hereby declared that any power conferred by this Act to include
incidental, consequential or supplemental provisions in any instrument
made under this Act includes a power to include transitional provisions in
that instrument.

Expenses
    44.—(1) There shall be paid out of moneys provided by Parliament any
sums payable by the Secretary of State in consequence of the provisions of
this Act.
    (2) Any sums payable under or by virtue of this Act to the Secretary of
State shall be paid into the Consolidated Fund.
    (3) In the application of section 4(1) of the Local Government (Scotland)
Act 1966 (variation of rate support grant orders) to a rate support grant
order made before the transfer date appointed under section 30 of this Act
for a grant period ending after that date, the Secretary of State shall take
into account any relief obtained, or likely to be obtained, by local
authorities—
    (*a*) which is attributable to the coming into operation of Part II of this
        Act, and
    (*b*) which was not taken into account in making the rate support grant
        order the variation of which is in question.
The provisions of this subsection are without prejudice to section 4(4) of
the said Act of 1966 (under which an order under that section may vary the
matters prescribed by a rate support grant order).

Interpretation
    45.—[1] (1) In this Act, unless the contrary intention appears—
    (*a*) references to a sheriff principal include reference to a temporary
        sheriff principal, and references to the office of sheriff principal
        include references to an appointment as a temporary sheriff
        principal;
    (*b*) references to a sheriff include references to a part-time sheriff
        and an honorary sheriff, and references to the office of sheriff
        include references to an appointment as a part-time sheriff and
        to the office of honorary sheriff;
    (*c*) references to an honorary sheriff are references to a person
        holding the office of honorary sheriff in his capacity as such.
    (2) In this Act—
    (*a*) "enactment" includes an order, regulation, rule or other
        instrument having effect by virtue of an Act;
    (*b*) any references to any enactment shall, unless the contrary
        intention appears, be construed as a reference to that enactment
        as amended or extended, and as including a reference thereto as
        applied, by or under any other enactment (including this Act).

D 90　　(3) Subject to the foregoing provisions of this section and to any other express provision of this Act, expressions used in this Act and in the Sheriff Courts (Scotland) Act 1907 shall have the same meanings in this Act as in that Act.

NOTE

[1] As amended by the Bail, Judicial Appointments etc. (Scotland) Act 2000 (asp 9), s.12 and Sched., para.1.

Amendment and repeal of enactments

46.—(1) Schedule 1 to this Act (which contains certain minor and consequential amendments of enactments) shall have effect.

(2) The enactments mentioned in Schedule 2 to this Act are hereby repealed to the extent specified in relation thereto in column 3 of that Schedule.

Short title, commencement and extent

47.—(1) This Act may be cited as the Sheriff Courts (Scotland) Act 1971.

[1] (2) This Act shall come into operation on such date as the Secretary of State may appoint by order made by statutory instrument, and different dates may be appointed for different provisions of this Act, or for different purposes.

Any reference in any provision of this Act to the commencement of this Act shall, unless otherwise provided by any such order, be construed as a reference to the date on which that provision comes into operation.

[2] (3) This Act, except section 4 (offices of sheriff principal and sheriff), shall extend to Scotland only.

NOTES

[1] See SI 1971/1582; SI 1973/276 and SI 1976/236. Power fully exercised.

[2] As amended by the House of Commons Disqualification Act 1975 (c. 24), Sch.3.

SCHEDULES

SCHEDULE 1

MINOR AND CONSEQUENTIAL AMENDMENT OF ENACTMENTS

General

1. In any enactment passed or made before the commencement of this Act, for any reference to a county, where it appears in relation to a sheriff or a sheriff substitute or in any similar context, there shall, unless the contrary intention appears, be substituted a reference to a sheriffdom.

———

NOTE

The remaining amendments are shown in the prints in *The Parliament House Book* of the Acts amended.

———

SCHEDULE 2

Repeal of Enactments

.　.　.　.　.　.

NOTE

Repeals of provisions of Acts printed in *The Parliament House Book* are shown in the prints of those Acts.

(1975 c. 20)

An Act to make provision as respects district courts . . . in Scotland . . . and for connected purposes.   [27th March 1975]

Abolition of existing inferior courts and establishment of district courts

1.—(1) On 16th May 1975 the inferior courts in Scotland existing immediately before that date (in this Act referred to as "the existing courts") shall cease to exist, and on that date there shall be established, in accordance with the provisions of this Act, a district court for each commission area except in the case of a commission area in respect of which the Secretary of State otherwise directs, having regard to the likely lack of business for such a court.

In this subsection, "inferior courts" means all justice of the peace courts, quarter sessions, burgh courts, police courts, and the court of the bailie of the river and firth of Clyde.

(2) On and after that date, all functions of burgh magistrates, not otherwise provided for, shall be exercisable by a justice of the peace.

(3) Where proceedings were instituted before that date in any existing court and those proceedings have not been completed by that date, then, for the purpose of enabling those proceedings to be continued on and after that date, and for preserving in other respects the continuity of the administration of justice—

(a) the district court having jurisdiction in the area where the proceedings were instituted shall be treated as succeeding to, and being the same court as, the existing court concerned, and any verdict, sentence, order, complaint, notice, citation, warrant, bail bond or other proceedings or document shall have effect accordingly; and

(b) the clerk and the prosecutor of the existing court shall transfer all records, productions and documents relating to those proceedings to the clerk or, as the case may be, the prosecutor of the district court concerned.

(4) Where proceedings were instituted after 14th May 1969 in any existing court and were completed on or before 15th May 1975, the clerk of that court shall transfer all complaints, minutes and other records relating thereto to the clerk of the district court concerned.

(5) In the case of any other record or document relating to proceedings in the existing courts, the person having custody of it shall, on request by or on behalf of a district court, release it to that court for the purpose of proceedings in that court, and any record or document so released shall be returned to the person who released it as soon as may be after it has ceased to be required for the said purposes.

Further provision as to establishment and disestablishment of district courts

¹ **1A.**—(1) Where it appears to the Secretary of State that—

(a) there is insufficient business for the district court in a particular commission area; and

(b) such insufficiency of business is likely to continue,

he may by order provide that the district court for that area cease to exist on a specified date.

(2) Where it appears to the Secretary of State that, in a commission area in which there is no district court, there is likely to be sufficient business to

D 92 justify the establishment of such a court, he may by order provide for the establishment of such a court in that area on a specified date.

(3) An order under subsection (1) or (2) above may contain all such provisions as appear to the Secretary of State to be necessary or expedient for rendering the order of full effect and any incidental, supplemental or consequential provisions which appear to him to be necessary or expedient for the purposes of the order, including, but without prejudice to the generality of the foregoing words, provisions amending, repealing or revoking any enactment (whether passed or made before or after the commencement of this enactment).

[2] (4) Before making an order under subsection (1) or (2) above, the Secretary of State shall consult the local authority for the area concerned, and such other persons as appear to him to have an interest in the proposed order.

(5) Orders under subsection (1) or (2) above shall be made by statutory instrument, which shall be subject to annulment in pursuance of a resolution of either House of Parliament.

NOTES
[1] Inserted by the Law Reform (Miscellaneous Provisions) (Scotland) Act 1985 (c. 73), s.33.
[2] As amended by the Local Government etc. (Scotland) Act 1994 (c. 39), Sch.13, para.96(2) (effective April 1, 1996: SI 1996/323).

District of, and exercise of jurisdiction by, district court

2. [Repealed by the Criminal Procedure (Consequential Provisions) (Scotland) Act 1995 (c. 40), Sched. 5 (effective 1st April, 1996: s. 7(2)).]

Jurisdiction and powers of district court

3. [Repealed by the Criminal Procedure (Consequential Provisions) (Scotland) Act 1995 (c. 40), Sched. 5 (effective 1st April, 1996: s. 7(2)).]

Procedure and practice in the district court

4. [Repealed by the Criminal Procedure (Consequential Provisions) (Scotland) Act 1995 (c. 40), Sched. 5 (effective 1st April, 1996: s. 7(2)).]

Stipendiary magistrates

5.—[1] (1) Subject to subsections (2) and (3) below, a local authority may appoint a stipendiary magistrate to sit in a district court, and the terms and conditions of such an appointment, including superannuation and other benefits, shall be those applicable to service in local government.

(2) A person shall not be appointed to be a stipendiary magistrate unless he is, and has been for at least five years, legally qualified, and for the purposes of this subsection a person shall be legally qualified if he is an advocate or a solicitor.

(3) A person shall not be appointed to be a stipendiary magistrate until the Secretary of State approves—

    (a) the establishment of the office of stipendiary magistrate in the district court concerned;

    (b) the salary which it is proposed should pertain to that office; and

    (c) the appointment of the person proposed for that office.

(4) Where it appears to the Secretary of State that it is expedient so to do in order to avoid delays in the administration of justice in any district court, he may direct the local authority concerned to appoint a person qualified to be so appointed to act as stipendiary magistrate in that court during such period as the Secretary of State thinks fit.

(5) Any person who immediately before 16th May 1975 holds office as stipendiary magistrate for any area shall, on that date, become stipendiary magistrate in the district court having jurisdiction in that area and shall be deemed in all respects to have been appointed by virtue of this section.

D 93 (6) The salary of any such stipendiary magistrate as is mentioned in subsection (5) above shall not be less than that payable to him immediately before 16th May 1975.

(7) Every stipendiary magistrate shall, by virtue of his office, be a justice of the peace for the commission area in which he is appointed.

(8) Section 12 of the Sheriff Courts (Scotland) Act 1971 (removal from office of sheriff) shall apply in relation to a stipendiary magistrate as it applies in relation to a sheriff.

NOTE
[1] See the Local Government etc. (Scotland) Act (c. 39), s.50 which provides for automatic appointment of existing stipendiary magistrates to new district courts on April 1, 1996.

District prosecutor
6. [Repealed by the Criminal Procedure (Consequential Provisions) (Scotland) Act 1995 (c. 40), Sched. 5 (effective April 1, 1996: s.7(2)).]

Clerk of district court
7.—(1) It shall be the duty of each local authority to appoint and employ, whether on a full-time or part-time basis, an officer to act as clerk of the district court for their area, who shall also act as legal assessor in that court, and any person so appointed shall be an advocate or a solicitor.

(2) There shall be transferred to the clerks of the district courts all functions hitherto exercisable by clerks of the existing courts.

(3) [Repealed by the Local Government etc. (Scotland) Act 1994 (c. 39), Sched. 13, para. 96(3) (effective April 1, 1996: SI 1996/323).]

Court houses for district court
8.—(1) Every local authority shall provide suitable and sufficient premises and facilities for the purposes of the district court.

(2) Without prejudice to subsection (1) above, every regional, islands, or district council having control of premises used to any extent for the purposes of the existing courts as at 15th May 1975 shall make those premises available for the purposes of the district court, and, where those premises include accommodation used by the prosecutor in the existing courts or in the district courts, that accommodation shall be made available to any procurator fiscal appointed by the Lord Advocate to serve in the district court for such period and at such times as the fiscal may require.

PART II

JUSTICES AND CLERKS OF THE PEACE

9–18. [Not printed.]

PART III

MISCELLANEOUS AND GENERAL

19–20. [Not printed.]

21–22. [Spent.]

· · · · · ·

General   **D 94**

Amendments and repeals
24. . . .

(3) The Secretary of State may by order amend, repeal or revoke any provision of an Act passed or an instrument under an Act made before 16th May 1975 if it appears to him that that provision is inconsistent with any provision of this Act or requires modification in consequence of this Act.

(4) Where any local enactment provides for any matter which is also provided for by any provision of this Act or of any order made thereunder, the provision of this Act, or, as the case may be, of that order, shall have effect in substitution for the local enactment, which shall cease to have effect.

(5) Any order made under this section shall be made by statutory instrument, which shall be subject to annulment in pursuance of a resolution of either House of Parliament.

Expenses

25. There shall be defrayed out of moneys provided by Parliament—
  (a) any expenses incurred by the Secretary of State under this Act; and
  (b) any increase attributable to the provisions of this Act in the sums payable out of moneys so provided under any other enactment.

Interpretation

26.—[1] (1) In this Act, unless the context otherwise requires—
  "clerk of the district court" includes such depute clerk as may be required for the purposes of any district court;
  [2] "commission area" means the area of a local authority;
  "district prosecutor" includes such depute or assistant district prosecutor as may be required for the purposes of any district court;
  "justice" or "justice of the peace" means a justice of the peace appointed under section 9 of this Act or deemed to have been so appointed;
  [2] "local authority" means a council substituted under section 2 of the Local Government etc. (Scotland) Act 1994;
  "prescribed" means prescribed by regulations made by the Secretary of State.

(2) Any power conferred by this Act to make an order shall include power, exercisable in like manner and subject to the same conditions, to vary or revoke the order by a subsequent order.

(3) Unless the context otherwise requires, any reference in this Act to any other enactment is a reference thereto as amended, extended or applied by or under any other enactment, including this Act.

NOTE
[1] As amended by the Licensing (Scotland) Act 1976 (c. 66), s.136 and Sch.8.
[2] Substituted by the Local Government etc. (Scotland) Act 1994 (c. 39), Sch.13, para.96(5) (effective April 1, 1996: SI 1996/323).

Short title, extent and commencement

27.—[1] (1) This Act may be cited as the District Courts (Scotland) Act 1975, and, except section 24(1) and subsection (2) below and the entries in Schedule 1 to this Act relating to section 18(1) of the Police (Scotland) Act 1967, extends to Scotland only.

(2) This Act, except sections 8, 10, 11, 14, 16, 17, 20, 23, 26 and this section, shall come into force on 16th May 1975.

NOTE
[1] As amended by the Criminal Law Act 1977 (c. 45), s.65 and Sch.13.

SCHEDULES

[Not reprinted]

(1976 c. 14)

An Act to make provision for Scotland for the holding of public inquiries in respect of fatal accidents, deaths of persons in legal custody, sudden, suspicious and unexplained deaths and deaths occurring in circumstances giving rise to serious public concern.
[13th April 1976.]

NOTE
[1] See the Anatomy Act 1984 (c. 14), s.4(6).

Investigation of death and application for public inquiry

1.—(1) Subject to the provisions of any enactment specified in Schedule 1 to this Act and subsection (2) below, where—

(a) in the case of a death to which this paragraph applies—
  (i) it appears that the death has resulted from an accident occurring in Scotland while the person who has died, being an employee, was in the course of his employment or, being an employer or self-employed person, was engaged in his occupation as such; or
  (ii) the person who has died was, at the time of his death, in legal custody; or
(b) it appears to the Lord Advocate to be expedient in the public interest in the case of a death to which this paragraph applies that an inquiry under this Act should be held into the circumstances of the death on the ground that it was sudden, suspicious or unexplained, or has occurred in circumstances such as to give rise to serious public concern,

the procurator fiscal for the district with which the circumstances of the death appear to be most closely connected shall investigate those circumstances and apply to the sheriff for the holding of an inquiry under this Act into those circumstances.

(2) Paragraph (a) of subsection (1) above applies to a death occurring in Scotland after the commencement of this Act (other than such a death in a case where criminal proceedings have been concluded against any person in respect of the death or any accident from which the death resulted, and the Lord Advocate is satisfied that the circumstances of the death have been sufficiently established in the course of such proceedings), and paragraph (b) of that subsection applies to a death occurring there at any time after the date three years before such commencement.

(3) An application under subsection (1) above—
(a) shall be made to the sheriff with whose sheriffdom the circumstances of the death appear to be most closely connected;
(b) shall narrate briefly the circumstances of the death so far as known to the procurator fiscal;
(c) may, if it appears that more deaths than one have occurred as a result of the same accident or in the same or similar circumstances, relate to both or all such deaths.

(4) For the purposes of subsection (1)(a)(ii) above, a person is in legal custody if—
(a) he is detained in, or is subject to detention in, a prison, remand centre, detention centre, borstal institution, or young offenders institution, all within the meaning of the Prisons (Scotland) Act 1952; or
(b) he is detained in a police station, police cell, or other similar place; or **D 96**
(c) he is being taken—

     (i) to any of the places specified in paragraphs (a) and (b) of this subsection to be detained therein; or

    (ii) from any such place in which immediately before such taking he was detained.

Citation of witnesses for precognition

    2.—(1) The procurator fiscal may, for the purpose of carrying out his investigation under section 1(1) of this Act, cite witnesses for precognition by him, and this section shall be sufficient warrant for such citation.

    (2) If any witness cited under subsection (1) above—

     (a) fails without reasonable excuse and after receiving reasonable notice to attend for precognition by the procurator fiscal at the time and place mentioned in the citation served on him; or

     (b) refuses when so cited to give information within his knowledge regarding any matter relevant to the investigation in relation to which such precognition is taken,

the procurator fiscal may apply to the sheriff for an order requiring the witness to attend for such precognition or to give such information at a time and place specified in the order; and the sheriff shall, if he considers it expedient to do so, make such an order.

   [1] (3) If the witness fails to comply with the order of the sheriff under subsection (2) above, he shall be liable to be summarily punished forthwith by a fine not exceeding level 3 on the standard scale or by imprisonment for any period not exceeding 20 days.

NOTE
[1] As amended by the Criminal Procedure (Consequential Provisions) (Scotland) Act 1995 (c. 40), Sch.4, para.10.

Holding of public inquiry

    3.—(1) On an application under section 1 of this Act being made to him, the sheriff shall make an order—

     (a) fixing a time and place for the holding by him of an inquiry under this Act (hereafter in this Act referred to as "the inquiry"), which shall be as soon thereafter as is reasonably practicable in such court-house or other premises as appear to him to be appropriate, having regard to the apparent circumstances of the death; and

     (b) granting warrant to cite witnesses and havers to attend at the inquiry at the instance of the procurator fiscal or of any person who may be entitled by virtue of this Act to appear at the inquiry.

    (2) On the making of an order under subsection (1) above, the procurator fiscal shall—

     (a) intimate the holding of the inquiry and the time and place fixed for it to the wife or husband or the nearest known relative and, in a case where the inquiry is being held in respect of such a death as is referred to in section 1(1)(a)(i) of this Act, to the employer, if any, of the person whose death is the subject of the inquiry, and to such other person or class of persons as may be prescribed in rules made under section 7(1)(g) of this Act; and

     (b) give public notice of the holding of the inquiry and of the time and place fixed for it.

D 97   (3) Where an application under section 1 of this Act relates to more than one death, the order made under subsection (1) above shall so relate; and in this Act references to a death shall include references to both or all deaths or to each death as the case may require, and in subsection (2)(a) above the reference to the person whose death is the subject of the inquiry shall include a reference to each person whose death is the subject of the inquiry.

Conduct of public inquiry

4.—(1) At the inquiry, it shall be the duty of the procurator fiscal to adduce evidence with regard to the circumstances of the death which is the subject of the inquiry.

(2) The wife or husband, or the nearest known relative, and, in a case where the inquiry is being held in respect of such a death as is referred to in section 1(1)(a)(i) of this Act, the employer, if any, of the person whose death is the subject of the inquiry, an inspector appointed under section 19 of the Health and Safety at Work etc. Act 1974 and any other person who the sheriff is satisfied has an interest in the inquiry may appear and adduce evidence at the inquiry.

(3) Subject to subsection (4) below, the inquiry shall be open to the public.

(4) Where a person under the age of 17 is in any way involved in the inquiry, the sheriff may, at his own instance or on an application made to him by any party to the inquiry, make an order providing that—

    (a) no report of the inquiry which is made in a newspaper or other publication or a sound or television broadcast shall reveal the name, address or school, or include any particulars calculated to lead to the identification of that person;

    (b) no picture relating to the inquiry which is or includes a picture of that person shall be published in any newspaper or other publication or televised broadcast.

[1] (5) Any person who contravenes an order made under subsection (4) above shall be guilty of an offence and shall be liable on summary conviction to a fine not exceeding level 4 on the standard scale in respect of each offence.

(6) The sheriff may, either at his own instance or at the request of the procurator fiscal or of any party who may be entitled by virtue of this Act to appear at the inquiry, summon any person having special knowledge and being willing to do so, to act as an assessor at the inquiry.

(7) Subject to the provisions of this Act and any rules made under section 7 of this Act, the rules of evidence, the procedure and the powers of the sheriff to deal with contempt of court and to enforce the attendance of witnesses at the inquiry shall be as nearly as possible those applicable in an ordinary civil cause brought before the sheriff sitting alone.

NOTE
[1] As amended by virtue of the Criminal Procedure (Scotland) Act 1975 (c. 21), ss.289F and 289G.

Criminal proceedings and compellability of witnesses

5.—(1) The examination of a witness or haver at the inquiry shall not be a bar to criminal proceedings being taken against him.

(2) No witness at the inquiry shall be compellable to answer any question tending to show that he is guilty of any crime or offence.

Sheriff's determination, etc.

6.—(1) At the conclusion of the evidence and any submissions thereon, or as soon as possible thereafter, the sheriff shall make a determination setting out the following circumstances of the death so far as they have been established to his satisfaction—

    (a) where and when the death and any accident resulting in the death took place;

    (b) the cause or causes of such death and any accident resulting in the **D 98** death;

    (c) the reasonable precautions, if any, whereby the death and any accident resulting in the death might have been avoided;

    (d) the defects, if any, in any system of working which contributed to the death or any accident resulting in the death; and

(e) any other facts which are relevant to the circumstances of the death.

(2) The sheriff shall be entitled to be satisfied that any circumstances referred to in subsection (1) above have been established by evidence, notwithstanding that that evidence is not corroborated.

(3) The determination of the sheriff shall not be admissible in evidence or be founded on in any judicial proceedings, of whatever nature, arising out of the death or out of any accident from which the death resulted.

(4) On the conclusion of the inquiry

    (a) the sheriff clerk shall send to the Lord Advocate a copy of the determination of the sheriff and, on a request being made to him, send to any Minister or Government Department or to the Health and Safety Commission, a copy of

        (i) the application made under section 1 of this Act;

        (ii) the transcript of the evidence;

        (iii) any report or documentary production used in the inquiry;

        (iv) the determination of the sheriff, and

    (b) the procurator fiscal shall send to the Registrar General of Births, Deaths and Marriages for Scotland the name and last known address of the person who has died and the date, place and cause of his death.

(5) Upon payment of such fee as may be prescribed in rules made under paragraph (i) of section 7(1) of this Act, any person—

    (a) may obtain a copy of the determination of the sheriff;

    (b) who has an interest in the inquiry may, within such period as may be prescribed in rules made under paragraph (j) of the said section 7(1), obtain a copy of the transcript of the evidence,

from the sheriff clerk.

Rules

[1] **7.**—(1) The Secretary of State may, by rules, provide in relation to inquiries under this Act—

    (a) as to the form of any document to be used in or for the purposes of such inquiries;

    (b) for the representation, on such conditions as may be specified in the rules, of any person who is entitled by virtue of this Act to appear at the inquiry;

    (c) for the authorisation by the sheriff of the taking and holding in safe custody of anything which it may be considered necessary to produce;

    (d) for the inspection by the sheriff or any person authorised by him of any land, premises, article, or other thing;

    (e) that written statements and reports may, on such conditions as may be specified in the rules, be admissible in lieu of parole evidence;

    (f) as to the duties, remuneration and other conditions of appointment of any assessor summoned under section 4 of this Act, and for keeping of lists of persons willing to act as such;

    (g) as to intimation of the holding of the inquiry;

    (h) as to the payment of fees to solicitors and expenses to witnesses and havers;

    (i) as to the payment of a fee by a person obtaining a copy of the determination of the sheriff or a copy of the transcript of the evidence;

D 99   (j) as to the period within which a person entitled may obtain a copy of the transcript of the evidence at the inquiry;

    (k) as to such other matters relating to procedure as the Lord Advocate thinks appropriate.

(2) The power to make rules conferred by any provision of this Act shall be exercisable by statutory instrument.

(3) Rules made by the Lord Advocate under this Act may contain such

incidental, consequential and supplemental provisions as appear to him to be necessary or proper for bringing the rules into operation and giving full effect thereto.

NOTE
[1] As amended by SI 1999/678, art.2, Sch. (effective May 19, 1999).

Minor and consequential amendments and repeals
    8. . . .

Application to continental shelf
    [1] **9.** For the purposes of this Act a death or any accident from which death has resulted which has occurred—
    (a) in connection with any activity falling within subsection (2) of section 11 of the Petroleum Act 1998; and
    (b) in that area, or any part of that area, in respect of which it is provided by Order in Council under subsection (1) of that section that questions arising out of acts or omissions taking place therein shall be determined in accordance with the law in force in Scotland,
shall be taken to have occurred in Scotland.

NOTE
[1] As amended by the Oil and Gas (Enterprise) Act 1982 (c. 23), Sch.3, para.34 and the Petroleum Act 1998 (c. 17), Sch.4 (effective February 15, 1999).

Interpretation, transitional, citation, commencement and extent
    [1] **10.**—(1) Any reference in this Act to any other enactment shall be construed as a reference to that enactment as amended by or under any other enactment including this Act.
    (2)–(3) [Repealed by the Statute Law (Repeals) Act 1989 (c. 43), Sched. 1, Pt I.]
    (4) This Act may be cited as the Fatal Accidents and Sudden Deaths Inquiry (Scotland) Act 1976.
    (5) [Repealed by the Statute Law (Repeals) Act 1989 (c. 43), Sched. 1, Pt I.]
    (6) This Act, other than subsections (4) and (5) of section 4 and section 9 of this Act, extends to Scotland only.

NOTE
[1] The Act was brought into force on March 1, 1977 by SI 1977/190.

Enforcement Abroad of Sheriff Court Judgments 1962

(SI 1962/1517)

[July 17, 1962]

The Lords of Council and Session, under and by virtue of the powers conferred upon them by section 34(1) of the Administration of Justice (Scotland) Act 1933 and of all other powers competent to them in that behalf, do hereby enact as follows:—

Interpretation
1. In this Act of Sederunt—
　"sheriff" includes sheriff-substitute;
　"sheriff clerk" includes sheriff clerk depute;
　"initial writ" means the statement of claim, petition, note of appeal, or
　　other document by which the action is initiated.
[1] **2.** An application for a certified copy of a judgment obtained in a sheriff court, made for the purpose of the enforcement of the judgment in a country other than a country to which Parts I and II of the Civil Jurisdiction and Judgments Act 1982 applies, shall be made in that sheriff court by minute lodged in the process in which the judgment was obtained. There shall be lodged with the minute either an extract decree setting forth the judgment or a copy of the judgment. The sheriff, on being satisfied, by affidavit or by other proper evidence, as to the purpose for which the application is being made, shall pronounce an order ordaining the sheriff clerk to issue a certified copy of the judgment. The certificate shall be in the following terms:—

　　　"I certify that the foregoing is a true copy of a judgment obtained
　　　in the　　　　　Sheriff Court and that this certificate is issued for the
　　　purpose of the enforcement of the judgment in a country other than a
　　　country to which Parts I and II of the Civil Jurisdiction and
　　　Judgments Act 1982 applies and in obedience to an order by the
　　　Sheriff of　　　　　dated

　　　　　　　　　　　　　　　　　　(Signed)
　　　　　　　　　　　　　　　　　　Sheriff Clerk."

NOTE
[1] As amended by SI 1986/1947.

3. There shall be issued along with the foregoing certificate the following further certificate also certified by the sheriff clerk—
　　A certificate, enumerating and identifying and having annexed to it; (1) a copy of the initial writ by which the proceedings were initiated, showing the manner in which the initial writ was served on the defender or respondent and whether the defender or respondent appeared thereto, and the objections made to the jurisdiction if any; (2) a copy of the pleadings, if any, in the proceedings; (3) a copy of the opinion or note, if any, of the sheriff, and (4) a statement of such other particulars as it may be necessary to give to the foreign tribunal in which it is sought to obtain execution of the judgment. Copies of the foregoing documents shall be supplied where necessary by the person making the application.

4. This Act of Sederunt may be cited as the Act of Sederunt (Enforcement Abroad of Sheriff Court Judgments) 1962, and shall come into operation on 17th July 1962.

Computer Evidence in the Sheriff Court 1969

(SI 1969/1643)

[18th November 1969]

The Lords of Council and Session, by virtue of the powers conferred upon them by section 34 of the Administration of Justice (Scotland) Act 1933 and section 15(6) of the Law Reform (Miscellaneous Provisions)(Scotland) Act 1968, do hereby enact and declare as follows:—

1. A party to any civil proceedings who wishes to rely on a statement contained in a document produced by a computer shall, not later than the date of closing the record, send to every other party to the proceedings a copy of the statement together with a notice in writing—
  (a) intimating that the party intends to rely on the statement;
  (b) stating that the statement is contained in a document produced by a computer; and
  [1] (c) informing the party to whom it is addressed that he may give a counter-notice in terms of paragraph 3 hereof;
and the party so giving notice may within fourteen days thereafter lodge in process a certificate in terms of section 13(4) of the Law Reform (Miscellaneous Provisions) (Scotland) Act 1968 relating to the document.

NOTE
[1] Substituted by SI 1970/456.

2. When a certificate in terms of section 13(4) of the Law Reform **D 235** (Miscellaneous Provisions) (Scotland) Act 1968 shall have been lodged in process, a copy thereof shall be sent to every other party to the proceedings within fourteen days after the date of the notice referred to in paragraph 1 hereof.

3. Any party who receives such a notice as is mentioned in paragraph 1 hereof may, within twenty-one days thereafter, by counter-notice in writing addressed to the party who served the notice, require him, within twenty-one days, to furnish him in writing with all or any of the following information—
  (a) any such information as might have been the subject of a certificate under section 13(4) of the Law Reform (Miscellaneous Provisions) (Scotland) Act 1968, except in so far as such information is the subject of a certificate lodged in process as aforesaid;
  (b) the name, occupation, business address and place of residence of a person occupying at the material time a responsible position in relation to each of (i) the operation of the device involved in the production of the document, (ii) the management of the activities for the purposes of which the computer was used to store or process information, (iii) the supply of information to the computer, (iv) the operation of the computer, and (v) the operation of any equipment by means of which the document containing the statement was produced by the computer; and
  (c) the name, occupation, business address and place of residence of the person who signed any certificate lodged in process in terms of

section 13(4) of the Law Reform (Miscellaneous Provisions) (Scotland) Act 1968.

4. Subject to the provisions of section 15(8) of the Law Reform (Miscellaneous Provisions) (Scotland) Act 1968, a party upon whom a counter-notice has been served in terms of paragraph 3 hereof shall not be entitled to rely upon the statement in the document to which the notice under paragraph 1 hereof related, unless the counter-notice shall have been withdrawn by the party who gave it or unless the court shall be satisfied that the counter-notice was complied with so far as was reasonably possible.

5. Any party to whom information is furnished under a counter-notice by virtue of paragraph 3 hereof may, not later than twenty-eight days before the date of the proof or trial, by notice in writing require that the party wishing to rely on the statement in the document produced by a computer should call as a witness any person of whom particulars were furnished under sub-paragraph (b) or (c) of paragraph 3 hereof.

6. (i) Subject to the provisions of section 15(8) of the Law Reform (Miscellaneous Provisions) (Scotland) Act 1968 a party who has been required to call any person as a witness in terms of paragraph 5 hereof shall not be entitled to rely upon the statement in the document to which the notice under paragraph 1 hereof related unless the notice requiring that person to be called as a witness shall have been withdrawn by the party who gave it, or unless that person shall be adduced as a witness, or unless the court shall be satisfied that such person is dead, or beyond the seas, or unfit by reason of his bodily or mental condition to attend as a witness, or cannot with reasonable diligence be identified or found, or cannot reasonably be expected (having regard to the passage of time and to all the circumstances) to have any recollection of matters relevant to the accuracy or otherwise of the statement in the document.

D 237   (ii) In the event that such person is not to be adduced as a witness for any reason aforesaid, the party wishing to rely on the statement in the document produced by a computer shall give notice in writing to every other party to the proceedings that such witness is not to be adduced and the reason therefor.

   (iii) The notice referred to in sub-paragraph (ii) hereof shall be given not later than fourteen days after the date of the notice under paragraph 5 hereof or, if such reason could not reasonably have become known to him within that period, immediately such reason shall become known.

7. This Act of Sederunt shall apply to all civil proceedings in the Sheriff Court.

8. This Act of Sederunt may be cited as the Act of Sederunt (Computer Evidence in the Sheriff Court) 1969, and shall come into operation on 1st December 1969.

D 253   **Interest in Sheriff Court Decrees or Extracts 1975**

(SI 1975/948)

[4th June 1975]

The Lords of Council and Session, under and by virtue of the powers conferred upon them by section 4 of the Administration of Justice (Scotland) Act 1972 and of all other powers competent to them in that behalf, do hereby enact and declare as follows:—

¹ **1.** In the case of any decree or extract in an action commenced on or after 1st July 1975 the provisions of section 9 of the Sheriff Courts (Scotland) Extracts Act 1892 as amended by the Act of Sederunt (Interest in Sheriff Court Decrees or Extracts) 1972 shall not apply. Instead there shall be substituted a new section 9 as follows:—

> "where interest is included in a decree or extract, it shall be deemed to be at the rate of eight *per centum per annum*, unless otherwise stated".

NOTE
¹ Twelve per cent substituted for eleven per cent, with effect from 5th April 1983, by SI 1983/409.

Fifteen per cent substituted for twelve per cent, with effect from 16th August 1985, by SI **D 254** 1985/1179.

Eight per cent substituted for fifteen per cent, with effect from 1st April 1993, by SI 1993/769.

2. This Act of Sederunt may be cited as the Act of Sederunt (Interest in Sheriff Court Decrees or Extracts) 1975, and shall come into operation on 2nd July 1975.

Fatal Accidents and Sudden Deaths Inquiry Procedure (Scotland) Rules 1977

(SI 1977/191)

[7th February 1977]

In exercise of the powers conferred on me by section 7(1) of the Fatal Accidents and Sudden Deaths Inquiry (Scotland) Act 1976 and of all other powers enabling me in that behalf I hereby make the following rules:—

Citation and commencement
1. These rules may be cited as the Fatal Accidents and Sudden Deaths Inquiry Procedure (Scotland) Rules 1977 and shall come into operation on 1st March 1977.

Interpretation
2.—(1) In these rules, unless the context otherwise requires,—
"the Act" means the Fatal Accidents and Sudden Deaths Inquiry (Scotland) Act 1976;
"inquiry" means an inquiry under the Act;
"officer of law" has the meaning assigned to it by section 462 of the Criminal Procedure (Scotland) Act 1975;
"procurator fiscal" has the meaning assigned to it by section 462 of the Criminal Procedure (Scotland) Act 1975;
"sheriff clerk" includes sheriff clerk depute and any person duly authorised to execute the duties of sheriff clerk.
(2) In these rules, unless the context otherwise requires, a reference to any enactment shall be construed as a reference to that enactment as amended or re-enacted by any subsequent enactment.
(3) The Interpretation Act 1889 shall apply for the interpretation of these rules as it applies for the interpretation of an Act of Parliament.

Application for holding of inquiry
3. The application for the holding of an inquiry in accordance with section 1(1) of the Act and the sheriff's first warrant thereon shall be in the case of such a death as is referred to in section 1(1)(a) of the Act in the form as nearly as may be of Form 1 of the Schedule to these rules, and in the case of

such a death as is referred to in section 1(1)(b) of the Act in the form as nearly as may be of Form 2 of the said Schedule.

D 294A *Notice of holding of inquiry*
   4.—(1) Intimation of the holding of an inquiry in accordance with section 3(2)(*a*) of the Act shall be made by notice in writing in the form as nearly as may be of Form 3 of the Schedule to these rules, given not less than 21 days before the date of the inquiry.
   (2) Such notice shall be given to the following persons, besides those specified in the said section 3(2)(*a*),—
   (*a*) in the case of such a death as is referred to in section 1(1)(*a*)(i) of the Act, to the Health and Safety Commission;
   (*b*) in the case of such a death as is referred to in section 1(1)(*a*)(ii) of the Act, to any minister, government department or other authority in whose legal custody the person who has died was at the time of his death;
   [1] (*c*) in the case of a death occurring in the circumstances specified in section 9 of the Act, or a death resulting from an accident occurring in those circumstances, to the Secretary of State for Employment;
   (*d*) in any case where it is competent for a minister or government department under any statute other than the Act to cause public inquiry to be made into the circumstances of the death, to such minister or government department.
   (3) Public notice of the holding of an inquiry in accordance with section 3(2)(*b*) of the Act shall be given by publishing in at least two newspapers circulating in the sheriff court district where the inquiry is to be held, not less than 21 days before the date of the inquiry, an advertisement in the form as nearly as may be of Form 4 of the Schedule to these rules.

NOTE
   [1] As amended by SI 1992/1568 (effective 3rd July 1992).

Custody of productions
   5. The sheriff may at the time of making an order for the holding of an inquiry or at any time thereafter, upon the application of the procurator
D 294/1 fiscal, or of any other person entitled to appear at the inquiry or at his own instance, grant warrant to officers of law to take possession of anything connected with the death which is the subject of inquiry and which it may be considered necessary to produce at the inquiry and to hold any such thing in safe custody, subject to inspection by any persons interested.

Inspection of land, premises, etc.
   6. The sheriff may at the time of making an order for the holding of an inquiry or at any time thereafter, upon the application of the procurator fiscal or of any other person entitled to appear at the inquiry or at his own instance, inspect or grant warrant for any person to inspect any land, premises, article or other thing the inspection of which the sheriff considers desirable for the purposes of the inquiry.

Representation
   7.—(1) The procurator fiscal may appear on his own behalf at an inquiry or be represented by an assistant or depute procurator fiscal or by Crown counsel.
   (2) Any person entitled to appear at an inquiry in terms of section 4(2) of the Act may appear on his own behalf or be represented by an advocate or a solicitor or, with the leave of the sheriff, by any other person.

Citation of witnesses or havers
   8. The citation of a witness or haver to appear at an inquiry shall be in the

form as nearly as may be of Form 5 of the Schedule to these rules, and an execution of citation in the form as nearly as may be of Form 6 of the said Schedule shall be sufficient evidence of such citation.

Adjournment of inquiry
9. The sheriff may at any time adjourn the inquiry to a time and place specified by him at the time of adjournment.

Written statements
10.—(1) The sheriff may admit in place of oral evidence by any person in an inquiry, to the like extent as such oral evidence, a written statement by that person signed by that person and sworn or affirmed to be true by that person before a notary public, commissioner for oaths or justice of the peace, or before a commissioner appointed by the sheriff for that purpose:
  Provided that such a statement may only be admitted if—
  (*a*) all persons who appear or are represented at the inquiry agree to its admission; or
  (*b*) the sheriff considers that its admission will not result in unfairness in the conduct of the inquiry to any person who appears or is represented at the inquiry.
  (2) A certificate that the statement has been so sworn and affirmed, annexed to the statement and signed by the person making the statement and by the person before whom it is sworn or affirmed, shall be sufficient evidence that it has been so sworn or affirmed.
  (3) Any statement which is admitted in evidence by virtue of this rule shall, unless the sheriff otherwise directs, be read aloud at the inquiry; and where the sheriff directs that a statement or any part of it shall not be read aloud he shall state his reason for so directing and, where appropriate, an account shall be given orally of what the sheriff has directed not to be read aloud.
  (4) Any document or object referred to as a production and identified in a written statement tendered in evidence under this rule shall be treated as if it had been produced and had been identified in court by the maker of the statement.

Sheriff's determination   D 294/2
11.—(1) The sheriff's determination shall be in writing and shall be signed by him.
  (2) The sheriff's determination shall, except in the circumstances specified in paragraph (3) of this rule, be read out by him in public.
  (3) Where the sheriff requires time to prepare his determination and considers that in the circumstances it is not reasonable to fix an adjourned sitting of the inquiry for the sole purpose of reading out the determination, the sheriff shall not be required to read out the determination, but the sheriff clerk shall send free of charge a copy of the determination, to the procurator fiscal and to any person who appeared or was represented at the inquiry and shall allow any person to inspect a copy of the determination at the sheriff clerk's office free of charge during the period of three months after the date when the determination was made.

Assessors
12.—(1) A request to the sheriff to summon a person to act as an assessor in terms of section 4(6) of the Act shall be made by written motion lodged with the sheriff clerk not less than seven days before the date of the inquiry.
  (2) The appointment of an assessor shall not affect the admissibility of expert evidence in the inquiry.

Recording of evidence

13. Evidence given in an inquiry shall be recorded in the same manner as evidence given in an ordinary civil cause in the sheriff court:

Provided that where the evidence shall have been taken down in shorthand it shall not be necessary to extend such evidence unless the sheriff shall so direct or unless a copy of the transcript of evidence shall be duly requested by any person entitled thereto in terms of the Act and these rules.

Time-limit for obtaining copy of transcript of evidence

14. A person shall be entitled to obtain a copy of the transcript of the evidence in accordance with section 6(5)(*b*) of the Act only if he makes application therefor to the sheriff clerk within a period of three months after the date when the sheriff's determination was made.

Fee on obtaining copy of determination, or of transcript of evidence

15.—(1) The fee payable upon obtaining a copy of the sheriff's determination in accordance with section 6(5)(*a*) of the Act shall be such fee as is payable to sheriff clerks for copying documents relating to civil proceedings in the sheriff court.

(2) The fee payable upon obtaining a copy of the transcript of the evidence in accordance with section 6(5)(*b*) of the Act shall be—

    (*a*) where the copy is made by a shorthand writer, such copying fee as is payable by the sheriff clerk to the shorthand writer;

    (*b*) where the copy is made by the sheriff clerk, such fee as is payable to sheriff clerks for copying documents relating to civil proceedings in the sheriff court.

Service of documents

16.—(1) The notice intimating the holding of an inquiry in accordance with section 3(2)(*a*) of the Act, the citation of a witness for precognition by the procurator fiscal, the citation of a witness or haver to attend at an inquiry, and any interlocutor, warrant or other order of the sheriff or writ following thereon issued in connection with an inquiry may be served on a person in any of the following manners:–

    (*a*) the procurator fiscal or the solicitor for any person entitled to appear at the inquiry, as appropriate, may post the document in a registered or recorded delivery letter addressed to the person on whom the document requires to be served at his residence or place of business or at any address specified by him for the purpose of receiving documents;

    (*b*) a police officer (where the document is issued by the procurator fiscal) or a sheriff officer may—

        (i) serve the document personally on the person on whom it requires to be served; or

        (ii) leave the document in the hands of an inmate or employee at that person's residence or place of business or any address specified by him for the purpose of receiving documents;

        (iii) introduce the document into that person's residence or place of business or any address so specified by means of a letterbox or other lawful means; or

        (iv) affix the document to the door of that person's residence or place of business or any place so specified;

D 294/3

Provided that when it proves difficult for any reason to serve any document on any person the sheriff, on being satisfied that all reasonable steps have been taken to serve it, may dispense with service of such document or order such other steps as he may think fit.

Dispensing power of sheriff
17. The sheriff may in his discretion relieve any person from the consequences of any failure to comply with the provisions of these rules if the failure resulted from mistake, oversight or any cause other than wilful non-observance of these rules and in granting such relief may impose such terms and conditions as appear to him to be just; and in any such case the sheriff may make such order as appears to him to be just regarding extension of time, lodging or amendment of papers or otherwise, so as to enable the inquiry to proceed as if such failure had not happened.

SCHEDULE

Rule 3   FORM 1

Under the Fatal Accidents and Sudden Deaths Inquiry (Scotland) Act 1976

To the Sheriff of   at (*place of court*)

The APPLICATION of the Procurator Fiscal for the District of

From information received by the applicant it appears that (*narrate briefly the apparent facts of the death*);

In terms of the said Act an inquiry requires to be held into the circumstances of said death.

May it therefore please your Lordship to fix a time and place for the holding by your Lordship of such in inquiry; to grant warrant to cite witnesses and havers to attend at such inquiry, at the instance of the applicant, and of any other person who may be entitled by virtue of said Act to appear thereat; to grant warrant to officers of law to take possession of, and hold in safe custody, subject to inspection by any person interested, anything which it may be considered necessary to produce at the inquiry.

According to Justice, &c.

(*Signature*)
Procurator Fiscal

(*Place and date*). The Sheriff having considered the foregoing application orders that inquiry into the circumstances of the death of   within designed, be held on the   day of   19 , at (*time*), within the Sheriff Court House at   ; grants warrant to cite witnesses and havers as craved; also grants warrant to officers of law to take possession of, and to hold in safe custody, subject to the inspection by any person interested, anything which it may be considered necessary to produce at the inquiry.

(*Signature*)

Rule 3   FORM 2   **D 294/4**

Under the Fatal Accidents and Sudden Deaths Inquiry (Scotland) Act 1976

To the Sheriff of   at (*place of court*)

The APPLICATION of the Procurator Fiscal for the District of

From information received by the applicant is appears that (*narrate briefly the apparent facts of the death*);

and it appears to the Lord Advocate to be expedient in the public interest that an inquiry under the said Act should be held into the circumstances of said death.
May it therefore please your Lordship to fix a time and place for the holding by your Lordship of such an inquiry; to grant warrant to cite witnesses and havers to attend at such inquiry, at the instance of the applicant and of any other person who may be entitled by virtue of said Act to appear thereat; to grant warrant to officers of law to take possession of, and hold in safe custody, subject to inspection by any person interested, anything which it may be considered necessary to produce at the inquiry.

According to Justice, &c.

(*Signature*)
Procurator Fiscal

(Place and date). The Sheriff having considered the foregoing application orders that inquiry into the circumstances of the death of   within designed, be held on the   day of   19 , at *(time)* within the Sheriff Court House at   ; grants warrant to cite witnesses and havers as craved; also grants warrant to officers of law to take possession of, and to hold in safe custody, subject to the inspection by any person interested, anything which it may be considered necessary to produce at the inquiry.

(Signature)

Rule 4(1)   FORM 3

(Address of procurator fiscal)

(Date)

(Name and address of person to whom notice is given)

Dear Sir

DEATH OF *(insert name of deceased)*

I have to intimate that an inquiry under the Fatal Accidents and Sudden Deaths Inquiry (Scotland) Act 1976 into the circumstances of the death of *(insert name and address of deceased)* will be held on   the   day of   at *(time)* within the Sheriff Court House at *(address)*.

* [You have the right to appear, call witnesses and lead evidence at the inquiry. You may attend in person or be represented by an advocate or a solicitor instructed by you or, with the leave of the sheriff, by some other person.]

Yours faithfully,

(Signature)
Procurator Fiscal

* To be inserted only when the person to whom notice is given is the wife, husband or nearest known relative, or the employer, of the deceased.

D 294/5 Rule 4(3)   FORM 4

ADVERTISEMENT

Under the Fatal Accidents and Sudden Deaths Inquiry (Scotland) Act 1976

The Sheriff of

will hold an inquiry on the   day of *(month)* 19 at *(time)* within the Sheriff Court House at *(address)* into the circumstances of the death of *(name, occupation, address)*.

(Signature)
Procurator Fiscal for the District of

Rule 8   FORM 5

To *(name and designation)*.

YOU are cited to attend at the Sheriff Court House at *(address)* on *(date)* at *(time)* as a witness at the instance of *(insert* "the Procurator Fiscal for the District of   " *or name and address of person calling witness)* at the INQUIRY then to be held into the circumstances of the DEATH of *(name and address of deceased)* [and are required to bring with you   ] and if you fail to attend you may be ordered to pay a penalty not exceeding*

(Signature and designation of procurator fiscal, police officer, sheriff officer or solicitor)

* (Insert penalty specified in rule [74(2)] of the First Schedule to the Sheriff Courts (Scotland) Act 1907 [as amended]).

Rule 8 FORM 6

I certify that on (*date*) I lawfully cited (*name and designation*) to attend at the Sheriff Court House at (*address*) on (*date*) at (*time*) as a witness at the instance of (*insert* "the Procurator Fiscal for the District of " *or name and address of person calling witness*) at the INQUIRY then to be held into the circumstances of the DEATH of (*name and address of deceased*) [and I required him to bring with him].

This I did by (*specify exactly how served*).

(*Signature and designation of procurator fiscal, police officer, sheriff officer or solicitor*)

Enforcement of Judgments under the Civil Jurisdiction and Judgments Act 1982, 1986

D 311

(S.I. 1986 No. 1947)

[13th November 1986]

The Lords of Council and Session, under and by virtue of the powers conferred on them by section 32 of the Sheriff Courts (Scotland) Act 1971, section 48 of the Civil Jurisdiction and Judgments Act 1982 and of all other powers enabling them in that behalf, do hereby enact and declare:—

Citation and commencement
1.—(1) This Act of Sederunt may be cited as the Act of Sederunt (Enforcement of Judgments under the Civil Jurisdiction and Judgments Act 1982) 1986 and shall come into operation on 1st January 1987.
(2) This Act of Sederunt shall be inserted in the Books of Sederunt.

Interpretation D 312
2.—[1] (1) In this Act of Sederunt—
"the 1982 Act" means the Civil Jurisdiction and Judgments Act 1982;
"the 1968 Convention" and "the Lugano Convention" have the meanings respectively assigned in section 1 of the 1982 Act;
"authentic instrument" means an instrument referred to in Articles 50 or 51 of the 1968 Convention and the Lugano Convention;
"court settlement" means a settlement referred to in Article 51 of the 1968 Convention and the Lugano Convention; and
"Ordinary Cause Rules" means the First Schedule to the Sheriff Courts (Scotland) Act 1907.
(2) A form referred to by number means the form so numbered in the Schedule to this Act of Sederunt or a form substantially to the same effect, with such variation as circumstances may require.

NOTE
[1] As amended by SI 1993/2346 (effective October 25, 1993).

Enforcement of sheriff court judgments in other parts of the United Kingdom (Money provisions)
3.—(1) An application for a certificate under paragraph 2 of Schedule 6 to the 1982 Act shall be made in writing to the sheriff clerk and shall be accompanied by an affidavit—
(a) stating the sum or aggregate of the sums, including expenses, payable and unsatisfied;
(b) verifying that the time for bringing an appeal against the judgment has expired and no appeal has been brought within that time, or that any appeal has been finally disposed of; and that enforcement of the

judgment has not been suspended and the time available for the enforcement has not expired; and

    (c) stating the address of the party entitled to enforce, and the usual or last known address of the party liable to execution on, the judgment.

    (2) A certificate under paragraph 4 of Schedule 6 to the 1982 Act shall be in Form 1 and be signed by the sheriff clerk.

Enforcement of sheriff court judgments in other parts of the United Kingdom (Non-money provisions)

    4.—(1) An application for a certified copy of an interlocutor or extract decree and, where appropriate, a copy of the note or opinion of the sheriff under paragraph 2 of Schedule 7 to the 1982 Act shall be made in writing to the sheriff clerk and shall be accompanied by an affidavit—

    (a) verifying that the time for bringing an appeal against the judgment has expired and no appeal has been brought within that time, or any appeal has been finally disposed of; and that enforcement of the judgment has not been suspended and the time available for the enforcement has not expired; and

    (b) stating the address of the party entitled to enforce, and the usual or last known address of the party liable to execution on, the judgment.

    (2) A copy of an interlocutor, decree, note or opinion issued under paragraph 4 of Schedule 7 to the 1982 Act shall have appended to it a certificate in Form 2 signed by the sheriff clerk.

Enforcement of sheriff court interlocutors and decrees in another Contracting State

    5.—[1] (1) Before an application is made under section 12 of the 1982 Act for a copy of a judgment or a certificate giving particulars relating to the judgment and the proceedings in which it was given, the party wishing to enforce the judgment shall serve the judgment on all parties against whom the judgment has been given in accordance with rule 5.4 or 5.5 of the Ordinary Cause Rules, as the case may be, accompanied by a notice in D 313 Form 4; and the execution of such service shall be in Form 5 unless a form of execution of service is provided by the person effecting service in the other Contracting State where service was effected.

    (2) An application under section 12 of the 1982 Act shall be made in writing to the sheriff clerk for—

    (*a*) a certificate in Form 3;

    (*b*) a certified copy interlocutor; and

    (*c*) if required, a certified copy of the opinion of the sheriff.

    (3) A certificate shall not be issued under sub-paragraph (2)(*a*) unless there is produced and lodged in the process of the cause an execution of service required under sub-paragraph (1).

NOTE

[1] As amended by SI 1993/2346 (effective 25th October 1993).

Recognition and enforcement in Scotland of foreign maintenance orders

    6.—[*Revoked by SI 1997/291, r.1.4, Sched. 2 (effective April 1, 1997).*]

    [1] **6A.**—(1) Paragraphs 5 and 6 shall apply to the recognition and enforcement of an authentic instrument or court settlement as they apply to the recognition and enforcement of a judgment under the 1982 Act, but with such modifications as circumstances may require.

    (2) Where paragraph 5 applies in relation to an authentic instrument, an application under section 12 of the 1982 Act shall be made, in writing, to the sheriff clerk for—

    (*a*) a certificate in Form 3A; and

    (*b*) a certified copy of the authentic instrument.

NOTE
¹ Inserted by SI 1993/2346 (effective October 25, 1993).

Consequential amendments
7.—(1) In paragraph 2 of the Act of Sederunt (Enforcement Abroad of Sheriff Court Judgments) 1962, for the word "abroad" wherever it occurs, substitute the words "in a country other than a country to which Parts I and II of the Civil Jurisdiction and Judgments Act 1982 applies".
(2) In rule 13(1) of the Act of Sederunt (Maintenance Orders (Reciprocal Enforcement) Act 1972 Rules) 1974, after the word "Act", where it second and third appears in that rule, insert the words "or any other enactment".

SCHEDULE D 315

Paragraph 3(2) FORM 1

CERTIFICATE BY SHERIFF CLERK UNDER SECTION 18 OF, AND PARAGRAPH 4(1) OF SCHEDULE 6 TO, THE CIVIL JURISDICTION AND JUDGMENTS ACT 1982

Sheriff Court (*address*)

.... (Pursuer) v. ....(Defender)

I,   Sheriff Clerk at   Sheriff Court,
hereby certify:—

1. That [AB] obtained judgment against [CD] in the above sheriff court on (*date*) for payment of   with   of expenses of which   is unsatisfied.

2. That the money provision in the judgment carries interest at the rate of   *per centum per annum* from the   day of   19   until payment.

3. That the time for appealing against the judgment has expired [and no appeal has been brought within that time] [*or* and an appeal having been brought within that time has been finally disposed of].

4. That enforcement of the judgment has not for the time being been suspended and that the time available for its enforcement has not expired.

5. That this certificate is issued under section 18 of, and paragraph 4(1) of Schedule 6 to, the Civil Jurisdiction and Judgments Act 1982 and paragraph 3(2) of the Act of Sederunt (Enforcement of Judgments under the Civil Jurisdiction and Judgments Act 1982) 1986.

Dated at (*place*) this   day of   19 .

(*Signed*)
Sheriff Clerk

Paragraph 4(2) FORM 2

CERTIFICATE BY SHERIFF CLERK UNDER SECTION 18 OF, AND PARAGRAPH 4(1)(B) OF SCHEDULE 7 TO, THE CIVIL JURISDICTION AND JUDGMENTS ACT 1982

Sheriff Court (*address*)

I,   Sheriff Clerk at   Sheriff Court,
hereby certify:—

1. That [AB] obtained judgment against [CD] in the above sheriff court on (*date*).

2. That the copy of the interlocutor attached is a true copy of the decree [*or other order*] [and that the copy of the note or opinion of the sheriff attached is a true copy thereof].

3. That the time for appealing against the interlocutor has expired [and no appeal has been brought within that time] [*or* and an appeal having been brought within that time has been finally disposed of].

4. That enforcement of the decree [*or other order*] has not for the time being been suspended and that the time available for its enforcement has not expired.

5. That this certificate is issued under section 18 of, and paragraph 4(1)(*b*) of Schedule 7 to, the Civil Jurisdiction and Judgments Act 1982 and paragraph 4(2) of the Act of Sederunt (Enforcement of Judgments under the Civil Jurisdiction and Judgments Act 1982) 1986.

Dated at (*place*) this   day of   19 .

(*Signed*)
Sheriff Clerk

D 316   **Paragraph 5(2)**   **FORM 3**

CERTIFICATE BY SHERIFF CLERK UNDER SECTION 12 OF THE CIVIL JURISDICTION AND JUDGMENTS ACT 1982

Sheriff Court (*address*)

.... (Pursuer) v. ....(Defender)

I,   Sheriff Clerk at   Sheriff Court,
hereby certify:—

1. That the initial writ raised by the pursuer, [AB] (*address*), was executed by citation of the defender, [CD] (*address*), served on him on the   day of   19 by (*state mode of service*).

2. That in the initial writ the pursuer sought [payment of the sum of £   in respect of (*state briefly the nature of the claim*) [and (*state other craves of the writ*)].

3. That [no] notice of intention to defend the action was lodged by the defender [on the   day of   19] [and lodged defences on the   day of   19].

4. That decree [*or other order*] was granted against the defender by the Sheriff of   at   for payment of the sum of £   [*or state briefly the terms of the interlocutor or opinion of the sheriff*] [and (*state briefly any other craves of the initial writ*)] together with expenses of the action in the sum of £   , all in terms of the certified copy interlocutor attached hereto.

5. That [no] objection to the jurisdiction of the court has been made [on the grounds that   ].

6. That the decree includes interest at the rate of   *per centum per annum* on the total of the sum of £   and expenses of £   from the   day of   19 until payment.

7. That the interlocutor containing the decree has been served on the defender.

8. That the time within which an appeal may be brought against the interlocutor [expires on   [*or* has expired]].

9. That an [*or* no] appeal against the interlocutor has been brought [and has been finally disposed of].

10. That enforcement of the decree has not for the time being been suspended and the time available for its enforcement has not expired.

11. That the whole pleadings of the parties are contained in the closed record [*or* initial writ] a copy of which is attached.

12. That the pursuer [*or* defender] benefited from legal aid.

13. That this certificate is issued under section 12 of the Civil Jurisdiction and Judgments Act 1982 and paragraph 5(2) of the Act of Sederunt (Enforcement of Judgments under the Civil Jurisdiction and Judgments Act 1982) 1986.

Dated at (*place*) this   day of   19

(*Signed*)
Sheriff Clerk

Paragraph 6A(2)   [1] FORM 3A

CERTIFICATE BY SHERIFF CLERK UNDER SECTION 12 OF THE CIVIL JURISDICTION AND JUDGMENTS ACT 1982 (AUTHENTIC INSTRUMENTS)

Sheriff Court (*address*)

Authentic Instrument between (*names of parties*)

I, (*name*) sheriff clerk at (*name of court*) Sheriff Court, (*address*) hereby certify:—   **D 316/1**

1. That the attached copy instrument is a true copy of an authentic instrument registered in the Sheriff Court Books on (*date*).

2. That a copy of the authentic instrument so registered was served on the said (*name of debtor*) on (*date*).

3. That (*state briefly the obligation contained in the authentic instrument*).

4. That enforcement of the authentic instrument has not for the time being been suspended and the time available for enforcement has not expired.

5. That this certificate is issued under section 12 of the Civil Jurisdiction and Judgments Act 1982 as modified by the Civil Jurisdiction and Judgments (Authentic Instruments and Court Settlements) Order 1993.

Dated at (*insert place*) this   day of   19   .

(*Signed*)
Sheriff Clerk

NOTE
[1] Inserted by SI 1993/2346 (effective October 25, 1993).

Paragraph 5(1)   FORM 4

NOTICE TO ACCOMPANY SERVICE COPY OF JUDGMENT

To [AB] (*address*)

You are hereby served with a copy of the interlocutor of the Sheriff of   at   given on the   day of   19   . [In terms of this interlocutor you are required to (*state requirements of interlocutor*). Your failure to do so may result in further steps being taken to enforce the interlocutor.]

(*Signed*)
(*Address*)
Solicitor [*or* Sheriff Officer]

(*Place and date*)

EXECUTION OF SERVICE OF JUDGMENT AND NOTICE WHERE SERVICE EFFECTED BY OFFICER OF COURT
OR SOLICITOR IN SCOTLAND

(place and date)

I, [AB] *(address)*, hereby certify that upon the   day of   19 , I duly served a
copy of this judgment together with notice in terms of paragraph 5(1) of the Act of Sederunt
(Enforcement of Judgments under the Civil Jurisdiction and Judgments Act 1982) 1986 upon
[CD], defender. This I did by posting *(set forth mode of service; if by officer and not by post,
add* in presence of EF *(address)* witness, hereto with me subscribing).

> *(Signed)*
> *(Address)*
> Solicitor for Pursuer
> [*or* Defender]
>
> [or
>
> *(Signed)*
> Sheriff Officer
>
> *(Signed)*
> Witness]

Paragraph 6(8)   FORM 6

[*Revoked by SI 1997/291, r.1.4, Sch.2 (effective April 1, 1997).*]

D 468   **Summary Suspension 1993**

(SI 1993/3128)

[December 10, 1993]

The Lords of Council and Session, under and by virtue of the powers
conferred on them by section 32 of the Sheriff Courts (Scotland) Act 1971
and of all other powers enabling them in that behalf, having approved, with
modifications, draft rules submitted to them by the Sheriff Court Rules
Council in accordance with section 34 of that Act, do hereby enact and
declare:

D 469 *Citation and commencement*
    1.—(1) This Act of Sederunt may be cited as the Act of Sederunt
(Summary Suspension) 1993 and shall come into force on 1st January 1994.
    (2) This Act of Sederunt shall be inserted in the Books of Sederunt.

Summary application for suspension of charge
    2. Where a charge for payment has been executed on any decree to which
section 5(5) of the Sheriff Courts (Scotland) Act 1907 applies the person so
charged may apply to the sheriff in the sheriff court having jurisdiction over
him for suspension of such charge and diligence.

Sist of diligence
    3.—(1) On sufficient caution being found or other security given for—
    (a) the sum charged for with interest and expenses, and
    (b) a further sum to be fixed by the sheriff in respect of expenses to be
         incurred in the suspension process.
the sheriff may sist diligence, order intimation and answers, and proceed to
dispose of the cause in a summary manner.

(2) The following rules of the Ordinary Cause Rules 1993 shall, with the necessary modifications, apply to an applicant under paragraph 2—
  rule 27.4 (methods of finding caution or giving security)
  rule 27.5 (cautioners and guarantors)
  rule 27.6 (forms of bonds of caution and other securities)
  rule 27.7 (sufficiency of caution or security and objections)
  rule 27.8 (insolvency or death of cautioner or guarantor).

Objections
4. Where objections are taken to the competency or regularity of suspension proceedings, the decision of the sheriff on such objections may be appealed to the sheriff principal whose decision shall be final and not subject to appeal.

Savings for proceedings arising out of causes already commenced
5. Nothing in this Act of Sederunt shall affect suspension proceedings arising out of causes commenced before the date of coming into force of this Act of Sederunt, which shall proceed according to the law and practice in force immediately before that date.

Act of Sederunt (Summary Applications, Statutory Applications and Appeals etc. Rules) 1999   D 502

(SI 1999/929)

[19th March 1999]

ARRANGEMENT OF RULES

CHAPTER 1: GENERAL

D 503   CHAPTER 3: RULES ON APPLICATIONS UNDER SPECIFIC STATUTES

PART I

ADMINISTRATION OF JUSTICE (SCOTLAND) ACT 1972

PART II

BETTING AND GAMING APPEALS

PART III

COAL MINING SUBSIDENCE ACT 1991

PART IV

CONVEYANCING AND FEUDAL REFORM (SCOTLAND) ACT 1970

PART V

COPYRIGHT, DESIGNS AND TRADE MARKS

PART VI

DRUG TRAFFICKING ACT 1994

PART VII

LICENSING (SCOTLAND) ACT 1976

PART VIII

D 504

MENTAL HEALTH (SCOTLAND) ACT 1984

PART IX

PROCEEDS OF CRIME (SCOTLAND) ACT 1995

PART X

RATING (DISABLED PERSONS) ACT 1978

PART XI

REPRESENTATION OF THE PEOPLE ACT 1983

PART XII

REQUESTS OR APPLICATIONS UNDER THE MODEL LAW ON INTERNATIONAL COMMERCIAL ARBITRATION

PART XIII

SEX DISCRIMINATION ACT 1975

PART XIV

ACCESS TO HEALTH RECORDS ACT 1990

PART XV

RACE RELATIONS ACT 1976

PART XVI

ADULTS WITH INCAPACITY (SCOTLAND) ACT 2000

PART XVII   **D 506**

ANTI-TERRORISM, CRIME AND SECURITY ACT 2001

PART XVIII

LOCAL GOVERNMENT (SCOTLAND) ACT 1973

PART IX

PROCEEDS OF CRIME ACT 2002

PART XXVII

ANTISOCIAL BEHAVIOUR ETC. (SCOTLAND) ACT 2004

D 506/2

PART XXVIII

LAND REFORM (SCOTLAND) ACT 2003

The Lords of Council and Session, under and by virtue of the powers conferred on them by Schedule 1, paragraphs 24(1), 28D and 28(2), Schedule 2, paragraph 7 and Schedule 3, paragraph 13(3) to the Betting Gaming and Lotteries Act 1963, Schedule 2, paragraphs 33(1), 34(1), 45 and 47, and Schedule 9, paragraph 15 to the Gaming Act 1968, section 32 of the Sheriff Courts (Scotland) Act 1971, sections 66(5A) and 75 of the Sex Discrimination Act 1975, section 39(9) of the Licensing (Scotland) Act 1976, Schedule 3, paragraph 12 to the Lotteries and Amusements Act 1976, sections 136, 139, 146, 147, 152, 153, 182(3) and 185 of the Representation of the People Act 1983, sections 114(3), 204(3) and 231(3) of the Copyright, Designs and Patents Act 1988, section 19(3) of the Trade Marks Act 1994, section 46 of the Drug Trafficking Act 1994, Regulation 5(3) of the Olympics Association Right (Infringement Proceedings) Regulations 1995, and sections 31(5) and 48 of, and Schedule 1, paragraph 11 to, the Proceeds of Crime (Scotland) Act 1995 and of all other powers enabling them in that behalf, having approved draft rules submitted to them by the Sheriff Court Rules Council in accordance with section 34 of the Sheriff Courts (Scotland) Act 1971, do hereby enact and declare:

CHAPTER 1

GENERAL

Citation and commencement
    1.1—(1) This Act of Sederunt may be cited as the Act of Sederunt (Summary Applications, Statutory Applications and Appeals etc. Rules) 1999 and shall come into force on 1st July 1999.
    (2) This Act of Sederunt shall be inserted in the Books of Sederunt.

Interpretation
    1.2—(1) In this Act of Sederunt, unless the context otherwise requires—
      "Ordinary Cause Rules" means the First Schedule to the Sheriff Courts (Scotland) Act 1907;
      "sheriff clerk" includes sheriff clerk depute; and
      "summary application" has the meaning given by section 3(p) of the Sheriff Courts (Scotland) Act 1907.
    (2) Unless the context otherwise requires, any reference in this Act of Sederunt to a specified Chapter, Part or rule shall be construed as a **D 506/3** reference to the Chapter, Part or rule bearing that number in this Act of Sederunt, and a reference to a specified paragraph, sub-paragraph or head shall be construed as a reference to the paragraph, sub-paragraph or head so numbered or lettered in the provision in which that reference occurs.
    (3) Any reference in this Act of Sederunt to a numbered Form shall, unless the context otherwise requires, be construed as a reference to the Form so numbered in Schedule 1 to this Act of Sederunt and includes a form substantially to the same effect with such variation as circumstances may require.

Revocation
    1.3 The Acts of Sederunt mentioned in column (1) of Schedule 2 to this Act of Sederunt are revoked to the extent specified in column (3) of that Schedule.

Application
    1.4 Unless otherwise provided in this Act of Sederunt or in any other enactment, any application or appeal to the sheriff shall be by way of summary application and the provisions of Chapter 2 of this Act of Sederunt shall apply accordingly.

CHAPTER 2

SUMMARY APPLICATION RULES

PART I

INTERPRETATION

Interpretation
    2.1 In this Chapter, unless the context otherwise requires—
      "decree" includes any judgment, deliverance, interlocutor, act, order, finding or authority which may be extracted;
      "defender" means any person other than the pursuer who is a party to a summary application; and
      "pursuer" means any person making a summary application.

PART II

GENERAL RULES

Application
2.2 This Part applies to summary applications.

Relief from failure to comply with rules
2.3—(1) The sheriff may relieve a party from the consequences of failure to comply with a provision in this Part which is shown to be due to mistake, oversight or other excusable cause, on such conditions as he thinks fit.

(2) Where the sheriff relieves a party from the consequences of a failure to comply with a provision in this Part of these Rules under paragraph (1), he may make such order as he thinks fit to enable the summary application to proceed as if the failure to comply with the provision had not occurred.

The initial writ
2.4—(1) Unless otherwise prescribed by any other enactment, a summary application shall be commenced by initial writ in Form 1.

(2) The initial writ shall be written, typed or printed on A4 size paper of durable quality and shall not be backed or folded.

(3) Where the pursuer has reason to believe that an agreement exists **D 507** prorogating jurisdiction over the subject-matter of the summary application to another court, the initial writ shall contain details of that agreement.

(4) Where the pursuer has reason to believe that proceedings are pending before another court involving the same cause of action and between the same parties as those named in the instance of the initial writ, the initial writ shall contain details of those proceedings.

(5) An article of condescendence shall be included in the initial writ averring—

 (a) the ground of jurisdiction; and

 (b) the facts upon which the ground of jurisdiction is based.

(6) Where the residence, registered office or place of business, as the case may be, of the defender is not known and cannot reasonably be ascertained, the pursuer shall set out in the instance of the initial writ that the whereabouts of the defender are not known and aver in the condescendence what steps have been taken to ascertain his present whereabouts.

(7) The initial writ shall be signed by the pursuer or his solicitor (if any) and the name and address of that solicitor shall be stated on the back of every service copy of that writ.

(8) The initial writ shall include averments about those persons who appear to the pursuer to have an interest in the application and in respect of whom a warrant for citation is sought.

[1] (9) Where warrant to arrest on the dependence is sought, the initial writ shall include averments to justify the grant of such a warrant.

NOTE
[1] Inserted by the Act of Sederunt (Ordinary Cause, Summary Application and Small Claim Rules) Amendment (Miscellaneous) 2004 (SSI 2004/197) (effective May 21, 2004), para.3(2).

Order for intimation to interested persons by sheriff
2.5 The sheriff may make an order for intimation to any person who appears to him to have an interest in the summary application.

Time limits
2.6—[1] (1) This rule applies to a summary application where the time within which the application being an appeal under statute or an application in the nature of an appeal may be made is not otherwise prescribed.

(2) An application to which this rule applies shall be lodged with the

sheriff clerk within 21 days after the date on which the decision, order, scheme, determination, refusal or other act complained of was intimated to the pursuer.

(3) On special cause shown, the sheriff may hear an application to which this rule applies notwithstanding that it was not lodged within the period prescribed in paragraph (2).

NOTE
[1] As amended by the Act of Sederunt (Ordinary Cause, Summary Application and Small Claim Rules) Amendment (Miscellaneous) 2004 (SSI 2004/197) (effective May 21, 2004), para.3(3).

Warrants, forms and certificate of citation
2.7—(1) Subject to paragraph (2), a warrant for citation or intimation may be signed by the sheriff or sheriff clerk.

[3] (1A) A warrant for arrestment on the dependence may be signed by the sheriff, if the sheriff considers it appropriate.

(2) A warrant containing a period of notice shorter than the period of notice to be given to a defender under rule 3.6(1)(a) or (b), as the case may be, of the Ordinary Cause Rules or any other warrant which the sheriff clerk may not sign, shall be signed by the sheriff.

D 508 (3) Where the sheriff clerk refuses to sign a warrant which he may sign, the party presenting the summary application may apply to the sheriff for the warrant.

(4) Where citation is necessary—
[1] (a) the warrant of citation shall, subject to paragraphs (5) and (7A)(a) and rule 3.18.3(1) (appeals under section 103J of the Local Government (Scotland) Act 1973), be in Form 2; and
[1] (b) citation shall, subject to paragraphs (7) and (7A)(b) and rules 2.13 (service where address of person is not known) and 3.18.3(2) (appeals under section 103J of the Local Government (Scotland) Act 1973), be in Form 3.

(5) Where a time to pay direction under the Debtors (Scotland) Act 1987 may be applied for by the defender, the warrant of citation shall be in Form 4.

(6) Where a warrant of citation in accordance with Form 4 is appropriate, there shall be served on the defender (with the initial writ and warrant) a notice in Form 5.

(7) Where a time to pay direction under the Debtors (Scotland) Act 1987 may be applied for by the defender, citation shall be in Form 6 which shall be attached to a copy of the initial writ and warrant of citation.

[2] (7A) In a summary application falling within section 1(1)(b) or (c) of the Mortgage Rights (Scotland) Act 2001—
(a) the warrant of citation shall be in Form 6A; and
(b) citation shall be in Form 6B which shall be attached to a copy of the initial writ and warrant of citation.

(8) Where citation is necessary, the certificate of citation shall be in Form 7 which shall be attached to the initial writ.

(9) Where citation is by a sheriff officer, one witness shall be sufficient for the execution of citation.

(10) Where citation is by a sheriff officer, the certificate of citation shall be signed by the sheriff officer and the witness and shall state—
(a) the method of citation; and
(b) where the method of citation was other than personal or postal citation, the full name and designation of any person to whom the citation was delivered.

(11) Where citation is executed under paragraph (3) of rule 2.11 (depositing or affixing by sheriff officer), the certificate shall include a statement—

(a) of the method of service previously attempted;
(b) of the circumstances which prevented such service being executed; and
(c) that a copy of the document was sent in accordance with the provisions of paragraph (4) of that rule.

NOTE
[1] As amended by the Act of Sederunt (Summary Applications, Statutory Applications and Appeals etc. Rules) Amendment (No.2) (Local Government (Scotland) Act 1973) 2002 (SSI 2002/130), para.2(2).
[2] Inserted by the Act of Sederunt (Amendment of Ordinary Cause Rules and Summary Applications, Statutory Applications and Appeals etc. Rules) (Applications under the Mortgage Rights (Scotland) Act 2001) 2002 (SSI 2002/7), para.3(2)(c).
[3] Inserted by the Act of Sederunt (Ordinary Cause, Summary Application and Small Claim Rules) Amendment (Miscellaneous) 2004 (SSI 2004/197) (effective May 21, 2004), para.3(4).

Orders against which caveats may be lodged
2.8 A person may lodge a caveat against an interim order (other than an order under section 1 of the Administration of Justice (Scotland) Act 1972 (orders for inspection of documents and other property, etc.)) sought before service of the initial writ.

Form, lodging and renewal of caveats   **D 508/1**
2.9—(1) A caveat shall be in Form 8 and shall be lodged with the sheriff clerk.
(2) A caveat shall remain in force for a period of one year from the date on which it was lodged and may be renewed on its expiry for a further period of one year and yearly thereafter.
(3) Where a caveat has been lodged and has not expired, no order in respect of which the caveat was lodged may be pronounced unless the sheriff is satisfied that all reasonable steps have been taken to afford the person who lodged the caveat an opportunity of being heard; and the sheriff may continue the hearing on such an order until he is satisfied that such steps have been taken.

Postal service or intimation
2.10—(1) In any summary application in which service or intimation of any document or citation of any person may be by recorded delivery, such service, intimation or citation shall be by the first class recorded delivery service.
(2) Notwithstanding the terms of section 4(2) of the Citation Amendment (Scotland) Act 1882 (time from which period of notice reckoned), where service or intimation is by post, any period of notice contained in the warrant of citation shall run from the beginning of the day after the date of posting.
(3) On the face of the envelope used for postal service or intimation under this rule there shall be written or printed the following notice:—
"This envelope contains a citation to or intimation from (*specify the court*). If delivery cannot be made at the address shown it is to be returned immediately to:— The Sheriff Clerk (*insert address of sheriff clerk's office*).".
(4) The certificate of citation or intimation in the case of postal service shall have attached to it any relevant postal receipts.

Service within Scotland by sheriff officer
2.11—(1) An initial writ, decree, charge, warrant or any other order or writ following upon such initial writ or decree served by a sheriff officer on any person shall be served—
(a) personally; or
(b) by being left in the hands of a resident at the person's dwelling place or an employee at his place of business.

(2) Where service is executed under paragraph (1)(b), the certificate of citation or service shall contain the full name and designation of any person in whose hands the initial writ, decree, charge, warrant or other order or writ, as the case may be, was left.

(3) Where a sheriff officer has been unsuccessful in executing service in accordance with paragraph (1), he may, after making diligent enquiries, serve the document question by—

    (a) depositing it in that person's dwelling place or place of business; or

    (b) affixing it to the door of that person's dwelling place or place of business.

(4) Subject to rule 2.18 (service of schedule of arrestment), where service is executed under paragraph (3), the sheriff officer shall, as soon as possible after such service, send a letter containing a copy of the document by ordinary first class post to the address at which he thinks it most likely that the person on whom service has been executed may be found.

[1] (5) Where the firm which employs the sheriff officer has in its possession—

D 509

    (a) the document or a copy of it certified as correct by the pursuer's solicitor, the sheriff officer may serve the writ upon the defender without having the document or certified copy in his possession, in which case he shall if required to do so by the person on whom service is executed and within a reasonable time of being so required, show the document or certified copy to the person; or

    (b) a certified copy of the interlocutor pronounced allowing service of the document, the sheriff officer may serve the document without having in his possession the certified copy interlocutor if he has in his possession a facsimile copy of the certified copy interlocutor (which he shall show, if required, to the person on whom service is executed).

NOTE

[1] Inserted by the Act of Sederunt (Ordinary Cause, Summary Application, Summary Cause and Small Claim Rules) Amendment (Miscellaneous) 2003 (SSI 2003/26), para.3(3) (effective January 24, 2003).

Service on persons furth of Scotland

[1,2] **2.12**—(1) Subject to the following provisions of this rule, an initial writ, decree, charge, warrant or any other order or writ following upon such initial writ or decree served on a person furth of Scotland shall be served—

    (a) at a known residence or place of business in England, Wales, Northern Ireland, the Isle of Man, the Channel Islands or any country with which the United Kingdom does not have a convention providing for service of writs in that country—

        (i) in accordance with the rules for personal service under the domestic law of the place in which service is to be executed; or

        (ii) by posting in Scotland a copy of the document in question in a registered letter addressed to the person at his residence or place of business;

    (b) in a country which is a party to the Hague Convention on the Service Abroad of Judicial and Extra-Judicial Documents in Civil or Commercial Matters dated 15th November 1965 or the Convention in Schedule 1 or 3C to the Civil Jurisdiction and Judgments Act 1982—

        (i) by a method prescribed by the internal law of the country where service is to be executed for the service of documents in domestic actions upon persons who are within its territory;

        (ii) by or through the central, or other appropriate, authority in the country where service is to be executed at the request of the Secretary of State for Foreign and Commonwealth Affairs;

        (iii) by or through a British Consular Office in the country where service is to be executed at the request of the Secretary of State for Foreign and Commonwealth Affairs;

  (iv) where the law of the country in which the person resides permits, by posting in Scotland a copy of the document in a registered letter addressed to the person at his residence; or

  (v) where the law of the country in which service is to be executed permits, service by an *huissier*, other judicial officer or competent official of the country where service is to be executed; or

(c) in a country with which the United Kingdom has a convention on the service of writs in that country other than the conventions mentioned in sub-paragraph (b), by one of the methods approved in the relevant convention.

[2] (1A) In a country to which the Council Regulation applies, service—

(a) may be effected by the methods prescribed in paragraph (1)(b)(ii) or (iii) only in exceptional circumstances; and

(b) is effected only if the receiving agency has informed the person that acceptance of service may be refused on the ground that the document has not been translated in accordance with paragraph (6). **D 510**

(2) Any document which requires to be posted in Scotland for the purposes of this rule shall be posted by a solicitor or a sheriff officer, and on the face of the envelope there shall be written or printed the notice set out in rule 2.10(3).

(3) In the case of service by a method referred to in paragraph (1)(b)(ii) and (iii), the pursuer shall—

(a) send a copy of the writ and warrant of service with citation attached, or other document, as the case may be, with a request for service by the method indicated in the request to the Secretary of State for Foreign and Commonwealth Affairs; and

(b) lodge in process a certificate signed by the authority which executed service stating that it has been, and the manner in which it was, served.

(4) In the case of service by a method referred to in paragraph (1)(b)(v), the pursuer or the sheriff officer shall—

(a) send a copy of the writ and warrant for service with citation attached, or other document, as the case may be, with a request for service by the method indicated in the request to the official in the country in which service is to be executed; and

(b) lodge in process a certificate of the official who executed service stating that it has been, and the manner in which it was, served.

(5) Where service is executed, in accordance with paragraph (1)(a)(i) or (1)(b)(i) other than on another party in the United Kingdom, the Isle of Man or the Channel Islands, the party executing service shall lodge a certificate by a person who is conversant with the law of the country concerned and who practises or has practised law in that country or is a duly accredited representative of the Government of that country, stating that the method of service employed is in accordance with the law of the place where service was executed.

(6) Every writ, document, citation or notice on the face of the envelope mentioned in rule 2.10(3) shall be accompanied by a translation in—

[2] (a) an official language of the country in which service is to be executed; or

(b) in a country to which the Council Regulation applies, a language of the member state of transmission that is understood by the person on whom service is being executed.

(7) A translation referred to in paragraph (6) shall be certified as correct by the person making it and the certificate shall—

(a) include his full name, address and qualifications; and

(b) be lodged with the execution of citation or service.

[2] (8) In this rule "the Council Regulation" means Council Regulation

(EC) No. 1348/2000 on the service in the Member States of judicial and extrajudicial documents in civil or commercial matters.

NOTE
[1] As amended by the Act of Sederunt (Ordinary Cause, Summary Application, Summary Cause and Small Claim Rules) Amendment (Miscellaneous) 2003 (SSI 2003/26), para.3(4) (effective January 24, 2003).
[2] As amended and inserted by the Act of Sederunt (Ordinary Cause, Summary Application and Small Claim Rules) Amendment (Miscellaneous) 2004 (SSI 2004/197) (effective May 21, 2004), para.3(4).

Service where address of person is not known
2.13—(1) Where the address of a person to be cited or served with a document is not known and cannot reasonably be ascertained, the sheriff shall grant warrant for citation or service upon that person by—

D 510/1
    (a) the publication of an advertisement in Form 9 in a specified newspaper circulating in the area of the last known address of that person; or
    (b) displaying on the walls of court a copy of the instance and crave of the initial writ, the warrant of citation and a notice in Form 10;
and any period of notice contained in the warrant of citation shall run from the date of publication of the advertisement or display on the walls of court, as the case may be.

(2) Where service requires to be executed under paragraph (1), the pursuer shall lodge a service copy of the initial writ and a copy of any warrant

D 511
of citation with the sheriff clerk from whom they may be uplifted by the person for whom they are intended.

(3) Where a person has been cited or served in accordance with paragraph (1) and, after the summary application has commenced, his address becomes known, the sheriff may allow the initial writ to be amended subject to such conditions as to re-service, intimation, expenses or transfer of the summary application as he thinks fit.

(4) Where advertisement in a newspaper is required for the purpose of citation or service under this rule, a copy of the newspaper containing the advertisement shall be lodged with the sheriff clerk by the pursuer.

(5) Where display on the walls of court is required under paragraph (1)(b), the pursuer shall supply to the sheriff clerk for that purpose a certified copy of the instance and crave of the initial writ and any warrant of citation.

Persons carrying on business under trading or descriptive name
2.14—(1) A person carrying on a business under a trading or descriptive name may be designed in the instance of the initial writ by such trading or descriptive name alone, and an extract of a—
    (a) decree pronounced in the sheriff court; or
    (b) decree proceeding upon any deed, decree arbitral, bond, protest of a bill, promissory note or banker's note or upon any other obligation or document on which execution may proceed, recorded in the sheriff court books,
against such person under such trading or descriptive name, shall be a valid warrant for diligence against such person.

(2) An initial writ, decree, charge, warrant or any other order or writ following upon such initial writ or decree in a summary application in which a person carrying on business under a trading or descriptive name is designed in the instance of the initial writ by that name shall be served—
    (a) at any place of business or office at which such business is carried on within the sheriffdom of the sheriff court in which the cause is brought; or
    (b) where there is no place of business within that sheriffdom, at any place where such business is carried on (including the place of

business or office of the clerk or secretary of any company, corporation or association or firm).

Endorsation unnecessary
2.15 An initial writ, decree, charge, warrant or any other order or writ following upon such initial writ or decree may be served, enforced or otherwise lawfully executed anywhere in Scotland without endorsation by a sheriff clerk and, if executed by a sheriff officer, may be so executed by a sheriff officer of the court which granted it or by a sheriff officer of the sheriff court district in which it is to be executed.

Re-service
2.16 Where it appears to the sheriff that there has been any failure or irregularity in citation or service on a person, he may order the pursuer to re-serve the initial writ on such conditions as the sheriff thinks fit.

No objection to regularity of citation, service or intimation
2.17—(1) A person who appears in a summary application shall not be entitled to state any objection to the regularity of the execution of citation, service or intimation on him, and his appearance shall remedy any defect in such citation, service or intimation.
(2) Nothing in paragraph (1) shall preclude a party from pleading that the court has no jurisdiction.

Service of schedule of arrestment **D 512**
2.18 If a schedule of arrestment has not been personally served on an arrestee, the arrestment shall have effect only if a copy of the schedule is also sent by registered post or the first class recorded delivery service to—
(a) the last known place of residence of the arrestee; or
(b) if such a place of residence is not known, or if the arrestee is a firm or corporation, to the arrestee's principal place of business if known, or, if not known, to any known place of business of the arrestee,
and the sheriff officer shall, on the certificate of execution, certify that this has been done and specify the address to which the copy of the schedule was sent.

Arrestment on dependence before service
2.19—(1) An arrestment on the dependence of a summary application used before service shall cease to have effect if the initial writ is not served within 20 days from the date of arrestment and either—
(a) in the case where the pursuer is entitled to minute for decree in absence on the expiry of a period of notice contained in the warrant of citation, decree in absence has not been pronounced within 20 days after the expiry of the period of notice; or
(b) in the case where the pursuer is not entitled to minute for decree in absence prior to the first hearing of the summary application, there is no appearance by the pursuer at the first hearing and the summary application drops from the roll.
(2) After such an arrestment has been executed, the party who executed it shall forthwith report the execution to the sheriff clerk.

Movement of arrested property
2.20—(1) Any person having an interest may apply by motion for a warrant authorising the movement of a vessel or cargo which is the subject of an arrestment to found jurisdiction or on the dependence of a summary application.
(2) Where the court grants a warrant sought under paragraph (1), it may make such further order as it thinks fit to give effect to that warrant.

Transfer to another sheriff court

2.21—(1) The sheriff may, on cause shown, remit a summary application to another sheriff court.

(2) Subject to paragraph (4), where a summary application in which there are two or more defenders has been brought in the sheriff court of the residence or place of business of one of them, the sheriff may transfer the summary application to any other sheriff court which has jurisdiction over any of the defenders.

(3) Subject to paragraph (4), where a plea of no jurisdiction is sustained, the sheriff may transfer the summary application to the sheriff court before which it appears to him the summary application ought to have been brought.

(4) The sheriff shall not transfer a summary application to another sheriff court under paragraph (2) or (3) except—

(a) on the motion of a party; and

(b) where he considers it expedient to do so having regard to the convenience of the parties and their witnesses.

(5) On making an or er under paragraph (1), (2) or (3), the sheriff—

(a) shall state his reasons for doing so in the interlocutor; and

(b) may make the order on such conditions as to expenses or otherwise as he thinks fit.

(6) The court to which a summary application is transferred under paragraph (1), (2) or (3) shall accept the summary application.

D 513	(7) A transferred summary application shall proceed in all respects as if it had been originally brought in the court to which it is transferred.

(8) An interlocutor transferring a summary application may, with leave of the sheriff, be appealed to the sheriff principal but shall not be subject to appeal to the Court of Session.

Applications for time to pay directions

2.22—(1) This rule applies to a summary application in which a time to pay direction may be applied for under the Debtors (Scotland) Act 1987.

(2) A defender may apply for a time to pay direction and, where appropriate, for recall or restriction of an arrestment—

(a) by appearing and making the appropriate motion at a diet fixed for hearing of the summary application;

(b) except where the warrant of citation contains a shorter period of notice than the period of notice to be given to a defender under rule 3.6(1)(a) or (b), as the case may be, of the Ordinary Cause Rules, by completing and returning the appropriate portion of Form 5 to the sheriff clerk at least seven days before the first diet fixed for hearing of the summary application or the expiry of the period of notice or otherwise, as the case may be in the warrant of citation; or

(c) by application to the court at any stage before final decree.

(3) The sheriff may determine an application under paragraph (2)(b) or (c) without the defender having to appear.

[1] *Applications under the Mortgage Rights (Scotland) Act 2001*

2.22A—(1) This rule applies to a summary application to which rule 2.7(7A) applies.

(2) Subject to paragraph (3), an application under either of the following provisions of the Mortgage Rights (Scotland) Act 2001 shall be made by minute in the summary application—

(a) section 1(2) (application to the court for an order under section 2);

(b) section 2(5) (application to vary or revoke an order or to further continue proceedings).

(3) A defender may apply orally for an order under section 2 when the summary application first calls in court or as the sheriff otherwise directs.

(4) A minute under paragraph (2) may be lodged by a person who is

entitled to make an application even although that person has not been called as a defender and such a person may appear or be represented at any hearing to determine the application made in the minute.

(5) Except where the sheriff otherwise directs, any such minute shall be lodged in accordance with, and regulated by, Chapter 14 of the Ordinary Cause Rules.

NOTE
[1] Inserted by the Act of Sederunt (Amendment of Ordinary Cause Rules and Summary Applications, Statutory Applications and Appeals etc. Rules) (Applications under the Mortgage Rights (Scotland) Act 2001) 2002 (SSI 2002/7), para.3(3).

Remuneration of assessors
2.23 Where an assessor is appointed by the sheriff to assist him in determining the summary application, the remuneration to be paid to such assessor shall be part of the expenses of the application.

Deposits for expenses
2.24 Where, under any enactment, the sheriff requires the pursuer to deposit a sum of money to cover the expenses of an appeal under the enactment, such sum shall, subject to the provisions of that enactment, not exceed an amount which is twenty-five times the amount of the fee payable at that time in respect of lodging the initial writ.

When decrees extractable   **D 514**
2.25—(1) Subject to the following paragraphs—
  (a) subject to sub-paragraph (c), a decree in absence may be extracted after the expiry of 14 days from the date of decree;
  (b) subject to sub-paragraph (c), any decree pronounced in a defended summary application may be extracted at any time after whichever is the later of the following—
      (i) the expiry of the period within which an application for leave to appeal may be made and no such application has been made;
      (ii) the date on which leave to appeal has been refused and there is no right of appeal from such refusal;
      (iii) the expiry of the period within which an appeal may be marked and no appeal has been marked; or
      (iv) the date on which an appeal has been finally disposed of; and
  (c) where the sheriff has, in pronouncing decree, reserved any question of expenses, extract of that decree may be issued only after the expiry of 14 days from the date of the interlocutor disposing of the question of expenses unless the sheriff otherwise directs.

(2) The sheriff may, on cause shown, grant a motion to allow extract to be applied for and issued earlier than a date referred to in paragraph (1).

(3) In relation to a decree referred to in paragraph (1)(b) or (c), paragraph (2) shall not apply unless—
  (a) the motion under that paragraph is made in the presence of the parties; or
  (b) the sheriff is satisfied of proper intimation of the motion has been made in writing to every party not present at the hearing of the motion.

(4) Nothing in this rule shall affect the power of the sheriff to supersede extract.

Form of extract decree
2.26 The extract of a decree shall be in Form 11.

Form of warrant for execution
2.27 An extract of a decree on which execution may proceed shall include a warrant for execution in the following terms:— "This extract is warrant for all lawful execution hereon.".

Date of decree in extract
2.28—(1) Where the sheriff principal has adhered to the decision of the sheriff following an appeal, the date to be inserted in the extract decree as the date of decree shall be the date of the decision of the sheriff principal.

(2) Where a decree has more than one date it shall not be necessary to specify in an extract what was done on each date.

Decrees in absence where defender furth of Scotland
2.29—(1) Where a defender is domiciled in another part of the United Kingdom or in another Contracting State, the sheriff shall not grant decree in absence until it has been shown that the defender has been able to receive the initial writ in sufficient time to arrange for his defence or that all necessary steps have been taken to that end, and for the purposes of this paragraph—

    (a) the question whether a person is domiciled in another part of the United Kingdom shall be determined in accordance with sections 41 and 42 of the Civil Jurisdiction and Judgments Act 1982;

    (b) the question whether a person is domiciled in another Contracting State shall be determined in accordance with Article 52 of the Convention in Schedule 1 or 3C to that Act, as the case may be; and

D 514/1   (c) the term "Contracting State" has the meaning assigned in section 1 of that Act.

(2) Where an initial writ has keen served in a country to which the Hague Convention on the Service Abroad of Judicial and Extra-Judicial Documents in Civil or Commercial Matters dated 15th November 1965 applies, decree shall not be granted until it is established to the satisfaction of the sheriff that the requirements of Article 15 of the Convention have been complied with.

Motion procedure
2.30 Except where the sheriff otherwise directs, any motion relating to a summary application shall be made in accordance with, and regulated by, Chapter. 15 of the Ordinary Cause Rules.

Power of sheriff to make orders
2.31 The sheriff may make such order as he thinks fit for the progress of a summary application in so far as it is not inconsistent with section 50 of the Sheriff Courts (Scotland) Act 1907.

D 515

CHAPTER 3

RULES ON APPLICATIONS UNDER SPECIFIC STATUTES

PART I

ADMINISTRATION OF JUSTICE (SCOTLAND) ACT 1972

Interpretation and application
[1] **3.1.1**—(1) In this Part,

    (a) "the Act" means the Administration of Justice (Scotland) Act 1972; and

    (b) "listed items" means a list of the documents and other property which the applicant in terms of rule 3.1.2 wishes to be made the subject of the order.

(2) This Part applies to applications under section 1(1) of the Act.

NOTE
[1] As amended by the Act of Sederunt (Summary Applications, Statutory Applications and Appeals etc. Rules) Amendment (No. 2) (Administration of Justice (Scotland) Act 1972 (SSI 2000/387 (effective November 20, 2000).

Applications under section 1(1) of the Act
[1] **3.1.2**—(1) An application for an order under section 1(1) of the Act (orders for inspection of documents and other property, etc.) shall be made by summary application where the proceedings in respect of which the application is made have not been commenced.

(2) The summary application shall contain—
(a) the listed items;
(b) the address of the premises within which the applicant believes the listed items are to be found; and
(c) the facts which give rise to the applicant's belief that, were the order not to be granted, the listed items, or any of them, would cease to be available for the purposes of section 1 of the Act.

Accompanying documents
3.1.3 The applicant shall lodge with the summary application—
(a) an affidavit supporting the averments in the summary application; and
(b) an undertaking by the applicant that he—
   (i) will comply with any order of the sheriff as to payment of compensation if it is subsequently discovered that the order, or the implementation of the order, has caused loss to the respondent or, where the haver is not the respondent, to the haver;
   (ii) will bring within a reasonable time of the execution of the order any proceedings which he decides to bring; and
   (iii) will not, without leave of the sheriff, use any information, documents or other property obtained as a result of the order, except for the purpose of any proceedings which he decides to bring and to which the order relates.

Modification of undertakings
3.1.4 The sheriff may, on cause shown, modify, by addition, deletion or substitution, the undertaking mentioned in rule 3.1.3.

Intimation and service of application
3.1.5—(1) Before granting the summary application, the sheriff may order such intimation or service of the summary application to be given or executed, as the case may be, as he thinks fit.

(2) Any person receiving intimation or service of the summary application by virtue of an order under paragraph (1) may appear and oppose the summary application. **D 516**

Form of order
3.1.6 An order made under this Part shall—
(a) be in Form 11A; and
(b) include in addition a warrant of citation in Form 2.

Caution and other security
3.1.7 On granting, in whole or in part, the summary application the sheriff may order the applicant to find such caution or other security as he thinks fit.

Execution of an order

3.1.8 The order made in terms of rule 3.1.6 shall be served by the Commissioner in person and it shall be accompanied by a copy of the affidavit referred to in rule 3.1.3(a).

Duties of a Commissioner

3.1.9 The Commissioner appointed by the sheriff shall, on executing the order—

(a) give to the haver a copy of the notice in Form 11B;
(b) explain to the haver—
    (i) the meaning and effect of the order; and
    (ii) that he may be entitled to claim that some or all of the listed items are confidential or privileged;
(c) inform the haver of his right to seek legal advice;
(d) enter the premises and take all reasonable steps to fulfil the terms of the order;
(e) where the order has authorised the recovery of any of the listed items, prepare an inventory of all the listed items to be recovered before recovering them; and
(f) send any recovered listed items to the sheriff clerk to await the further order of the sheriff.

Confidentiality

3.1.10—(1) Where confidentiality is claimed for any listed item, that listed item shall, where practicable, be enclosed in a sealed envelope.

(2) A motion to have such a sealed envelope opened may be made by the party who obtained the order and he shall intimate the terms of the motion, by registered post or first class recorded delivery, to the person claiming confidentiality.

(3) A person claiming confidentiality may oppose a motion made under paragraph (2).

Restrictions on service

3.1.11—(1) Except on cause shown, the order may be served on Monday to Friday only, between the hours of 9am and 5pm only.

(2) The order shall not be served at the same time as a search warrant granted in the course of a criminal investigation.

(3) The Commissioner may be accompanied only by—

(a) any person whom he considers necessary to assist him to execute the order;
(b) such representatives of the applicant as are named in the order,

and if it is likely that the premises will be occupied by an unaccompanied female and the Commissioner is not female, one of the people accompanying the Commissioner shall be female.

D 516/1 (4) If it appears to the Commissioner when he comes to serve the order that the premises are occupied by an unaccompanied female and the Commissioner is neither female nor accompanied by a female, the Commissioner shall not enter the premises.

Right of haver to consult

3.1.12 The haver may seek legal or other professional advice of his choice and where the purpose of seeking this advice is to help him to decide whether to ask the sheriff to vary the order the Commissioner shall not commence to search for or to take any other steps to take possession of or preserve the listed items.

NOTE

[1] As amended by the Act of Sederunt (Summary Applications, Statutory Applications and Appeals etc. Rules) Amendment (No. 2) (Administration of Justice (Scotland) Act 1972 (SSI 2000/387) (effective November 20, 2000).

PART II

BETTING AND GAMING APPEALS

Interpretation
3.2.1 In this Part—
"the 1963 Act" means the Betting Gaming and Lotteries Act 1963;
"the 1968 Act" means the Gaming Act 1968; and
"the 1976 Act" means the Lotteries and Amusements Act 1976.

Appeals under Part I of the 1963 Act
3.2.2—(1) This rule applies to—
(a) appeals under paragraph 24(1) of Schedule 1 to the 1963 Act against the decision of a licensing board refusing to grant or renew a bookmaker's permit, betting agency permit or betting office licence;
(b) appeals under paragraph 28(2) of Schedule 1 to the 1963 Act against a decision of a licensing board ordering that a bookmaker's permit be forfeited or cancelled;
(c) appeals under paragraph 28D of Schedule 1 to the 1963 Act against the decision of a licensing board ordering that a betting office licence be forfeited and cancelled;
(d) appeals under paragraph 7 of Schedule 2 to the 1963 Act against the decision of a registering authority to refuse to register that appellant as a pools promoter, or to revoke his registration as a pools promoter; and
(e) appeals under paragraph 13(3) of Schedule 3 to the 1963 Act against the decision of a licensing authority to revoke a track betting licence.
(2) The appellant shall serve a copy of the initial writ on—
(a) the clerk to the licensing board, registering authority or licensing authority, as the case may be;
(b) all parties who appeared at the hearing before the licensing board, registering authority or licensing authority, as the case may be; and
(c) in the case of an appeal against the forfeiture and cancellation of a bookmaker's permit or of a betting office licence, the applicant for forfeiture and cancellation.
(3) The clerk to the licensing board, registering authority or licensing authority, as the case may be shall, within 7 days after the date of service on him of a copy of the initial writ, send a written statement setting out the reasons for the decision of the licensing board, registering authority or licensing authority, as the case may be to—
(a) the sheriff clerk; and   **D 516/2**
(b) each of the persons on whom service of a copy initial writ is required to be made in terms of paragraph (2).

Appeals by applicants under Part II of the 1968 Act
3.2.3—(1) This rule applies to—
(a) appeals under paragraph 33(1) of Schedule 2 to the 1968 Act against the decision of a licensing board refusing to grant or renew a licence for gaming to take place on premises or imposing restrictions on such a licence; and
(b) appeals under paragraph 45 of that Schedule against the decision of a licensing board cancelling such a licence.
(2) The appellant shall serve a copy of the initial writ on—
(a) the clerk to the licensing board;
(b) all parties who appeared at the hearing before the licensing board;
(c) the Gaming Board;
(d) the appropriate collector of duty; and
(e) the appropriate officer of police.
(3) The clerk to the licensing board shall within 7 days after the date of

service on him of a copy of the initial writ, send a written statement setting out the reasons for the decision of the licensing board to—
    (a) the sheriff clerk; and
    (b) each of the persons on whom service of a copy initial writ is required to be made in terms of paragraph (2).

Appeals by the Gaming Board under Part II of the 1968 Act
    3.2.4—(1) This rule applies to—
    (a) appeals under paragraph 34(1) of Schedule 2 to the 1968 Act against the decision of a licensing board to grant or renew a licence for gaming to take place on premises, with or without restrictions; and
    (b) appeals under paragraph 47(1) of that Schedule against the decision of a licensing board refusing to cancel such a licence.
    (2) Where a licensing board, after hearing any objections or representations made by or on behalf of the Gaming Board or any other person—
    (a) grants or renews a licence for gaming to take place on premises, with or without imposing restrictions; or
    (b) refuses an application for the cancellation of such a licence,
the clerk to the licensing board shall forthwith give notice of the decision of the licensing board to the Gaming Board.
    (3) The appellant shall serve a copy of the initial writ on—
    (a) the clerk to the licensing board;
    (b) the applicant;
    (c) all parties who appeared at the hearing before the licensing board;
    (d) the Gaming Board;
    (e) the appropriate collector of duty; and
    (f) the appropriate officer of police.
    (4) The clerk to the licensing board shall within 7 days after the date of service on him of a copy of the initial writ, send a written statement setting out the reasons for the decision of the licensing board to—
    (a) the sheriff clerk; and
    (b) each of the persons on whom service of a copy initial writ is required to be made in terms of paragraph (3).

Appeals under Part III of the 1968 Act and Part III of the 1976 Act
    3.2.5—(1) This rule applies to—
    (a) appeals under paragraph 15 of Schedule 9 to the 1968 Act against the decision of the appropriate authority refusing to grant or renew a permit for the provision of machines for amusement purposes on premises, or to grant such a permit subject to a condition; and
    (b) appeals under paragraph 12 of Schedule 3 to the 1976 Act against the decision of the appropriate authority refusing to grant or renew a permit for the provision of amusements with prizes or to grant or renew such a permit subject to a condition.
    (2) The appellant shall serve a copy of the initial writ on—
    (a) the clerk to the authority;
    (b) the applicant;
    (c) all parties who appeared at the hearing before the authority;
    (d) the Gaming Board;
    (e) the appropriate collector of duty; and
    (f) the appropriate officer of police.

D 517

PART III

COAL MINING SUBSIDENCE ACT 1991

Interpretation and application
    3.3.1—(1) In this Part—
        "the Act" means the Coal Mining Subsidence Act 1991;

"agreement or consent" means the agreement or consent referred to in section 41 of the Act);

"person" means a person referred to in section 41 of the Act;

"any person with responsibility for subsidence affecting any land" has the meaning given in section 43 of the Coal Industry Act 1994.

(2) This Part applies to proceedings under section 41 of the Act.

Applications under section 41 of the Act

3.3.2—(1) An application under section 41 of the Act (disputes about withholding of agreement or consent) shall specify—

(a) the person with whom any person with responsibility for subsidence affecting any land has reached agreement and from whom any person with responsibility for subsidence affecting any land obtained consent; and

(b) the steps which have been taken to obtain the agreement or consent of the person who is withholding such agreement or consent.

(2) An application under section 41 of the Act made in relation to the exercise of a power under section 5(3) or (5) of the Act, shall, when lodged with the sheriff clerk, be accompanied by the notice of proposed remedial action under section 4(2) of the Act.

PART IV

CONVEYANCING AND FEUDAL REFORM (SCOTLAND) ACT 1970

Application

3.4.1—(1) In this Part, "the Act" means the Conveyancing and Feudal Reform (Scotland) Act 1970.

(2) This Part applies to applications and counter applications under Part II of the Act.

Disposal of applications under Part II of the Act

3.4.2 An interlocutor of the sheriff disposing of an application or counter application under Part II of the Act shall be final and not subject to appeal except as to a question of title or as to any other remedy granted.

PART V   D 518

COPYRIGHT, DESIGNS AND TRADE MARKS

Interpretation

3.5.1 In this Part—

"the 1988 Act" means the Copyright, Designs and Patents Act 1988;

"the 1994 Act" means the Trade Marks Act 1994; and

"the 1995 Regulations" means the Olympics Association Right (Infringement Proceedings) Regulations 1995.

Orders for delivery up, forfeiture, destruction or other disposal

3.5.2 An application to the sheriff made under sections 99, 114, 195, 204, 230, 231 or 298 of the 1988 Act, under sections 16 or 19 of the 1994 Act or under Regulation 3 or 5 of the 1995 Regulations, shall be made—

(a) by motion or incidental application, as the case may be, where proceedings have been commenced; or

(b) by summary application where no proceedings have been commenced.

Service of notice on interested persons
3.5.3. Where an application has been made under section 114, 204, 231 or 298 of the 1988 Act, section 19 of the 1994 Act or Regulation 5 of the 1995 Regulations—

  (a) the application shall—
    (i) specify the name and address of any person known or believed by the applicant to have an interest in the subject matter of the application; or
    (ii) state that to the best of the applicant's knowledge and belief no other person has such an interest; and
  (b) the sheriff shall order that there be intimated to any person who has such an interest, a copy of the pleadings and any motion, incidental application or summary application, as the case maybe.

Procedure where leave of court required
3.5.4—(1) Where leave of the court is required under the 1988 Act before the action may proceed, the pursuer shall lodge along with the initial writ or summons a motion or incidental application, as the case may be, stating the grounds upon which leave is sought.

(2) The sheriff may hear the pursuer on the motion or incidental application and may grant or refuse it or make such other order in relation to it as he considers appropriate prior to determination.

(3) Where such motion or incidental application is granted, a copy of the sheriff's interlocutor shall be served upon the defender along with the warrant of citation.

[1] PART VI

DRUG TRAFFICKING ACT 1994

NOTE
[1] Revoked by the Act of Sederunt (Summary Applications, Statutory Applications and Appeals etc. Rules) Amendment (No.5) (Proceeds of Crime Act 2002) 2002 (SSI 2002/563), para.2(3) (effective December 30, 2002), subject to savings outlined in para.2(3).

D 519

PART VII

LICENSING (SCOTLAND) ACT 1976

Interpretation and application
3.7.1—(1) In this Part, "the Act" means the Licensing (Scotland) Act 1976.

(2) This Part applies to appeals under section 39 of the Act.

Service
3.7.2 The appellant shall serve a copy of the initial writ on—
  (a) the clerk to the licensing board and the chief constable;
  (b) if he was the applicant at the hearing before the licensing board, upon all parties who appeared at the hearing; and
  (c) if he was an objector at the hearing, upon the applicant.

Statement of reasons of licensing board
3.7.3—(1) Where the appellant has received from the licensing board a statement of reasons for its decision, he shall lodge a copy thereof with the sheriff clerk along with the initial writ.

(2) The sheriff may, at any time prior to pronouncing a final interlocutor, require the licensing board to state the ground of refusal of an application and to give their reasons for finding such ground to be established.

PART VIII

MENTAL HEALTH (SCOTLAND) ACT 1984

Interpretation and application
3.8.1.—(1) In this Part, "the Act" means the Mental Health (Scotland) Act 1984.
(2) This Part applies to—
(a) applications for admission submitted to a sheriff under section 21 of the Act;
(b) guardianship applications submitted to a sheriff under section 40 of the Act; and
(c) community care applications submitted under section 35A of the Act.

Appointment of hearing
3.8.2—(1) On an application being submitted, the sheriff shall appoint a hearing subject, in the case of an application for admission, to section 21(3A) of the Act.
(2) The sheriff may, where he considers it appropriate in all the circumstances, appoint that the hearing of an application shall take place in a hospital or other place.

Service of application
3.8.3—(1) The sheriff clerk shall serve or cause to be served on the patient a copy of the application, with the exception of any medical recommendation, together with a notice in Form 12.
(2) Where the patient is not a resident patient in a hospital, the notice and copy application shall be served on him personally by sheriff officer.
(3) Where the patient is a resident patient in a hospital, the notice and copy application shall be served together with a notice in Form 13 on his responsible medical officer—
(a) by first class recorded delivery service; or
(b) personally by sheriff officer.
(4) Where the patient is already the subject of a guardianship order, the notice and copy application (including any medical recommendations) shall, **D 520** in addition to any other service required by this rule, be served on the guardian—
(a) by first class recorded delivery service; or
(b) personally a sheriff officer.

Duties of responsible medical officer
3.8.4—(1) On receipt of a notice in Form 13 the responsible medical officer shall, subject to rule 3.8.5(1)—
(a) deliver the notice in Form 12 to the patient; and
(b) as soon as practicable thereafter, complete and return to the court a certificate of such delivery in Form 14.
[1] (2) Where, in the opinion of the responsible medical officer, it would be prejudicial to the patient's health or treatment if the patient were to be present during the proceedings—
(a) in an application to which rule 3.8.3(3) applies, the responsible medical officer shall set forth his reasons for his opinion in the certificate in Form 14; and
(b) in any other case, the responsible medical officer or the special medical officer, as the case may be, shall set forth his reasons for his opinion in writing and send them to the sheriff clerk.

NOTE
[1] As amended by SSI 2003/26, para.3(5) (clerical error).

Appointment of curator ad litem
3.8.5—(1) Where two medical certificates are produced stating that it would be prejudicial to the health or treatment of the patient if personal service were effected in terms of rule 3.8.3(2) or 3.8.4(1) the sheriff—
   (a) may dispense with such service; and
   (b) if he does so, shall appoint a curator *ad litem* to receive the application and represent the interest of that patient.
(2) The sheriff may appoint a curator *ad litem* to represent the interests of the patient where he is satisfied that—
   (a) the patient should be excluded from the whole or any part of the proceedings under section 113(2) of the Act; or
   (b) in any other case, it is in all the circumstances appropriate to do so.
(3) The sheriff clerk shall serve the application on the curator *ad litem* by handing, or sending by first class recorded delivery service, to him a copy of the application and of the order appointing him as the curator.

Appointment of solicitor by court
3.8.6 Where the patient has indicated that he wishes to be represented at the hearing but has not nominated a representative, the sheriff may appoint a solicitor to take instructions from the patient.

Intimation to representatives
3.8.7 Where in any proceedings under the Act, the sheriff clerk is aware that the patient is represented by any person and that representative would not otherwise receive intimation of any diet, a copy of the notice served on the patient shall be intimated to the representative by the sheriff clerk by first class recorded delivery service.

Service by sheriff officer
3.8.8—(1) Where a copy of an application and any notice has been served personally by sheriff officer, he shall prepare and return to the court an execution of such service setting forth in detail the manner and circumstances of such service.
D 521 (2) Where a sheriff officer has been unable to effect personal service under this Part, he shall report to the court the reason why service was not effected.

Variation of conditions of community care order
3.8.9—(1) Where, after consulting the persons referred to in subsections (1) and (2) of section 35D of the Act (variation of conditions of community care order), an application is made by the special medical officer for the variation of a community care order under that section, the special medical officer shall—
   (a) complete Form 22 in Schedule 2 to the Mental Health (Prescribed Forms) (Scotland) Regulations 1996; and
   (b) lodge that form with the sheriff clerk, together with a certified copy of the community care order to which the application for variation relates.

Hearing
3.8.10—(1) Any hearing to determine an application under rule 3.8.9 shall take place within 28 days after receipt by the sheriff clerk of Form 22 and the community care order referred to in that rule.
(2) Intimation of the date of the hearing referred to in paragraph (1) shall be given by the Stationery sheriff clerk by first class recorded delivery service to such persons as the sheriff may direct; and any intimation of such date to the patient shall be made personally by sheriff officer.

Appeal against community care order
   3.8.11 An application by way of appeal for the revocation of a community care order under section 35F of the Act shall be in Form 15.

PART IX

PROCEEDS OF CRIME (SCOTLAND) ACT 1995

Interpretation and application
   3.9.1—(1) In this Part—
      "the Act" means the Proceeds of Crime (Scotland) Act 1995; and
      "administrator" means the person appointed under paragraph 1(1) of
         Schedule 1 to Act.
   (2) This Part applies to proceedings under sections 28, 29, 30, 31 and 33 of, and paragraphs 1, 2, 4, 6 and 12 of Schedule 1 to, the Act.

Service of restraint orders
   3.9.2 Where the sheriff pronounces an interlocutor making a restraint order under section 28(1) of the Act (application for restraint order), the prosecutor shall serve a copy of that interlocutor on every person named in the interlocutor as restrained by the order.

Recall or variation of restraint orders
   3.9.3.—(1) An application to the sheriff under any of the following provisions of the Act shall be made by note in the process containing the interlocutor malting the restraint order to which the application relates—
      (a) section 29(4) or (5) (recall of restraint orders in relation to realisable
         property);
      (b) section 30(3) or (4) (recall of restraint orders in relation to forfeitable
         property);
      (c) section 31(1) (variation or recall of restraint order).
   (2) In respect of an application by note under paragraph (1)(c) by a person having an interest for an order for variation or recall under section 31(1)(b) of the Act—
      (a) the note shall be lodged in process within 21 days after service of the
         restraint order on that person or within such other period as the **D 522**
         sheriff thinks fit; and
      (b) the period of notice for lodging answers to the note shall be 14 days
         or such other period as the sheriff thinks fit.

Applications for interdict
   3.9.4—(1) An application to the sheriff under section 28(8) of the Act (interdict) may be made—
      (a) in the application made under section 28(1) of the Act; or
      (b) if made after a restraint order has been made, by note in the process
         of the application for that order.
   (2) An application under section 28(8) of the Act by note under paragraph (1)(b) shall not be intimated, served or advertised before that application is granted.

Applications in relation to arrestment   **D 523**
   3.9.5—(1) An application to the sheriff under section 33(1) of the Act (arrestment of property affected by restraint order by the prosecutor for warrant for arrestment may be made—
      (a) in the application made under section 28(1) of the Act; or
      (b) if made after a restraint order has been applied for, by note in the
         process of the application for that order.
   (2) An application to the sheriff under section 33(2) of the Act, to loose,

restrict or recall an arrestment shall be made by note in the process of the application for the restraint order.

(3) An application to the sheriff under section 33(4) of the Act (recall or restriction of arrestment) shall be made by note in the process containing the interlocutor making the restraint order to which the application relates.

Appeals to the Court of Session
3.9.6—(1) This rule applies to appeals against an interlocutor of the sheriff refusing, varying or recalling or refusing to vary or recall a restraint order.

(2) An appeal to which this rule applies shall be marked within 14 days after the date of the interlocutor concerned.

(3) An appeal to which this rule applies shall be marked by writing a note of appeal on the interlocutor sheet, or other written record containing the interlocutor appealed against, or on a separate sheet lodged with the sheriff clerk, in the following terms:— "The applicant appeals to the Court of Session.".

(4) A note of appeal to which this rule applies shall—
(a) be signed by the appellant;
(b) bear the date on which it is signed; and
(c) where the appellant is represented, specify the name and address of the solicitor or other agent who will be acting for him in the appeal.

(5) The sheriff clerk shall transmit the process within 4 days after the appeal is marked to the Deputy Principal Clerk of Session.

(6) Within the period specified in paragraph (5), the sheriff clerk shall—
(a) send written notice of the appeal to every other party; and
(b) certify on the interlocutor sheet that he has done so.

(7) Failure of the sheriff clerk to comply with paragraph (6) shall not invalidate the appeal.

Applications for appointment of administrators
3.9.7—(1) An application to the sheriff under paragraph 1 of Schedule 1 to the Act (appointment of administrators) shall be made—
(a) where made after a restraint order has been made, by note in the process of the application for that order; or
(b) in any other case, by summary application.

(2) The notification to be made by the sheriff clerk under paragraph 1 (3)(a) of Schedule 1 to the Act shall be made by intimation of a copy of the interlocutor to the person required to give possession of property to an administrator.

Incidental applications in an administration
3.9.8—(1) An application to the sheriff under any of the following provisions of Schedule to the Act shall be made by note in the process of the application for appointment of the administrator—
(a) paragraph 1(1) with respect to an application after appointment of an administrator to require a person to give property to him;
(b) paragraph 1(4) (making or altering a requirement or removal of administrator);
(c) paragraph 1(5) (appointment of new administrator on death, resignation or removal of administrator);
(d) paragraph 2(1)(n) (directions as to functions of administrator);
(e) paragraph 4 (directions for application of proceeds).

D 524 (2) An application to the sheriff under any of the following provisions of Schedule 1 to the Act shall be made in the application for appointment of an administrator under paragraph 1(1) of that Schedule or, if made after the application has been made, by note in the process—
(a) paragraph 2(1)(o) (special powers of administrator);
(b) paragraph 2(3) (vesting of property in administrator);
(c) paragraph 12 (order to facilitate the realisation of property).

Requirements where order to facilitate realisation of property considered
3.9.9 Where the sheriff considers making an order under paragraph 12 of
Schedule 1 to the Act (order to facilitate the realisation of property)—
   (a) the sheriff shall fix a date for a hearing in the first instance; and
   (b) the applicant or noter, as the case may be, shall serve a notice in
       Form 16 on any person who has an interest in the property.

Documents for Accountant of Court
3.9.10—(1) A person who has lodged any document in the process of an
application for the appointment of an administrator shall forthwith send a
copy of that document to the Accountant of Court.
   (2) The sheriff clerk shall transmit to the Accountant of Court any part of
the process as the Accountant of Court may request in relation to an
administration which is in dependence before the sheriff unless such part of
the process is, at the time of request, required by the sheriff.

Procedure for fixing and finding caution
3.9.11 Rules 9 to 12 of the Act of Sederunt (Judicial Factors Rules) 1992
(fixing and finding caution in judicial factories) shall, with the necessary
modifications, apply to the fixing and finding of caution by an administrator
under this Part as they apply to the fixing and finding of caution by a
judicial factor.

Administrator's title to act
3.9.12 An administrator appointed under this Part shall not be entitled to
act until he has obtained a copy of the interlocutor appointing him.

Duties of administrator
3.9.13—(1) The administrator shall, as soon as possible, but within three
months after the date of his appointment, lodge with the Accountant of
Court—
   (a) an inventory of the property in respect of which he has been
       appointed;
   (b) all vouchers, securities, and other documents which are in his
       possession; and
   (c) a statement of that property which he has in his possession or intends
       to realise.
   (2) An administrator shall maintain accounts of his intromissions with the
property in his charge and shall, subject to paragraph (3)—
   (a) within six months after the date of his appointment; and
   (b) at six monthly intervals after the first account during the subsistence
       of his appointment,
lodge with the Accountant of Court an account of his intromissions in such
form, with such supporting vouchers and other documents, as the
Accountant of Court may require.
   (3) The Accountant of Court may waive the lodging of an account where
the administrator certifies that there have been no intromissions during a
particular accounting period.

State of funds and scheme of division
3.9.14—(1) The administrator shall—
   (a) where there are funds available for division, prepare a state of funds
       after application of sums in accordance with paragraph 4(2) of
       Schedule 1 to the Act, and a scheme of division amongst those who **D 525**
       held property which has been realised under the Act and lodge them
       and all relevant documents with the Accountant of Court; or
   (b) where there are no funds available for division, prepare a state of
       funds only and lodge it with the Accountant of Court, and give to the
       Accountant of Court such explanations as he shall require.

(2) The Accountant of Court shall—

(a) make a written report on the state of funds and any scheme of division including such observations as he considers appropriate for consideration by the sheriff; and

(b) return the state of funds and any scheme of division to the administrator with his report.

(3) The administrator shall, on receiving the report of the Accountant of Court—

(a) lodge in process the report, the state of funds and any scheme of division;

(b) intimate a copy of it to the prosecutor; and

(c) intimate to each person who held property which has been realised under the Act a notice stating—

(i) that the state of funds and scheme of division or the state of funds only, as the case may be, and the report of the Accountant of Court, have been lodged in process; and

(ii) the amount for which that person has been ranked, and whether he is to be paid in full, or by a dividend, and the amount of it, or that no funds are available for payment.

Objections to scheme of division

3.9.15—(1) A person wishing to be heard by the sheriff in relation to the distribution of property under paragraph 4(3) of Schedule 1 to the Act shall lodge a note of objection in the process to which the scheme of division relates within 21 days of the date of the notice intimated under rule 3.9.14(3)(c).

(2) After the period for lodging a note of objection has expired and no note of objection has been lodged, the administrator may apply by motion for approval of the scheme of division and state of funds, or the state of funds only, as the case may be.

(3) After the period for lodging a note of objection has expired and a note of objection has been lodged, the sheriff shall dispose of such objection after hearing any objector and the administrator and making such inquiry as he thinks fit.

(4) If any objection is sustained to any extent, the necessary alterations shall be made to the state of funds and any scheme of division and shall be approved by the sheriff.

Application for discharge of administrator

3.9.16—(1) Where the scheme of division is approved by the sheriff and the administrator delivered or conveyed to the persons entitled the sums or receipts allocated to them in the scheme, the administrator may apply for his discharge.

(2) An application to the sheriff for discharge of the administrator shall be made by note in the process of the application under paragraph 1(1) of Schedule 1 to the Act.

Appeals against determination of outlays and remuneration

3.9.17 An appeal to the sheriff under paragraph 6(2) of Schedule 1 to the Act (appeal against a determination by the Accountant of Court) shall be made by note in the process of the application in which the administrator was appointed.

PART X

RATING (DISABLED PERSONS) ACT 1978

Interpretation and application
3.10.1—(1) In this Part, "the Act" means the Rating (Disabled Persons) Act 1978.
(2) This Part applies to appeals under section 6(5) or 6(5A) of the Act.

Appeals under section 6(5) or 6(5A) of the Act
3.10.2 Any appeal under this Part shall be lodged within 42 days of the date on which the application to the rating authority is refused by the authority.

PART XI

REPRESENTATION OF THE PEOPLE ACT 1983

Interpretation and application
3.11.1—(1) In this Part—
"sheriff clerk" means, except in rule 3.11.2, the sheriff clerk of the sheriff court district where the trial of the election petition is to take place;
"the Act" means the Representation of the People Act 1983.
(2) This Part applies to election petitions under the Act.

Initiation of proceedings
3.11.2—(1) The election petition shall be lodged with the sheriff clerk of a sheriff court district within which the election questioned has taken place.
(2) The sheriff clerk shall without delay transmit it to the sheriff principal who shall forthwith appoint—
(a) the time and place for trial of the petition;
(b) the amount of the security to be given by the petitioner; and
(c) if he thinks fit, answers to be lodged within a specified time after service.
(3) Service in terms of section 136(3) of the Act (security for costs) shall be effected—
(a) personally within—
(i) 5 days; or
(ii) such other period as the sheriff principal may appoint,
of the giving of security; or
(b) by first class recorded delivery post within—
(i) 5 days; or
(ii) such other period as the sheriff principal may appoint,
of the giving of security.

Security for expenses by bond of caution
3.11.3—(1) If the security proposed is in whole or in part by bond of caution, it shall be given by lodging with the sheriff clerk a bond for the amount specified by the sheriff principal.
(2) Such bond shall—
(a) recite the nature of the petition; and
(b) bind and oblige the cautioner and the petitioner jointly and severally, and their respective heirs, executors and successors whomsoever, that the petitioner shall make payment of all costs, charges and expenses that may be payable by him to any person by virtue of any order or decree pronounced in the petition.
(3) The sufficiency of the cautioner must be attested to the satisfaction of the sheriff clerk, as in the case of judicial bonds of caution.

Objections to bond of caution

3.11.4—(1) Objections to a bond of caution shall be lodged with the sheriff clerk within 14 days of service in terms of section 136(3) of the Act.

(2) Objections shall be heard and disposed of by the sheriff clerk.

(3) If any objection is allowed, it may be removed by a deposit of such sum of money as the sheriff clerk shall determine, made in the manner provided in rule 3.11.5 and within 5 days after the date of the sheriff clerk's determination.

Security by deposit

3.11.5—(1) Security tendered in whole or in part by deposit of money shall be made in such bank the sheriff clerk may select.

(2) The deposit receipt shall be—

(a) taken in joint name of the petitioner and the sheriff clerk;

(b) handed to the sheriff clerk; and

(c) held by the sheriff clerk subject to the orders of the court in the petition.

Amendment of pleadings

3.11.6—(1) Subject to paragraph (2), the sheriff principal shall have power at any stage to allow petition and any answers to be amended upon such condition as to expenses or otherwise as he shall think fit.

(2) No amendment altering the ground upon which the election was questioned in the petition as presented shall be competent, except to the extent sanctioned by section 129(6) of the Act (time for presentation or amendment of petition questioning local election).

Notice of date and place of trial

3.11.7—(1) The sheriff clerk shall, as soon as he receives intimation of the time and place fixed for trial—

(a) display a notice thereof on the walls of his principal office; and

(b) send by first class post one copy of such notice to—

(i) the petitioner;

(ii) the respondent;

(iii) the Lord Advocate; and

(iv) the returning officer.

(2) The returning officer on receipt of notice from the sheriff clerk shall forthwith publish the time and place fixed for trial in the area for which the election questioned was held.

(3) Subject to paragraph (4), display of a notice in accordance with paragraph (1)(a) shall be deemed to be notice in the prescribed manner within the meaning of section 139(1) of the Act (trial of petition) and such notice shall not be vitiated by any miscarriage of or relating to all or any copies sent by post.

(4) At any time before the trial it shall be competent for any party interested to bring any miscarriage of notice sent by post before the sheriff principal, who shall deal therewith as he may consider fit.

Clerk of court

3.11.8 The sheriff clerk shall attend and act as clerk of court at the trial of the petition.

Shorthand writer's charges

3.11.9 The shorthand writer's charges, as approved by the sheriff principal, shall be paid in the first instance by the petitioner.

Appeals

3.11.10 The application to state a special case referred to in section 146(1) of the (special case for determination of the Court of Session) shall be made by minute in the petition proceedings.

List of votes objected to and of objections   **D 528**
    3.11.11—(1) When a petitioner claims the seat for an unsuccessful candidate, alleging that such candidate had a majority of lawful votes, he and the respondent shall, 5 days before the day fixed for the trial, respectively deliver to the sheriff clerk, and send by first class post to the other party and the Lord Advocate, a list of the votes intended to be objected to, and of the objections to each such vote.
    (2) The sheriff clerk shall allow inspection of such list to all parties concerned.
    (3) No evidence shall be allowed to be given against any vote or in support of any objection not specified in such list, except by leave of the sheriff principal granted upon such terms as to the amendment of the list, postponement of the trial, and payment of expenses as to him may seem fit.

Petition against undue return
    3.11.12—(1) When on the trial of a petition complaining of an undue return and claiming the office for some person, the respondent intends to give evidence to prove that that person was not duly elected, such respondent shall, 5 days before the day appointed for the trial, deliver to the sheriff clerk, and send by first class post to the petitioner and the Lord Advocate, a list of the objections to the election upon which he intends to rely.
    (2) No evidence shall be allowed to be given by a respondent in support of any objection to the election not specified in such list except by leave of the sheriff principal granted upon such terms as to the amendment of the list, postponement of the trial, and payment of expenses as to him may seem fit.

Prescribed officer
    3.11.13 The sheriff clerk shall be the prescribed officer for the purposes of sections 143(1) (expense of witnesses) and 155(2) (neglect or refusal to pay costs) of the Act.

Leave to abandon
    3.11.14—(1) Application for leave to withdraw a petition in terms of section 147(1) of the Act (withdrawal of petition), shall be made by minute in Form 17 and shall be preceded by written notice of the intention to make it, sent by first class post to—
    (a) the respondent;
    (b) the Lord Advocate; and
    (c) the returning officer.
    (2) The returning officer shall forthwith publish the fact of his having received such notice in the area for which the election questioned was held.
    (3) The sheriff principal, upon the application being laid before him, shall by interlocutor, fix the time, not being earlier than 8 days after the date of the interlocutor, and place for hearing it.
    (4) The petitioner shall, at least 6 days before the day fixed for the hearing, publish in a newspaper circulating in the district named in the interlocutor a notice in Form 18.

Death of petitioner
    3.11.15—(1) In the event of the death of the sole petitioner, or of the last survivor of several petitioners, the sheriff clerk shall forthwith, upon the fact being brought to his knowledge, insert in a newspaper circulating in the district a notice in Form 19.
    (2) The time within which any person who might have been a petitioner in respect of the election may apply to the court by minute in the petition

proceedings to be substituted as a petitioner shall be 21 days from the date of publication of such notice.

D 529 *Notice by respondent that he does not oppose petition*

3.11.16—(1) Notice that a respondent does not intend to oppose a petition shall be given by leaving a written notice to that effect at the office of the sheriff clerk at least 6 days (exclusive of the day of leaving such notice) before the day fixed for the trial.

(2) On such notice being left with the sheriff clerk, or on its being brought to his knowledge that a respondent other than a returning officer has died, resigned, or otherwise ceased to hold the office to which the petition relates, the sheriff clerk shall forthwith—

   (a) advertise the fact once in a newspaper circulating in the district; and
   (b) send intimation thereof by first class post to—
      (i) the petitioner;
      (ii) the Lord Advocate; and
      (iii) the returning officer, who shall publish the fact in the district.

(3) The advertisement to be made by the sheriff clerk shall state the last day on which, under this Part, application to be admitted as a respondent to oppose the petition can be made.

Application to be admitted as respondent

3.11.17 Application to be admitted as a respondent to oppose a petition on the occurrence of any of the events mentioned in section 153(1) of the Act (withdrawal and substitution of respondents before trial) must be made by minute in the petition proceedings within 10 days after the date of publication of the advertisement mentioned in rule 3.11.16, unless the sheriff principal on cause shown sees fit to extend the time.

Public notice of trial not proceeding

3.11.18—(1) This rule applies where after the notice of trial has been published the sheriff clerk receives notice

   (a) the petitioner's intention to apply for leave to withdraw;
   (b) the respondent's intention not to oppose;
   (c) the abatement of the petition by death; or
   (d) the occurrence of any of the events mentioned in section 153(1) of the Act.

(2) Where this rule applies the sheriff clerk shall forthwith give notice by advertisement inserted once in a newspaper circulating in the district, that the trial will not proceed on the day fixed.

Notice to a party's agent sufficient

3.11.19 Where a party to proceedings under this Part is represented by a solicitor any reference to such party shall, where appropriate, be construed as a reference to the solicitor representing that party and a notice sent to his solicitor shall be held to be notice to the party.

Cost of publication

3.11.20 Where under this Part the returning officer or the sheriff clerk requires to have published a notice or advertisement, the cost shall be paid in the first instance by the petitioner or in the case of a notice under rule 3.11.15 from the estate of the sole or last surviving petitioner and shall form part of the general expenses of the petition.

Expenses

3.11.21 The expenses of petitions and other proceedings under the Act shall be taxed by the auditor of the sheriff court.

REQUESTS OR APPLICATIONS UNDER THE MODEL LAW ON INTERNATIONAL
COMMERCIAL ARBITRATION

Interpretation
3.12.1 In this Part, "the Model Law" means the United Nations
Commission on International Trade Law Model Law on International
Commercial Arbitration as set out in Schedule 7 to the Law Reform
(Miscellaneous Provisions) (Scotland) Act 1990.

Application
3.12.2—(1) Subject to sub-paragraph (2), any request or application
which may be made to the sheriff under the Model Law shall be made by
summary application.
(2) Where proceedings involving the same arbitration and the same
parties are already pending before the sheriff under this Part, a further
application or request may be made by note in the same process.
(3) The sheriff shall order service of such summary application or note to
be made on such persons as he considers appropriate.

Recognition and enforcement of awards
3.12.3—(1) There shall be lodged along with an application under Article
35 of the Model Law—
    (a) the original arbitration agreement or certified copy thereof;
    (b) the duly authenticated original award or certified copy thereof and
    (c) where appropriate, a duly certified translation in English of the
        agreement and award.
(2) An application under this paragraph shall specify whether to the
knowledge of the applicant—
    (a) the arbitral award has been recognised, or is being enforced, in any
        other jurisdiction; and
    (b) an application for setting aside or suspension of the arbitral award
        has been made to a court of the country in which or under whose law
        the award was made.
(3) Where the sheriff is satisfied that an arbitral award should be
recognised and enforced, he shall so order and shall instruct the sheriff clerk
to register the award in the Books of the Sheriff Court for execution.

Part XIII

SEX DISCRIMINATION ACT 1975

Interpretation
3.13.1 In this Part—
    "the Act" means the Sex Discrimination Act 1975; and
    "the Commission" means the Equal Opportunities Commission
        established under section 53 of the Act.

Application
3.13.2 This Part shall apply to the following proceedings under the Act:—
    (a) an application by the Commission under section 59(4) for an order
        requiring a person to comply with a notice served on him under
        section 59(1);
    (b) an appeal by a person under section 68(1) against a requirement of a
        non-discrimination notice served on him under section 67;
    (c) an application by the Commission under section 71(1) for an order
        restraining a person from doing any of the acts referred to in that
        section;

(d) an application by the Commission under section 72(2) for a decision whether an alleged contravention of section 38, 39 or 40 has occurred;

(e) an application by the Commission under section 72(4) for an order restraining a person from doing any of the acts referred to in that section; and

(f) an application by a person under section 77(5) for an order removing or modifying any term of a contract made unenforceable by section 77(2).

Taxation of Commission expenses

3.13.3 The expenses incurred by the Commission within the meaning and for the purposes of section 75(3) of the Act shall be taxed by the auditor of the sheriff court in which the proceedings under the Act were taken or would have been taken but for any compromise or settlement, as if they were outlays incurred by a solicitor on behalf of the applicant.

Proceedings under section 66 of the Act

3.13.4—(1) In a cause in which a breach of statutory duty under section 66(1) of the Act (proceedings for act of discrimination) is averred, the sheriff may, of his own motion or on the motion of any party, appoint an assessor.

(2) An assessor appointed under paragraph (1) shall be a person who the sheriff considers has special qualifications to be of assistance in determining a cause referred to in that paragraph.

(3) In a cause referred to in paragraph (1), the pursuer shall send a copy of the initial writ by post by first class recorded delivery service to the Commission.

[1] PART XIV

ACCESS TO HEALTH RECORDS ACT 1990

NOTE
[1] Inserted by the Act of Sederunt (Summary Applications, Statutory Applications and Appeals etc. Rules) Amendment 2000 (SSI 2000/148), para.2(2) (effective July 3, 2000).

Interpretation and application

3.14.1(1) In this Part—

"the Act" means the Access to Health Records Act 1990; and

"the Reg" means the Access to Health Records (Steps to Secure Compliance and Complaints Procedures) (Scotland) Regulations 1991.

(2) This Part applies to applications under section 8(1) of the Act (applications to the court for order to comply with requirement of the Act).

Accompanying documents

3.14.2 An application shall specify those steps prescribed in the Regulations which have been taken by the person concerned to secure compliance with any requirement of the Act, and when lodged in process shall be accompanied by—

(a) a copy of the application under section 3 of the Act (applications for access to a health record);

(b) a copy of the complaint under regulation 3 or 4 of the Regulations (complaint about non-compliance with the Act); and

(c) if applicable, a copy of the report under regulation 6 of the Regulations (report in response to complaint).

Time of making application

3.14.3 The application shall be made where the applicant—

(a) has received a report in accordance with regulation 6 of the **D 532** Regulations, within one year of the date of the report;

(b) has not received such a report, within 18 months of the date of the complaint.

[1] PART XV

RACE RELATIONS ACT 1976

NOTE
[1] Inserted by the Act of Sederunt (Summary Applications, Statutory Applications and Appeals etc. Rules) Amendment 2000 (SSI 2000/148), para.2(2) (effective July 3, 2000).

Interpretation
3.15.1 In this Part—
"the Act" means the Race Relations Act 1976; and
"the Commission" means the Commission for Racial Equality established under section 43 of the Act.

Application
3.15.2 This Part shall apply to the following proceedings under the Act:—

(a) an application by the Commission under section 50(4) for an order requiring a person to comply with a notice served on him under section 50(1);

(b) an appeal by a person under section 59(1) against the requirement of a non discrimination notice served on him under section 58;

(c) an application by the Commission under section 62(1) for an order restraining a person from doing any of the acts referred to in that section;

(d) an application by the Commission under section 63(2) for a decision whether an alleged contravention of section 29, 30 or 31 has occurred;

(e) an application by the Commission under section 63(4) for an order restraining a person from doing any of the acts referred to in that section;

[1] (ea) an application by the Commission under section 71E for an order requiring a person to furnish any information required by a compliance notice; and

(f) an application by a person under section 72(5) for an order removing or modifying any term of a contract made unenforceable by section 72(2).

NOTE
[1] Inserted by the Act of Sederunt (Ordinary Cause, Summary Application and Small Claim Rules) Amendment (Miscellaneous) 2004 (SSI 2004/197) (effective May 21, 2004), para.3(6).

Intimation of proceedings
3.15.3 When any proceedings are brought under section 57 of the Act the applicant shall send by recorded delivery post a copy of the initial it initiating the action to the Commission

Taxation
3.15.4 The expenses incurred by the Commission within the meaning and for the purposes of section 66(5) of the Act, shall be taxed or assessed by the Auditor of the Sheriff Court in which proceedings under the Act were taken or would have been taken but for any compromise or settlement, as if they were outlays incurred by a solicitor on behalf of the applicant.

Adults with Incapacity (Scotland) Act 2000

NOTE
[1] Inserted by the Act of Sederunt (Summary Applications, Statutory Applications and Appeals etc. Rules) Amendment (Adults with Incapacity) 2001 (SSI 2001/142), r.3(2).

Interpretation
3.16.1 In this Part—
 "the 1984 Act" means the Mental Health (Scotland) Act 1984;
 "the 2000 Act" means the Adults with Incapacity (Scotland) Act 2000;
 "adult" means a person who has attained the age of 16 years and who is the subject of an application under the 2000 Act;
 "authorised establishment" has the meaning ascribed to it in section 35(2) of the 2000 Act;
 "continuing attorney" means a person on whom there has been conferred a power of attorney granted under section 15(1) of the 2000 Act;
 [1] "guardianship order" means an order made under section 58(4) of the 2000 Act;
 "incapable" has the meaning ascribed to it at section 1(6) of the 2000 Act, and "incapacity" shall be construed accordingly;
 [1] "intervention order" means an order made under section 53(1) of the 2000 Act;
 [1] "local authority" has the meaning ascribed to it by section 87(1) of the 2000 Act;
 "managers" has the meaning ascribed to it in paragraph 1 of Schedule 1 to the 2000 Act;
 [1] "Mental Welfare Commission" has the meaning ascribed to it by section 87(1) of the 2000 Act;
 "nearest relative" means, subject to section 87(2) of the 2000 Act, the person who would be, or would be exercising the functions of, the adult's nearest relative under sections 53 to 57 of the 1984 Act if the adult were a patient within the meaning of that Act and notwithstanding that the person neither is or was caring for the adult for the purposes of section 53(3) of that Act;
 "power of attorney" includes a factory and commission;
 "primary carer" means the person or organisation primarily engaged in caring for an adult;
 "Public Guardian" shall be construed in accordance with section 6 of the 2000 Act; and
 "welfare attorney" means a person on whom there has been conferred a power of attorney granted under section 16(1) of the 2000 Act.

NOTE
[1] As amended by the Act of Sederunt (Summary Applications, Statutory Applications and Appeals etc. Rules) Amendment (No.3) (Adults with Incapacity) 2002 (SSI 2002/146), r.2(2).

Appointment of hearing
3.16.2 On an application or other proceedings being submitted under or in pursuance of the 2000 Act the sheriff shall—
 (a) fix a hearing;
 (b) order answers to be lodged (where he considers it appropriate to do so) within a period that he shall specify; and
 (c) appoint service and intimation of the application or other proceedings.

Place, and privacy, of any hearing D 532/2
[1] **3.16.3** The sheriff may, where he considers it appropriate in all the circumstances, appoint that the hearing of an application or other proceedings shall take place—
  (a) in a hospital, or any other place than the court building;
  (b) in private.

NOTE
[1] Inserted by the Act of Sederunt (Ordinary Cause, Summary Application and Small Claim Rules) Amendment (Miscellaneous) 2004 (SSI 2004/197) (effective May 21, 2004), para.3(7).

Service of application
3.16.4—(1) Service of the application or other proceedings shall be made in Form 20 on—
  (a) the adult;
  (b) the nearest relative of the adult;
  (c) the primary carer of the adult (if any);
  (d) any guardian, continuing attorney or welfare attorney of the adult who has any power relating to the application or proceedings;
  (e) the Public Guardian;
[1] (ea) where appropriate, the Mental Welfare Commission;
[1] (eb) where appropriate, the local authority;
  (f) any other person directed by the sheriff.
  (2) Where the applicant is an individual person without legal representation service shall be effected by the sheriff clerk.
  (3) Where the adult is in an authorised establishment the person effecting service shall not serve Form 20 on the adult under paragraph (1)(a) but shall instead serve Forms 20 and 21, together with Form 22, on the managers of that authorised establishment by—
  (a) first class recorded delivery post; or
  (b) personal service by a sheriff officer.
  (4) On receipt of Forms 20 and 21 in terms of paragraph (3) the managers of the authorised establishment shall, subject to rule 3.16.5—
  (a) deliver the notice in Form 20 to the adult; and
  (b) as soon as practicable thereafter complete and return to the sheriff clerk a certificate of such delivery in Form 22.
  (5) Where the application or other proceeding follows on a remit under rule 3.16.9 the order for service of the application shall include an order for service on the Public Guardian or other party concerned.
[1] (6) Where the application is for an intervention order or a guardianship order, copies of the reports lodged in accordance with section 57(3) of the 2000 Act (reports to be lodged in court along with application) shall be served along with Forms 20, 21 and 22 as the case may be.

NOTE
[1] As amended by the Act of Sederunt (Summary Applications, Statutory Applications and Appeals etc. Rules) Amendment (No.3) (Adults with Incapacity) 2002 (SSI 2002/146), r.2(2).

Dispensing with service on adult
3.16.5—(1) Where, in relation to any application or proceeding under or in pursuance of the 2000 Act, two medical certificates are produced stating that intimation of the application or other proceeding, or notification of any interlocutor relating to such application or other proceeding, would be likely to pose a serious risk to the health of the adult the sheriff may dispense with such intimation or notification.
  (2) Any medical certificates produced under paragraph (1) shall be prepared by medical practitioners independent of each other.
  (3) In any case where the incapacity of the adult is by reason of mental disorder, one of the two medical practitioners must be a medical practitioner D 532/2/1

approved for the purposes of section 20 of the 1984 Act as having special experience in the diagnosis or treatment of mental disorder.

Hearing
3.16.6—[1] (1) A hearing to determine any application or other proceeding shall take place within 28 days of the interlocutor fixing the hearing under rule 3.16.2 unless any person upon whom the application is to be served is outside Europe.

(2) At the hearing referred to in paragraph (1) the sheriff may determine the application or other proceeding or may order such further procedure as he thinks fit.

NOTE
[1] As amended by the Act of Sederunt (Summary Applications, Statutory Applications and Appeals etc. Rules) Amendment (No.3) (Adults with Incapacity) 2002 (SSI 2002/146), r.2(2).

Prescribed forms of application
3.16.7—(1) An application submitted to the sheriff under or in pursuance of the 2000 Act, other than an appeal or remitted matter, shall be in Form 23.

(2) An appeal to the sheriff under or in pursuance of the 2000 Act shall be in Form 24.

Subsequent applications
3.16.8—[1] (1) Unless otherwise prescribed in the Part or under the 2000 Act, any application or proceedings subsequent to an initial application or proceeding considered by the sheriff including an application to renew an existing order, shall take the form of a minute lodged in the process.

[1] (1A) Except where the sheriff otherwise directs, any such minute shall be lodged in accordance with, and regulated by, Chapter 14 of the Ordinary Cause Rules.

(2) Where any subsequent application or proceedings under paragraph (1) above are made to a court in another sheriffdom the sheriff clerk shall transmit the court process to the court dealing with the current application or proceeding.

(3) Transmission of the process in terms of paragraph (2) shall be made within 4 days of it being requested by the sheriff clerk of the court in which the current application or proceedings have been raised.

[1] (4) Where the application is for renewal of a guardianship order, copies of the reports lodged in accordance with section 57(3) shall be served along with the minute.

NOTE
[1] As amended the Act of Sederunt (Summary Applications, Statutory Applications and Appeals etc. Rules) Amendment (No.3) (Adults with Incapacity) 2002 (SSI 2002/146), r.2(2).

Remit of applications by the Public Guardian etc.
3.16.9 Where an application is remitted to the sheriff by the Public Guardian or by any other party authorised to do so under the 2000 Act the party remitting the application shall, within 4 days of the decision to remit, transmit the papers relating to the application to the sheriff clerk of the court where the application is to be considered.

NOTE
[1] As amended by the Act of Sederunt (Summary Applications, Statutory Applications and Appeals etc. Rules) Amendment (No.3) (Adults with Incapacity) 2002 (SSI 2002/146), r.2(2).

Caution
[1] **3.16.10**—(1) Where the sheriff requires a person authorised under an intervention order or any variation of an intervention order, or appointed as a guardian, to find caution he shall specify the amount and period within which caution is to be found in the interlocutor authorising or appointing the person or varying the order (as the case may be).

(2) The sheriff may, on application made by motion before the expiry of the period for finding caution and on cause shown, allow further time for finding caution in accordance with paragraph (1).

(3) Caution shall be lodged with the Public Guardian.

(4) Where caution has been lodged to the satisfaction of the Public Guardian he shall notify the sheriff clerk.

(5) The sheriff may at any time while a requirement to find caution is in **D 532/4** force—

    (a) increase the amount of, or require the person to find new, caution; or

    (b) authorise the amount of caution to be decreased.

NOTE
[1] Inserted by the Act of Sederunt (Summary Applications, Statutory Applications and Appeals etc. Rules) Amendment (No.3) (Adults with Incapacity) 2002 (SSI 2002/146), r.2(2).

Appointment of interim guardian
[1] **3.16.11** An application under section 57(5) of the 2000 Act (appointment of interim guardian) may be made in the crave of the application for a guardianship order to which it relates or, if made after the submission of the application for a guardianship order, by motion in the process of that application.

NOTE
[1] Inserted by the Act of Sederunt (Summary Applications, Statutory Applications and Appeals etc. Rules) Amendment (No.3) (Adults with Incapacity) 2002 (SSI 2002/146), r.2(2).

Registration of intervention order or guardianship order relating to heritable property
[1] **3.16.12** Where an application for an intervention order or a guardianship order seeks to vest in the person authorised under the order, or the guardian, as the case may be, any right to deal with, convey or manage any interest in heritable property which is recorded or capable of being recorded in the General Register of Sasines or is registered or capable of being registered in the Land Register of Scotland, the applicant must specify the necessary details of the property in the application to enable it to be identified in the Register of Sasines or the Land Register of Scotland, as the case may be.

NOTE
[1] Inserted by the Act of Sederunt (Summary Applications, Statutory Applications and Appeals etc. Rules) Amendment (No.3) (Adults with Incapacity) 2002 (SSI 2002/146), r.2(2).

Non-compliance with decisions of guardians with welfare powers
[1] **3.16.13**—(1) Where the court is required under section 70(3) of the 2000 Act to intimate an application for an order or warrant in relation to non-compliance with the decision of a guardian with welfare powers, the sheriff clerk shall effect intimation in Form 20 in accordance with paragraphs (2) and (3).

(2) Intimation shall be effected—

    (a) where the person is within Scotland, by first class recorded delivery post, or, in the event that intimation by first class recorded delivery post is unsuccessful, by personal service by a sheriff officer; or

(b) where the person is furth of Scotland, in accordance with rule 2.12 (service on persons furth of Scotland).

(3) Such intimation shall include notice of the period within which any objection to the application shall be lodged.

NOTE
[1] Inserted by the Act of Sederunt (Summary Applications, Statutory Applications and Appeals etc. Rules) Amendment (No.3) (Adults with Incapacity) 2002 (SSI 2002/146), r.2(2).

D 532/5   [1] PART XVII

ANTI-TERRORISM, CRIME AND SECURITY ACT 2001

NOTE
[1] Inserted by the Act of Sederunt (Summary Applications, Statutory Applications and Appeals etc. Rules) Amendment (Detention and Forfeiture of Terrorist Cash) 2002 (SSI 2002/129), para.2(2).

Interpretation
3.17.1 In this Part, any reference to a specified paragraph shall be construed as a reference to the paragraph bearing that number in Schedule 1 to the Anti-terrorism, Crime and Security Act 2001.

Applications for extended detention of cash
3.17.2—(1) An application to the sheriff for an order under paragraph 3(2) (extended detention of seized cash) shall be made by summary application.

(2) An application for any further order for the detention of cash under paragraph 3(2) shall be made by minute in the original process and shall be proceeded with in accordance with sub-paragraph (3) below.

(3) On the lodging of an application for any further order the sheriff shall—
(a) fix a date for determination of the application; and
(b) order service of the application together with notice of such date for determination on any persons whom he considers may be affected.

Applications for release of detained cash
3.17.3—(1) An application to the sheriff under paragraph 5(2) (application for release of detained cash) or under paragraph 9(1) (application by person who claims that cash belongs to him) shall, where the court has made an order under paragraph 3(2), be made by minute in the original process of the application for that order, and in any other case shall be made by summary application.

(2) On the lodging of such an application the sheriff shall—
(a) fix a date for a hearing; and
(b) order service of the application together with notice of such hearing on the procurator fiscal and any other person whom he considers may be affected by the granting of such an application.

Applications for forfeiture of detained cash
3.17.4—(1) An application to the sheriff under paragraph 6(1) (application for forfeiture of detained cash) shall, where the court has made an order under paragraph 3(2), be made by minute in the original process of the application for that order, and in any other case shall be made by summary application.

(2) On the lodging of such an application the sheriff shall—
(a) fix a date for a hearing; and
(b) order service of the application together with notice of such hearing on any person whom he considers may be affected by the granting of such an application.

Applications for compensation
  3.17.5—(1) An application to the sheriff under paragraph 10(1) (application for compensation) shall, where the court has made an order under paragraph 3(2), be made by minute in the original process of the application for that order, and in any other case shall be made by summary application.
  (2) On the lodging of such an application the sheriff shall—
  (a) fix a date for a hearing; and   **D 532/6**
  (b) order service of the application together with notice of such hearing on any person whom he considers may be affected by the granting of such an application.

[1] PART XVIII

LOCAL GOVERNMENT (SCOTLAND) ACT 1973

NOTE
  [1] Inserted by the Act of Sederunt (Summary Applications, Statutory Applications and Appeals etc. Rules) Amendment (No.2) (Local Government (Scotland) Act 1973) 2002 (SSI 2002/130), para.2(3).

Application
  3.18.1—This Part applies to appeals to the sheriff principal under section 103J of the Local Government (Scotland) Act 1973 (appeals from the Accounts Commission for Scotland).

Appeals
  3.18.2—(1) An appeal under this Part shall be made by summary application.
  (2) A summary application made under paragraph (1) shall include grounds of appeal stating—
  (a) the finding or sanction or suspension being appealed;
  (b) reasons why the appeal should be allowed; and
  (c) the date of sending of the finding or imposition of the sanction or suspension concerned,
and shall be accompanied by a copy of such finding, sanction or suspension.

Warrant and form of citation
  3.18.3—(1) A warrant for citation in an appeal under this Part shall be in Form 2A and shall state—
  (a) the date by which answers should be lodged; and
  (b) the date and time when the appeal will call.
  (2) Citation in respect of a warrant granted under paragraph (1) shall be in Form 3A.
  (3) Where a party on whom service has been made lodges answers under paragraph (1)(a) that party shall, at the same time, send a copy to the applicant.
  (4) In Schedule 1 (forms)—
  (a) after Form 2 insert Form 2A; and
  (b) after Form 3 insert Form 3A,
as set out in the Schedule to this Act of Sederunt.

[1] PART XIX

PROCEEDS OF CRIME ACT 2002

NOTE
  [1] Inserted by the Act of Sederunt (Summary Applications, Statutory Applications and Appeals etc. Rules) Amendment (No.5) (Proceeds of Crime Act 2002) 2002 (SSI 2002/563), para.2(2) (effective December 30, 2002).

Interpretation and application

[1] **3.19.1.**—(1) In this Part—

"the Act" means the Proceeds of Crime Act 2002;

references to an administrator are to an administrator appointed under section 125(1) or 128(3);

a reference to a specified section is a reference to the section bearing that number in the Act; and any reference to a specified paragraph in a specified Schedule is a reference to the paragraph bearing that number in the Schedule of that number in the Act.

(2) This Part applies to applications to the sheriff under Parts 3, 5 and 8 of the Act; but it only applies to applications under Part 8 in relation to property that is the subject of a civil recovery investigation.

NOTE

[1] Substituted by the Act of Sederunt (Summary Applications, Statutory Applications and Appeals etc. Rules) Amendment (No.6) (Proceeds of Crime Act 2002) 2003 (SSI 2003/98), para.2(2)(a) (effective March 24, 2003).

Recovery of cash in summary proceedings

Applications for extended detention of cash

3.19.2.—(1) An application to the sheriff for an order under sections 295(2) and (7) (extended detention of seized cash) shall be made by summary application.

(2) An application for any further order for the detention of cash under section 295(2) shall be made by minute in the process of the original application for extended detention of seized cash and shall be proceeded with in accordance with sub-paragraph (3) below.

(3) On the lodging of an application for any further order the sheriff shall—

(a) fix a date for determination of the application; and

(b) order service of the application together with notice of such date for determination on any persons whom he considers may be affected.

Applications for release of detained cash

3.19.3.—(1) An application to the sheriff under section 297(3) (application for release of detained cash) or under section 301(1) (application by person who claims that cash belongs to him) shall, where the court has made an order under section 295(2), be made by minute in the process of the application for that order, and in any other case shall be made by summary application in the course of the proceedings or at any other time.

(2) On the lodging of such an application the sheriff shall—

(a) fix a date for a hearing; and

(b) order service of the application together with notice of such hearing on the procurator fiscal and any other person whom he considers may be affected by the granting of such an application.

Applications for forfeiture of detained cash

3.19.4.—(1) An application to the sheriff under section 298(1)(b) (application by the Scottish Ministers for forfeiture of detained cash) shall, where the court has made an order under section 295(2), be made by minute in the process of the application for that order, and in any other case shall be made by summary application.

(2) On the lodging of such an application the sheriff shall—

(a) fix a date for a hearing; and

(b) order service of the application together with notice of such hearing on any person whom he considers may be affected by the granting of such an application.

Applications for compensation
3.19.5.—(1) An application to the sheriff under section 302(1) (application for compensation) shall, where the court has made an order under section 295(2), be made by minute in the process of the application for that order, **D 532/8** and in any other case shall be made by summary application.

(2) On the lodging of such an application the sheriff shall—
(a) fix a date for a hearing; and
(b) order service of the application together with notice of such hearing on any person whom he considers may be affected by the granting of such an application.

[1] *Restraint and administration orders*

Service of restraint orders
[1] **3.19.6.** The intimation to be made by the prosecutor under section 121(3) shall be made by serving a copy of the interlocutor granting a restraint order on every person named in the interlocutor as restrained by the order.

Recall or variation of restraint orders
[1] **3.19.7.** An application to the sheriff under section 121(5) (variation or recall of restraint order) shall be made by minute in the process of the application for the restraint order.

Appeals to the Court of Session
[1] **3.19.8.**—(1) An appeal against an interlocutor of the sheriff refusing, varying or recalling or refusing to vary or recall a restraint order shall be marked within 14 days after the date of the interlocutor concerned.

(2) Such an appeal shall be marked by writing a note of appeal on the interlocutor sheet, or other written record containing the interlocutor appealed against, or on a separate sheet lodged with the sheriff clerk, in the following terms—
"The applicant appeals to the Court of Session.".

(3) The note of appeal shall—
(a) be signed by the appellant;
(b) bear the date on which it is signed; and
(c) where the appellant is represented, specify the name and address of the solicitor or other agent who will be acting for him in the appeal.

(4) The sheriff clerk will transmit the process within 4 days after the appeal is marked to the Deputy Principal Clerk of Session.

(5) Within the period specified in paragraph (4), the sheriff clerk shall—
(a) send written notice of the appeal to every other party; and
(b) certify on the interlocutor sheet that he has done so.

(6) Failure of the sheriff clerk to comply with paragraph (5) shall not invalidate the appeal.

Applications in relation to arrestment
[1] **3.19.9.**—(1) An application to the sheriff under section 124(1) (arrestment of property affected by restraint order) by the prosecutor for warrant for arrestment may be made—
(a) in the application made under section 121(2) (application for restraint order); or
(b) if made after a restraint order has been applied for, by minute in the process of the application for that order.

(2) An application to the sheriff under section 124(3) (recalling, loosing or restricting arrestment) or under section 124(6) (recall or restriction of arrestment) shall be made by minute in the process of the application for the restraint order.

Applications for appointment of administrators

[1] **3.19.10.**—(1) An application to the sheriff under section 125(1) (appointment of management administrator) shall be made by minute in the process of the application for the restraint order.

(2) An application to the sheriff under section 128(2) (appointment of enforcement administrator) shall be made—

    (a) where made after a restraint order has been made, by minute in the process of the application for that order; or

    (b) in any other case, by summary application.

(3) The notification to be made by the sheriff clerk under section 125(3) or 128(8) (as the case may be) shall be made by intimation of a copy of the interlocutor to the accused and the persons subject to the order.

Incidental applications in relation to an administration

[1] **3.19.11.** An application to the sheriff subsequent to the appointment of an administrator relating to any matter incidental to that appointment shall be made by minute in the process of the application in which the administrator was appointed.

Documents for Accountant of Court

[1] **3.19.12.**—(1) A person who has lodged any document in the process of an application for the appointment of an administrator shall forthwith send a copy of that document to the Accountant of Court.

(2) The sheriff clerk shall transmit to the Accountant of Court any part of the process as the Accountant of Court may request in relation to an administration which is in dependence before the sheriff unless such part of the process is, at the time of request, required by the sheriff.

Procedure for fixing and finding caution

[1] **3.19.13.**—(1) The Accountant of Court shall forthwith, on receiving intimation of an application for the appointment of an administrator, fix the caution to be found in the event of appointment being made and shall notify the amount to the sheriff clerk and the applicant.

(2) During the subsistence of the appointment of the administrator, the Accountant of Court may, at any time—

    (a) require the administrator to increase the amount of or find new or additional caution; or

    (b) authorise the administrator to decrease the amount of existing caution.

Time for finding caution

[1] **3.19.14.**—(1) Where the time within which caution is to be found is not stipulated in the interlocutor appointing the administrator, the time allowed for finding caution shall be, subject to paragraph (2) of this rule, limited to one calendar month from the date of the interlocutor.

(2) The sheriff may, on application made before the expiry of the period for finding caution, and, on cause shown, allow further time for finding caution.

Procedure on finding caution

[1] **3.19.15.**—(1) Caution shall be lodged with the Accountant of Court.

(2) Where caution has been found to the satisfaction of the Accountant of Court, he shall notify the sheriff clerk.

Issue of certified copy interlocutor
  [1] **3.19.16.**—(1) A certified copy interlocutor of appointment of an administrator shall not be issued by the sheriff clerk until he receives notification from the Accountant of Court in accordance with rule 3.19.15(2).

Administrator's title to act
  [1] **3.19.17.** An administrator shall not be entitled to act until he has obtained a certified copy of the interlocutor appointing him.

Accounts   D 532/10
  [1] **3.19.18.**—(1) An administrator shall maintain accounts of his intromissions with the property in his charge and shall, subject to paragraph (2)—
  (a) within six months after the date of his appointment; and
  (b) at six monthly intervals after the first account during the subsistence of his appointment,
lodge with the Accountant of Court an account of his intromissions in such form, with such supporting vouchers and other documents, as the Accountant of Court may require.
  (2) The Accountant of Court may waive the lodging of an account where the administrator certifies that there have been no intromissions during a particular accounting period.

Application for discharge of administrator
  [1] **3.19.19.** An application to the sheriff for discharge of an administrator shall be made by minute in the process of the application in which the administrator was appointed.

Appeals against determination of outlays and remuneration
  [1] **3.19.20.** An appeal to the sheriff under paragraph 9(1) of Schedule 3 (appeal against a determination by the Accountant of Court) shall be made by minute in the process of the application in which the administrator was appointed.

NOTE
  [1] Inserted by the Act of Sederunt (Summary Applications, Statutory Applications and Appeals etc. Rules) Amendment (No.6) (Proceeds of Crime Act 2002) 2003 (SSI 2003/98), para.2(2)(b) (effective March 24, 2003).

[1] *Civil recovery investigations*

Production orders
  [1] **3.19.21.**—(1) An application to the sheriff under section 382(2) (order to grant entry to premises) may be made—
  (a) in the application for the production order; or
  (b) if made after the production order has been made, by minute in the process of the application for that order.
  (2) A report to the sheriff under section 385(4) (report of failure to bring production order made in relation to an authorised government department to the attention of the officer concerned) shall take the form of a letter to the sheriff clerk.
  (3) An application to the sheriff under section 386(4) (discharge or variation of a production order or an order to grant entry) shall be made by minute in the process of the application for the production order.

Search warrants
  [1] **3.19.22.** An application to the sheriff under section 387(1) (search warrant) shall be in the form of a summary application.

Customer information orders
    [1] **3.19.23**. An application under section 403(4) (discharge or variation of a customer information order) shall be made by minute in the process of the application for the customer information order.

Account monitoring orders
    [1] **3.19.24**. An application under section 408(4) (discharge or variation of an account monitoring order) shall be made by minute in the process of the application for the account monitoring order.

D 532/11 NOTE
    [1] Inserted by the Act of Sederunt (Summary Applications, Statutory Applications and Appeals etc. Rules) Amendment (No.6) (Proceeds of Crime Act 2002) 2003 (SSI 2003/98), para.2(2)(b) (effective February 24, 2003).

[1] PART XX

INTERNATIONAL CRIMINAL COURT (SCOTLAND) ACT 2001

NOTE
    [1] Inserted by the Act of Sederunt (Summary Applications, Statutory Applications and Appeals etc. Rules) Amendment (International Criminal Court) 2003 (SSI 2003/27), para.2(2) (effective January 24, 2003).

General

Interpretation and application
    3.20.1.—(1) In this Part—
        "the Act" means the International Criminal Court (Scotland) Act 2001;
        "ICC crime" has the same meaning as in section 28(1) of the Act; and a reference to a specified section is a reference to the section bearing that number in the Act, and any reference to a specified paragraph in a specified schedule is a reference to the paragraph bearing that number in the schedule of that number to the Act.
    (2) This Part applies to applications to the sheriff under Parts 1 and 2 of schedule 5 to the Act.

Investigations of proceeds of ICC crime

Production or access orders
    3.20.2.—(1) An order under Part 1 of schedule 5 to the Act may be made by the sheriff on a summary application by a person authorised for the purpose under section 19 of the Act.
    (2) Any such application may be made on an ex parte application to a sheriff in chambers.
    (3) Any such application must set out reasonable grounds for suspecting—
        (a) that a specified person has benefited from an ICC crime; and
        (b) that the material to which the application relates is likely to be of substantial value (whether by itself or together with other material) to the investigation for the purposes of which the application is made.
    (4) Any application for variation or discharge of an order under Part 1 of schedule 5 to the Act shall be made by minute.

Search warrants
    3.20.3.—(1) On a summary application by a person authorised under section 19 of the Act to the sheriff sitting as a court of civil jurisdiction, the sheriff may issue a warrant under Part 2 of the Act.

(2) Any such application must set out grounds sufficient to satisfy the sheriff—

    (a) that a production or access order made in relation to material on the premises has not been complied with;

    (b) that—

        (i) there are reasonable grounds for suspecting that a specified person has benefited from an ICC crime;

        (ii) there are grounds for making a production and access order in relation to material on the premises; and

        (iii) it would not be appropriate to make a production and access order in relation to the material for any of the reasons specified in paragraph 10(4) of schedule 5 to the Act; or

                                                              D 532/12

    (c) that—

        (i) there are reasonable grounds for suspecting that a specified person has benefited from an ICC crime;

        (ii) there are reasonable grounds for suspecting that there is material on the premises which cannot be particularised at the time of the application, but which—

            (aa) relates to the specified person, or to the question of whether that person has benefited from an ICC crime, or to any question as to the extent or whereabouts of the proceeds of an ICC crime; and

            (bb) is likely to be of substantial value (whether by itself or together with other material) to the investigation for the purposes of which the application is made; and

        (iii) any of the circumstances specified in paragraph 10(6) of schedule 5 to the Act applies.

[1] PART XXI

IMMIGRATION AND ASYLUM ACT 1999

NOTE

[1] Inserted by the Act of Sederunt (Summary Applications, Statutory Applications and Appeals etc. Rules) Amendment (Immigration and Asylum) 2003 (SSI 2003/261), para.2(2) (effective May 24, 2003).

Interpretation

3.21.1. In this Part—

"the Act" means the Immigration and Asylum Act 1999; and

"an appeal" means an appeal to the sheriff under section 35A(1) or section 40B(1) of the Act.

Appeals

3.21.2.—(1) A person making an appeal against a decision by the Secretary of State to impose a penalty under section 32 or a charge under section 40 of the Act must, subject to paragraph (2), bring an appeal within 21 days after receiving the penalty notice or charge notice.

(2) Where the appellant has given notice of objection to the Secretary of State under section 35(4) or section 40A(3) of the Act within the time prescribed for doing so, he must bring an appeal within 21 days after receiving notice of the Secretary of State's decision under section 35(7) or section 40A(6) respectively of the Act in response to the notice of objection.

[1] PART XXII

CRIME AND DISORDER ACT 1998

NOTE

[1] Inserted by the Act of Sederunt (Summary Applications, Statutory Applications and Appeals etc. Rules) Amendment (Anti-social Behaviour Orders) 2003 (SSI 2003/319), para.2(2) (effective June 27, 2003).

Interpretation

3.22.1. In this Part—

"the Act" means the Crime and Disorder Act 1998;

"interim ASBO" means an ASBO made under section 19(2A) of the Act; and

"ASBO" means an anti-social behaviour order made under section 19(3) of the Act.

D 532/13 *Application for an interim ASBO*

3.22.2.—(1) An application for an interim ASBO shall be made by crave in the initial writ in which an ASBO is sought.

(2) An application for an interim ASBO once craved shall be moved by motion to that effect.

(3) The sheriff shall not consider an application for an interim ASBO until after service of the initial writ has been effected on the person in respect of whom that application is made.

Intimation of an ASBO

3.22.3. The pursuer shall forthwith intimate the making or recall of an ASBO or an interim ASBO to the relevant Chief Constable.

[1] PART XXIII

ETHICAL STANDARDS IN PUBLIC LIFE ETC. (SCOTLAND) ACT 2000

NOTE

[1] Inserted by the Act of Sederunt (Summary Applications, Statutory Applications and Appeals etc. Rules) Amendment (Standards Commission for Scotland) 2003 (SSI 2003/346), para.2(2) (effective July 4, 2003).

Application

3.23.1. This Part applies to appeals to the sheriff principal under sections 22 (appeals from commission) or 26 (appeals by water industry commissioner) of the Ethical Standards in Public Life etc. (Scotland) Act 2000.

Appeals

3.23.2.—(1) An appeal under this Part shall be made by summary application.

(2) A summary application made under paragraph (1) shall include grounds of appeal stating—

(a) which of the findings of, or sanction or suspension imposed by, the Standards Commission for Scotland is being appealed;

(b) reasons why the appeal should be allowed; and

(c) the date of the sending of that finding, or imposition of that sanction or suspension,

and shall be accompanied by a copy of that finding, sanction or suspension.

Warrant and form of citation

3.23.3.—(1) A warrant for citation in an appeal under this Part shall be in Form 2A, or a form as near thereto as circumstances permit, and shall state—

    (a) the date by which answers should be lodged; and

    (b) the date and time when the appeal will call.

    (2) Citation in respect of a warrant granted under paragraph (1) shall be in Form 3A, or a form as near thereto as circumstances permit.

    (3) Where a party on whom service has been made lodges answers under paragraph (1)(a) that party shall, at the same time, send a copy to the appellant.

[1] PART XXIV

INTERNATIONAL PROTECTION OF ADULTS

NOTE

[1] Inserted by the Act of Sederunt (Summary Applications, Statutory Applications and Appeals etc.Rules) Amendment (International Protection of Adults) 2003 (SSI 2003/556), para.2(2) (effective November 14, 2003).

Interpretation   **D 532/14**

    3.24.1. In this Part—

    "the Act" means the Adults with Incapacity (Scotland) Act 2000;

    "the Convention" means the Hague Convention of 13th January 2000 on the International Protection of Adults;

    "international measure" means any measure taken under the law of a country other than Scotland for the personal welfare, or the protection of property, of an adult with incapacity, where—

        (a) jurisdiction in the other country was based on the adult's habitual residence there; or

        (b) the other country and the United Kingdom were when that measure was taken parties to the Convention, and jurisdiction in that other country was based on a ground of jurisdiction in the Convention; and

    "Public Guardian" shall be construed in accordance with section 6 (the public guardian and his functions) of the Act.

Application

    3.24.2—(1) An application to register an international measure under paragraph 8(1) of schedule 3 to the Act shall be by summary application made under this Part.

    (2) The original document making the international measure, or a copy of that document duly certified as such by an officer of the issuing or a requesting body, shall be lodged with an application under paragraph (1), together with (as necessary) an English translation of that document and that certificate.

    (3) Any translation under paragraph (2) must be certified as a correct translation by the person making it, and the certificate must contain the full name, address and qualifications of the translator.

Intimation of application

    3.24.3.—(1) The sheriff shall order intimation of an application to register an international measure—

        (a) except where the sheriff is satisfied that the person to whom the international measure relates had an opportunity to be heard in the country where that measure was taken, to that person;

        (b) which if registered would have the effect of placing the adult to whom the international measure relates in an establishment in Scotland, to the—

            (i) Scottish Central Authority; and

            (ii) Mental Welfare Commission;

        (c) to the Public Guardian; and

(d) to any other person whom the sheriff considers appropriate.

(2) In this rule—

(a) "Scottish Central Authority" means an authority—
   (i) designated under Article 28 of the Convention for the purposes of acting as such; or
   (ii) appointed by the Scottish Ministers for the purposes of carrying out the functions to be carried out under schedule 3 of the Act by the Scottish Central Authority, where no authority is designated for the purposes of sub paragraph (i); and
(b) "Mental Welfare Commission" means the Mental Welfare Commission for Scotland continued in being by section 2 of the Mental Health (Scotland) Act 1984.

Notice to the Public Guardian

3.24.4. The sheriff clerk shall within 7 days after the date of an order registering an international measure, provide the Public Guardian with—

D 532/15

(a) a copy of that order; and

(b) a copy of the international measure, and of any translation.

Register of recognised foreign measures

3.24.5.—(1) There shall be a register of international measures ("the register") registered by order under this Part.

(2) The register shall include—

(a) the nature of the international measure;

(b) the date of the international measure;

(c) the date of the order under this Part granting recognition of the international measure;

(d) the name and address of—
   (i) the person who applied for recognition of the international measure under this Part;
   (ii) the person in respect of whom the international measure was taken; and
   (iii) if applicable, the person on whom any power is conferred by the international measure; and

(e) a copy of the international measure, and of any translation.

(3) The Public Guardian shall maintain the register, and make it available during normal office hours for inspection by members of the public.

(4) The Public Guardian shall if requested by any person certify that an international measure registered under this Part has been entered in the register.

[1] PART XXV

SEXUAL OFFENCES ACT 2003

NOTE

[1] Inserted by the Act of Sederunt (Summary Applications, Statutory Applications and Appeals etc. Rules) Amendment (Sexual Offences Act 2003) 2004 (SSI 2004/222), para.2(2) (effective May 21, 2004).

Interpretation

3.25.1. In this Part—

"the Act" means the Sexual Offences Act 2003.

Time limit for service of a notice under section 99(3)

3.25.2. If the person in respect of whom a notification order is sought wishes to serve on the applicant a notice under section 99(3) of the Act, that person must do so no later than 3 working days before the hearing date for the application for the relevant notification order.

Time limit for service of a notice under section 106(11)

3.25.3. If the person in respect of whom a sexual offences prevention order is sought wishes to serve on the applicant a notice under section 106(11) of the Act, that person must do so no later than 3 working days before the hearing date for the application for the relevant sexual offences prevention order.

Time limit for service of a notice under section 116(6)

3.25.4. If the person in respect of whom a foreign travel order is sought wishes to serve on the applicant a notice under section 116(6) of the Act, that person must do so no later than 3 working days before the hearing date for the application for the relevant foreign travel order.

Remit of original process under section 108(1)

3.25.5. Where an application is made under section 108(1) of the Act for an order varying, renewing or discharging a sexual offences prevention order (a "section 108 order") to a sheriff other than a sheriff of the sheriff court which granted the sexual offences prevention order in respect of which the relevant section 108 order is sought (in this rule, the "granting sheriff court")— **D 532/16**

(a) the sheriff court to which the application for the relevant section 108 order has been made (in this rule, the "requesting sheriff court") shall notify the granting sheriff court of such application; and

(b) the granting sheriff court shall, within 4 days of receipt of such notification, remit to the requesting sheriff court the original process relating to the relevant sexual offences prevention order.

Remit of original process under section 118(1)

3.25.6. Where an application is made under section 118(1) of the Act for an order varying, renewing or discharging a foreign travel order (a "section 118 order") to a sheriff other than a sheriff of the sheriff court which granted the foreign travel order in respect of which the relevant section 118 order is sought (in this rule, the "granting sheriff court")—

(a) the sheriff court to which the application for the relevant section 118 order has been made (in this rule, the "requesting sheriff court") shall notify the granting sheriff court of such application; and

(b) the granting sheriff court shall within 4 days of receipt of such notification, remit to the requesting sheriff court the original process relating to the foreign travel order.

[1] PART XXVI

PROTECTION OF CHILDREN (SCOTLAND) ACT 2003

NOTE

[1] Inserted by the Act of Sederunt (Summary Applications, Statutory Applications and Appeals etc. Rules) Amendment (Protection of Children (Scotland) Act 2003) 2004 (SSI 2004/ 334), para.2(2) (effective July 30, 2004).

Interpretation

3.26.1. In this Part—

"the Act" means the Protection of Children (Scotland) Act 2003; and

"the list" means the list of individuals considered unsuitable to work with children kept by the Scottish Ministers under section 1(1) of the Act, and cognate expressions shall be construed accordingly.

Application

3.26.2. An application under section 7(6) or 14(1) or an appeal under section 15(1) of the Act shall be made by summary application.

Provisional inclusion in the list
3.26.3. The sheriff may consider and dispose of an application by the Scottish Ministers under section 7(6) of the Act without intimation to, or representation by, any other person.

Applications for removal from the list
3.26.4.—(1) A listed individual shall combine in a single application—
  (a) a request for leave to make an application under section 14(1) of the Act;
  (b) the grounds on which that individual considers that the sheriff should grant leave; and
  (c) the grounds on which that individual considers that the sheriff should grant such an application.
(2) An application under paragraph (1) shall be intimated to the Scottish Ministers.

(3) The sheriff shall consider and dispose of at a preliminary hearing that part of an application relating to the request for leave under paragraph (1)(a).

Appeal: inclusion in lists under section 5 or 6 of the Act
3.26.5. An appeal under section 15(1) of the Act against inclusion in the list in terms of section 5 or 6 of the Act shall be intimated to the Scottish Ministers.

Appeals: to the sheriff principal or to the Inner House of the Court of Session
3.26.6. An appeal under section 15(4) of the Act to the sheriff principal or an appeal under section 15(6)(a) of the Act to the Inner House of the Court of Session shall be intimated to the Scottish Ministers.

[1] PART XXVII

ANTISOCIAL BEHAVIOUR ETC. (SCOTLAND) ACT 2004

Interpretation
3.27.1.—(1) In this Part—
  "the Act" means the Antisocial Behaviour etc. (Scotland) Act 2004;
  "ASBO" means an antisocial behaviour order under section 4(1) of the Act;
  "interim ASBO" means an interim ASBO under section 7(2) of the Act;
  "parenting order" means a parenting order under section 13 or 102 of the Act; and
  "the Principal Reporter" means the Principal Reporter appointed under section 127 of the Local Government etc. (Scotland) Act 1994.
(2) Any reference to a section shall, unless the context otherwise requires, be a reference to a section of the Act.

Applications for variation or revocation of ASBOs to be made by minute in the original process
3.27.2.—(1) An application under section 5 (variation and revocation of antisocial behaviour orders) shall be made by minute in the original process of the application for the ASBO in relation to which the variation or revocation is sought.
(2) Where the person subject to the ASBO is a child, a written statement containing the views of the Principal Reporter on the application referred to in rule 3.27.2(1) shall, where practicable, be lodged with that application.

Application for an interim ASBO

3.27.3.—(1) An application for an interim ASBO shall be made by crave in the initial writ in which an ASBO is sought.

(2) An application for an interim ASBO once craved shall be moved by motion to that effect.

(3) The sheriff shall not consider an application for an interim ASBO until after the initial writ has been intimated to the person in respect of whom that application is made and, where that person is a child, a written statement containing the views of the Principal Reporter on that application has been lodged.

Notification of making etc. of ASBOs and interim ASBOs

3.27.4.—(1) Where a person is present in court at the time an ASBO or interim ASBO is made or an ASBO to which that person is subject is varied, service of a copy of the order making the ASBO or interim ASBO or varying the ASBO, as the case may be, shall be made under section 8(5)(a) or (b) and may be effected by the sheriff clerk—

(a) giving such copy to and obtaining a receipt therefor from that person; or **D 532/18**

(b) sending such copy to that person by recorded delivery letter or registered post.

(2) Where a person is not present in court at the time an ASBO or interim ASBO is made or an ASBO to which that person is subject is varied, service of a copy of the order making the ASBO or interim ASBO or varying the ASBO, as the case may be, shall be made under section 8(5)(b) and shall be effected by such copy being sent to the person subject to the ASBO or interim ASBO by recorded delivery letter or registered post.

Parenting orders

3.27.5.—(1) Where a sheriff is considering making a parenting order under section 13 (sheriff's power to make parenting order), the sheriff shall order the applicant for the ASBO to—

(a) intimate to any parent in respect of whom the parenting order is being considered—

   (i) that the court is considering making a parenting order in respect of that parent;

   (ii) that if that parent wishes to oppose the making of such a parenting order, he or she may attend or be represented at the hearing at which the sheriff considers the making of the parenting order;

   (iii) the place, date and time of the hearing set out in sub-paragraph (a)(ii) above; and

   (iv) that if that parent fails to appear and is not represented at the hearing, a parenting order may be made in respect of the parent; and

(b) serve on any parent in respect of whom the parenting order is being considered a copy of the initial writ in which the ASBO is sought.

(2) Any parent in respect of whom a parenting order under section 13 is being considered may be sisted as a party to the action on their own motion, on the motion of either party or by the sheriff of his own motion.

Closure notice

3.27.6.—(1) A closure notice served under section 27 (service etc.) shall be in the form of Form 25 and shall (in addition to the requirements set out in section 27(5))—

(a) state that it has been authorised by a senior police officer;

(b) specify the date, time and place of the hearing of the application for a closure order under section 28; and

(c) state that any person living on or having control of, responsibility for or an interest in the premises to which the closure notice relates who wishes to oppose the application should attend or be represented.

(2) Certification of service of a copy of the closure notice to all persons identified in accordance with section 27(2)(b) shall be in the form of Form 26.

Application for closure orders
3.27.7. An application to the sheriff for a closure order under section 28 shall be in the form of Form 27.

Application for extension of closure orders
3.27.8. An application to the sheriff for an extension of a closure order under section 32 shall be by minute in the form of Form 28 lodged in the original process of the application for the closure order in relation to which the extension is sought and shall be lodged not less than 21 days before the closure order to which it relates is due to expire.

D 532/19 #### Application for revocation of closure order
3.27.9. An application to the sheriff for revocation of a closure order under section 33 shall be by minute in the form of Form 29 lodged in the original process of the application for the closure order in relation to which the revocation is sought.

Application for access to premises
3.27.10. An application to the sheriff for an order for access to premises under section 34 shall be by minute in the form of Form 30 lodged in the original process of the application for the closure order in relation to which the access order is sought.

Applications by summary application
3.27.11. An application under section 35 (Reimbursement of expenditure), 63 (Appeal against graffiti removal notice) or 64 (Appeal against notice under section 61(4)) shall be by summary application.

3.27.12. An application under section 71 (Failure to comply with notice: order as to rental income), 74 (Failure to comply with notice: management control order) or 97 (Appeals against notice under section 94) shall be by summary application.

Revocation and suspension of order as to rental income
3.27.13. An application under section 73(2) for the revocation or suspension of an order relating to rental income shall be by minute lodged in the original process of the application for the order relating to rental income in relation to which the order for revocation or suspension is sought.

Revocation of management control order
3.27.14. An application under section 76(1) for the revocation of a management control order shall be by minute lodged in the original process of the application for the management control order in relation to which the order for revocation is sought.

Review of parenting order
3.27.15.—(1) An application under section 105(1) for revocation or variation of a parenting order shall be by minute lodged in the original process of the application for the parenting order in relation to which the order for revocation or variation is sought.

(2) Where the court that made a parenting order makes an order under section 105(5) that court shall within 4 days transmit the original process relating to the parenting order to the court specified in that order.

Procedural requirements relating to parenting orders

3.27.16. Where the sheriff is considering making a parenting order, or a revocation or variation of a parenting order, and it is practicable, having regard to the age and maturity of the child to—

(a) give the child an opportunity to indicate whether the child wishes to express views; and

(b) if the child so wishes, give the child an opportunity to express those views,

the sheriff shall order intimation in the form of Form 31 to the child in respect of whom the order was or is proposed to be made.

3.27.17. Where the sheriff is considering making a parenting order or revoking or varying a parenting order and does not already have sufficient information about the child, the sheriff shall order intimation in the form of Form 32 to the local authority for the area in which the child resides.

Enforcement of local authorities' duties under section 71 of the Children D 532/20 *(Scotland) Act 1995*

3.27.18. An application under section 71A(2) of the Children (Scotland) Act 1995 by the Principal Reporter shall be by summary application to the sheriff principal of the Sheriffdom in which the principal office of the local authority is situated.

NOTE
[1] Inserted by SSI 2004/455, Art.2(4) (effective as follows: Rule 3.27.18 comes into force January 31, 2005; Rules 3.27.5 and 3.27.15 to 3.27.17 come into force April 4, 2005; Rules 3.27.12 to 3.27.14 come into force November 15, 2005).

[1] PART XXVIII

LAND REFORM (SCOTLAND) ACT 2003

Interpretation

3.28.1. In this Part—

"the Act" means the Land Reform (Scotland) Act 2003.

Public notice of appeal against section 14(2) remedial notice

3.28.2. Where an owner of land appeals by summary application under section 14(4) of the Act against a notice served on him under section 14(2) of the Act, the owner must at the same time as, or as closely in time as practicable to, the lodging of the application, advertise by publication of an advertisement in a newspaper circulating in the area of the land details of the application including details of the notice appealed against.

Restriction on number of persons being party to section 14(4) application

3.28.3. Persons interested in the exercise of access rights over the land to which a summary application under section 14(2) of the Act relates, and persons or bodies representative of such persons, may be parties to the summary application proceedings, but the court may order that any one or more of the persons or bodies who have the same interests and no others, may take an active part in the proceedings.

Public notice and restriction on number of parties to section 15 application

3.28.4. The provisions in rules 3.28.2 and 3.28.3 above apply with necessary modifications to a summary application appealing against a notice served under section 15(2) of the Act.

Public notice and restriction on number of parties to section 28 application

3.28.5.—(1) The provisions in rules 3.28.2 and 3.28.3 above apply with necessary modifications to a summary application for a declaration under section 28(1) or (2) of the Act.

(2) A summary application under section 28(1) or (2) of the Act may be made at any time.

NOTE

[1] Inserted by the Act of Sederunt (Summary Applications, Statutory Applications and Appeals, etc. Rules) Amendment (Land Reform) (Scotland) Act 2005 (SSI 2005/61), para.2(2) (effective February 9, 2005).

D 532/20/1 **Rule 1.2(3)**   SCHEDULE 1

FORMS

Rule 2.4(1)   FORM 1

FORM OF INITIAL WRIT

SUMMARY APPLICATION UNDER (*title & section of statute or statutory instrument*)

INITIAL WRIT

SHERIFFDOM OF (*insert name of sheriffdom*)

AT (*insert place of sheriff court*)

[A.B.] (*design and state any special capacity in which the pursuer is suing*) Pursuer

against

[C.D.] (*design and state any special capacity in which the defender is being sued*) Defender

The Pursuer craves the court (*here state the specific decree, warrant or order sought*)

CONDESCENDENCE

(*State in numbered paragraphs the facts which form the ground of action*)

PLEAS-IN-LAW

(*State in numbered sentences*)

> Signed
> [A.B.], Pursuer
> or [X.Y.], solicitor for the Pursuer
> (*state designation and business address*)

Rule 2.7(4)(a)   FORM 2

FORM OF WARRANT OF CITATION

(*Insert place and date*). Grants warrant to cite the defender (*insert name and address*) by serving upon him [*or her*] a copy of the writ and warrant [on a period of notice of (*insert period of notice*) days], [and ordains him [*or her*] to answer within the Sheriff Court House (*insert place of sheriff court*) [in Room No. , or in Chambers, *or otherwise, as the case may be*], on the   day of   at   o'clock   noon] [*or otherwise, as the case may be*] [and grants warrant to arrest on the dependence].

> Signed
> Sheriff [*or sheriff clerk*]

Rule 3.18.3(1)   [1] FORM 2A   **D 532/21**

FORM OF WARRANT OF CITATION

(*Insert place and date*). Grants warrant to cite (*insert name and address of parties specified by sheriff principal*) by serving upon them a copy of the writ and warrant on a period of notice of 21 days and ordains them if they wish to oppose the application—

   (a) to lodge answers within the period of notice; and

   (b) to be represented within the Sheriff Court House (*insert place and address of sheriff court*) [in Room No. , *or otherwise, as the case may be*], on the   day of at   o'clock   noon [*or otherwise, as the case may be*].

Signed
Sheriff [or sheriff clerk]

NOTE
[1] Inserted by the Act of Sederunt (Summary Applications, Statutory Applications and Appeals etc. Rules) Amendment (No.2) (Local Government (Scotland) Act 1973) 2002 (SSI 2002/130), para.2(4) and Sch.

Rule 2.7(4)(b)   FORM 3

FORM OF CITATION FOR SUMMARY APPLICATION

CITATION FOR SUMMARY APPLICATION

SHERIFFDOM OF (<i>insert name of sheriffdom</i>)

AT (<i>insert place of sheriff court</i>)

[A.B.], (<i>insert designation and address</i>) Pursuer

against

[C.D.], (<i>insert designation and address</i>) Defender

Court ref. no.

(*Insert place and date*). You [C.D.] are hereby served with this copy writ and warrant, and are required to answer it.

IF YOU ARE UNCERTAIN AS TO WHAT ACTION TO TAKE you should consult a solicitor. You may be eligible for legal aid depending on your income, and you can get information about legal aid from a solicitor. You may also obtain advice from any Citizens' Advice Bureau or other advice agency.

PLEASE NOTE THAT IF YOU DO NOTHING IN ANSWER TO THIS DOCUMENT the court may regard you as admitting the claim made against you and the pursuer may obtain decree against you in your absence.

Signed
[PQ.], Sheriff Officer,
or [X.Y] (add designation and business address)
Solicitor for the Pursuer

¹ FORM 3A

FORM OF CITATION FOR SUMMARY APPLICATION

CITATION FOR SUMMARY APPLICATION

SHERIFFDOM OF *(insert name of sheriffdom)*

AT *(insert place of sheriff court)*

[A.B.], *(insert designation and address)*, Applicant

against

[C.D.], *(insert designation and address)*, Respondent

Court ref. no.

(Insert place and date). You [C.D.] are hereby served with this copy writ and warrant, and are required to answer it.

If you wish to oppose the application, you—

(a) must lodge answers with the sheriff clerk at *(insert place and address of sheriff court)* sheriff court, *(insert address)* not later than *(insert date)*, and at the same time, send a copy of the answers to the Applicant; and

(b) should be represented within the Sheriff Court House *(insert place and address of sheriff court)* [in Room No.   , or otherwise, as the case may be] on the day of   at   o'clock   noon [*or otherwise as the case maybe*].

PLEASE NOTE THAT IF YOU DO NOTHING IN ANSWER TO THIS DOCUMENT the court may regard you as admitting the appeal and the Applicant may obtain decree against you in your absence.

> Signed
> [P.Q.], Sheriff Officer, or [X.Y.]
> *(add designation and business address)*
> Solicitor for the Applicant

NOTE
¹ Inserted by the Act of Sederunt (Summary Applications, Statutory Applications and Appeals etc. Rules) Amendment (No.2) (Local Government (Scotland) Act 1973) 2002 (SSI 2002/130), para.2(4) and Sch.

Rule 2.7(5)   FORM 4

FORM OF WARRANT OF CITATION WHERE TIME TO PAY DIRECTION MAY BE APPLIED FOR

(Insert place and date). *Grants warrant to cite the defender (insert name and address)* by serving a copy of the writ and warrant, together with Form 5, [on a period of notice of *(insert period of notice)* days] and ordains him [*or* her] if he [*or* she]—

(a) intends to defend the action or make any claim [to answer within the Sheriff Court House *(insert place and address of sheriff court)* [in Room No.   , or in Chambers, *or otherwise, as the case may be*], on the   day of   at   o'clock   noon] [*or otherwise, as the case may be*] or

(b) admits the claim and intends to apply for a time to pay direction (and where appropriate apply for recall or restriction of an arrestment) [either to appear at that diet and make such application or] to lodge the appropriate part of Form 5 duly completed with the sheriff clerk at *(insert place of sheriff court)* at least seven days before [the diet *or* the expiry of the period of notice *or otherwise*, as the case may be] [and grants warrant to arrest on the dependence].

> Signed
> Sheriff [*or* sheriff clerk]

Rule 2.7(6) and 2.22(2)(b)   FORM 5   **D 533**

ACTION IN SUMMARY APPLICATION BY

_____   _____

_____   _____

_____   _____

_____   _____

PURSUER   DEFENDER

AT   SHERIFF COURT

(including address)

_____

COURT REF. NO _____ [DATE OF FIRST HEARING]

_____

_____ [EXPIRY OF PERIOD OF NOTICE]

THIS SECTION MUST BE COMPLETED BY THE PURSUER BEFORE SERVICE

The Debtors (Scotland) Act 1987 gives you the right to apply to the court for a "time to pay direction" which is an order permitting you to pay any sum of money you are ordered to pay to the pursuer (which may include interest and court expenses) either by way of instalments or deferred lump sum. A deferred lump sum means that you must pay all the amount at one time within a period specified by the court.

When making a time to pay direction the court may recall or restrict an arrestment made on your property by the pursuer in connection with the action or debt (for example your bank account may have been frozen).

HOW TO APPLY FOR A TIME TO PAY DIRECTION WHERE YOU ADMIT THE CLAIM AND YOU DO NOT WANT TO DEFEND THE ACTION.

What must I do?

You must complete box 1 of Section A below giving details of the offer you are making to pay the claim and details of your income and outgoings. You must sign your name against the word "signature" in box 1 below. If you wish to apply to have an arrestment recalled or restricted you should also sign box 2 below.

After completing the form it should be returned to the Sheriff Court at least seven days before the date of the first hearing or expiry of the period of notice or otherwise, as the case may be, in the warrant of citation. The address of the court is shown in Section B below.

You should retain the copy initial writ and any other pages that have been served on you as you may need them at a later stage.

For further information or in the event of any difficulty you may contact the local sheriff clerk's office, any solicitor, Citizen's Advice Bureau or other advice agency.

D 534 *What happens if my offer to pay is accepted?*

If your application for time to pay is accepted by the pursuer, the court will make an order for payment against you. A copy of the order (called an extract decree) will be served on you by the pursuer's solicitor telling you when instalment payments should start or deferred payment is to be made.

What happens If my offer to pay is rejected?

If your application for time to pay is objected to by the pursuer, the Sheriff Clerk will advise you in writing.

You may attend the first hearing and give reasons to the sheriff why your application for time to pay should be granted. You will be expected to address the Sheriff directly, giving reasons why your application should be granted. Before coming to court you should prepare what you are going to say. You should bring any papers that you will be referring to with you.

If you do not attend, your application will still be considered by the Sheriff.

You will find the first hearing date in the warrant of citation attached to the initial writ.

SECTION A

ADMIT THE CLAIM AND APPLY FOR TIME TO PAY

BOX 1   **APPLICATION IN WRITING FOR A TIME TO PAY DIRECTION UNDER THE DEBTORS (SCOTLAND) ACT 1987**
(payment by instalments or deferred lump sum)

My outgoings are	weekly	fort-nightly	monthly	My income is	weekly	fort-nightly	monthly	My capital assets are:
Rent/Mortgage	£			Wage/Pensions	£			Value of house—
Heating	£			Social Security	£			(minus mortgage)
Food	£			Other (specify)	£			Amount in Bank
HP	£				£			Amount in Building
Other (specify)	£				£			Society
	£				£			Shares
	£				£			Other (specify)
Total	£			Total	£			

if necessary attach a separate sheet

DEPENDENTS—CHILDREN—How Many _____   **Others—How Many** _____

I am a defender in the action by the pursuer named in Section B. I admit the claim and make application

    (1) To pay by instalments of £_____ each week/fortnight/month*

    or

    (2) To pay the sum ordered in one payment within _____ weeks/months*

SIGNATURE _____   ***DELETE AS APPROPRIATE**

BOX 2   **D 535**
APPLICATION FOR RECALL OR RESTRICTION OF AN ARRESTMENT

I wish to apply for the recall/restriction of the arrestment being served on (insert the date the arrestment was made) of which the details are as follows:—

SIGNATURE _____

_____

_____

SECTION B This section must be completed before service	**SHERIFF COURT** (including address) _____	_____
	_____	Court Ref No: _____
	_____	
	_____	First
	_____	Hearing Date _____
_____		_____
_____	**COURT STAMP** (OFFICIAL USE ONLY)	_____
_____		_____
_____		_____
		_____

PURSUER'S FULL NAME AND ADDRESS   DEFENDER'S FULL NAME AND ADDRESS

Rule 2.7(7)   FORM 6

FORM OF CITATION WHERE TIME TO PAY DIRECTION MAY BE APPLIED FOR IN SUMMARY APPLICATION

SHERIFFDOM OF (*insert name of sheriffdom*)

AT (*insert place of sheriff court*)

[A.B.], (*insert designation and address*) Pursuer

against

[C.D.], (*insert designation and address*) Defender

Court ref. no.

(*Insert place and date*). You [C.D.], are hereby served with this copy writ and warrant, together with Form 5 (application for time to pay direction in summary application).

Form 5 is served on you because it is considered that you may be entitled to apply for a time to pay direction [and for the recall or restriction of an arrestment used on the dependence of the action or in security of the debt referred to in the copy writ]. See Form 5 for further details.

IF YOU ADMIT THE CLAIM AND WISH TO APPLY FOR A TIME TO PAY DIRECTION, you must complete Form 5 and return it to the sheriff clerk at the above address at least 7 days before the hearing or the expiry of the period of notice or otherwise, as the case may be, in the warrant of citation.

IF YOU ADMIT THE CLAIM AND WISH TO AVOID A COURT ORDER BEING MADE AGAINST YOU, the whole sum claimed including interest and any expenses due should be paid to the pursuer or his solicitor by the court date.

IF YOU ARE UNCERTAIN AS TO WHAT ACTION TO TAKE you should consult a solicitor. You may be eligible for legal aid depending on your income, and you can get information about legal aid from a solicitor. You may also obtain advice from any **D 536** Citizens' Advice Bureau, or other advice agency.

PLEASE NOTE THAT IF YOU DO NOTHING IN ANSWER TO THIS DOCU-MENT the court may regard you as admitting the claim made against you and the pursuer may obtain decree against you in your absence.

> Signed
> [P.Q.], Sheriff Officer,
> or [X.Y.] (*add designation and business address*)
> Solicitor for the Pursuer

Rule 2.7(7A)(a)   [1] FORM 6A

FORM OF WARRANT OF CITATION IN AN APPLICATION TO WHICH RULE 2.7(7A) APPLIES

(*Insert place and date*). Grants warrant to cite the defender (*insert name and address*) by serving a copy of the writ and warrant together with Form 6B [on a period of notice of (*insert period of notice*) days] and ordains him [*or* her] if he [*or* she]—

(a) intends to defend the action or make any claim to answer within the Sheriff Court House (*insert place and address of sheriff court*) [in Room No , *or in chambers, or otherwise, as the case may be*] on the day of at o'clock noon] [*or otherwise, as the case may be*]; or

(b) intends to apply for an order under section 2 of the Mortgage Rights (Scotland) Act 2001 to be present or represented at that diet.

Rule 2.7(7A)(b)   [1] FORM 6B

FORM OF CITATION IN AN APPLICATION TO WHICH RULE 2.7(7A) APPLIES

SHERIFFDOM OF (*insert name of sheriffdom*)

AT (*insert place of sheriff court*)

[A.B.], (*insert designation and address*) Pursuer

against

[C.D.], (*insert designation and address*) Defender

Court ref. no:

(Insert place and date). You [C.D.], are hereby served with this copy writ and warrant, and you are required to answer it.

IF YOU WISH TO MAKE AN APPLICATION FOR AN ORDER UNDER SECTION 2 OF THE MORTGAGE RIGHTS (SCOTLAND) ACT 2001 you should be present or represented at the diet on (*insert date and time*) within (*insert name and address of sheriff court*)

IF YOU ARE UNCERTAIN AS TO WHAT ACTION TO TAKE you should consult a solicitor. You may be eligible for legal aid depending on your income, and you can get information about legal aid from a solicitor. You may also obtain advice from any Citizens' Advice Bureau, or other advice agency.

PLEASE NOTE THAT IF YOU DO NOTHING IN ANSWER TO THIS DOCUMENT the court may regard you as admitting the claim made against you and the pursuer may obtain decree against you in your absence.

> Signed
> [P.Q.], Sheriff Officer,
> or [X.Y.] (*add designation and business address*)
> Solicitor for the Applicant

FORM OF CERTIFICATE OF CITATION

CERTIFICATE OF CITATION

(Insert place and date) I, hereby certify that upon the day of I duly cited [C.D.], Defender, to answer the foregoing writ. I did this by (*state method of service; [if by officer and not by post, add*: in the presence of [L.M.], (*insert designation*), witness hereto with me subscribing;] *and where service executed by post state whether by registered post or the first class recorded delivery service*).

(*In actions in which a time to pay direction may be applied for, state whether Form 4 and Form 5 were sent in accordance with rule 2.7(5) and (6)*.)

(*In actions in which an order under section 2 of the Mortgage Rights (Scotland) Act 2001 may be applied for, state whether Form 6B was sent in accordance with rule 2.7(7A)(b)*.)

> Signed
> [P.Q.], Sheriff Officer
> [L.M.], witness
> or [X.Y.] (*add designation and business address*)
> Solicitor for the Pursuer

NOTE
[1] Inserted by the Act of Sederunt (Amendment of Ordinary Cause Rules and Summary Applications, Statutory Applications and Appeals etc. Rules) (Applications under the Mortgage Rights (Scotland) Act 2001) 2002 (SSI 2002/7), para.3(4) and Sch.2.

Rule 2.9(1)   FORM 8

FORM OF CAVEAT

SHERIFFDOM OF (*insert name of sheriffdom*)

AT (*insert place of sheriff court*)

CAVEAT for [A.B.] (*insert designation and address**)

Should any application be made for (*here specify the nature of the application(s) to which this caveat is to apply*) prior to service of the initial writ, it is requested that intimation be made to the caveator before any order is pronounced.

Date (*insert date*)   Signed
                                        [A.B.]

                                        or [X.Y] Solicitor for [A.B.] (*add designation and business address*)

Caveator's telephone and fax number (*insert where caveat is not lodged by solicitor*)

Solicitor (*insert name and address, telephone and fax number and reference*)

Out of hours contacts:

1. (*insert name and telephone number*)

2. (*insert name and telephone number*)

*State whether the caveat is lodged in an individual capacity, or a specified representative capacity (*e.g.* as trustee of a named trust) or both. Where appropriate, state also the nature of the caveator's interest (*e.g.* shareholder, debenture holder).

D 537 Rule 2.13(1)(a)

FORM 9

FORM OF ADVERTISEMENT

NOTICE TO [C.D.]

Court ref. no.

An action has been raised in   Sheriff Court by [A.B.], Pursuer calling as a Defender [C.D.], whose last known address was (*insert last known address of defender*).

If [C.D.] wishes to defend the action he [*or* she] should immediately contact the sheriff clerk (*insert address*) from whom the service copy initial writ may be obtained. If he [*or* she] fails to do so decree may pass against him [*or* her] [when the case calls in court on (*date*) or on the expiry of the period of notice *or otherwise, as the case may be in the warrant of citation*].

> Signed
> [X.Y.], (*add designation and*
> business address)
> Solicitor for the Pursuer
> or [P.Q.] (*add business address*)

Rule 2.13(1)(b)

FORM 10

FORM OF NOTICE FOR WALLS OF COURT

NOTICE TO [C.D.]

Court ref. no.

An action has been raised in   Sheriff Court by [A.B.], Pursuer calling as a Defender [C.D.], whose last known address was (*insert last known address of defender*).

If [C.D.] wishes to defend the action he [*or* she] should immediately contact the sheriff clerk at (*insert address*) from whom the service copy initial writ may be obtained. If he [*or* she] fails to do so decree may pass against him [*or* her] [when the case calls in court on (*date*) or on the expiry of the period of notice *or otherwise, as the case may be in the warrant of citation*].

Date (*insert date*)

> Signed
> Sheriff clerk (*depute*)
> Telephone no. (*insert telephone number*
> *of sheriff clerk's office*)

Rule 2.26

FORM 11

FORM OF EXTRACT DECREE

EXTRACT DECREE

Sheriff Court	Court Ref. No.
Date of decree	*In absence
Pursuer(s)	Defender(s)

The Sheriff

and granted decree against the   for payment of expenses of £

This extract is warrant for all lawful execution hereon.

Date (*insert date*)   Sheriff clerk (*depute*)

*Delete as appropriate

FORM OF ORDER FOR RECOVERY OF DOCUMENTS ETC. UNDER PART I OF CHAPTER 3 OF ACT OF SEDERUNT (SUMMARY APPLICATIONS, STATUTORY APPLICATIONS AND APPEALS ETC. RULES) 1999

SHERIFFDOM OF (*insert name of sheriffdom*)

AT (*insert place of sheriff court*)

in the Summary Application

of

[A.B.] (*designation and address*)

Applicant

against

[C.D.] (*designation and address*)

Respondent

Date: (*date of interlocutor*)

To: (*name and address of party or parties or named third party haver, from whom the documents and other property are sought to be recovered*)

THE SHERIFF having heard the applicant and being satisfied that it is appropriate to make an order under section 1 of the Administration of Justice (Scotland) Act 1972:

ORDERS the Summary Application to be served upon the person(s) named and designed therein;

APPOINTS (*name and designation of Commissioner*) to be Commissioner of the court;

GRANTS commission and diligence;

ORDERS the Commissioner to explain to the haver on executing the order—
    (1) the meaning and effect of the order;
    (2) that the haver may be entitled to claim that certain of the documents and other property are confidential or privileged; and
    (3) that the haver has a right to seek legal or other professional advice of his choice,
and to give to the haver a copy of the Notice in Form 11B of Schedule 1 to the Act of Sederunt (Summary Applications, Statutory Applications and Appeals etc. Rules) 1999.

GRANTS warrant to and authorises the said Commissioner, whether the haver has allowed entry or not—
    (1) to enter, between the hours of 9am and 5pm on Monday to Friday, (*or, where the court has found cause shown under rule 3.1.11(1), otherwise specify the time and day*) the premises at (*address of premises*) and any other place in Scotland owned or occupied by the haver at which it appears to the Commissioner that any of the items set out in the statement of facts in the application to the court (the "listed items") may be located; and
    (2) unless the haver is taking legal or other professional advice on the question of having the order varied—
        (a) to search for and take all other steps which he considers necessary to take possession of or preserve (*specify the listed items*); and
        (b) to take possession of and to preserve all or any of the listed items and to consign them with the Sheriff Clerk at (*enter name and address of sheriff court*) to be held by him pending the further order of the sheriff,
and for that purpose,

ORDERS the haver or his servants or agents to allow the Commissioner, any person whom the Commissioner considers necessary to assist him, and the Applicant's representatives to enter the premises named in the order and, unless the haver has sought legal or other professional advice on the question of having the order varied, to allow them—

(1) to search for the listed items and take such other steps as the Commissioner considers it is reasonable to take to execute the order;

(2) to provide access to information stored on any computer owned or used by him by supplying or providing the means to overcome any and all security mechanisms inhibiting access thereto;

(3) to allow the Commissioner, any person whom the Commissioner considers necessary to assist him, and the Applicant's representatives to remain in the premises until such time as the search is complete, including allowing them to continue the search on subsequent days if necessary;

(4) to inform the Commissioner immediately of the whereabouts of the listed items; and

(5) to provide the Commissioner with a list of the names and addresses of everyone who has supplied him with any of the listed items and of the names and addresses of everyone to whom he has given any of the listed items,

and not to destroy, conceal or tamper with any of the listed items except in accordance with the terms of this order;

FURTHER AUTHORISES (*specify the representatives*) to be the sole representatives of the Applicant to accompany the Commissioner for the purpose of identification of the said documents and other property.

SCHEDULE TO THE ORDER

Undertakings given by Applicant

The Applicant has given the following undertakings:—

1. That he will comply with any order of the court as to payment of compensation if it is subsequently discovered that the order, or the implementation of the order, has caused loss to the respondent or, where the respondent is not the haver, to the haver.

2. That he will bring within a reasonable time of the execution of the order any proceedings which he decides to bring.

3. That he will not, without leave of the court, use any information, documents or other property obtained as a result of the order, except for the purpose of any proceedings which he decides to bring and to which the order relates.
(*or as modified under rule 3.1.4*)

Rule 3.1.9(a)   FORM 11B

Notice to accompany order in Form 11A when served by Commissioner

IMPORTANT
NOTICE TO PERSON ON WHOM THIS ORDER IS SERVED

1. This order orders you to allow the person appointed and named in the order as Commissioner to enter your premises to search for, examine and remove or copy the items mentioned in the order.

2. It also allows entry to the premises to any person appointed and named in the order as a representative of the person who has been granted the order and to any person accompanying the Commissioner to assist him.

3. No one else is given authority to enter the premises.

4. You should read the order immediately.

5. You have the right to seek legal or other professional advice of your choice and you are advised to do so as soon as possible.

6. Consultation under paragraph 5 will not prevent the Commissioner from entering your premises for the purposes mentioned in paragraph 1 but if the purpose of your seeking advice is to help you to decide if you should ask the court to vary the order he will not be able to search the premises.

7. The Commissioner is obliged to explain the meaning and effect of the order to you.

8. He is also obliged to explain to you that you are entitled to claim that the items, or some of **D 538/2** them, are protected as confidential or privileged.

9. You are entitled to ask the court to vary the order provided that—
you take steps to do so at once; and
you allow the Commissioner, any person appointed as a representative of the person who has been granted the order and any person accompanying the Commissioner to assist him, to enter the premises—but not to start the search—meantime.

10. The Commissioner and the people mentioned as representatives or assistants have a right to enter the premises even if you refuse to allow them to do so, unless—
you are female and alone in the premises and there is no female with the Commissioner (where the Commissioner is not female), in which case they have no right to enter the premises;
the Commissioner serves the order before 9am or after 5pm on a weekday or at any time on a Saturday or Sunday (except where the court has specifically allowed this, which will be stated in the order);
in which cases you should refuse to allow entry.

11. You are entitled to insist that there is no one (*or* no one other than*insert name of person*) present who could gain commercially from anything which might be read or seen on your premises.

12. You are required to hand over to the Commissioner any of the items mentioned in the order which are in your possession.

13. You may be found liable for contempt of court if you refuse to comply with the order.

Rule 3.8.3(1)   FORM 12

FORM OF NOTICE TO BE SERVED ON PERSON WHO IS SUBJECT OF HOSPITAL ORDER, GUARDIANSHIP
ORDER OR COMMUNITY CARE ORDER

To [*name and address of patient*]
Attached to this notice is a copy of—

*an application to the managers of [*name of hospital*] for your admission to that hospital in accordance with section 21 of the Mental Health (Scotland) Act 1984.

*an application to the sheriff at [*name of Sheriff Court*] for a Community Care Order in accordance with section 35A of the Mental Health (Scotland) Act 1984.

*an application to the [*name of local authority*] for your reception into guardianship in accordance with Section 40 of the Mental Health (Scotland) Act 1984.

The hearing will be held at [*place*]   **on** [*date*]   **at** [*time*].

You may appear personally at the hearing of this application unless the court decides otherwise on medical recommendations.

In any event, if you are unable or do not wish to appear personally you may request any person to appear on your behalf.

If you do not appear personally or by representative, the sheriff will consider the application in the absence of you or your representative.

[*Signed*]
Sheriff Clerk

[*Place and date*]
**delete as appropriate*

D 538/3 Rule 3.8.3(3)   FORM 13

FORM OF NOTICE TO RESPONSIBLE MEDICAL OFFICER

To [*name and address of responsible medical officer*]

In accordance with the Mental Health (Scotland) Act 1984, a copy of the application and notice of hearing is sent with this notice.

1. You are requested to deliver it personally to [*name of patient*] and to explain the contents of it to him.

2. You are also required to arrange if the patient so wishes, for the attendance of [*name of patient*] at the hearing at [*place of hearing*] on [*date*] so that he may appear and be heard in person.

3. You are further requested to complete and return to me in the enclosed envelope the certificate appended hereto before the date of the hearing.

4. If in your opinion it would be prejudicial to the patient's health or treatment for him to appear and be heard personally you may so recommend in writing, with reasons on the certificate.

[*Signed*]
Sheriff Clerk

[*Place and date*]

D 539 Rule 3.8.4(1)(b) and   FORM 14
       3.8.4(2)(a)

FORM OF CERTIFICATE OF DELIVERY BY RESPONSIBLE MEDICAL OFFICER

I, [*name and designation*], certify that—

1. I have on the   day of   personally delivered to [*name of patient*] a copy of the application and the intimation of the hearing; and have explained the contents or purport to him [*or her*].

2. The patient does [not] wish to attend the hearing.

3. The patient does [not] wish to be represented at the hearing [and has nominated [*name and address of representative*] to represent him].

4. I shall arrange for the attendance of the patient at the hearing [*or* in my view it would be prejudicial to the patient's health or treatment for him [*or* her] to appear and be heard in person for the following reasons [*give reasons*]].

[*Signature and designation*]

[*Address and date*]

Rule 3.8.11   FORM 15

FORM OF APPEAL FOR REVOCATION OF A COMMUNITY CARE ORDER UNDER SECTION 35F OF THE
MENTAL HEALTH (SCOTLAND) ACT 1984

SHERIFFDOM OF *(insert name of sheriffdom)*

AT *(insert name of Sheriff Court)*

I, [*insert name and address of applicant*],

appeal to the sheriff for revocation of a community care order made on [*insert date of order*] on
the following grounds:—

[*State grounds on which appeal is to proceed*]

The community care order was renewed under section 35C(5) of the Mental Health (Scotland)
Act 1984 on [*insert date of renewal*] and is still in force.

The special medical officer specified in the community care order is [*insert name and address of
special medical officer*].

> [*Signed*]
> Applicant
> [*or* Solicitor for Applicant]
> [*Insert designation and address*]

Rule 3.9.9(b)   FORM 16   **D 540**

FORM OF NOTICE TO PERSON WITH INTEREST IN PROPERTY SUBJECT OT AN APPLICATION FOR AN
ORDER UNDER PARAGRAPH 12 OF SCHEDULE 1 TO THE PROCEEDS OF CRIME (SCOTLAND) ACT 1995

IN THE SHERIFF COURT

in the

PETITION [*or* NOTE]

of

[A.B.] *(name and address)*

for an order under paragraph 12 of Schedule 1 to the
Proceeds of Crime (Scotland) Act 1995

in respect of the estates of [C.D.] *(name and address)*

Court Ref No.

Date: *(date of posting or other method of service)*

To: (name and address of person on whom notice is to be served)

This Notice—
    (a) gives you warning that an application has been made to the sheriff court for an order
        which may affect your interest in property; and
    (b) informs you that you have an opportunity to appear and make representations to the
        court before the application is determined.

TAKE NOTICE

1. That on (*date*) in the sheriff court at (*place*) a confiscation order was made under section 1 of the Proceeds of Crime (Scotland) Act 1995 in respect of [C.D.] (*name and address*).

2. That on (*date*) the administrator appointed under paragraph 1(1)(a) of Schedule 1 to the Proceeds of Crime (Scotland) Act 1995 on (*date*) was empowered to realise property belonging to [C.D.].

or

2. That on (*date*) the administrator was appointed under paragraph 1 (1)(b) of Schedule 1 to the Proceeds of Crime (Scotland) Act 1995 on (*date*) to realise property belonging to [C.D.].

3. That application has been made by petition [or note] for an order under paragraph 12 of Schedule 1 to the Proceeds of Crime (Scotland) Act 1995 (*here set out briefly the nature of the order sought*). A copy of the petition [*or* note] is attached.

4. That you have the right to appear before the court in person or by counsel or other person having a right of audience and make such representations as you may have in respect of the order applied for. The court has fixed (*insert day and date fixed for hearing the application*), at (*insert time and place fixed for hearing*) as the time when you should appear to do this.

5. That if you do not appear or are not represented on the above date, the order applied for may be made in your absence.

IF YOU ARE UNCERTAIN ABOUT THE EFFECT OF THIS NOTICE, you should consult a Solicitor, Citizen's Advice Bureau or other local advice agency or adviser immediately.

> (*Signed*)
> Sheriff Officer
> [*or* Solicitor [*or* Agent] for petitioner
> [*or* noter]]
> (*Address*)

D 541 Rule 3.11.14(1)   FORM 17

Representation of the People Act 1983

In the petition questioning the election for the   of   , in which   is petitioner and   is respondent.

The petitioner desires to withdraw his petition on the following grounds [*state grounds*], and craves that a diet may be appointed for hearing his application. He has, in compliance, with rule 3.11.14 of the Act of Sederunt (Summary Applications, Statutory Applications and Appeals etc. Rules) 1999, given the written notice of his intention to present this application to the respondent, to the Lord Advocate, and to the returning officer.

[To be signed by the petitioner or his solicitor.]

Rule 3.11.14(4)   FORM 18

Representation of the People Act 1983

In the petition questioning the election for the   of   , in which   is the petitioner and   is respondent.

Notice is hereby given that the above petitioner has applied for leave to withdraw his petition, and that the sheriff principal has, by interlocutor dated the   day of   , assigned the   day of   at   o'clock   noon within the   as a diet for hearing the application.

Notice is further given that under the Act any person who might have been a petitioner in respect of the said election may at the above diet apply to the sheriff principal to be substituted as a petitioner.

[To be signed by the petitioner or his solicitor.]

Rule 3.11.15(1)   FORM 19

Representation of the People Act 1983

In the petition questioning the election for the   of   , in
which   was the petitioner [*or* last surviving petitioner] and   is the
respondent.

Notice is hereby given that the above petition stands abated by the death of the petitioner [*or*
last surviving petitioner], and that any person who might have been a petitioner in respect of the
said election and who desires to be substituted as a petitioner must, within 21 days from this
date, lodge with the undersigned sheriff clerk of [*name sheriff court district*], a minute craving to
be so substituted.

Date (*insert date*)

[*To be signed by the sheriff clerk*]

Rule 3.16.4(1)   [1] FORM 20

FORM OF NOTICE OF AN APPLICATION UNDER THE ADULTS WITH INCAPACITY (SCOTLAND) ACT 2000

To (*insert name and address*)

Attached to this notice is a copy of an application for (*insert type of application*) under the
Adults with Incapacity (Scotland) Act 2000.

The hearing will be held at (insert place) on (insert date) at (insert time)

You may appear personally at the hearing of this application.   **D 542**

In any event, if you are unable or do not wish to appear personally you may appoint a legal
representative to appear on your behalf.

If you are uncertain as to what action to take you should consult a solicitor. You may be eligible
for legal aid, and you can obtain information about legal aid from any solicitor. You may also
obtain information from any Citizens Advice Bureau or other advice agency.

If you do not appear personally or by legal representative, the sheriff may consider the
application in the absence of you or your legal representative.

(*insert place and date*)   (*signed*)
                                             Sheriff Clerk
                                             or
                                             [P.Q.] Sheriff Officer
                                             or
                                             [X.Y.],Solicitor

Rule 3.16.4(3)   [1] FORM 21

FORM OF NOTICE TO MANAGERS

To (*insert name and address of manager*)

A copy of an application made under the Adults with Incapacity (Scotland) Act 2000 and notice
of hearing is sent with this notice.

1. You are requested to deliver it personally to (name of adult) and to explain the contents of it
to him or her.

2. You are further requested to complete and return to the sheriff clerk in the enclosed envelope
the certificate (Form 22) appended hereto before the date of the hearing.

(insert place and date)

(*signed*)
Sheriff Clerk
or
[P.Q.], Sheriff Officer
or
[X.Y.], Solicitor

Rule 3.16.4(4)   [1] FORM 22

FORM OF CERTIFICATE OF DELIVERY BY MANAGER

I, *(insert name and designation)*, certify that—

I have on *(insert date)* personally delivered to (name of adult) a copy of the application and the intimation of the hearing and have explained the contents to him/her.

Date *(insert date)*

(*signed*)
Manager
(add designation and address)

Rule 3.16.7(1)   [1] FORM 23

SUMMARY APPLICATION UNDER THE ADULTS WITH INCAPACITY (SCOTLAND) ACT 2000

SHERIFFDOM OF *(insert name of sheriffdom)*

AT *(insert place of Sheriff Court)*

D 542/1 [A.B.] *(design and state capacity in which the application is made)*, Pursuer

The applicant craves the court *(state here the specific order(s) sought by reference to the provisions in the Adults with Incapacity (Scotland) Act 2000.)*

STATEMENTS OF FACT

(State in numbered paragraphs the facts on which the application is made, including:

1. *The designation of the adult concerned (if other than the applicant).*

   (a)   *the adult's nearest relative;*
   (b)   *the adult's primary carer;*
   (c)   *any guardian, continuing attorney or welfare attorney of the adult; and*
   (d)   *any other person who may have an interest in the application.*

3. *The adult's place of habitual residence and/or the location of the property which is the subject of the application.)*

(insert place and date)

(*signed*)
[A.B.], Pursuer or
[X.Y.], *(state designation and business address)*
Solicitor for the Pursuer

Note. This Form should not be used for appeals to the Sheriff. Appeals should be made in Form 24.

Rule 3.16.7(2)   [1] FORM 24

APPEAL TO THE SHERIFF UNDER THE ADULTS WITH INCAPACITY (SCOTLAND) ACT 2000

SHERIFFDOM OF *(insert name of sheriffdom)*

AT *(insert place of Sheriff Court)*

[A.B.] *(design and state capacity in which the appeal is being made)*, Pursuer

This appeal is made in respect of *(state here the decision concerned, the date on which it was intimated to the pursuer, and refer to the relevant provisions in the Adults with Incapacity (Scotland) Act 2000).*

(State here, in numbered paragraphs:

1. *The designation of the adult concerned (if other than the applicant).*

2. *The designation of:*

     (a) *the adult's nearest relative;*
     (b) *the adult's primary carer;*
     (c) *any guardian, continuing attorney or welfare attorney of the adult; and*
     (d) *any other person who may have an interest in the application.*

3. *The adult's place of habitual residence and/or the location of the property which is the subject of the application.)*

The pursuer appeals against the decision on the following grounds *(state here in separate paragraphs the grounds on which the appeal is made).*

The pursuer craves the court *(state here orders sought in respect of appeal).*   **D 542/2**

(insert place and date)   *(signed)*
                               [A.B.], Pursuer
                               or
                               [X.Y.], *(state designation and business address)*
                               Solicitor for the Pursuer

NOTE
[1] Inserted by the Act of Sederunt (Summary Applications, Statutory Applications and Appeals etc. Rules) Amendment (Adults with Incapacity) 2001 (SSI 2001/142), r.3(3) and Sch.

Rule 3.27.6(1)   [1]FORM 25

ANTISOCIAL BEHAVIOUR ETC. (SCOTLAND) ACT 2004

CLOSURE NOTICE

Section 27

1. The service of this closure notice is authorised by a senior police officer under section 26(1) of the Antisocial Behaviour etc. (Scotland) Act 2004 ("the Act").

2. The premises to which this closure notice relates are: *(specify premises).*

3. Access to those premises by any person other than—
     (a) a person who habitually resides in the premises; or

(b) the owner of the premises,
is prohibited.

4. Failure to comply with this notice is an offence which may result in a fine of up to £2,500 or imprisonment for a term of up to 3 months (or both). The penalties may be higher for repeated failure to comply with this (or any other) closure notice.

5. An application for the closure of these premises will be made under section 28 of the Act and will be considered at *(insert place including Room No. if appropriate)* on the   day of   at am/pm.

6. On such an application as set out in paragraph 5 being made, the sheriff may make a closure order under section 29 of the Act in respect of these premises.

7. The effect of the Closure Order in respect of these premises would be to close the premises to all persons (other than any person expressly authorised access by the sheriff in terms of section 29(3) of the Act) for such period not exceeding 3 months as is specified in the order. Measures may be taken to ensure that the premises are securely closed against entry by any person.

8. If you live on or have control of, responsibility for or an interest in the premises to which this closure notice relates and wish to oppose the application for a closure order, you should attend or be represented at the hearing mentioned in paragraph 5 of this notice.

9. If you would like further information or advice about housing or legal matters you can contact—

(specify at least two persons or organisations (including name and means of contacting) based in the locality of the promises who or which will be able to provide advice about housing and legal matters). You also have a legal right to advice from your local authority should you be threatened with possible homelessness.

D 542/3 Rule 3.27.6(2)   FORM 26

ANTISOCIAL BEHAVIOUR ETC. (SCOTLAND) ACT 2004

CERTIFICATION OF SERVICE

Section 27

I *(insert designation, including address and rank, of police officer)* certify that a copy of the closure notice which was authorised by *(insert designation of senior police officer)* on *(insert date on which closure notice was authorised)* in respect of *(insert details of the premises to which closure notice relates)* was served on: *(insert name and address of each person to whom a copy of the notice was given, including date)*

_____

_____

_____

_____

by *(insert designation, including address and rank, of police officer who served the copy or copies of the closure notice and, if more than one, indicate which police officer served a copy of the notice on which of the persons listed above).*

Signed

(insert designation, including rank, of police officer)

Rule 3.27.7 FORM 27

ANTISOCIAL BEHAVIOUR ETC. (SCOTLAND) ACT 2004

Section 28

Sheriff Court . . . . 20. . . . .

(Court Ref No.)

PART A

APPLICATION FOR CLOSURE ORDER IN RESPECT OF PREMISES AT:

_____

_____

_____

("the Premises")

PART B

1. This application is made [by/on behalf of] *(delete as appropriate)* *(insert name and rank of senior police officer)* of *(insert details of police force)*.

2. Service of a closure notice on the Premises was authorised by *(insert details of senior police officer)* on the   day of   . A copy of [the authorisation/written confirmation of such authorisation] *(delete as appropriate)* is attached.

3. A copy of the closure notice was, on the   day of   ,—   **D 542/4**
   (a) fixed to:
        (insert details of all locations in, or used as part of, the Premises, to which a copy of the notice was fixed)

_____

_____

_____

_____

_____

_____

   (b) given to:
        (insert name and address of each person to whom a copy of the notice was given)

_____

_____

_____

_____

_____

_____

4. Certification in the prescribed form of service of the closure notice to the persons described at paragraph 3(b) above is attached.

5. This application is made on the following grounds:

(insert reasons for making application)

_____

_____

_____

_____

_____

_____

6. The following evidence is [attached/supplied] *(delete as appropriate)* in respect of this application *(insert short details of supporting evidence)*.

PART C

7. The applicant asks the court to—
     (a) assign the hearing for the   day of   at   am/pm; and
     (b) make a closure order in respect of the Premises.

. . . . Signed

Senior Police Officer for [Police Force] (Applicant)

or [X.Y.] Solicitor for Senior Police Officer

(add designation and business address)

D 542/5 FORM OF INTERLOCUTOR

Sheriff Court . . . . 20 . . . .

(Court Ref No.)

The sheriff having considered this application assigns . . . . at . . . . within .
. . . . as a hearing, this date having been previously intimated to known interested persons and published in the closure notice.

. . . . Signed

Sheriff

FORM OF INTERLOCUTOR

Sheriff Court . . . . 20 . . . .

(Court Ref No.)

The sheriff having heard *(insert details of parties who attended the hearing)* and having considered the application [, being satisfied that the conditions mentioned in section 30(2) of the Antisocial Behaviour etc. (Scotland) Act 2004 are met] *(delete as appropriate)* and having regard to the matters mentioned in section 30(3) of the Antisocial Behaviour etc. (Scotland) Act 2004 ("the Act"),

*1. makes an order under section 29(1) of the Act that the premises at *(insert details of premises)* are closed to all persons for a period of *(insert period)*.

*2. directs intimation of this interlocutor to *(insert details of all known interested persons)* and by posting a copy thereof at prominent places on the premises at *(indicate where copies have been posted)*.

*3. refuses to make a closure order in respect of the premises at *(insert details of premises)*.

*4. postpones the determination of the application until *(insert date)* at *(insert time)* within *(insert location)*.

*delete as appropriate

. . . . Signed

Sheriff

Rule 3.27.8   FORM 28

ANTISOCIAL BEHAVIOUR ETC. (SCOTLAND) ACT 2004

Minute

Section 32

Application for extension of closure order

Sheriff Court . . . . :   . . . . 20. . . . .

(Court Ref No.)

PART A

PREMISES IN RESPECT OF WHICH CLOSURE ORDER HAS BEEN MADE:

_____

_____   **D 542/6**

_____

("the Premises")

PART B

1. This application is made [by/on behalf of] *(delete as appropriate) (insert name and rank of senior police officer)* of *(insert details of police force)*.

2. A copy of the closure order made in respect of the Premises is attached. The closure order has effect until *(enter date)*.

3. The applicant believes that it is necessary to extend the period for which the closure order has effect for the purpose of preventing relevant harm, on the following grounds: *(specify reasons for extension)*.

4. *(Insert details of local authority)* has been consulted about the applicant's intention to make this application.

PART C

5. The applicant asks the court to—
    (c) fix a hearing;
    (d) order the applicant to intimate this application and the date of the hearing to such persons as the sheriff considers appropriate; and
    (e) extend the closure order in respect of the Premises for a period of   [months/days] *(delete as appropriate)* or for such period not exceeding 6 months as the court may consider appropriate.

. . . . Signed

Senior Police Officer for [Police Force] (Applicant)

or [X.Y.] Solicitor for Senior Police Officer

(add designation and business address)

FORM OF INTERLOCUTOR

Sheriff Court . . . . 20. . . . .

(Court Ref No.)

The sheriff having considered this minute orders the applicant to intimate this application and interlocutor to . . . ., assigns . . . . at . . . . within . . . . as a hearing and directs any person wishing to oppose the granting of the application to appear or be represented at the hearing to show cause why the application should not be granted.

. . . . Signed

Sheriff

FORM OF INTERLOCUTOR

Sheriff Court . . . . 20. . . . .

(Court Ref No.)

The sheriff having heard *(insert details of parties who attended the hearing)* [and] having considered this minute [and being satisfied that the condition mentioned in section 32(1) of the Antisocial Behaviour etc. (Scotland) Act 2004 is met] *(delete as appropriate)*,

D 542/7   *1. makes an order extending the closure order made under section 29(1) of the Antisocial Behaviour etc. (Scotland) Act 2004 in respect of the premises at *(insert details of premises)* for a period of *(insert period)*.

*2. directs intimation of this interlocutor to *(insert details of persons to whom sheriff considers it to be appropriate to intimate)* and by posting a copy thereof at prominent places on the premises at *(indicate where copies have been posted)*.

*3. refuses to make an order extending the closure order in respect of the premises at *(insert details of premises)*.

*4. postpones the determination of the application until *(insert date)* at *(insert time)* within *(insert location)*.

*delete as appropriate

. . . . Signed

Sheriff

Rule 3.27.9   FORM 29

Antisocial Behaviour etc. (Scotland) Act 2004

Minute

Section 33

Application for revocation of closure order

Sheriff Court . . . . 20. . . . .

(Court Ref No.)

PART A

PREMISES IN RESPECT OF WHICH CLOSURE ORDER HAS BEEN MADE:

_____

_____

_____

("the Premises")

The applicant is *(insert name and address of applicant)* who is:

*1. a senior police officer of the police force for the area within which the Premises (or part thereof) are situated.

*2. the local authority for the area within which the Premises or part thereof are situated.

*3. a person on whom a copy of the closure notice relating to the Premises in respect of which the closure order has effect was served under section 27(2)(b) or (3) of the Antisocial Behaviour etc. (Scotland) Act 2004.

*4. a person who has an interest in these premises but on whom the closure notice was not served.

*delete as appropriate.

PART B   D 542/8

1. A copy of the closure order made in respect of the Premises is attached.

2. The applicant believes that a closure order in respect of the Premises is no longer necessary to prevent the occurrence of relevant harm for the following reasons *(specify grounds for application for revocation)*.

PART C

3. The applicant asks the court to:
    (a) fix a hearing;
    (b) order the applicant to intimate this application and the date of the hearing to such persons as the sheriff considers appropriate and, where the applicant is not a senior police officer, to such senior police officer as the sheriff considers appropriate; and
    (c) order the revocation of the closure order.

. . . . Signed

Applicant *(include full designation)*

or [X.Y.] Solicitor for Applicant *(include full designation and business address)*

FORM OF INTERLOCUTOR

Sheriff Court . . . . 20. . . . .

(Court Ref No.)

The sheriff having considered this minute orders the applicant to intimate this application and interlocutor to . . . ., assigns . . . . within . . . . as a hearing and directs any person wishing to oppose the granting of the application to appear or be represented at the hearing to show cause why the application should not be granted.

. . . . Signed

Sheriff

FORM OF INTERLOCUTOR

Sheriff Court . . . . 20. . . . .

(Court Ref No.)

The sheriff having heard *(insert details of parties who attended the hearing)* [and] having considered this minute [and being satisfied that a closure order is no longer necessary to prevent the occurrence of relevant harm] *(delete as appropriate)*,

*1. makes an order revoking the closure order made under section 29(1) of the Antisocial Behaviour etc. (Scotland) Act 2004 in respect of the premises at *(insert details of the premises)*.

*2. directs intimation of this interlocutor to *(insert details of persons to whom sheriff considers it to be appropriate to intimate)*.

*3. refuses to make an order revoking the closure order in respect of the premises at *(insert details of the premises)*.

*4. postpones the determination of the application until *(insert date)* at *(insert time)* within *(insert location)*.

*delete as appropriate

. . . . Signed

Sheriff

D 542/9 Rule 3.27.10   FORM 30

ANTISOCIAL BEHAVIOUR ETC. (SCOTLAND) ACT 2004

Minute

Section 34

Application for access to premises in respect of which a closure order is in force

Sheriff Court . . . . 20. . . . .

(Court Ref No.)

PART A

PREMISES IN RESPECT OF WHICH CLOSURE ORDER HAS BEEN MADE:

("the Premises")

PREMISES IN RESPECT OF WHICH APPLICATION FOR ACCESS IS BEING MADE:

PART B

1. A copy of the closure order made in respect of the Premises is attached. The closure order has effect until *(insert date)*.

2. The applicant *(insert details of applicant)* [owns/occupies] *(delete as appropriate)* the following [part of] *(delete as appropriate)* building or structure in which the Premises are situated and in respect of which the closure order does not have effect.

PART C

3. The applicant asks the court to:
   (a) fix a hearing;
   (b) order the applicant to intimate this application and the date of the hearing to such persons as the sheriff considers appropriate and, where the applicant is not a senior police officer, to such senior police officer as the sheriff considers appropriate; and
   (c) make an order allowing access *(detail access provisions requested)*.

. . . . Signed

Applicant *(include full designation)*

or [X.Y.] Solicitor for Applicant *(include full designation and business address)*

FORM OF INTERLOCUTOR

Sheriff Court . . . . 20. . . . .

(Court Ref No.)

The sheriff having considered this minute orders the applicant to intimate this application and **D 542/10**
interlocutor to . . . ., assigns . . . . at . . . . within . . . .
as a hearing and directs any person wishing to oppose the granting of the application to appear or be represented at the hearing to show cause why the application should not be granted.

. . . . Signed

Sheriff

FORM OF INTERLOCUTOR

Sheriff Court . . . . 20. . . . .

(Court Ref No.)

The sheriff having heard *(insert details of parties who attended the hearing)* and having considered this minute,

*1. makes an order an order allowing *(insert name and address)*

_____

_____

_____

access to the following part or parts of the premises at *(insert details of premises)* in relation to which a closure order has been made under section 29(1) of the Antisocial Behaviour etc. (Scotland) Act 2004: *(insert details of parts of premises to which access order is to apply)*

_____

_____

_____

*2. directs intimation of this interlocutor to *(insert details of all known interested persons to whom the sheriff considers it to be appropriate to intimate)*.

*3. refuses to make an access order in respect of the premises at *(insert details of premises)*.

*4. postpones the determination of the application until *(insert date)* at *(insert time)* within *(insert location)*.

*delete as appropriate

. . . . Signed

Sheriff

Rule 3.27.16   FORM 31

ANTISOCIAL BEHAVIOUR ETC. (SCOTLAND) ACT 2004

Section 13, 102 or 105

Intimation that court may make or revoke or vary a parenting order

Sheriff Court . . . . 20. . . . .

(Court Ref No.)

D 542/11   PART A

This part must be completed by the applicant's solicitor in language a child is capable of understanding

To **(1)**

The Sheriff (the person who has to decide about the parenting order) has been asked by **(2)** to decide:—
  (a) **(3)** and **(4)**;
  (b) **(5)**;
  (c) **(6)**.

If you want to tell the Sheriff what you think about the things **(2)**   has asked the Sheriff to decide about your future you should complete Part B of this form and send it to the Sheriff Clerk at **(7)** by **(8)**   . An envelope which does not need a postage stamp is enclosed for you to use to return the form.

IF YOU DO NOT UNDERSTAND THIS FORM OR IF YOU WANT HELP TO COMPLETE IT you may get free help from a SOLICITOR or contact the SCOTTISH CHILD LAW CENTRE ON the FREE ADVICE TELEPHONE LINE ON 0800 317 500.

If you return the form it will be given to the Sheriff. The Sheriff may wish to speak with you and may ask you to come and see him or her.

NOTES FOR COMPLETION

(1) Insert name and address of child.	(2) Insert description of party making the application to the court.
(3) Insert appropriate wording for parenting order sought.	(4) Insert appropriate wording, if relevant, for Antisocial Behaviour Order.
(5) Insert appropriate wording for contact.	(6) Insert appropriate wording for any other order sought or determinations to be made by sheriff.
(7) Insert address of sheriff clerk.	(8) Insert the date occurring 21 days after the date on which intimation is given.
(9) Insert court reference number.	(10) Insert name and address of parties to the action.

PART B

IF YOU WISH THE SHERIFF TO KNOW YOUR VIEWS ABOUT THE PARENTING ORDER YOU SHOULD COMPLETE THIS PART OF THE FORM

To the Sheriff Clerk, **(7)**

Court Ref. No. **(9)**

(10) . . . .

QUESTION (1): DO YOU WISH THE SHERIFF TO KNOW WHAT YOUR VIEWS ARE ABOUT THE PARENTING ORDER?

(PLEASE TICK BOX)

YES	
NO	

If you have ticked YES please also answer Question (2) *or* (3)

QUESTION (2): WOULD YOU LIKE A FRIEND, RELATIVE OR OTHER PERSON TO   D 542/12 TELL THE SHERIFF YOUR VIEWS ABOUT THE PARENTING ORDER?

(PLEASE TICK BOX)

YES	
NO	

If you have ticked YES please write the name and address of the person you wish to tell the Sheriff your views in Box (A) below. You should also tell that person what your views are about the parenting order.

BOX A:	(NAME)				
	(ADDRESS)				
	Is this person—	A friend?		A relative?	
		A teacher?		Other?	

OR

QUESTION (3): WOULD YOU LIKE TO WRITE TO THE SHERIFF AND TELL HIM WHAT YOUR VIEWS ARE ABOUT THE PARENTING ORDER?

(PLEASE TICK BOX)

YES	
NO	

If you decide that you wish to write to the Sheriff you can write what your views are about the parenting order in Box (B) below or on a separate piece of paper. If you decide to write your views on a separate piece of paper you should send it along with this form to the Sheriff Clerk in the envelope provided.

BOX B:	WHAT I HAVE TO SAY ABOUT THE PARENTING ORDER:—

NAME: . . . .

ADDRESS: . . . .

DATE: . . . .

D 542/13 Rule 3.27.17   FORM 32

ANTISOCIAL BEHAVIOUR ETC. (SCOTLAND) ACT 2004

Section 13, 102 or 105

Form of notice to local authority requesting a report in respect of a child

Sheriff Court . . . . 20 . . . .

(Court Ref No.)

To *(insert name and address)*

1. YOU ARE GIVEN NOTICE that in an action in the Sheriff Court at *(insert address)* an application for [the variation/revocation of] *(delete as appropriate)* a parenting order is being considered in respect of a parent of the child *(insert name of child)*. A copy of the application is enclosed.

2. You are required to submit to the court a report on all the circumstances of the child, including but not limited to:—
    (a) the current or proposed arrangements for the case and upbringing of the child;
    (b) information about the family circumstances of the parent; and

(c) the likely effect of a parenting order on the family circumstances of the parent and the child.

3. This report should be sent to the Sheriff Court at . . . . on or before . . . . *(insert date)*.

Date *(insert date)*

. . . . Signed:

Applicant *(include full designation)*

or [X.Y.] Solicitor for Applicant *(include full designation and business address)*

or Sheriff Clerk

Rule 1.3   SCHEDULE 2

REVOCATIONS

(1) *Act of Sederunt*	*(2)* *Reference*	*(3)* *Extent of Revocation*
Codifying Act of Sederunt 1913	SR & O 1913/638	Book L, Chapter X (proceedings under the Representation of the People Act 1983)
Codifying Act of Sederunt 1913	SR & O 1913/638	Book L, Chapter XI (appeals to the Court under the Pilotage Act 1913)
Act of Sederunt Regulating Appeals under the Pharmacy and Poisons Act 1933	SR & O 1935/1313	The whole Act of Sederunt
Act of Sederunt (Betting, Gaming and Lotteries Act Appeals) 1965)	1965/1168	The whole Act of Sederunt
Act of Sederunt (Housing Appeals) 1966	1966/845	The whole Act of Sederunt
Act of Sederunt (Sheriff Court Procedure under Part IV of the Housing (Scotland) Act 1969) 1970	1970/1508	The whole Act of Sederunt
Act of Sederunt (Proceedings under Sex Discrimination Act 1975) 1976	1976/374	The whole Act of Sederunt
Act of Sederunt (Proceedings under Sex Discrimination Act 1975) No 2 1976	1976/1851	The whole Act of Sederunt
Act of Sederunt (Proceedings under Sex Discrimination Act 1975) 1977	1977/973	The whole Act of Sederunt
Act of Sederunt (Appeals under the Licensing (Scotland) Act 1976) 1977	1977/1622	The whole Act of Sederunt
Act of Sederunt (Betting and Gaming Appeals) 1978	1978/229	The whole Act of Sederunt
Act of Sederunt (Appeals under the Rating (Disabled Persons) Act 1978) 1979	1979/446	The whole Act of Sederunt
Act of Sederunt (Copyright, Deisgns and Patents) 1990	1990/380	The whole Act of Sederunt
Act of Sederunt (Proceedings in the Sheriff Court under the Model Law on International Commercial Arbitration) 1991	1991/2214	The whole Act of Sederunt
Act of Sederunt (Coal Mining Subsidence Act 1991) 1992	1992/798	The whole Act of Sederunt
Act of Sederunt (Applications under Part III of the Criminal Justice (International Co-operation) Act 1990) 1992	1992/1077	The whole Act of Sederunt
Act of Sederunt (Sheriff Court Summary Application Rules) 1993	1993/3240	The whole Act of Sederunt

(1) Act of Sederunt	(2) Reference	(3) Extent of Revocation
Act of Sederunt (Mental Health Rules) 1996	1996/2149	The whole Act of Sederunt
Act of Sederunt (Proceeds of Crime Rules) 1996	1996/2446	The whole Act of Sederunt

D 543   **Act of Sederunt (Proceedings for Determination of Devolution Issues Rules) 1999**

(S.I. 1999 No. 1347)

The Lords of Council and Session, under and by virtue of the powers conferred on them by section 32 of the Sheriff Courts (Scotland) Act 1971, paragraph 37 of Schedule 6 to the Scotland Act 1998, paragraph 38 of Schedule 10 to the Northern Ireland Act 1998 and paragraph 36 of Schedule 8 to the Government of Wales Act 1998 and of all other powers enabling them in that behalf, having approved, draft rules submitted to them by the Sheriff Court Rules Council in accordance with section 34 of the Sheriff Courts (Scotland) Act 1971, do hereby enact and declare:

Citation
1.—(1) This Act of Sederunt may be cited as the Act of Sederunt (Proceedings for Determination of Devolution Issues Rules) 1999 and shall come into force on 6th May 1999.
(2) This Act of Sederunt shall be inserted in the Books of Sederunt.

Interpretation
2.—(1) In this Act of Sederunt—
"Advocate General" means the Advocate General for Scotland;
"devolution issue" means a devolution issue within the meaning of—
   (a) Schedule 6 to the Scotland Act 1998;
   (b) Schedule 10 to the Northern Ireland Act 1998; or
   (c) Schedule 8 to the Government of Wales Act 1998;
"initiating document" means the initial writ, summons, petition or other document by which the proceedings are initiated;
"the Judicial Committee" means the Judicial Committee of the Privy Council;
"relevant authority" means the Advocate General and—
   (a) in the case of a devolution issue within the meaning of Schedule 6, the Lord Advocate;
   (b) in the case of a devolution issue within the meaning of Schedule 10, the Attorney General for Northern Ireland, the First Minister and the deputy First Minister;
   (c) in the case of a devolution issue within the meaning of Schedule 8, the National Assembly for Wales.
(2) Any reference in this Act of Sederunt to a numbered Form shall be construed as a reference to the Form so numbered in Schedule 1 to this Act of Sederunt, and any reference to a rule shall be a reference to the rule so numbered in this Act of Sederunt.

Proceedings for determination of a devolution issue
3. Where the initiating document contains an averment or crave which raises a devolution issue, the initiating document shall include a crave for warrant to intimate it to the relevant authority, unless he is a party to the action.

Time for raising devolution issue
4. It shall not be competent for a party to any proceedings to raise a devolution issue after proof is commenced, unless the sheriff, on cause shown, otherwise determines.

Specification of devolution issue
5.—(1) Any party raising a devolution issue shall specify—
(a) where he initiates the action, in the initiating document;
(b) in the written defences or answers; or
(c) in any other case, in Form 1,

D 544

the facts and circumstances and contentions of law on the basis of which it is alleged that the devolution issue arises in sufficient detail to enable the sheriff to determine whether such an issue arises in the proceedings.
(2) Where a pay wishes to raise a devolution issue after lodging any writ mentioned in paragraph (1) above he shall do so—
(a) by way of adjustment or minute of amendment; or
(b) in proceedings in which there is no procedure for adjustment or amendment, in Form 1,
so as to provide specification of the matters mentioned in that paragraph.

Intimation of devolution issue
6.—(1) Intimation of a devolution issue shall be given to the relevant authority (unless he is a party to the proceedings) in accordance with this rule.
(2) Where the devolution issue is raised in the initiating document, the sheriff shall order intimation of the devolution issue as craved in the warrant for service.
(3) In any case other than that described in paragraph (2) above, the party raising the devolution issue shall lodge a motion or incidental application, as the case may be, craving a warrant for intimation of the devolution issue on the relevant authority, and on considering the motion or incidental application, where it appears to the sheriff that a devolution issue arises, he shall order such intimation of the devolution issue.
(4) Where intimation is ordered in accordance with paragraphs (2) or (3) above, such intimation shall be in Form 2 and be made in such manner as the sheriff considers appropriate in the circumstances.
(5) The intimation of a devolution issue shall specify 14 days, or such other period as the sheriff thinks fit, as the period within which the relevant authority may enter appearance as a party in the proceedings.

Response to intimation of devolution issue
7.—(1) This rule applies where the relevant authority receives intimation of a devolution issue.
(2) Where the relevant authority intends to enter an appearance as a party in the proceedings, he shall lodge a minute stating that he intends to do so.
(3) Upon receipt of the minute lodged in accordance with paragraph (2) above, the sheriff shall sist the relevant authority as a party to the action.
(4) Upon the relevant authority being sisted as a party in accordance with paragraph (3) above, the sheriff shall order the relevant authority to lodge a note of his written submissions in respect of the devolution issue specifying those matters mentioned in rule 5(1) within 7 days, or such other period as the sheriff thinks fit.
(5) A copy of the minute lodged in accordance with paragraph (2) above and a copy of any note lodged in accordance with paragraph (4) above shall, at the same time as lodging the minute or any note, be intimated by the party lodging such to all other parties in the proceedings.
(6) At any time after the note mentioned in paragraph (4) above has been lodged, the sheriff may regulate such further procedure in the proceedings as he thinks fit.

_Intimation under section 102 of the Scotland Act 1998, section 81 of the
Northern Ireland Act 1998 or section 110 of the Government of Wales
Act 1998_

8.—(1) This rule applies to orders made under—
(a) section 102 of the Scotland Act 1998 (powers of courts or tribunals to
vary retrospective decisions);

(b) section 81 of the Northern Ireland Act 1998 (powers of courts or
tribunals to vary retrospective decisions); or
(c) section 110 of the Government of Wales Act 1998 (power to vary
retrospective decisions).

(2) Where the sheriff is considering whether to make an order under any
of the provisions mentioned in paragraph (1) above, he shall order
intimation of that fact to be given to every person to whom intimation is
required to be given by that provision.

(3) The intimation mentioned in paragraph (2) above shall—
(a) be made forthwith by the sheriff clerk in Form 3 by first class
recorded delivery post; and
(b) specify 14 days, or such other period as the sheriff thinks fit, as the
period within which a person may enter an appearance as a party in
the proceedings so far as they relate to the making of the order.

Response to intimation of order under rule 8

9.—(1) This rule applies where a person receives intimation in accordance
with rule 8.

(2) Where a person intends to enter an appearance as a party in the
proceedings, he shall lodge a minute stating that he intends to do so.

(3) Upon receipt of the minute lodged in accordance with paragraph (2)
above, the sheriff shall sist the person as a party to the action.

(4) Upon a person being sisted as a party in accordance with paragraph
(3) above, the sheriff shall order the person to lodge a note of his written
submissions in respect of the making of the order within 7 days, or such
other period as the sheriff thinks fit.

(5) A copy of the minute lodged in accordance with paragraph (2) above
and a copy of any note lodged in accordance with paragraph (4) above shall,
at the same time as lodging the minute or any note, be intimated by the
party lodging such to all other parties in the proceedings.

(6) At any time after the note mentioned in paragraph (4) above has been
lodged, the sheriff may regulate such further procedure in the proceedings as
he thinks fit.

_Reference of devolution issue to Inner House of the Court of Session or
Judicial Committee_

10.—(1) This rule applies where—
(a) any reference of a devolution issue is made to the Inner House of the
Court of Session; or
(b) the sheriff is required by the relevant authority to refer a devolution
issue to the Judicial Committee.

(2) Where a reference is made in accordance with paragraph (1) above, the
sheriff shall pronounce an interlocutor giving directions about the manner
and time in which the reference is to be drafted and adjusted.

(3) When the reference has been drafted and adjusted in accordance with
paragraph (2) above, the sheriff shall sign the reference.

(4) The reference shall include such matters as are prescribed in Schedule
2 to this Act of Sederunt, and shall have annexed to it the interlocutor
making the reference and any other order of the court in the cause.

(5) The sheriff clerk shall send a copy of the reference by first class
recorded delivery post to—
(a) the parties to the proceedings; and

(b) the relevant authority (if he is not already a party) who may have a
      potential interest in the proceedings,
and shall certify on the back of the principal reference that a copy has been
sent and to whom.

Sist of cause on reference to Inner House of the Court of Session or Judicial **D 546**
  Committee
  11. On a reference being made in accordance with rule 10, the cause shall,
unless the sheriff when making the reference otherwise orders, be sisted until
the devolution issue has been determined.

Interim Orders
  12.—(1) Notwithstanding the reference of a devolution issue to the Inner
House of the Court of Session or to the Judicial Committee in accordance
with rule 10, the sheriff shall have power to make any interim order which a
due regard to the interests of the parties may require.
  (2) The sheriff may recall a sist made under rule 11 for the purpose of
making the interim order mentioned in paragraph (1) above.

Transmission of reference
  13.—(1) The sheriff clerk shall forthwith transmit the principal copy of
the reference—
  (a) to the Deputy Principal Clerk of the Court of Session; or
  (b) together with seven copies, to the Registrar of the Judicial
       Committee,
as the case may be.
  (2) Unless the sheriff otherwise directs, the principal copy of the reference
shall not be transmitted in accordance with paragraph (1) above, where an
appeal against the making of the reference is pending.
  (3) For the purpose of paragraph (2) above, an appeal shall be treated as
pending—
  (a) until the expiry of the time for making that appeal; or
  (b) where an appeal has been made, until that appeal has been determined.

Procedure following determination on reference or appeal
  14.—(1) This rule applies where either the Inner House of the Court of
Session or the Judicial Committee have determined—
  (a) a devolution issue referred to them in accordance with rule 10; or
  (b) an appeal ma to them.
  (2) Upon receipt of the determination of the Inner House of the Court of
Session or the Judicial Committee, as the case may be, the sheriff clerk shall
forthwith place before the sheriff a copy of the determination and the court
process.
  (3) The sheriff may *ex proprio motu* or shall upon the lodging of a motion
or incidental application by any of the parties to the proceedings, pronounce
an interlocutor ordering such further procedure as may be required.
  (4) Where the sheriff *ex proprio motu* pronounces an interlocutor in
accordance with paragraph (3) above, the sheriff clerk shall forthwith
intimate a copy of the interlocutor to all parties in the proceedings.

Rule 2(2) SCHEDULE 1

Rules 5(1)(c) and 5(2)(b) FORM 1

FORM OF SPECIFICATION OF DEVOLUTION ISSUE

SHERIFFDOM OF (*insert name of sheriffdom*)

AT (*insert place of sheriff court*) Court Ref No.

In the action of

[A.B.] (*designation and address*)

Pursuer

against

[C.D.] (*designation and address*)

Defender

D 547 **1.** The *Pursuer/Defender (*if other please specify*) wishes to raise a devolution issue in the above action.

[*The Pursuer or Defender or other party, as the case may be, should then insert the following information—*

- *the facts and circumstances and contentions of law on the basis of which it is alleged that the devolution issue arises in sufficient detail to enable the sheriff to determine whether such an issue arises in the proceedings;*
- *details of the relevant law including the relevant provisions of the Scotland Act 1998, the Government of Wales Act 1998 or the Northern Ireland Act 1998, as the case may be; and*
- *the reason why the resolution of the devolution issue is considered necessary for the purpose of disposing of the proceedings*].

Date (*insert date*) (*Signed*)

Solicitor for the *Pursuer/Defender (*if other please specify*)

*Delete as appropriate

Rule 6(4) FORM 2

FORM OF INTIMATION TO RELEVANT AUTHORITY OF A DEVOLUTION ISSUE RAISED IN CIVIL
PROCEEDINGS IN THE SHERIFF COURT

To (*insert name and address*) Court Ref No

1. You are given notice that in the Sheriff Court at (*insert address*),

*an action has been raised which includes a crave in respect of a devolution issue;

*a devolution issue has been raised in an action;

A copy of the * initial writ/pleadings in the case (*as adjusted*) is enclosed. A copy of the interlocutor appointing intimation is also enclosed.

2. If you wish to enter appearance as a party to the proceedings, you must lodge with the Sheriff Clerk (*insert name and address*) a notice in writing stating that you intend to appear as a party in the proceedings. The notice must be lodged within 14 days of (*insert date on which intimation was given*).

Date (*insert date*)

(*Signed*)

Solicitor for *Pursuer/Defender

*Delete as appropriate.

Rule 8(3) FORM 3

FORM OF INTIMATION UNDER *SECTION 102 OF THE SCOTLAND ACT 1998/SECTION 81 OF THE
NORTHERN IRELAND ACT 1998/SECTION 110 OF THE GOVERNMENT OF WALES ACT 1998

To (*insert name and address*) Court Ref No

1. You are given notice that in an action raised in the Sheriff Court at (*insert address*), the sheriff has decided

*that an Act/provision of an Act of the Scottish Parliament is not within the legislative competence of the Parliament;

*a member of the Scottish Executive does not have the power to make, confirm or approve a provision of subordinate legislation he has purported to make, confirm or approve;

A copy of the *initial writ/pleadings in the case (*as adjusted*) is enclosed. A copy of the interlocutor appointing intimation is also enclosed.

2. The sheriff is considering whether to make an order under *section 102 of the Scotland Act 1998/section 81 of the Northern Ireland Act 1998/section 110 of the Government of Wales Act 1998 either removing or limiting the retrospective effect of the decision, or suspending the effect of the decision to allow the defect to be corrected.

3. If you wish to enter appearance as a party to the proceedings so far as they relate to the **D 548** making of the order, you must lodge with the sheriff clerk (*insert name and address*) a notice in writing stating that you intend to appear as a party in the proceedings. The notice must be lodged within 14 days of (*insert date on which intimation was given*).

Date (*insert date*)

(*Signed*)
Sheriff Clerk

*Delete as appropriate

Rule 10(4) SCHEDULE 2

DETAILS TO BE INCLUDED WHERE REFERENCE MADE TO *THE
INNER HOUSE OF THE COURT OF SESSION/JUDICIAL COMMITTEE

1. The question(s) referred.

2. The addresses of the parties.

3. A concise statement of the background to the matter, including—
  (i) the facts of the case, including any relevant findings of fact by the referring court; and
  (ii) the main issues in the case and contentions of the parties with regard to them.

4. The relevant law including the relevant provisions of the *Scotland Act 1998/Government of Wales Act 1998/Northern Ireland Act 1998.

5. The reasons why an answer to the question(s) *is/are considered necessary for the purpose of disposing of the proceedings.

Note: A copy of the interlocutor making the reference and a copy of any judgment in the proceedings must be annexed to the reference.

*Delete as appropriate.

Act of Sederunt (Summary Cause Rules) 2002

(SI 2002 No. 132)

The Lords of Council and Session, under and by virtue of the powers conferred by section 32 of the Sheriff Courts (Scotland) Act 1971 (a) and of all other powers enabling them in that behalf, having approved draft rules submitted to them by the Sheriff Court Rules Council in accordance with section 34 of the said Act of 1971, do hereby enact and declare:

Citation and commencement

1.—(1) This Act of Sederunt may be cited as the Act of Sederunt (Summary Cause Rules) 2002 and shall come into force on 10th June 2002.

(2) This Act of Sederunt shall be inserted in the Books of Sederunt.

Summary Cause Rules

2. The provisions of Schedule 1 to this Act of Sederunt shall have effect for the purpose of providing rules for a summary cause other than a small claim.

Transitional provision

3. Nothing in Schedule 1 to this Act of Sederunt shall apply to a summary cause commenced before 10th June 2002 and any such action shall proceed according to the law and practice in force immediately before that date.

Revocation

4. The Acts of Sederunt mentioned in column (1) of Schedule 2 to this Act of Sederunt are revoked to the extent specified in column (3) of that Schedule except—

(a) in relation to any summary cause commenced before 10th June 2002; and

(b) for the purposes of the Act of Sederunt (Small Claim Rules) 1988.

SCHEDULE 1   **Paragraph 2**

SUMMARY CAUSE RULES 2002

ARRANGEMENT OF RULES

Chapter 1

Citation, interpretation and application

1.1. Citation, interpretation and application

Chapter 2

Representation

2.1. Representation

Chapter 3

Relief from failure to comply with rules

3.1. Dispensing power of sheriff

D 554

Chapter 17

Productions and documents

Chapter 18

Recovery of evidence and attendance of witnesses

Chapter 19

Challenge of documents

Chapter 20

European Court

Chapter 21

Abandonment

Chapter 22   D 555

Decree by default

Chapter 23

Decrees, extracts, execution and variation

Chapter 28

Chapter 29

Action of count, reckoning and payment

Chapter 30

Recovery of possession of heritable property

Chapter 31

Action of sequestration for rent

Chapter 32

Action for aliment

Chapter 33

Child Support Act 1991

Chapter 34

Action of damages for personal injury

Electronic transmission of documents

APPENDIX 1

FORMS

APPENDIX 2

GLOSSARY

CHAPTER 1   **D 559**

CITATION, INTERPRETATION AND APPLICATION

Citation, interpretation and application
1.1—(1) These Rules may be cited as the Summary Cause Rules 2002.
(2) In these Rules—
"the 1907 Act" means the Sheriff Courts (Scotland) Act 1907;
"the 1971 Act" means the Sheriff Courts (Scotland) Act 1971;
"the 1975 Act" means the Litigants in Person (Costs and Expenses) Act 1975;
"authorised lay representative" means a person to whom section 32(1) of the Solicitors (Scotland) Act 1980 (offence to prepare writs) does not apply by virtue of section 32(2)(a) of that Act;
"small claim" has the meaning assigned to it by section 35(2) of the 1971 Act;
"summary cause" has the meaning assigned to it by section 35(1) of the 1971 Act.
(3) Any reference to a specified Chapter or rule shall be construed as a reference to the Chapter or rule bearing that number in these Rules, and a reference to a specified paragraph, subparagraph or head shall be construed as a reference to the paragraph, sub-paragraph or head so numbered or lettered in the provision in which that reference occurs.
(4) A form referred to by number means the form so numbered in Appendix 1 to these Rules or a form substantially of the same effect with such variation as circumstances may require.
(5) The glossary in Appendix 2 to these Rules is a guide to the meaning of certain legal expressions used in these Rules, but is not to be taken as giving those expressions any meaning which they do not have in law generally.
(6) These Rules shall apply to a summary cause other than a small claim.

CHAPTER 2

REPRESENTATION

Representation
  2.1.—(1) A party may be represented by an advocate, solicitor or, subject to the following provisions of this rule, an authorised lay representative.
  (2) An authorised lay representative shall not appear in court on behalf of a party except at the hearing held in terms of rule 8.2(1) and, unless the sheriff otherwise directs, any subsequent or other calling where the action is not defended on the merits or on the amount of the sum due.
  (3) Subject to the provisions of this rule, an authorised lay representative may, in representing a party, do everything for the preparation and conduct of an action as may be done by an individual conducting his own action.
  (4) If the sheriff finds that the authorised lay representative is—
    (a) not a suitable person to represent the party; or
    (b) not in fact authorised to do so,
that person must cease to represent the party.
  (5) A party may be represented by a person other than an advocate or solicitor at any stage of any proceedings under the Debtors (Scotland) Act 1987, other than appeals to the sheriff principal, if the sheriff is satisfied that that person is a suitable person to represent the party at that stage and is authorised to do so.

CHAPTER 3

RELIEF FROM FAILURE TO COMPLY WITH RULES

Dispensing power of sheriff
  3.1.—(1) The sheriff may relieve any party from the consequences of any failure to comply with the provisions of these Rules which is shown to be due to mistake, oversight or other excusable cause, on such conditions as he thinks fit.
  (2) Where the sheriff relieves a party from the consequences of the failure to comply with a provision in these Rules under paragraph (1), he may make such order as he thinks fit to enable the action to proceed as if the failure to comply with the provision had not occurred.

CHAPTER 4

COMMENCEMENT OF ACTION

Form of summons
  4.1.—(1) A summary cause action shall be commenced by summons, which shall be in Form 1.
D 560   (2) The form of claim in a summons may be in one of Forms 2, 3, 4, 5, 6, 7, 8 or 9.

Statement of claim
  4.2. The pursuer must insert a statement of his claim in the summons to give the defender fair notice of the claim; and the statement must include-
    (a) details of the basis of the claim including relevant dates; and
    (b) if the claim arises from the supply of goods or services, a description of the goods or services and the date or dates on or between which they were supplied and, where relevant, ordered.

Defender's copy summons
  4.3. A copy summons shall be served on the defender—
    (a) where the action is for, or includes a claim for, payment of money—
      (i) in Form 1a where an application for a time to pay direction under the Debtors (Scotland) Act 1987 or time order under the Consumer Credit Act 1974 may be applied for; or
      (ii) in Form 1b in every other case;
    (b) where the action is not for, and does not include a claim for, payment of money, in Form 1c; or
    (c) in an action of multiplepoinding, in Form 1d.

Authentication and effect of summons
  4.4.—(1) A summons shall be authenticated by the sheriff clerk in some appropriate manner except where—

    (a) he refuses to do so for any reason;

    (b) the defender's address is unknown; or

    (c) a party seeks to alter the normal period of notice specified in rule 4.5(2); or

[1] (d) a warrant for arrestment on the dependence, or to found jurisdiction, is sought.

    (2) If any of paragraphs (1)(a) to (d) applies, the summons shall be authenticated by the sheriff, if he thinks it appropriate.

    (3) The authenticated summons shall be warrant for—

    (a) service on the defender; and

    (b) where the appropriate warrant has been sought in the summons—

        (i) arrestment on the dependence; or

        (ii) arrestment to found jurisdiction,

    as the case may be.

[1] (4) Where a warrant for arrestment on the dependence, or to found jurisdiction, is sought, averments to justify that warrant must be included in the statement of claim.

NOTE

[1] Inserted by the Act of Sederunt (Ordinary Cause, Summary Application and Small Claim Rules) Amendment (Miscellaneous) 2004 (SSI 2004/197) (effective May 21, 2004), para.4(2).

Period of notice

    4.5.—(1) An action shall proceed after the appropriate period of notice of the summons has been given to the defender prior to the return day.

    (2) The appropriate period of notice shall be—

    (a) 21 days where the defender is resident or has a place of business within Europe; or

    (b) 42 days where the defender is resident or has a place of business outwith Europe.

    (3) The sheriff may, on cause shown, shorten or extend the period of notice on such conditions as to the form of service as he may direct, but in any case where the period of notice is reduced at least two days' notice must be given.

    (4) If a period of notice expires on a Saturday, Sunday, public or court holiday, the period of notice shall be deemed to expire on the next day on which the sheriff clerk's office is open for civil court business.

    (5) Notwithstanding the terms of section 4(2) of the Citation Amendment (Scotland) Act 1882, where service is by post the period of notice shall run from the beginning of the day next following the date of posting.

    (6) The sheriff clerk shall insert in the summons—

    (a) the return day, which is the last day on which the defender may return a form of response to the sheriff clerk; and

    (b) the calling date, which is the date set for the action to call in court.

    (7) The calling date shall be seven days after the return day.

Intimation   **D 561**

    4.6. Any provision in these Rules requiring papers to be sent to or any intimation to be made to any party, applicant or claimant shall be construed as if the reference to the party, applicant or claimant included a reference to the solicitor representing that party, applicant or claimant.

CHAPTER 5

REGISTER OF SUMMARY CAUSES, SERVICE AND RETURN OF THE SUMMONS

Register of Summary Causes

    5.1.—(1) The sheriff clerk shall keep a register of summary cause actions and incidental applications made in such actions, which shall be known as the Register of Summary Causes.

    (2) There shall be entered in the Register of Summary Causes a note of all actions, together with a note of all minutes under rule 24.1(1) (recall of decree) and the entry for each action or minute must contain the following particulars where appropriate:-

    (a) the names, designations and addresses of the parties;

    (b) whether the parties were present or absent at any hearing, including an inspection, and the names of their representatives;

    (c) the nature of the action;

    (d) the amount of any claim;

    (e) the date of issue of the summons;

    (f) the method of service;

    (g) the return day;

    (h) the calling date;

    (i) whether a form of response was lodged and details of it;

    (j) the period of notice if shortened or extended in accordance with rule 4.5(3);

    (k) details of any minute by the pursuer regarding an application for a time to pay direction or time order, or minute by the pursuer requesting decree or other order;

    (l) details of any interlocutors issued;

   (m) details of the final decree and the date of it; and

    (n) details of any variation or recall of a decree.

(3) There shall be entered in the Register of Summary Causes in the entry for the action to which they relate details of incidental applications including, where appropriate—

    (a) whether parties are present or absent at the hearing of the application, and the names of their representatives;

    (b) the nature of the application; and

    (c) the interlocutor issued or order made.

(4) The Register of Summary Causes must be—

    (a) authenticated in some appropriate manner by the sheriff in respect of each day any order is made or application determined in an action; and

    (b) open for inspection during normal business hours to all concerned without fee.

(5) The Register of Summary Causes may be kept in electronic or documentary form.

Persons carrying on business under trading or descriptive name

5.2.—(1) A person carrying on a business under a trading or descriptive name may sue or be sued in such trading or descriptive name alone.

(2) An extract of—

    (a) a decree pronounced in an action; or

    (b) a decree proceeding upon any deed, decree arbitral, bond, protest of a bill, promissory note or banker's note or upon any other obligation or document on which execution may proceed, recorded in the sheriff court books, against such person under such trading or descriptive name shall be a valid warrant for diligence against such person.

(3) A summons, decree, charge or other document following upon such summons or decree in an action in which a person carrying on business under a trading or descriptive name sues or is sued in that name may be served—

    (a) at any place of business or office at which such business is carried on within the sheriffdom of the sheriff court in which the action is brought; or

    (b) if there is no place of business within that sheriffdom, at any place where such business is carried on (including the place of business or office of the clerk or secretary of any company, corporation or association or firm).

Form of service and certificate thereof

5.3.—(1) Subject to rule 5.5 (service where address of defender is unknown), a form of service in Form 11 must be enclosed with the defender's copy summons.

D 562   (2) After service has been effected a certificate of execution of service in Form 12 must be prepared and signed by the person effecting service.

(3) When service is by a sheriff officer, the certificate of execution of service must—

    (a) be signed by him; and

    (b) specify whether the service was personal or, if otherwise, the mode of service and the name of any person to whom the defender's copy summons was delivered.

(4) If service is effected in accordance with rule 5.4(2), the certificate must also contain a statement of—

    (a) the mode of service previously attempted; and

    (b) the circumstances which prevented such service from being effected.

Service within Scotland by sheriff officer

5.4.—(1) A sheriff officer may validly serve any summons, decree, charge or other document following upon such summons or decree issued in an action by—

    (a) personal service; or

    (b) leaving it in the hands of—

        (i) an inmate at the person's dwelling place; or

       (ii) an employee at the person's place of business.

(2) If a sheriff officer has been unsuccessful in effecting service in accordance with paragraph (1), he may, after making diligent inquiries, serve the document—

    (a) by depositing it in the person's dwelling place or place of business by means of a letter box or by other lawful means; or

    (b) by affixing it to the door of the person's dwelling place or place of business.

(3) Subject to the requirements of rule 6.1 (service of schedule of arrestment), if service is effected in accordance with paragraph (2), the sheriff officer must thereafter send by ordinary

post to the address at which he thinks it most likely that the person may be found a letter containing a copy of the document.

(4) In proceedings in or following on an action, it shall be necessary for any sheriff officer to be accompanied by a witness except where service, citation or intimation is to be made by post.

(5) Where the firm which employs the sheriff officer has in its possession—
- (a) the document or a copy of it certified as correct by the pursuer's solicitor, the sheriff officer may serve the document upon the defender without having the document or certified copy in his possession (in which case he shall if required to do so by the person on whom service is executed and within a reasonable time of being so required, show the document or certified copy to the person); or
- (b) a certified copy of the interlocutor pronounced allowing service of the document, the sheriff officer may serve the document without having in his possession the certified copy interlocutor if he has in his possession a facsimile copy of the certified copy interlocutor (which he shall show, if required, to the person on whom service is executed).

Service on persons whose address is unknown

5.5.—(1) If the defender's address is unknown to the pursuer and cannot reasonably be ascertained by him, the sheriff may grant warrant to serve the summons—
- (a) by the publication of an advertisement in Form 13 in a newspaper circulating in the area of the defender's last known address; or
- (b) by displaying on the walls of court a notice in Form 14.

(2) Where a summons is served in accordance with paragraph (1), the period of notice, which must be fixed by the sheriff, shall run from the date of publication of the advertisement or display on the walls of court, as the case may be.

(3) If service is to be effected under paragraph (1), the pursuer must lodge a service copy of the summons with the sheriff clerk.

(4) The defender may uplift from the sheriff clerk the service copy of the summons lodged in accordance with paragraph (3).

(5) If display on the walls of court is required under paragraph (1)(b), the pursuer must supply to the sheriff clerk for that purpose a completed copy of Form 14.

(6) In every case where advertisement in a newspaper is required for the purpose of service, a copy of the newspaper containing said advertisement must be lodged with the sheriff clerk.

(7) If service has been made under this rule and thereafter the defender's address becomes known, the sheriff may allow the summons to be amended and, if appropriate, grant warrant for reservice subject to such conditions as he thinks fit.

Service by post

5.6.—(1) If it is competent to serve or intimate any document or to cite any person by recorded delivery, such service, intimation or citation, must be made by the first class recorded delivery service.

(2) On the face of the envelope used for postal service under this rule, there must be written or **D 563** printed a notice in Form 15.

(3) The certificate of execution of postal service must have annexed to it any relevant postal receipt.

Service on persons outwith Scotland

5.7.—(1) If any summons, decree, charge or other document following upon such summons or decree, or any charge or warrant, requires to be served outwith Scotland on any person, it must be served in accordance with this rule.

(2) If the person has a known home or place of business in—
- (a) England and Wales, Northern Ireland, the Isle of Man or the Channel Islands; or
- (b) any country with which the United Kingdom does not have a convention providing for service of writs in that country,

the document must be served either—
- (i) by posting in Scotland a copy of the document in question in a registered letter addressed to the person at his residence or place of business; or
- (ii) in accordance with the rules for personal service under the domestic law of the place in which the document is to be served.

(3) Subject to paragraph (4), if the document requires to be served in a country which is a party to the Hague Convention on the Service Abroad of Judicial and Extra-Judicial Documents in Civil or Commercial Matters dated 15th November 1965 or the European Convention on Jurisdiction and Enforcement of Judgments in Civil and Commercial Matters as set out in Schedule 1 or 3C to the Civil Jurisdiction and Judgments Act 1982, it must be served—
- (a) by a method prescribed by the internal law of the country where service is to be effected

for the service of documents in domestic actions upon persons who are within its territory;

(b) by or through a British consular authority at the request of the Secretary of State for Foreign and Commonwealth Affairs;

(c) by or through a central authority in the country where service is to be effected at the request of the Secretary of State for Foreign and Commonwealth Affairs;

(d) where the law of the country in which the person resides permits, by posting in Scotland a copy of the document in a registered letter addressed to the person at his residence; or

(e) where the law of the country in which service is to be effected permits, service by an *huissier*, other judicial officer or competent official of the country where service is to be made.

[1] (4) If the document requires to be served in a country to which the Council Regulation applies, service—

(a) may be effected by the methods prescribed in paragraph (3)(b) or (c) only in exceptional circumstances; and

(b) is effected only if the receiving agency has informed the person that acceptance of service may be refused on the ground that the document has not been translated in accordance with paragraph (12).

(5) If the document requires to be served in a country with which the United Kingdom has a convention on the service of writs in that country other than the conventions specified in paragraph (3) or the regulation specified in paragraph (4), it must be served by one of the methods approved in the relevant convention.

(6) Subject to paragraph (9), a document which requires to be posted in Scotland for the purposes of this rule must be posted by a solicitor or a sheriff officer, and the form of service and certificate of execution of service must be in Forms 11 and 12 respectively.

(7) On the face of the envelope used for postal service under this rule there must be written or printed a notice in Form 15.

(8) Where service is effected by a method specified in paragraph (3)(b) or (c), the pursuer must—

(a) send a copy of the summons and warrant for service with form of service attached, or other document, with a request for service to be effected by the method indicated in the request to the Secretary of State for Foreign and Commonwealth Affairs; and

(b) lodge in process a certificate of execution of service signed by the authority which has effected service.

(9) If service is effected by the method specified in paragraph (3)(e), the pursuer must—

(a) send to the official in the country in which service is to be effected a copy of the summons and warrant for service, with citation attached, or other document, with a request for service to be effected by delivery to the defender or his residence; and

(b) lodge in process a certificate of execution of service by the official who has effected service.

D 564 (10) Where service is executed in accordance with paragraph (2)(b)(ii) or (3)(a) other than on another party in—

(a) the United Kingdom;

(b) the Isle of Man; or

(c) the Channel Islands, the party executing service must lodge a certificate stating that the form of service employed is in accordance with the law of the place where the service was executed.

(11) A certificate lodged in accordance with paragraph (10) shall be given by a person who is conversant with the law of the country concerned and who—

(a) practises or has practised law in that country; or

(b) is a duly accredited representative of the government of that country.

(12) Every summons or document and every citation and notice on the face of the envelope referred to in paragraph (7) must be accompanied by a translation

(a) an official language of the country in which service is to be executed; or

(b) in a country to which the Council Regulation applies, a language of the member state of transmission that is understood by the person on whom service is being executed.

(13) A translation referred to in paragraph (12) must be certified as a correct translation by the person making it and the certificate must contain the full name, address and qualifications of the translator and be lodged along with the execution of such service.

[1] (14) In this rule "the Council Regulation" means Council Regulation (EC) No. 1348/2000 on the service in the Member States of judicial and extrajudicial documents in civil or commercial matters.

NOTE

[1] As amended and inserted by the Act of Sederunt (Ordinary Cause, Summary Application and Small Claim Rules) Amendment (Miscellaneous) 2004 (SSI 2004/197) (effective May 21, 2004), para.4(3).

Endorsation by sheriff clerk of defender's residence not necessary

5.8. Any summons, decree, charge or other document following upon a summons or decree may be served, enforced or otherwise lawfully executed in Scotland without endorsation by a sheriff clerk and, if executed by a sheriff officer, may be so executed by a sheriff officer of the court which granted the summons, or by a sheriff officer of the sheriff court district in which it is to be executed.

Contents of envelope containing defender's copy summons

5.9. Nothing must be included in the envelope containing a defender's copy summons except—

    (a) the copy summons;

    (b) a response or other notice in accordance with these Rules; and

    (c) any other document approved by the sheriff principal.

Re-service

5.10.—(1) If it appears to the sheriff that there has been any failure or irregularity in service upon a defender, the sheriff may order the pursuer to re-serve the summons on such conditions as he thinks fit.

(2) If re-service has been ordered in accordance with paragraph (1) or rule 5.5(7) the action shall proceed thereafter as if it were a new action.

Defender appearing barred from objecting to service

5.11.—(1) A person who appears in an action shall not be entitled to state any objection to the regularity of the execution of service or intimation on him and his appearance shall remedy any defect in such service or intimation.

(2) Nothing in paragraph (1) shall preclude a party pleading that the court has no jurisdiction.

Return of summons

5.12.—(1) If any appearance in court is required on the calling date in respect of any party—

    (a) the summons; and

    (b) the relevant certificate of execution of service, shall be returned to the sheriff clerk not later than two days before the calling date.

(2) If no appearance by any party is required on the calling date, only the certificate of execution of service need be returned to the sheriff clerk, not later than two days before the calling date.

(3) If the pursuer fails to proceed in accordance with paragraph (1) or (2) as appropriate, the sheriff may dismiss the action.

CHAPTER 6

D 565

ARRESTMENT

Service of schedule of arrestment

6.1. If a schedule of arrestment has not been personally served on an arrestee, the arrestment shall have effect only if a copy of the schedule is also sent by registered post or the first class recorded delivery service to—

    (a) the last known place of residence of the arrestee; or

    (b) if such place of residence is not known, or if the arrestee is a firm or corporation, to the arrestee's principal place of business if known, or, if not known, to any known place of business of the arrestee,

and the sheriff officer must, on the certificate of execution, certify that this has been done and specify the address to which the copy of the schedule was sent.

Arrestment before service

6.2.—(1) An arrestment to found jurisdiction or an arrestment on the dependence of an action used prior to service shall cease to have effect, unless the summons is served within 21 days from the date of execution of the arrestment.

(2) When such an arrestment as is referred to in paragraph (1) has been executed, the party using it must forthwith report the execution to the sheriff clerk.

Recall and restriction of arrestment

6.3—(1) The sheriff may order that an arrestment on the dependence of an action or counterclaim shall cease to have effect if the party whose funds or property are arrested—

(a) pays into court; or

(b) finds caution to the satisfaction of the sheriff clerk in respect of, the sum claimed together with the sum of £50 in respect of expenses.

(2) Without prejudice to paragraph (1), a party whose funds or property are arrested may at any time apply to the sheriff to exercise his powers to recall or restrict an arrestment on the dependence of an action or counterclaim, with or without consignation or caution.

(3) An application made under paragraph (2) must be intimated by the applicant to the party who instructed the arrestment.

(4) On payment into court in accordance with paragraph (1), or if the sheriff recalls or restricts an arrestment on the dependence of an action in accordance with paragraph (2) and any condition imposed by the sheriff has been complied with, the sheriff clerk must—

(a) issue to the party whose funds or property are arrested a certificate in Form 16 authorising the release of any sum or property arrested to the extent ordered by the sheriff; and

(b) send a copy of the certificate to—

(i) the party who instructed the arrestment; and

(ii) the party who has possession of the funds or property that are arrested.

CHAPTER 7

UNDEFENDED ACTION

Undefended action

7.1.—(1) Subject to paragraphs (4), (5) and (6), where the defender has not lodged a form of response on or before the return day—

(a) the action shall not require to call in court on the calling date; and

(b) the pursuer must lodge a minute in Form 17 before the sheriff clerk's office closes for business on the second day before the calling date.

(2) If the pursuer does not lodge a minute in terms of paragraph (1), the sheriff must dismiss the action.

(3) If the sheriff is not prepared to grant the order requested in Form 17, the sheriff clerk must—

(a) fix a date, time and place for the pursuer to be heard; and

(b) inform the pursuer of—

(i) that date, time and place; and

(ii) the reasons for the sheriff wishing to hear him.

(4) Where no form of response has been lodged in an action—

(a) for recovery of possession of heritable property; or

D 566   (b) of sequestration for rent, the action shall call in court on the calling date and the sheriff shall determine the action as he thinks fit.

(5) Where no form of response has been lodged in an action of multiplepoinding the action shall proceed in accordance with rule 27.9(1)(a).

(6) Where no form of response has been lodged in an action of count, reckoning and payment the action shall proceed in accordance with rule 29.2.

(7) If the defender does not lodge a form of response in time or if the sheriff is satisfied that he does not intend to defend the action on the merits or on the amount of the sum due, the sheriff may grant decree with expenses against him.

Application for time to pay direction or time order

7.2.—(1) If the defender admits the claim, he may, where competent—

(a) make an application for a time to pay direction (including, where appropriate, an application for recall or restriction of an arrestment) or a time order by completing the appropriate part of the form of response contained in the defender's copy summons and lodging it with the sheriff clerk on or before the return day; or

(b) lodge a form of response indicating that he admits the claim and intends to apply orally for a time to pay direction (including, where appropriate, an application for recall or restriction of an arrestment) or time order.

(2) Where the defender has lodged an application in terms of paragraph (1)(a), the pursuer may intimate that he does not object to the application by lodging a minute in Form 18 before

the time the sheriff clerk's office closes for business on the day occurring two days before the calling date stating that he does not object to the defender's application and seeking decree.

(3) If the pursuer intimates in accordance with paragraph (2) that he does not object to the application—

    (a) the sheriff may grant decree on the calling date;

    (b) the parties need not attend; and

    (c) the action will not call in court.

(4) If the pursuer wishes to oppose the application for a time to pay direction or time order made in accordance with paragraph (1)(a), he must lodge a minute in Form 19 before the time the sheriff clerk's office closes for business on the day occurring two days before the calling date.

(5) Where the pursuer objects to an application in terms of paragraph (1)(a) or the defender has lodged a form of response in accordance with paragraph (1)(b), the action shall call on the calling date when the parties may appear and the sheriff must decide the application and grant decree accordingly.

(6) The sheriff shall decide an application in accordance with paragraph (5) whether or not any of the parties appear.

(7) Where the defender has lodged an application in terms of paragraph (1)(a) and the pursuer fails to proceed in accordance with either of paragraphs (2) or (4) the sheriff may dismiss the claim.

Decree in actions to which the Hague Convention or Civil Jurisdiction and Judgements Act 1982 apply

7.3.—(1) If the summons has been served in a country to which the Hague Convention on the Service Abroad of Judicial and Extra-Judicial Documents in Civil or Commercial Matters dated 15th November 1965 applies, decree must not be granted until it is established to the satisfaction of the sheriff that the requirements of Article 15 of that Convention have been complied with.

(2) Where a defender is domiciled in another part of the United Kingdom or in another Contracting State, the sheriff shall not grant decree until it has been shown that the defender has been able to receive the summons in sufficient time to arrange his defence or that all necessary steps have been taken to that end.

(3) For the purposes of paragraph (2)—

    (a) the question whether a person is domiciled in another part of the United Kingdom shall be determined in accordance with sections 41 and 42 of the Civil Jurisdiction and Judgments Act 1982;

    (b) the question whether a person is domiciled in another Contracting State shall be determined in accordance with Article 52 of the Convention in Schedule 1 or 3C to that Act; and

    (c) the term "Contracting State" has the meaning assigned in section 1 of that Act.

CHAPTER 8   **D 567**

DEFENDED ACTION

Response to summons

8.1.—(1) If the defender intends—

    (a) to challenge the jurisdiction of the court or the competency of the action;

    (b) to defend the action (whether as regards the amount claimed or otherwise); or

    (c) state a counterclaim,

he must complete and lodge with the sheriff clerk on or before the return day the form of response contained in the defender's copy summons including a statement of his response which gives fair notice to the pursuer.

(2) The sheriff clerk must upon receipt intimate to the pursuer a copy of any response lodged under paragraph (1).

Procedure in defended action

8.2.—(1) Where the defender has lodged a form of response in accordance with rule 8.1(1) the action will call in court for a hearing.

(2) The hearing shall be held on the calling date.

(3) The sheriff may continue the hearing to such other date as he considers appropriate.

(4) The defender must either be present or be represented at the hearing.

(5) Where the defender—

    (a) does not appear or is not represented; and

    (b) the pursuer is present or is represented,

decree may be granted against the defender in terms of the summons.

(6) Where at the hearing—

    (a) the pursuer does not appear or is not represented; and

    (b) the defender is present or represented, the sheriff shall dismiss the action and may grant decree in terms of any counterclaim.

(7) If all parties fail to appear at the hearing, the sheriff shall, unless sufficient reason appears to the contrary, dismiss the action and any counterclaim.

Purpose of hearing

8.3.—(1) If, at the hearing, the sheriff is satisfied that the action is incompetent or that there is a patent defect of jurisdiction, he must grant decree of dismissal in favour of the defender or, if appropriate, transfer the action in terms of rule 16.1(2).

(2) At the hearing, the sheriff shall—

    (a) ascertain the factual basis of the action and any defence, and the legal basis on which the action and defence are proceeding; and

    (b) seek to negotiate and secure settlement of the action between the parties.

(3) If the sheriff cannot secure settlement of the action between the parties, he shall—

    (a) identify and note on the summons the issues of fact and law which are in dispute;

    (b) note on the summons any facts which are agreed;

    (c) where it appears that the claim as stated or any defence stated in response to it is not soundly based in law in whole or in part, hear parties forthwith on that matter and may grant decree in favour of any party; and

    (d) if satisfied that the claim and any defence have or may have a sound basis in law and that the dispute between the parties depends upon resolution of disputed issues of fact, fix a diet of proof or, alternatively, if satisfied that the claim and any defence have a sound basis in law and that the facts of the case are sufficiently agreed, hear parties forthwith on the merits of the action and may grant decree in whole or in part in favour of any party.

(4) Where the sheriff fixes a proof, the sheriff clerk shall make up a folder for the case papers.

Remit to person of skill

8.4.—(1) The sheriff may, on an incidental application by any party or on a joint application, remit to any person of skill, or other person, to report on any matter of fact.

(2) If a remit under paragraph (1) is made by joint application or of consent of all parties, the report of such person shall be final and conclusive with respect to the matter of fact which is the subject of the remit.

(3) If a remit under paragraph (1) is made—

    (a) on the application of one of the parties, the expenses of its execution must, in the first instance, be met by that party; or

    (b) on a joint application or of consent of all parties, the expenses must, in the first instance, be met by the parties equally, unless the sheriff otherwise orders.

D 568   *Inspection and recovery of documents*

8.5.—(1) Each party shall, within 28 days after the date of the fixing of a proof, intimate to every other party, and lodge with the sheriff clerk, a list of documents, which are or have been in his possession or control which he intends to use or put in evidence at the proof, including the whereabouts of those documents.

(2) A party who has received a list of documents from another party under paragraph (1) may inspect those documents which are in the possession or control of the party intimating the list at a time and place fixed by that party which is reasonable to both parties.

(3) Nothing in this rule shall affect—

    (a) the law relating, or the right of a party to object, to the inspection of a document on the ground of privilege or confidentiality; or

    (b) the right of a party to apply under rule 18.1 for a commission and diligence for recovery of documents or under rule 18.3 for an order under section 1 of the Administration of Justice (Scotland) Act 1972.

Exchange of lists of witnesses

8.6.—(1) Within 28 days after the date of the fixing of a proof, each party shall intimate to every other party, and lodge with the sheriff clerk, a list of witnesses, including any skilled witnesses, whom he intends to call to give evidence.

(2) A party who seeks to call as a witness a person not on his list intimated and lodged under paragraph (1) shall, if any other party objects to such a witness being called, seek leave of the sheriff to call that person as a witness; and such leave may be granted on such conditions, if any, as the sheriff thinks fit.

(3) The list of witnesses intimated under paragraph (1) shall include the name, occupation (where known) and address of each intended witness.

Exchange of reports of skilled witnesses

8.7.—(1) Not less than 28 days before the diet of proof, a party shall—

(a) disclose to every other party in the form of a written report the substance of the evidence of any skilled person whom he intends to call as a witness; and

(b) lodge a copy of that report in process.

(2) Except on special cause shown, a party may only call as a skilled witness any person the substance of whose evidence has been disclosed in accordance with paragraph (1).

Evidence generally

8.8. Where possible, the parties shall agree photographs, sketch plans, and any statement or document not in dispute.

Hearing parts of action separately

8.9.—(1) In any action which includes a claim for payment of money, the sheriff may—

(a) of his own accord; or

(b) on the incidental application of any party,

order that proof on liability or any specified issue be heard separately from proof on any other issue and determine the order in which the proofs shall be heard.

(2) The sheriff shall pronounce such interlocutor as he thinks fit at the conclusion of the first proof of any action ordered to be heard in separate parts under paragraph (1).

Returning borrowed parts of process before proof

8.10. All parts of process which have been borrowed must be returned to process not later than noon on the day preceding the proof.

Conduct of proof

8.11. The pursuer must lead in the proof unless the sheriff, on the incidental application of any of the parties which has been intimated to the other parties not less than seven days before the diet of proof, directs otherwise.

Administration of oath or affirmation to witness

8.12. The sheriff must administer the oath to a witness in Form 20 or, where the witness elects to affirm, the affirmation in Form 21.

Noting of evidence, etc.

8.13.—(1) The sheriff who presides at the proof may make a note of any facts agreed by the parties since the hearing held in terms of rule 8.2(1).

(2) The parties may, and must if required by the sheriff, lodge a joint minute of admissions of **D 569** the facts upon which they have reached agreement.

(3) The sheriff must—

(a) make for his own use notes of the evidence led at the proof, including any evidence the admissibility of which is objected to, and of the nature of any such objection; and

(b) retain these notes until after any appeal has been disposed of.

Parties to be heard at close of proof

8.14.—(1) After all the evidence has been led relevant to the particular proof, the sheriff must hear parties on the evidence.

(2) At the conclusion of that hearing, the sheriff may—

(a) pronounce his decision; or

(b) reserve judgment.

Objections to admissibility of evidence

8.15. If in the course of a proof an objection is made to the admissibility of any evidence and that line of evidence is not abandoned by the party pursuing it, the sheriff must except where—

(a) he is of the opinion that the evidence is clearly irrelevant or scandalous; or

(b) it is an objection falling within rule 8.16(1),

note the terms of the objection and allow the evidence to be led reserving the question of its admissibility to be decided by him at the close of the proof.

Incidental appeal against rulings on confidentiality of evidence and production of documents

8.16.—(1) Where a party or any other person objects to the admissibility of oral or documentary evidence on the ground of confidentiality or to the production of a document on any ground, he may, if dissatisfied with the ruling of the sheriff on the objection, express immediately his formal dissatisfaction with the ruling and, with leave of the sheriff, appeal to the sheriff principal.

(2) The sheriff principal shall dispose of an appeal under paragraph (1) with the least possible delay.

(3) Except as provided in paragraph (1), no appeal may be made during a proof against any decision of the sheriff as to the admissibility of evidence or the production of documents.

(4) The appeal referred to in paragraph (1) shall not remove the action from the sheriff who may proceed with the action in relation to any issue which is not dependent on the ruling appealed against.

Application for time to pay direction or a time order in defended action

8.17. A defender in an action which proceeds as defended may, where it is competent to do so, make a incidental application or apply orally at any hearing, at any time before decree is granted, for a time to pay direction (including where appropriate, an order recalling or restricting an arrestment on the dependence) or time order.

Pronouncement of decision

8.18.—(1) If the sheriff pronounces his decision at the end of the hearing held in terms of rule 8.2(1) or any proof, he must state briefly the grounds of his decision, including the reasons for his decision on any question of law or of admissibility of evidence.

(2) If the sheriff pronounces his decision after reserving judgement, he must give to the sheriff clerk within 28 days—

(a) a statement of his decision; and

(b) a brief note of the matters mentioned in paragraph (1).

(3) The sheriff clerk must send copies of the documents mentioned in paragraphs (2)(a) and (b) to each of the parties.

CHAPTER 9

INCIDENTAL APPLICATIONS AND SISTS

General

9.1.—(1) Except where otherwise provided, any incidental application in an action may be made—

(a) orally with the leave of the sheriff during any hearing of the action; or

(b) by lodging the application in written form with the sheriff clerk.

(2) An application lodged in accordance with paragraph (1)(b) may only be heard after not less than two days' notice has been given to the other party.

(3) Where the party receiving notice of an incidental application lodged in accordance with paragraph (1)(b) intimates to the sheriff clerk and the party making the application that the application is not opposed, the application shall not require to call in court unless the sheriff so directs.

D 570 (4) Any intimation made under paragraph (3) shall be made not later than noon on the day before the application is due to be heard.

Application to sist action

9.2.—(1) Where an incidental application to sist an action is made, the reason for the sist—

(a) shall be stated by the party seeking the sist; and

(b) shall be recorded in the Register of Summary Causes and on the summons.

(2) Where an action has been sisted, the sheriff may, after giving parties an opportunity to be heard, recall the sist.

CHAPTER 10

COUNTERCLAIM

Counterclaim

10.1.—(1) If a pursuer intends to oppose a counterclaim, he must lodge answers within seven days of the lodging of the form of response.

(2) The pursuer must at the same time as lodging answers intimate a copy of any answers to every other party.

(3) The defender may apply for warrant to arrest on the dependence of a counterclaim.

(4) An application under paragraph (3) must be made by appending to the counterclaim the words "warrant for arrestment on the dependence applied for".

[1] (4A) Where an application under paragraph (3) is made—
   (a) the counterclaim must include averments to justify the grant of the warrant sought; and
   (b) the sheriff may grant the application if he thinks it appropriate.
(4B) If the sheriff grants an application under paragraph (3), then the sheriff shall add to the counterclaim the words "Warrant granted as craved", and authenticate the counterclaim in an appropriate manner.
(5) Any such warrant shall have the like effect as it would have in any summons.

NOTE
[1] As amended and inserted by the Act of Sederunt (Ordinary Cause, Summary Application and Small Claim Rules) Amendment (Miscellaneous) 2004 (SSI 2004/197) (effective May 21, 2004), para.4(4).

CHAPTER 11

THIRD PARTY PROCEDURE

Application for third party notice
   11.1.—(1) Where in an action a defender claims that—
   (a) he has in respect of the subject matter of the action a right of contribution, relief or indemnity against any person who is not a party to the action; or
   (b) a person whom the pursuer is not bound to call as a defender should be made a party to the action along with the defender in respect that such person is—
      (i) solely liable, or jointly or jointly and severally liable with the defender to the pursuer in respect of the subject matter of the action; or
      (ii) liable to the defender in respect of the claim arising from or in connection with the liability, if any, of the defender to the pursuer,
   he may apply by incidental application for an order for service of a third party notice upon that other person.
   (2) An application for service of a third party notice shall be made at the time when the defender lodges a form of response, unless the sheriff on cause shown shall permit a later application.
   (3) Where—
   (a) a pursuer against whom a counterclaim is made; or
   (b) a third party convened in the action,
seeks, in relation to the claim against him, to make against a person who is not a party, a claim mentioned in paragraph (1) as a claim which could be made by a defender against a third party, he shall apply by incidental application for an order for service of a third party notice; and rules 11.2 and 11.3 shall, with the necessary modifications, apply to such a claim as they apply in relation to a counterclaim by a defender.

Procedure
   11.2.—(1) If an application in terms of rule 11.1 is granted, the sheriff shall—
   (a) fix a date on which he will regulate further procedure; and
   (b) grant warrant to serve on the third party—
      (i) a copy of the summons;
      (ii) a copy of the grounds upon which it is claimed that the third party is liable; and **D 571**
      (iii) a notice in Form 22 and a copy of Form 23.
   (2) A copy of the third party notice, and any certificate of execution of service, shall be lodged by the defender before the hearing fixed under paragraph (1)(a).
   (3) A third party seeking to answer the claim against him shall complete and lodge the form of response no later than seven days before the hearing fixed under paragraph (1)(a).
   (4) The sheriff clerk must upon receipt intimate to the other parties a copy of any response lodged under paragraph (3).

Warrants for diligence on third party notice
   11.3.—(1) A defender who applies for an order for service of a third party notice may apply for a warrant for arrestment to found jurisdiction or for arrestment on the dependence which would have been permitted had the warrant been sought in a separate action.
   (2) A certified copy of the interlocutor granting warrant for diligence shall be sufficient authority for execution of the diligence.

SUMMARY DECREE

Application of chapter
12.1. This chapter applies to any action other than an action of multiplepoinding.

Application for summary decree
12.2.—(1) A pursuer may at any time after a defender has lodged a form of response apply by incidental application for summary decree against any defender on the ground that there is no defence to the action or any part of it.

(2) In applying for summary decree the pursuer may ask the sheriff to dispose of the whole or part of the subject matter of the action.

(3) The pursuer shall intimate an application under paragraph (1) by registered or recorded delivery post to every other party not less than seven days before the date fixed for the hearing of the application.

(4) On an application under paragraph (1), the sheriff may ordain any party, or a partner, director, officer or office-bearer of any party—
    (a) to produce any relevant document or article; or
    (b) to lodge an affidavit in support of any assertion of fact made in the action or at the hearing of the incidental application.

(5) Notwithstanding the refusal of an application for summary decree, a subsequent application may be made on a change of circumstances.

Summary decree in a counterclaim etc.
12.3. Rule 12.2 shall apply with the necessary modifications to an application by any other party for summary decree.

CHAPTER 13

ALTERATION OF SUMMONS ETC.

Alteration of summons etc.
13.1.—(1) The sheriff may, on the incidental application of a party, allow amendment of the summons, form of response, counterclaim or answers to a counterclaim and adjust the note of disputed issues at any time before final judgment is pronounced on the merits.

(2) In an undefended action, the sheriff may order the amended summons to be re-served on the defender on such period of notice as he thinks fit.

(3) Paragraph (1) includes amendment for the following purposes:-
    (a) increasing or reducing the sum claimed;
    (b) seeking a different remedy from that originally sought;
    (c) correcting or supplementing the designation of a party;
    (d) enabling a party to sue or be sued in a representative capacity; and
    (e) sisting a party in substitution for, or in addition to, the original party.

(4) Where an amendment sists an additional or substitute defender to the action the sheriff shall order such service and regulate further procedure as he thinks fit.

D 572

CHAPTER 14

ADDITIONAL DEFENDER

Additional defender
14.1—(1) Any person who has not been called as a defender may apply by incidental application to the sheriff for leave to enter an action as a defender, and to state a defence.

(2) An application under this rule must specify—
    (a) the applicant's title and interest to enter the action; and
    (b) the grounds of the defence which he proposes to state.

(3) On the lodging of an application under this rule—
    (a) the sheriff must appoint a date for hearing the application; and
    (b) the applicant must forthwith serve a copy of the application and of the order for a hearing on the parties to the action.

(4) After hearing the applicant and any party to the action the sheriff may, if he is satisfied that the applicant has shown title and interest to enter the action, grant the application.

(5) Where an application is granted under paragraph (4)—

(a) the applicant shall be treated as a defender; and

(b) the sheriff must forthwith consider whether any decision already taken in the action on the issues in dispute between the parties requires to be reconsidered in light of the terms of the application.

CHAPTER 15

APPLICATION FOR SIST OF PARTY AND TRANSFERENCE

Application for sist of party and transference
15.1.—(1) If a party dies or becomes legally incapacitated while an action is depending, any person claiming to represent that party or his estate may apply by incidental application to be sisted as a party to the action.

(2) If a party dies or becomes legally incapacitated while an action is depending and the provisions of paragraph (1) are not invoked, any other party may apply by incidental application to have the action transferred in favour of or against, as the case may be, any person who represents that party or his estate.

CHAPTER 16

TRANSFER AND REMIT OF ACTIONS

Transfer to another court
16.1.—(1) The sheriff may transfer an action to any other sheriff court, whether in the same sheriffdom or not, if the sheriff considers it expedient to do so.

(2) If the sheriff is satisfied that the court has no jurisdiction, he may transfer the action to any sheriff court in which it appears to the sheriff that it ought to have been brought.

(3) An action so transferred shall proceed in all respects as if it had been brought originally in the court to which it is transferred.

Remit between procedures
16.2.—(1) If the sheriff makes a drection that an action is to be treated as an ordinary cause, he must, at the time of making that direction—

(a) direct the pursuer to lodge an initial writ, and intimate it to every other party, within 14 days of the date of the direction;

(b) direct the defender to lodge defences within 28 days of the date of the direction; and

(c) fix a date and time for an Options Hearing and that date shall be the first suitable court day occurring not sooner than ten weeks, or such lesser period as he considers appropriate, after the last date for lodging the initial writ.

(2) If the sheriff directs that an ordinary cause or small claim is to be treated as an action under these rules—

(a) he must specify the next step of procedure to be followed in the action; and

(b) in the case of an ordinary cause, the initial writ shall be deemed to be a summary cause summons.

Remit from Court of Session   **D 573**
16.3. On receipt of the process in an action which has been remitted from the Court of Session under section 14 of the Law Reform (Miscellaneous Provisions) (Scotland) Act 1985, the sheriff clerk must—

(a) record the date of receipt in the Register of Summary Causes;

(b) fix a hearing to determine further procedure on the first court day occurring not earlier than 14 days after the date of receipt of the process; and

(c) forthwith send written notice of the date of the hearing fixed under paragraph (b) to each party.

CHAPTER 17

PRODUCTIONS AND DOCUMENTS

Lodging of productions
17.1.—(1) A party who intends to rely at a proof upon any documents or articles in his possession, which are reasonably capable of being lodged with the court, must—

(a) lodge them with the sheriff clerk together with a list detailing the items no later than 14 days before the proof; and

(b) at the same time send a copy of the list to the other party.

(2) The documents referred to in paragraph (1) include any affidavit or other written statement admissible under section 2 (1) of the Civil Evidence (Scotland) Act 1988.

(3) A party lodging a document under this rule must send a copy of it to every other party, unless it is not practicable to do so.

(4) Subject to paragraph (5), only documents or articles produced—

> (a) in accordance with paragraph (1) (and, if it was a document to which rule 8.5 (1) applies, was on the list lodged in accordance with that rule);
> (b) at a hearing under rule 8.2; or
> (c) under rule 18.2 (2) or (3), may be used or put in evidence.

(5) Documents other than those mentioned in paragraph (4) may be used or put in evidence only with the—

> (a) consent of the parties; or
> (b) permission of the sheriff on cause shown, and on such terms as to expenses or otherwise as to him seem proper.

Copy productions

17.2.—(1) A copy of every production, marked with the appropriate number of process of the principal production, must be lodged for the use of the sheriff at a proof not later than 48 hours before the diet of proof.

(2) Each copy production consisting of more than one sheet must be securely fastened together by the party lodging it.

Borrowing of productions

17.3.—(1) Any productions borrowed must be returned not later than noon on the day preceding the date of the proof.

(2) A receipt for any production borrowed must be entered in the list of productions and that list must be retained by the sheriff clerk.

(3) Subject to paragraph (4), productions may be borrowed only by—

> (a) a solicitor; or
> (b) his authorised clerk for whom he shall be responsible.

(4) A party litigant or an authorised lay representative may borrow a production only with permission of the sheriff and subject to such conditions as the sheriff may impose.

(5) Productions may be inspected within the office of the sheriff clerk during normal business hours, and copies may be obtained by a party litigant, where practicable, from the sheriff clerk.

Penalty for failure to return productions

17.4.—(1) If a solicitor has borrowed a production and fails to return it for any diet at which it is required, the sheriff may impose upon such solicitor a fine not exceeding £50.

(2) A fine imposed under paragraph (1) shall—

> (a) be payable to the sheriff clerk; and
> (b) be recoverable by civil diligence.

(3) An order imposing a fine under this rule shall not be subject to review except that the sheriff who granted it may, on cause shown, recall it.

D 574 ### Documents lost or destroyed

17.5.—(1) This rule applies to any—

> (a) summons;
> (b) form of response;
> (c) answers to a counterclaim;
> (d) third party notice or answers to a third party notice;
> (d) Register of Summary Causes; or
> (e) other document lodged with the sheriff clerk in connection with an action.

(2) Where any document mentioned in paragraph (1) is—

> (a) lost; or
> (b) destroyed,

a copy of it, authenticated in such manner as the sheriff may require, may be substituted and shall, for the purposes of the action including the use of diligence, be equivalent to the original.

Documents and productions to be retained in custody of sheriff clerk

17.6.—(1) This rule applies to all documents or other productions which have at any time been lodged or referred to during a hearing or proof.

(2) The sheriff clerk must retain in his custody any document or other production mentioned in paragraph (1) until—

> (a) after the expiry of the period during which an appeal is competent; and

(b) any appeal lodged has been disposed of.

(3) Each party who has lodged productions in an action shall—

    (a) after the final determination of the claim, where no appeal has been lodged, within 14 days after the appeal period has expired; or

    (b) within 14 days after the disposal of any appeal lodged on the final determination of the action, uplift the productions from the sheriff clerk.

(4) Where any production has not been uplifted as required by paragraph (3), the sheriff clerk shall intimate to—

    (a) the solicitor who lodged the production; or

    (b) where no solicitor is acting, the party himself or such other party as seems appropriate, that if he fails to uplift the production within 28 days after the date of such intimation, it will be disposed of in such manner as the sheriff directs.

CHAPTER 18

RECOVERY OF EVIDENCE AND ATTENDANCE OF WITNESSES

Diligence for recovery of documents

18.1.—(1) At any time after a summons has been served, a party may make an incidental application in writing to the sheriff to grant commission and diligence to recover documents.

(2) A party who makes an application in accordance with paragraph (1) must list in the application the documents which he wishes to recover.

(3) A copy of the incidental application made under paragraph (1) must be intimated by the applicant to—

    (a) every other party; and

    (b) where necessary, the Advocate General for Scotland or the Lord Advocate (and if there is any doubt, both).

(4) The Advocate General for Scotland and the Lord Advocate may appear at the hearing of any incidental application under paragraph (1).

(5) The sheriff may grant commission and diligence to recover those documents in the list mentioned in paragraph (2) which he considers relevant to the action.

Optional procedure before executing commission and diligence

18.2.—(1) Any party who has obtained a commission and diligence for the recovery of documents may, at any time before executing it, serve by first class recorded delivery post on the person from whom the documents are sought to be recovered (or on his known solicitor or solicitors) an order with certificate attached in Form 24.

(2) Documents recovered in response to an order under paragraph (1) must be sent to, and retained by, the sheriff clerk who shall, on receiving them, advise the parties that the documents are in his possession and may be examined within his office during normal business hours.

(3) If the party who served the order is not satisfied that full production has been made under the specification, or that adequate reasons for non-production have been given, he may execute the commission and diligence in normal form, notwithstanding his adoption in the first instance of the foregoing procedure by order.

(4) At the commission, the commissioner shall—   **D 575**

    (a) administer the appropriate oath or affirmation to any clerk and any shorthand writer appointed for the commission; and

    (b) administer to the haver the oath in Form 20, or where the haver elects to affirm, the affirmation in Form 21.

(5) Documents recovered under this rule may be tendered as evidence at any hearing or proof without further formality, and rules 18.4(2), (3) and (4) shall apply to such documents.

Applications for orders under section 1 of the Administration of Justice (Scotland) Act 1972

18.3.—(1) An application by a party for an order under section 1 of the Administration of Justice (Scotland) Act 1972, must be made by incidental application in writing.

(2) At the time of lodging an incidental application under paragraph (1), a specification of—

    (a) the document or other property sought to be inspected, photographed, preserved, taken into custody, detained, produced, recovered, sampled or experimented with or upon, as the case may be; or

    (b) the matter in respect of which information is sought as to the identity of a person who might be a witness or a defender, must be lodged in process.

(3) A copy of the specification lodged under paragraph (2) and the incidental application made under paragraph (1) must be intimated by the applicant to—

    (a) every other party;

    (b) any third party haver; and

(c) where necessary, the Advocate General for Scotland or the Lord Advocate (and if there is any doubt, both).

(4) If the sheriff grants an incidental application under paragraph (1) in whole or in part, he may order the applicant to find such caution or give such other security as he thinks fit.

(5) The Advocate General for Scotland and the Lord Advocate may appear at the hearing of any incidental application under paragraph (1).

Confidentiality

18.4.—(1) Confidentiality may be claimed for any evidence sought to be recovered under rule 18.2 or 18.3.

(2) Where confidentiality is claimed under paragraph (1), the documents or property in respect of which confidentiality is claimed shall be enclosed in a separate, sealed packet.

(3) A sealed packet referred to in paragraph (2) shall not be opened except by authority of the sheriff obtained on the incidental application of the party who sought the commission and diligence or order.

(4) The incidental application made under paragraph (3) must be intimated by the applicant to the party or parties from whose possession the documents specified in the commission and diligence or order were obtained.

(5) Any party received intimation under paragraph (4) may appear at the hearing of the application.

Preservation and obtaining of evidence

18.5.—(1) Evidence in danger of being lost may be taken to be retained until required and, if satisfied that it is desirable so to do, the sheriff may, upon the application of any party at any time, either take it himself or grant authority to a commissioner to take it.

(2) The interlocutor granting such a commission shall be sufficient authority for citing the witness to appear before the commission.

(3) The evidence of any witness who—

 (a) is resident beyond the sheriffdom;

 (b) although resident within the sheriffdom, resides at some place remote from the court in which the proof is to be held; or

 (c) is by reason of illness, age, infirmity or other sufficient cause unable to attend the proof, may be taken in the same manner as is provided in paragraph (1).

(4) On special cause shown, evidence may be taken from any witness or haver on a ground other than one mentioned in paragraph (1) or (3).

(5) Evidence taken under paragraph (1), (3) or (4) may be taken down by—

 (a) the sheriff;

 (b) the commissioner; or

 (c) a clerk or shorthand writer nominated by the sheriff or commissioner, and such evidence may be recorded in narrative form or by question and answer as the sheriff or commissioner shall direct and the extended notes of such evidence certified by such clerk or shorthand writer shall be the notes of such oral evidence.

(6) At the commission, the commissioner shall or where the sheriff takes evidence himself, the sheriff shall—

D 576

 (a) administer the appropriate oath or affirmation to any clerk and any shorthand writer appointed for the commission; and

 (b) administer to the witness the oath in Form 20, or where the witness elects to affirm, the affirmation in Form 21.

Warrants for production of original documents from public records

18.6.—(1) If a party seeks to obtain from the keeper of any public record production of the original of any register or deed in his custody for the purposes of an action, he must apply to the sheriff by incidental application.

(2) Intimation of an incidental application under paragraph (1) must be given to the keeper of the public record concerned at least seven days before the incidental application is lodged.

(3) In relation to a public record kept by the Keeper of the Registers of Scotland or the Keeper of the Records of Scotland—

 (a) where it appears to the sheriff that it is necessary for the ends of justice that an incidental application under this rule should be granted, he must pronounce an interlocutor containing a certificate to that effect; and

 (b) the party applying for production may apply by letter (enclosing a copy of the interlocutor duly certified by the sheriff clerk), addressed to the Deputy Principal Clerk of Session, for an order from the Court of Session authorising the Keeper of the Registers or the Keeper of the Records, as the case may be, to exhibit the original of any register or deed to the sheriff.

(4) The Deputy Principal Clerk of Session must submit the application sent to him under paragraph (3) to the Lord Ordinary in chambers who, if satisfied, shall grant a warrant for production or exhibition of the original register or deed sought.

(5) A certified copy of the warrant granted under paragraph (4) must be served on the keeper of the public record concerned.

(6) The expense of the production or exhibition of such an original register or deed must be met, in the first instance, by the party who applied by incidental application under paragraph (1).

Letter of request

18.7.—(1) This rule applies to an application for a letter of request to a court or tribunal outside Scotland to obtain evidence of the kind specified in paragraph (2), being evidence obtainable within the jurisdiction of that court or tribunal, for the purpose of an action depending before the sheriff.

(2) An application to which paragraph (1) applies may be made in relation to a request—
  (a) for the examination of a witness;
  (b) for the inspection, photographing, preservation, custody, detention, production or recovery of, or the taking of samples of, or the carrying out of any experiment on or with, a document or other property, as the case may be;
  (c) for the medical examination of any person;
  (d) for the taking and testing of samples of blood from any person; or
  (e) for any other order for obtaining evidence, for which an order could be obtained from the sheriff.

(3) Such an application must be made by minute in Form 25 together with a proposed letter of request in Form 25a.

(4) It shall be a condition of granting a letter of request that any solicitor for the applicant, or a party litigant, as the case may be, is to be personally liable, in the first instance, for the whole expenses which may become due and payable in respect of the letter of request to the court or tribunal obtaining the evidence and to any witness who may be examined for the purpose; and he must consign into court such sum in respect of such expenses as the sheriff thinks fit.

(5) Unless the court or tribunal to which a letter of request is addressed is a court or tribunal in a country or territory—
  (a) where English is an official language; or
  (b) in relation to which the sheriff clerk certifies that no translation is required, then the applicant must, before the issue of the letter of request, lodge in process a translation of that letter and any interrogatories and cross-interrogatories into the official language of that court or tribunal.

(6) The letter of request when issued, any interrogatories and cross-interrogatories and the translations (if any) must be forwarded by the sheriff clerk to the Foreign and Commonwealth Office or to such person and in such manner as the sheriff may direct.

Citation of witnesses

18.8.—(1) The citation of a witness or haver must be in Form 26 and the certificate of it must be in Form 26a.

(2) A party shall be responsible for securing the attendance of his witnesses or havers at a **D 577** hearing and shall be personally liable for their expenses.

(3) The summons or the copy served on the defender shall be sufficient warrant for the citation of witnesses and havers.

(4) The period of notice given to witnesses or havers cited in terms of paragraph (3) must be not less than seven days.

(5) A witness or haver shall be cited—
  (a) by registered post or the first class recorded delivery service by the solicitor for the party on whose behalf he is cited; or
  (b) by a sheriff officer—
    (i) personally;
    (ii) by a citation being left with a resident at the person's dwelling place or an employee at his place of business;
    (iii) by depositing it in that person's dwelling place or place of business;
    (iv) by affixing it to the door of that person's dwelling place or place of business; or
    (v) by registered post or the first class recorded delivery service.

(6) Where service is effected under paragraph (5) (b) (iii) or (iv), the sheriff officer shall, as soon as possible after such service, send by ordinary post to the address at which he thinks it most likely that the person may be found, a letter containing a copy of the citation.

Citation of witnesses by party litigants

18.9.—(1) Where a party to an action is a party litigant he shall—

(a) not later than 28 days before the diet of proof apply to the sheriff by incidental application to fix caution for expenses in such sum as the sheriff considers reasonable having regard to the number of witnesses he proposes to cite and the period for which they may be required to attend court; and

(b) before instructing a solicitor or a sheriff officer to cite a witness, find caution in the sum fixed in accordance with paragraph (1).

(2) A party litigant who does not intend to cite all the witnesses referred to in his application under paragraph 1(a), may apply by incidental application for variation of the amount of caution.

Witnesses failing to attend

18.10.—(1) A hearing must not be adjourned solely on account of the failure of a witness to appear unless the sheriff, on cause shown, so directs.

(2) A witness or haver who fails without reasonable excuse to answer a citation after having been properly cited and offered his travelling expenses if he has asked for them may be ordered by the sheriff to pay a penalty not exceeding £250.

(3) The sheriff may grant decree for payment of a penalty imposed under paragraph (2) above in favour of the party on whose behalf the witness or haver was cited.

(4) The sheriff may grant warrant for the apprehension of the witness or haver and for bringing him to court.

(5) A warrant mentioned in paragraph (4) shall be effective in any sheriffdom without endorsation and the expenses of it may be awarded against the witness or haver.

CHAPTER 19

CHALLENGE OF DOCUMENTS

Challenge of documents

19.1.—(1) If a party relies on a deed or other document to support his case, any other party may object to the deed or document without having to bring an action of reduction.

(2) If an objection is made, the sheriff may order the objector, if an action of reduction would otherwise have been competent, to find caution or to consign with the sheriff clerk a sum of money as security.

CHAPTER 20

EUROPEAN COURT

Interpretation of rules 20.2 to 20.5

20.1.—(1) In rules 20.2 to 20.5—

"the European Court" means the Court of Justice of the European Communities;

D 578   "reference" means a reference to the European Court for—

(a) a preliminary ruling under Article 234 of the E.E.C. Treaty, Article 150 of the Euratom Treaty or Article 41 of the E.C.S.C. Treaty; or

(b) a ruling on the interpretation of the Conventions, as defined in section 1(1) of the Civil Jurisdiction and Judgments Act 1982, under Article 3 of Schedule 2 to that Act.

(2) The expressions "E.E.C. Treaty", "Euratom Treaty" and "E.C.S.C. Treaty" have the meanings assigned respectively in Schedule 1 to the European Communities Act 1972.

Application for reference

20.2.—(1) The sheriff may, on the application of a party or of his own accord make a reference.

(2) A reference must be made in the form of a request for a preliminary ruling of the European Court in Form 27.

Preparation of case for reference

20.3.—(1) If the sheriff decides that a reference shall be made, he must within four weeks draft a reference.

(2) On the reference being drafted, the sheriff clerk must send a copy to each party.

(3) Within four weeks after the date on which copies of the draft have been sent to parties, each party may—

(a) lodge with the sheriff clerk; and

(b) send to every other party, a note of any adjustments he seeks to have made in the draft reference.

(4) Within 14 days after the date on which any such note of adjustments may be lodged, the sheriff, after considering any such adjustments, must make and sign the reference.

(5) The sheriff clerk must forthwith intimate the making of the reference to each party.

Sist of action

20.4.—(1) Subject to paragraph (2), on a reference being made, the action must, unless the sheriff when making the reference otherwise orders, be sisted until the European Court has given a preliminary ruling on the question referred to it.

(2) The sheriff may recall a sist made under paragraph (1) for the purpose of making an interim order which a due regard to the interests of the parties may require.

Transmission of reference

20.5. A copy of the reference, certified by the sheriff clerk, must be transmitted by the sheriff clerk to the Registrar of the European Court.

CHAPTER 21

ABANDONMENT

Abandonment of action

21.1.—(1) A pursuer may before an order granting absolvitor or dismissing the action has been pronounced, offer to abandon the action.

(2) Where the pursuer offers to abandon the action in accordance with paragraph (1), the sheriff clerk shall, subject to the approval of the sheriff, fix the amount of the defender's expenses to be paid by the pursuer in accordance with rule 23.3 and the action must be continued to the first appropriate court occurring not sooner than 14 days after the amount has been fixed.

(3) If before the continued diet the pursuer makes payment to the defender of the amount fixed under paragraph (2), the sheriff must dismiss the action unless the pursuer consents to absolvitor.

(4) If before the continued diet the pursuer fails to pay the amount fixed under paragraph (2), the defender shall be entitled to decree of absolvitor with expenses.

CHAPTER 22

DECREE BY DEFAULT

Decree by default

22.1.—(1) If, after a proof has been fixed under rule 8.3(3)(d), a party fails to appear at a hearing where required to do so, the sheriff may grant decree by default.

(2) If all parties fail to appear at a hearing or proof where required to do so, the sheriff must, **D 579** unless sufficient reason appears to the contrary, dismiss the action and any counterclaim.

(3) If, after a proof has been fixed under rule 8.3(3)(d), a party fails to implement an order of the court, the sheriff may, after giving him an opportunity to be heard, grant decree by default.

(4) The sheriff shall not grant decree by default solely on the ground that a party has failed to appear at the hearing of an incidental application.

CHAPTER 23

DECREES, EXTRACTS, EXECUTION AND VARIATION

Decree

23.1. The sheriff must not grant decree against—

(a) a defender or a third party in respect of a claim; or

(b) a pursuer in respect of a counterclaim, under any provision of these Rules unless satisfied that a ground of jurisdiction exists.

Final decree

[1] **23.2.** The final decree of the sheriff principal or the sheriff shall be granted, where expenses

are awarded, only after expenses have been dealt with in accordance with rules 23.3, 23.3A and 23.3B.

NOTE
[1] As amended by the Act of Sederunt (Summary Cause Rules) (Amendment) 2002 (SSI 2002/516), para.2(2) (effective January 1, 2003) (applies only to summary cause actions commenced after that date).

Expenses
23.3.—(1) Subject to rule 23.3A and paragraphs (2) to (4), the sheriff clerk must, with the approval of the sheriff, assess the amount of expenses including the fees and outlays of witnesses awarded in any cause, in accordance with the statutory table of fees of solicitors appropriate to the action.

(2) A party litigant, who is not represented by a solicitor or advocate and who would have been entitled to expenses if he had been so represented, may be awarded any outlays or expenses to which he might be found entitled by virtue of the 1975 Act or any enactment under that Act.

(3) A party who is or has been represented by an authorised lay representative and who would have been found entitled to expenses if he had been represented by a solicitor or an advocate may be awarded any outlays or expenses to which a party litigant might be found entitled in accordance with paragraph (2).

(4) A party who is not an individual, and—
(i) is or has been represented by an authorised lay representative;
(ii) if unrepresented, could not represent itself; and
(iii) would have been found entitled to expenses if it had been represented by a solicitor or an advocate,
may be awarded any outlays to which a party litigant might be found entitled under the 1975 Act or any enactment made under that Act.

(5) Except where an account of expenses is allowed to be taxed under rule 23.3A, in every case including an appeal where expenses are awarded, the sheriff clerk shall hear the parties or their solicitors on the claims for expenses including fees, if any, and outlays.

(6) Except where the sheriff principal or the sheriff has reserved judgment or where he orders otherwise, the hearing on the claim for expenses must take place immediately upon the decision being pronounced.

(7) When that hearing is not held immediately, the sheriff clerk must—
(a) fix the date, time and place when he shall hear the parties or their solicitors; and
(b) give all parties at least 14 days' notice in writing of the hearing so fixed.

(8) The party awarded expenses must—
(a) lodge his account of expenses in court at least seven days prior to the date of any hearing fixed under paragraph (7); and
(b) at the same time forward a copy of that account to every other party.

(9) The sheriff clerk must—
(a) fix the amount of the expenses; and
(b) report his decision to the sheriff principal or the sheriff in open court for his approval at a diet which the sheriff clerk has intimated to the parties.

(10) The sheriff principal or the sheriff, after hearing parties or their solicitors if objections are stated, must pronounce final decree including decree for payment of expenses as approved by him.

D 580 (11) In an appeal, the sheriff may pronounce decree under paragraph (10) on behalf of the sheriff principal.

(12) Failure by—
(a) any party to comply with any of the foregoing provisions of this rule; or
(b) the successful party or parties to appear at the hearing on expenses, must be reported by the sheriff clerk to the sheriff principal or the sheriff at a diet which the sheriff clerk has intimated to the parties.

(13) In either of the circumstances mentioned in paragraphs (12)(a) or (b), the sheriff principal or sheriff must, unless sufficient cause be shown, pronounce decree on the merits of the action and find no expenses due to or by any party.

(14) A decree pronounced under paragraph (13) shall be held to be the final decree for the purposes of these Rules.

(15) The sheriff principal or sheriff may, if he thinks fit, on the application of the solicitor of any party to whom expenses may be awarded, made at or before the time of the final decree being pronounced, grant decree in favour of that solicitor for the expenses of the action.

NOTE
[1] As amended by the Act of Sederunt (Summary Cause Rules) (Amendment) 2002 (SSI 2002/

516), para.2(3) (effective January 1, 2003) (applies only to summary cause actions commenced after that date).

Taxation
   [1] **23.3A.**—(1) Either—
   (a) the sheriff, on his own motion or on the motion of any party; or
   (b) the sheriff clerk on cause shown,
may allow an account of expenses to be taxed by the auditor of court instead of being assessed by the sheriff clerk under rule 23.3.
   (2) Where an account of expenses is lodged for taxation, the account and process shall be transmitted by the sheriff clerk to the auditor of court.
   (3) The auditor of court shall—
   (a) assign a diet of taxation not earlier than 7 days from the date he receives the account from the sheriff clerk; and
   (b) intimate that diet forthwith from to the party who lodged the account.
   (4) The party who lodged the account of expenses shall, on receiving intimation from the auditor of court under paragraph (3)—
   (a) send a copy of the account; and
   (b) intimate the date, time and place of the diet of taxation,
to every other party.
   (5) After the account has been taxed, the auditor of court shall transmit the process with the account and his report to the sheriff clerk.
   (6) Where the auditor of court has reserved consideration of the account at the date of the taxation, he shall intimate his decision to the parties who attended the taxation.
   (7) Where no objections are lodged under rule 23.3B (objections to auditor's report), the sheriff may grant decree for the expenses as taxed.

NOTE
   [1] Inserted by the Act of Sederunt (Summary Cause Rules) (Amendment) 2002 (SSI 2002/ 516), para.2(4) (effective January 1, 2003) (applies only to summary cause actions commenced after that date).

Objections to auditor's report
   [1] **23.3B.**—(1) A party may lodge a note of objections to an account as taxed only where he attended the diet of taxation.
   (2) Such a note shall be lodged within 7 days after—
   (a) the diet of taxation; or
   (b) where the auditor of court reserved consideration of the account under paragraph (6) of rule 23.3A, the date on which the auditor of court intimates his decision under that paragraph.
   (3) The sheriff shall dispose of the objection in a summary manner, with or without answers.

NOTE
   [1] Inserted by the Act of Sederunt (Summary Cause Rules) (Amendment) 2002 (SSI 2002/ 516), para.2(4) (effective January 1, 2003) (applies only to summary cause actions commenced after that date).

Correction of interlocutor or note   D 580/1
   23.4. At any time before extract, the sheriff may correct any clerical or incidental error in an interlocutor or note attached to it.

Taxes on funds under control of the court
   23.5.—(1) Subject to paragraph (2), in an action in which money has been consigned into court under the Sheriff Court Consignations (Scotland) Act 1893, no decree, warrant or order for payment to any person shall be granted until there has been lodged with the sheriff clerk a certificate by an authorised officer of the Inland Revenue stating that all taxes or duties payable to the Commissioners of Inland Revenue have been paid or satisfied.
   (2) In an action of multiplepoinding, it shall not be necessary for the grant of a decree, warrant or order for payment under paragraph (1) that all of the taxes or duties payable on the estate of a deceased claimant have been paid or satisfied.

Extract of decree
   23.6.—(1) Extract of a decree signed by the sheriff clerk may be issued only after the lapse of 14 days from the granting of the decree unless the sheriff on application orders earlier extract.

(2) In an action (other than an action to which rule 30.2 applies) where an appeal has been lodged, the extract may not be issued until the appeal has been disposed of.

(3) The extract decree—

    (a) may be written on the summons or on a separate paper;

    (b) may be in one of Forms 28 to 28k; and

    (c) shall be warrant for all lawful execution.

Charge

23.7.—(1) The period for payment specified in any charge following on a decree for payment granted in an action shall be—

    (a) 14 days if the person on whom it is served is within the United Kingdom; and

    (b) 28 days if he is outside the United Kingdom or his whereabouts are unknown.

(2) The period in respect of any other form of charge on a decree in an action shall be 14 days.

Service of charge where address of defender is unknown

23.8.—(1) If the address of a defender is not known to the pursuer, a charge shall be deemed to have been served on the defender if it is—

    (a) served on the sheriff clerk of the sheriff court district where the defender's last known address is located; and

    (b) displayed by the sheriff clerk on the walls of court for the period of the charge.

(2) On receipt of such a charge, the sheriff clerk must display it on the walls of court and it must remain displayed for the period of the charge.

(3) The period specified in the charge shall run from the first date on which it was displayed on the walls of court.

(4) On the expiry of the period of charge, the sheriff clerk must endorse a certificate in Form 29 on the charge certifying that it has been displayed in accordance with this rule and must then return it to the sheriff officer by whom service was executed.

Diligence on decree in actions for delivery

23.9.—(1) In an action for delivery, the court may, when granting decree, grant warrant to search for and take possession of goods and to open shut and lockfast places.

(2) A warrant granted under paragraph (1) shall only apply to premises occupied by the defender.

Applications in same action for variation, etc. of decree

23.10.—(1) If by virtue of any enactment the sheriff, without a new action being initiated, may order that—

D 581   (a) a decree granted be varied, discharged or rescinded; or

    (b) the execution of that decree in so far as it has not already been executed be sisted or suspended,

the party requesting the sheriff to make such an order must do so by lodging a minute to that effect, setting out briefly the reasons for the application.

(2) On the lodging of such a minute by the pursuer, the sheriff clerk must grant warrant for service upon the defender (provided that the pursuer has returned the extract decree).

(3) On the lodging of such a minute by the defender, the sheriff clerk must grant warrant for service upon the pursuer ordaining him to return the extract decree and may, where appropriate, grant interim sist of execution of the decree.

(4) Subject to paragraph (5), the minute shall not be heard in court unless seven days' notice of the minute and warrant has been given to the other parties by the party lodging the minute.

(5) The sheriff may, on cause shown, alter the period of seven days referred to in paragraph (4) but may not reduce it to less than two days.

(6) This rule shall not apply to any proceedings under the Debtors (Scotland) Act 1987 or to proceedings which may be subject to the provisions of that Act.

CHAPTER 24

RECALL OF DECREE

Recall of decree

24.1.—(1) A party may apply for recall of a decree granted under rule 7.1 or 8.2(5), (6) or (7) by lodging with the sheriff clerk a minute in Form 30, explaining the party's failure to appear and in the case of—

    (a) a defender; or

(b) where decree has been granted in respect of a counterclaim, a pursuer, stating, where he has not already done so—
   (i) his proposed defence, in the case of a defender; or
   (ii) his proposed answer, in the case of a pursuer responding to a counterclaim.
(2) A party may apply for recall of a decree in the same action on one occasion only.
(3) Except in relation to an application to which paragraph (4) applies, a minute by a pursuer under paragraph (1) must be lodged within 14 days of the grant of the decree.
(4) A minute lodged by—
   (a) a pursuer in respect of a decree granted in terms of a counterclaim;
   (b) a defender; or
   (c) a third party, shall be lodged—
      (i) if the action was served on the party seeking recall outwith the United Kingdom under rule 5.7, within a reasonable time after he had knowledge of the decree against him or in any event before the expiry of one year from the date of that decree; or
      (ii) in any other case, within 14 days of the execution of a charge or execution of arrestment, whichever first occurs, following on the grant of decree.
(5) On the lodging of a minute for recall of a decree, the sheriff clerk must fix a date, time and place for a hearing of the minute.
(6) If a hearing has been fixed under paragraph (5), the party seeking recall must serve upon the other party not less than seven days before the date fixed for the hearing—
   (a) a copy of the minute in Form 30a; and
   (b) a note of the date, time and place of the hearing.
(7) At a hearing fixed under paragraph (5), the sheriff shall recall the decree so far as not implemented and the hearing shall then proceed in terms of rule 8.3.
(8) A minute for recall of a decree, when lodged and served in terms of this rule, shall have the effect of preventing any further action being taken by the other party to enforce the decree.
(9) On receipt of the copy minute for recall of a decree, any party in possession of an extract decree must return it forthwith to the sheriff clerk.
(10) If it appears to the sheriff that there has been any failure or irregularity in service of the minute for recall of a decree, he may order re-service of the minute on such conditions as he thinks fit.

CHAPTER 25   **D 582**

APPEALS

Appeals
25.1.—(1) An appeal to the sheriff principal, other than an appeal to which rule 25.4 applies, must be by note of appeal in Form 31 lodged with the sheriff clerk not later than 14 days after the date of final decree—
   (a) requesting a stated case; and
   (b) specifying the point of law upon which the appeal is to proceed.
(2) The appellant must, at the same time as lodging a note of appeal, intimate a copy of it to every other party.
(3) The sheriff must, within 28 days of the lodging of a note of appeal, issue a draft stated case containing—
   (a) findings in fact and law or, where appropriate, a narrative of the proceedings before him;
   (b) appropriate questions of law; and
   (c) a note stating the reasons for his decisions in law,
and the sheriff clerk must send a copy of the draft stated case to the parties.
(4) In an appeal where questions of admissibility or sufficiency of evidence have arisen, the draft stated case must contain a description of the evidence led at the proof to which these questions relate.
(5) Within 14 days of the issue of the draft stated case—
   (a) a party may lodge with the sheriff clerk a note of any adjustments which he seeks to make;
   (b) a respondent may state any point of law which he wishes to raise in the appeal; and
   (c) the note of adjustment and, where appropriate, point of law must be intimated to every other party.
(6) The sheriff may, on the motion of a party or of his own accord, and must where he proposes to reject any proposed adjustment, allow a hearing on adjustments and may provide for such further procedure under this rule prior to the hearing of the appeal as he thinks fit.
(7) The sheriff must, within 14 days after—

    (a) the latest date on which a note of adjustments has been or may be lodged; or

    (b) where there has been a hearing on adjustments, that hearing, and after considering such note and any representations made to him at the hearing, state and sign the case.

    (8) If the sheriff is temporarily absent from duty for any reason, the sheriff principal may extend any period specified in paragraphs (3) or (7) for such period or periods as he considers reasonable.

    (9) The stated case signed by the sheriff must include questions of law, framed by him, arising from the points of law stated by the parties and such other questions of law as he may consider appropriate.

    (10) After the sheriff has signed the stated case, the sheriff clerk must—

    (a) place before the sheriff principal all documents and productions in the case together with the stated case; and

    (b) send to the parties a copy of the stated case together with a written note of the date, time and place of the hearing of the appeal.

Effect of and abandonment of appeal

    25.2.—(1) When a note of appeal has been lodged, it may be insisted on by all other parties in the action although they may not have lodged separate appeals.

    (2) After a note of appeal has been lodged, the appellant shall not be at liberty to withdraw it, except—

    (a) with the consent of the other parties which may be incorporated in a joint minute; or

    (b) by leave of the sheriff principal and on such terms as to expenses or otherwise as to him seem proper.

Hearing of appeal

    25.3.—(1) The sheriff principal shall hear the parties or their solicitors orally on all matters connected with the appeal including liability for expenses, but if any party moves that the question of liability for expenses be heard after the sheriff principal has given his decision the sheriff principal may grant that motion.

    (2) In the hearing of an appeal, a party shall not be allowed to raise questions of law of which notice has not been given except on cause shown and subject to such conditions as to expenses or otherwise as the sheriff principal may consider appropriate.

D 583   (3) The sheriff principal may permit a party to amend any question of law or to add any new question in accordance with paragraph (2).

    (4) The sheriff principal may—

    (a) adhere to or vary the decree appealed against;

    (b) recall the decree appealed against and substitute another therefor; or

    (c) remit, if he considers it desirable, to the sheriff, for any reason other than to have further evidence led.

    (5) At the conclusion of the hearing, the sheriff principal may either pronounce his decision or reserve judgment in which latter case he must within 28 days thereof give his decision in writing and the sheriff clerk must forthwith intimate it to the parties.

Appeal in relation to a time to pay direction

    25.4.—(1) This rule applies to appeals to the sheriff principal or to the Court of Session which relate solely to any application in connection with a time to pay direction.

    (2) Rules 25.1, 25.2, 25.3(2) and (3) and 25.7 shall not apply to appeals under this rule.

    (3) An application for leave to appeal against a decision in an application for a time to pay direction or any order connected therewith must—

    (a) be made in Form 32 within seven days of that decision, to the sheriff who made the decision; and

    (b) must specify the question of law upon which the appeal is to proceed.

    (4) If leave to appeal is granted, the appeal must be lodged in Form 33 and intimated by the appellant to every other party within 14 days of the order granting leave and the sheriff must state in writing his reasons for his original decision.

    (5) An appeal under this rule to the sheriff principal shall proceed in accordance with paragraphs (1), (4) and (5) of rule 25.3.

Sheriff to regulate interim possession

    25.5—(1) Notwithstanding an appeal, the sheriff shall have power—

    (a) to regulate all matters relating to interim possession;

    (b) to make any order for the preservation of any property to which the action relates or for its sale, if perishable;

    (c) to make any order for the preservation of evidence; or

(d) to make in his discretion any interim order which a due regard for the interests of the parties may require.

(2) An order under paragraph (1) shall not be subject to review except by the appellate court at the hearing of the appeal.

Provisions for appeal in actions for recovery of heritable property to which rule 30.2 applies
25.6. In an action to which rule 30.2 applies—
(a) it shall not be competent to shorten or dispense with the period for appeal specified in rule 25.1;
(b) it shall be competent to appeal within that period for appeal irrespective of the early issue of an extract decree; and
(c) the lodging of a note of appeal shall not operate so as to suspend diligence unless the sheriff directs otherwise.

Appeal to the Court of Session
25.7.—(1) A certificate that an action is suitable for appeal to the Court of Session may be applied for by completing and lodging an application in Form 34 with the sheriff clerk.

(2) An application made in accordance with paragraph (1) must be lodged within 14 days of the date of the final decree.

(3) The sheriff clerk must put the application before the sheriff principal who, after hearing the parties or their solicitors, shall grant or refuse the certificate.

CHAPTER 26

MANAGEMENT OF DAMAGES PAYABLE TO PERSONS UNDER LEGAL DISABILITY

Orders for payment and management of money
26.1.—(1) In an action of damages in which a sum of money becomes payable, by virtue of a decree or an extra-judicial settlement, to or for the benefit of a person under legal disability (other than a person under the age of 18 years), the sheriff shall make such order regarding the payment and management of that sum for the benefit of that person as he thinks fit.

(2) Any order required under paragraph (1) shall be made on the granting of decree for **D 584** payment or of absolvitor.

Methods of management
26.2. In making an order under rule 26.1(1), the sheriff may—
(a) order the money to be paid to—
(i) the Accountant of Court; or
(ii) the guardian of the person under legal disability, as trustee, to be applied, invested or otherwise dealt with and administered under the directions of the sheriff for the benefit of the person under legal disability;
(b) order the money to be paid to the sheriff clerk of the sheriff court district in which the person under legal disability resides, to be applied, invested or otherwise dealt with and administered, under the directions of the sheriff of that district, for the benefit of the person under legal disability; or
(c) order the money to be paid directly to the person under legal disability.

Subsequent orders
26.3.—(1) If the sheriff has made an order under rule 26.1(1), any person having an interest may apply for an order under rule 26.2, or any other order for the payment or management of the money, by incidental application.

(2) An application for directions under rule 26.2(a) or (b) may be made by any person having an interest by incidental application.

Management of money paid to sheriff clerk
26.4.—(1) A receipt in Form 35 by the sheriff clerk shall be a sufficient discharge in respect of the amount paid to him under rules 26.1 to 26.3.

(2) The sheriff clerk shall, at the request of any competent court, accept custody of any sum of money in an action of damages ordered to be paid to, applied, invested or otherwise dealt with by him, for the benefit of a person under legal disability.

(3) Any money paid to the sheriff clerk under rules 26.1 to 26.3 must be paid out, applied, invested or otherwise dealt with by the sheriff clerk only after such intimation, service and enquiry as the sheriff may order.

(4) Any sum of money invested by the sheriff clerk under rules 26.1 to 26.3 must be invested

in a manner in which trustees are authorised to invest by virtue of the Trustee Investments Act 1961.

Management of money payable to children
26.5. If the sheriff has made an order under section 13 of the Children (Scotland) Act 1995, an application by a person for an order by virtue of section 11(1)(d) of that Act must be made in writing.

CHAPTER 27

ACTION OF MULTIPLEPOINDING

Application of Chapter
27.1. This Chapter applies to an action of multiplepoinding.

Application of other rules
27.2.—(1) Rule 8.1 shall not apply to an action of multiplepoinding.
(2) Rules 8.2 to 8.17 shall only apply to an action of multiplepoinding in accordance with rule 27.7.

Pursuer in multiplepoinding
27.3. An action of multiplepoinding may be raised by any party holding or having an interest in or claim on the fund or subject *in medio*.

Parties
27.4. The pursuer must call as defenders—
    (a) all persons so far as known to him as having an interest in the fund or subject *in medio*; and
    (b) where he is not the holder of the fund or subject, the holder of that fund or subject.

D 585 *Statement of fund or subject in medio*
27.5.—(1) Where the pursuer is the holder of the fund or subject *in medio* he shall include a statement of the fund or subject in his statement of claim.
(2) Where the pursuer is not the holder of the fund or subject *in medio*, the holder shall, before the return day—
    (a) lodge with the sheriff clerk a statement in Form 5a providing—
        (i) a statement of the fund or subject;
        (ii) a statement of any claim or lien which he may profess to have on the fund or subject; and
      [1] (iii) a list of all persons known to him as having an interest in the fund or subject; and
    (b) intimate the statement in Form 5a to the pursuer, the defenders and all persons listed in the statement as having an interest in the fund or subject.

NOTE
[1] As amended by SSI 2003/26, para.4(3) (clerical error).

Response to summons
27.6.—(1) If a defender intends to—
    (a) challenge the jurisdiction of the court or the competency of the action;
    (b) object to the extent of the fund or subject *in medio*; or
    (c) make a claim on the fund, he must complete and lodge with the sheriff clerk on or before the return day the form of response contained in the defender's copy summons as appropriate, including a statement of his response which gives fair notice to the pursuer.
(2) The sheriff clerk must upon receipt intimate to the pursuer a copy of any response lodged under paragraph (1).

Procedure where response lodged
27.7. Where in a form of response a defender states a defence in accordance with rule 27.6(1)(a)—
    (a) the provisions of rules 8.2 to 8.17 shall, with the necessary modifications, apply to the resolution of the issues raised under that sub-paragraph; and
    (b) rules 27.8 to 27.10 shall apply only once those issues have been so dealt with.

Objections to fund or subject in medio

27.8.—(1) If objections to the fund or subject *in medio* have been lodged, the sheriff must, after disposal of any defence—

(a) fix a hearing; and

(b) state the order in which the claimants shall be heard at the hearing.

(2) If no objections to the fund or subject *in medio* have been lodged, or if objections have been lodged and disposed of, the sheriff may approve the fund or subject and if appropriate find the holder liable only in one single payment.

Claims hearing

27.9.—(1) This rule applies where—

(a) no defence or objection to the extent of the fund or subject *in medio* has been stated;

(b) any defence stated has been repelled; or

(c) any such objection stated has been dealt with.

(2) The sheriff must—

(a) order claims in Form 5b to be lodged within 14 days; and

(b) must fix a claims hearing at which all parties may appear or be represented.

(3) The sheriff clerk must intimate to the parties, the order for claims and the date and time of any claims hearing fixed in terms of paragraph (2).

Procedure at claims hearing

27.10.—(1) If there is no competition between the claimants who appear at the claims hearing, the sheriff may order the holder of the fund or subject *in medio*, or the sheriff clerk if it is consigned with him in terms of rule 27.12, to make it over to the claimants in terms of their claims or otherwise and subject to such provisions as to expenses as he directs.

(2) If the sheriff is unable at the claims hearing to resolve competing claims, he shall pronounce an order—

(a) fixing a date, time and place for a further hearing; and

(b) regulating the nature and scope of the hearing and the procedure to be followed.

(3) The sheriff may require that evidence be led at the further claims hearing fixed under paragraph (2).

(4) The sheriff clerk must intimate to all claimants the date, time and place of any hearing fixed under paragraph (2).

(5) At the conclusion of the claims hearing or the further claims hearing fixed under **D 586** paragraph (2), the sheriff may either pronounce his decision or reserve judgement in which case he must give his decision in writing within 28 days and the sheriff clerk must forthwith intimate it to the parties.

(6) In giving his decision under paragraph (5) the sheriff—

(a) must dispose of the action;

(b) may order the holder of the fund or subject *in medio*, or the sheriff clerk if it is consigned with him in terms of rule 27.12, to make it over to such claimants and in such quantity or amount as he may determine; and

(c) must deal with all questions of expenses.

Advertisement

27.11. If it appears to the sheriff at any stage in the multiplepoinding that there may be other potential claimants who are not parties to the action, he may order such advertisement or intimation of the order for claims as he thinks proper.

Consignation and discharge of holder

27.12.—(1) At any stage in an action of multiplepoinding the sheriff may order that—

(a) the fund or subject *in medio* be consigned in the hands of the sheriff clerk; or

(b) any subject *in medio* be sold and the proceeds of sale consigned in the hands of the sheriff clerk.

(2) After such consignation the holder of the fund or subject may apply for his exoneration and discharge.

(3) The sheriff may allow the holder of the fund or subject, on his exoneration and discharge, his expenses out of the fund as a first charge on the fund.

Action of furthcoming

Expenses included in claim

28.1. The expenses of bringing an action for furthcoming, including the expenses of the arrestment, shall be deemed to be part of the arrestor's claim which may be paid out of the arrested fund or subject.

Chapter 29

Action of count, reckoning and payment

Response to summons

29.1. If a defender wishes to admit liability to account in an action for count, reckoning and payment, this must be stated on the form of response.

Accounting hearing

29.2.—(1) This rule applies where in an action of count, reckoning and payment—

    (a) no form of response has been lodged;

    (b) the defender has indicated on the form of response that he admits liability to account; or

    (c) any defence stated has been repelled.

(2) Where paragraph 1(a) or (b) applies, the pursuer must lodge with the sheriff clerk a minute in Form 17 before close of business on the second day before the calling date.

(3) If the pursuer does not lodge a minute in accordance with paragraph (2), the sheriff must dismiss the action.

(4) Where the pursuer has lodged a minute in accordance with paragraph (2), or any defence stated has been repelled, the sheriff shall pronounce an order—

    (a) for the lodging of accounts within 14 days and objections within such further period as the sheriff may direct;

    (b) fixing a date, time and place for an accounting hearing; and

    (c) regulating the nature and scope of the accounting hearing and the procedure to be followed.

(5) The sheriff may require that evidence be led at an accounting hearing fixed under paragraph (4) to prove the accounts and in support of any objection taken.

(6) The sheriff clerk must intimate to all claimants the date, time and place of any hearing fixed under paragraph (4).

D 587

Chapter 30

Recovery of possession of heritable property

Action raised under section 38 of the 1907 Act

30.1. An action for the recovery of possession of heritable property made in terms of section 38 of the 1907 Act may be raised by—

    (a) a proprietor;

    (b) his factor; or

    (c) any other person authorised by law to pursue a process of removing.

Action against persons in possession of heritable property without right or title

30.2.—(1) Subject to paragraph (2), this rule applies only to an action for recovery of possession of heritable property against a person or persons in possession of heritable property without right or title to possess the property.

(2) This rule shall not apply with respect to a person who has or had a title or other right to occupy the heritable property and who has been in continuous occupation since that title or right is alleged to have come to an end.

(3) Where the name of a person in occupation of a heritable property is not known and cannot reasonably be ascertained, the pursuer shall call that person as a defender by naming him as an "occupier".

(4) Where the name of a person in occupation of the heritable property is not known and cannot reasonably be ascertained, the summons shall be served (whether or not it is also served on a named person), unless the sheriff otherwise directs, by an officer of the court—

    (a) affixing a copy of the summons and a citation in Form 11 addressed to "the occupiers"

to the main door or other conspicuous part of the premises, and if practicable, depositing a copy of each of those documents in the premises; or
  (b) in the case of land only, inserting stakes in the ground at conspicuous parts of the occupied land to each of which is attached a sealed transparent envelope containing a copy of the summons and a citation in Form 11 addressed to "the occupiers".
  (5) In an action to which this rule applies, the sheriff may in his discretion, and subject to rule 25.6, shorten or dispense with any period of time provided anywhere in these rules.
  (6) An application by a party under this rule to shorten or dispense with any period may be made orally and the provisions in rule 9.1 shall not apply, but the sheriff clerk must enter details of any such application in the Register of Summary Causes.

Effect of decree
30.3. When decree for the recovery of possession is granted, it shall have the same force and effect as—
  (a) a decree of removing;
  (b) a decree of ejection;
  (c) a summary warrant of ejection;
  (d) a warrant for summary ejection in common form; or
  (e) a decree pronounced in a summary application for removing, in terms of sections 36, 37 and 38 respectively of the 1907 Act.

Preservation of defender's goods and effects
30.4. When decree is pronounced and the defender is neither present nor represented, the sheriff may give such directions as he deems proper for the preservation of the defender's goods and effects.

Action of removing where fixed term of removal
30.5.—(1) Subject to section 21 of the Agricultural Holdings (Scotland) Act 1991—
  (a) if the tenant has bound himself to remove by writing, dated and signed—
      (i) within 12 months after the term of removal; or
      (ii) where there is more than one ish, after the ish first in date to remove, an action of removing may be raised at any time; and
  (b) if the tenant has not bound himself, an action of removing may be raised at any time, but—
      (i) in the case of a lease of lands exceeding two acres in extent for three years and upwards, an interval of not less than one year nor more than two years must elapse between the date of notice of removal and the term of removal first in date;
      (ii) in the case of a lease of lands exceeding two acres in extent, whether written or oral, held from year to year or under tacit relocation, or for any other period less than three years, an interval of not less than six months must elapse between the **D 588** date of notice of removal and the term of removal first in date; and
      (iii) in the case of a house let with or without land attached not exceeding two acres in extent, as also of land not exceeding two acres in extent without houses, as also of mills, fishings, shootings, and all other heritable subjects excepting land exceeding two acres in extent and let for a year or more, 40 days at least must elapse between the date of notice of removal and the term of removal first in date.
  (2) In any defended action of removing, the sheriff may order the defender to find caution for violent profits.

Form of notices and letter
30.6.—(1) A notice under section 34, 35 or 36 of the 1907 Act must be in Form 3a.
  (2) A notice under section 37 of the 1907 Act must be in Form 3b.
  (3) A letter of removal must be in Form 3c.

Giving notice of removal
30.7.—(1) A notice under section 34, 35, 36, 37 or 38 of the 1907 Act may be given by—
  (a) a sheriff officer;
  (b) the person entitled to give such notice; or
  (c) the solicitor or factor of such person,
posting the notice by registered post or the first class recorded delivery service at any post office within the United Kingdom in time for it to be delivered at the address on the notice before the last date on which by law such notice must be given, addressed to the person entitled to receive such notice, and bearing the address of that person at the time, if known, or, if not known, to the last known address of that person.
  (2) A sheriff officer may also give notice under any section of the 1907 Act mentioned in

paragraph (1) in any manner in which he may serve an initial writ; and, accordingly, rule 5.4 shall, with the necessary modifications, apply to the giving of notice under this paragraph as it applies to service of a summons.

Evidence of notice to remove
30.8.—(1) It shall be sufficient evidence that notice has been given if—
  (a) a certificate of the sending of notice under rule 30.7 dated and endorsed on the lease or an extract of it, or on the letter of removal, is signed by the sheriff officer or the person sending the notice, his solicitor or factor; or
  (b) an acknowledgement of the notice is endorsed on the lease or an extract of it, or on the letter of removal, by the party in possession or his agent.
(2) If there is no lease, a certificate of the sending of such notice must be endorsed on a copy of the notice or letter of removal.

CHAPTER 31

ACTION OF SEQUESTRATION FOR RENT

General
31.1. An action of sequestration for rent or in security of rent may be brought as a summary cause whether it be brought before or after the term of payment.

Appraisal inventory and execution of citation
31.2.—(1) The sheriff officer when he executes the warrant for sequestration shall have the effects appraised by one person who may also be a witness to the sequestration.
(2) A notice in accordance with Form 4a and an inventory or list of sequestrated effects with the appraisal in accordance with Part 1 of Form 4b shall be given to or left for the tenant who shall be cited thereafter in accordance with Chapter 5.
(3) After executing the sequestration the sheriff officer shall—
  (a) prepare and sign the certificate of execution of sequestration contained in Part 2 of Form 4b; and
  (b) return Form 4b (including the inventory and appraisal in Part 1) to the sheriff clerk within seven days of execution of the sequestration.

Procedure
31.3.—(1) After hearing the cause the sheriff shall dispose of it as he thinks fit and may either recall the sequestration in whole or in part, or grant decree for the rent found due and grant warrant for the sale of the sequestrated effects.
D 589 (2) Where warrant for sale of the sequestered effects has been granted the sale shall be carried out by an officer of court or by such other person as the sheriff may direct by public roup at such place as the sheriff may direct and after—
  (a) advertisement in a newspaper circulating in the district; and
  (b) display, until the sale has been concluded, of a copy of the warrant on the walls of the court which granted it.
(3) Any proceeds of the sale surplus to the sum decerned for, the expenses awarded and the expenses of the sale, shall be returned to the owner, or if he cannot be found, consigned in the hands of the sheriff clerk.
(4) If the effects are not sold, they shall be delivered to the creditor at the appraised value to the amount of the sum decerned for and expenses, and the expenses of the sequestration and sale.

Sale to be reported within 14 days
31.4. A report of the proceedings in the sequestration and sale of proceeds, or of delivery of the effects, shall be made by the officer to the sheriff clerk within 14 days of the date of sale or delivery.

Recall of sequestration
31.5. If the tenant—
  (a) pays to the landlord the rent due, with the expenses of raising the summons and sequestrating; or
  (b) consigns the rent due, with a sum determined by the sheriff clerk to cover expenses, in the hands of the sheriff clerk,
the sheriff clerk shall recall the sequestration by appropriately endorsing the summons or the defender's copy thereof.

Warrant to eject and re-let where premises displenished

31.6.—(1) If the officer who has executed a warrant for sale, or who was instructed to execute such a warrant, reports to the court that the premises are displenished the landlord may apply to the court to obtain a warrant to cite the defender to a fixed diet at which the sheriff may make such order as appropriate.

(2) Where a warrant to re-let is granted the rent accruing thereafter shall only be exigible for such period as the tenant continues to occupy the premises.

Warrant to sequestrate, etc.

31.7. All warrants to sequestrate, inventory, sell, eject or re-let shall be deemed to include authority, if need be, to open shut and lockfast places for the purpose of carrying such warrants into execution.

CHAPTER 32

ACTION FOR ALIMENT

Recall or variation of decree for aliment

32.1.—(1) Applications for the recall or variation of any decree for payment of aliment pronounced in the small debt court under the Small Debt Acts or in a summary cause under the 1971 Act must be made by summons.

(2) The sheriff may make such interim orders in relation to such applications or in relation to actions brought under section 3 of the Sheriff Courts (Civil Jurisdiction and Procedure) (Scotland) Act 1963 as he thinks fit.

(3) In paragraph (1) "the Small Debt Acts" means and includes the Small Debt (Scotland) Acts 1837 to 1889 and Acts explaining or amending the same.

Warrant and forms for intimation

32.2. In the summons in an action brought under section 3 of the Sheriff Courts (Civil Jurisdiction and Procedure) (Scotland) Act 1963, the pursuer must include an application for a warrant for intimation—

    (a) in an action where the address of the defender is not known to the pursuer and cannot reasonably be ascertained, to—

        (i) every child of the marriage between the parties who has reached the age of 16 years; and

        (ii) one of the next-of-kin of the defender who has reached that age,

        unless the address of such a person is not known to the pursuer and cannot reasonably be ascertained, and a notice of intimation in Form 36 must be attached to the copy of **D 590** the summons intimated to any such person; or

    (b) in an action where the defender is a person who is suffering from a mental disorder, to—

        (i) those persons mentioned in paragraphs (a)(i) and (ii), unless the address of such person is not known to the pursuer and cannot reasonably be ascertained; and

        (ii) the guardian of, the defender, if one has been appointed, and a notice in Form 37 must be attached to the copy of the summons intimated to any such person.

CHAPTER 33

CHILD SUPPORT ACT 1991

Interpretation of rules 33.2 to 33.4

33.1. In rules 33.2 to 33.4 below—

    "the 1991 Act" means the Child Support Act 1991;

    "child" has the meaning assigned in section 55 of the 1991 Act;

    "claim relating to aliment" means a crave for decree of aliment in relation to a child or for recall or variation of such a decree; and

    "maintenance calculation" has the meaning assigned in section 54 of the 1991 Act.

Statement of claim

33.2.—(1) Any summons or counterclaim which contains a claim relating to aliment and to which section 8(6), (7), (8) or (10) of the 1991 Act applies must—

    (a) state, where appropriate—

        (i) that a maintenance calculation under section 11 of the 1991 Act (maintenance calculations) is in force;

    (ii) the date of the maintenance calculation;

    (iii) the amount and frequency of periodical payments of child support maintenance fixed by the maintenance calculation; and

    (iv) the grounds on which the sheriff retains jurisdiction under section 8(6), (7), (8) or (10) of the 1991 Act; and

  (b) unless the sheriff on cause shown otherwise directs, be accompanied by any document issued by the Secretary of State to the party intimating the making of the maintenance calculation referred to in sub-paragraph (a).

(2) Any summons or counterclaim which contains a claim relating to aliment and to which section 8(6), (7), (8) or (10) of the 1991 Act does not apply must include a statement—

  (a) that the habitual residence of the absent parent, person with care or qualifying child, within the meaning of section 3 of the 1991 Act, is outwith the United Kingdom; or

  (b) that the child is not a child within the meaning of section 55 of the 1991 Act.

(3) A summons or counterclaim which involves parties in respect of whom a decision has been made in any application, review or appeal under the 1991 Act must—

  (a) include in the statement of claim statements to the effect that such a decision has been made and give details of that decision; and

  (b) unless the sheriff on cause shown otherwise directs, be accompanied by any document issued by the Secretary of State to the parties intimating that decision.

Effect of maintenance calculations

33.3.—(1) On receiving notification that a maintenance calculation has been made, cancelled or has ceased to have effect so as to affect an order of a kind prescribed for the purposes of section 10 of the 1991 Act, the sheriff clerk must enter in the Register of Summary Causes in respect of that order a note to that effect.

(2) The note mentioned in paragraph (1) must state that—

  (a) the order ceases or ceased to have effect from the date two days after the making of the maintenance calculation; or

  (b) the maintenance calculation has been cancelled or has ceased to have effect.

Effect of maintenance calculations on extacts of decrees relating to aliment

33.4—(1) Where a decree relating to aliment is affected by a maintenance calculation, any extract of that decree issued by the sheriff clerk must be endorsed with the following certificate:—

"A maintenance calculation having been made under the Child Support Act 1991 on *(insert date)*, this order, in so far as it relates to the making or securing of periodical payments to or for the benefit of *(insert name(s) of child/children)*, ceases to have effect from *(insert date two days after the date on which the maintenance calculation was made)*.".

D 591

(2) Where a decree relating to aliment has ceased to have effect on the making of a maintenance calculation and that maintenance calculation is later cancelled or ceases to have effect, any extract of that order issued by the sheriff clerk must be endorsed also with the following certificate:—

"The jurisdiction of the child support officer under the Child Support Act 1991 having terminated on *(insert date)*, this order, in so far as it relates to *(insert name(s) of child/children)*, again shall have effect as of *(insert date of termination of child support officer's jurisdiction)*.".

CHAPTER 34

ACTION OF DAMAGES FOR PERSONAL INJURY

Application of Chapter and disapplication of certain rules

34.1.—(1) This Chapter applies to an action of damages for personal injuries or the death of a person from personal injuries.

(2) In this Chapter "personal injuries" includes any disease or impairment of physical or mental condition.

(3) The following rules shall not apply to an action of damages for personal injuries or death:—

Rule 4.2, other than the requirement to give fair notice of the claim; and

Rule 8.1.

(4) Rules 8.2 to 8.17 shall only apply to an action of damages for personal injuries or death in accordance with rule 34.3(2).

Form of summons

34.2.—(1) The statement of claim in the summons shall be in Form 10 and shall include—

(a) a concise statement of the grounds of action, and the facts relied upon to establish the claim;

(b) the date of birth and where applicable National Insurance number of the pursuer; and

(c) the names of every medical practitioner from whom, and every hospital, or other institution in which, the pursuer, or in an action in respect of the death of a person, the deceased, received treatment for injuries sustained or for disease suffered by him.

(2) There shall be lodged along with the summons—

(a) all medical reports then available to the pursuer on which he intends, or intends to reserve the right, to rely in the action or a statement that there are no such medical reports; and

(b) a statement of valuation of claim (which shall include a list of supporting documents) in Form 10c.

(3) An application for an order under section 12(2)(a) of the Administration of Justice Act 1982 (provisional damages for personal injuries) shall be made by including in the summons a claim for provisional damages in Form 10a, and where such application is made, a concise statement as to the matters referred to in paragraphs (a) and (b) of section 12(1) of that Act shall be included in the statement of claim.

(4) In paragraph (3) above "provisional damages" means the damages referred to in section 12(4)(a) of the Administration of Justice Act 1982.

(5) A summons may include—

(a) an application for warrants for intimation in so far as permitted under these Rules; and

(b) a specification of documents containing such of the calls in Form 10e as the pursuer considers appropriate.

(6) Where a summons includes a specification of documents in accordance with paragraph (5)(b), it must, where necessary, be intimated to the Advocate General for Scotland or the Lord Advocate (and if there is any doubt, both) when lodged.

(7) A copy of Form 10b and a copy of the statement of valuation of claim lodged by the pursuer in Form 10c shall accompany the defender's copy summons when it is served on the defender.

Response to summons

34.3.—(1) A defender wishing to defend the action shall complete and lodge with the sheriff clerk on or before the return day the form of response in Form 10b stating, in a manner which gives the pursuer fair notice, the grounds of fact and law on which the defender intends to resist the claim together with a brief statement of the facts upon which the defender relies in his **D 592** defence.

(2) Where a defender lodges a form of response in accordance with paragraph (1), the provisions of rules 8.2 to 8.17 shall apply with the necessary modifications.

Inspection and recovery of documents

34.4.—(1) This rule applies where the summons includes a specification of documents in accordance with rule 34.2 (5)(b).

(2) Subject to paragraph (5), where a response in Form 10b is lodged stating a defence to the action, the sheriff clerk shall make an order granting commission and diligence for the production and recovery of the documents mentioned in the specification.

(3) An order under paragraph (2) shall be treated for all purposes as an interlocutor of the court granting commission and diligence signed by the sheriff.

(4) Nothing in this rule shall affect the right of a party to apply under rule 18.1 for a commission and diligence for recovery of documents or under rule 18.3 for an order under section 1 of the Administration of Justice (Scotland) Act 1972 in respect of any document or other property not mentioned in the specification included in the summons.

(5) Where the defender, or where appropriate, the Advocate General for Scotland or the Lord Advocate, objects to the specification of documents, he shall make such objection by incidental application.

(6) An incidental application under paragraph (5) shall be—

(a) lodged on or before the return day; and

(b) determined at the hearing held in terms of rule 8.2(1).

Statement of valuation of claim

34.5.—(1) Each party to an action who is not required elsewhere in these rules to do so shall make a statement of valuation of claim (which shall include a list of supporting documents) in Form 10c in accordance with the following paragraphs of this rule.

(2) A statement of valuation of claim made in terms of paragraph (1) shall be lodged with the sheriff clerk.

(3) Each party on lodging a statement of valuation of claim in terms of paragraph (2), shall give written intimation to every other party of the statement and the list of documents contained in the statement of valuation of claim.

(4) A party who fails to lodge a statement of valuation of claim not later than 28 days before the date fixed for proof shall be liable to any other party for the expenses of proving the quantification of the claim, unless the sheriff, on special cause shown, otherwise directs.

Intimation to connected persons

34.6.—(1) This rule applies to an action of damages in which, following the death of any person from personal injuries, damages are claimed—

    (a) by the executor of the deceased, in respect of the injuries from which the deceased died; or

    (b) by any relative of the deceased, in respect of the death of the deceased.

(2) In this rule—

"connected person" means a person, not being a party to the action, who has title to sue the defender in respect of the personal injuries from which the deceased died or in respect of his death; and

"relative" has the meaning assigned to it in Schedule 1 to the Damages (Scotland) Act 1976.

(3) The pursuer shall state in the summons, as the case may be—

    (a) that there are no connected persons;

    (b) that there are connected persons, being the persons specified in the application for warrant for intimation; or

    (c) that there are connected persons in respect of whom intimation should be dispensed with on the ground that—

        (i) the names or whereabouts of such persons are not known to, and cannot reasonably be ascertained by, the pursuer; or

        (ii) such persons are unlikely to be awarded more than £200 each.

(4) Where the pursuer makes statements under rule 34.6(3)(b) he shall include an application for warrant in the summons for intimation to any such person.

(5) A notice of intimation in Form 10d shall be attached to the copy of the summons, and a copy of Form 10c shall accompany the summons, where intimation is given on a warrant under paragraph (4).

(6) Where the pursuer makes statements under rule 34.6(3)(c), he shall apply in the summons for an order to dispense with intimation.

D 593 (7) In determining an application under paragraph (6), the sheriff shall have regard to—

    (a) the desirability of avoiding a multiplicity of actions; and

    (b) the expense, inconvenience or difficulty likely to be involved in taking steps to ascertain the name or whereabouts of the connected person.

(8) Where the sheriff is not satisfied that intimation to a connected person should be dispensed with, he may—

    (a) order intimation to a connected person whose name and whereabouts are known;

    (b) order the pursuer to take such further steps as he may specify in the interlocutor to ascertain the name or whereabouts of any connected person; and

    (c) order advertisement in such manner, place and at such times as he may specify in the interlocutor.

(9) Where the name or whereabouts of a person, in respect of whom the sheriff has dispensed with intimation on a ground specified in rule 34.6(3)(c), subsequently becomes known to the pursuer, the pursuer shall apply to the sheriff by incidental application for a warrant for intimation to such a person; and such intimation shall be made in accordance with rule 34.6(5).

(10) A connected person may apply by incidental application to be sisted as an additional pursuer to the action.

(11) Such an incidental application shall also seek leave of the sheriff to adopt the existing grounds of action, and to amend the claim.

(12) The period within which answers to an incidental application under paragraph (10) may be lodged shall be 14 days from the date of intimation of the incidental application.

(13) There shall be lodged along with the incidental application a statement of valuation of claim (which shall include a list of supporting documents) in Form 10c.

(14) The statement of valuation of claim lodged in accordance with paragraph (13) shall be intimated to the other parties at the same time as the incidental application.

(15) Where a connected person to whom intimation is made—

    (a) does not apply to be sisted as an additional pursuer to the action;

(b) subsequently raises a separate action against the same defender in respect of the same personal injuries or death; and

(c) would, apart from this rule, be awarded the expenses or part of the expenses of that action,

he shall not be awarded those expenses except on cause shown.

Application for further damages

34.7.—(1) An application for further damages by a pursuer in respect of whom an order under section 12(2)(b) of the Administration of Justice Act 1982 has been made shall be made by lodging a minute with the sheriff clerk in Form 10f, which minute shall include—

(a) a claim for further damages;

(b) a concise statement of the facts supporting that claim;

(c) an application for warrant to serve the minute on—

(i) every other party; and

(ii) where such other parties are insured or otherwise indemnified, their insurer or indemnifier, if known to the pursuer; and

(d) a request for the court to fix a hearing on the application.

(2) A notice of intimation in Form 10g shall be attached to every copy of the minute served on a warrant granted under paragraph (1)(c).

(3) At the hearing fixed under paragraph (1)(d) above, the sheriff may determine the application or order such further procedure as he thinks fit.

CHAPTER 35

ELECTRONIC TRANSMISSION OF DOCUMENTS

Extent of provision

35.1.—(1) Any document referred to in these rules which requires to be—

(a) lodged with the sheriff clerk;

(b) intimated to a party; or

(c) sent by the sheriff clerk,

may be in electronic or documentary form, and if in electronic form may be lodged, intimated or sent by e-mail or similar means.

(2) Paragraph (1) does not apply to any certificate of execution of service, citation or arrestment, or to a decree or extract decree of the court.

(3) Where any document is lodged by e-mail or similar means the sheriff may require any principal document to be lodged.

Time of lodgement   **D 594**

35.2. The time of lodgement, intimation or sending shall be the time when the document was sent or transmitted.

APPENDIX 1

FORMS

Rule 4.1(1)

FORM 1

Summons

FORM 1

	OFFICIAL USE ONLY
	SUMMONS No.

Summary Cause Summons

Action for/of

(state type, e.g. payment of money)

Sheriff Court (name, address, e-mail and telephone no.)	**1**
Name and address of person raising the action (**pursuer**)	**2**
Name and address of person against whom action raised (**defender, arrestee, etc.**)	**3**
Name(s) and address(s) of any interested party (eg. connected person)	**3a**
Claim (form of decree or other order sought)	**4**
Name, full address, telephone no, and e-mail address of pursuer's solicitor or representative (if any) acting in the case	**5**
Fee Details (Enter these only if forms sent electronically to court)	**5a**

6	RETURN DAY	20		
	CALLING DATE	20	at	am.

***Sheriff Clerk to**

delete as appropriate

The pursuer is authorised to serve a copy summons in form *1a/1b/1c, on the defender, and give intimation to any interested party, not less than * 21/42 days before the **RETURN DAY** shown in the box above. The summons is warrant for service, *arrestment on the dependence and for citation of witnesses to attend court on any future date at which evidence may be led.

Court Authentication

Sheriff clerk depute (name)   Date: 20

NOTE: The pursuer should complete boxes 1 to 5a above and box 7 on page 2. The sheriff clerk will complete box 6.

7. **STATE DETAILS OF CLAIM HERE (all cases) and PARTICULARS OF ARRESTMENT (furthcoming actions only)**
(To be completed by the pursuer. If space is insufficient, a separate sheet may be attached)

The details of the claim are:

FOR OFFICIAL USE ONLY

Sheriff's notes as to:

1. Issues of fact and law in dispute
2. Facts agreed
3. Reasons for any final disposal at the hearing held on the calling date.

Rule 4.3(a)

FORM 1a

Defender's copy summons – claim for or including claim for payment of money where time to pay direction or time order may be applied for

FORM 1a

Summary Cause Summons
Action for/of
(state type, e.g. payment of money)

> OFFICIAL USE ONLY
> SUMMONS No.

DEFENDER'S COPY: Claim for or including payment of money (where time to pay direction or time order may be applied for)

Sheriff Court (name, address, e-mail and telephone no.)	**1**	
Name and address of person raising the action (**pursuer**)	**2**	
Name and address of person against whom action raised (**defender, arrestee, etc.**)	**3**	
Name(s) and address(s) of any interested party (e.g. connected person)	**3a**	
Claim (form of decree or other order sought)	**4**	
Name, full address, telephone no, and e-mail address of pursuer's solicitor or representative (if any) acting in the case	**5**	

6				
RETURN DAY	20			
CALLING DATE	20	at		am.

NOTE: You will find details of claim on page 2.

---

7.   **STATEMENT OF CLAIM**
     PARTICULARS OF ARRESTMENT (furthcoming actions only)
     (To be completed by the pursuer. If space is insufficient, a separate sheet may be attached)

     The details of the claim are:

8.   **SERVICE ON DEFENDER**

                 (Place)   (Date)

          To: (defender)

          You are hereby served with a copy of the above summons.

                                              Solicitor / sheriff officer
                                              delete as appropriate

---

NOTE: The pursuer should complete boxes 1 to 6 on page 1, the statement of claim in box 7 on page 2 and section A on page 5 before service on the defender. The person serving the Summons will complete box 8.

WHAT MUST I DO ABOUT THIS SUMMONS?

Decide whether you wish to dispute the claim, admit any liability for the claim and whether you owe any money or not, and how you wish to proceed. Then, look at the 4 options listed below. Find the one which covers your decision and follow the instructions given there. You will find the RETURN DAY and the CALLING DATE on page one of the summons.

Written guidance on summary cause procedure can be obtained from the sheriff clerk at any sheriff clerk's office. Advice can also be obtained by contacting any of the following:

Citizen's Advice Bureau, Consumer Advice Centre, Trading Standards or Consumer Protection Department or a solicitor. (Addresses can be found in the guidance booklets.)

OPTIONS

1.   **ADMIT LIABILITY FOR THE CLAIM and settle it with the pursuer now.**

If you wish to avoid the possibility of a court order passing against you, you should settle the claim (including any question of expenses) with pursuer or his representative **in good time before the return day.** Please do not send any payment direct to the court. Any payment should be made to the pursuer or his representative.

2.   **ADMIT LIABILITY FOR THE CLAIM and make <u>written</u> application to pay by instalments or by <u>deferred</u> lump sum.**

Complete Box 1 of section B on page 5 of this form and return pages 5 and 7 to the court **to arrive on or before the return day.** You should then contact the court to find out whether or not the pursuer has accepted your offer. If he has not accepted it, the case will then call in court on the calling date, when the court will decide how the amount claimed is to be paid.

NOTE: If you fail to return pages 5 and 7 as directed, or if, having returned them, you fail to attend or are not represented at the calling date if the case is to call, the court will almost certainly decide the claim in your absence.

3.   **ADMIT LIABILITY FOR THE CLAIM and <u>attend at court</u> to make application to pay by instalments or deferred lump sum.**

Complete Box 2 on page 5. Return page 5 to the court so that it arrives **on or before the return day.**

You must attend personally, or be represented, at court on the calling date. Your representative may be a Solicitor, or someone else having your authority. It may be helpful if you or your representative bring pages 1 and 2 of this form to the court.

NOTE: If you fail to return page 5 as directed, or if, having returned it, you fail to attend or are not represented at the calling date, the court will almost certainly decide the claim in your absence.

4.   **DISPUTE THE CLAIM and <u>attend at court</u> to do any of the following:**

- Challenge the jurisdiction of the court or the competency of the action
- Defend the action (whether as regards the sum claimed or otherwise)
- State a counterclaim

Complete Box 3 on page 5. Return page 5 to the court so that it arrives **on or before the return day. You must attend personally, or be represented, at court on the calling date.**

D 600

Your representative may be a solicitor, or someone else having your authority. It may be helpful if you or your representative bring pages 1 and 2 of this form to the court.

NOTE: If you fail to return page 5 as directed, or if, having returned it, you fail to attend or are not represented at the calling date, the court will almost certainly decide the claim in your absence.

WRITTEN NOTE OF PROPOSED DEFENCE

You must send to the court by the return day a written note of any proposed defence, or intimate that you intend to dispute the sum claimed or wish to dispute the court's jurisdiction. You must also attend or be represented at court on the calling date.

PLEASE NOTE

If you do nothing about this summons, the court will almost certainly, where appropriate, grant decree against you and order you to pay the pursuer the sum claimed, including any interest and expenses found due.

YOU ARE ADVISED TO KEEP PAGES 1 AND 2, AS THEY MAY BE USEFUL AT A LATER STAGE OF THE CASE.

D 601

SECTION A This section must be completed before service	Summons No Return Day Calling Date
SHERIFF COURT (Including address)	
PURSUER'S FULL NAME AND ADDRESS	DEFENDER'S FULL NAME AND ADDRESS

SECTION B **DEFENDER'S RESPONSE TO THE SUMMONS**
** **Delete those boxes which do __not__ apply**

**Box 1

ADMIT LIABILITY FOR THE CLAIM and make __written__ application to pay by instalments or by __deferred__ lump sum.

I do not intend to defend the case but admit liability for the claim.

I wish to make a written application about payment.

I have completed the application form on page 7.

**Box 2

ADMIT LIABILITY FOR THE CLAIM and __attend at court__ to make application to pay by instalments or deferred lump sum.

I admit liability for the claim.

I intend to appear or be represented at court on the calling date.

**Box 3

DISPUTE THE CLAIM (or the amount due) and attend at court
* I intend to challenge the jurisdiction of the court.
* I intend to challenge the competency of the action.
* I intend to defend the action.
* I wish to dispute the amount due only.

* I apply for warrant to serve a third party notice (see page 8).

I intend to appear or be represented in court on the calling date.
----
*I attach a note of my proposed defence/counterclaim.
OR
* I return form 10b (personal injury cases only).

* *delete as necessary*

WRITTEN NOTE OF PROPOSED DEFENCE / COUNTERCLAIM
State which facts in the statement of claim are admitted:

State briefly any facts regarding the circumstances of the claim on which you intend to rely:

State details of counterclaim, if any:

PLEASE REMEMBER: You must send your response to the court to **arrive on or before the return day** if you have completed a response in Section B. If you have admitted the claim, please do not send any payment direct to the court. **Any payments you wish to make should be made to the pursuer or his solicitor.**

APPLICATION IN WRITING FOR A TIME TO PAY DIRECTION
UNDER THE DEBTORS (SCOTLAND) ACT 1987 OR A TIME ORDER
UNDER THE CONSUMER CREDIT ACT 1974

I WISH TO APPLY FOR A* TIME TO PAY DIRECTION/TIME ORDER
* delete whichever does not apply

I admit the claim and make application to pay as follows:

    (1) by instalments of £ _____ per *week / fortnight / month

            OR

    (2) In one payment within _____ *weeks / months from the date of the court order

To help the court please provide details of your financial position in the boxes below
*Please also indicate whether payments/receipts are weekly, fortnightly or monthly

My outgoings are:	*Weekly / fortnightly / monthly	My income is	*Weekly / fortnightly / monthly
Rent/Mortgage	£	Wages/Pensions £	
Council Tax	£	Social Security £	
Gas/Electricity etc	£	Other	
Food	£		
Loans and Credit Agreements	£		
Other	£		

Number of Dependent Children – [   ]   Number of Dependent Relatives [   ]

Please list details of all capital held. Eg. Value of house; amount in savings account, shares or other investments:

Notes: TIME TO PAY DIRECTIONS AND TIME ORDERS
(1) Time to pay directions
The Debtors (Scotland) Act 1987 gives you the right to apply to the court for a 'time to pay direction'. This is an order which allows you to pay any sum which the court orders you to pay either in instalments or by deferred lump sum. A 'deferred lump sum' means that you will be ordered by the court to pay the whole amount at one time within a period which the court will specify.

If the court makes a time to pay direction it may also recall or restrict any arrestment made on your property by the pursuer in connection with the action or debt (for example, your bank account may have been frozen).

D 604

No court fee is payable when making an application for a time to pay direction.

If a time to pay direction is made, a copy of the court order (called an extract decree) will be sent to you by the pursuer telling you when payment should start or when it is you have to pay the lump sum.

If a time to pay direction is not made, and an order for immediate payment is made against you, an order to pay (called a charge) may be served on you if you do not pay.

(2) Time Orders

The Consumer Credit Act 1974 allows you to apply to the court for a 'time order' during a court action. A time order is similar to a time to pay direction, but can only be applied for in certain circumstances, e.g., in relation to certain types of credit agreement. Payment under a time order can only be made by instalments, so that you cannot apply to pay by deferred lump sum.

---

*APPLICATION FOR RECALL OR RESTRICTION OF AN ARRESTMENT
I seek the recall or restriction of the arrestment of which the details are as follows:-

Date:
Delete if inapplicable

APPLICATION FOR SERVICE OF A THIRD PARTY NOTICE

NOTE:
You can apply to have another party added to the action if:

(A)   You think that, as regards the matter which the action is about, that other party has a duty to:
      1.   Indemnify you; or
      2.   Make a contribution in respect of the matter; or
      3.   Relieve you from any responsibility as regards it.
              or
(B)   You think that other party is:
      1.   Solely liable to the pursuer; or
      2.   Liable to the pursuer along with you; or
      3.   Has a liability to you as a result of the pursuer's claim against you.

You may apply for warrant to found jurisdiction or to arrest on the dependence of the action if you wish to do so.

D 605

FORM OF APPLICATION

(TO BE RETURNED TO THE COURT ALONG WITH YOUR RESPONSE)

I request the court to grant warrant for service of a third party notice on the following party:
Name   :

Address   :

The reason I wish a third party notice to be served on the party mentioned above is as follows:
(Give details below of the reasons why you wish the party to be made a defender in the action.)

* **I apply for warrant to arrest on the dependence/to found jurisdiction**

* delete as appropriate

Date   :

FORM 1b

Defender's copy summons – claim for or including payment of money (where time to pay direction or time order may not be applied for)

FORM 1b

	OFFICIAL USE ONLY SUMMONS No.

Summary Cause Summons
Action for/of
(state type, e.g. payment of money)

DEFENDER'S COPY: Claim for or including payment of money (where time to pay direction or time order may not be applied for)

Sheriff Court (name, address, e-mail and telephone no.)	**1**	
Name and address of person raising the action (**pursuer**)	**2**	
Name and address of person against whom action raised (**defender, arrestee, etc.**)	**3**	
Name(s) and address(s) of any interested party (e.g. connected person)	**3a**	
Claim (Form of decree or other order sought)	**4**	
Name, full address, telephone no., and e-mail address of pursuer's solicitor or representative (if any)	**5**	

6	RETURN DAY	20		
	CALLING DATE	20	at	am.

NOTE: You will find details of claim on page 2.

---

7.   **STATEMENT OF CLAIM**
    PARTICULARS OF ARRESTMENT (furthcoming actions only.)
    (To be completed by the pursuer. If space is insufficient, a separate sheet may be attached)

    The details of the claim are:

8.   **SERVICE ON DEFENDER**

            (Place)   (Date)

            To: (defender)

            You are hereby served with a copy of the above summons.

                                    Solicitor / sheriff officer
                                    delete as appropriate

NOTE: The pursuer should complete boxes 1 to 6 on page 1, the statement of claim in box 7 on page 2 and section A on page 5 before service on the defender. The person serving the Summons will complete box 8.

WHAT MUST I DO ABOUT THIS SUMMONS?

Decide whether you wish to dispute the claim, or admit any liability for the claim and whether you owe any money or not, and how you wish to proceed. Thereafter, look at the 2 options listed below. Find the one which covers your decision and follow the instructions given there. You will find the RETURN DAY and the CALLING DATE on page one of the summons.

Written guidance on summary cause procedure can be obtained from the sheriff clerk at any sheriff clerk's office. Further advice can also be obtained by contacting any of the following:

   Citizen's Advice Bureau, Consumer Advice Centre, Trading Standards or Consumer Protection Department or a Solicitor. (Addresses can be found in the guidance booklets)

OPTIONS

1.   **ADMIT LIABILITY FOR THE CLAIM and settle it with the pursuer now.**

   If you wish to avoid the possibility of a court order passing against you, you should settle the claim (including any question of expenses) with pursuer or his representative **in good time before the return day**. Please do not send any payment direct to the court. Any payment should be made to the pursuer or his representative.

2.   **DISPUTE THE CLAIM and <u>attend at court</u> to do any of the following:**

   - Challenge the jurisdiction of the court or the competency of the action
   - Defend the action
   - Dispute the sum claimed
   - State a counterclaim

   Complete Section B on page 4. Return your response to the court so that it arrives **on or before the return day. You must attend personally, or be represented, at court on the calling date.**

   Your representative may be a solicitor, or someone else having your authority. It may be helpful if you or your representative bring pages 1 and 2 of this form to the court.

   NOTE: If you fail to return your response as directed, or if, having returned it, you fail to attend or are not represented at the calling date, the court will almost certainly decide the claim in your absence.

WRITTEN NOTE OF PROPOSED DEFENCE

   You must send to the court by the return day a written note of any proposed defence, or intimate that you intend to dispute the sum claimed or wish to challenge the court's jurisdiction. You must also attend or be represented at court on the calling date.

PLEASE NOTE:

If you do nothing about this summons, the court will almost certainly, where appropriate, grant decree against you and order you to pay the pursuer the sum claimed, including any interest and expenses found due.

YOU ARE ADVISED TO KEEP PAGES 1 AND 2, AS THEY MAY BE USEFUL AT A LATER STAGE OF THE CASE.

D 609

SECTION A		Summons No
This section must		
be completed		Return Day
before service		
		Calling Date

SHERIFF COURT (Including address)

PURSUER'S FULL NAME AND ADDRESS

DEFENDER'S FULL NAME AND ADDRESS

SECTION B   **DEFENDER'S RESPONSE TO THE SUMMONS**

DISPUTE THE CLAIM (or the amount due) and attend at court
* I intend to challenge the jurisdiction of the court.
* I intend to challenge the competency of the action.
* I intend to defend the claim.
* I wish to dispute the amount due only.
* I apply for warrant to serve a third party notice (see page 6).

I intend to appear or be represented in court on the calling date.
----
*I attach a note of my proposed defence/counterclaim (see page 5).
OR
* I return Form 10b (personal injury cases only).

* *delete as necessary*

WRITTEN NOTE OF PROPOSED DEFENCE / COUNTERCLAIM
State which facts in the statement of claim are admitted:

State briefly any facts regarding the circumstances of the claim on which you intend to rely:

State details of counterclaim, if any:

PLEASE REMEMBER: You must send your response to the court to **arrive on or before the return day** if you have completed a response in Section B. If you have admitted the claim, please do not send any payment direct to the court. **Any payments you wish to make should be made to the pursuer or his solicitor.**

APPLICATION FOR SERVICE OF A THIRD PARTY NOTICE

NOTE:
You can apply to have another party added to the action if:

(A)   **You think that, as regards the matter which the action is about, that other party has a duty to:**
1.   Indemnify you; or
2.   Make a contribution in respect of the matter; or
3.   Relieve you from any responsibility as regards it.
                         or
(B)   You think that other party is:
4.   Solely liable to the pursuer; or
5.   Liable to the pursuer along with you; or
6.   Has a liability to you as a result of the pursuer's claim against you.

You may apply for warrant to found jurisdiction or to arrest on the dependence of the action if you wish to do so.

FORM OF APPLICATION

(TO BE RETURNED TO THE COURT ALONG WITH YOUR RESPONSE)

I request the court to grant warrant for service of a third party notice on the following party:
Name   :

Address   :

The reason I wish a third party notice to be served on the party mentioned above is as follows:
(Give details below of the reasons why you wish the party to be made a defender in the action.)

* **I apply for warrant to arrest on the dependence/to found jurisdiction**

* delete as appropriate

Rule 4.3(b) **D 612**

FORM 1c

Defender's copy summons – non monetary claim

FORM 1c

**Summary Cause Summons
Action for/of**
(state type, e.g. delivery)

OFFICIAL USE ONLY
SUMMONS No.

DEFENDER'S COPY: Non Monetary Claim

Sheriff Court (name, address, e-mail and telephone no.)	1	
Name and address of person raising the action (**pursuer**)	2	
Name and address of Person against whom Action raised (**defender**)	3	
Claim (Form of decree or other order sought)	4	
Name, full address, telephone no, and e-mail address of pursuer's solicitor or representative (if any)	5	

6	RETURN DAY	20		
	CALLING DATE	20	at	am.

NOTE: You will find details of claim on page 2.

7.   **STATE DETAILS OF CLAIM HERE OR ATTACH A STATEMENT OF CLAIM**
       (to be completed by the pursuer. If space is insufficient, a separate sheet may be attached)

The details of the claim are:

8.   **SERVICE ON DEFENDER**

       (Place)   (Date)

       To: (defender)

       You are hereby served with a copy of the above summons.

                                        * Solicitor / sheriff officer
                                          (delete as appropriate)

NOTE: The pursuer should complete boxes 1 to 6 on page 1, the statement of claim in box 7 on page 2 and
section A on page 5 before service on the defender. The person serving the Summons will complete box 8.

WHAT MUST I DO ABOUT THIS SUMMONS?

Decide whether you wish to dispute the action and how you wish to proceed. Thereafter, look at the 2 options listed below. Find the one which covers your decision and follow the instructions given there. You will find the RETURN DAY and the CALLING DATE on page one of the summons.

Written guidance on summary cause procedure can be obtained from the sheriff clerk at any sheriff clerk's office. Further advice can also be obtained by contacting any of the following:

Citizen's Advice Bureau, Consumer Advice Centre, Trading Standards or Consumer Protection Department or a Solicitor. (Addresses can be found in the guidance booklets)

OPTIONS

1.   **ADMIT LIABILITY FOR THE CLAIM and settle it with the pursuer now.**

If you wish to avoid the possibility of a court order passing against you, you should settle the claim (including any liability for expenses) with the pursuer or his representative **in good time before the return day.**

2.   **DISPUTE THE CLAIM and <u>attend at court</u> to do any of the following:**

- Challenge the jurisdiction of the court or the competency of the action
- Defend the action
- State a counterclaim

Complete Section B on page 4. Return page 4 to the court so that it arrives **on or before the return day. You must attend personally, or be represented, at court on the calling date.**

Your representative may be a solicitor, or someone else having your authority. It may be helpful if you or your representative bring pages 1 and 2 of this form to the court.

NOTE: If you fail to return page 4 as directed, or if, having returned it, you fail to attend or are not represented at the calling date, the court will almost certainly decide the claim in your absence.

WRITTEN NOTE OF PROPOSED DEFENCE

You must send to the court by the return day a written note of any proposed defence, or intimate that you wish to challenge the jurisdiction of the court. You must also attend or be represented at court on the calling date.

PLEASE NOTE

If you do nothing about this summons, the court will almost certainly, where appropriate, grant decree against you, including any interest and expenses found due.

YOU ARE ADVISED TO KEEP PAGES 1 AND 2, AS THEY MAY BE USEFUL AT A LATER STAGE OF THE CASE.

D 615

SECTION A
This section must
Be completed
Before service

Summons No
Return Day
Calling Date

SHERIFF COURT (Including address)

PURSUER'S FULL NAME AND ADDRESS

DEFENDER'S FULL NAME AND
ADDRESS

SECTION B   **DEFENDER'S RESPONSE TO THE SUMMONS**

DISPUTE THE CLAIM and attend at court
* I intend to challenge the jurisdiction of the court.
* I intend to challenge the competency of the court.
* I wish to defend the action.
* I apply for warrant to serve a third party notice (see page 6).

I intend to appear or be represented in court on the calling date.
*I attach a note of my proposed defence/counterclaim (see page 5).

* *delete as necessary*

WRITTEN NOTE OF PROPOSED DEFENCE / COUNTERCLAIM
State which facts in the statement of claim are admitted:

State briefly any facts regarding the circumstances of the claim on which you intend to rely:

State details of counterclaim, if any:

PLEASE REMEMBER: You must send your response to the court to **arrive on or before the return day** if you have completed a response in Section B.

APPLICATION FOR SERVICE OF A THIRD PARTY NOTICE

NOTE:
You can apply to have another party added to the action if:

(A)   **You think that, as regards the matter which the action is about, that other party has a duty to:**
1.   Indemnify you; or
2.   Make a contribution in respect of the matter; or
3.   Relieve you from any responsibility as regards it.
or

(B)   You think that other party is:
4.   Solely liable to the pursuer; or
5.   Liable to the pursuer along with you; or
6.   Has a liability to you as a result of the pursuer's claim against you.

You may apply for warrant to found jurisdiction or to arrest on the dependence of the action if you wish to do so.

FORM OF APPLICATION

(TO BE RETURNED TO THE COURT ALONG WITH YOUR RESPONSE)

I request the court to grant warrant for service of a third party notice on the following party:
Name   :

Address   :

The reason I wish a third party notice to be served on the party mentioned above is as follows:
(Give details below of the reasons why you wish the party to be made a defender in the action.)

* I apply for warrant to arrest on the dependence/to found jurisdiction

delete as appropriate

Rule 4.3(c)   **D 618**

FORM 1d

Defender's copy summons - multiplepoinding

FORM 1d

Summary Cause Summons

Action of Multiplepoinding

DEFENDER'S COPY

Sheriff Court
(name, address, e-mail
and telephone no.)   **1**

Name and address
of person raising
the action (**pursuer**)   **2**

Name and address of
persons against whom
action raised (**defenders**)   **3**

Claim (Form of decree or
other order sought – see
Form 5)   **4**

Name, full address, telephone
no., and e-mail address of
pursuer's solicitor (if any)   **5**

6

RETURN DAY	20		
CALLING DATE	20	at	am.

NOTE: You will find details of claim on page 2.

7.   **STATE DETAILS OF CLAIM HERE OR ATTACH A STATEMENT OF CLAIM**
           (to be completed by the pursuer. If space is insufficient, a separate sheet may be attached)

        The details of the claim are:

8.   **SERVICE ON DEFENDER**

        (Place)   (Date)

        To: (Defender.)

        You are hereby served with the above summons. The pursuer has been authorised by
        the court to serve it on you.

                                        Solicitor / sheriff officer
                                      (delete as appropriate)

NOTE: The Pursuer should complete boxes 1 to 6 on page 1, the statement of claim in box 7 on page 2 and section A on page 5 before service on the defender. The person serving the Summons will complete box 8.

<u>**WHAT MUST I DO ABOUT THIS SUMMONS?**</u>

Decide whether you wish to dispute the action and how you wish to proceed. Thereafter, look at the 2 options listed below. Find the one which covers your decision and follow the instructions given there. You will find the RETURN DAY and the CALLING DATE on page one of the summons.

Written guidance on summary cause procedure can be obtained from the sheriff clerk at any sheriff clerk's office. Further advice can also be obtained by contacting any of the following:

Citizen's Advice Bureau, Consumer Advice Centre, Trading Standards or Consumer Protection Department or a solicitor. (Addresses can be found in the guidance booklets)

OPTIONS

1.   **ADMIT LIABILITY FOR THE CLAIM and settle it with the pursuer now.**

   If you wish to avoid the possibility of a court order passing against you, you should attempt to settle the claim (including any liability for expenses) with the pursuer or his Solicitor **in good time before the return day.**

2.   **DISPUTE THE CLAIM and <u>attend at court</u> to do any of the following:**

   - Challenge the jurisdiction of the court or the competency of the action.
   - Object to the extent of the fund or subject detailed in the statement of claim on page 2.
   - Make a claim on the fund or subject.

   Complete Section B on page 4. Return page 4 to the court so that it arrives **on or before the return day. You must attend personally, or be represented, at court on the calling date.**

   Your representative may be a Solicitor, or someone else having your authority. It may be helpful if you or your representative bring pages 1 and 2 of this form to the court.

   NOTE: If you fail to return page 4 as directed, or if, having returned it, you fail to attend or are not represented at the calling date, the court will almost certainly deal with the action in your absence.

NOTES:

1.   If you do nothing about this summons, the court will almost certainly deal with the action in your absence.

2.   **IF YOU ARE THE HOLDER OF THE FUND,** you must complete the enclosed form 5a and send it to the sheriff clerk before the return day. You must also, before the return day, send a copy of form 5a to the pursuer, the other defenders in the action and to all the persons you have listed in form 5a as having an interest in the fund or subject.

YOU ARE ADVISED TO KEEP PAGES 1 AND 2, AS THEY MAY BE USEFUL AT A LATER STAGE OF THE CASE.

D 621

SECTION A

This section must
be completed
Before service

SHERIFF COURT (Including address)

Summons No
Return Day
Calling Date

PURSUER'S FULL NAME AND ADDRESS

DEFENDER'S FULL NAME AND
ADDRESS

SECTION B   **DEFENDER'S RESPONSE TO THE SUMMONS**

DISPUTE THE CLAIM and attend at court

I intend to:

*   (1)   Challenge the jurisdiction of the court or the competency of the action.
*   (2)   Object to the extent of the fund or subject detailed in the statement
        of claim.
*   (3)   Make a claim on the fund or subject.

      I intend to appear or be represented in court on the calling date.

*   *delete as necessary*

**Please give below brief details of your reason(s) for disputing the claim in
accordance with your response to 1, 2 or 3 above:**

Rule 4.1(2) FORM 2

FORM OF CLAIM IN A SUMMONS FOR PAYMENT OF MONEY

The pursuer claims from the defender(s) the sum of £   with   interest on that sum at the rate of   annually from the date of service, together with the expenses of bringing the action.

Rule 4.1(2) FORM 3

FORM OF CLAIM IN A SUMMONS FOR RECOVERY OF POSSESSION OF HERITABLE PROPERTY

The pursuer claims that, in the circumstances described in the statement contained on page 2 of this copy summons, he is entitled to recover possession of the property at *(address)*, and that you refuse or delay to remove from said property.

The pursuer therefore asks the court to grant a decree against you, removing you, and your family, sub-tenants and dependants (if any) with your goods and possessions from the said property.

The pursuer also claims from you the expenses of bringing the action.

Rule 30.6(1) FORM 3A

FORM OF NOTICE OF REMOVAL UNDER SECTIONS 34, 35 OR 36 OF THE SHERIFF COURTS (SCOTLAND) ACT 1907

To: *(name, designation and address of party in possession)*

You are hereby required to remove from *(describe subjects)* at the term of *(or, if different terms, state them and the subjects to which they apply)*, in terms of *(describe lease, terms of letter of removal or otherwise)*.

(date)   *(signature, designation and address)*

Rule 30.6(2) FORM 3B

FORM OF NOTICE OF REMOVAL UNDER SECTION 37 OF THE SHERIFF COURTS (SCOTLAND) ACT 1907

NOTICE OF REMOVAL UNDER SECTION 37 OF THE SHERIFF COURTS (SCOTLAND) ACT 1907

To: *(name, designation and address)*

You are hereby required to remove from *(describe subjects)* at the term of *(Whitsunday or Martinmas)*, *(date)*.

(date)   *signature, designation and address)*

Rule 30.6(3) FORM 3C

FORM OF LETTER OF REMOVAL

To: *(name, designation and address)*

(place and date). I am to remove from (describe subjects by usual name or give a short description sufficient for identification) at the term of *(insert term and date)*.

(date)   *(signature, designation and address)*

D 623 Rule 4.1(2)   FORM 4

FORM OF CLAIM IN A SUMMONS OF SEQUESTRATION FOR RENT

The pursuer claims that, in the circumstances described in the statement contained on page 2 of this copy summons, you owe, (*and/or will owe*) him the sum of £   as rent for the premises at (*address*), and that you refuse or delay to make payment of said sums.

The pursuer therefore asks the court to grant warrant to list, value, sequestrate and, if necessary, secure the goods and effects within the said premises.

The pursuer also asks the court to grant a decree against you ordering you to pay the said sum to him.

The pursuer also claims from you the expenses of bringing the action.

The court hereby authorises the pursuer to sequestrate, inventory and appraise your effects.

Rule 31.2(2)   FORM 4A

NOTICE INFORMING DEFENDER OF RIGHT TO APPLY FOR CERTAIN ORDERS UNDER THE DEBTORS (SCOTLAND) ACT 1987

Where articles are sequestrated in an action for sequestration for rent, you have the right to apply to the sheriff for the following orders under the Debtors (Scotland) Act 1987:

(1) You may apply to the sheriff within 14 days from the date upon which the articles were sequestrated for an order releasing any of said articles on either of the following grounds:

    (a) that it is exempt from the process of sequestration for rent. Articles which are exempt are listed in section 16 of the Debtors (Scotland) 1987;
       or

    (b) its inclusion in the process of sequestration for rent (or its subsequent sale) is unduly harsh.

(2) Where a mobile home, such as a caravan, is your only, or principal, residence and it has been sequestrated for rent, you may apply to the sheriff, before a warrant to sell is granted, for an order that, for a specified period, no further steps shall be taken in the sequestration.

Any enquiry relating to the above rights should be made to a solicitor, Citizens Advice Bureau or other local advice centre, or to any sheriff clerk's office.

Rule 31.2(2)   FORM 4B

CERTIFICATE OF SEQUESTRATION

PART 1—Inventory and appraisal

1 ITEM NO.	2 DESCRIPTION OF EFFECTS	3 APPRAISED AT £ p

PART 2—Certificate of execution

By virtue of the authority contained in the summary cause summons no.(*insert number*) lodged at (*insert place*) Sheriff Court in the case of (*insert names of parties*) in which warrant for citation was granted on (*insert date*).

On the   day of   20   , I, (*insert name, designation and address*), accompanied by (*insert name, designation and address of witness/person appraising the effects*) attended at the premises at (*insert address of premises*), mentioned in the summons.

I there sequestrated the effects listed in column 1 above, all of which were found within or at **D 624** those premises, and had them appraised, on oath, at the values shown in column 3 above.

I *gave a copy of this form to/left a copy of this form for the tenant on (*insert date*).

**delete as appropriate*

(*Signature of sheriff officer*)   (*Signature of witness/appraiser*)

Date: Date:

NOTE: This form should be returned to the sheriff clerk within seven days of the date of the sequestration.

Rule 4.1(2) FORM 5

FORM OF CLAIM IN A SUMMONS OF MULTIPLEPOINDING

The pursuer claims that, in the circumstances described in the statement contained on page 2 of this copy summons, the (*state party*) is the holder of a fund (*or subject*) valued at £   on which competing claims are being made by the defenders.

The pursuer therefore asks the court to grant a decree finding the holder of the said fund or subject liable to make payment of, or to deliver, same to the party found by the court to be entitled thereto.

The pursuer also asks that the expenses of bringing the action be deducted from the value of the said fund or subject before payment is made.

Rule 27.5(2)(a) FORM 5A

FORM OF STATEMENT BY HOLDER OF FUND OR SUBJECT WHEN NOT THE PURSUER

(1) I, (*name, address*), hereby state that the fund or subject in the summary cause summons raised at the instance of AB (*design*) against CD, (*EF and GH*) (*design*) is as follows: (*description and details of fund or subject*).

(2) I have the following claim or lien on said fund or subject (give details, including a reference to any document founded upon in support of the claim).

(3) I am aware that the persons listed below have an interest in the said fund/subject:

(*list names and addresses*)

(4) I certify that I have today intimated a copy of this statement to each of the persons contained in the list at (3) above.

(*date*)

Rule 27.9(2)(a) FORM 5B

FORM OF CLAIM ON THE FUND OR SUBJECT IN ACTION OF MULTIPLEPOINDING

I, EF, claim to be preferred on the fund in the multiplepoinding raised in the name of AB against CD, EF etc. for the sum of £   by reason of (*state ground of claim, including a reference to any document founded upon in support thereof*) with interest thereon from (*date*).

I also claim any appropriate court expenses which I may incur by appearing in this action.

(*signature*)

Rule 4.1(2) FORM 6

FORM OF CLAIM IN A SUMMONS OF FURTHCOMING

The pursuer claims that, in the circumstances described in the statement contained on page 2 of this copy summons, the said (*name of common debtor*) is due to him the sum of £   .

D 625 He further claims that he has lawfully arrested in the hands of the said (*name of arrestee*) the goods or money valued at £   and described in the said statement of claim, which ought to be made furthcoming to him.

He therefore asks the court to order that you make furthcoming and deliver to him the said arrested goods or money or so much thereof as will satisfy (*or part satisfy*) the said sum of £   owing to him.

The pursuer also claims from you the expenses of bringing this action. If the value of the arrested funds are insufficient to meet the sum owing to the pursuer plus the expenses of the action, the pursuer claims those expenses from the said (*name of common debtor*).

Rule 4.1(2)   **FORM 7**

FORM OF CLAIM IN A SUMMONS FOR DELIVERY

The pursuer claims that, in the circumstances described in the statement contained on page 2 of this copy summons, he has right to the possession of the article(s) described therein.

He therefore asks the court to grant a decree ordering you to deliver the said articles to the pursuer.

Alternatively, if you do not deliver said articles, the pursuer asks the court to grant a decree ordering you to pay to him the sum of £   with interest on that sum at the rate of   % annually from (*date*) until payment.

The pursuer also claims from you the expenses of bringing the action.

Rule 4.1(2)   **FORM 8**

FORM OF CLAIM IN A SUMMONS FOR IMPLEMENT OF AN OBLIGATION

The pursuer claims that, in the circumstances described in the statement contained on page 2 of this copy summons, you are obliged to

He therefore asks the court to grant a decree ordering you to implement the said obligation.

Alternatively, if you do not fulfil the obligation, the pursuer asks the court to grant a decree ordering you to pay to him the sum of £   with interest on that sum at the rate of   % annually from (*date*) until payment.

The pursuer also claims from you the expenses of bringing the action.

Rule 4.1(2)   **FORM 9**

FORM OF CLAIM IN A SUMMONS FOR COUNT, RECKONING AND PAYMENT

The pursuer claims that, in the circumstances described in the statement contained on page 2 of this copy summons, you have intromitted with (*describe briefly the fund or estate*), in which he has an interest.

He therefore asks the court to grant a decree ordering you to produce a full account of your intromissions therewith, and for payment to him of the sum of £   , or such other sum as appears to the court to be the true balance due by you, with interest thereon at the rate of   % annually from (*date*) until payment.

Alternatively, if you do not produce such an account, the pursuer asks the court to grant a decree ordering you to pay to him the said sum of £   with interest thereon at the rate of   % annually from (*date*) until payment.

The pursuer also claims from you the expenses of bringing the action.

Rule 34.2(1)   **FORM 10**

FORM OF STATEMENT OF CLAIM IN A SUMMONS FOR DAMAGES FOR PERSONAL INJURY

1. The pursuer is (*state designation, address, occupation, date of birth and National Insurance number of the pursuer*). (*In an action arising out of the death of a relative state designation of the deceased and relation to the pursuer.*)

2.   The defender is (*state designation, address and occupation of the defender*).   **D 626**

3.   The court has jurisdiction to hear this claim against the defender because (*state briefly ground of jurisdiction*).

4.   (*State briefly the facts necessary to establish the claim*).

5.   (*State briefly the personal injuries suffered and give the names and addresses of medical practitioners and hospitals and other institutions in which the person injured received treatment; and specify every medical practitioner from whom, and hospital and other institution in which the pursuer or the deceased received treatment in respect of injury or disease to which the action relates*).

6.   (*State whether claim based on fault at common law or breach of statutory duty, or other basis of liability; if breach of statute, state provision of enactment*).

*It is not necessary to include in the statement of claim the amount(s) claimed. This should be done by completing a valuation of claim in Form 10c.

Rule 34.2(3)   FORM 10A

FORM OF CLAIM FOR PROVISIONAL DAMAGES

For payment to the pursuer by the defender of the sum (*amount in words and figures*) as provisional damages.

(*Statements to include risk that pursuer will as result of cause of action develop serious disease or deterioration of condition in future; and that defender public authority or corporation or insured or indemnified in respect of claim*).

Rules 34.2(7) and 34.3(1)   FORM 10B

FORM OF RESPONSE

SHERIFF COURT OF

(Action for damages: personal injuries)

[AB] (*designation and address*), pursuer

against

[CD] (*designation and address*), defender

RESPONSE TO STATEMENT OF CLAIM

Question	Response
1. Is it intended to dispute the description and designation of the pursuer? If so, why?	
2. Is the description and designation of the defender disputed? If so, why?	
3. Is there any dispute that the court has jurisdiction to hear the claim. If so, why?	
4. (a) State which facts in paragraph 4 of the statement of claim are admitted.	
(b) State any facts regarding the circumstances of the claim upon which the defender intends to rely.	
5. (a) State whether the nature and extent of the pursuer's injuries is disputed and whether medical reports can be agreed.	
(b) If the defender has a medical report upon which he intends to rely to contradict the pursuer's report in any way, state the details.	

D 627 (c) State whether the claims for other losses are disputed in whole or in part.

(d) State any other facts in relation to the quantification claim upon which the defender intends to rely.

6. (a) Does the defender accept that the common law duty or duties in the statement of claim were incumbent upon the defender in the circumstances? If not, state why.

(b) Does the defender accept that the statutory duty or duties alleged in the statement of claim were incumbent upon them in the circumstances? If not, state why.

(c) State any other provisions or propositions upon which the defender proposes to rely in relation to the question of his liability for the accident including, if appropriate, details of any allegation of contributory negligence.

(d) Does the defender allege that the accident was caused by any other wrongdoer? If so, give details.

(e) Does the defender allege that he is entitled to be indemnified or relieved from any liability he might have to the pursuer? If so, give details.

Rules 34.2(2)(b), 34.5(1) and 34.6(13)   FORM 10C

FORM OF STATEMENT OF VALUATION OF CLAIM

SHERIFF COURT OF

(Action for damages: personal injuries)

[AB] (*designation and address*), pursuer

against

[CD] (*designation and address*), defender

Head of Claim	Components	Valuation
Solatium	Past	£x
	Future	£x
Interest on past solatium	Percentage applied to past solatium. State percentage rate.	£x
Past wage loss	Date from which wage loss claimed	£x
	(............)	
	Date to which wage loss claimed	
	(............)	
	Rate of net wage loss (per week, per month or per annum)	
Interest on past wage loss	Percentage applied to past wage loss (State percentage rate)	£x
Past services Specify nature, duration, and components of calculation	Total amount claimed	£x
	(............)	
	Interest	

Future losses including wages, disadvantage on the labour market, services or loss of capacity to provide services. Specify which and provide details.

Other financial losses	Specify	£x
	TOTAL	£x

DEFENDER ONLY.

The defender should adapt the form as appropriate.

Where the defender is unable to state a valuation of any part of the claim because of the absence of information properly and reasonably sought in writing from the pursuer, please explain and produce with this form a copy of the relative request.

Rule 34.6(5)   FORM 10D

FORM OF INTIMATION TO CONNECTED PERSONS

Court ref. no.

To: (*insert name and address as in warrant*)

You are hereby given notice that an action has been raised against (*name*), your (*insert relationship, e.g., father, brother or other relative as the case may be*). A copy of the summons is enclosed.

It is believed that you may have a title or interest to sue the said (*name of defender*) in this action, which is based upon (*the injuries from which the late (insert name and designation) died*) (*or the death of the late (name and designation)*). You may therefore be entitled to enter this action as an additional pursuer.

If you wish to appear as a party in the action, or are uncertain about what action to take, you should contact a solicitor. You may, depending on your financial circumstances, be entitled to legal aid, and you can get information about legal aid from a solicitor.

You may also obtain advice from any Citizen's Advice Bureau, other advice agency or any sheriff clerk's office.

Rule 34.6(5)   FORM 10E

SPECIFICATION OF DOCUMENTS

SPECIFICATION OF DOCUMENTS

1. All books, medical records reports, charts, X-rays, notes and other documents of (*specify name of each medical practitioners named in summons in accordance with rule 34.2(1)(c)*), and relating to the pursuer [*or as the case may be the deceased*], in order that excerpts may be taken therefrom at the sight of the Commissioner of all entries showing or tending to show the nature, extent and cause of the pursuer's [*or, as the case may be, the deceased's*] injuries when he attended his doctor on or after (*specify date*) and the treatment received by him since that date.

2. All books, medical records reports, charts, X-rays, notes and other documents of (*specify name of each institution named in summons in accordance with rule 34.2(1)(c)*), and relating to the pursuer [*or, as the case may be, the deceased*], in order that excerpts may be taken therefrom at the sight of the Commissioner of all entries showing or tending to show the nature, extent and cause of all injuries from which the pursuer [*or, as the case may be,* the deceased] was suffering when he was admitted to that institution on or about (*specify date*), the treatment received by him since that date and his certificate of discharge, if any.

3. All wage books, cash books, wage sheets, computer records and other earnings information held by or on behalf of the defenders, for the period (*specify dates*) in order that excerpts may be taken therefrom at the sight of the Commissioner of all entries showing or tending to show (a) the pursuer's [*or, as the case may be, the deceased's*] earnings, both gross and net, over the said period and (b) the earnings of other employees in the same or similar employment over the said period.

D 629 4.   All accident reports, memoranda or other written communications made to the defenders or anyone on their behalf by an employee of the defenders at or about the time at which the pursuer [*or, as the case may be,* the deceased] sustained the injuries in respect of which the summons in this cause was issued and relevant to the matters contained in the statement of claim.

5.   Failing principals, drafts, copies or duplicates of the above or any of them.

Rule 34.7(1)   FORM 10F

FORM OF MINUTE—APPLICATION FOR FURTHER DAMAGES

Court ref. no.:

Sheriff Court at (*insert place of court*)

APPLICATION FOR FURTHER DAMAGES

in the cause

(AB) (*insert designation and address*), pursuer

against

(CD) (*insert designation and address*), defender

The pursuer claims payment from the defender of the sum (*amount in words and figures*) as further damages.

(*Insert concise statement of facts supporting claim for further damages*).

The pursuer requests the court to fix a hearing on this minute and applies for warrant to serve the minute on—

(*Here state names and addresses of other parties to the action; and, where such other parties are insured or otherwise indemnified, their insurers or indemnifiers, if known to the pursuer*).

Rule 34.7(3)   FORM 10G

FORM OF NOTICE OF APPLICATION FOR FURTHER DAMAGES

Date:

To:

TAKE NOTICE

(*Pursuer's name and address*), pursuer, raised an action against (*defender's name and address*), defender, in the sheriff court at (*insert place of court*).

In the action, the sheriff on (*date*) made an award of provisional damages in favour of the pursuer against (*you or* name of party). [The sheriff specified that the pursuer may apply for an award of further damages at any time before (*date*)]. The pursuer has applied by minute for an award of further damages against you [or name of party]. A copy of the minute is attached.

A hearing on the minute has been fixed for (*date and time*) at (*place of sheriff court*). If you wish to be heard on the minute, you should attend or be represented at court on that date.

Rule 5.3(1)   FORM 11

FORM OF SERVICE

XY, you are hereby served with a copy of the above (or attached) summons.

(*signature of solicitor or sheriff officer*)

Rule 5.3(2)   FORM 12   **D 630**

FORM OF CERTIFICATE OF EXECUTION OF SERVICE

Case name:

Court ref: no:

(*Place and date*)

I,   , hereby certify that on the   day of   , 20   , I duly cited XY to answer the foregoing summons. This I did by (*set forth the mode of service*).

(*Signature of solicitor or sheriff officer*)

Rule 5.5(1)(a)   FORM 13

SERVICE ON PERSON WHOSE ADDRESS IS UNKNOWN FORM OF ADVERTISEMENT

A summary cause action has been raised in the sheriff court at   by AB, pursuer against CD, defender, whose last known address was

If the said CD wishes to defend the action he should immediately contact the sheriff clerk's office at the above court.

    Address of court:
    Telephone no:
    Fax no:
    E-mail address:

Rule 5.5(1)(b)   FORM 14

SERVICE ON PERSON WHOSE ADDRESS IS UNKNOWN
FORM OF NOTICE TO BE DISPLAYED ON THE WALLS OF COURT

A summary cause action has been raised in this court by AB, pursuer against CD, defender, whose last known address was

If the said CD wishes to defend the action he should immediately contact the sheriff clerk's office.

(*Date*)   Displayed on the walls of court of this date.

Sheriff clerk depute

Rule 5.6(2)   FORM 15

SERVICE BY POST—FORM OF NOTICE

This letter contains a citation to or intimation from the sheriff court at

If delivery cannot be made the letter must be returned immediately to the sheriff clerk at (*insert full address*).

Rule 6.3(4)(a)   FORM 16

RECALL OR RESTRICTION OF ARRESTMENT
CERTIFICATE AUTHORISING THE RELEASE OF ARRESTED FUNDS OR PROPERTY

Sheriff court, (*place*)

Court ref. no.:   AB (pursuer) against CD (defender)

I, (*name*), hereby certify that the sheriff on (*date*) authorised the release of the funds or property arrested on the *dependence of the action/counterclaim/third party notice to the following extent:

D 631   (*details of sheriff's order*)

(*Date*)   Sheriff clerk depute

*delete as appropriate

Copy to:
>   Party instructing arrestment
>   Party possessing arrested funds/property

Rule 7.1(1)   FORM 17

FORM OF MINUTE—NO FORM OF RESPONSE LODGED BY DEFENDER

Sheriff court, (*place*)

Calling date:

In respect that the defender(s) has/have failed to lodge a form of response to the summons, the pursuer respectfully craves the court to make the orders specified in the following case(s):

Court ref. No   Name(s) of defender(s)   Minute(s)

Rule 7.1(2)   [1] FORM 18

FORM OF MINUTE—PURSUER NOT OBJECTING TO APPLICATION FOR A TIME TO PAY DIRECTION
OR TIME ORDER

Sheriff court, (*place*)

Court ref. no.:

Name(s) of defender(s)

Calling date:

I do not object to the defender's application for

>   *a time to pay direction
>   *recall or restriction of an arrestment
>   *a time order

The pursuer requests the court to grant decree or other order in terms of the following minute(s)

*delete as appropriate

NOTE
[1] As amended by the Act of Sederunt (Ordinary Cause, Summary Application, Summary Cause and Small Claim Rules) Amendment (Miscellaneous) 2003 (SSI 2003/26), para.4(4)(b) (effective January 24, 2003).

Rule 7.2(4)   FORM 19

FORM OF MINUTE—PURSUER OPPOSING AN APPLICATION FOR A TIME TO PAY DIRECTION
OR TIME ORDER

Sheriff court, (*place*)

Court ref. no.:

Name(s) of defender(s)

Calling date:

I oppose the defender's application for

*a time to pay direction
*recall or restriction of an arrestment
*a time order

*delete as appropriate

Rule 8.12   FORM 20   **D 632**

FORM OF OATH FOR WITNESSES

I swear by Almighty God that I will tell the truth, the whole truth and nothing but the truth.

Rule 8.12   FORM 21

FORM OF AFFIRMATION FOR WITNESSES

I solemnly, sincerely and truly declare and affirm that I will tell the truth, the whole truth and nothing but the truth.

Rule 11.2(1)(b)(iii)   FORM 22

FORM OF THIRD PARTY NOTICE

Court ref. no.

SHERIFF COURT, (*place*)

THIRD PARTY NOTICE

in the cause

(AB) (*insert designation and address*), pursuer

against

(CD) (*insert designation and address*), defender

To (EF)

You are given notice by (CD) of an order granted by the sheriff at (*insert place of court*) in which (AB) is the pursuer and (CD) is the defender. A copy of the order is enclosed herewith.

In the action, the pursuer claims from the defender (*insert a brief account of the circumstances of the claim*) as more fully appears in the copy summons enclosed.

The defender claims that,   (**delete as appropriate*).

*if he is liable to the pursuer, you are liable to relieve him wholly/partially of his liability, as more fully appears in the copy grounds upon which the defender relies for this, which are also enclosed.

*he is not liable to the pursuer for the claim made against him. He maintains that any liability to the pursuer in respect of this claim rests solely on you, as more fully appears in the copy grounds upon which the defender relies for this, which are also enclosed.

*if he is liable to the pursuer in respect of this claim, he shares that liability with you, as more fully appears in the copy grounds upon which the defender relies for this, which are also enclosed.

*You are liable to him in respect of the claim, as more fully appears in the copy grounds upon which the defender relies for this, which are also enclosed.

If you wish to resist the claim(s) made by the defender as detailed above, you must—
    (a) return the form of response enclosed to the sheriff clerk at (*address*) by (*date seven days before the date of hearing*); and
    (b) attend or be represented at a hearing on (*date and time*).

(Date)   *(Signature of person serving notice)*

D 633 Rule 11.2(1)(b)(iii)   FORM 23

<small>FORM OF RESPONSE TO THIRD PARTY NOTICE</small>

in the cause

(AB) (*insert designation and address*), pursuer

against

(CD) (*insert designation and address*), defender

I wish to answer the claim made against me by (CD), defender. (*here state briefly the grounds of opposition to the defender's claim.*)

(*date*)

Rule 18.2(1)   FORM 24

<small>ORDER BY THE COURT AND CERTIFICATE IN OPTIONAL PROCEDURE FOR RECOVERY OF DOCUMENTS</small>

Sheriff Court, (*place and address*)

In the cause (court ref. no.)

in which

AB (*design*) is the pursuer

and

CD (*design*) is the defender

To: (*name and designation of party or haver from whom the documents are sought to be recovered.*)

You are required to produce to the sheriff clerk at (address) within
days of the service upon you of this order.

(1) This order itself (which must be produced intact);

(2) The certificate marked 'B' attached;

(3) All documents within your possession covered by the specification which is enclosed; and

(4) A list of those documents.

You can produce the items listed above either:

(a) by delivering them to the sheriff clerk at the address shown above; or

(b) sending them to the sheriff clerk by registered or recorded delivery post.

(*date*)   (*Signature, name, address and designation of person serving order*)

PLEASE NOTE:

If you claim confidentiality for any of the documents produced by you, you must still produce them. However, they may be placed in a separate envelope by themselves, marked 'confidential' The court will, if necessary, decide whether the envelope should be opened or not.

CERTIFICATE

Sheriff Court, (*place and address*)

In the cause (court ref. no.)

in which

AB (*design*) is the pursuer

and

CD (*design*) is the defender.

Order for recovery of documents dated . . . .

With reference to the above order and relative specification of documents, I certify:

*delete as appropriate

*that the documents produced herewith and the list signed by me which accompanies them are all the documents in my possession which fall under the specification.

*I have no documents in my possession falling under the specification.

*I believe that there are other documents falling within the specification which are not in my possession. These documents are (*list the documents as described in the specification.*) These documents were last seen by me on (*date*) in the possession of (*name and address of person/ company, if known*).

*I know of no documents falling within the specification which are in the possession of any other person.

(*name*)   (*date*)

Rule 18.7(3)   FORM 25

FORM OF MINUTE IN AN APPLICATION FOR LETTER OF REQUEST

Sheriff Court, (*place and address*)

MINUTE

for (*designation*)

In the cause (court ref. no.)

in which

AB (*design*) is the pursuer

and

CD (*design*) is the defender.

The minuter states to the court that the evidence specified in the proposed letter of request lodged with this minute is required for the purpose of this cause. The minuter respectfully asks the court to issue a letter of request in terms of the proposed letter of request to (*specify the court or tribunal having power to obtain the evidence*) in order to obtain the evidence so specified.

(*designation of minuter*)

Rule 18.7(3)   FORM 25A

FORM OF LETTER OF REQUEST

PART A—items to be included in every letter of request

D 635 1. Sender   *(Identity and address)*...........................
....

2. Central authority of the   *(Identity and address)*...........................
....

3. Persons to whom the executed request is *(Identity and address)*...........................
to be returned   ....

4. The undersigned applicant has the honour
to submit the following request:

5. a. Requesting Judicial authority   *(Identity and address)*...........................
                      ....

  b. To the competent authority   *(the requested state)*...........................
                      ....

6. Names and addresses of the parties and
their representatives
a. pursuer   ....
b. defender   ....
c. other parties   ....

7. Nature and purpose of the proceedings ....
and summary of the facts   ....

8. Evidence to be obtained or other judicial ....
act to be performed   ....

PART B—items to be completed where applicable
9. Identity and address of any person to be ....
examined   ....

10. Questions to be put to the person to be *(or, see attached list)*...........................
examined, or statement of the subject ....
matter about which they are to be   ....
examined

11. Documents or other property to be   *(specify whether to be produced, copied,*
inspected   *valued etc.)*...........................

12. Any requirement that the evidence be *(in the event that the evidence cannot be*
given on oath or affirmation and any *taken in the manner requested, specify*
special form to be used   *whether it is to be taken in such manner*
                      as provided by local law for the formal
                      taking of evidence)

13. Special methods or procedure to be   ....
followed   ....

14. Request for notification of the time and ....
place for the execution of the request and ....
identity and address of any person to be ....
notified   ....

15. Request for attendance or participation of ....
judicial personnel of the requesting   ....
authority at the execution of the letter of ....
request   ....

16. Specification of privilege or duty to refuse ....
to give evidence under the law of the state ....
of origin   ....

17.   The fees and expenses incurred will be   (*identity and address*)............................ **D 636**
        borne by   ....

PART C—to be included in every letter of request
18.   Date of request, signature and seal of the   ....
        requesting authority   ....

Rule 18.8(1)   FORM 26

FORM OF WITNESS CITATION

SHERIFF COURT, (*insert place*)

TO AB (*design*)

You are required to attend at (*full name and address of court*) on (*day,* (*date*) at (*time*) as a witness for the (*party*) in the action at the instance of AB (*design*) against CD (*design*) (and required to bring with you ....).

If you fail to attend, warrant may be granted for your arrest.

(*date*)   (*signature of solicitor or sheriff officer*)

    Name of person/firm serving citation
    Address
    Telephone no.
    Fax no.
    E-mail address

NOTE: Within certain specified limits, a claim for any necessary outlays and loss of earnings incurred by your attendance at court as a witness will be met. Claims should be made to the person who has cited you to attend court. Proof of any expenses incurred may be requested and should be given to that person.

If you wish your travelling expenses to be paid prior to your attendance, you should apply for payment to the person who has cited you.

If you fail to attend without reasonable cause, having requested and been paid your travelling expenses, you may be ordered to pay a penalty not exceeding £250.

Rule 18.8(1)   FORM 26A

FORM OF CERTIFICATE OF WITNESS CITATION

I certify that on (*date*) I duly cited AB (*design*) to attend at (*name of court*) on (*date*) at (*time*) as a witness for the (*design party*) in the action at the instance of CD (*design*) against EF (*design*) (and I required him to bring with him ....). This I did by ....

                            (*Signature of solicitor or sheriff officer*)

Rule 20.2(2)   FORM 27

FORM OF REFERENCE TO THE EUROPEAN COURT

REQUEST

for

PRELIMINARY RULING

of

THE COURT OF JUSTICE OF THE EUROPEAN COMMUNITIES

from

THE SHERIFFDOM OF (*insert name of sheriffdom*) at (*insert place of court*)

In the cause

AB (*insert designation and address*),

Pursuer

Against

CD (*insert designation and address*)

Defender

(*Here set out a clear and succinct statement of the case giving rise to the request for a ruling of the European Court in order to enable the European Court to consider and understand the issues of Community law raised and to enable governments of Member states and other interested parties to submit observations. The statement of the case should include*:

(*a*) particulars of the parties;

(*b*) the history of the dispute between the parties;

(*c*) the history of the proceedings;

(*d*) the relevant facts as agreed by the parties or found by the court or, failing such agreement or finding, the contentions of the parties on such facts;

(*e*) the nature of the issues of law and fact between the parties;

(*f*) the Scots law, so far as relevant;

(*g*) the Treaty provisions or other acts, instruments or rules of Community law concerned;

(*h*) an explanation of why the reference is being made).

The preliminary ruling of the Court of Justice of the European Communities is accordingly requested on the following questions:

1,2,etc.   (*Here set out the question(s) on which the ruling is sought, identifying the Treaty provisions or other acts, instruments or rules of Community law concerned.*)

Dated the   day of   20

Rule 23.6(3) FORM 28

FORM OF EXTRACT DECREE—BASIC

Sheriff Court Court ref. no.
Date of decree *in absence
Pursuer(s) Defender(s)
The sheriff

and granted decree against the   for payment of expenses of £   against the (name of party).

This extract is warrant for all lawful execution thereon.

Date Sheriff clerk depute

*delete as appropriate

Rule 23.6(3) FORM 28A

FORM OF EXTRACT DECREE—PAYMENT

Sheriff Court Court ref. no.
Date of decree *in absence
Pursuer(s) Defender(s)

The sheriff granted decree against the   for payment to the   the undernoted sums: **D 638**

(1) Sum(s) decerned for: £

(2) Interest at   per cent per year from (*date*) until payment.

(3) Expenses of £   against the (*name of party*).

*A time to pay direction was made under section 1(1) of the Debtors (Scotland) Act 1987.

*A time order was made under section 129(1) of the Consumer Credit Act 1974.

*The amount is payable by instalments of £percommencing within

*days/weeks/months of intimation of this extract decree.

*The amount is payable by lump sum within*days/weeks/months of intimation of this extract decree.

This extract is warrant for all lawful execution thereon.

Date   Sheriff clerk depute

delete as appropriate

Rule 23.6(3)   **FORM 28B**

FORM OF EXTRACT DECREE—RECOVERY OF POSSESSION OF HERITABLE PROPERTY

Sheriff Court   Court ref. no.

Date of decree   *in absence

Pursuer(s)   Defender(s)

The sheriff

(1) granted warrant for ejecting the defender (and others mentioned in the summons) from the premises at   , such ejection being not sooner than (*date*) at 12 noon.

(2) granted decree against the defender for payment to the pursuer of the sum of £   of expenses.

This extract is warrant for all lawful execution thereon.

Date   Sheriff clerk depute

Rule 23.6(3)   **FORM 28C**

FORM OF EXTRACT DECREE AND WARRANT TO SELL IN SEQUESTRATION FOR RENT AND SALE

Sheriff Court   Court ref. no.

Date of decree   *in absence

Pursuer(s)   Defender(s)

The sheriff granted decree against the   for payment to the   of the undernoted sums:

(1) Sum(s) decerned for: £

(2) Interest at   per cent per year from (*date*) until payment.

(3) Expenses of £   against the (*name of party*).

*A time to pay direction was made under section 1(1) of the Debtors (Scotland) Act 1987.

*A time order was made under section 129(1) of the Consumer Credit Act 1974.

*The amount is payable by instalments of £   per   commencing within

*days/weeks/monthsof intimation of this extract decree.   **D 639**

*The amount is payable by lump sum within   *days/weeks/months of intimation of this extract decree.

Further, the sheriff granted warrant to any officer of court or to AB (*design*)   to sell, by public roup, at (*name of premises*) as much of the sequestrated effects as shall satisfy and pay (1) the said sum decerned for and (2) the expenses occasioned by the sale.

This extract is warrant for all lawful execution thereon.

Date

Sheriff clerk depute

*delete as appropriate

Rule 23.6(3)   FORM 28D

FORM OF EXTRACT—WARRANT FOR EJECTION AND TO RE-LET IN SEQUESTRATION FOR RENT AND SALE

Sheriff Court

Court ref. no.

Date of decree

*in absence

Pursuer(s)

Defender(s)

The sheriff

(1) granted warrant for ejecting the defender from the premises at (*address*), they being displenished.

(2) granted warrant to the pursuer to re-let the said premises.

(3) granted decree for expenses of £   against the defender.

This extract is warrant for all lawful execution thereon.

Date

Sheriff clerk depute

*delete as appropriate

Rule 23.6(3)   FORM 28E

FORM OF EXTRACT DECREE—FURTHCOMING

Sheriff Court

Court ref. no.

Date of decree

*in absence

Date of original decree

Pursuer(s)

Defender(s)/Arrestee(s)

Common debtor

The sheriff granted decree

(1) against the arrestee(s) for payment of £, or such other sum(s) as may be owing by the arrestee(s) to the common debtor(s) by virtue of the original decree mentioned above in favour of the pursuer(s) against the common debtor(s).

(2) for expenses of £

*payable out of the arrested fund.

*payable by the common debtor.

*delete as appropriate

D 640 This extract is warrant for all lawful execution thereon.

Date

Sheriff clerk depute

Rule 23.6(3) FORM 28F

FORM OF EXTRACT DECREE—DELIVERY

Sheriff Court Court ref. no.

Date of decree *in absence

Pursuer(s)

Defender(s)

The sheriff granted decree against the defender

(1) for delivery to the pursuer of (*specify articles*)

(2) for expenses of £

*Further, the sheriff granted warrant to officers of court to (1) open shut and lockfast places occupied by the defender and (2) search for and take possession of said goods in the possession of the defender.

delete as appropriate

This extract is warrant for all lawful execution thereon.

Date Sheriff clerk depute

Rule 23.6(3) FORM 28G

FORM OF EXTRACT DECREE—DELIVERY—PAYMENT FAILING DELIVERY

Sheriff Court Court ref. no.

Date of decree *in absence

Pursuer(s)

Defender(s)

The sheriff, in respect that the defender has failed to make delivery in accordance with the decree granted in this court on (*date*), granted decree for payment against the defender of the undernoted sums:

(1) Sum(s) decerned for: £ , being the alternative crave claimed.

(2) Interest at per cent per year from (*date*) until payment.

(3) Expenses of £ against the (*name of party*).

*A time to pay direction was made under section 1(1) of the Debtors (Scotland) Act 1987.

*A time order was made under section 129(1) of the Consumer Credit Act 1974.

*The amount is payable by instalments of £ per .commencing within *days/weeks/months of intimation of this extract decree.

*The amount is payable by lump sum within *days/weeks/months of intimation of this extract decree.

delete as appropriate

This extract is warrant for all lawful execution thereon.

Date Sheriff clerk depute

      FORM 28H

FORM OF EXTRACT DECREE—ALIMENT

Sheriff Court   Court ref. no.

Date of decree   *in absence

Pursuer(s)

Defender(s)

The sheriff

Granted decree against the defender for payment to the pursuer of aliment at the rate of £   per *week/month.

*delete as appropriate

This extract is warrant for all lawful execution thereon.

Date   Sheriff clerk depute

Rule 23.6(3)   FORM 28I

FORM OF EXTRACT DECREE—AD FACTUM PRAESTANDUM

Sheriff Court   Court ref. no.

Date of decree   *in absence

Pursuer(s)

Defender(s)

The sheriff

(1) ordained the defender(s)

(2) granted decree for payment of expenses of £against the defender(s).

*delete as appropriate

This extract is warrant for all lawful execution thereon.

Date   Sheriff clerk depute

Rule 23.6(3)   FORM 28J

FORM OF EXTRACT DECREE—ABSOLVITOR

Sheriff Court   Court ref. no.

Date of decree   *in absence

Pursuer(s)

Defender(s)

The sheriff

(1) absolved the defender(s)

(2) granted decree for payment of expenses of £   against the   **D 642**

*delete as appropriate

This extract is warrant for all lawful execution thereon.

Date   Sheriff clerk depute

Rule 23.6(3)   FORM 28K

FORM OF EXTRACT DECREE—DISMISSAL

Sheriff Court   Court ref. no.
Date of decree   *in absence
Pursuer(s)
Defender(s)

The sheriff

 (1) dismissed the action against the defender(s)

*(2) granted decree for payment of expenses of £   against the

*(3) found no expenses due to or by either party

*delete as appropriate

This extract is warrant for all lawful execution thereon.

Date   Sheriff clerk depute

Rule 23.8(4)   FORM 29

FORM OF CERTIFICATE BY SHERIFF CLERK
SERVICE OF CHARGE WHERE ADDRESS OF DEFENDER IS UNKNOWN

I certify that the foregoing charge was displayed on the walls of court on (*date*) and that it remained so displayed for a period of (*period of charge*) from that date.

(*date*)   Sheriff clerk depute

Rule 24.1(1)   FORM 30

MINUTE FOR RECALL OF DECREE

Sheriff Court: (place)

Court ref. no.:

AB (*pursuer*) against CD (*defender(s)*)

The *(*pursuer/defender*) moves the court to recall the decree pronounced on (*date*) in this case * and in which execution of a charge/arrestment was effected on (*date*)

Reason for failure to appear or be represented:

Proposed defence/answer:

*delete as appropriate

       FORM 30A

MINUTE FOR RECALL OF DECREE—SERVICE COPY

Sheriff Court: (*place*)

Court ref. no.:

AB (*pursuer*) against CD (*defender(s)*)

The *(*pursuer/defender*) moves the court to recall the decree pronounced on (*date*) in this case * and in which execution of a charge/arrestment was effected on (*date*)

Reason for failure to appear or be represented:

Proposed defence/answer:

*delete as appropriate

NOTE: You must return the summons to the sheriff clerk at the court mentioned at the top of this form by (*insert date 2 days before the date of the hearing.*)

     Rule 25.1(1)   FORM 31

FORM OF NOTE OF APPEAL TO THE SHERIFF PRINCIPAL

SHERIFF COURT (*place*)

Court ref. no.   AB (pursuer) against CD (defender)

The pursuer/defender appeals the sheriff's interlocutor of (*date*) to the sheriff principal and requests the sheriff to state a case.

The point(s) of law upon which the appeal is to proceed is/are: (*give brief statement*)

(*date*)

     Rule 25.4(3)(a)   FORM 32

APPLICATION FOR LEAVE TO APPEAL AGAINST TIME TO PAY DIRECTION

SHERIFF COURT (*place*)

Court ref. no.   AB (pursuer) against CD (defender)

The pursuer/defender requests the sheriff to grant leave to appeal the decision made on (*date*) in respect of the defender's application for a time to pay direction to the sheriff principal/Court of Session.

The point(s) of law upon which the appeal is to proceed is/are: (*give brief statement*)

(*date*)

     Rule 25.4(4)   FORM 33

APPEAL AGAINST TIME TO PAY DIRECTION

SHERIFF COURT (*place*)

Court ref. no.   AB (pursuer) against CD (defender)

The pursuer/defender appeals the decision made on (*date*) in respect of the defender's application for a time to pay direction to the sheriff principal/Court of Session.

(*date*)

Rule 25.7(1)   FORM 34   **D 644**

APPLICATION FOR CERTIFICATE OF SUITABILITY FOR APPEAL TO THE COURT OF SESSION

The pursuer/defender in the summary cause at the instance of AB against CD hereby moves the sheriff principal to certify that the cause is suitable for appeal to the Court of Session.

Rule 26.4(1)   FORM 35

FORM OF RECEIPT FOR MONEY PAID TO THE SHERIFF CLERK

In the sheriff court of (*name of sheriffdom*) at (*place of sheriff court*).

In the cause (*state names of parties or other appropriate description*)

AB (*designation*) has this day paid into court the sum of £   , being a payment made in terms of rule 26(4)(1) of the Summary Cause Rules 2002.

*Custody of this money has been accepted at the request of (*insert name of court making the request*)

*delete as appropriate

(Date)   Sheriff clerk depute

Rule 32.2(a)   FORM 36

ACTION FOR ALIMENT
FORM OF NOTICE OF INTIMATION TO CHILDREN AND NEXT OF KIN
WHERE ADDRESS OF DEFENDER IS UNKNOWN

Court ref. no.

To: (*insert name and address as in warrant*)

You are hereby given notice that an action for aliment has been raised against (*name*), your (*insert relationship, e.g, father, brother or other relative as the case may be*). A copy of the summons is enclosed.

If you know of his/her present address, you are requested to inform the sheriff clerk at (*insert full address*) in writing immediately.

If you wish to appear as a party in the action, or are uncertain about what action to take, you should contact a solicitor. You may, depending on your financial circumstances, be entitled to legal aid, and you can get information about legal aid from a solicitor.

You may also obtain advice from any Citizen's Advice Bureau, other advice agency or any sheriff clerk's office.

Rule 32.2(b)   FORM 37

ACTION FOR ALIMENT
FORM OF NOTICE OF INTIMATION TO CHILDREN, NEXT OF KIN AND GUARDIAN WHERE
DEFENDER SUFFERS FROM MENTAL DISORDER

Court ref. no.

To: (*insert name and address as in warrant*)

You are hereby given notice that an action for aliment has been raised against (*name*), your (*insert relationship, e.g, father or other relative, or ward, as the case may be*). A copy of the summons is enclosed.

If you wish to appear as a party in the action, or are uncertain about what action to take, you should contact a solicitor immediately. You may, depending on your financial circumstances, be **D 645** entitled to legal aid, and you can get information about legal aid from a solicitor.

You may also obtain advice from any Citizen's Advice Bureau, other advice agency or any sheriff clerk's office.

APPENDIX 2

GLOSSARY

Absolve
To find in favour of and exonerate the defender.

Absolvitor
An order of the court granted in favour of and exonerating the defender which means that the pursuer is not allowed to bring the same matter to court again.

Action of count, reckoning and payment
A legal procedure for requiring someone to account for their dealings with assets under their stewardship. For example, a trustee might be subject to such an action.

Action of furthcoming
A final stage of diligence or enforcement. It results in whatever has been subject to arrestment being made over to the person who is suing. For example, where a bank account has been arrested this results in the appropriate amount being transferred to the pursuer.

Appellant
A person making an appeal against the sheriff's decision. This might be the pursuer or the defender.

Arrestee
A person subject to an arrestment.

Arrestment on the dependence
A court order to freeze the goods or bank account of the defender until the court has heard the case.

Arrestment to found jurisdiction
A court order to used against a person who has goods or other assets in Scotland to give the court jurisdiction to hear a case. This is achieved by preventing anything being done with the goods or assets until the case has been disposed of.

Authorised lay representative
A person other than a lawyer who represents a party to a summary cause.

Calling date
The date on which the case will first be heard in court.

Cause
Another word for case or claim.

Caution (pronounced kay-shun)
A security, usually a sum of money, given to ensure that some obligation will be carried out.

Certificate of execution of service
The document recording that an application to, or order or decree of, the court for service of documents has been effected.

Charge
An order to obey a decree of a court. A common type is one served on the defender by a sheriff officer on behalf of the pursuer who has won a case demanding payment of a sum of money.

Claim
The part of the summons which sets out the legal remedy which the pursuer is seeking.

Commission and diligence
Authorisation by the court for someone to take the evidence of a witness who cannot attend court or to obtain the production of documentary evidence. It is combined with a diligence authorising the person appointed to require the attendance of the witness and the disclosure of documents.

Consignation
The deposit in court, or with a third party, of money or an article in dispute.

Continuation
An order made by the sheriff postponing the completion of a hearing until a later date or dates.

Contribution, Right of
The right of one person who is legally liable to pay money to someone to claim a proportionate share from others who are also liable.

Counterclaim
A claim made by a defender in response to the pursuer's case and which is not necessarily a defence to that case. It is a separate but related case against the pursuer which is dealt with at the same time as the pursuer's case.

Damages
Money compensation payable for a breach of contract or some other legal duty.

Declarator of irritancy of a lease
A decision of a court finding that a tenant has failed to observe a term of a lease which may lead to the termination of the lease.

Decree
An order of the court containing the decision of the case in favour of one of the parties and granting the remedy sought or disposing of the case.

Decree of ejection
A decree ordering someone to leave land or property which they are occupying. For example, it is used to remove tenants in arrears with their rent.

Decree of removing
A court order entitling someone to recover possession of heritable property and ordering a person to leave land which he is occupying. For example, it is used to remove tenants in arrears with their rent.

Defender
Person against whom a summary cause is started.

Deliverance
A decision or order of a court.

Diet
Date for a court hearing.

Diligence
The collective term for the procedures used to enforce a decree of a court. These include arrestment of wages, goods or a bank account.

Dismissal
An order bringing to an end the proceedings in a summary cause. It is usually possible for a new summary cause to be brought if not time barred.

Domicile
The place where a person is normally resident or where, in the case of a company, it has its place of business or registered office.

Execution of service
See *Certificate of execution of service.*

D 647 *Execution of a charge*
The intimation of the requirement to obey a decree or order of a court.

Execution of an arrestment
The carrying out of an order of arrestment.

Expenses
The costs of a court case.

Extract decree
The document containing the order of the court made at the end of the summary cause. For example, it can be used to enforce payment of a sum awarded.

Fund in medio
See *Multiplepoinding.*

Haver
A person who holds documents which are required as evidence in a case.

Heritable property
Land and buildings as opposed to moveable property.

Huissier
An official in France and some other European countries who serves court documents.

Incidental application
An application that can be made during the course of a summary cause for certain orders. Examples are applications for the recovery of documents or to amend the statement of claim.

Interlocutor
The official record of the order or judgment of a court.

Interrogatories
Written questions put to someone in the course of a court case and which must be answered on oath.

Intimation
Giving notice to another party of some step in a summary cause.

Jurisdiction
The authority of a court to hear particular cases.

Ish
The date on which a lease terminates.

Letter of request
A document issued by the sheriff court requesting a foreign court to take evidence from a specified person within its jurisdiction or to serve Scottish court documents on that person.

Messenger at arms
Officers of court who serve documents issued by the Court of Session.

Minute
A document produced in the course of a case in which a party makes an application or sets out his position on some matter.

Minute for recall
A form lodged with the court by one party asking the court to recall a decree.

Multiplepoinding (pronounced "multiple pinding")
A special type of summary cause in which the holder of property, etc. (referred to as the fund *in medio*) requires claimants upon it to appear and settle claims in court. For example, where the

police come into possession of a stolen car of which two or more people claim to be owner this **D 648** procedure could be used.

Options Hearing
A preliminary stage in an ordinary cause action.

Ordinary cause
Another legal procedure for higher value cases available in the sheriff court.

Party litigant
A person who conducts his own case.

Process
The court file containing the collection of documents relating to a case.

Productions
Documents or articles which are used in evidence.

Pursuer
The person who starts a summary cause.

Recall of an arrestment
A court order withdrawing an arrestment.

Restriction of an arrestment
An order releasing part of the money or property arrested.

Recall of a decree
An order revoking a decree which has been granted.

Recovery of documents
The process of obtaining documentary evidence which is not in the possession of the person seeking it (e.g. hospital records necessary to establish the extent of injuries received in a road accident).

Remit between procedures
A decision of the sheriff to transfer the summary cause to another court procedure e.g. small claim or ordinary cause procedure.

Respondent
When a decision of the sheriff is appealed against, the person making the appeal is called the appellant. The other side in the appeal is called the respondent.

Return day
The date by which the defender must send a written reply to the court and, where appropriate, the pursuer must return the summons to court.

Schedule of arrestment
The list of items which may be arrested.

Serve / service
Sending a copy of the summons or other court document to the defender or another party.

Sheriff clerk
The court official responsible for the administration of the sheriff court.

Sheriff officer
A person who serves court documents and enforces court orders.

Sist of action
The temporary suspension of a court case by court order.

D 649 *Sist as a party*
To add another person as a litigant in a case.

Small claim
Another legal procedure in the sheriff court for claims having a lower value than summary cause.

Specification of documents
A list lodged in court of documents for the recovery of which a party seeks a court order.

Stated case
An appeal procedure where the sheriff sets out his findings and the reasons for his decision and states the issues on which the decision of the sheriff principal is requested.

Statement of claim
The part of the summons in which pursuers set out details of their cases against defenders.

Summons
The form which must be filled in to begin a summary cause.

Time to pay direction
A court order for which a defender who is an individual may apply permitting a sum owed to be paid by instalments or by a single payment at a later date.

Time order
A court order which assists debtors who have defaulted on an agreement regulated by the Consumer Credit Act 1974 (c.39) and which may be applied for during a court action.

Warrant for diligence
Authority to carry out one of the diligence procedures.

Writ
A legally significant writing.

REVOCATIONS

(1) *Act of Sederunt*	(2) *Reference*	(3) *Extent of revocation*
Act of Sederunt (Summary Cause Rules, Sheriff Court) 1976	S.I. 1976/476	The whole Act of Sederunt
Act of Sederunt (Summary Cause Rules, Sheriff Court) (Amendment) 1978	S.I. 1978/112	The whole Act of Sederunt
Act of Sederunt (Summary Cause Rules, Sheriff court) (Amendment no. 2) 1978	S.I. 1978/1805	The whole Act of Sederunt
Act of Sederunt (Summary Cause Rules, Sheriff Court) (Amendment) 1980	S.I. 1980/455	The whole Act of Sederunt
Act of Sederunt (Ordinary Cause Rules, Sheriff Court) 1983	S.I. 983/747	Paragraph 4
Act of Sederunt (Civil Jurisdiction of the Sheriff Court) 1986	S.I. 1986/1946	Paragraph 3
Act of Sederunt (Miscellaneous Amendments) 1986	S.I. 1986/1966	Paragraph 3
Act of Sederunt (Small Claim Rules)1988	S.I. 1988/1976	Paragraph 3
Act of Sederunt (Amendment of Sheriff Court Ordinary Cause, and Summary Cause, Rules) 1988	S.I. 1988/1978	Paragraphs 19 to 35 and Schedule 2
Act of Sederunt (Amendment of Ordinary Cause and Summary Cause Rules) (Written Statements) 1989	S.I. 1989/436	Paragraph 3
Act of Sederunt (Amendment of Sheriff Court Ordinary Cause, Summary Cause and Small Claim, Rules) 1990	S.I. 1990/661	Paragraph 3
Act of Sederunt (Amendment of Sheriff Court Ordinary Cause, Summary Cause and Small Claim, Rules) (No. 2) 1990	S.I. 1990/2105	Paragraph 3
Act of Sederunt (Amendment of Summary Cause and Small Claim Rules) 1991	S.I. 1991/821	The whole Act of Sederunt
Act of Sederunt (Amendment of Ordinary Cause, Summary Cause and Small Claim Rules) 1992	S.I. 1992/249	Paragraph 3
Act of Sederunt (Child Support Act 1991) (Amendment of Ordinary Cause and Summary Cause Rules) 1993	S.I. 1993/919	Paragraph 4
Act of Sederunt (Sheriff Court Ordinary Cause Rules) 1993	S.I. 1993/1956	Paragraph 3

Act of Sederunt (Small Claim Rules) 2002

(SI 2002/133)

The Lords of Council and Session, under and by virtue of the powers conferred by section 32 of the Sheriff Courts (Scotland) Act 1971 and of all other powers enabling them in that behalf, having approved draft rules submitted to them by the Sheriff Court Rules Council in accordance with section 34 of the said Act of 1971, do hereby enact and declare:

Citation and commencement
1.—(1) This Act of Sederunt may be cited as the Act of Sederunt (Small Claim Rules) 2002 and shall come into force on 10th June 2002.
(2) This Act of Sederunt shall be inserted in the Books of Sederunt.

Small Claim Rules
2. The provisions of Schedule 1 to this Act of Sederunt shall have effect for the purpose of providing rules for the form of summary cause process known as a small claim.

Transitional provision
3. Nothing in Schedule 1 to this Act of Sederunt shall apply to a small claim commenced before 10th June 2002 and any such claim shall proceed according to the law and practice in force immediately before that date.

Revocation
4. The Acts of Sederunt mentioned in column (1) of Schedule 2 to this Act of Sederunt are revoked to the extent specified in column (3) of that Schedule except in relation to any small claim commenced before 10th June 2002.

SCHEDULE 1

SMALL CLAIM RULES 2002

ARRANGEMENT OF RULES

Chapter 1

Citation, interpretation and application

1.1. Citation, interpretation and application

Chapter 2

Representation

2.1. Representation

Chapter 3

Relief from failure to comply with rules

3.1. Dispensing power of sheriff

Chapter 4

Commencement of claim

4.1. Form of summons
4.2. Statement of claim

D 653

Chapter 19

Abandonment

Chapter 20

Decree by default

Chapter 21

Decrees, extracts, execution and variation

Chapter 22

Recall of decree

Chapter 23

Appeals

Chapter 24

Management of damages payable to persons under legal disability

Chapter 25   **D 655**

Electronic transmission of documents

APPENDIX 1

FORMS

1   Small claim summons
1a   Small claim summons—defender's copy—claim for or including payment of
     money (where time to pay direction or time order may be applied for)
1b   Small claim summons—defender's copy—all other claims
2   Claim in a summons for payment of money
3   Claim in a summons for delivery
4   Claim in a summons for implement of an obligation
5   From of service
6   Certificate of execution of service
7   Postal service—form of notice
8   Service on person who address is unknown—form of advertisement
9   Service on person whose address is unknown—form of notice to be displayed on
     the walls of court
10   Recall or restriction of arrestment—certificate authorising the release of arrested
     funds or property
11   Minute—no form of response lodged by defender
12   Minute—pursuer not objecting to application for a time to pay direction or time
     order
13   Minute—pursuer opposing an application for a time to pay direction or time
     order
14   Counterclaim—form of intimation by sheriff clerk where pursuer fails to appear
15   Order by the court and certificate in optional procedure for recovery of
     documents
16   Witness citation
16a Certificate of execution of witness citation
17   Reference to the European Court
18   Extract decree—(basic)
18a Extract decree—payment
18b Extract—delivery
18c Extract decree—delivery—payment failing delivery
18d Extract decree—recovery of possession of moveable property
18e Extract decree—recovery of possession of moveable property—payment failing
     recovery
18f Extract decree—*ad factum praestandum*
18g Extract decree—*ad factum praestandum*—payment upon failure to implement
     obligation
18h Extract decree—absolvitor
18i Extract decree—dismissal
19   Certificate by sheriff clerk—service of charge were address of defender is
     unknown
20   Minute for recall of decree
20a Minute for recall of decree—service copy
21   Note of appeal to the sheriff principal
22   Application for leave to appeal against time to pay direction
23   Appeal against time to pay direction
24   Form of receipt for money paid to sheriff clerk

APPENDIX 2

GLOSSARY

CHAPTER 1

CITATION, INTERPRETATION AND APPLICATION

Citation, interpretation and application
   1.1.—(1) These Rules may be cited as the Small Claim Rules 2002.
   (2) In these rules—
       "the 1971 Act" means the Sheriff Courts (Scotland) Act 1971;
       "the 1975 Act" means the Litigants in Person (Costs and Expenses) Act 1975;

"authorised lay representative" means a person to whom section 32(1) of the Solicitors (Scotland) Act 1980 (offence to prepare writs) does not apply by virtue of section 32(2)(a) of that Act;

"small claim" has the meaning assigned to it by section 35(2) of the 1971 Act;

"summary cause" has the meaning assigned to it by section 35(1) of the 1971 Act.

(3) Any reference in these Rules to a specified rule shall be construed as a reference to the rule bearing that number in these Rules, and a reference to a specified paragraph, sub-paragraph or head shall be construed as a reference to the paragraph, sub-paragraph or head so numbered or lettered in the provision in which that reference occurs.

(4) A form referred to by number in these Rules means the form so numbered in Appendix 1 to these rules or a form substantially of the same effect with such variation as circumstances may require.

(5) The glossary in Appendix 2 to these Rules is a guide to the meaning of certain legal expressions used in these Rules, but is not to be taken as giving those expressions any meaning which they do not have in law generally.

(6) These Rules shall apply to a small claim.

CHAPTER 2

REPRESENTATION

Representation

2.1.—(1) A party may be represented by an advocate, solicitor or, subject to paragraph (3), an authorised lay representative.

(2) An authorised lay representative may in representing a party do everything for the preparation and conduct of a small claim as may be done by an individual conducting his own claim.

(3) If the sheriff finds that the authorised lay representative is—

(a) not a suitable person to represent the party; or

(b) not in fact authorised to do so,

that person must cease to represent the party.

CHAPTER 3

RELIEF FROM FAILURE TO COMPLY WITH RULES

Dispensing power of sheriff

3.1.—(1) The sheriff may relieve any party from the consequences of any failure to comply with the provisions of these Rules which is shown to be due to mistake, oversight or other excusable cause, on such conditions as he thinks fit.

(2) Where the sheriff relieves a party from the consequences of the failure to comply with a provision in these Rules under paragraph (1), he may make such order as he thinks fit to enable the claim to proceed as if the failure to comply with the provision had not occurred.

CHAPTER 4

COMMENCEMENT OF CLAIM

Form of summons

4.1.—(1) A small claim shall be commenced by summons, which shall be in Form 1.

(2) The claim in a small claim summons may be in one of Forms 2 to 4.

Statement of claim   **D 657**

4.2. The pursuer must insert a statement of his claim in the summons to give the defender fair notice of the claim; and the statement must include—

(a) details of the basis of the claim including relevant dates; and

(b) if the claim arises from the supply of goods or services, a description of the goods or services and the date or dates on or between which they were supplied and, where relevant, ordered.

Defender's copy summons

4.3. A copy summons shall be served on the defender—

(a) in Form 1a where—

(i) the small claim is for, or includes a claim for, payment of money; and

    (ii) an application for a time to pay direction under the Debtors (Scotland) Act 1987 or time order under the Consumer Credit Act 1974 may be applied for;
    or
    (b) in Form 1b in every other case.

Authentication and effect of summons
    4.4.—(1) A summons shall be authenticated by the sheriff clerk in some appropriate manner except where—
    (a) he refuses to do so for any reason;
    (b) the defender's address is unknown; or
    (c) a party seeks to alter the normal period of notice specified in rule 4.5(2); or
[1] (d) a warrant for arrestment on the dependence, or to found jurisdiction, is sought
    (2) If any of paragraphs (1)(a) to (d) applies, the summons shall be authenticated by the sheriff, if he thinks it appropriate.
    (3) The authenticated summons shall be warrant for—
    (a) service on the defender; and
    (b) where the appropriate warrant has been sought in the summons—
        (i) arrestment on the dependence; or
        (ii) arrestment to found jurisdiction,
as the case may be.
[1] (4) Where a warrant for arrestment on the dependence, or to found jurisdiction, is sought, averments to justify that warrant must be included in the statement of claim.

---

[1] As amended and inserted by the Act of Sederunt (Ordinary Cause, Summary Application and Small Claim Rules) Amendment (Miscellaneous) 2004 (SSI 2004/197) (effective May 21, 2004), para.5(2).

Period of notice
    4.5.—(1) A claim shall proceed after the appropriate period of notice of the summons has been given to the defender prior to the return day.
    (2) The appropriate period of notice shall be—
    (a) 21 days where the defender is resident or has a place of business within Europe; or
    (b) 42 days where the defender is resident or has a place of business outwith Europe.
    (3) The sheriff may, on cause shown, shorten or extend the period of notice on such conditions as to the form of service as he may direct, but in any case where the period of notice is reduced at least two days' notice must be given.
    (4) If a period of notice expires on a Saturday, Sunday, public or court holiday, the period of notice shall be deemed to expire on the next day on which the sheriff clerk's office is open for civil court business.
    (5) Notwithstanding the terms of section 4(2) of the Citation Amendment (Scotland) Act 1882, where service is by post the period of notice shall run from the beginning of the day next following the date of posting.
    (6) The sheriff clerk shall insert in the summons—
    (a) the return day, which is the last day on which the defender may return a form of response to the sheriff clerk; and
    (b) the hearing date, which is the date set for the hearing of the claim.

Intimation
    4.6. Any provision in these Rules requiring papers to be sent to or any intimation to be made to any party or applicant shall be construed as if the reference to the party or applicant included a reference to the solicitor representing that party or applicant.

D 658

CHAPTER 5

REGISTER OF SMALL CLAIMS

Register of Small Claims
    5.1.—(1) The sheriff clerk shall keep a register of claims and incidental applications made in claims, which shall be known as the Register of Small Claims.
    (2) There shall be entered in the Register of Small Claims a note of all claims, together with a note of all minutes under rule 22.1(1) (recall of decree) and the entry for each claim or minute must contain the following particulars where appropriate:-
    (a) the names, designations and addresses of the parties;

(b) whether the parties were present or absent at any hearing, including an inspection, and the names of their representatives;

(c) the nature of the claim;

(d) the amount of any claim;

(e) the date of issue of the summons;

(f) the method of service;

(g) the return day;

(h) the hearing date;

(i) whether a form of response was lodged and details of it;

(j) the period of notice if shortened or extended in accordance with rule 4.5(3);

(k) details of any minute by the pursuer regarding a time to pay direction or time order, or minute by the pursuer requesting decree or other order;

(l) details of any interlocutors issued;

(m) details of the final decree and the date of it; and

(n) details of any variation or recall of a decree by virtue of the Debtors (Scotland) Act 1987.

(3) There shall be entered in the Register of Small Claims, in the entry for the claim to which they relate, details of incidental applications including, where appropriate—

(a) whether parties are present or absent at the hearing of the application, and the names of their representatives;

(b) the nature of the application; and

(c) the interlocutor issued or order made.

(4) The Register of Small Claims must be—

(a) authenticated in some appropriate manner by the sheriff in respect of each day any order is made or application determined in a claim; and

(b) open for inspection during normal business hours to all concerned without fee.

(5) The Register of Small Claims may be kept in electronic or documentary form.

CHAPTER 6

SERVICE AND RETURN OF THE SUMMONS

Persons carrying on business under trading or descriptive name

6.1.—(1) A person carrying on a business under a trading or descriptive name may sue or be sued in such trading or descriptive name alone.

(2) An extract of a decree pronounced in a claim against such person under such trading or descriptive name shall be a valid warrant for diligence against that person.

(3) A summons, decree, charge or other document following upon such summons or decree in a claim in which a person carrying on business under a trading or descriptive name sues or is sued in that name may be served—

(a) at any place of business or office at which such business is carried on within the sheriffdom of the sheriff court in which the claim is brought; or

(b) if there is no place of business within that sheriffdom, at any place where such business is carried on (including the place of business or office of the clerk or secretary of any company, corporation or association or firm).

Form of service

6.2.—(1) Subject to rule 6.6 (service where address of defender is unknown), a form of service in Form 5 must be enclosed with the defender's copy summons.

(2) After service has been effected a certificate of execution of service in Form 6 must be prepared and signed by the person effecting service.

(3) When service is effected by a sheriff officer the certificate of execution of service must specify whether the service was personal or, if otherwise, the mode of service and the name of any person to whom the defender's copy summons was delivered.

(4) If service is effected in accordance with rule 6.4(2) (service within Scotland by sheriff **D 659** officer where personal service etc. unsuccessful) the certificate must also contain a statement of—

(a) the mode of service previously attempted; and

(b) the circumstances which prevented the service from being effected.

Service of the summons

6.3.—(1) Subject to rule 6.5 (service on persons outwith Scotland), a copy summons may be served on the defender—

(a) by the pursuer's solicitor, a sheriff officer or the sheriff clerk sending it by first class recorded delivery post; or

(b) in accordance with rule 6.4 (service within Scotland by sheriff officer).

(2) On the face of the envelope used for postal service in terms of this rule, there must be printed or written a notice in Form 7.

(3) The certificate of execution of service in the case of postal service must have annexed to it any relevant postal receipt.

(4) If the pursuer requires the sheriff clerk to effect service on his behalf by virtue of section 36A of the 1971 Act (pursuer not being a partnership, body corporate or acting in a representative capacity) under paragraph (1), he may require the sheriff clerk to supply him with a copy of the summons.

Service within Scotland by sheriff officer

6.4.—(1) A sheriff officer may validly serve any summons, decree, charge or other document following upon such summons or decree issued in a claim by—

(a) personal service; or
(b) leaving it in the hands of—
    (i) an inmate at the person's dwelling place; or
    (ii) an employee at the person's place of business.

(2) If a sheriff officer has been unsuccessful in effecting service in accordance with paragraph (1), he may, after making diligent inquiries, serve the document—

(a) by depositing it in the person's dwelling place or place of business by means of a letter box or by other lawful means; or
(b) by affixing it to the door of the person's dwelling place or place of business.

(3) If service is effected in accordance with paragraph (2), the sheriff officer must thereafter send by ordinary post to the address at which he thinks it most likely that the person may be found a letter containing a copy of the document.

(4) In proceedings in or following on a claim, it shall be necessary for any sheriff officer to be accompanied by a witness except where service, citation or intimation is to be made by post.

(5) Where the firm which employs the sheriff officer has in its possession—

(a) the document or a copy of it certified as correct by the pursuer's solicitor or the sheriff clerk, the sheriff officer may serve the document upon the defender without having the document or certified copy in his possession (in which case he shall if required to do so by the person on whom service is executed and within a reasonable time of being so required, show the document or certified copy to the person); or
(b) a certified copy of the interlocutor pronounced allowing service of the document, the sheriff officer may serve the document without having in his possession the certified copy interlocutor if he has in his possession a facsimile copy of the certified copy interlocutor (which he shall show, if required, to the person on whom service is executed).

(6) If the pursuer requires the sheriff clerk to effect service of the summons on his behalf by virtue of section 36A of the 1971 Act, the sheriff clerk may instruct a sheriff officer to effect service in accordance with this rule on payment to the sheriff clerk by the pursuer of the fee prescribed by order of the Scottish Ministers.

Service on persons outwith Scotland

6.5.—(1) If any summons, decree, charge or other document following upon such summons or decree, or any charge or warrant, requires to be served outwith Scotland on any person, it must be served in accordance with this rule.

(2) If the person has a known home or place of business in—

(a) England and Wales, Northern Ireland, the Isle of Man or the Channel Islands; or
(b) any country with which the United Kingdom does not have a convention providing for service of writs in that country,

the document must be served either—

(i) by posting in Scotland a copy of the document in question in a registered letter addressed to the person at his residence or place of business; or
D 660   (ii) in accordance with the rules for personal service under the domestic law of the place in which the document is to be served.

(3) Subject to paragraph (4), if the document requires to be served in a country which is a party to the Hague Convention on the Service Abroad of Judicial and Extra-Judicial Documents in Civil or Commercial Matters dated 15th November 1965 or the European Convention on Jurisdiction and Enforcement of Judgments in Civil and Commercial Matters as set out in Schedule 1 or 3C to the Civil Jurisdiction and Judgments Act 1982, it must be served—

(a) by a method prescribed by the internal law of the country where service is to be effected for the service of documents in domestic actions upon persons who are within its territory;

(b) by or through a British consular authority at the request of the Secretary of State for Foreign and Commonwealth Affairs;

(c) by or through a central authority in the country where service is to be effected at the request of the Secretary of State for Foreign and Commonwealth Affairs;

(d) where the law of the country in which the person resides permits, by posting in Scotland a copy of the document in a registered letter addressed to the person at his residence; or

(e) where the law of the country in which service is to be effected permits, service by an *huissier*, other judicial officer or competent official of the country where service is to be made.

[1] (4) If the document requires to be served in a country to which the Council Regulation applies, service—

(a) may be effected by the methods prescribed in paragraph (3)(b) or (c) only in exceptional circumstances; and

(b) is effected only if the receiving agency has informed the person that acceptance of service may be refused on the ground that the document has not been translated in accordance with paragraph (12).

(5) If the document requires to be served in a country with which the United Kingdom has a convention on the service of writs in that country other than the conventions specified in paragraph (3) or the regulation specified in paragraph (4), it must be served by one of the methods approved in the relevant convention.

(6) Subject to paragraph (9), a document which requires to be posted in Scotland for the purposes of this rule must be posted by a solicitor, the sheriff clerk or a sheriff officer, and the form for service and the certificate of execution of service must be in Forms 5 and 6 respectively.

(7) On the face of the envelope used for postal service under this rule there must be written or printed a notice in Form 7.

(8) Where service is effected by a method specified in paragraph (3)(b) or (c), the pursuer must—

(a) send a copy of the summons and warrant for service with form of service attached, or other document, with a request for service to be effected by the method indicated in the request to the Secretary of State for Foreign and Commonwealth Affairs; and

(b) lodge in process a certificate of execution of service signed by the authority which has effected service.

(9) If service is effected by the method specified in paragraph (3)(e), the pursuer must—

(a) send to the official in the country in which service is to be effected a copy of the summons and warrant for service, with citation attached, or other document, with a request for service to be effected by delivery to the defender or his residence; and

(b) lodge in process a certificate of execution of service by the official who has effected service.

(10) Where service is executed in accordance with paragraph (2)(b)(ii) or (3)(a) other than on another party in—

(a) the United Kingdom;

(b) the Isle of Man; or

(c) the Channel Islands,

the party executing service must lodge a certificate stating that the form of service employed is in accordance with the law of the place where the service was executed.

(11) A certificate lodged in accordance with paragraph (10) shall be given by a person who is conversant with the law of the country concerned and who—

(a) practises or has practised law in that country; or

(b) is a duly accredited representative of the government of that country.

(12) Every summons or document and every citation and notice on the face of the envelope referred to in paragraph (7) must be accompanied by a translation in—

[1] (a) an official language of the country in which service is to be executed; or

(b) in a country to which the Council Regulation applies, a language of the member state of transmission that is understood by the person on whom service is being executed.

(13) A translation referred to in paragraph (12) must be certified as a correct translation by **D 661** the person making it and the certificate must contain the full name, address and qualifications of the translator and be lodged along with the execution of such service.

(14) If the pursuer requires the sheriff clerk to effect service on his behalf under this rule by virtue of section 36A of the 1971 Act (pursuer not a partnership, body corporate or acting in a representative capacity)—

(a) the cost must be borne by the pursuer;

(b) no service shall be instructed by the sheriff clerk until such cost has been paid to him by the pursuer; and

(c) the pursuer may require the sheriff clerk to supply him with a copy of the summons.

[1] (15) In this rule "the Council Regulation" means Council Regulation (EC) No. 1348/2000

on the service in the Member States of judicial and extrajudicial documents in civil or commercial matters.

---

[1] As amended and inserted by the Act of Sederunt (Ordinary Cause, Summary Application and Small Claim Rules) Amendment (Miscellaneous) 2004 (SSI 2004/197) (effective May 21, 2004), para.5(3).

Service where address of defender is unknown
6.6.—(1) If the defender's address is unknown to the pursuer and cannot reasonably be ascertained by him, the sheriff may grant warrant to serve the summons—
  (a) by the publication of an advertisement in Form 8 in a newspaper circulating in the area of the defender's last known address; or
  (b) by displaying on the walls of court a copy of a notice in Form 9.
(2) Where a summons is served in accordance with paragraph (1), the period of notice, which must be fixed by the sheriff, shall run from the date of publication of the advertisement or display on the walls of court, as the case may be.
(3) If service is to be effected under paragraph (1), the pursuer must lodge a defender's copy summons with the sheriff clerk.
(4) The defender may uplift from the sheriff clerk the copy summons lodged in accordance with paragraph (3).
(5) If the pursuer requires the sheriff clerk to effect service on his behalf under paragraph (1) by virtue of section 36A of the 1971 Act (pursuer not a partnership, body corporate or acting in a representative capacity)—
  (a) the cost of any advertisement required under sub-paragraph (a) of that paragraph must be borne by the pursuer;
  (b) no advertisement required under sub-paragraph (a) of that paragraph shall be instructed by the sheriff clerk until such cost has been paid to him by the pursuer; and
  (c) the pursuer may require the sheriff clerk to supply him with a copy of the summons.
(6) A copy of the newspaper containing the advertisement referred to in paragraph (1)(a) must be lodged with the sheriff clerk unless the sheriff clerk instructed such advertisement.
(7) If display on the walls of court is required under paragraph (1)(b), the pursuer must supply to the sheriff clerk for that purpose a completed copy of Form 9.
(8) If service has been made under this rule and thereafter the defender's address becomes known, the sheriff may allow the summons to be amended and, if appropriate, grant warrant for resservice subject to such conditions as he thinks fit.

Endorsation by sheriff clerk of defender's residence not necessary
6.7. Any summons, decree, charge or other document following upon a summons or decree may be served, enforced or otherwise lawfully executed in Scotland without endorsation by a sheriff clerk and, if executed by a sheriff officer, may be so executed by a sheriff officer of the court which granted the summons, or by a sheriff officer of the sheriff court district in which it is to be executed.

Contents of envelope containing defender's copy summons
6.8. Nothing must be included in the envelope containing a defender's copy summons except—
  (a) the copy summons;
  (b) a response or other notice in accordance with these Rules; and
  (c) any other document approved by the sheriff principal.

Re-service
6.9.—(1) If it appears to the sheriff that there has been any failure or irregularity in service
D 662 upon a defender, the sheriff may order the pursuer to re-serve the summons on such conditions as he thinks fit.
(2) If re-service has been ordered in accordance with paragraph (1) or rule 6.6(8), the claim shall proceed thereafter as if it were a new claim.

Defender appearing barred from objecting to service
6.10.—(1) A person who appears in any claim shall not be entitled to state any objection to the regularity of the execution of service or intimation on him and his appearance shall remedy any defect in such service or intimation.
(2) Nothing in paragraph (1) shall preclude a party pleading that the court has no jurisdiction.

Return of summons and execution
6.11.—(1) If—
(a) someone other than the sheriff clerk has served the summons; and
(b) the case requires to call in court for any reason on the hearing date, the pursuer must return the summons and the certificate of execution of service to the sheriff clerk at least two days before the hearing date.

(2) If the case does not require to call in court on the hearing date, the pursuer must return the certificate of execution of service to the sheriff clerk by the date mentioned in paragraph (1) above.

(3) If the pursuer fails to return the summons or certificate of execution of service in accordance with paragraph (1) or (2) as appropriate, the sheriff may dismiss the claim.

CHAPTER 7

ARRESTMENT

Service of schedule of arrestment
7.1. If a schedule of arrestment has not been personally served on an arrestee, the arrestment shall have effect only if a copy of the schedule is also sent by registered post or the first class recorded delivery service to—
(a) the last known place of residence of the arrestee; or
(b) if such place of residence is not known, or if the arrestee is a firm or corporation, to the arrestee's principal place of business if known, or, if not known, to any known place of business of the arrestee,
and the sheriff officer must, on the certificate of execution, certify that this has been done and specify the address to which the copy of the schedule was sent.

Arrestment before service
7.2.—(1) An arrestment to found jurisdiction or an arrestment on the dependence of a claim used prior to service shall cease to have effect, unless the summons is served within 21 days from the date of execution of the arrestment.

(2) When such an arrestment as is referred to in paragraph (1) has been executed, the party using it must forthwith report the execution to the sheriff clerk.

Recall and restriction of arrestment
7.3.—(1) The sheriff may order that an arrestment on the dependence of a claim or counterclaim shall cease to have effect if the party whose funds or property are arrested—
(a) pays into court; or
(b) finds caution to the satisfaction of the sheriff clerk in respect of, the sum claimed together with the sum of £50 in respect of expenses.

(2) Without prejudice to paragraph (1), a party whose funds or property are arrested may at any time apply to the sheriff to exercise his powers to recall or restrict an arrestment on the dependence of a claim or counterclaim, with or without consignation or caution.

(3) An application made under paragraph (3) must be intimated by the applicant to the party who instructed the arrestment.

(4) On payment into court or the finding of caution to the satisfaction of the sheriff clerk in accordance with paragraph (1), or if the sheriff recalls or restricts an arrestment on the dependence of a claim in accordance with paragraph (2) and any condition imposed by the sheriff has been complied with, the sheriff clerk must—
(a) issue to the party whose funds or property are arrested a certificate in Form 10 authorising the release of any sum or property arrested to the extent ordered by the sheriff; and
(b) send a copy of the certificate to— **D 663**
(i) the party who instructed the arrestment; and
(ii) the party who has possession of the funds or property that are arrested.

CHAPTER 8

UNDEFENDED CLAIM

Undefended claim
8.1.—(1) Where the defender has not lodged a form of response on or before the return day, the claim shall not require to call in court.

(2) Where paragraph (1) applies, the pursuer must lodge a minute in Form 11 before the sheriff clerk's office closes for business on the second day before the date set for the hearing.

(3) Where the pursuer has lodged a minute in accordance with paragraph (2), the sheriff may grant decree or other competent order sought in terms of that minute.

(4) Where the pursuer has not lodged a minute in accordance with paragraph (2), the sheriff must dismiss the claim.

Application for time to pay direction or time order

8.2.—(1) If the defender admits the claim, he may, where competent—

    (a) make an application for a time to pay direction (including, where appropriate, an application for recall or restriction of an arrestment) or a time order by completing the appropriate parts of the Form 1a and lodging it with the sheriff clerk on or before the return day; or

    (b) lodge a form of response indicating that he admits the claim and intends to apply orally for a time to pay direction (including, where appropriate, an application for recall or restriction of an arrestment) or time order.

(2) Where the defender has lodged an application in terms of paragraph (1)(a), the pursuer may intimate that he does not object to the application by lodging a minute in Form 12 before the time the sheriff clerk's office closes for business on the day occurring two days before the hearing date stating that he does not object to the defender's application and seeking decree.

(3) If the pursuer intimates in accordance with paragraph (2) that he does not object to the application—

    (a) the sheriff may grant decree on the hearing date;

    (b) the parties need not attend; and

    (c) the action will not call in court.

(4) If the pursuer wishes to oppose the application for a time to pay direction or time order made in accordance with paragraph (1)(a), he must lodge a minute in Form 13 before the time the sheriff clerk's office closes for business on the day occurring two days before the hearing date.

(5) Where the pursuer objects to an application in terms of paragraph (1)(a) or the defender has lodged a form of response in accordance with paragraph (1)(b), the action shall call in court on the hearing date when the parties may appear and the sheriff must decide the application and grant decree accordingly.

(6) The sheriff shall decide an application in accordance with paragraph (5) whether or not any of the parties appear.

(7) Where the defender has lodged an application in terms of paragraph (1)(a) and the pursuer fails to proceed in accordance with either of paragraphs (2) or (4) the sheriff may dismiss the claim.

Decree in claims to which the Hague Convention or the Civil Jurisdiction and Judgments Act 1982 apply

8.3.—(1) If the summons has been served in a country to which the Hague Convention on the Service Abroad of Judicial and Extra-Judicial Documents in Civil or Commercial Matters dated 15th November 1965 applies, decree must not be granted until it is established to the satisfaction of the sheriff that the requirements of Article 15 of that Convention have been complied with.

(2) Where a defender is domiciled in another part of the United Kingdom or in another Contracting State, the sheriff shall not grant decree until it has been shown that the defender has been able to receive the summons in sufficient time to arrange his defence or that all necessary steps have been taken to that end.

(3) For the purposes of paragraph (2)—

    (a) the question whether a person is domiciled in another part of the United Kingdom shall be determined in accordance with sections 41 and 42 of the Civil Jurisdiction and Judgments Act 1982;

    (b) the question whether a person is domiciled in another Contracting State shall be determined in accordance with Article 52 of the Convention in Schedule 1 or 3C to that Act; and

    (c) the term "Contracting State" has the meaning assigned in section 1 of that Act.

D 664

CHAPTER 9

DEFENDED CLAIM

The Hearing

9.1.—(1) Where a defender intends to—

    (a) challenge the jurisdiction of the court;

(b) state a defence (including, where appropriate, a counterclaim); or

(c) dispute the amount of the claim, he must complete the form of response part of Form 1a or 1b as appropriate indicating that intention and lodge it with the sheriff clerk on or before the return day.

(2) Where the defender has lodged a form of response in accordance with paragraph (1) the claim will call in court for a hearing ("the Hearing").

(3) The Hearing shall be held on the hearing date which shall be seven days after the return day.

(4) If the claim is not resolved at the Hearing, the sheriff may continue the Hearing to such other date as he considers to be appropriate.

(5) The defender must attend or be represented at the Hearing and the sheriff shall note any challenge, defence or dispute, as the case may be, on the summons.

(6) Where at the Hearing the defender—

(a) does not appear or is not represented; and

(b) the pursuer is present or is represented, decree may be granted against the defender in terms of the summons.

(7) Where at the Hearing—

(a) the pursuer does not appear or is not represented; and

(b) the defender is present or represented, the sheriff may grant decree of dismissal.

(8) If all parties fail to appear at the Hearing, the sheriff shall, unless sufficient reason appears to the contrary, dismiss the claim.

Purpose of the Hearing

9.2.—(1) If, at the Hearing, the sheriff is satisfied that the claim is incompetent or that there is a patent defect of jurisdiction, he must grant decree of dismissal in favour of the defender or, if appropriate, transfer the claim in terms of rule 15.1(2).

(2) At the Hearing, the sheriff shall—

(a) ascertain the factual basis of the claim and any defence, and the legal basis on which the claim and defence are proceeding; and

(b) seek to negotiate and secure settlement of the claim between the parties.

(3) If the sheriff cannot secure settlement of the claim between the parties, he shall—

(a) identify and note on the summons the issues of fact and law which are in dispute;

(b) note on the summons any facts which are agreed; and

(c) if possible reach a decision on the whole dispute on the basis of the information before him.

(4) Where evidence requires to be led for the purposes of reaching a decision on the dispute, the sheriff shall—

(a) direct parties to lead evidence on the disputed issues of fact which he has noted on the summons;

(b) indicate to the parties the matters of fact that require to be proved, and may give guidance on the nature of the evidence to be led; and

(c) fix a hearing on evidence for a later date for that purpose.

Conduct of hearings

9.3.—(1) Any hearing in a claim shall be conducted in accordance with the following paragraphs of this rule.

(2) A hearing shall be conducted as informally as the circumstances of the claim permit.

(3) The procedure to be adopted at a hearing shall be such as the sheriff considers—

(a) to be fair;

(b) best suited to the clarification and determination of the issues before him; and

(c) gives each party sufficient opportunity to present his case.

(4) Before proceeding to hear evidence, the sheriff shall explain to the parties the form of procedure which he intends to adopt.

(5) Having considered the circumstances of the parties and whether (and to what extent) they **D 665** are represented, the sheriff—

(a) may, in order to assist resolution of the disputed issues of fact, put questions to parties and to witnesses; and

(b) shall (if he considers it necessary for the fair conduct of the hearing) explain any legal terms or expressions which are used.

(6) Evidence will normally be taken on oath or affirmation but the sheriff may dispense with that requirement if it appears reasonable to do so.

Inspection of places and objects

9.4.—(1) If, at any hearing, a disputed issue noted by the sheriff is the quality or condition of an object, the sheriff may inspect the object in the presence of the parties or their representatives in court or, if it is not practicable to bring the object to court, at the place where the object is located.

(2) The sheriff may, if he considers it appropriate, inspect any place that is material to the disputed issues in the presence of the parties or their representatives.

Remit to determine matter of fact

9.5.—(1) The sheriff may, where parties agree, remit to any suitable person to report on any matter of fact.

(2) Where a remit is made under paragraph (1) above, the report of such person shall be final and conclusive with respect to the matter of fact which is the subject of the remit.

(3) A remit shall not be made under paragraph (1) of this rule unless parties have previously agreed the basis upon which the fees, if any, of such person shall be met.

Noting of evidence

9.6. The sheriff must make notes of the evidence at a hearing for his own use and must retain these notes until after any appeal has been disposed of.

Application for time to pay direction or time order in defended claim

9.7. A defender in a claim which proceeds as defended may, where it is competent to do so, make an incidental application or apply orally at any hearing, at any time before decree is granted, for a time to pay direction (including where appropriate, an order recalling or restricting an arrestment on the dependence) or a time order.

Pronouncement of decision

9.8.—(1) The sheriff must, where practicable, give his decision and a brief statement of his reasons at the end of the hearing of a claim, or he may reserve judgment.

(2) If the sheriff reserves judgment, he must, within 28 days of the hearing, give his decision in writing together with a brief note of his reasons, and the sheriff clerk must send a copy to the parties.

(3) After giving his judgment, the sheriff must—

    (a) deal with the question of expenses and, where appropriate, make an award of expenses; and

    (b) grant decree as appropriate

(4) The decree of the sheriff shall be a final decree.

CHAPTER 10

INCIDENTAL APPLICATIONS AND SISTS

General

10.1.—(1) Except where otherwise provided, any incidental application in a claim may be made—

    (a) orally with the leave of the sheriff during any hearing of the claim; or

    (b) by lodging the application in written form with the sheriff clerk.

(2) An application lodged in accordance with paragraph (1)(b) may only be heard after not less than two days' notice has been given to the other party.

(3) A party who is not—

    (a) a partnership or a body corporate; or

    (b) acting in a representative capacity, and is not represented by a solicitor, may require the sheriff clerk to intimate to the other party a copy of an incidental application.

(4) Where the party receiving notice of an incidental application lodged in accordance with paragraph (1)(b) intimates to the sheriff clerk and the party making the application that it is not opposed, the application shall not require to call in court unless the sheriff so directs.

D 666

(5) Any intimation under paragraph (4) shall be made not later than noon on the day before the application is due to be heard.

Application to sist claim

10.2.—(1) Where an incidental application to sist a claim is made, the reason for the sist—

    (a) shall be stated by the party seeking the sist; and

    (b) shall be recorded in the Register of Small Claims and on the summons.

(2) Where a claim has been sisted, the sheriff may, after giving parties an opportunity to be heard, recall the sist.

Chapter 11

Counterclaim

Counterclaim
11.1.—(1) If a defender intends to state a counterclaim he must—
  (a) indicate that on the form of response; and
  (b) state the counterclaim—
    (i) in writing on the form of response; or
    (ii) orally at the Hearing.
(2) Where a defender states a counterclaim in accordance with paragraph (1)(b)(i) he must at the same time send a copy of the form of response to—
  (a) the pursuer; and
  (b) any other party.
[1] (3) Where a counterclaim stated in accordance with paragraph (1)(b)(i) seeks a warrant for arrestment on the dependence, the sheriff may authenticate the warrant if—
  (a) averments to justify the grant of the warrant are included in the counterclaim; and
  (b) the sheriff considers that appropriate.
(5) Where a defender has indicated in terms of paragraph (1)(a) that he intends to state a counterclaim orally at the Hearing the sheriff may continue the Hearing to allow an answer to the counterclaim to be stated.
(6) The defender may state a counterclaim after—
  (a) the Hearing; or
  (b) any continuation of the Hearing,
as the case may be, only with the leave of the sheriff.
(7) If a counterclaim has been stated orally at any hearing at which the pursuer fails to appear or be represented the sheriff may continue that hearing after noting the counterclaim and the factual basis of it to allow the pursuer to appear.
(8) Intimation of a continued hearing fixed under paragraph (7) shall be given to the pursuer by the sheriff clerk in Form 14 advising him that if he fails to appear or be represented at the continued hearing decree may be granted in terms of the counterclaim.

---

[1] As amended and inserted by the Act of Sederunt (Ordinary Cause, Summary Application and Small Claim Rules) Amendment (Miscellaneous) 2004 (SSI 2004/197) (effective May 21, 2004), para.5(4).

Chapter 12

Alteration of summons etc.

Alteration of summons etc.
12.1.—(1) The sheriff may, on the incidental application of a party allow amendment of the summons, form of response or any counterclaim, and adjust the note of disputed issues at any time before final judgment is pronounced on the merits.
(2) In an undefended claim, the sheriff may order the amended summons to be re-served on the defender on such period of notice as he thinks fit.

Chapter 13   **D 666/1**

Additional defender

Additional defender
13.1.—(1) Any person who has not been called as a defender may apply by incidental application to the sheriff for leave to enter a claim as a defender, and to state a defence.
(2) An application under this rule must specify—
  (a) the applicant's title and interest to enter the claim; and
  (b) the grounds of the defence which he proposes to state.
(3) On the lodging of an application under this rule—
  (a) the sheriff must fix a date for hearing the application; and
  (b) the applicant must forthwith serve a copy of the application and of the order for a hearing on the parties to the claim.
(4) After hearing the applicant and any party to the claim the sheriff may, if he is satisfied that **D 667** the applicant has shown title and interest to enter the claim, grant the application.

(5) Where an application is granted under paragraph (4)—

    (a) the applicant shall be treated as a defender; and

    (b) the claim shall proceed against him as if was the Hearing in terms of rule 9.2.

CHAPTER 14

APPLICATIONS FOR SIST OF PARTY AND TRANSFERENCE

Application for sist of party and transference

14.1.—(1) If a party dies or becomes legally incapacitated while a claim is depending, any person claiming to represent that party or his estate may apply by incidental application to be sisted as a party to the claim.

(2) If a party dies or becomes legally incapacitated while a claim is depending and the provisions of paragraph (1) are not invoked, any other party may apply by incidental application to have the claim transferred in favour of or against, as the case may be, any person who represents that party or his estate.

CHAPTER 15

TRANSFER AND REMIT OF CLAIMS

Transfer to another court

15.1.—(1) The sheriff may transfer a claim to any other sheriff court, whether in the same sheriffdom or not, if the sheriff considers it expedient to do so.

(2) If the sheriff is satisfied that the court has no jurisdiction, he may transfer the claim to any sheriff court in which it appears to the sheriff that it ought to have been brought.

(3) A claim so transferred shall proceed in all respects as if it had been brought originally in the court to which it is transferred.

Remit between procedures

15.2.—(1) If the sheriff makes a direction that a claim is to be treated as an ordinary cause, he must, at the time of making that direction—

    (a) direct the pursuer to lodge an initial writ, and intimate it to every other party, within 14 days of the date of the direction;

    (b) direct the defender to lodge defences within 28 days of the date of the direction; and

    (c) fix a date and time for an Options Hearing and that date shall be the first suitable court day occurring not sooner than ten weeks, or such lesser period as he considers appropriate, after the last date for lodging the initial writ.

(2) If the sheriff directs that a claim is to be treated as a summary cause he must specify the next step of procedure to be followed.

(3) If the sheriff directs that an ordinary cause or a summary cause is to be treated as a claim under these rules it shall call for the Hearing held in terms of rule 9.1(2).

CHAPTER 16

PRODUCTIONS AND DOCUMENTS

Lodging of productions

16.1.—(1) A party who intends to rely at a hearing at which evidence is to be led, upon any documents or articles in his possession, which are reasonably capable of being lodged with the court, must—

    (a) lodge them with the sheriff clerk together with a list detailing the items no later than 14 days before the hearing; and

    (b) at the same time send a copy of the list to the other party.

(2) The documents referred to in paragraph (1) include any affidavit or other written statement admissible under section 2(1) of the Civil Evidence (Scotland) Act 1988.

(3) Subject to paragraph (4), only documents or articles produced—

    (a) in accordance with paragraph (1);

    (b) at an earlier hearing; or

    (c) under rule 17.2(3) or (4), may be used or put in evidence.

(4) Documents other than those mentioned in paragraph (3) may be used or put in evidence only with the—

    (a) consent of the parties; or

(b) permission of the sheriff on cause shown, and on such terms as to expenses or otherwise as to him seem proper.

Borrowing of productions
  16.2.—(1) Any productions borrowed must be returned not later than noon on the day preceding the date of any hearing.
  (2) A receipt for any production borrowed must be entered in the list of productions and that list must be retained by the sheriff clerk.
  (3) Subject to paragraph (4), productions may be borrowed only by—
  (a) a solicitor; or
  (b) his authorised clerk for whom he shall be responsible.
  (4) A party litigant or an authorised lay representative may borrow a production only with permission of the sheriff and subject to such conditions as the sheriff may impose.
  (5) Productions may be inspected within the office of the sheriff clerk during normal business hours, and copies may be obtained by a party litigant, where practicable, from the sheriff clerk.

Documents lost or destroyed
  16.3.—(1) This rule applies to any—
  (a) summons;
  (b) form of response;
  (c) counterclaim;
  (d) Register of Small Claims; or
  (e) other document lodged with the sheriff clerk in connection with a claim.
  (2) Where any document mentioned in paragraph (1) is—
  (a) lost; or
  (b) destroyed,
a copy of it, authenticated in such manner as the sheriff may require, may be substituted and shall, for the purposes of the claim including the use of diligence, be equivalent to the original.

Documents and productions to be retained in custody of sheriff clerk
  16.4.—(1) This rule applies to all documents or other productions which have at any time been lodged or referred to during a hearing.
  (2) The sheriff clerk must retain in his custody any document or other production mentioned in paragraph (1) until—
  (a) after the expiry of the period during which an appeal is competent; and
  (b) any appeal lodged has been disposed of.
  (3) Each party who has lodged productions in a claim shall—
  (a) after the final determination of the claim, where no appeal has been lodged, within 14 days after the appeal period has expired; or
  (b) within 14 days after the disposal of any appeal lodged on the final determination of the claim, uplift the productions from the sheriff clerk.
  (4) Where any production has not been uplifted as required by paragraph (3), the sheriff clerk shall intimate to—
  (a) the solicitor who lodged the production; or
  (b) where no solicitor is acting, the party himself or such other party as seems appropriate, that if he fails to uplift the production within 28 days after the date of such intimation, it will be disposed of in such manner as the sheriff directs.

CHAPTER 17

RECOVERY OF DOCUMENTS AND ATTENDANCE OF WITNESSES

Diligence for recovery of documents
  17.1—(1) At any time after a summons has been served, a party may make an incidental application in writing to the sheriff to grant commission and diligence to recover documents.
  (2) A party who makes an application in accordance with paragraph (1) must list in the application the documents which he wishes to recover.
  (3) The sheriff may grant commission and diligence to recover those documents in the list mentioned in paragraph (2) which he considers relevant to the claim.

Optional procedure before executing commission and diligence
  17.2.—(1) Any party who has obtained a commission and diligence for the recovery of documents may, at any time before executing it, serve by first class recorded delivery post on the

D 669 person from whom the documents are sought to be recovered (or on his known solicitor or solicitors) an order with certificate attached in Form 15.

(2) If in a claim the party in whose favour the commission and diligence has been granted is not—

(a) a partnership or body corporate; or

(b) acting in a representative capacity, and is not represented by a solicitor, service under paragraph (1) must be effected by the sheriff clerk posting a copy of the order together with a certificate in Form 15 by first class recorded delivery post or, on payment of the fee prescribed by the Scottish Ministers by order, by sheriff officer.

(3) Documents recovered in response to an order under paragraph (1) must be sent to, and retained by, the sheriff clerk who shall, on receiving them, advise the parties that the documents are in his possession and may be examined within his office during normal business hours.

(4) If the party who served the order is not satisfied that—

(a) full production has been made under the specification; or

(b) that adequate reasons for non-production have been given, he may execute the commission and diligence in normal form, notwithstanding his adoption in the first instance of the procedure in paragraph (1) above.

(5) Documents recovered under this rule may be submitted as evidence at any hearing without further formality, and rule 17.3(3) and (4) shall apply to such documents.

Confidentiality of documents

17.3.—(1) In any claim where a party has obtained a commission and diligence to recover documents and the documents have been produced either—

(a) before the execution of the commission and diligence; or

(b) following execution of the commission and diligence, confidentiality may be claimed for any document produced.

(2) Where confidentiality is claimed under paragraph (1), the documents in respect of which confidentiality is claimed shall be enclosed in a separate, sealed packet.

(3) A sealed packet referred to in paragraph (2) shall not be opened except by authority of the sheriff obtained on the application of the party who sought the commission and diligence.

(4) Before the sheriff grants an application made in accordance with paragraph (3), he shall offer to hear the party or parties from whose possession the documents specified in the commission and diligence were obtained.

Witnesses

17.4.—(1) A party shall be responsible for securing the attendance of his witnesses or havers at a hearing and shall be personally liable for their expenses.

(2) The summons or the copy served on the defender shall be sufficient warrant for the citation of witnesses or havers.

(3) The citation of a witness or haver must be in Form 16 and the certificate of execution of citation must be in Form 16a.

(4) The period of notice given to witnesses or havers cited in terms of paragraph (3) must be not less than seven days.

(5) A witness or haver shall be cited—

(a) by registered post or the first class recorded delivery service by the solicitor for the party on whose behalf he is cited;

(b) by a sheriff officer—

(i) personally;

(ii) by a citation being left with a resident at the person's dwelling place or an employee at his place of business;

(iii) by depositing it in that person's dwelling place or place of business;

(iv) by affixing it to the door of that person's dwelling place or place of business; or

(v) by registered post or the first class recorded delivery service.

(6) Where service is effected under paragraph 5(b)(iii) or (iv), the sheriff officer shall, as soon as possible after such service, send by ordinary post to the address at which he thinks it most likely that the person may be found, a letter containing a copy of the citation.

Citation of witnesses by party litigants

17.5.—(1) Where a party to a claim is a party litigant he shall—

(a) not later than 28 days before any hearing on evidence apply to the sheriff to fix caution for expenses in such sum as the sheriff considers reasonable having regard to the number of witnesses he proposes to cite and the period for which they may be required to attend court; and

(b) before instructing a solicitor or a sheriff officer to cite a witness, find the sum fixed in accordance with paragraph (1)(a).

(2) A party litigant who does not intend to cite all the witnesses referred to in his application **D 670**
under paragraph (1)(a) may apply for variation of the amount of caution.

Witnesses failing to attend
   17.6.—(1) A hearing must not be adjourned solely on account of the failure of a witness to
appear unless the sheriff, on cause shown, so directs.
   (2) A witness or haver who fails without reasonable excuse to answer a citation after having
been properly cited and offered his travelling expenses if he has asked for them may be ordered
by the sheriff to pay a penalty not exceeding £250.
   (3) The sheriff may grant decree for payment of a penalty imposed under paragraph (2) above
in favour of the party on whose behalf the witness or haver was cited.
   (4) The sheriff may grant warrant for the apprehension of the witness or haver and for
bringing him to court.
   (5) A warrant mentioned in paragraph (4) shall be effective in any sheriffdom without
endorsation and the expenses of it may be awarded against the witness or haver.

CHAPTER 18

EUROPEAN COURT

Interpretation of rules 18.2 to 18.5
   18.1.—(1) In rules 18.2 to 18.5—
   "the European Court" means the Court of Justice of the European Communities;
   "reference" means a reference to the European Court for—
      (a) a preliminary ruling under Article 234 of the E.E.C. Treaty, Article 150 of the Euratom
           Treaty or Article 41 of the E.C.S.C. Treaty; or
      (b) a ruling on the interpretation of the Conventions, as defined in section 1(1) of the Civil
           Jurisdiction and Judgments Act 1982, under Article 3 of Schedule 2 to that Act.
   (2) The expressions "E.E.C. Treaty", "Euratom Treaty" and "E.C.S.C. Treaty" have the
meanings assigned respectively in Schedule 1 to the European Communities Act 1972.

Application for reference
   18.2.—(1) The sheriff may, on the incidental application of a party, or of his own accord,
make a reference.
   (2) A reference must be made in the form of a request for a preliminary ruling of the
European Court in Form 17.

Preparation of case for reference
   18.3.—(1) If the sheriff decides that a reference shall be made, he must within four weeks
draft a reference.
   (2) On the reference being drafted, the sheriff clerk must send a copy to each party.
   (3) Within four weeks after the date on which copies of the draft have been sent to parties,
each party may—
      (a) lodge with the sheriff clerk; and
      (b) send to every other party, a note of any adjustments he seeks to have made in the draft
           reference.
   (4) Within 14 days after the date on which any such note of adjustments may be lodged, the
sheriff, after considering any such adjustments, must make and sign the reference.
   (5) The sheriff clerk must forthwith intimate the making of the reference to each party.

Sist of claim
   18.4.—(1) Subject to paragraph (2), on a reference being made, the claim must, unless the
sheriff when making the reference otherwise orders, be sisted until the European Court has
given a preliminary ruling on the question referred to it.
   (2) The sheriff may recall a sist made under paragraph (1) for the purpose of making an
interim order which a due regard to the interests of the parties may require.

Transmission of reference
   18.5. A copy of the reference, certified by the sheriff clerk, must be transmitted by the sheriff
clerk to the Registrar of the European Court.

ABANDONMENT

Abandonment of claim

19.1.—(1) At any time prior to decree being granted, the pursuer may offer to abandon the claim.

(2) If the pursuer offers to abandon, the sheriff clerk must assess the expenses payable by the pursuer to the defender on such basis as the sheriff may direct subject to the provisions of section 36B of the 1971 Act and rule 21.6, and the claim must be continued to the first appropriate court occurring not sooner than 14 days thereafter.

(3) If before the continued diet the pursuer makes payment to the defender of the amount fixed under paragraph (2), the sheriff must dismiss the action unless the pursuer consents to absolvitor.

(4) If before the continued diet the pursuer fails to pay the amount fixed under paragraph (2), the defender shall be entitled to decree of absolvitor with expenses.

CHAPTER 20

DECREE BY DEFAULT

Decree by default

20.1.—(1) If, after the sheriff has fixed a hearing on evidence under rule 9.2(4), any party fails to appear or be represented at a hearing, the sheriff may grant decree by default.

(2) If all parties fail to appear or be represented at a hearing referred to at paragraph (1) the sheriff must, unless sufficient reason appears to the contrary, dismiss the claim and any counterclaim.

(3) If, after a defence has been stated, a party fails to implement an order of the court, the sheriff may, after giving him an opportunity to be heard, grant decree by default.

(4) The sheriff shall not grant decree by default solely on the ground that a party has failed to appear at the hearing of an incidental application.

CHAPTER 21

DECREES, EXTRACTS, EXECUTION AND VARIATION

Decree

21.1.—(1) The sheriff must not grant decree against—
  (a) a defender in respect of a claim; or
  (b) a pursuer in respect of a counterclaim,
under any provision of these Rules unless satisfied that a ground of jurisdiction exists.

Decree for alternative claim for payment

21.2.—(1) If the sheriff has granted decree for—
  (a) delivery;
  (b) recovery of possession of moveable property; or
  (c) implement of an obligation,
and the defender fails to comply with that decree, the pursuer may lodge with the sheriff clerk an incidental application for decree in terms of the alternative claim for payment.

(2) If the pursuer lodges an incidental application in terms of paragraph (1), he must intimate it to the defender at or before the time it is lodged with the sheriff clerk.

(3) The pursuer must appear at the hearing of an incidental application under paragraph (1).

Taxes on funds under control of the court

21.3. In a claim in which money has been consigned into court under the Sheriff Court Consignations (Scotland) Act 1893, no decree, warrant or order for payment to any person shall be granted until there has been lodged with the sheriff clerk a certificate by an authorised officer of the Inland Revenue stating that all taxes or duties payable to the Commissioners of Inland Revenue have been paid or satisfied.

Correction of interlocutor or note

21.4. At any time before extract, the sheriff may correct any clerical or incidental error in an interlocutor or note attached to it.

Extract of decree

21.5.—(1) Unless the sheriff on application authorises earlier extract, extract of a decree signed by the sheriff clerk may be issued only after the lapse of 14 days from the granting of the decree.

(2) An application for early extract shall be made by incidental application.

(3) In a claim where an appeal has been lodged, the extract may not be issued until the appeal has been disposed of.

(4) The extract decree—

    (a) may be written on the summons or on a separate paper;

    (b) may be in one of Forms 18 to 18i; and

    (c) shall be warrant for all lawful execution.

Expenses

21.6.—(1) This rule applies, subject to section 36B of the 1971 Act, to the determination of expenses—

    (a) in a claim, where the defender has—

        (i) not stated a defence;

        (ii) having stated a defence, has not proceeded with it; or

        (iii) having stated a defence, has not acted in good faith as to its merits; and

    (b) in an appeal to the sheriff principal.

(2) Subject to paragraphs (3) to (5), the sheriff clerk must, with the approval of the sheriff, assess the amount of expenses including the fees and outlays of witnesses awarded in any claim, in accordance with the statutory table of fees of solicitors appropriate to a summary cause.

(3) Paragraph (4) applies to a party who—

    (a) represents himself;

    (b) is represented by an authorised lay representative; or

    (c) is not an individual and—

        (i) is represented by an authorised lay representative; and

        (ii) if unrepresented could not represent itself.

(4) A party mentioned in paragraph (3) who, if he had been represented by a solicitor or advocate would have been entitled to expenses, may be awarded any outlays or expenses to which he might be found entitled by virtue of the 1975 Act or any enactment under that Act.

(5) In every case including an appeal where expenses are awarded, the sheriff clerk shall hear the parties or their solicitors on the claims for expenses including fees, if any, and outlays.

(6) Except where the sheriff principal or the sheriff has reserved judgment or where he orders otherwise, the hearing on the claim for expenses must take place immediately upon the decision being pronounced.

(7) When that hearing is not held immediately, the sheriff clerk must—

    (a) fix the date, time and place when he shall hear the parties or their solicitors; and

    (b) give all parties at least 14 days' notice in writing of the hearing so fixed.

(8) The party awarded expenses must—

    (a) lodge his account of expenses in court at least seven days prior to the date of any hearing fixed under paragraph (7); and

    (b) at the same time forward a copy of that account to every other party.

(9) The sheriff clerk must—

    (a) fix the amount of the expenses; and

    (b) report his decision to the sheriff principal or the sheriff in open court for his approval at a diet which the sheriff clerk has intimated to the parties.

(10) The sheriff principal or the sheriff, after hearing parties or their solicitors if objections are stated, must pronounce final decree including decree for payment of expenses as approved by him.

(11) In an appeal, the sheriff may pronounce decree under paragraph (10) on behalf of the sheriff principal.

(12) Failure by—

    (a) any party to comply with any of the foregoing provisions of this rule; or

    (b) the successful party or parties to appear at the hearing on expenses, must be reported by the sheriff clerk to the sheriff principal or the sheriff at a diet which the sheriff clerk has intimated to the parties.

(13) In either of the circumstances mentioned in paragraphs (12)(a) or (b), the sheriff principal or sheriff must, unless sufficient cause be shown, pronounce decree on the merits of the claim and find no expenses due to or by any party.

(14) A decree pronounced under paragraph (13) shall be held to be the final decree for the purposes of these Rules.

(15) The sheriff principal or sheriff may, if he thinks fit, on the application of the solicitor of

any party to whom expenses may be awarded, made at or before the time of the final decree being pronounced, grant decree in favour of that solicitor for the expenses of the claim.

D 673 *Charge*

21.7.—(1) The period for payment specified in any charge following on a decree for payment granted in a claim shall be—

    (a) 14 days if the person on whom it is served is within the United Kingdom; and

    (b) 28 days if he is outside the United Kingdom or his whereabouts are unknown.

(2) The period in respect of any other form of charge on a decree granted in a claim shall be 14 days.

Service of charge where address of defender is unknown

21.8.—(1) If the address of a defender is not known to the pursuer, a charge shall be deemed to have been served on the defender if it is—

    (a) served on the sheriff clerk of the sheriff court district where the defender's last known address is located; and

    (b) displayed by the sheriff clerk on the walls of court for the period of the charge.

(2) On receipt of such a charge, the sheriff clerk must display it on the walls of court and it must remain displayed for the period of the charge.

(3) The period specified in the charge shall run from the first date on which it was displayed on the walls of court.

(4) On the expiry of the period of charge, the sheriff clerk must endorse a certificate in Form 19 on the charge certifying that it has been displayed in accordance with this rule and must thereafter return the charge to the sheriff officer by whom service was executed.

Diligence on decree in claim for delivery

21.9.—(1) In a claim for delivery, the court may, when granting decree, grant warrant to search for and take possession of goods and to open shut and lockfast places.

(2) A warrant granted under paragraph (1) shall only apply to premises occupied by the defender.

Applications in same claim for variation, etc. of decree

21.10.—(1) If by virtue of any enactment the sheriff, without a new action being initiated, may order that—

    (a) a decree granted be varied, discharged or rescinded; or

    (b) the execution of that decree in so far as it has not already been executed be sisted or suspended, the party requesting the sheriff to make such an order must do so by lodging a minute to that effect, setting out briefly the reasons for the application.

(2) On the lodging of such a minute by the pursuer, the sheriff clerk must grant warrant for service upon the defender (provided that the pursuer has returned the extract decree).

(3) On the lodging of such a minute by the defender, the sheriff clerk must grant warrant for service upon the pursuer ordaining him to return the extract decree and may, where appropriate, grant interim sist of execution of the decree.

(4) Subject to paragraph (5), the minute shall not be heard in court unless seven days' notice of the minute and warrant has been given to the other parties by the party lodging the minute.

(5) The sheriff may, on cause shown, alter the period of seven days referred to in paragraph (4) but may not reduce it to less than two days.

(6) This rule shall not apply to any proceedings under the Debtors (Scotland) Act 1987 or to proceedings which may be subject to the provisions of that Act.

CHAPTER 22

RECALL OF DECREE

Recall of decree

22.1.—(1) A party may apply for recall of a decree granted under rule 8.1(3), rule 9.1(6), (7) or (8) or rule 11.1(8) by lodging with the sheriff clerk a minute in Form 20, explaining the party's failure to appear and in the case of—

    (a) a defender; or

    (b) where decree has been granted in respect of a counterclaim, a pursuer, stating, where he has not already done so—

        (i) his proposed defence, in the case of a defender; or

        (ii) his proposed answer, in the case of a pursuer responding to a counterclaim.

(2) A party may apply for recall of a decree in the same claim on one occasion only.

(3) Except in relation to an application to which paragraph (4) applies, a minute by a pursuer under paragraph (1) must be lodged within 14 days of the grant of the decree.

(4) A minute lodged by—
- (a) a pursuer in respect of a decree granted in terms of a counterclaim; or
- (b) a defender, shall be lodged—
  - (i) if the claim has been served outwith the United Kingdom under rule 6.5, within a reasonable time after he had knowledge of the decree against him or in any event before the expiry of one year from the date of that decree; or   **D 674**
  - (ii) in any other case, within 14 days of the execution of a charge or execution of arrestment, whichever first occurs, following on the grant of decree.

(5) On the lodging of a minute for recall of a decree, the sheriff clerk must fix a date, time and place for a hearing of the minute.

(6) If a hearing has been fixed under paragraph (5), the party seeking recall must serve upon the other party not less than seven days before the date fixed for the hearing—
- (a) a copy of the minute in Form 20a; and
- (b) a note of the date, time and place of the hearing.

(7) If the party seeking recall—
- (a) is not a partnership or body corporate;
- (b) is not acting in a representative capacity; and
- (c) is not represented by a solicitor,

the sheriff clerk must assist that party to complete and lodge the minute for recall and must arrange service of it—
  - (i) by first class recorded delivery post; or
  - (ii) on payment of the fee prescribed by the Scottish Ministers by order, by sheriff officer.

(8) At a hearing fixed under paragraph (5), the sheriff shall recall the decree so far as not implemented and the hearing shall then proceed as the Hearing held in terms of rule 9.1(2).

(9) A minute for recall of a decree, when lodged and served in terms of this rule, shall have the effect of preventing any further action being taken by the other party to enforce the decree.

(10) On receipt of the copy minute for recall of a decree, any party in possession of an extract decree must return it forthwith to the sheriff clerk.

(11) If it appears to the sheriff that there has been any failure or irregularity in service of the minute for recall of a decree, he may order re-service of the minute on such conditions as he thinks fit.

CHAPTER 23

APPEALS

Appeals
23.1.—(1) An appeal to the sheriff principal, other than an appeal to which rule 23.4 applies, must be by note of appeal in Form 21 and lodged with the sheriff clerk not later than 14 days after the date of final decree—
- (a) requesting a stated case; and
- (b) specifying the point of law upon which the appeal is to proceed.

(2) The appellant must, at the same time as lodging a note of appeal, intimate a copy of it to every other party.

(3) The sheriff must, within 28 days of the lodging of a note of appeal, issue a draft stated case containing—
- (a) findings in fact and law or, where appropriate, a narrative of the proceedings before him;
- (b) appropriate questions of law; and
- (c) a note stating the reasons for his decisions in law, and the sheriff clerk must send a copy of the draft stated case to the parties.

(4) Within 14 days of the issue of the draft stated case—
- (a) a party may lodge with the sheriff clerk a note of any adjustments which he seeks to make;
- (b) a respondent may state any point of law which he wishes to raise in the appeal; and
- (c) the note of adjustment and, where appropriate, point of law must be intimated to every other party.

(5) The sheriff may, on the motion of a party or of his own accord, and must where he proposes to reject any proposed adjustment, allow a hearing on adjustments and may provide for such further procedure under this rule prior to the hearing of the appeal as he thinks fit.

(6) The sheriff must, within 14 days after—
- (a) the latest date on which a note of adjustments has been or may be lodged; or

(b) where there has been a hearing on adjustments, that hearing, and after considering such note and any representations made to him at the hearing, state and sign the case.

(7) If the sheriff is temporarily absent from duty for any reason, the sheriff principal may extend any period specified in paragraphs (3) or (6) for such period or periods as he considers reasonable.

D 675 (8) The stated case signed by the sheriff must include questions of law, framed by him, arising from the points of law stated by the parties and such other questions of law as he may consider appropriate.

(9) After the sheriff has signed the stated case, the sheriff clerk must—
  (a) place before the sheriff principal all documents and productions in the case together with the stated case; and
  (b) send to the parties a copy of the stated case together with a written note of the date, time and place of the hearing of the appeal.

Effect of and abandonment of appeal
23.2.—(1) When a note of appeal has been lodged, it may be insisted on by all other parties in the claim although they may not have lodged separate appeals.

(2) After a note of appeal has been lodged, the appellant shall not be at liberty to withdraw it, except—
  (a) with the consent of the other parties which may be incorporated in a joint minute; or
  (b) by leave of the sheriff principal and on such terms as to expenses or otherwise at to him seem proper.

Hearing of appeal
23.3.—(1) The sheriff principal shall hear the parties or their solicitors orally on all matters connected with the appeal including liability for expenses, but if any party moves that the question of liability for expenses be heard after the sheriff principal has given his decision the sheriff principal may grant that motion.

(2) In the hearing of an appeal, a party shall not be allowed to raise questions of law of which notice has not been given except on cause shown and subject to such conditions as to expenses or otherwise as the sheriff principal may consider appropriate.

(3) The sheriff principal may permit a party to amend any question of law or to add any new question in accordance with paragraph (2).

(4) The sheriff principal may—
  (a) adhere to or vary the decree appealed against;
  (b) recall the decree appealed against and substitute another therefor; or
  (c) remit, if he considers it desirable, to the sheriff, for any reason other than to have further evidence led.

(5) At the conclusion of the hearing, the sheriff principal may either pronounce his decision or reserve judgment in which case he must give his decision in writing within 28 days and the sheriff clerk must forthwith intimate it to the parties.

Appeal in relation to a time to pay direction
23.4.—(1) This rule applies to appeals to the sheriff principal or to the Court of Session which relate solely to any application in connection with a time to pay direction.

(2) Rules 23.1, 23.2 and 23.3(2) and (3) shall not apply to appeals under this rule.

(3) An application for leave to appeal against a decision in an application for a time to pay direction or any order connected therewith must—
  (a) be made in Form 22, within seven days of that decision, to the sheriff who made the decision; and
  (b) must specify the question of law upon which the appeal is to proceed.

(4) If leave to appeal is granted, the appeal must be lodged in Form 23 and intimated by the appellant to every other party within 14 days of the order granting leave and the sheriff must state in writing his reasons for his original decision.

(5) An appeal under this rule to the sheriff principal shall proceed in accordance with paragraphs (1), (4) and (5) of rule 23.3.

Sheriff to regulate interim possession
23.5.—(1) Notwithstanding an appeal, the sheriff shall have power—
  (a) to regulate all matters relating to interim possession;
  (b) to make any order for the preservation of any property to which the claim relates or for its sale, if perishable;
  (c) to make any order for the preservation of evidence; or
  (d) to make in his discretion any interim order which a due regard for the interests of the parties may require.

(2) An order under paragraph (1) shall not be subject to review except by the appellate court at the hearing of the appeal.

Chapter 24

D 676

Management of damages payable to persons under legal disability

Orders for payment and management of money
    24.1.—(1) In a claim of damages in which a sum of money becomes payable, by virtue of a decree or an extra-judicial settlement, to or for the benefit of a person under legal disability (other than a person under the age of 18 years), the sheriff shall make such order regarding the payment and management of that sum for the benefit of that person as he thinks fit.
    (2) Any order required under paragraph (1) shall be made on the granting of decree for payment or of absolvitor.

Methods of management
    24.2. In making an order under rule 24.1 (1), the sheriff may—
        (a) order the money to be paid to—
            (i) the Accountant of Court, or
            (ii) the guardian of the person under legal disability, as trustee, to be applied, invested or otherwise dealt with and administered under the directions of the sheriff for the benefit of the person under legal disability;
        (b) order the money to be paid to the sheriff clerk of the sheriff court district in which the person under legal disability resides, to be applied, invested or otherwise dealt with and administered, under the directions of the sheriff of that district, for the benefit of the person under legal disability; or
        (c) order the money to be paid directly to the person under legal disability.

Subsequent orders
    24.3.—(1) If the sheriff has made an order under rule 24.1(1), any person having an interest may apply for an order under rule 24.2, or any other order for the payment or management of the money, by incidental application.
    (2) An application for directions under rule 24.2(a) or (b) may be made by any person having an interest by incidental application.

Management of money paid to sheriff clerk
    24.4.—(1) A receipt in Form 24 by the sheriff clerk shall be a sufficient discharge in respect of the amount paid to him under rules 24.1 to 24.3.
    (2) The sheriff clerk shall, at the request of any competent court, accept custody of any sum of money in an claim of damages ordered to be paid to, applied, invested or otherwise dealt with by him, for the benefit of a person under legal disability.
    (3) Any money paid to the sheriff clerk under rules 24.1 to 24.3 must be paid out, applied, invested or otherwise dealt with by the sheriff clerk only after such intimation, service and enquiry as the sheriff may order.
    (4) Any sum of money invested by the sheriff clerk under rules 24.1 to 24.3 must be invested in a manner in which trustees are authorised to invest by virtue of the Trustee Investments Act 1961.

Management of money payable to children
    24.5. If the sheriff has made an order under section 13 of the Children (Scotland) Act 1995, an application by a person for an order by virtue of section 11(1)(d) of that Act must be made in writing.

Chapter 25

Electronic transmission of documents

Extent of provision
    25.1.—(1) Any document referred to in these rules which requires to be—
        (a) lodged with the sheriff clerk;
        (b) intimated to a party; or
        (c) sent by the sheriff clerk, may be in electronic or documentary form, and if in electronic form may be lodged, intimated or sent by e-mail or similar means.

(2) Paragraph (1) does not apply to any certificate of execution of service, citation or arrestment, or to a decree or extract decree of the court.

(3) Where any document is lodged by e-mail or similar means the sheriff may require any principal document to be lodged.

D 677 *Time of lodgement*
25.2. The time of lodgement, intimation or sending shall be the time when the document was sent or transmitted.

D 678
Rule 1.1(4)

APPENDIX 1

FORMS
Rule 4.1(1)

FORM 1

Summons

FORM 1

	OFFICIAL USE ONLY SUMMONS No.

Small Claim Summons
Action for/of
(state type, e.g., payment of money)

Sheriff Court (name, address, e-mail and telephone no.)	**1**	
Name and address of person making the claim (**pursuer**)	**2**	
Name and address of person against whom claim made (**defender**)	**3**	
Claim (form of decree or other order sought)	**4**	
Name, full address, telephone no, and e-mail address of pursuer's solicitor or authorised lay representative (if any) acting in the claim	**5**	
Fee Details (Enter these only if forms sent electronically to court)	**5a**	

6	RETURN DAY	20		
	HEARING DATE	20	at	am.

*Sheriff Clerk to

delete as appropriate

The pursuer is authorised to serve a copy summons in Form *1a/1b, on the defender(s) not less than *21/42 days before the **RETURN DAY** shown in the box above. The summons is warrant for service, *arrestment on the dependence and for citation of witnesses to attend court on any future date at which evidence may be led.

Court Authentication

NOTE: The pursuer should complete boxes 1 to 5a, and the statement of claim on page 2. The sheriff clerk will complete box 6.

---

7.   STATE DETAILS OF CLAIM HERE OR ATTACH A STATEMENT OF CLAIM
(To be completed by the pursuer. If space is insufficient, a separate sheet may be attached)

The details of the claim are:

FOR OFFICIAL USE ONLY

Sheriff's notes as to:

1. Issues of fact and law in dispute
2. Facts agreed
3. Directions and guidance upon evidence to be led

FORM 1a

Defender's copy summons – claim for or including claim for payment of money where time to pay direction or time order may be applied for

FORM 1a

Small Claim Summons
Action for/of
(state type, e.g., payment of money)

| OFFICIAL USE ONLY |
| SUMMONS No. |

DEFENDER'S COPY: Claim for or including payment of money (where time to pay direction or time order may be applied for)

Sheriff Court (name, address, e-mail and telephone no.)	**1**	
Name and address of person making the claim (**pursuer**)	**2**	
Name and address of person against whom claim made (**defender**)	**3**	
Claim (form of decree or other order sought – *complete as in section 4 of Form 1*)	**4**	
Name, full address, telephone no, and e-mail address of pursuer's solicitor or authorised lay representative (if any) acting in the claim	**5**	

6	RETURN DAY	20		
	HEARING DATE	20	at	am.

NOTE: You will find details of claim on page 2.

7. **STATE DETAILS OF CLAIM HERE OR ATTACH A STATEMENT OF CLAIM**
    (To be completed by the pursuer. If space is insufficient, a separate sheet may be attached)

    The details of the claim are:

8. **SERVICE ON DEFENDER**

    (Place)   (Date)

    To: (defender)

    You are hereby served with a copy of the above summons.

                         Solicitor / sheriff officer
                         delete as appropriate

NOTE: The pursuer should complete boxes 1 to 6 on page 1, the statement of claim in box 7 on page 2 and section A on page 5 before service on the defender. The person serving the summons will complete box 8.

WHAT MUST I DO ABOUT THIS SUMMONS?

Decide whether you wish to dispute the claim and/or whether you owe any money or not, and how you wish to proceed. Then, look at the 4 options listed below. Find the one which covers your decision and follow the instructions given there. You will find the RETURN DAY and the HEARING DATE on page one of the summons.

Written guidance on small claims procedure can be obtained from the sheriff clerk at any sheriff clerk's office. Further advice can also be obtained by contacting any of the following:

> **Citizen's Advice Bureau, Consumer Advice Centre, Trading Standards or Consumer Protection Department or a Solicitor. (Addresses can be found in the guidance booklets.)**

OPTIONS

1.   **ADMIT LIABILITY FOR THE CLAIM and settle it with the pursuer now.**

If you wish to avoid the possibility of a court order passing against you, you should settle the claim (including any question of expenses) with pursuer or his representative **in good time before the return day.** Please do not send any payment direct to the court. Any payment should be made to the pursuer or his representative.

2.   **ADMIT LIABILITY FOR THE CLAIM and make a <u>written</u> application to pay by instalments or by <u>deferred</u> lump sum.**

Complete box 1 of section B on page 5 of this form and return pages 5 and 6 to the court **to arrive on or before the return day.** You should then contact the court to find out whether or not the pursuer has accepted your offer. If he has not accepted it, the case will then call on the hearing date and the court will decide how the amount claimed is to be paid.

If the claim is for delivery, or implement of an obligation, and you wish to pay the alternative amount claimed, you may also wish to make an application about the method of payment. If so, follow the instructions in the previous paragraph.

NOTE: If you fail to return pages 5 and 6 as directed, or if, having returned them, you fail to attend or are not represented at the hearing date if the case is to call, the court will almost certainly decide the claim in your absence.

3.   **ADMIT LIABILITY FOR THE CLAIM and <u>attend at court</u> to make application to pay by instalments or deferred lump sum.**

Complete box 2 on page 5. Return page 5 to the court so that it arrives **on or before the return day**.

If the claim is for delivery, or implement of an obligation, you may wish to pay the alternative amount claimed, and attend at court to make an application about the method of payment.

You must attend personally, or be represented, at court on the hearing date. Your representative may be a solicitor, or someone else having your authority. It may be helpful if you or your representative bring pages 1 and 2 of this form to the court.

NOTE: If you fail to return page 5 as directed, or if, having returned it, you fail to attend or are not represented on the hearing date, the court will almost certainly decide the claim in your absence.

4.   **DISPUTE THE CLAIM and <u>attend at court</u> to do any of the following:**

- Challenge the jurisdiction of the court
- State a defence
- State a counterclaim
- Dispute the amount of the claim

Complete box 3 on page 5. Return page 5 to the court so that it arrives **on or before the return day. You must attend personally, or be represented, at court on the hearing date.**

Your representative may be a solicitor, or someone else having your authority. It may be helpful if you or your representative bring pages 1 and 2 of this form to the court.

NOTE: If you fail to return page 5 as directed, or if, having returned it, you fail to attend or are not represented on the hearing date, the court will almost certainly decide the claim in your absence.

WRITTEN NOTE OF PROPOSED COUNTERCLAIM

You may send to the court a written note of any counterclaim. If you do, you should also send a copy to the pursuer. You must also attend or be represented at court on the hearing date.

PLEASE NOTE

If you do nothing about this summons, the court will almost certainly, where appropriate, grant decree against you and order you to pay to the pursuer the sum claimed, including any interest and expenses found due.

If the summons is for delivery, or implement of an obligation, the court may order you to deliver the article or perform the duty in question within a specified period. If you fail to do so, the court may order you to pay to the pursuer the alternative amount claimed, including interest and expenses.

YOU ARE ADVISED TO KEEP PAGES 1 AND 2, AS THEY MAY BE USEFUL AT A LATER STAGE OF THE CASE.

SECTION A		Summons No
This section must be completed before service		Return Day
		Hearing Date

SHERIFF COURT (Including address)

PURSUER'S FULL NAME AND ADDRESS

DEFENDER'S FULL NAME AND ADDRESS

SECTION B

DEFENDER'S RESPONSE TO THE SUMMONS
** Delete whichever boxes do <u>not</u> apply

**Box 1

ADMIT LIABILITY FOR THE CLAIM and make <u>written</u> application to pay by instalments or by <u>deferred</u> lump sum.

I do not intend to defend the case but admit liability for the claim and wish to pay the sum of money claimed.

I wish to make a written application about payment.

I have completed the application form on page 6.

**Box 2

ADMIT LIABILITY FOR THE CLAIM and attend at court.

I admit liability for the claim.

I wish to make application to pay the sum claimed by instalments or by deferred lump sum.

I intend to appear or be represented at court.

**Box 3

DISPUTE THE CLAIM (or the amount due) and attend at court
* I wish to dispute the amount due only.
* I intend to challenge the jurisdiction of the court.
* I intend to state a defence.
* I intend to state a counterclaim.

I intend to appear or be represented in court.

* I attach a note of my proposed counterclaim which has been copied to the pursuer.

* delete as necessary

NOTE: Please remember to send your response to the court to arrive on or before the return day if you have completed any of the responses above.

APPLICATION IN WRITING FOR A TIME TO PAY DIRECTION
OR A TIME ORDER

I WISH TO APPLY FOR A *TIME TO PAY DIRECTION/TIME ORDER
* delete whichever does not apply

I admit the claim and make application to pay as follows:

    (1)   by instalments of £ _____ per *week / fortnight / month

          OR

    (2)   In one payment within _____ *weeks / months from the date of
          the court order

To help the court, please provide details of your financial position in the boxes below
*Please also indicate whether payments/receipts are weekly, fortnightly or monthly

My outgoings are:	*Weekly / fortnightly / monthly	My income is:	*Weekly / fortnightly / monthly
Rent/Mortgage £		Wages/Pensions £	
Council tax £		Social Security £	
Gas/electricity etc £		Other	
Food £			
Loans and credit agreements £			
Other			
TOTAL		**TOTAL**	

Number of dependent children – [   ]   Number of dependent relatives [   ]

Please list details of all capital held. eg. value of house; amount in savings account, shares or other investments:

---

*APPLICATION FOR RECALL OR RESTRICTION OF AN ARRESTMENT

I seek the recall or restriction of the arrestment of which the details are as follows:-

Date:
*Delete if inapplicable

NOTES: APPLICATION FOR A TIME TO PAY DIRECTION OR TIME ORDER

(1) Time to pay directions

The Debtors (Scotland) Act 1987 gives you the right to apply to the court for a 'time to pay direction'. This is an order which allows you to pay any sum which the court orders you to pay either in instalments or by deferred lump sum. A 'deferred lump sum' means that you will be ordered by the court to pay the whole amount at one time within a period which the court will specify.

If the court makes a time to pay direction it may also recall or restrict any arrestment made on your property by the pursuer in connection with the action or debt (for example, your bank account may have been frozen).

No court fee is payable when making an application for a time to pay direction.

If a time to pay direction is made, a copy of the court order (called an extract decree) will be sent to you by the pursuer telling you when payment should start or when it is you have to pay the lump sum.

If a time to pay direction is not made, and an order for immediate payment is made against you, an order to pay (called a charge) may be served on you if you do not pay.

(2) Time Orders

The Consumer Credit Act 1974 allows you to apply to the court for a 'time order' during a court action. A time order is similar to a time to pay direction, but can only be applied for in certain circumstances, e.g., in relation to certain types of credit agreement. Payment under a time order can only be made by instalments, so that you cannot apply to pay by deferred lump sum.

FORM 1b

Defender's copy summons – all other claims

FORM 1b

OFFICIAL USE ONLY
SUMMONS No.

Small Claim Summons
Action for/of
(state type, e.g., payment of money)

DEFENDER'S COPY: (Claim other than claim for or including payment of money where time to pay direction or time order may be applied for)

Sheriff Court (name, address, e-mail and telephone no.)	**1**	
Name and address of person making the claim (**pursuer**)	**2**	
Name and address of person against whom claim made (**defender**)	**3**	
Claim (Form of decree or other order sought - *complete as in section 4 of Form 1*)	**4**	
Name, full address, telephone no, and e-mail address of pursuer's solicitor or authorised lay representative (if any)	**5**	

6	RETURN DAY	20		
	HEARING DATE	20	at	am.

NOTE: You will find details of claim on page 2.

7.   **STATE DETAILS OF CLAIM HERE OR ATTACH A STATEMENT OF CLAIM**
        (To be completed by the pursuer. If space is insufficient, a separate sheet may be attached)

        The details of the claim are:

8.   **SERVICE ON DEFENDER**

                (Place)   (Date)

                To: (defender)

                You are hereby served with a copy of the above summons.

                                                        Solicitor / sheriff officer
                                                        delete as appropriate

The pursuer should complete boxes 1 to 6 on page 1, the statement of claim in box 7 on page 2 and section A
on page 4 before service on the defender. The person serving the summons will complete box 8.

WHAT MUST I DO ABOUT THIS SUMMONS?

Decide whether you wish to dispute the claim and/or whether you owe any money or not, and how you wish to proceed. Then, look at the 2 options listed below. Find the one which covers your decision and follow the instructions given there. You will find the RETURN DAY and the HEARING DATE on page one of the summons.

Written guidance on small claims procedure can be obtained from the sheriff clerk at any Sheriff Clerk's office.

Further advice can also be obtained by contacting any of the following:

Citizen's Advice Bureau, Consumer Advice Centre, Trading Standards or Consumer Protection Department or a solicitor. (Addresses can be found in the guidance booklets).

OPTIONS

1. **ADMIT LIABILITY FOR THE CLAIM and settle it with the pursuer now.**

   If you wish to avoid the possibility of a court order passing against you, you should settle the claim (including any question of expenses) with pursuer or his representative **in good time before the return day**. Please do not send any payment direct to the court. Any payment should be made to the pursuer or his representative.

2. **DISPUTE THE CLAIM and <u>attend at court</u> to do any of the following:**

   - Challenge the jurisdiction of the court
   - State a defence
   - State a counterclaim
   - Dispute the amount of the claim

   Complete Section B on page 4. Return page 4 to the court so that it arrives **on or before the return day. You must attend personally, or be represented, at court on the hearing date.**

   Your representative may be a solicitor, or someone else having your authority. It may be helpful if you or your representative bring pages 1 and 2 of this form to the court.

   NOTE: If you fail to return page 4 as directed, or if, having returned it, you fail to attend or are not represented at the hearing date, the court will almost certainly decide the claim in your absence.

WRITTEN NOTE OF PROPOSED COUNTERCLAIM

You may send to the court a written note of any counterclaim. If you do, you should also send a copy to the pursuer. You must also attend or be represented at court on the hearing date.

PLEASE NOTE

If you do nothing about this summons, the court will almost certainly, where appropriate, grant decree against you and order you to pay to the pursuer the sum claimed, including any interest and expenses found due.

If the summons is for delivery, or implement of an obligation, the court may order you to deliver the article or perform the duty in question within a specified period. If you fail to do so, the court may order you to pay to the pursuer the alternative amount claimed, including interest and expenses.

YOU ARE ADVISED TO KEEP PAGES 1 AND 2, AS THEY MAY BE USEFUL AT A LATER STAGE OF THE CASE.

D 690

SECTION A This section must be completed before service		Summons No Return Day Hearing Date
	SHERIFF COURT (Including address)	
	PURSUER'S FULL NAME AND ADDRESS	DEFENDER'S FULL NAME AND ADDRESS

SECTION B   **DEFENDER'S RESPONSE TO THE SUMMONS**

> **DISPUTE THE CLAIM (or the amount due) and attend at court**
> * I wish to dispute the amount due only.
> * I intend to challenge the jurisdiction of the court.
> * I intend to state a defence.
> * I intend to state a counterclaim.
>
> I intend to appear or be represented in court.
>
> * I attach a note of my proposed counterclaim which has been copied to the pursuer.
>
> ** delete as necessary*

PLEASE REMEMBER: You must send this page to the court **to arrive on or before the return day** if you have completed Section B above.

If you have admitted the claim, please do not send any payment direct to the court. Any payment should be made to the pursuer or his solicitor.

Rule 4.1(2)   FORM 2

FORM OF CLAIM IN A SUMMONS FOR PAYMENT OF MONEY

The pursuer claims from the defender(s) the sum of £   with interest on that sum at the rate of   % annually from the date of service, together with the expenses of bringing the claim.

Rule 4.1(2)   FORM 3

FORM OF CLAIM IN A SUMMONS FOR DELIVERY

The pursuer claims that, in the circumstances described in the statement contained on page 2 of this copy summons, he has right to the possession of the article(s) described therein.

He therefore asks the court to grant a decree ordering you to deliver the said articles to the pursuer.

Alternatively, if you do not deliver said articles, the pursuer asks the court to grant a decree ordering you to pay to him the sum of £   with interest on that sum at the rate of   % annually from   until payment.

The pursuer also claims from you the expenses of bringing the claim.

Rule 4.1(2)   FORM 4

FORM OF CLAIM IN A SUMMONS FOR IMPLEMENT OF AN OBLIGATION

The pursuer claims that, in the circumstances described in the statement contained on page 2 of the summons, you are obliged to

He therefore asks the court to grant a decree ordering you to implement the said obligation.

Alternatively, if you do not fulfil the obligation, the pursuer asks the court to grant a decree ordering you to pay to him the sum of £   with interest on that sum at the rate of   % annually from   until payment.

The pursuer also claims from you the expenses of bringing the claim.

Rule 6.2(1)   FORM 5

FORM OF SERVICE

XY, you are hereby served with a copy of the above (or attached) summons.

                              (*signature of solicitor or sheriff officer*)

Rule 6.2(2)   FORM 6

FORM OF CERTIFICATE OF EXECUTION OF SERVICE

(*place and date*)

I,   , hereby certify that on the   day of   20 ,I duly cited XY to answer the foregoing summons. This I did by (*set forth the mode of service*)

                              (*signature of solicitor or sheriff officer*)

Rule 6.3(2)   FORM 7

POSTAL SERVICE—FORM OF NOTICE

This letter contains a citation to or intimation from the sheriff court at

If delivery cannot be made the letter must be returned immediately to the sheriff clerk at (*insert full address*).

Rule 6.6(1)(a) FORM 8

SERVICE ON PERSON WHOSE ADDRESS IS UNKNOWN

FORM OF ADVERTISEMENT

A small claim has been raised in the sheriff court at   , by AB., pursuer, against CD, defender, whose last known address was   .

If the said CD wishes to defend the claim he should immediately contact the sheriff clerk's office at the above court, from whom the defender's copy summons may be obtained.

    Address of court:
    Telephone no:
    Fax no:
    E mail address:

Rule 6.6(1)(b) FORM 9

SERVICE ON PERSON WHOSE ADDRESS IS UNKNOWN

FORM OF NOTICE TO BE DISPLAYED ON THE WALLS OF COURT

A small claim has been raised in this court by AB, pursuer against CD, defender, whose last known address was   .

If the said CD wishes to defend the claim he should immediately contact the sheriff clerk's office, from whom the defender's copy summons may be obtained.

(*date*)Displayed on the walls of court of this date.

Sheriff clerk depute

Rule 7.3(4)(a) FORM 10

RECALL OR RESTRICTION OF ARRESTMENT CERTIFICATE AUTHORISING THE RELEASE OF ARRESTED FUNDS OR PROPERTY

Sheriff court at (*place*)

Court ref. no.:

AB (pursuer) against CD (defender)

I, (*name*), hereby certify that the sheriff on (*date*) authorised the release of the funds or property arrested on the *dependence of the action / counterclaim to the following extent:

(*details of sheriff's order*)

(*date*) Sheriff clerk depute

delete as appropriate

Copy to:
    Party instructing arrestment
    Party possessing arrested funds/property

Rule 8.1(2) FORM 11

FORM OF MINUTE—NO FORM OF RESPONSE LODGED BY DEFENDER

Sheriff court at (*place*)

Hearing date:

In respect that the defender(s) has/have failed to lodge a form of response to the summons, the pursuer requests the court to make the orders specified in the following case(s):

Court ref. no.:   Name(s) of defender(s)   Minute(s)

Rule 8.2(2)   [1] FORM 12   **D 693**

<small>FORM OF MINUTE—PURSUER NOT OBJECTING TO APPLICATION FOR A TIME TO PAY DIRECTION OR TIME ORDER</small>

Sheriff court at (*place*)

Court ref. no.:

Name(s) of defender(s)

Hearing date:

I do not object to the defender's application for

    *a time to pay direction
    *recall or restriction of an arrestment
    *a time order

The pursuer requests the court to grant decree or other order in terms of the following minute(s)

*delete as appropriate

NOTE
[1] As amended by the Act of Sederunt (Ordinary Cause, Summary Application, Summary Cause and Small Claim Rules) Amendment (Miscellaneous) 2003 (SSI 2003/26), para.5(2)(b) (effective January 24, 2003).

Rule 8.2(4)   FORM 13

<small>FORM OF MINUTE—PURSUER OPPOSING AN APPLICATION FOR A TIME TO PAY DIRECTION OR TIME ORDER</small>

Sheriff court at (*place*)

Court ref. no.:

Name(s) of defender(s)

Hearing date:

I oppose the defender's application for

    *a time to pay direction
    *recall or restriction of an arrestment
    *a time order

*delete as appropriate

Rule 11.1(8)   FORM 14

<small>COUNTERCLAIM—FORM OF INTIMATION BY SHERIFF CLERK WHERE PURSUER FAILS TO APPEAR</small>

Court ref. no.:

(AB) (insert address), pursuer

against

(CD) (insert address), defender

When the above case called in court on (*insert date*), the defender appeared (or was represented) and stated a counterclaim to the claim made by you against him.

The court continued the case until (*date*) at (*time*).

Please note that, if you fail to appear or be represented at the continued diet, the court may grant decree against you in terms of the counterclaim.

(*date*)   Sheriff clerk depute

Rule 17.2(1)   FORM 15

ORDER BY THE COURT AND CERTIFICATE IN OPTIONAL PROCEDURE FOR RECOVERY OF DOCUMENTS

Sheriff court at (*place*)

In the claim (*court ref. no.*)

in which

AB (*design*) is the pursuer

and

C.D. (*design*) is the defender

To: (*name and designation of party or haver from whom the documents are sought to be recovered*).

You are hereby required to produce to the sheriff clerk at (address) within days of the service upon you of this order:

1. This order itself (which must be produced intact);

2. The certificate marked 'B' attached;

3. All documents within your possession covered by the specification which is enclosed; and

4. A list of those documents.

You can produce the items listed above either:

(a) by delivering them to the sheriff clerk at the address shown above; or

(b) sending them to the sheriff clerk by registered or recorded delivery post.

(date)   (*signature, name, address and designation of person serving order*)

PLEASE NOTE:

If you claim confidentiality for any of the documents produced by you, you must still produce them. However, they may be placed in a separate envelope by themselves, marked 'confidential' The court will, if necessary, decide whether the envelope should be opened or not.

CERTIFICATE

Sheriff Court at (*place*)

In the claim (*court ref. no.*)

in which

AB (*design*) is the pursuer

and

CD (*design*) is the defender

Order for recovery of documents dated (*insert date*).

With reference to the above order and relative specification of documents, I hereby certify:

*that the documents produced herewith and the list signed by me which accompanies them are all the documents in my possession which fall under the specification.

*I have no documents in my possession falling under the specification.

*I believe that there are other documents falling within the specification which are not in my possession. These documents are (list the documents as described in the specification.) These documents were last seen by me on (date) in the possession of (name and address of person/ company, if known).

*I know of no documents falling within the specification which are in the possession of any other person.

delete as appropriate

(*name*)   (*date*)

Rule 17.4(3)   FORM 16

FORM OF WITNESS CITATION

Sheriffdom of (*insert name of sheriffdom*)

at (*insert place of sheriff court*)

to AB (*design*)

You are required to attend at (*full name and address of court*) on (*day*), (*date*) at (*time*) as a   **D 695**
witness for the (*party*) in the action at the instance of CD (*design*) against EF (*design*) (*and
required to bring with you*   ).

If you fail to attend, warrant may be granted for your arrest.

(*date*)   (*signature of solicitor or sheriff officer*)

> Name of person/firm serving citation
> Address
> Telephone no.
> Fax no.
> E mail address

NOTE: Within certain specified limits claims for necessary outlays and loss of earnings incurred
by your attendance at court as a witness will be met. Claims should be made to the person who
has cited you to attend court. Proof of any expenses incurred may be requested and should be
given to that person.

If you wish your travelling expenses to be paid prior to your attendance, you should apply for
payment to the person who has cited you.

**If you fail to attend without reasonable cause, having requested and been paid your travelling
expenses, you may be ordered to pay a penalty not exceeding £250.**

Rule 17.4(3)   FORM 16A

FORM OF CERTIFICATE OF EXECUTION OF WITNESS CITATION

I certify that on (*date*) I duly cited AB (*design*) to attend at (*name of court*) on (*date*) at (*time*) as
a witness for the (*design party*) in the action at the instance of CD (*design*) against EF (*design*)
(*and I required him to bring with him*   ). This I did by

                                    (*signature of solicitor or sheriff officer*)

Rule 18.2(2)   FORM 17

FORM OF REFERENCE TO THE EUROPEAN COURT

REQUEST

for

PRELIMINARY RULING

of

THE COURT OF JUSTICE OR THE EUROPEAN COMMUNITIES

from

THE SHERIFFDOM OF (*insert name of sheriffdom*) at (*insert place of court*)

in the cause

AB (*insert designation and address*), pursuer

against

CD (*insert designation and address*), defender

(*Here set out a clear and succinct statement of the case giving rise to the request for a ruling of the
European Court in order to enable the European Court to consider and understand the issues of
Community law raised and to enable governments of Member states and other interested parties to
submit observations. The statement of the case should include:*

(*a*) particulars of the parties;
(*b*) the history of the dispute between the parties;
(*c*) the history of the proceedings;

D 696 (*d*) the relevant facts as agreed by the parties or found by the court or, failing such agreement or finding, the contentions of the parties on such facts;
(*e*) the nature of the issues of law and fact between the parties;
(*f*) the Scots law, so far as relevant;
(*g*) the Treaty provisions or other acts, instruments or rules of Community law concerned;
(*h*) an explanation of why the reference is being made).

The preliminary ruling of the Court of Justice of the European Communities is accordingly requested on the following questions:

1,2, etc. (*Here set out the question(s) on which the ruling is sought, identifying the Treaty provisions or other acts, instruments or rules of Community law concerned.*)

Dated the   day of   20

Rule 21.5(4)(b)   FORM 18

FORM OF EXTRACT DECREE (BASIC)

Sheriff court   Court ref. no.:

Date of decree   *in absence

Pursuer(s)   Defender(s)

The sheriff

and granted decree against the   for payment of expenses of
£   against the (name of party).

This extract is warrant for all lawful execution thereon.

Date   Sheriff clerk depute

delete as appropriate

Rule 21.5(4)(b)   FORM 18A

FORM OF EXTRACT DECREE FOR PAYMENT

Sheriff court   Court ref. no.

Date of decree   *in absence

Pursuer(s)   Defender(s)

The sheriff granted decree against the   for payment to
the   of the undernoted sums:

(1) Sum(s) decerned for: £

(2) Interest at per cent per year from (*date*) until payment.

(3) Expenses of £   against the (*name of party*).

*A time to pay direction was made under section 1(1) of the Debtors (Scotland) Act 1987.

*A time order was made under section 129 (1) of the Consumer Credit Act 1974.

*The amount is payable by instalments of £   per   commencing

within   *days/weeks/months of intimation of this extract decree.

*The amount is payable by lump sum within   *days/weeks/months of intimation of this extract decree.

This extract is warrant for all lawful execution thereon.

Date   Sheriff clerk depute

delete as appropriate

Rule 21.5(4)(b)   FORM 18B   **D 697**

F<small>ORM OF EXTRACT DECREE IN AN ACTION OF DELIVERY</small>

Sheriff court   Court ref. no.:

Date of decree   *in absence

Pursuer(s)

Defender(s)

The sheriff granted decree against the defender

(1) for delivery to the pursuer of (*specify articles*)

(2) for expenses of £

* Further, the sheriff granted warrant to officers of court to (1) open shut and lockfast places occupied by the defender and (2) search for and take possession of said goods in the possession of the defender.

*delete as appropriate

This extract is warrant for all lawful execution thereon.

Date   Sheriff clerk depute

Rule 21.5(4)(b)   FORM 18C

F<small>ORM OF EXTRACT DECREE IN AN ACTION OF DELIVERY</small>—P<small>AYMENT FAILING DELIVERY</small>

Sheriff court   Court ref. no.:

Date of decree   *in absence

Pursuer(s)

Defender(s)

The sheriff, in respect that the defender has failed to make delivery in accordance with the decree granted in this court on (*date*), granted decree for payment against the defender of the undernoted sums:

(1) Sum(s) decerned for: £ , being the alternative amount claimed.

(2) Interest at per cent per year from (*date*) until payment.

(3) Expenses of £ against the (*name of party*).

*A time to pay direction was made under section 1 (1) of the Debtors (Scotland) Act 1987.

*The amount is payable by instalments of £ per   commencing within

  *days/weeks/monthsof intimation of this extract decree.

*The amount is payable by lump sum within *days/weeks/months of intimation of this extract decree.

*delete as appropriate

This extract is warrant for all lawful execution thereon.

Date   Sheriff clerk depute

Rule 21.5(4)(b)   FORM 18D

F<small>ORM OF EXTRACT DECREE</small> R<small>ECOVERY OF POSSESSION OF MOVEABLE PROPERTY</small>

Sheriff court   Court ref. no.:

Date of decree   *in absence

Pursuer(s)   Defender(s)

D 698 The sheriff granted decree against the defender:

(1) Finding the pursuer entitled to recovery of possession of the article(s) (*specify*)

(2) for expenses of £

* Further, the sheriff granted warrant to officers of court to (1) open shut and lockfast places occupied by the defender and (2) search for and take possession of said goods in the possession of the defender.

**delete as appropriate*

This extract is warrant for all lawful execution thereon.

Date   Sheriff clerk depute

Rule 21.5(4)(b)   FORM 18E

FORM OF EXTRACT DECREE

Recovery of possession of moveable property—payment failing recovery

Sheriff court   Court ref. no.:

Date of decree   *in absence

Pursuer(s)   Defender(s)

The sheriff, in respect that the defender has failed to recover possession in accordance with the decree granted in this court on (*date*), granted decree for payment against the defender of the undernoted sums:

Sum(s) decerned for: £   , being the alternative amount claimed.

Interest at   per cent per year from (*date*) until payment.

Expenses of £   against the (*name of party*).

*A time to pay direction was made under section 1 (1) of the Debtors (Scotland) Act 1987.

*The amount is payable by instalments of £   per   commencing within

                    *days/weeks/monthsof intimation of this extract decree.

*The amount is payable by lump sum within   *days/weeks/months of intimation of this extract decree.

**delete as appropriate*

This extract is warrant for all lawful execution thereon.

Date   Sheriff clerk depute

Rule 21.5(4)(b)   FORM 18F

FORM OF EXTRACT DECREE AD FACTUM PRAESTANDUM

Sheriff court   Court ref. no.:

Date of decree   *in absence

Pursuer(s)

Defender(s)

The sheriff

(1) ordained the defender(s)

(2) granted decree for payment of expenses of £   against the defender(s).

This extract is warrant for all lawful execution thereon.

Date   Sheriff clerk depute

Rule 21.5(4)(b)   FORM 18G   **D 699**

FORM OF EXTRACT DECREE AD FACTUM PRAESTANDUM—PAYMENT UPON FAILURE TO
IMPLEMENT OBLIGATION

Sheriff court   Court ref. no.:

Date of decree   *in absence

Pursuer(s)

Defender(s)

The sheriff, in respect that the defender has failed to implement the obligation contained in and in accordance with the decree granted in this court on (*date*), granted decree for payment against the defender of the undernoted sums:

(1) Sum(s) decerned for: £   ,being the alternative amount claimed.

(2) Interest at   per cent per year from (*date*) until payment.

(3) Expenses of £   against the (*name of party*).

*A time to pay direction was made under section 1(1) of the Debtors (Scotland) Act 1987.

*The amount is payable by instalments of £   per   commencing within

           *days/weeks/monthsof intimation of this extract decree.

*The amount is payable by lump sum within   *days/weeks/months of intimation of this extract decree.

**delete as appropriate*

This extract is warrant for all lawful execution thereon.

Date   Sheriff clerk depute

Rule 21.5(4)(b)   FORM 18H

FORM OF EXTRACT DECREE OF ABSOLVITOR

Sheriff court   Court ref. no.:

Date of decree   *in absence

Pursuer(s)

Defender(s)

The sheriff

(1) absolved the defender(s).

(2) granted decree for payment of expenses of £   against the

This extract is warrant for all lawful execution thereon.

Date   Sheriff clerk depute

Rule 21.5(4)(b)   FORM 18I

FORM OF EXTRACT DECREE OF DISMISSAL

Sheriff court   Court ref. no.:

Date of decree   *in absence

Pursuer(s)

Defender(s)

D 700 The sheriff

(1) dismissed the action against the defender(s).

(2) granted decree for payment of expenses of £   against the

This extract is warrant for all lawful execution thereon.

Date   Sheriff clerk depute

Rule 21.8(4)   FORM 19

FORM OF CERTIFICATE BY SHERIFF CLERK
SERVICE OF CHARGE WHERE ADDRESS OF DEFENDER IS UNKNOWN

I certify that the foregoing charge was displayed on the walls of court on (*date*) and that it remained so displayed for a period of (*period of charge*) from that date.

(*date*)   Sheriff clerk depute

Rule 21.1(1)   FORM 20

MINUTE FOR RECALL OF DECREE

Sheriff court: (*place*)

Court ref. no.:

AB (*pursuer*) against CD (*defender(s)*)

The *(*pursuer/defender*) moves the court to recall the decree pronounced on (*date*) in this case * and in which execution of a charge/arrestment was effected on (*date*).

Reason for failure to appear or be represented:

Proposed defence/answer:

Date

*delete as appropriate

Rule 22.1(6)   FORM 20A

MINUTE FOR RECALL OF DECREE—SERVICE COPY

Sheriff court: (*place*)

Court ref. no.:

AB (*pursuer*) against CD (*defender(s)*)

The *(*pursuer/defender*) moves the court to recall the decree pronounced on (*date*) in this case * and in which execution of a charge/arrestment was effected on (*date*).

Reason for failure to appear or be represented:

Proposed defence/answer:

Date

*delete as appropriate

NOTE: You must return the summons to the sheriff clerk at the court mentioned at the top of this form by (insert date 2 days before the date of the hearing).

Rule 23.1(1) FORM 21 **D 700/1**

<small>FORM OF NOTE OF APPEAL TO THE SHERIFF PRINCIPAL</small>

Sheriff court (*place*)

Court ref. no:

AB (pursuer) against CD (defender(s))

The pursuer/defender appeals the sheriff's interlocutor of (*date*) to the sheriff principal and requests the sheriff to state a case.

The point(s) of law upon which the appeal is to proceed is/are: (*give brief statement*).

(*date*)

Rule 23.4(3)(a) FORM 22

<small>APPLICATION FOR LEAVE TO APPEAL AGAINST TIME TO PAY DIRECTION</small>

Sheriff court (*place*)

Court ref. no.:

AB (pursuer) against CD (defender(s))

The pursuer/defender requests the sheriff to grant leave to appeal the decision made on (*date*) in respect of the defender's application for a time to pay direction to the sheriff principal/Court of Session.

The point(s) of law upon which the appeal is to proceed is/are: (*give brief statement*).

(*date*)

Rule 23.4(4) FORM 23

<small>APPEAL AGAINST TIME TO PAY DIRECTION</small>

Sheriff court (*place*)

Court ref. no.:

AB (pursuer) against CD (defender(s))

The pursuer/defender appeals the decision made on (*date*) in respect of the defender's application for a time to pay direction to the sheriff principal/Court of Session.

(*date*)

Rule 24.4(1) FORM 24

<small>FORM OF RECEIPT FOR MONEY PAID TO SHERIFF CLERK</small>

In the sheriff court of (*name of sheriffdom*) at (*place of sheriff court*).

In the claim (*state names of parties or other appropriate description*)

AB (*designation*) has this day paid into court the sum of £   , being a payment made in terms of Chapter 24 of the Small Claim Rules 2002.

*Custody of this money has been accepted at the request of (*insert name of court making the request*).

**delete as appropriate*

(Date)   Sheriff clerk depute

Glossary

Absolve
To find in favour of and exonerate the defender.

Absolvitor
An order of the court granted in favour of and exonerating the defender which means that the pursuer is not allowed to bring the same matter to court again.

Appellant
A person making an appeal against the sheriff's decision. This might be the pursuer or the defender.

Arrestee
A person subject to an arrestment.

Arrestment on the dependence
A court order to freeze the goods or bank account of the defender until the court has heard the case.

Arrestment to found jurisdiction
A court order used against a person who has goods or other assets in Scotland to give the court jurisdiction to hear a claim. This is achieved by preventing anything being done with the goods or assets until the case has been disposed of.

Authorised lay representative
A person other than a lawyer who represents a party to a small claim.

Cause
Another word for case or claim, used for cases under the summary cause procedure.

Caution (pronounced kay-shun)
A security, usually a sum of money, given to ensure that some obligation will be carried out.

Certificate of execution of service
The document recording that an application to, or order or decree of, the court for service of documents has been effected.

Charge
An order to obey a decree of a court. A common type is one served on the defender by a sheriff officer on behalf of the pursuer who has won a case demanding payment of a sum of money.

Commission and diligence
Authorisation by the court for someone to take the evidence of a witness who cannot attend court or to obtain the production of documentary evidence. It is combined with a diligence authorising the person appointed to require the attendance of the witness and the disclosure of documents.

Consignation
The deposit in court, or with a third party, of money or an article in dispute.

Continuation
An order made by the sheriff postponing the completion of a hearing until a later date or dates.

Counterclaim
A claim made by a defender in response to the pursuer's claim and which is not a defence to that claim. It is a separate but related claim against the pursuer which is dealt with at the same time as the pursuer's claim.

Damages
Money compensation payable for a breach of contract or some other legal duty.

Decree
An order of the court containing the decision of the claim in favour of one of the parties and granting the remedy sought or disposing of the claim.

Defender
Person against whom a claim is made.

Deliverance
A decision or order of a court.

Depending
A case is said to be depending when it is going through a court procedure. Technically, this begins with citation of the defender and ends with any final appeal.

Diet
Date for a court hearing.

Diligence
The collective term for the procedures used to enforce a decree of a court. These include arrestment of wages, goods or a bank account.

Dismissal
An order bringing to an end the proceedings in a claim. It is usually possible for a new claim to be brought if not time barred.

Domicile
The place where a person is normally resident or where, in the case of a company, it has its place of business or registered office.

Execution of service
See *Certificate of execution of service.*

Execution of a charge
The intimation of the requirement to obey a decree or order of a court.

Execution of an arrestment
The carrying out of an order of arrestment.

Expenses
The costs of a court case.

Extra-judicial settlement
An agreement between the parties to a case to settle it themselves rather than to await a decision by the sheriff.

Extract decree
The document containing the order of the court made at the end of the claim. For example, it can be used to enforce payment of a sum awarded.

Haver
A person who holds documents which are required as evidence in a case.

Huissier
An official in France and some other European countries who serves court documents.

Incidental application
An application that can be made during the course of a small claim for certain orders. Examples are applications for the recovery of documents or to amend the statement of claim.

Interlocutor
The official record of the order or judgment of a court.

D 700/4 *Intimation*
Giving notice to another party of some step in the small claim.

Jurisdiction
The authority of a court to hear particular cases.

Messenger at arms
Officers of court who serve documents issued by the Court of Session.

Minute
A document produced in the course of a case in which a party makes an application or sets out his position on some matter.

Minute for recall
A form lodged with the court by one party asking the court to recall a decree.

Options Hearing
A preliminary stage in an ordinary cause action.

Ordinary cause
Another legal procedure for higher value claims available in the sheriff court.

Party litigant
A person who conducts his own case.

Productions
Documents or articles which are used in evidence.

Pursuer
The person making a claim.

Recall of an arrestment
A court order withdrawing an arrestment.

Restriction of an arrestment
An order releasing part of the money or property arrested.

Recall of a decree
An order revoking a decree which has been granted.

Recovery of documents
The process of obtaining documentary evidence which is not in the possession of the person seeking it (e.g. hospital records necessary to establish the extent of injuries received in a road accident).

Remit between procedures
A decision of the sheriff to transfer the claim to another court procedure e.g. summary cause or ordinary cause procedure.

Respondent
When a decision of the sheriff is appealed against, the person making the appeal is called the appellant. The other side in the appeal is called the respondent.

Return day
The date by which the defender must send a written reply to the court and, where appropriate, the pursuer must return the summons to court.

Schedule of arrestment
The list of items which may be arrested.

Serve/Service
Sending a copy of the summons or other court document to the defender or another party.

Sheriff clerk
The court official responsible for the administration of the sheriff court.

Sheriff officer
A person who serves court documents and enforces court orders.

Sist of action
The temporary suspension of a court case by court order.

Sist as a party
To add another person as a litigant in a case.

Stated case
An appeal procedure where the sheriff sets out his findings and the reasons for his decision and states the issues on which the decision of the sheriff principal is requested.

Statement of claim
The part of the summons in which pursuers set out details of their claims against defenders.

Summary cause
Another legal procedure available in the Sheriff Court. It is used for certain types of claim usually having a higher value than small claims though less than those dealt with as ordinary causes.

Summons
The form which must be filled in to begin a small claim.

Time to pay direction
A court order for which a defender who is an individual may apply permitting a sum owed to be paid by instalments or by a single payment at a later date.

Time order
A court order which assists debtors who have defaulted on an agreement regulated by the Consumer Credit Act 1974 (c.39) and which may be applied for during a court action.

Warrant for diligence
Authority to carry out one of the diligence procedures.

Writ
A legally significant writing.

Paragraph 4   SCHEDULE 2

REVOCATIONS

(1) *Act of Sederunt*	*(2)* *Reference*	*(3)* *Extent of revocation*
Act of Sederunt (Small Claim Rules) 1988	S.I. 1988/1976	The whole Act of Sederunt
Act of Sederunt (Amendment of Sheriff Court Ordinary Cause, Summary Cause and Small Claim, Rules) 1990	S.I. 1990/661	Paragraph 4
Act of Sederunt (Amendment of Sheriff Court Ordinary Cause, Summary Cause and Small Claim, Rules) (No. 2) 1990	S.I. 1990/2105	Paragraph 4
Act of Sederunt (Amendment of Summary Cause and Small Claim Rules) 1991	S.I. 1991/821	Paragraph 3
Act of Sederunt (Amendment of Ordinary Cause, Summary Cause and Small Claim Rules) 1992	S.I. 1992/249	Paragraph 3
Act of Sederunt (Sheriff Court Ordinary Cause Rules) 1993	S.I. 1993/1956	Paragraph 4